LUCY HUGHES-HALLETT
HEROES

Lucy Hughes-Hallett is a critic for *The Sunday Times* (London) and the author of *Cleopatra: Histories, Dreams, and Distortions*. She lives in London with her husband and daughters and is at work on a book about Gabriele d'Annunzio and the origins of Italian fascism.

14

HEROES

HE

ROES

LUCY HUGHES-HALLETT

ANCHOR BOOKS
A DIVISION OF RANDOM HOUSE, INC.
NEW YORK

FIRST ANCHOR BOOKS EDITION, DECEMBER 2006

Copyright © 2004 by Lucy Hughes-Hallett

All rights reserved. Published in the United States by Anchor Books, a division of Random House, Inc., New York. Originally published in Great Britain by Fourth Estate, an imprint of HarperCollins Publishers, London, in 2004, and subsequently in hardcover in the United States by Alfred A. Knopf, a division of Random House, Inc., New York, in 2005.

Anchor Books and colophon are registered trademarks of Random House, Inc.

The Library of Congress has cataloged the Knopf edition as follows:
Hughes-Hallett, Lucy, [date].
Heroes / by Lucy Hughes-Hallett.
p. cm.
Includes bibliographical references and index.
1. Heroes—Biography.   2. Heroes—Mythology.   3. Courage.   I. Title.
CT105.H785 2005
920.02—dc22
2004061557 [B]

Vintage ISBN-10: 1-4000-7979-9
Vintage ISBN-13: 978-1-4000-7979-7

Author photograph © Jerry Bauer
Book design by Pamela G. Parker

www.anchorbooks.com

Printed in the United States of America
10   9   8   7   6   5   4   3   2   1

For Dan

CONTENTS

HEROES

PROLOGUE

"Rage!" The first word of the *Iliad*, the word that inaugurates Europe's literary culture and introduces one of its dominant themes. The rage not of Agamemnon, king and commander, but of Achilles, the semidivine delinquent, the paradigmatic hero whose terrible choice of glory at the price of an early death has haunted the collective imagination of the West for two and a half millennia.

Heroes are dynamic, seductive people—they wouldn't be heroes otherwise—and heroic rage is thrilling to contemplate. It is the expression of a superb spirit. It is associated with courage and integrity and a disdain for the cramping compromises by means of which the unheroic majority manage their lives—attributes which are widely considered noble. It is also profoundly disruptive of any civil state. Homer's Achilles was the "the best of the Achaeans," the preeminent Greek warrior, but his rage was directed against Agamemnon, leader of the Greeks. The *Iliad* is a celebration of Achilles' lethal glamour; it is also the story of how he came close to occasioning the defeat of the community of which he was the most brilliant representative.

This book is about Achilles and some of his real-life successors (whether Homer's hero really lived we are unlikely ever to know for certain). It takes the form of a series of brief lives of people who have been considered by their contemporaries to be so exceptionally gifted as to be capable of something momentous—the defeat of an enemy, the salvation of a race, the preservation of a political system, the completion of a voyage—which no one else could have accomplished. In 411 BC the people of Athens resolved to recall Alcibiades, whom they had once condemned to death and who had subsequently fought with devastating success for their opponents, because, as one of their commanders told the Assembly, he was "the only person living" who could save their state. So the eleventh century King Alfonso VI of Castile turned to Rodrigo Díaz de Vivar, known as the Cid—a man he had twice banished—when African invaders poured into Spain, because whatever threat the Cid posed to the stability of the kingdom he was known to have been "born in a lucky hour" and could therefore never be defeated. And so in 1630 the Holy Roman Emperor Ferdinand II, having first nerved himself to dismiss his over-weening and intransigent general, Albrecht von Wallenstein, had then to humble himself by imploring Wallenstein to resume his command and save the empire from the onslaught of the invading Swedes, something that, by common consent of all his enemies (he had few friends), Wallenstein alone could hope to do.

Cometh the hour, cometh the man. It is in times of emergency that heroes are looked for, and found. Bertolt Brecht wrote, famously, that it is an unhappy land that looks for heroes. The dictum is ambiguous, and works both ways. A land without heroes may be fortunate in their absence, for a hero is a menace to any state's equilibrium. "The Argonauts left Heracles behind," noted Aristotle, for the same reason that the Athenians took to ostracizing and sending into exile outstanding citizens, "so the Argos would not have on board one so vastly bigger than the rest of the crew." But only a fortunate land is confident enough to dispense with heroes. Now it is fashionable to lament the littleness of those accorded celebrity within our culture—so many football players and rock stars and models, so few great spirits—but such collective frivolity should be cherished as one of the privileges of peace. It is desperation that prompts people to crave a champion, a protector, or a redeemer and, hav-ing identified one, to offer him their worship.

Virtue is not a necessary qualification for heroic status: a hero is not a role model. On the contrary, it is of the essence of a hero to be unique and therefore inimitable. Some of the people whose stories are told in this book were irreproachable, others were scoundrels. Cato had the highest moral standards and adhered to them as nearly always as could possibly be expected. Garibaldi was a man of signal sincerity. (Although he was not quite so transparently simple as his admirers imagined. Alfred, Lord Tennyson, meeting him in 1864, was delighted to recognize in him the "divine stupidity of a hero." In fact Garibaldi was far from dumb: he just didn't speak English.) But Alcibiades was an arrogant libertine and a turn-coat several times over. The Cid was a predatory warlord, Drake was a pirate and a terrorist, and Wallenstein was a profiteer prone to apparently psychotic rages whose contemporaries believed him to be in league with the devil. But heroes are not required to be altruistic, or honest, or even competent. They are required only to inspire confidence and to appear, not good necessarily, but great.

This book is rooted in ambivalence. Thomas Carlyle, who wrote one on the same subject and with the same structure a century and half ago, declared that there was "no nobler feeling" than hero worship. "Heartfelt prostrate admiration, submission, burning, boundless, for a noblest god-like Form of Man . . . it is to this hour and at all hours the vivifying influence in a man's life." I disagree. An exaggerated veneration for an exceptional individual poses an insidious temptation. It allows worshipers to abnegate responsibility, looking to the great man for salvation or for fulfillment which they should more properly be working to accomplish for themselves. Carlyle approvingly called it "the germ . . . of all religion hitherto known," but to make a fellow human the object of religious devotion is unwise. Hero worshipers, as the stories in this book repeatedly demonstrate, are frequently disappointed in, and lay themselves open to abuse by, the heroes of their choice.

The notion of the hero—that some men are born special—is radically inegalitarian. It can open the way for tyranny. "Beware of the pursuit of the Superhuman," wrote George Bernard Shaw. "It leads to an indiscriminate contempt for the Human." True. Carlyle's friend Ralph Waldo Emerson, who wrote, "Life is sweet and tolerable only in our belief in great men," saw the prime function of the great man as that of rendering "indemnification for populations of pigmies," while humanity en masse seemed to him "disgusting, like moving cheese, like hills of ants or of fleas." Such a revulsion from the majority of one's fellow beings, combined with an exaggerated admiration for the exceptional few, makes a politically poisonous mix.

But a wariness of the potentially pernicious effects of hero worship hasn't made me immune to the intoxicating allure of the hero. The people I have written about here are all compelling personalities whose life stories have been told and retold over centuries, in some cases millennia, because they are so dramatic, so full of complex resonance and so profoundly moving. The idea of the hero would not be so emotionally disturbing or so politically dangerous were it not so potent.

I am not a debunker, more a collector and analyst of bunk. I shall repeatedly be pointing to discrepancies between the ascertainable facts about heroes and the legends that grew up around them. I do so not as an iconoclast but because the process whereby heroes' characters and curricula vitae are adjusted to suit the moral values and emotional needs of those who adore them is a fascinating one. That most idols have feet of clay is a banality; what is interesting is the question why, knowing it, we are still enthralled by them. Cato was an inept politician who repeatedly handed advantages to his opponents, but his contemporaries thought him a man in ten thousand and his admirers in the next generation revered him as a god. Francis Drake turned aside from the pursuit of the Spanish Armada to grab a disabled ship as his own prize, imperiling the entire English fleet by doing so, but his popularity was undiminished by the action; on the contrary, when the news reached London bonfires were lit in celebration. Byron and Keats had both read their Plutarch: they knew all about Alcibiades' treachery. Yet Byron wrote that "no name comes down from antiquity with a more general charm than that of Alcibiades," while to Keats "Alcibiades, leaning on his crimson couch in his galley, his broad shoulders imperceptibly heaving with the sea" was the embodiment of the abstract idea of the heroic, "large, prominent, round and coloured with magnificence."

Heroes are insubordinate: that is part of their glamour. Several of the people I have written about followed Achilles in defying their political masters: in doing so they were acting within a well-established heroic tradition. There are men, wrote Aristotle, so godlike, so exceptional, that they naturally, by right of their extraordinary gifts, transcend all moral judgment or constitutional control: "There is no law which embraces men of that calibre: they are themselves law." Such a man inevitably clashes with the established powers which his inordinate personal prestige subverts. The legendary Persian hero Rustum quarreled with his king and refused his services. Horatio Nelson is at his most heroic with his telescope clamped to his blind eye. George Custer was court-martialed barely a week after he graduated from West Point and afterwards he so frequently annoyed his superiors that he would have been excluded from the Little Big Horn campaign had not a storm of public protest obliged President Grant to restore him to his command.

One who has become the object of hero worship is hard to accommodate in a well-ordered state. Established authority has often been highly (and justifiably) suspicious of the heroes that served it. The Cid and Wallenstein were both dismissed by the royal masters who feared and envied them. Garibaldi was and is revered as the valiant creator of a united Italy, but he was repeatedly imprisoned or blockaded on his tiny island home by the state he had brought into being.

Most heroes are rebels. A startling number are actually traitors.

Achilles, having quarreled with Agamemnon, prayed that his fellow Greeks might be defeated. Lancelot was the most complete knight at Arthur's Round Table but brought about the collapse of the civilization of which he was paragon. Of my six historical heroes five fought at some point against their compatriots (a fact which didn't prevent their passing into legend as nationalist heroes). Drake is the exception—but though he never had political power enough to precipitate a confrontation with his queen, he frequently disobeyed her.

Hero worship is the cult of the individual, and the hero is always imagined standing alone. The heroes of classical mythology were homeless wanderers and so are those of modern legend, be they cowboys or police officers, vigilantes or secret agents. They are brilliant mavericks, outsiders coming in from elsewhere to handle an emergency before riding off into the sunset. The wanderer seems to the settled majority to be free and invulnerable. As Herodotus wrote of the nomadic Scythians: "This people has no cities or settled forts: they carry their houses with them and shoot with bows from horseback: they live off herds of cattle, not from tillage, and their dwellings are on their wagons. How then can they fail to be invincible?" Much more can be expected of a stranger, whose unfamiliarity makes him a blank screen for the projection of fantasies, than could ever be asked of someone familiar. Historical heroes, whose hero status depends at least in part on the public's identification of them with legendary counterparts, have frequently been people with no fixed position in the society which expected such great things of them. Wallenstein, the protector of the Austro-Hungarian-German empire, was a Czech. Garibaldi, the maker of Italy, was born in France, wore the costume of a South American gaucho, and until the end of his life still needed a dictionary by him when writing in Italian.

The responsibilities of government don't combine well with the individualism expected of the hero. Achilles, wrote Aristotle, was that rare, not-quite-human creature, a nonpolitical man, "a non-co-operator like an isolated piece in a game of draughts." None of my subjects were heads of state (although, the Cid, at the end of his life, created a new state for himself). They are the successors, not of Agamemnon but of Achilles, not of Arthur but of Lancelot, not of Jehovah but of Jesus Christ. In the 1880s Friedrich Nietzsche defined the state—any state—as "a fearful tyranny, a remorseless machine of oppression" against which he opposed the heroic figure of the "superman." Nietzsche's superman is "like a star thrown forth into empty space and into the icy breath of solitude." He has no community within which to hide, no religion, legal system, or moral code as guide, no group or institution to share the responsibility for his choices. He is terrifyingly exposed. "Can you furnish yourself with your own good and evil and hang up your own will above yourself as a law?" asks Nietzsche's Zarathustra. "Can you be judge of yourself and avenger of your law?" Achilles took it upon himself to do so, repudiating his allegiance to Agamemnon, denying any obligation to his fellow Greeks, choosing to answer to no human authority save his own and insisting on his right to determine when and on whose behalf he would exercise his devastating skills. And although some of my subjects—Cato, with his embarrassing clothes and persnickety accountancy; tubby, venal Drake—are scarcely the kind of resplendent figures Nietzsche had in mind, the same proud rejection of a communal identity has been the mark of the hero throughout the millennia covered by this book.

My subjects are all Europeans. There are many correspondences between the Western heroic tradition and those of some Asian and African cultures, but I have not attempted to trace them, partly for practical reasons—this book is plenty long enough as it is—and partly because the tradition I describe is a continuous and self-referential one. Achilles in his tent sang of the exploits of heroes dead and gone, tales which shaped his concept of himself and his role just as his own story was to condition posterity's idea of what a hero might be. Cato prepared himself for his own suicide by reading Plato's account of the death of Socrates. Even when heroes were not themselves aware of the parallels between their careers and those of their celebrated antecedents, the people who told and modified their stories frequently were. Those stories, as they have come down to us, are therefore full of echoes and presentiments—Drake is a latter-day Jason, Wallenstein a Mars. Cato (despite having died half a century before the Christian era began) is a precursor of Christ. To Alexander Herzen, Garibaldi seemed "a hero of antiquity, a figure out of the Aeneid." As heroes are shaped by the past, so in turn they shape the future. In the 1930s, when Europe was once more in crisis, my heroes (except for Alcibiades, whose offenses against his birthplace rendered him anathema in the age of nationalism) were resurrected and put to political use.

They are all white Westerners and, for different reasons, they are all male. Heroes' stories resemble women's stories in that the hero is simultaneously adored and marginalized, being more often an object of veneration than a holder of power, but the vast majority of the people accorded hero status in Western history have been men. Of course there are women I might have included, but to have done so would have been to obscure the lamentable fact that people of my sex have, throughout most of recorded time, been considered incapable of running a country, let alone saving one. To have chosen a female subject would have been to imply that one-sixth of historical heroes were women. That kind of emollient falsification, in my opinion, does women no service.

When Agamemnon sent out a call for all the men of Greece to join him in attacking Troy, Achilles' father, anxious to save his wonderful boy from conscription, dressed him as a girl and hid him in the women's quarters. Odysseus heard of it and came visiting, bringing a load of magnificent gifts. The women of the court crowded round, exclaiming over the embroidered cloths and golden cups, the robes and the jewels, but Achilles, unable to suppress his true nature, seized upon a sword. At once Odysseus knew him. Achilles abandoned his pretense, acknowledged his manhood, and accepted his heroic destiny. So Odysseus himself, in Homer's account of his journey home, has to extricate himself from Calypso's island, the tempting domain of the feminine where he enjoys every comfort and every pleasure, before the tale of his adventures can begin. Alcibiades dreamed shortly before he was murdered that he was wearing his mistress's clothes and she was making up his face with pigments and white lead like a woman's. Plutarch recounts the dream as though it should be read as a premonition of the hero's death: to lose one's masculinity is tantamount, for a traditional hero, to losing life itself.

The definition of that masculinity has fluctuated. Homer's heroes fume and weep, indulging their emotions in ways commentators from Plato onwards have found disgracefully unmanly, and they are immensely proud and careful of their magnificent bodies, shamelessly indulging a level of physical vanity that latter ages would consider contemptibly effeminate. Charles Baudelaire identified Alcibiades as being among the first of the dandies: the tradition of heroic self-adornment is ancient. The warriors of ancient Sparta decorated their clothes and weapons with ornaments: they wore their hair long and plaited it intricately before going into battle wreathed with flowers. Beauty breeds valor. The troops who traveled on the Armada's ships in 1588 were not required to wear uniforms, explained a Spanish military expert in 1610, because their morale was much enhanced by the gorgeousness of their own clothes: "It is the finery, the plumes and bright colours which give spirit and strength to a soldier so that he can with furious resolution overcome any difficulty or accomplish any valorous exploit." Napoleon's Marshal Murat was as noted for his red boots and extravagant epaulettes as he was for his fearlessness. But although the heroic tradition encompasses areas of human experience identified for most of the recent past as feminine, it is nonetheless sexually exclusive. Even Joan of Arc, perhaps the most obvious female candidate for inclusion in this book, renounced her sex and its perceived limitations by cross-dressing, tacitly acknowledging that the pantheon of heroes admits men only.

So what makes a hero? And what are heroes for? In narrating the lives of a handful of heroes, in attempting to re-create their contemporaries' expectations of them and tracing the way posterity responded to and reshaped their stories, I hope to give a kaleidoscopic answer to each question. Simple, single ones would be impossible. The hero's nature and function have repeatedly shifted along with the mentality of the culture which produced them, and so have the attributes ascribed to the hero, the exploits expected of him, and his place within political structures and society at large.

Each era has a different theory as to how some men come to be, or to seem, superhuman. Often ideas about the hero are religious: the hero is the son of a god, or a saint, or a hubristic challenger of divine authority, or a god himself. Or his extraordinary talents may be less legitimately supernatural: he may be a witch. Class is important, though not always in predictable ways. Many heroes' social status is indeterminate and wavering, like that of the English folk hero Robin Hood, who is now the dispossessed lord of Locksley Hall, now the comrade of common criminals. The majority of heroes throughout history have been, or pretended to be, or aspired to become aristocrats. But heroes, especially dead ones, are usefully malleable: their images have been pressed into service as often by revolutionaries as by defenders of authoritarianism. There is a vigorous countertradition celebrating the popular hero, the man of the people who challenges elitist power and privilege, the plucky little fellow who slays the giant with nothing but a pebble in a sling, the common sailor or the carpenter's son who lays low principalities and powers.

There is an erotic dimension to hero worship. Beauty, charm, and sex appeal are useful assets for a hero; in their absence a dashing style or a commanding presence will do. People were dazzled by Alcibiades, besotted with Garibaldi, terrified by Wallenstein. A hero must be able either to seduce or intimidate: either way he needs an outsize personality and a talent for projecting it. Heroism is theatrical. Heroes must look, and act, the part. They must swagger and preen, or, if their public's taste inclines the other way, they must make a show of their humility, as Cato did, going indecently underdressed to the Forum. Heroic gestures are frequently histrionic, which is not to say they are frivolous: a symbolic gesture can have substantial consequences. When it was suggested to General Gordon that his brightly illuminated headquarters in Khartoum provided too easy a target for the Mahdi's guns, he called for an immense candelabrum, lit its twenty-four candles with his own hands, and stationed himself beside it at a great arched window, saying, "Go tell the people of Khartoum that Gordon fears nothing." He died anyway, but he had made a stirring spectacle of his own defeat. The capacity to stage a splendid tableau is a more important qualification for admission to the gallery of heroes than either survival or success.

Appearances matter, and not only because "defeat in battle," as Tacitus wrote, "always begins with the eye." "What is he [Achilles] more than another?" asks Ajax in Shakespeare's bitterly antiheroic version of the Troy story, *Troilus and Cressida*. "No more than what he thinks he is," replies Agamemnon. Heroic status depends on the hero's self-confidence and often also on the confidence trick he (or his sponsors and advocates) pulls on others in persuading them of his superhuman potency. Some heroes' reputations are manufactured or enlarged by others. Drake's power and ferocity were magnified by Spaniards motivated by anger at the humiliations to which he had subjected them. Garibaldi was surprised, on returning to Europe in 1848, to find that Mazzini had made him an international celebrity. Others are self-created: Alcibiades' most audacious and ingenious publicist was himself. But whether by his own or others' will a hero inevitably acquires an artificial public persona. Shakespeare's Achilles is addressed as "thou picture of what thou seemest," a doubled image of inauthenticity. But an image is what a hero inevitably becomes. In 1961 Anthony Mann, with General Franco's enthusiastic support (the Spanish army was placed at his disposal for the battle scenes), made a stirring film of *El Cid*. At the end of it the Cid is killed fighting but his grieving wife and followers, knowing that without the inspiration his presence provides their armies will never succeed in beating off the hordes of the enemy, keep his death secret. His corpse is dressed and armed and strapped upright in the saddle of his great white charger. The trusty horse gallops out at the head of the Cid's army. Believing that their great leader is still with them, his men win a marvelous victory before the horse, with its lifeless but still invincible burden, disappears over the horizon.

The story was made up on purpose for the film—there is no medieval legend, let alone chronicle, in which it appears in that form—but the thinking behind it is sound. A hero's appearance is sometimes all that is required of him. He can win a battle, or quell a riot, or raise a revolution simply by being seen. He doesn't have to be active; he doesn't even have to be alive. Indeed, it isn't necessary that he be really present: it is enough that he should be so apparently. Achilles sent Patroclus out to fight disguised in his armor, knowing that the mere simulacrum of himself would be terrifying enough to send the Trojans hurtling back towards their walls. Julius Caesar used to wear a cloak of a striking and unusual color into battle to advertise his presence and at Thapsus, when he himself was overtaken by an attack of "his usual sickness" (probably epilepsy), he sent a surrogate onto the field in that cloak. Nobody noticed: victory came quickly. A hero, once his fame reaches a certain pitch, becomes a totem, an object of magical potency which need take no action in order to achieve results. Garibaldi, serving France when he was old and crippled by arthritis, was carried around the battlefield on a stretcher: his presence was all the same reckoned to have been invaluable. And where the actual hero, active or inert, is unavailable, an effigy, an understudy, or a corpse will do as well.

It follows that a hero is not always, even in his lifetime, and certainly not thereafter, responsible for the uses to which his image is put. Frequently, as the stories I have to tell demonstrate, a hero is—consciously or unconsciously—the chief actor in a spectacle scripted and directed by others. As Elizabeth and Walsingham used Drake, so Victor Emmanuel II and Cavour used Garibaldi. And once dead a hero becomes an infinitely adaptable symbol. Cato's repeated metamorphoses, from conservative oligarch to Christian saint to martyr in the cause of liberty to Whig parliamentarian, have parallels in most heroes' afterlives. Every retelling of a heroic story is colored by the politics and predilections of the teller, whether that teller's intentions are deliberately propagandist or ostensibly innocent. Looking at heroes, we find what we seek.

What that is exactly depends on the time and place from which we are looking. In telling my heroes' stories I demonstrate how various are the ways in which heroes appeal to us. Heroes may challenge or comfort; they may offer the elation of victory or the infantilizing luxury of being taken care of by a superhuman protector. They may constitute models of courage or integrity, or they may set enticing examples of transgression and license. But one thing is constant: they all provide ways of thinking about mortality.

"Madam," Francis Drake purportedly told Queen Elizabeth, "the wings of opportunity are fledged with the feathers of death." Heroes expose themselves to mortal danger in pursuit of immortality. Sophocles, writing while Alcibiades was a boy, has the heroically intransigent Antigone tell her sister, Ismene, "You chose life, but I chose death." Ismene is preparing to compromise her principles, bowing to the powers that be in order to secure herself a safe place in the world, but Antigone would rather die than do so, and so her name will long outlive them both. "Many men," wrote Sallust, "being slaves to appetite and sleep, have passed through life like mere wayfarers . . . The lives and deaths of such men is about alike, since no record is made of either." But a few rise above the sordid limitations of physical existence, the repetitive and futile cycle of consumption and excretion and slow decay. Sallust considered Cato, who was his contemporary, to be one of those exceptional beings whose greatness lifts them above the common ruck, who transcend their pitifully ephemeral physical nature, thus holding out the profoundly consoling vision of an existence in which oblivion can be averted and a mortal may escape time's scythe.

A hero may sacrifice himself so that others might live, or so that he himself may live forever in other's memories. But even when his exploits are undertaken for purely selfish and temporal motives of ambition or greed the very fact of his enduring fame is a token of immortality. Since the prospect of death is something with which we all have to come to terms, the stories of heroes will never lose their fascination. Dead heroes escape the degeneration that awaits the rest of us. "They shall not grow old as we that are left grow old," and it seems to those who survive them that they can even evade death. "Being dead they have not died," wrote Simonides of the Spartans who died at Thermopylae; "their excellence raised them gloriously out of the house of Hades."

Hero worship still plays a vital part in our political lives. It inspires both terrorists and those who combat them. It shapes the rhetoric of our election campaigns. It helps determine the choices made by democratic voters and it eases dictators' ascent to power. I have chosen not to play the game of spot-the-hero among the people whose names now fill our screens and newspapers, but I hope that, while reading this book, others will. Garibaldi, the most recent of my subjects, died in 1882: I have traced the alterations in his and the others' reputations only up to the outbreak of the Second World War. But although the stories I have to tell are legendary or historical, each one of them is to be read as a parable about the way we live now.

There is an odd kind of inverted vanity which persuades people to imagine that some of our collective follies are brand new, peculiar to the age of mass media. Wrong. As the stories I have told here demonstrate, there is nothing new about the cult of personality, about the calculated manipulation of news for political ends, about the ways in which celebrity and sexual charisma can be translated into power, about the suggestibility of a populace who in a time of fear or overexcited enthusiasm can be tempted to hand over their political rights to a glorious superman. On September 12, 2001, a group of people were photographed near the ruins of the World Trade Center holding up a banner reading WE NEED HEROES NOW. This book is first and foremost a collection of extraordinary stories, but it is also an attempt to examine that need, to acknowledge its urgency, and to warn against it.

I

ACHILLES

Homer's Troy. Achilles, paragon of warriors, consents to enter the fight. Ready for battle in the armor made for him by the smith god Hephaestus, he glitters like the sun. His teeth grind, his eyes flash fire. With a voice as plangent as a trumpet's he calls out to his immortal horses which no other man can master and one of them replies. Yes, says the beast, this time the team will bring their master safely back to the Greek camp, but the day of his death already hovers near and when it comes, even were they to have the speed and power of the west wind, they would not be able to save him: "You are doomed to die violently, Achilles." Achilles' reply is impatient: "Don't waste your breath, I know, well I know." With a terrifying yell he sends his chariot hurtling into the front line.

Of all the warriors who fight at Troy Achilles is the only one who is bound to die there. He is not courting risk: he is confronting certainty, and he himself must take responsibility for his own end. His mother, the goddess Thetis, has told him of the two destinies between which he must choose. He can stay peaceably in his father's house, and if he does so his life will be long and fruitful. He can marry and have children. He can use his wealth and amass more. He can exploit his strength and exercise his intellect. He can inherit and rule his father's kingdom, enjoying the satisfactions of power and, in due time, the respect accorded to an elder. Or he can fight. If he chooses the latter he will be killed before the war's end, but first he will win such glory that his name will live in song forevermore.

He chooses death, buying immortality at the cost of his life. And so he becomes the paradigmatic hero, one whose traits and actions are echoed, with infinite variations, in the life stories of subsequent heroes both legendary and actual. His beauty, his swiftness and ferocity, his unrivaled talent for killing his fellow men, his uncompromising commitment both to honesty and to honor and, above all, the pathos of his freely accepted death combine to invest him with an ineffable glamour.

His choice is not easy. There is an alternative. There is another Homeric epic and another hero, Odysseus, who chooses life, and who is so determined to hang on to all that Achilles has renounced that he will lie, cheat, and steal for it. Odysseus is an intriguer, a shapeshifter, a warrior like Achilles but one noted primarily not for his actions but for his words. Achilles' foil, he repeatedly calls into question the values Achilles represents—both tacitly, by his very existence as one who has taken the opposite path, and explicitly on the several occasions when the two confront each other. In the stories of the heroes who come after them the characteristics of Odysseus and Achilles combine and alternate, but for Achilles himself there can be no half measures, no partial sacrifice. His choice is absolute and tragic. The brilliance with which his prowess and his physical splendor invest him is simultaneously shadowed and intensified by his inconsolable grief at the prospect of his own end, by his pity for his father and mother in the anguish his death must bring them, and his mourning for all that he might have been. Throughout the *Iliad* Homer imagines him questioning the bargain he has made (and which he can at any moment revoke—three days' sailing would take him home), asking at each setback, "Was it for this" that he decided to forgo so much? He neither despises life nor belittles death. The former he knows to be worth more than all the wealth in the world. The prospect of the latter is dreadful to him. He describes the underworld habitations of the dead as "dank moldering horrors / that fill the deathless gods themselves with loathing," and he dwells obsessively on the ignominies to which dead flesh is subject.

If Achilles ever lived (something unlikely ever to be proven) he inhabited a culture separated from us by over three millennia, by tremendous changes in belief, in accepted morality, in technology, in human knowledge. Yet his story, as told by Homer, addresses questions as troubling now as they were when Agamemnon's host laid siege to Troy. "Like the generations of leaves, the lives of mortal men," so a Trojan warrior tells a Greek, as they prepare to fight to the death. The Greek has asked to know his antagonist's identity. The Trojan's point is that the question is otiose. If each individual is as expendable and replaceable as this year's leaves, it scarcely matters who anyone might be. Before the fact of mortality any achievement seems futile, any quarrel petty. Death would make nihilists of us all, were it not for the passion with which humans struggle against its reductive, equalizing influence. Achilles will give anything, including life itself, to assert his own uniqueness, to endow his particular life with significance, and to escape oblivion.

A non-Homeric legend tells how Achilles' divine mother sought to make her baby invulnerable by dipping him in the waters of the Styx, the river over which the souls of the dead were ferried to the underworld. The attempt was unsuccessful. The heel by which Thetis held Achilles remained dry, and it was in that heel that he eventually received his fatal wound. Thetis could not keep her son alive, but he was to find his own way to life eternal, a way closely analogous to the one she tried. Just as she had sought to save him from dying by immersing him in the waters of death's river, so he cheated death by embracing it, voluntarily dying in his quest for everlasting life.

The *Iliad* begins with a quarrel over a girl. Two female prisoners have been awarded, by the consent of the full Greek army, one to Agamemnon, king and commander-in-chief, and one to the supreme warrior Achilles, as part of the prize due to each for their exploits in the war. The girl given to Agamemnon is the daughter of a priest of Apollo. The angry god retaliates by sending down a plague. An assembly is called. Reluctantly Agamemnon agrees to return the girl to her father, but demands compensation. If he cannot keep his own prize he will take someone else's. Achilles, who is not only the paragon of warriors but also the scrupulous guardian of the warriors' code of honor, protests that to do so would be disgraceful. Agamemnon is defiant. He is the overlord: he will have his way regardless of another's opinion: "Let that man I go visit choke with rage." Achilles, beside himself, declares that he will sail for home if Agamemnon perpetrates such an outrage against the code of conduct they all observe. Agamemnon rounds on him and declares his intention of taking Achilles' own prize, the girl Briseis. For a moment Achilles is ready to kill him, but he is restrained by the voice of wisdom, Pallas Athena. Instead he swears a great oath that he will not fight again in the quarrels of the house of Atreus. Leaving the assembly he goes to his tent, way out at the end of the Greek lines, and there he stays. The rage of Achilles, the passion which is at once so disastrous and so magnificent, and which has earned his immortality, is not the savage bloodthirst which drives him on the battlefield, but the principled fury which keeps him off it.

This argument is far more than a squabble over possession of a slave. It is a dispute over the nature of superiority. Agamemnon tells Achilles he will take his girl "so you can learn just how much greater I am than you." But is a man's worth dependent on his power, or on his talent? Is it a function of his social and political relationships, or can an individual possess a value independent of his place in the community? Is Agamemnon, as old Nestor says, the more to be honored "because he rules more men"? Or might Achilles, whose claim to supremacy lies entirely in himself, in his own particular, unsurpassed brilliance, be the greater man? These questions are fundamental. Their answers must affect the conduct both of individuals and of states, determining the relationship between political institutions and the people of whom they are constituted.

Achilles is a divinely created aristocrat, a living demonstration that men are not born equal. The son of a goddess and repeatedly described by Homer as being himself "godlike," he is innately superior to his fellows. Pindar, the fifth-century BC poet who was classical Athens' most eloquent upholder of the class system, celebrated his prowess, his "hands like Ares', his feet like lightning." In the *Iliad* he is physically magnificent. When he loses his armor he cannot borrow more from any of his fellow Greeks, for none of them, with the possible exception of Ajax, is as tall as he. The perfection of his body is sublime, the loveliness of his features flawless. His beauty, potently erotic, marks him, like Helen, as a superhuman being. He is "brilliant," literally: in armor he shines like the sun. He is faster than any of his peers and therefore more deadly in battle. When he chases Hector three times round the walls of Troy, hunting him as a hawk hunts a terrified dove, it is his speed as much as his courage and his strength which makes him invincible. Destined never to grow old, he has a young man's splendor and a young man's energy. His emotions are extreme, his responses passionate, his actions devastating. For all these reasons he is unique among the Homeric warriors. Nestor may be wiser, Odysseus more astute and articulate, Ajax stronger in a hand-to-hand fight, but Achilles is, by common consent, the "best of the Achaeans." Only Agamemnon disputes his right to that title, and he does so on political grounds. He doesn't claim that he is a greater individual than Achilles. He bases his challenge on the assumption that no individual can count for as much as a community, and that therefore the ruler of that community is, by definition and regardless of his or anybody else's personal qualities, the greatest person in it. Extraordinary as Achilles' gifts may be, they are easily outweighed, in Agamemnon's view, by the latter's authority as overlord. Agamemnon tells him, "You are nothing to me!"

That would be enough to enrage Achilles, but there is more. Beyond the competition between Agamemnon the king and Achilles the hero—embodiments respectively of the power of the collective and the brilliance of the individual—lies the question of the legitimacy or otherwise of the war in which they are engaged. The disputed women are prizes, not booty. (They are also, of course, human beings whose rights, judged by modern standards, are being grossly violated—but let that be.) They have been awarded to the two men as marks of honor. They are not mere chattels to be passed from tent to tent, any more than a medal awarded for valor is only a coin on a ribbon, or an athlete's gold cup just an expensive drinking vessel. A prize which has been awarded to one cannot be appropriated by another without its meaning being erased and the symbolic code within which it existed being called into question. In demanding Briseis Agamemnon is acting not like a warrior eager for glory, but like a bandit greedy for loot. In doing so he shames not only himself, but the whole Greek army. In the gruesome setting of the battlefield, a situation where men are all too easily reduced to the level of beasts of prey, or to carrion, it is essential to hold fast to the elusive concept of honor as a talisman against horror and despair. Achilles came to Troy to avenge the insult done to Agamemnon and his brother Menelaus when the Trojan prince Paris abducted Helen, Menelaus's wife—to protect their honor. But if Agamemnon seizes Briseis then he is an abductor, just as Paris is. The Greeks' invasion of Priam's kingdom is revealed to be no more than a predatory attack on a wealthy victim and Achilles is no longer a warrior in a noble cause but the underling of an unprincipled looter. If he dies he will do so ignominiously, in the prosecution of a stupid, brutal war, and the eternal fame for which he hoped will be denied him. As he later tells those who come to implore him to return to the field, there is no point in doing so once Agamemnon has robbed fighting of its meaning. The king's rapacity has leveled all value, trivialized all achievement. In a world in which the distinction between the noble warrior and the thug has been erased, "the same honour waits for the coward and the brave. They both go down to death."

When it becomes clear that the Greeks will continue to obey Agamemnon, Achilles turns his back on them, becoming, like so many subsequent heroes, a voluntary outcast from a society he despises. Self-exiled, he is isolated. His only companion is Patroclus, the beloved friend who has followed him to Troy. Always exceptional, he is now unassimilable. He respects no human jurisdiction. He defers to no one; he fears no one. In Homer's telling of his story he is the champion of individualism against the compromising demands of the community, the defender of the loner's purity against the complex imperfections of the group. In that role he is superb, but potentially lethal to any ordered state. When an embassy comes to him from Agamemnon, imploring him to rejoin the fighting, promising him splendid gifts and the restoration of his honor, he rejects the offer: "I say my honour lies in the great decree of Zeus." He asks nothing of his fellows now, nor does he acknowledge any claim they might make on him. In a ferociously apocalyptic vision he prays that Greeks and Trojans alike may cut each other to pieces, leaving no one at all alive but Patroclus and himself, so that the two of them might, alone, bring Troy's towers toppling down. In his tent he plays the lyre and sings to himself of "the famous deeds of fighting heroes." He acknowledges allegiance now not to any living society, but only to his dead peers, each one exceptional, brilliant mavericks like himself.

While Achilles broods, his fellow Greeks fight on. Slowly, inexorably, over several days, the Trojans, led by Hector, force them back across the coastal plain. Their leaders—Agamemnon, Diomedes, Odysseus—are all wounded. They throw up a rampart of rocks and clay to protect their ships. The Trojans breach the rampart. The two armies are fighting hand to hand on and around the ships, the beach is black with blood and the air full of the scorching heat and ferocious crackle of the firebrands when Patroclus comes weeping to Achilles, begging his friend to relent, to save the Greeks from defeat and from the horror of being marooned in a hostile land, their ships burned, to be massacred or enslaved. Achilles is moved, but he has sworn he will not join the battle unless the Trojans menace his own ships, still secure at the furthest end of the Greek lines. He will hold to his vow. He will not fight in person. But he agrees to a compromise: he will lend Patroclus his armor and send him out to battle in his stead.

Encased in the magnificent star-emblazoned, silver-studded bronze armor which is immediately identifiable to Greek and Trojan alike as that of the terrible Achilles, with a great crest of horsehair tossing on his helmet's crest, Patroclus leads out the Myrmidons, "hungry as wolves that rend and bolt raw flesh, / hearts filled with battle-frenzy that never dies." Seeing him, the Trojans quake, their columns waver. Achilles appears to have returned, bearing with him "sudden, plunging death." Shrieking, wild as storm clouds driven by a cyclone, the Trojan army stampedes back and away from the Greek ships, back toward the safety of their own walls.

In the fighting that follows, Hector kills Patroclus, and strips from his corpse the armor of Achilles. When the news is brought to Achilles he lays aside his quarrel with Agamemnon. In the frenzy of his mourning all scruples about propriety, about honor, about the sanctity of vows, are forgotten. He resolves to fight the next day, but first he displays himself to his enemy. As twilight descends he climbs alone and unarmed onto the rampart before the Greek ships. Pallas Athena, whose favorite he is, crowns him with a diadem of fire which blazes from his head to the sky, and slings around him a shield of flaring storm. Furious with grief for his slaughtered friend, he lets loose three times a war cry so piercing and terrible that the Trojans whirl round in panic. "Twelve of their finest fighters died then and there, crushed by chariots, impaled on their own spears," killed by the mere sight and sound of the awful Achilles.

"The man who is incapable of working in common, or who in his self-sufficiency has no need of others, is no part of the community," wrote Aristotle. Such a man is "like an animal or a god." Achilles, who has divorced himself from the fellowship of the army, who looks to Zeus alone for the validation of his claim to honor, has made himself independent of his fellow men. He reenters the battle not to save his compatriots but in pursuit of a private revenge. In the cataclysmic battle that follows he is both subhuman and superhuman, both bestial and divine. He is likened to a forest fire, to a massive ox threshing barley, to a lion (repeatedly), to the Dog Star that rains down pestilence, to the frenzied god of war. He kills and kills and kills until the earth is drenched with blood and the river that flows before the walls of Troy is choked with corpses. His rampage is outrageous, so transgressive in the extremity of its violence that earth and heaven alike are angered by it. The river rises up against the desecration of its waters: a tremendous tidal wave threatens to engulf Achilles and sweep him away. Hephaestus, to protect him, hurls a great fireball down from heaven. The blaze races across the plain, blasting trees and corpses and scorching the river banks until the river is all but dried. The conflict is elemental, apocalyptic, and at its center Homer places Achilles, a figure from a nightmare, trumpet-tongued, gigantic, shrieking out his rage, his sharp-hoofed stallions trampling on corpses, sending up sprays of blood, blood on his wheels, blood on his chariot's handrail, "bloody filth splattering both his invincible arms."

In this war the Trojans are at home. At night they retire from the battlefield to well-built halls, to wives and children. They belong to a polity. Even the bravest warrior among them must defer to the civil authority, King Priam. They have temples and priests. The landscape in which they do battle with the Greeks is one they have tamed and made productive. Their horses have grazed the earth now slippery with blood. The spring past which Achilles chases Hector has been their washing place. Their babies wave to them as they advance through the Scaean gates. Their parents and elders line the city walls, watching the fighting from a position of security. Hector is husband, father, son, and brother, as well as being the protector of his home and his fellow citizens. In the frenzy of battle he may become, as Achilles does, as fierce as a wild beast, but he is essentially domestic. On the day of his death his wife Andromache sits weaving as she waits for him, within earshot of the fight, and her women have the water heated ready for his bath.

The Greeks, by contrast, are far from home, from family, from women, from the sources of their culture. They may have come from a civilization, but they are no longer part of it. For nine years and more they have been encamped on the windy plain with the gray sea behind them. They are cut off from parents and children, isolated from the continuum of generation. All male, all adult, only a few of them old, they form, as any army does, a pathologically unbalanced community. They are raiders, cattle rustlers; they neither grow nor produce anything. Homeless and predatory, they circle the walls of Troy like hungry wolves.

This existence, the life of a vagrant marauder, of a dangerous and perpetually endangered outsider, is what Achilles chose when he picked the path that would lead to his early and glorious death. The Trojans fight because it is their civic duty to do so, to "form a wall before our loving parents, wives and sons / to defend Troy." Achilles fights because he has a lust for "the bloody grind of war." Freud would recognize Hector as a devotee of Eros, the creative deity "whose purpose is to combine single human individuals, and after that families, then races, peoples and nations, in one great unity, the unity of mankind." In battle he is courageous and terrible, but his fighting is a service performed for the sake of the community. It is a function of the relationships by which he defines himself. Achilles the loner, by contrast, is an agent of Thanatos, the force which divides man from man and which drives its acolytes to seek their own and others' deaths. He is one of the wild ones, one who has rejected the restrictions as well as the rewards of civilian life, whose readiness to risk his own death has accorded him unlimited license. At large on the plains outside the Trojan walls he is a terrifying apparition, the personification of cruelty and brute force. But he is also, always, even when crazy-eyed and cloaked in others' blood, dazzlingly beautiful.

Everything about him is exciting, even when (especially when) he is at his most psychotic. He is the first of the lordly delinquents, the charismatic outcasts by whom law-abiding citizens have always been fascinated as well as scared witless. Off the battlefield, arguing in the assembly or in his tent, he exhilarates by his uncompromising integrity and his emotional extremism. In the thick of the fighting he generates a related but darker response. His titanic energy, his lethal skill, his pitilessness ring out like another, harsher, kind of truth telling. "Come friend," he says to a Trojan prince who clasps his knees, unarmed, abjectly begging for mercy. "You too must die. Why moan about it so? / . . . Look, you see how handsome and powerful I am? . . . Even for me I tell you / death and the strong force of fate are waiting. / There will come a dawn or sunset or high noon / when a man will take my life in battle too." This is the truth. The coolness with which Achilles faces it is connected with the deplorable but intoxicating fury with which he slaughters his fellow men.

Such courage and such rage are not human. "The salt grey sunless ocean gave you birth / and the towering blank rocks," Patroclus tells him, reproaching him for his indifference to his fellows' fate. Before their final duel Hector proposes a pact binding the winner to return the victim's corpse to his own people for decent burial. Hector is dressed in the armor he stripped from Patroclus's dead body, the armor of Achilles. He looks just like Achilles; he is nearly his equal in arms. He is what Achilles might be if he chose to respect the conventions governing human intercourse and rendering its useful continuance possible. Achilles answers by disowning any connection between his wild self and his civilized double. "Don't talk to me of pacts. There are no binding oaths between men and lions." He acknowledges no obligation now to anyone or to any power other than his own rage. He is ready to shuffle off his humanity altogether, to become completely bestial. He would like to eat Hector's flesh. He has already consented to his own death, a decision of inhuman bravado which has emancipated him even from what Tacitus called "that hindrance to all mighty enterprises, the desire for survival." Death may be immortality's opposite, but it confers a similar invulnerability. Death dealing and bent on dying, Achilles has achieved absolute freedom.

Panic-stricken, the Trojans flee before him, racing for the security of the city. At last only Hector is left outside the walls. The two champions confront each other. Achilles is deadly as the Dog Star, brilliant as the blazing sun. Hector, the noble, all but invincible Hector, loses his nerve and runs. Three times the great runner Achilles chases him round the walls of Troy. Hector is humiliated, pathetic, as feeble as a cringing dove. At last he turns to fight and be killed. With his last breath he foretells Achilles' own death, but Achilles, as impervious to fear as he is to compassion, taunts him: "Die, die! For my own death, I'll meet it freely." As soon as the Trojan is still, the rest of the Greeks run up. In a scene of horrible frenzy each one of them stabs Hector's corpse, until Achilles calls them off. He, the killer, will also be the prime desecrator of Hector's body. He pierces the tendons in the Trojan prince's ankles (the tendons later to be known by his own name) and lashes them to the back of his chariot. As he whips his horses to a gallop and races over the plain back to the Greek camp, Hector's head, so handsome once, is dragged bouncing in the dust behind him. From the walls of Troy the watchers, Hector's parents among them, scream out their horror and their despair.

This agent of mass slaughter and perpetrator of atrocity, this "monstrous man" as Priam justly calls him, Achilles, is still "the best of the Achaeans," the supreme exemplar of heroic virtue. Back in camp he presides at splendid funeral games for Patroclus. As instigator of the games and giver of the prizes he does not compete: were he to do so, he would, of course, be unbeatable. He consoles the losers, arbitrates wherever there is a dispute, sends all home happy with the generosity of his awards. His rage has left him. When Agamemnon wishes to compete as spear thrower, risking an embarrassing situation if he loses, Achilles intervenes to prevent him by tactful flattery, acknowledging, as he once so passionately refused to do, his commander's superiority: "You are the best by far." Even his deference is princely. He is courteous, judicious, munificent, a lord among men. In a warrior culture, nobility coexists comfortably with a capacity for mass murder.

For twelve days Hector's body lies unburied. For twelve days Achilles mourns for Patroclus, wandering distraught along the beach, or time and again lashing his enemy's corpse to his chariot and dragging it three times around his beloved's tomb. At last the gods intervene. Thetis comes to tell her son that it is Zeus's will he return the body. That night, helped by Hermes, who has led him unseen past the Greek sentries, old King Priam appears in Achilles' tent, and begs to be allowed to ransom Hector's body. He offers in exchange magnificent gifts: twelve of the brocaded robes for which the weavers of Troy are celebrated all over the known world, tripods and cauldrons, ten bars of gold, a priceless Thracian cup. Achilles, who has repeatedly spurned Agamemnon's attempts to conciliate him with rich gifts, accepts.

His doing so is a signal that he may be ready to exchange the quasi-divinity of the warrior enraged for the compromised condition of the socialized human being. On the wonderful shield Hephaestus forged for him two cities are depicted, two visions juxtaposed. One is that of a world of war, where even allies quarrel over tactics, where animals and men alike are promiscuously and wastefully killed, where the only way of resolving differences is by the slaughter of opponents. The other is a microcosm of civilized life, typified first by weddings and dancing, emblems of union and cooperative creation, and, most pointedly, by the detailed representation of a dispute resolved, not by violence, but by argument culminating in financial payment. A man has been murdered. The killer and the victim's kinsman have come into the marketplace so that the case may be publicly debated. The killer offers to pay the blood price. The other refuses to accept it. Both ask for a judge to "cut the knot" of their antagonism, to save them from the horrors of vendetta. The elders of the city, in turn, propose solutions. Money, not blood, will end this quarrel.

Mercenary exchange has frequently been held to be antithetical to the heroic ideal. One who allows himself to be bought off forfeits his claim to glory. Plato censured Homer for showing the great Achilles trading a corpse for gifts. A hero should not be represented as suffering from the "disease of mean-spirited avarice." Sallust, the Roman historian, praised the great men of Rome's early days for their disdain for gold, their preference for fame: "To be seen of all while doing a splendid deed, this they considered riches." Virgil, whose hero was the Trojan prince Aeneas, cast Achilles as the archenemy, not only of Troy but of civilization in general, and took every opportunity of discrediting him: in the *Aeneid* the events of the *Iliad* are conflated so as to suggest that Achilles was driven by financial greed, that he killed Hector with the ignoble intention of selling him. The distaste for deal making has proved persistent. At the beginning of the twentieth century members of the European nobility still thought twice before marrying their children to nouveaux riches who had made their fortunes in trade.

The heroes of the *Iliad* have no such scruples. In the terrifyingly belligerent world Homer describes, the making of a financial deal seems like a blessed release from the otherwise inevitable cycle of killing and counterkilling. As Ajax argues, "Any man will accept the blood-price paid / for a brother murdered, a child done to death." Once the price has been paid, the murderer can be reincorporated into society and the injured man must "curb his pride, his smouldering, vengeful spirit." Such transactions may run counter to the individual's craving for vengeance, but they are necessary to the preservation of the community. Far from being dishonorable, they are manifestations of praiseworthy forbearance. Achilles' refusal to accept Agamemnon's gifts along with his apology is a sign that he is still death-bent, an enemy of his own kind, a "hard, ruthless man."

He accepts the exchange Priam proposes because the old king asks it not only for his own sake but also for that of Achilles' father, who will some day grieve as he does now for the loss of a glorious son. Touched at last, Achilles weeps with him. The rage which had made him emotionally inviolable is passed. He feels pity, for Priam, for his own father, for Patroclus, for himself. He is no longer isolated, no longer either superhuman or subhuman, but part of a family, part of a race. He urges Priam to eat, as Odysseus and Thetis have each on earlier occasions urged him, the need for food being something which humbles people, reminds them of their vulnerability and of the imperative need for cooperation. He seems almost ready to countenance the compromises and sacrifices a social existence requires, to accept the limitations physicality sets to a human's behavior. Ever since Briseis was taken from him he has been set on a suicidal course. "Only death submits to no man," says Agamemnon, infuriated by his obduracy, but Achilles has been as implacable as death, and implacably set on dying. Perhaps, if it were open to him to chose again, he might this time chose survival. But he is given no second chance. Priam returns to Troy with Hector's body. For twelve days both sides observe a truce while the Trojans celebrate the funeral rites. Shortly after the fighting resumes Achilles falls.

The Romans had a legend that in earliest times a chasm opened up in the center of the Forum, threatening to yawn wide enough to swallow the city. The terrified citizens consulted the oracles, which told them that the horrid mouth would close only if Rome's greatest treasure were cast into it. A splendid young man named Curtius, handsome, brave, and nobly born, at once sprang upon his horse, and, fully armed as though for battle, put his spurs to its sides and leapt into the abyss. The earth closed over him. The city was saved. Similarly the death of Achilles, "the best of the Achaeans," opens the way for a Hellenic victory. Once their supreme warrior, their greatest treasure, has been sacrificed, the Greeks take Troy.

When the war is over, when the fabled towers of Troy are shattered, its riches plundered and its people slaughtered or enslaved, when the Greeks at last have sailed away, Poseidon and Apollo throw down the massive rampart that protected the Greek ships. The proper sacrifices were not made before building began. The prodigious wall is an impious defacement of the landscape. The gods call upon the waters of the earth to wash it away. Rivers in flood, torrential rain, the sea's breakers all batter against it until there is nothing left of that desperate labor. This war, the most celebrated in human history, is to leave no trace upon the face of the earth.

"You'd think me hardly sane," says Apollo to a fellow god, "[i]f I fought with you for the sake of wretched mortals. / Like leaves, no sooner flourishing, full of the sun's fire, / feeding on earth's gifts, than they waste away and die." Human affairs, viewed *sub specie aeternitatis*, are of gnatlike insignificance. Human aspirations are absurd. Human quarrels are petty and the human life span as short as summer's lease.

For Homer's heroes life's pathetic brevity renders it all the more precious. They have no faith in a sublime afterlife to compensate for this one's evanescence. The souls of the dead survive, but once parted from their bodies their existence is shadowy and mournful. When a warrior dies his soul goes "winging down to the House of Death, / wailing its fate, leaving his manhood far behind, / his young and supple strength." Physical beauty, the marvelous vigor and grace of the human body, these are life's splendors. The pleasures of the intellect, of stratagem and storytelling and debate, are prized as well, but they too are a part of corporeal life, dependent for their very existence on ear and tongue and brain.

Achilles and his fellows treat bodies, alive or dead, with reverence and tenderness—or with a violence which deliberately outrages the body's acknowledged sanctity. More than half of the fighting described in the *Iliad* consists of battles over corpses, as a warrior's enemies try to strip his fallen body of armor (which, poignantly, is far more durable than its wearers) while his comrades struggle to defend him from such posthumous indignity, giving their lives sometimes to save one already dead. It is the flesh that is precious; without it the spirit is of little consequence. Funerals are awesome, long drawn out, and prodigally expensive. Funeral games honor the dead by celebrating the survivors' bodily strength and swiftness and skill, insisting, even in commemoration of one who has lost it, that the breath of life is of ineffable value. And once gone it is irretrievable. Achilles refuses all Agamemnon's proffered presents, and he would refuse them even if they were as numberless as the sand, for all the world's wealth is worth less than his little time in the sun. "A man's life's breath cannot come back again once it slips through a man's clenched teeth."

But just as the disincarnate spirit is a sad and paltry thing, so the inanimate flesh is gross and open to the most squalid abuse. The dignity of embodied man is exquisitely precarious. "Oh my captains," cries Patroclus, grieving over the beleaguered Greeks. "How doomed you are . . . to glut with your shining fat / the wild dogs of battle here in Troy." The Homeric warriors, who have lived for over nine years by a battlefield, the horrors of war perpetually before their eyes, are haunted by the knowledge that the strong arms, the tireless shoulders, the springy knees in which they take such pride are also so much grease to be melted and swallowed up by the impartial earth, so many joints of meat. In one of this harsh poem's most desolating passages King Priam foresees his own death: "The dogs before my doors / Will eat me raw . . . The very dogs / I bred in my own halls to share my table . . . mad, rabid at heart they'll lap their master's blood." Death cancels all relationship, annuls all status. "The dogs go at the grey head and the grey beard / and mutilate the genitals." Even a king like Priam, his life's breath gone, is reduced to unlovely matter, defenseless, disgusting. When Zeus sees Achilles' immortal horses weeping for Patroclus he apologizes to them for having sent them to live with mortals, whose inevitable destiny is so pitiful, so degrading: "There is nothing alive more agonised than man."

There is one way to salvage something from the brutal fact of death. To the Homeric warriors it seemed that the fearless confrontation of violence with more violence might be a way to transform themselves from destructible things into indestructible memories. A man without courage is mere evanescent matter. "You can all turn to earth and water—rot away," Menelaus tells the Greeks when none among them is brave enough to take up Hector's challenge to single combat. But a man ready to go out and meet death, cheats it. The battlefield, as Homer tells us over and over again, is where "men win glory," and the winning of glory, for the ancients, had a precise and urgent purpose. "Ah my friend," says Sarpedon to his comrade, "if you and I could escape this fray and live forever, never a trace of age, immortal, / I would never fight on the front lines again / or command you to the field where men win fame. / But now as it is, the fates of death await us / . . . and not a man alive / Can flee them or escape—so in we go for the attack! / Give our enemy glory or win it for ourselves." Only glory could palliate the grim inexorability of death. The man who attained it distinguished himself in life from the mass of his fellows, and when he died he escaped oblivion.

Achilles' surpassing beauty is precious not because of any erotic advantage it may give him but because, along with his strength and prowess, it renders him outstanding. His celebrity is profoundly important to him, as it would be to any of his peers. It is not frivolous vanity that makes him prize it so. A man who is praised and honored while he is alive may be remembered even after his body is reduced to ashes and his spirit has gone down into the dark. To be forgotten is to die utterly. To Agamemnon, facing defeat as the Trojans close on the Greek ships, the most terrible aspect of the fate awaiting him and his army is that, once they have been massacred so far from home, their memory will be "blotted out." The only moment in the *Iliad* when Achilles shows fear is when the river Xanthus comes close to overpowering him, to sweeping him away ignominiously "like some boy, some pig-boy" and threatens to bury him in slime and silt so deep that his bones will never be found, and no fine burial mound will ensure his lasting fame.

St. Augustine understood the ancients' craving for fame, and what seemed to him their overvaluation of the "windy praise of men." Looking back from the standpoint of one to whom Christ's death had offered the hope of Heaven, he wrote forgivingly of the folly with which they tried to extend and to give significance to their pathetically finite lives: "Since there was no eternal life for them what else were they to love apart from glory, whereby they chose to find even after death a sort of life on the lips of those who sang their praise?"

That windy afterlife could be attained by killing. Better still, it could be achieved by being killed in battle. In the *Odyssey* Achilles' shade and that of Agamemnon meet in the underworld. Agamemnon who, alive, insisted so vehemently on his supremacy, now defers to the other, paying tribute to Achilles' glorious end. Rank confers honor, but only a soldier's death brings glory. Murdered on his return to Mycenae by his wife Clytemnestra, Agamemnon, as the victim of a squalid and abhorrent crime, is degraded in perpetuity. He wishes, and Achilles agrees that he is right to do so, that he had been killed at Troy. Enviously he describes Achilles' funeral, the eighteen days of unbroken mourning and somber ceremony, the tears, the dirges, the burnt offerings, the games, the long cortege of men in battle armor, the resounding roar that went up when the pyre was lit, the great tomb built over the hero's bones. "Even in death your name will never die. / Great glory is yours, Achilles, / for all time, in the eyes of all mankind."

The gods held to their side of the bargain Achilles made. His fame has yet to die. For the Greeks of the classical era, for the Romans after them, and—after a lapse of nearly a thousand years during which the Greek language was all but forgotten in the West—for every educated European gentleman (and a few ladies) from the Renaissance until the beginning of the twentieth century, the two Homeric epics were the acknowledged foundations of Western culture, and "the best of the Achaeans" the prototypical hero.

In 334 BC Alexander, the twenty-two-year-old king of Macedonia, already remarkable for his daring and his vast ambition, chose to make his first landfall in Asia on the beach traditionally held to be the one where, some nine centuries earlier, the Greeks' black ships were drawn up throughout the ten harrowing years that they laid siege to Troy. Alexander slept every night with a copy of the *Iliad*, which he called his "journey-book of excellence in war," beneath his pillow along with a dagger. He claimed that his mother was descended from Achilles. He encouraged his courtiers to address him by Achilles' name. As his fleet neared the shore he dressed himself in full armor and took the helm of the royal trireme. Before embarking on his world-subduing campaign Alexander had come to pay tribute to his model.

At Troy, at this period a mere village, he refused the citizens' offer of the instrument on which Paris (also known as Alexander) used to serenade Helen. "For that lyre," he told them, "I care little. I have come for the lyre of Achilles, with which, as Homer says, he would sing of the prowess and glories of brave men." Achilles sang to himself in his tent, evoking the reputation of the heroes dead and gone among whom he wished to be numbered: so Alexander, at this momentous starting point, solemnly honored his great forerunner. Stripped naked, and anointed with oil, he ran with his companions to lay a garland on the mound believed to be Achilles' tomb.

That a young Hellenic king, ambitious of military conquest in Asia and intent on creating for himself the reputation of a warrior to compare with those of the legendary past, should choose Achilles as model and patron is perhaps predictable. But two generations earlier a great man of a very different stamp had also invoked his name. In 399 BC the seventy-year-old philosopher Socrates was put on trial in Athens, accused of refusing to recognize the city's gods, introducing new deities, and corrupting the young. He was summoned before a court consisting of five hundred of his peers, and invited to make his defense. He proceeded not to answer the charges against him but to mock them. Then, midway through his defense (as it was written down by Plato some years after the event), his tone altered. For a while his famous irony and his provocative sangfroid alike were laid aside. He was unpopular, he said, he realized that, and he had known for some time that he risked incurring a capital charge. But to one who might ask him why, in that case, he persisted in a course which was so evidently irritating to the authorities he said that he would answer, "You are mistaken, my friend, if you think that a man who is worth anything ought to spend his time weighing up the prospects of life and death. He has only one thing to consider in performing any action; that is whether he is acting justly or unjustly." If he were offered acquittal—and with it his life—on the condition that he would refrain in the future from the kind of philosophical inquiry he was accustomed to practice, he would refuse the offer. "I am not going to alter my conduct, not even if I have to die a hundred deaths."

There was an uproar in the court. Unabashed, Socrates reiterated his defiance, alluding to the passage in the *Iliad* when Thetis tells Achilles that if he reenters the fighting he will die soon, for he is doomed to fall shortly after Hector. " 'Let me die forthwith,' said [Achilles], '. . . rather than remain here by the beaked ships to be mocked, a burden on the ground.' Do you suppose that he gave a thought to death and danger?" The quotation was inaccurate but the sentiment is authentically Homeric. Achilles, like Socrates after him, refused to be a "burden on the earth," a mere lump of animated matter, obedient to the stupid or immoral decrees of others. Wherever he went, Socrates told his judges, established authority would persecute him if he continued to question it, and he would never cease to do so. A life in which he was not free to think and speak as he pleased was "not worth living." To die was preferable.

A vote was called for. Socrates was found guilty by 280 votes to 220. He spoke again. His accusers demanded the death penalty. According to Athenian law it was for the defendant to propose another, lesser punishment. Socrates believed, and most historians agree with him, that if he had asked for banishment it would have been granted. He disdained to do so. The sentence of death was voted on, and approved by a substantially larger majority than the verdict (indicating that there were more people in court who wanted Socrates dead than there were people who believed him to be guilty as charged). He spoke again, asserting that he was content because the satisfaction of acting rightly, according to one's own lights of reason and moral discrimination, was so great as to eclipse any suffering: "Nothing can harm a good man either in life or after death." Defiant, courageous, intransigent, he had proved himself equal to the example he invoked in court, Achilles.

A man of violence who admitted that he was easily bested in debate, whose passions were hectic and whose thought processes were frequently incoherent, who spoke his mind at all times and despised subterfuge, Achilles was in many ways a bizarre model for the philosopher who strove unceasingly to subject emotion to reason, who was a master of irony and a brilliant manipulator of men's minds. But the classical philosopher and the legendary warrior were, for all their differences, soulmates.

Alexander, world conqueror in the making, sought to associate himself with Achilles' youthful valor and invincibility, with the glittering, deadly warrior whose brilliance rivaled the splendor of the midday sun. But when Socrates, the impecunious, pug-nosed, incorrigible old worrier of complacent authority and scourge of dishonest thinking, claimed Achilles as a predecessor, he did so in appreciation of the fact that Achilles was more than a killer of unparalleled charisma, that he could be taken as a model in peace as well as in war, as one who insisted that his life should be worthy of his own estimation of his own tremendous value as an individual, and who would pay the price required to invest that life with significance and dignity, even if the price were life itself. Socrates defied convention and eventually fell foul of the law because he would submit to no other dictates than those of his intellect and of his private daemon. Achilles rebelled against Agamemnon's overlordship, and looked on relentless while his countrymen were slaughtered rather than compromise his honor. Both were stubborn and self-destructive, to the exasperation of their enemies and the dismay of their friends. Both insisted on valuing their own personal integrity higher than any service or disservice they might do the community. Both have been condemned for their culpable pride, and venerated for their courage and their superb defiance.

In his tent at the extreme end of the Greek encampment, sworn to inaction, isolated by his own rage and by others' fear of it, Achilles set himself at odds with the fractured, fudged-together thing that society necessarily is. Any human group, be it a family, a city, an army, or a nation, depends for its continued existence on its members' willingness to bend and yield, to compromise, to accept what is possible rather than demand what is perfect. But a society which loses sight of the standard of perfection is a dangerously unstable one: from the accommodating to the corrupt is an easy slide. Achilles and others who, like him, have stood firm, however willfully and self-destructively, on a point of principle have generally been revered by onlookers and by posterity as wholeheartedly as they have been detested by the authorities they challenge. "Become who you are!" wrote Pindar, Socrates' contemporary. It is not an easy injunction. For a man to become who he is takes a ruthless lack of concern for others' interests, monstrous solipsism, and absolute integrity. Achilles, who hated a dissembler worse than the gates of death, had the courage to make the attempt, and so died.

II

ALCIBIADES

In 405 BC the Peloponnesian War, which had lasted for a quarter of a century and set the entire Hellenic world at odds, ended with the comprehensive defeat of the Athenians at Aegospotami on the Hellespont. The fleet on which Athens depended for its security and its food supply was destroyed. Lysander, commanding the victorious Spartans, had all the defeated Athenian troops slaughtered. The ship bearing the news reached the Athenian port of Piraeus at nightfall. The wailing began down in the harbor. As the news was passed from mouth to mouth it spread gradually all along the defensive walls linking city to sea until it reached the darkened streets around the Acropolis and the whole city was heard to cry out like an enormous beast in its agony. "That night," wrote Xenophon, "no one slept. They mourned for the lost, but more still for their own fates."

The Athenians had good cause to mourn. Within a matter of months they had been blockaded and starved into submission. Their democracy had been replaced by a murderous puppet government, an oligarchy known as the Thirty Tyrants. They lived in fear, of the Spartans who were now their overlords, and of each other, for every formerly prominent person was under suspicion, informers were so active that none dared trust his neighbor, and Critias, leader of the Thirty, "began to show a lust for putting people to death." And yet, according to Plutarch, "in the midst of all their troubles a faint glimmer of hope yet remained, that the cause of Athens could never be utterly lost so long as Alcibiades was alive."

Alcibiades! The name was a charm, and its workings, like all magical processes, were beyond reason. The man on whom the Athenians, in their extremity, pinned their hopes was one whom they had three times rejected, a traitor who had worked so effectively for their enemies that there were those who held him personally responsible for Athens' downfall. Exiled from Athens for the second time, he was now living among the barbarians in Thrace. There, in a heavily fortified stronghold, with a private army at his command, he led the life of an independent warlord or bandit chief. There was no substantial reason to suppose that he could do anything for the Athenian democracy, and no certainty that he would wish to help even were it in his power to do so. And yet, as the first-century BC historian Cornelius Nepos noted, Alcibiades was a man from whom miracles, whether malign or beneficent, had always been expected: "The people thought there was nothing he could not accomplish."

Plato, who knew Alcibiades, elaborates in *The Republic* what he calls a "noble lie," a fable in which he suggests that all men are made from earth, but that in a few the earth has been mixed with gold, rendering them inherently superior to their fellow men, and fit to wield power. This lie, Plato suggests, is a politically useful one. In his ideal republic, he would like to "indoctrinate" the mass of the people with a belief in it, in order that they might be the more easily governed. It would probably not be hard to do so. The belief that some people are innately different from and better than others pervades all pagan mythology and classical legend and surfaces as well in folk tales and fairy stories. The foundling whose white skin proclaims her noble birth, the favored younger son who survives his ordeals assisted by the birds and beasts who recognize his privileged status, the emperor-to-be whose birth is attended by tremendous omens— all spring, as Plato's men of gold do, from a profoundly anti-egalitarian collective belief in, and yearning for, the existence of a naturally occurring elite, of exceptional beings capable of leading their subordinates to victory, of averting evil and playing savior, or simply of providing by their prodigious feats a spectacle capable of exhilarating and inspiring the humdrum multitude. In Alcibiades the Athenians found their golden man.

That Alcibiades was indeed an extraordinary person is well attested. All his life he had a quality, which his contemporaries were at a loss to define or explain, which inspired admiration, fear, and vast irrational hopes. "No one ever exceeded Alcibiades," wrote Nepos, "in his faults or in his virtues." His contemporaries recognized in him something demonic and excessive which both alarmed and excited them. Plutarch likened him to the fertile soil of Egypt, so rich that it brings forth wholesome drugs and poisons in equally phenomenal abundance. He was a beauty and a bully, an arrogant libertine and a shrewd diplomat, an orator as eloquent when urging on his troops as when lying to save his life, a traitor three or four times over with a rare and precious gift (essential to a military commander) for winning his men's love. There was a time when his prodigious energy and talents terrified many Athenians, who feared that a man so exceptional must surely aim to make himself a tyrant, but in their despair they looked to him as a redeemer.

His adult life coincided almost exactly with the duration of the Peloponnesian War, which began in 431 BC, when he was nineteen, and ended with the fall of Athens in 405, the year before his death. Throughout that period, with brief interludes, the Spartans and their allies (known collectively as the Peloponnesians) struggled against the Athenians, with their allies and colonies, for ascendancy, while lesser powers repeatedly shifted allegiance, tilting the balance of power first that way, then this. Sparta was a rigidly conservative state with a curious and ancient constitution in which two hereditary kings ruled alongside, and were outranked by, a council of grandees, the ephors, selected from a handful of noble families. Spartan colonies had oligarchic governments imposed upon them. Athens was a democracy, and founded democracies in its colonies. The war had an ideological theme, but it was also a competition between two aggressively expansionist rival powers for political and economic dominance of the eastern Mediterranean. From 412 onwards it was complicated by the intervention of the Persians, whose empire dwarfed both the Hellenic alliances. Athens' successful colonization of the Aegean islands and the coastal regions of Asia Minor deprived the Persian Great King of revenue. His regional governors, the satraps, sided first with Spartans, later with Athens, in an attempt to reestablish control of the area. Alcibiades, who had Odysseus' cunning as well as Achilles' brilliance, was a skillful actor in the complex, deadly theater of the war. As a general he was swift, subtle, and daring. As a diplomat he proved himself to be a confidence trickster of genius.

In his youth he was the golden boy of Athens' golden age. His family was rich, aristocratic (they claimed descent from Homer's Nestor), and well connected not only in Athens but all over the Greek world. In constitutional terms every free male citizen of Athens was equal to every other, but in practice the nobility still dominated the government as they did the city's economic and social life. "The splendour running in the blood has much weight," wrote Pindar. When Alcibiades was still a child his father was killed in battle, and he was taken to live in the household of his guardian Pericles, who was for thirty years effective ruler of Athens. He could scarcely have been given a better start in life.

Nature was as kind to him as fortune had been. Like Achilles, he was dazzlingly beautiful. To Plutarch, writing five hundred years after his death, his loveliness was still so much of a byword that "we need say no more about it, than that it flowered at each season of his growth in turn." In the homoerotic society of Athens such good looks made him an instant celebrity. As a boy he was "surrounded and pursued by many admirers of high rank ... captivated by the brilliance of his youthful beauty." Whether he actually had sexual relations with any of them is unclear, but gossip maintained that he did. If so, few of his contemporaries would therefore have considered him either immoral or effete. Aeschylus, in the generation before Alcibiades, and Plato, his contemporary, both believed Achilles to be Patroclus's lover (something Homer does not suggest), but neither of them thought any the less of him for it. On the contrary Plato's Phaedus cites Achilles' "heroic choice to go and rescue Patroclus" as an example of the way in which love can ennoble a man, earning him "the extreme admiration of the Gods."

Among those smitten by Pericles' ward was Socrates, who told a disciple that the two great loves of his life were philosophy and Alcibiades. The philosopher had gathered around himself a group of aristocratic young men, nonpaying students of whom Alcibiades was certainly not the most serious but of whom he was the most highly favored. Plato (another of them) testifies that the relationship between the ugly middle-aged philosopher and the radiantly beautiful teenager remained chaste, but it surely was, at least on Socrates' part, physically motivated. Alcibiades' appearance marked him out, just as Achilles' had done, as a superior being. In the second century AD the Roman emperor Hadrian, a connoisseur and devotee of male beauty as ardent as any Athenian, set up an image of Alcibiades in Parian marble and commanded that an ox should be sacrificed to him every year. In his lifetime as well his looks made him an object not only of lust but also of worship. And lovely as he was, his charm was as potent as his physical attractions. His personal magnetism, according to Plutarch, "was such that no disposition could wholly resist it, and no character remain unaffected." The events of his extraordinary career confirm the claim.

As a young man he was showy, extravagant, outrageous. He wore his hair as long as a woman's, spoke with a provocative lisp, and strutted through the marketplace trailing his long purple robe. He was a ringleader, a setter of trends. Eupolis reports that he started a fashion for drinking in the morning. When he appeared in a new style of sandal all his contemporaries had copies made, and called them "Alcibiades." He was proud and unbiddable, touchily conscious of his dignity as a nobleman. Plutarch relates an anecdote about him as a child playing in the street, first refusing to interrupt a game of dice in order to allow a cart to go by, and then lying down in the vehicle's path to show his defiance of the driver's threats, risking his life rather than take orders from a common carter. He refused to learn to play the flute, on the grounds that flutists made themselves look ridiculous by pursing their lips: flute playing at once went out of fashion among the smart Athenian youth. As an adolescent, according to his son, he disliked the favorite Athenian sport of wrestling because "some of the athletes were of low birth." As an adult he was a keen breeder and trainer of horses, an amusement open only to the rich. He carried himself as one who knows himself to be a superior being, by virtue of his class but also because his gifts fitted him for a splendid destiny and because his gargantuan vitality would settle for no less. Plato records Socrates saying to him, "You appear to me such that if any god were to say to you, 'Are you willing, Alcibiades, to live having what you now do, or would you choose to die instantly unless you were permitted greater things?' you would prefer to die." Socrates was not talking about material possessions. "Further, if the same god said, 'You can be master here in Europe, but will not be allowed to pass over into Asia,' it appears to me that you would not even on those terms be willing to live, unless you could fill the mouths of all men with your name and power." Like Achilles, Alcibiades, according to those intimate with him, had no use for an unremarkable life.

The device on his extravagantly splendid ivory and gold shield showed Eros with a thunderbolt, an image combining aggressive sexuality with elemental violence, which nicely encapsulates the impression he made. He was prodigally, flashily generous. It was customary for wealthy Athenians with political ambitions to woo the populace by subsidizing choral performances and other public shows; Alcibiades' were always the most lavish. His first public action was, characteristically, an act of munificence. He happened to be passing the place of assembly and overheard the applause with which citizens who had made voluntary contributions to the treasury were being received. He was carrying a live quail under his cloak but, undeterred, he went in, pledged a large sum, and at the same time inadvertently released the bird. There was laughter and a scramble which ended in a seaman named Antiochus catching the quail and handing it back to Alcibiades. (The meeting was to prove a fateful one. Antiochus's next appearance in recorded history is in the role of catalyst for Alcibiades' downfall.) The rich young dilettante whose mind was on sport had demonstrated that he could, if he chose, be of substantial service to the state.

While still in his teens Alcibiades served his stint in the army, as all Athenians were obliged to, sharing a tent with Socrates. Philosopher and disciple each acquitted himself well but when Socrates saved the younger man's life, fighting off the enemy when he lay wounded, it was Alcibiades who was awarded a crown and suit of armor as a prize for valor—an injustice which owes something to Socrates' selflessness, something to the generals' snobbery, and something as well to Alcibiades' frequently noted gift for gaining the credit for more than he had actually performed. His actions were as ostentatious as his appearance. "Love of distinction and desire for fame" were, according to Plutarch, the engines that drove him. But courageous he certainly was, and popular with both the common soldiers and those who commanded him.

Warfare provided an outlet for his prodigious energies. In civilian life, they festered. Cornelius Nepos praises his accomplishments and abilities but goes on: "but yet, so soon as he relaxed his efforts and there was nothing that called for mental exertion, he gave himself again to extravagance, indifference, licentiousness, depravity." He had voracious appetites, for sex, for drink, for luxury of all kinds, and he had the money to indulge them all. Already very rich himself, he married Hipparete, one of the wealthiest heiresses in Athens. The wedding seems to have scarcely interrupted his scandalous series of liaisons with courtesans. Scurrilous gossip later accused him of incest with his sister, mother, and illegitimate daughter. The charges are lurid and unconvincing (there is no other evidence that he even had a sister), but his reputation for promiscuity was undoubtedly well founded.

He was a high-handed swaggerer, someone by whom others were readily intimidated and who took pleasure in trying his power. He was jealous. Even Socrates said of him, albeit teasingly, "I am really quite scared by his mad behaviour and the intensity of his affections." He was violent. As a boy he had beaten up a teacher who confessed to owning no copy of Homer's works (an assault which was generally agreed—such was the mystique accorded the two epics—to redound to the perpetrator's credit). He once struck his father-in-law simply for a wager. He thrashed a political rival. He was rumored to have killed a servant. When he wanted his house decorated with murals he abducted the distinguished painter Agatharchus, locked him up in the house until he had done the work, then sent him home with a cartload of gold. Annoyed by one of the many older men who doted on him, he refused an invitation to dinner but then arrived at the party, late and visibly drunk, with a gang of slaves whom he ordered to seize half of the gold and silver vessels laid out to impress the guests. When Hipparete, rendered desperate by his shameless infidelities, appeared before the magistrates to petition for a divorce, Alcibiades interrupted the proceedings, seized her, and carried her home through the marketplace "and not a soul dared oppose him or take her from him." Such delinquency in one so high placed and privileged was unnerving. It threatened to disrupt not only the lives of his immediate circle, but that of the whole community which observed him, fascinated and fearful. Timon, the notorious misanthrope, once accosted Alcibiades in the street, shook him by the hand, and said, "You are doing well, my boy! Go on like this and you will soon be big enough to ruin the lot of them."

As befitted Pericles' ward, he soon began to make his mark in the Assembly, displaying, according to the great Demosthenes himself, an "extraordinary power" of oratory. Pericles had died in 429 BC. By 421 Alcibiades, though not yet thirty, was one of the two most influential men in the city. The other, Nicias, was in nearly every way his opposite. Older than his rival by twenty years, Nicias was cautious, timid, and notoriously superstitious. Alcibiades' indiscretions were brazen; Nicias used to shut himself up in his house at night rather than waste time or risk being duped by a spy. Alcibiades liked to dazzle the public; Nicias was careful to ascribe his success to the favor of the gods in order to avoid provoking envy. Most importantly, Alcibiades saw the by now protracted war against the Spartans as a splendid opportunity for the aggrandizement of himself and of his city; Nicias longed only to end it.

In 421 BC he succeeded temporarily in doing so. He negotiated a treaty whereby the Peloponnesians and the Athenians agreed to exchange prisoners and to restore all of each other's captured territory. But, as Plutarch records, "No sooner had [Nicias] set his country's affairs on the path of safety than the force of Alcibiades' ambition bore down upon him like a torrent, and all was swept back into the tumult of war." There were disputes about the procedure for restoring the conquered cities and fortresses, disputes which Alcibiades aggravated and exploited. A Spartan delegation arrived in Athens. Alcibiades tricked them and undermined their standing, ensuring that the Assembly would refuse to deal with them and sending them home humiliated and enraged. Nicias followed after them but was unable to repair the damage: the Spartans rejected his overtures, and the Athenians had lost their enthusiasm for the peace. Alcibiades was elected general—for one year, as was the custom. He forged an alliance with Mantinea, Elis, and Argos, and took Athens back to war.

There were those who accused him of making war for personal gain. Certainly there were prizes to be won which he would have welcomed. He had a reputation for financial rapacity. His father-in-law (or brother-in-law: accounts differ) was so afraid of him that he entrusted his enormous fortune to the state, lest Alcibiades might be tempted to kill him for it. He had already, after demanding a dowry of unprecedented size, extorted a second equally enormous sum from his wife's family on the birth of their first child. His wealth was immense, but so was his expenditure. "His enthusiasm for horse-breeding and other extravagances went beyond what his fortune could supply," wrote Thucydides. Besides, in the Athenian democracy (as in several of the modern democracies for which Athens is a model), only the very rich could aspire to the highest power. Alcibiades needed money to pay for choruses, for largesse, for personal display designed not solely to gratify his personal vanity but to advertise his status as a great man.

But the war offered him far more than money. It provided him with a task hard and exhilarating enough to channel even his fantastic vitality, and it afforded an opportunity for him to satisfy the driving ambition Socrates had seen in him. Nicias, his rival, understood him well, and paid backhanded tribute to his eagerness for glory when he told the Athenian Assembly to "beware of [Alcibiades] and do not give him the chance of endangering the state in order to live a brilliant life of his own."

As advocate for the war, Alcibiades was spokesman for the young and restless, and also for the lower classes. He probably belonged to one of the clubs of wealthy young Athenians, clubs which were generally (and correctly) suspected to be breeding places of oligarchic conspiracy, but there is no evidence he had any such sympathies. Haughty and spectacularly overprivileged as he was, his political affiliations were democratic. In his personal life he defied class divisions. Homer's lordly Achilles detests the insolent commoner Thersites, and in an extra-Homeric version of the tale of Troy he kills him, thus upholding the dignity of the warrior caste and silencing the mockery of the people. Alcibiades would not have done so. He earned the disapproval of his peers by consorting with actors and courtesans and other riffraff, and he was to remain friends for most of his life with Antiochus, the common seaman who caught his quail. Politically he followed the example of his guardian Pericles in establishing his power base among the poorer people, who tended to favor war. Military conflict was expensive for the upper classes, who were obliged to pay for men and ships, but it offered employment, decent pay, and a chance of booty to the masses. According to Diodorus Siculus it was the youthful Alcibiades who urged Pericles to embroil Athens in the Peloponnesian War as a way of enhancing his own standing and diverting popular attention from his misdemeanors. Certainly Alcibiades would have learned from observing his guardian's career that, as Diodorus puts it, "in time of war the populace has respect for noble men because of their urgent need of them . . . whereas in time of peace they keep bringing false accusations against the very same men, because they have nothing to do and are envious."

The Athenian alliance was defeated in 418 BC at the battle of Mantinea, but its failure cannot be blamed on Alcibiades, whose term as general had elapsed. During the following years he loomed ever larger in the small world of Athens, menacing those who mistrusted him, dazzling his many admirers. Everything about him was excessive—his wildness, his glamour, his ambition, his self-regard, the love he inspired. In a society whose watchword was "Moderation in all things" he was a fascinatingly transgressive figure, an embodiment of riskiness, of exuberance, of latent power. "The fact was," writes Plutarch, "that his voluntary donations, the public shows he supported, his unrivalled munificence to the state, the fame of his ancestry, the power of his oratory and his physical strength and beauty, together with his experience and prowess in war, all combined to make the Athenians forgive him everything else."

The dinner party described in Plato's *Symposium*, which contains the fullest contemporary description of Alcibiades, dates from this period. The host is the poet Agathon, who is celebrating having won the tragedian's prize. As the wine goes round, the guests, each in turn, talk about love. They are serious, competitive, rapt. At last it is Socrates' turn. In what has proved one of the most influential speeches ever written, he enunciates his deadly vision of a love divested in turn of physicality, of human affection, of any reference whatsoever to our material existence. He finishes. There is some applause and then—right on cue—comes a loud knocking at the door. There is an uproar in the courtyard, the sounds of a flute and of a well-known voice shouting, and suddenly there in the doorway is the living refutation of Socrates' austere transcendentalism. The philosopher has been preaching against the excitements of the flesh and the elation attendant on temporal power. To mock him comes Alcibiades, wild with drink, his wreath of ivy and violets slanted over his eyes, flirtatious, arrogant, alarming, a figure of physical splendor and worldly pride forcing himself into that solemn company like a second Dionysus. No wonder, as Nepos wrote, Alcibiades filled his fellow Athenians "with the highest hopes, but also with profound apprehension."

In 416 BC, when he was thirty-four, he entered no fewer than seven chariots in the games at Olympia—something no one, commoner or king, had ever done before him—and carried off three prizes. Euripides wrote a celebratory ode: "Victory shines like a star, but yours eclipses all victories." The games were far more than a sporting event: they were festivals of great religious and political significance attended by crowds from all over the Greek world. Alcibiades celebrated his triumph with superb ostentation, drawing on the resources of his far-flung clients and dependents, pointedly making a display of a network of personal influence spreading all the way across the eastern Mediterranean. "The people of Ephesus erected a magnificently decorated tent for him. Chios supplied fodder for his horses and large number of animals for sacrifice, while Lesbos presented him with wine and other provisions which allowed him to entertain lavishly." Alcibiades was only a private citizen, but with his wealth and his pan-Hellenic connections he formed, on his own, a political entity which looked like rivalling Athens itself.

It was too much. On the plain before Troy Achilles had measured his status as an outstandingly gifted individual against Agamemnon's regal authority. At Olympia Alcibiades, in parading his wealth, his influence, and his talent, seemed to be issuing a parallel challenge to the state of which he was part but which he threatened to eclipse. So, anyway, his contemporaries understood the spectacle. He was accused of having the city's gold and silver ceremonial vessels carried in his triumphal procession and of having used them at his own table "as if they were his own." Non-Athenians, maintained one of his critics, "laughed at us when they saw one man showing himself superior to the entire community." Answering the grumblers Alcibiades asserted that in making himself splendid he was doing a service to his country, that a city needs its illustrious men to personify its power. "There was a time when the Hellenes imagined that our city had been ruined by the war, but they came to consider it even greater than it really is because of the splendid show I made as its representative at the Olympic games. . . . Indeed this is a very useful kind of folly, when a man spends his own money not only to benefit himself but his city as well." Not everyone was convinced. After Alcibiades won another victory at the Nemean Games, the great painter Aristophon exhibited a portrait of him. Any visual representation of him, it should be remembered, would have paid tribute to his striking beauty, and beauty, in fifth-century Athens, was commonly understood to make a man eligible for far more than mere sexual conquest. "This much is clear," wrote Aristotle in the next generation, "suppose that there were men whose bodily physique showed the same superiority as is shown by the statues of the gods, then all would agree that the rest of mankind would deserve to be their slaves." The people crowded to see Aristophon's painting, but there were those who "thought it a sight fit only for a tyrant's court and an insult to the laws of Athens." There was no place within a democracy for an Alcibiades. "Men of sense," warned a contemporary orator in an address entitled "Against Alcibiades," "should beware of those of their fellows who grow too great, remembering it is such as they that set up tyrannies."

In the winter of 416/415 BC Alcibiades was at last presented with an adventure commensurate with his ambition. A delegation arrived in Athens from Sicily, asking the Athenians to intervene in a war between their own colonists there and the people of Syracuse, which was a colony and powerful ally of the Spartans. The careful Nicias put forward sound arguments against undertaking such a risky and unnecessary venture, but Alcibiades was all for action, and, according to Plutarch, he "dazzled the imagination of the people and corrupted their judgement with the glittering prospects he held out." All Athens caught his war fever. The young men in the wrestling schools and the old men in the meeting places sat sketching maps of Sicily in the sand, intoxicating themselves with visions of conquest and of glory. The projected invasion of Sicily was not expedient, it was not prudent, it was not required by any treaty or acknowledged code of obligation, but its prospect offered excitement, booty, and the intangible rewards of honor. In the Assembly Alcibiades, the man of whom it was said that without some great enterprise to engage his energies he became decadent, self-destructive, and a danger to others, ascribed to the state a character to match his own: "My view is that a city which is active by nature will soon ruin itself if it changes its nature and becomes idle." He argued that, like himself, Athens was the object of envy and resentment, impelled for its own safety to make itself ever greater and greater. "It is not possible for us to calculate, like housekeepers, exactly how much empire we want to have." At Olympia, he claimed, Alcibiades was identified with Athens. Now, in urging the war in Sicily, he was offering Athens the chance to identify with Alcibiades, to be, like him, bold and reckless and superbly overweening.

He won fervent support. Nicias, in a last attempt to halt the folly, pointed out that the subduing of all the hostile cities in Sicily would require a vast armada, far larger and more expensive than the modest expeditionary force initially proposed. But the Assembly had by this time cast parsimony as well as prudence to the winds. They voted to raise and equip an army and navy commensurate with their tremendous purpose.

The generals appointed to command the expedition were one Lamachus, the appalled and reluctant Nicias, and Alcibiades.

The resulting host's might was matched by its splendor. The captains (gentlemanly amateurs whose civic duty it was to outfit their own ships) had "gone to great expense on figureheads and general fittings, every one of them being as anxious as possible that his own ships should stand out from the rest for its fine looks and for its speed." Those who would fight on land had taken an equally competitive pride in their handsome armor. When the fleet lay ready off Piraeus it was, according to Thucydides, "by a long way the most costly and finest-looking force of Hellenic troops that up to that time had ever come from a single city."

On the appointed day, shortly after midsummer, almost the entire population of Athens went down to the waterfront to watch the fleet sail. A trumpet sounded for silence. A herald led all of the vast crowds on ship and shore in prayer. The men poured libations of wine from gold and silver bowls into the sea. A solemn hymn was sung. Slowly the ships filed out of the harbor, then, assembling in open sea, they raced each other southwards. All the onlookers marveled at the expedition's setting out, at "its astonishing daring and the brilliant show it made," and were awed at the "demonstration of the power and greatness of Athens," and incidentally the power and greatness of Alcibiades, the expedition's instigator and co-commander. This was a triumph to make his victory at Olympia seem trivial, or it would have been, but that by the time he sailed out at the head of the great fleet Alcibiades' downfall was already accomplished. The brilliant commander was also a suspected criminal on parole. The Athenians, who had entrusted the leadership of this grand and perilous enterprise to Alcibiades, had given him notice that on his return he must stand trial for his life. In his story the pride and the fall are simultaneous.

One morning, shortly before the armada was due to sail, the Athenians awoke to find that overnight all the hermae, the familiar idols which stood everywhere, on street corners, in the porches of private houses, in temples, had been mutilated. A wave of shock and terror ran through the city. The hermae represented the god Hermes. Often little more than crude blocks of stone topped with a face and displaying an erect penis in front, they were objects both of affection and of reverence. Thucydides called them "a national institution." Now their faces had been smashed, and, according to Aristophanes, their penises hacked off. The outrage threatened the Athenians at every level. The gods must be angry, or if not angry before they would certainly have been enraged by the sacrilege. This was the worst possible omen for the projected expedition. Besides it was terrifying to imagine the presence in the city of a hostile group numerous enough to perpetrate such a laborious outrage in a single night. There were panic-stricken rumors. Some held the city had been infiltrated by enemies from elsewhere—possibly Corinthians. Others asserted that the culprits were treacherous Athenians, that the desecration was the first manifestation of a conspiracy to overthrow the democracy. An investigation was launched. Rewards were offered to anyone coming forward with useful information and informers' immunity was guaranteed. One Andocides accused himself and other members of his club, which may well have been an association of would-be oligarchs, but Thucydides (along with most other ancient sources) seems to have considered his confession a false one: "Neither then nor later could anyone say with certainty who had committed the deed."

In the atmosphere of panic and universal suspicion, other dark doings came to light. It was a fine time for the undoing of reputations. Alcibiades had many opponents. Nicias's supporters resented his popularity. So did the radical demagogues, especially one Androcles, who was instrumental in finding, and perhaps bribing, slaves and foreigners ready to testify to the investigators. Three separate informers, apparently seeing one form of sacrilege as being much the same as another, told stories of the Eleusinian Mysteries—the sacred rites of Demeter which none but the initiated might witness—being enacted, or rather parodied, at the houses of various aristocratic young men. On all three occasions Alcibiades was said to have been present, and at one he was alleged to have played the part of the high priest. The punishment for such a impious action could only be death.

The allegation was, and remains, credible. Fourteen years later Socrates was to die on a charge of failing to honor the city's gods, a charge against which he scarcely deigned to defend himself, and Socrates had been Alcibiades' mentor. It is unlikely the young general was in any conventional sense devout, and his "insolence" and readiness to breach taboos were well known. Gossip had it that he had even staged a mock murder, shown the corpse to his friends and asked them to help conceal the crime. If he was ready to make a game of the solemnity of death, why should he be expected to stop short of blaspheming against the gods?

Whatever the truth, Alcibiades vociferously asserted his innocence, and declared his readiness to stand trial and clear his name. His opponents demurred. He was the charismatic leader of the expedition from which all Athenians were hoping for so much. His popularity was at its height. Thucydides writes that his enemies feared that the people would be overlenient with him were he to come to trial. They probably feared more than that. "All the soldiers and sailors who were about to embark for Sicily were on his side, and the force of 1,000 Argive and Mantinean infantry had openly declared that it was only on Alcibiades' account they were going to cross the sea and fight in a distant land." The expeditionary force was, in effect, his army. To impeach him while it lay in the harbor would trigger a mutiny. To put him to death might well start a civil war. His accusers temporized. They did not wish to delay the fleet's departure, they said. Alcibiades would sail, but the charges against him remained outstanding. On his return, whatever happened in Sicily, he would face his accusers.

Perhaps a quick victory might have made it possible for him to win his case and salvage his position, but that victory was not forthcoming. The money, essential for the maintenance of the expeditionary force, that had been promised by the Athenian colonies in Sicily had never existed. Cities they had thought their allies refused to let them land. Alcibiades managed to take Catania, but it was a small gain and it came too late. At home in Athens more informers had been coming forward. With so many of the fighting men who admired him absent on campaign he had fewer supporters left in the city. Without his presence to dazzle or intimidate them the Assembly turned against him. In August, only weeks after he had sailed out of Piraeus with such pomp, the *Salaminia*, the state ship, arrived at Catania bringing orders recalling him at once to Athens to answer the charges against him.

This, Alcibiades' first fall, was brought about in part by himself—whether or not he was guilty as charged, he had undoubtedly been reckless in his defiance of conventional propriety and arrogant in his disdain for the public's opinion of his wild ways—and in part by the intrigues of his political rivals. But beyond those immediate causes of his downfall lies something more nebulous and more fundamental. Alcibiades was a hero. He had the charisma and the prodigious talents of his legendary predecessors. And the Athenians feared their heroes as fervently as they worshiped them, and they feared even more the tendency to hero worship in themselves.

Months before his fall Alcibiades had told the Assembly he knew full well that "people whose brilliance has made them prominent" aroused suspicion and dislike. Aristotle expressed a popular sentiment when he described a polity which contained an outstanding individual as being as ill proportioned as a portrait in which one foot was gigantic. Alcibiades had already been subjected to one of the methods by which the Athenians rid themselves of those grown too great. In 417 BC an ostracism had been proposed. "They employ this measure from time to time," wrote Plutarch, "in order to cripple and drive out any man whose power and reputation in the city may have risen to exceptional heights." Each citizen wrote a name on a potsherd. The unfortunate winner of most votes was banished for ten years. The target in this case was either Alcibiades or Nicias, but the two joined forces and by vigorous campaigning contrived that the majority of votes went to a comparative nonentity (who was probably the instigator of the ostracism). It was, for Alcibiades, a warning of how wary his compatriots were of their great men. There were plenty of other instances to underline the point. In Alcibiades' lifetime Phidias, the sculptor and designer of the Parthenon, was jailed on a charge of sacrilege. Pericles himself was stripped of his command and fined the enormous sum of fifteen talents when the Assembly agreed to blame him for the plague (a decision which, in ascribing to him a power to rival that of Providence, was in itself a kind of tribute to his superhuman capacity). The astronomer Anaxagoras was imprisoned, Euripides was so slighted that he left Athens for Macedonia, and five years after Alcibiades died his mentor and the love of his youth, Socrates, was put to death. "The people were ready to make use of men who excelled," wrote Plutarch, "but they still looked on them with suspicion and constantly strove to humble their pride."

Alcibiades was not only exceptional; he was also bellicose. The Athenians were a fighting people, but they were also justly proud of their great creation, a civilization based on the resolution of differences by nonviolent dispute. The heroes of old were still worshiped in classical Athens. Hero cults were numerous, and attracted distinguished devotees: Alcibiades' contemporary Sophocles was a priest in the cult of the hero Halon. But the heroes were fierce spirits who had to be propitiated. They were thirsty for blood, which was poured, after dark, into trenches at the supposed site of their burials, and if they were not appeased their anger was terrible.

"Let me seize great glory," Homer's Achilles begs his mother, "and drive some woman of Troy . . . / to claw with both hands at her tender cheeks and wipe away / her burning tears as the sobs come choking from her throat." Homer's warriors know full well that their splendid exploits are the cause of others' grief; they may regret the fact, but they do not balk at it. To later generations, though, their ruthlessness came to seem

savage and abhorrent. In the *Iliad* Achilles sacrifices twelve Trojan prisoners on Patroclus's pyre, slaughtering them in cold blood and hacking their
bodies to pieces. Homer reports his action briefly and without condem-
nation, but to Euripides, who had celebrated Alcibiades' Olympic victory
with a song, Achilles' human sacrifices were monstrous. In his *Hecuba*
Achilles' ghost demands the slaughter of the Trojan princess Polyxena on
his grave. In *Iphigenia at Aulis* Achilles is associated with Agamemnon's
sacrifice of his daughter. If she were not killed there would be no wind to
carry the black ships to Troy, no war in which Achilles could demonstrate
his valor. The death of the innocent girl is the necessary prerequisite for
the fulfillment of the warrior's glorious destiny: both the hero and his
glory are tainted with her blood. In the second century AD Flavius Philostratus told a story about Achilles' ghost appearing to a merchant and
demanding a slave girl who boasted of being descended from King Priam.
The merchant, terrified, handed her over. The spectral hero fell upon her
and tore her to pieces. In the light cast backwards across time by these
horrific stories Homer's account of Achilles' rage takes on a different
shading. The brilliant warrior is also the serial killer, the slaughterer of
fathers, husbands, farmers, councillors, the enemy of all women, the
destroyer of civilized society.

The shattered hermae were not the only ominous sight in the streets
of Athens at the time the Sicilian expedition sailed out with Alcibiades as
one of its commanders. It was the festival of Adonis, and groups of
women dressed as though in deep mourning were carrying effigies of the
dead youth, the beautiful young man whom Venus had loved, through
the streets, wailing as they went. Later, when the terrible outcome of the
expedition was known, the somber processions were remembered as
presages of what was to come and, more particularly, as reminders of the
price to others of one man's glory. If the campaign was to fulfill what
Socrates had identified as being Alcibiades' ambition, "to fill the mouths
of all men with your name and power," it would do so only at the cost of
many other young men's lives. It was a price the Athenians did not pay
gladly. In one of the reversals frequent in the history of Athenian democracy the people first allowed themselves to be seduced by Alcibiades' high
talk of glorious conquest, and then, in a fit of self-disgust and revulsion,
punished him for their own lapse into irrationality.

Alcibiades was not placed under arrest when the *Salaminia* arrived in
Sicily. His opponents still feared provoking a mutiny, and as Plutarch
remarked, Alcibiades "might very easily have brought this about if he had
wished." But he preferred the role of exile to that of rebel. Apparently

docile, he agreed to follow the *Salaminia* home in his own ship. In southern Italy he put ashore, and vanished. The Athenian Assembly tried him in his absence and condemned him to death. His estate was confiscated. His name was inscribed on a stele set up on the Acropolis as a monument to his disgrace. All the priests and priestesses of Athens were ordered to call down curses on him. A reward of a talent (a considerable fortune) was offered to anyone who could bring him in, dead or alive. Three months after he had sailed from Athens with such pomp and splendor he was an outcast, a hunted man with a price on his head.

What Alcibiades did next has identified him, in the opinion of many latter-day historians, as an unprincipled scoundrel. When he heard of the death sentence pronounced against him he is reported to have said grimly, "I will show them I am still alive." Achilles turned traitor after his quarrel with Agamemnon, praying that his fellow Greeks should be beaten back to their ships. So, now, did Alcibiades. Before he even left Sicily he had begun his treachery. The Athenians had contacted an opposition group in the Sicilian city of Messina and arranged that they should open the gates to an Athenian attack. Alcibiades informed the pro-Spartan authorities in Messina of the plot. The attack was thwarted and the conspirators were put to death. From Italy Alcibiades crossed to the Peloponnese, and after first sending to ask for a guarantee of his safety, he made his way to Sparta. There he offered his services to his hosts, his native city's archenemies. He urged them to intervene in Sicily (which they did, with devastating consequences for the Athenians). He also suggested that they do what the Athenians had for years been dreading that they might do, fortify the stronghold of Decelea in the mountains north of Athens which commanded the route whereby the revenue from the silver mines, the tribute money from the offshore colonies, and, most importantly, food supplies reached Athens. The Spartans acted on his advice. "It was this, more than any other single action," remarks Plutarch, "which wore down the resources of Athens, and finally ruined her."

Such a betrayal, surely, could never be forgiven. Yet this was the same Alcibiades whom the Athenians were to welcome back seven years later with garlands and embraces and cries of joy, whom they crowned with a golden crown and elected general with supreme powers on both land and sea, the same Alcibiades of whom it was said that while he lived Athens could not die.

. . .

We live in a postnationalist age, one in which Alcibiades' disloyalty to his native city seems an absolute disqualification from the pantheon of heroes. But treason has not always been judged the action of the mean-spirited. A hero may demonstrate his grandeur as an individual by the disdain with which he ignores or transgresses the obligations which bind ordinary people to each other or to the state. Achilles despised the kind of status attainable by allegiance to a community of petty mortals, looking to Zeus alone for confirmation of his honor. So, after the Athenians condemned him to death, Alcibiades, as far as his motives can be guessed at, acted for the rest of his life for himself alone, serving now Athens' enemies, now Athens herself again, true only to himself and his limitless ambition. His Athenian contemporaries intermittently feared and distrusted him. Some hated him. But, traitor though he was, they did not despise him.

The relationship between the individual and the community in fifth-century Athens was an unstable one. The democratic Assembly was terrifyingly fickle, inclined to turn savagely on its own servants. The generals who later replaced Alcibiades (after he was stripped of his command for the second time in 406 BC) were all put to death for alleged misconduct during a battle which they had won for Athens. And just as the state could and did abandon its citizens, so citizens could quit the state. Both of the two great Athenian historians who wrote as contemporaries of Alcibiades, Thucydides and Xenophon, were to spend the majority of their adult lives away from the city, the former exiled for a military failure, the latter leaving of his own free will to serve first the Persian pretender Cyrus and subsequently the Spartans. Alcibiades' defection would not have outraged his contemporaries to anything like the extent that it has shocked posterity.

Nor, given the influences to which he had been exposed, was it entirely unpredictable. The nurse who cared for him in his earliest childhood was a Spartan woman. His family had long had Spartan connections. One of his first political acts was to claim for himself the position of the Spartans' representative in Athens, a job which had traditionally been performed by his forebears. When the Spartan delegates came to Athens to negotiate peace terms in 421 BC Alcibiades enjoyed privileged access to the most powerful of them, the ephor Endius, with whom he had family connections. The two states might be deadly enemies, but they were also near neighbors, and the links between upper-class families, in classical Greece as in medieval and early modern Europe, transcended national boundaries.

Besides, as an adolescent Alcibiades had been Socrates' best-beloved disciple. Socrates was said to be the only person who could manage him, the only one whose opinion Alcibiades valued and whose advice he took. It is unclear how much influence the philosopher maintained over him once he was an adult, but unless Plato's *Symposium* is entirely fictional (which is unlikely) they were still close friends in the year before the Sicilian expedition embarked. Much later, when the philosopher was on trial for his life, his friends were at pains to point out that he could not be held responsible for the actions of his followers, but that he influenced their thinking seems indisputable. In *The Birds* Aristophanes describes a group of unpatriotically pro-Spartan youths as having been "socratified." The jibe was amply justified. The philosopher's most prominent disciples included not only the traitor Alcibiades but also several others who were passionate admirers of all things Spartan. Xenophon the historian, who was one of Socrates' devoted followers, fought for the Spartans against Persia, accepted an estate in recognition of his services from the Spartan King Agesilaus II, and lived happily on it for twenty years. When Sparta was defeated by the Thebans in 371 BC he was obliged to leave, but he did not return to Athens. Critias, the collaborator who was set up by the Spartans as leader of the oligarchic regime of the Thirty Tyrants in Athens in 404 BC, was another of Socrates' circle. And so of course was Plato, a nobleman who had relatives among the Thirty and whose ideal state, as described in *The Republic*, has a constitution which resembles that of Sparta far more closely than it resembles the Athenian democracy. It has been argued that when the restored Athenian democracy accused Socrates of "corrupting the youth," and put him to death for it, the charge had a precise political meaning. He was being accused of being a Spartan sympathizer. The heroic stand he made at his trial, which has earned him the admiration of generations of libertarians and defenders of free speech and free inquiry, was made, if this theory is correct, in assertion of his right to commend one of the most repressive and secretive regimes in recorded history.

Sparta is the classical model for all subsequent totalitarian states, just as Athens is for democracies. It was a warrior society, dedicated with grim exclusivity to its own preservation and aggrandizement. The Spartans were a Dorian people who had invaded the Peloponnese from the north and had reduced the indigenous population, known as helots, to a state of serfdom. The helots had not submitted tamely. Their repeated uprisings were brutally suppressed. New ephors, on taking office, routinely declared war on them "in order that there might be no impiety in slaying them." The state maintained a corps of helot killers, whose operations Plutarch describes: "They would be armed with daggers and supplied with basic rations, but nothing else. . . . At night they came down onto the roads and, if they found a helot, would cut his throat." The state's much-admired stability was guaranteed only by the omnipresence within it of violence and sudden death.

The helots were obliged to provide food for the master race. The Spartans, thus freed from the labor of providing for themselves, were able to devote themselves single-mindedly to the business of warfare. "The Spartans are, of all men, those who admire poetry and poetic glory least," noted Pausanias. "They did not understand how to be at leisure," wrote Aristotle, "and never engaged in any kind of training higher than training for war."

It was forbidden for any Spartan to travel abroad except for purposes of conquest, and foreigners were not made welcome, for Lycurgus, the Spartans' mythical lawgiver, had wished the society he created should remain permanently intact and unchanged and "along with strange people strange doctrines must come in." Trade was virtually nonexistent, each Spartan living off the produce of his own allotted plot of land. Lycurgus had forbidden luxury of all sorts. The staple Spartan food was a black broth famous throughout Greece for its nastiness. Spartan houses were all identical, and so crudely built that (according to a patronizing Athenian joke) a Spartan visiting Corinth was astonished to see wooden planks, and asked whether the trees in that region had square trunks. Spartan dress was austerely simple. Even Spartan speech was limited and deliberately brusque. The people maintained a "general habit of silence," a "laconicism" (the word means simply "Spartan") which combined the caution of those whose rigidly conservative, authoritarian state permitted them no political voice and the dumbness of those whose every personal response was suppressed or put to public use.

The state was all-encompassing. Spartans, according to Plutarch, had "neither the time nor the ability to live for themselves; but like bees they were to make themselves integral parts of the whole community." The city was like a military encampment, where each person had allotted duties. All personal relationships were subordinated to that between the individual and the state. Male babies were inspected by the elders at birth. If they were not perfectly healthy they were thrown into a ravine. Those who passed muster were cared for by their parents until at the age of seven they entered the school, a vast boot camp whose curriculum consisted almost entirely of gymnastics, where they learned obedience to discipline, indifference to pain, and the rigid suppression of private emotion.

The boys were systematically underfed, and encouraged to steal to satisfy their perpetual hunger, but if they were caught in the act they were ruthlessly flogged. The young men lived in all-male dormitories but were permitted to marry. A bride was abducted by force from her family home. Her hair was cropped back to her scalp by a "bridesmaid," who then stripped her and left her lying alone on the floor of a darkened room to await her husband, who came late at night and stayed only long enough to perform his reproductive duty before returning to the men's house. The couple's subsequent encounters would be equally swift and furtive, and always nocturnal, so that a woman might give birth to several children before seeing her husband's face. All men, whatever their age, took their meals in the communal mess (women ate separately, and were rationed to about one-sixth the quantity of food allowed to their menfolk). Men who refused to marry were punished and publicly shamed. Husbands who failed to impregnate their wives were pressured into inviting other men to do so. Jealousy was despised, along with all other manifestations of strong personal feeling. A mother who expressed contempt for a cowardly son was especially esteemed. Sparta was a place of throttled emotion, suppressed individuality, of willed dumbness. Spartans coupled sightlessly. The men never carried lights when they returned from the mess to their sleeping quarters. "When the Spartans kill," writes Herodotus, "they do so at night."

This place of darkness was widely admired even by its enemies. Socrates joked about the fashionable Athenian Spartophiles who wore short tunics and leather bands around their legs and mutilated their ears in the Spartan style. Spartans were praised for their frugality and their physical fitness, for the fortitude with which they bore pain, for their indifference to all forms of pleasure and their readiness to sacrifice themselves for the common good. To many Athenians they seemed, not enviable of course, but admirable, models of ascetic virtue, time travelers from a simpler but more dignified age. The austerity of their lifestyle made an aesthetic appeal even to those who would not themselves have wished to drink black broth. The authoritarianism of their rulers was insidiously seductive to those weary of the endless argument and counter-argument of the democratic process, a process which frequently deteriorated into time-wasting, irresponsible chatter. Pindar wrote in praise of Sparta, its venerable council of elders, its young men's conquering spears. And Plato, while overtly rejecting the Spartan system of government as being debased, incorporated many Spartan institutions and Spartan values into his ideal Republic, thus ensuring that Lycurgus's program for converting an individual into a useful component part of a state which existed not for its people's benefit but for the perpetuation of its own power has become intrinsic to the Western ideals of manliness, of good citizenship, and of heroic virtue.

A totalitarian state whose ordinary citizens are denied almost all self-expression provides, paradoxical as it may seem, a hospitable habitat for exceptional great men. Plutarch likened Sparta to a colony of bees, and every bee swarm has its queen. The subjugation of many empowers and liberates the few. In Sparta Alcibiades, Socrates' student, was to describe Athenian democracy as "a system which is generally recognized as absurd," and although he was undoubtedly attempting to curry favor with his anti-Athenian audience it is also possible that he spoke from the heart. He had proved a brilliant manipulator of the democratic Athenian Assembly, with powers of persuasion equal to those of the demagogues he despised, but once the Assembly turned against him he had strong personal reasons to reject not only that particular gathering but the political system of which it was the foremost example. As an aristocrat he may have found the oligarchic Spartan system congenial. As a young and famously beautiful military commander he must have responded to the Spartan cult of the warrior: "In time of war they relaxed the severity of the young men's discipline and permitted them to beautify their hair and ornament their arms and clothing, rejoicing to see them, like horses, prance and neigh for the contest." He had felt in Athens what it was like to be at the mercy of people he considered his inferiors. He had been condemned by his own city for reasons which probably seemed to him pettifogging and stupid. Sparta may have seemed to him a home more fit for heroes.

Certainly it suited him to give his hosts that impression. He arrived in Sparta a penniless fugitive whose life depended on his winning the protection of his former enemies. Never again would he dazzle and intimidate in his youthful role of spoiled, swaggering dandy. In Athens he had made a mock of public opinion. In Sparta he was tactful, accommodating, charming. In Athens he glittered like Achilles; in Sparta he showed that he could bend and change like Odysseus, Homer's "man of twists and turns." Achilles is absolutely self-consistent, totally transparent. He says he hates the man "who says one thing but hides another in his heart" as he hates the Gates of Death. Odysseus says the same thing in almost identical words but he says it in the course of a speech we know to be a concatenation of lies. He is a diplomat and intriguer, a master of disguise and dissimulation, the godson of Autolychus, the divine master of "thievery and subtle shifty oaths," a compulsive fabulist who speaks as often, in the

Odyssey, in an assumed character as he does in his own. Alcibiades was like him. He was a chameleon, a brilliant role player. He possessed, says Plutarch, "one special gift which surpassed all the rest and served to attach men to him, namely that he could assimilate and adapt himself to the pursuits and the manner of living of others."

He was an outcast now, and those deprived of their rooted identity are free to reinvent themselves. The second-century theologian Justin Martyr described the lineage of Cain, those outsiders of Hebrew legend, as shapeshifters who could become at will birds, serpents, or quadrupeds. Alcibiades, an accursed exile like Cain, had the same protean gift, mark both of his untrustworthiness and his uncanny brilliance. In Athens his lifestyle had been luxurious to the point of decadence. Sailing to Sicily, he astonished his peers by having part of the deck of his trireme cut away so that he could sling up a hammock, instead of sleeping, as all his compatriots did, wrapped in his cloak on the wooden deck. Now he became an ascetic. "By adopting Spartan customs in his everyday life he captivated the people and brought them under his spell." He grew his hair long in the Spartan fashion, took cold baths, and ate coarse bread with the notorious black broth. (Ironically, this playacting won him the accolade of comparison with the hero who was never anything but himself: "In Sparta, so far as all the externals went, one could say of him 'this is no son of Achilles, but Achilles himself.'") A marked man, he could no longer afford the self-indulgence of spontaneity. For the rest of his life, for all the glory and acclaim that still lay before him, he would have to please his audience, to mind his manners and watch his back.

He had to present himself to his new masters as something more than a renegade with an exhaustible fund of useful information. He could probably, had he been content to live a modest and private life, have bought himself sanctuary at the price of a few minor betrayals, but the restless, self-castigating ambition that Socrates had identified in him made such a solution to his problems inconceivable. When he arrived in Sparta in the winter of 415/414 BC he had yet to score any notable military successes. But, deprived as he was of his social position, without his wealth, without an army, the only way he could win a role consonant with the "love of distinction and desire for fame" which drove him all his life was to project an image of himself as a superman, one capable in his own person of accomplishing mighty deeds. In Sparta he began the creation of that image.

He had a quick eye for the main chance. Odysseus is "never at a loss" and Thomas Carlyle was to define a hero as "a man with an almost mythical awareness of what needed to be done." Alcibiades was one such. The philosopher Theophrastus, who lived a century after him, thought that he "possessed in a higher degree than any of his contemporaries the faculty of discerning and grasping what was required in a given situation." Delegations arrived in Sparta from Sicily asking for help against the Athenians. Alcibiades seized his opportunity. He spoke in the Sicilians' support, using the occasion to make his formal entry into Spartan public life. His speech, as reported by Thucydides, is a brilliant exercise in self-justification and self-aggrandizement. In it he publicly declares, for the first time, a tremendous program of conquest and colonization of which the Sicilian expedition was to have been only the beginning. From Sicily, he told the Spartans, he would have led the Athenians on to Italy and, that territory once conquered, would have launched an attack on Carthage and its empire. Then, with all the might of their new western conquests to draw on, the Athenians would have returned to crush the Peloponnesians, and emerged as masters of the entire Mediterranean world.

Probably Alcibiades had entertained such intentions: they are entirely consonant with his well-attested ambition, his vast self-confidence, and his pleasure in the superlative gesture (his seven chariot teams, his three prizes). But it is unlikely that such a grand design ever existed outside of his imagination. It is inconceivable that Nicias would have consented to it. When Alcibiades told the Spartan assembly, "The generals who are left will, if they can, continue just the same to carry out these plans," he was certainly lying. But the lie went undetected. The Spartans were persuaded. They decided to intervene in Sicily. And from then onwards, in their eyes and in posterity's, the audacity and grandeur of those tremendous projected conquests attached themselves to Alcibiades, lending him the aura of a great man—one who, had he not been thwarted by his ungrateful compatriots, might have become, five years before Alexander of Macedon was born, a world-conquering Greek. The modern historian Donald Kagan pays tribute to his performance on this occasion: "One can only marvel at his boldness, his imagination, his shrewd psychological understanding, and the size of his bluff."

For the next two and a half years Alcibiades lived in Sparta. Plutarch speaks pityingly of him wandering aimlessly about the city, but there is no evidence that he was humiliated by his hosts. The only story we have about his sojourn in Sparta is that of his liaison with Queen Timea, wife of Agis II, one of Sparta's two kings. Agis was abstaining from sex after an earthquake—which he took to be a divine warning—had interrupted his lovemaking with Timea, and he was anyway absent on campaign when a second earthquake shook the palace and a man was seen escaping from the queen's bedroom. That man, according to ancient gossip, was Alcibiades. Nine months later Timea gave birth to a son. The story may be scurrilous (Agis's other heirs would have had a motive for alleging the baby was illegitimate), but it is perfectly credible. Alcibiades was as attractive as ever and unused to sexual continence. The child was later barred from succession. When challenged about his alleged paternity Alcibiades is reported to have said with his characteristic arrogance "that he had not done this as a mere insult, nor simply to gratify his appetite, but to ensure that his descendants would one day rule over the Spartans."

While Alcibiades dallied in Sparta the Athenians' campaign in Sicily ended in horror. The fleet was annihilated. The entire army was either slaughtered or enslaved. The venture for which Alcibiades was largely responsible and which he had envisioned as the first phase of a glorious series of conquests left Athens crippled, without money, without ships, without fighting men. At once her colonies began to contemplate secession.

During the winter of 413/412 BC, two years after Alcibiades had arrived in Sparta, the Spartans were twice approached by rebellious oligarchic factions within Athenian colonies asking for support. In both cases the rebels already had Persian backing. The Great King was, or rather his satraps in the region were, eager to exploit any weakness within the Athenian empire. Alcibiades was among those who advocated sending a fleet to support the rebels on the island of Chios. He must, after two years' stagnation, have been craving action and the chance to make a brilliant show. King Agis, who had presumably heard the stories in circulation about Queen Timea's surprising pregnancy, was by now openly hostile towards him. Unless he could do the Spartans some signal service Sparta would not much longer be a safe refuge for him. He embarked on the second phase of his self-mythologizing. He personally, he told the ephors, and he alone, would be able to break Athens' hold on the cities of the eastern Mediterranean. "He said he would easily persuade the cities to revolt by informing them of the weakness of Athens and of the active policy of Sparta; and they would regard his evidence as being particularly reliable."

The ephors were persuaded. A small fleet was assembled. The first group of ships to set out blundered into the Athenian fleet and were defeated. The commander was killed and the surviving ships blockaded off Epidaurus. The Spartans hesitated. Many were so discouraged by this first setback they were ready to abandon the venture entirely, but Alcibiades succeed in holding them to their purpose. A second group of five ships, commanded by the Spartan Chalcides but with Alcibiades on board as mastermind, dashed to Chios, arriving before the news of the first party's defeat. Any seaman they encountered on the voyage they arrested and took with them to ensure secrecy. They sailed up to the city while its council was sitting. Alcibiades and Chalcides disembarked and marched into the Assembly. To the consternation of the pro-Athenian party they announced that they were the vanguard of a Peloponnesian fleet (but omitted to mention that the rest of the aforesaid fleet was trapped several hundred miles away). The ruse was successful: their opponents capitulated. First Chios, then the neighboring cities of Erythrae and Clazomenae, switched allegiance, and prepared to resist the Athenians.

The suborning of Chios was a brilliant coup, and one typical of Alcibiades. It bears all his trademarks: swiftness, audacity, a dependence on his own charisma and histrionic powers, flamboyant deception. Like the great runner Achilles he knew the value of speed, the way an army, or even a man, appearing where they are not looked for, where the rules of probability decree they cannot possibly be, can be as shocking and awesome as a supernatural apparition, demoralizing opposition and lending fresh courage to allies. Later that same year, after fighting all day in a desperate and unsuccessful attempt to repel the Athenians at Miletus, Alcibiades took horse and galloped southward through the night to meet the Peloponnesian fleet as it came into harbor and urge its captains to turn and sail on till morning. At dawn the next day, thanks to his despatch, the fleet appeared off Miletus and the Athenians slunk away "without realizing the fruit of their victory." A masterly manipulator of the facts with which circumstances presented him, Alcibiades was one who could conjure up an illusion of victory, and use it to make that victory real.

His cunning and theatricality as a commander have their parallels in the political games he was obliged to play throughout the last ten years of his life to keep himself alive and in command. He was instrumental in the making of a treaty between the Persians and the Spartans which heavily favored the former. There were suspicions in Sparta (quite possibly justified) that he was not a faithful servant to his adopted masters, masters who had a reputation for summarily and secretly killing those inconvenient to them. "The most powerful and ambitious of the Spartans were by now both jealous and tired of him," says Plutarch. After the battle of Miletus the Spartan admiral received orders, which probably originated with King Agis, to have Alcibiades put to death. Somehow, possibly warned by Queen Timea, who was so recklessly in love with him that in private she called her baby son by his name, Alcibiades heard of the order even before the admiral received it. A condemned man now in both halves of the Greek world, he slipped away from the Peloponnesian fleet and, turning his back not only on his native city but on his native culture, took refuge with the Persian satrap Tissaphernes at Sardis.

The satrap received him well. Plutarch describes Tissaphernes as one "who was naturally inclined to malice and enjoyed the company of rogues, being anything but straightforward himself," and adds that he "admired intensely Alcibiades' versatility and exceptional cleverness." The Persian and the Athenian, two schemers and conjurors with the truth, became—at least apparently—fast friends. Once again Alcibiades played the chameleon, adopting (possibly with more enthusiasm than he had adopted Spartan asceticism) Persian luxury and Persian pomp. Once again his extraordinary charm worked its spell. "Even those who feared and envied him could not help taking pleasure in his company," writes Plutarch. Tissaphernes was so delighted with his guest that he named a pleasure garden, "decorated in regal and extravagant style," after him, one "famous for its refreshing streams and meadows and pavilions and pleasances." Alcibiades "became his adviser in all things," says Thucydides. But his position was terrifyingly insecure, dependent as it was on a web of deceptions. Tissaphernes welcomed him initially on the understanding that he offered advice on behalf of the Spartans, the people who in fact now sought his death. Over the next year he was to play a perilous game of bluff and double bluff with Persians and Greeks alike, borrowing others' authority to cloak his real situation, which was that of an impotent and resourceless fugitive, and seeking to impress each party by laying claim to vast influence over another who at best distrusted him, at worst wanted him dead.

Achilles, rejected by his own people but still the inveterate enemy of their enemies, prayed that Achaeans and Trojans might cut each other to pieces, leaving no one alive but himself and his beloved Patroclus to stride together across the corpses into the shattered ruins of Troy. Alcibiades, doubly rejected and doubly a renegade, gave Tissaphernes advice which echoes Achilles' ferocious wish: "Let the Hellenes wear each other out among themselves." The Persian had been subsidizing the Peloponnesian fleet. Alcibiades suggested that he reduce the level of his support, lest the Spartans become a colonial power potentially as troublesome to Persia as Athens had been. The advice was shrewd. It was typical of Alcibiades, who preferred guile to bloodshed. It forcefully expresses his disengagement from all things Greek, from both of the two warring parties each of which had first made use of him and subsequently sought his death. It also, paradoxically, marks the beginning of his return to Greece. In Thucydides' opinion he "gave this advice not only because he thought it was the best he could offer, but also because he was looking out for a way to be recalled to his own country." He must have been acutely aware of the precariousness of his position in Sardis. Sparta was now closed to him. Tissaphernes's favor offered him a chance of returning to Athens, where he had once been so popular and influential, where in times gone by the young men had imitated his sandals and their elders had looked to him to win for them an empire in the west. That chance depended on his ability to persuade the Athenians that he might be able to come back to them not as the impotent exile he really was, begging for their mercy, but as one who could call on all the vast resources of Persia's Great King, and who might, on his own terms, use those resources to Athens' advantage.

The Athenians, in his long absence, had had cause to question their wisdom in rejecting him. After his recall from Sicily Nicias was left in the unenviable position of commanding a massive aggressive campaign which he himself had advised against from its inception. Irresolute, in pain from a diseased kidney, repeatedly terrified by ominous portents, he dithered and procrastinated through a war which ended in horror. The survivors straggled back to Athens, months or years after the final defeat, to recount their terrible experiences. They told of the repeated slaughters, of the infernal scene at the river Assinarus, where parched Athenians trampled over one another's corpses to get a palmful of water fouled by their own compatriots' blood, of the months after the surrender during which the survivors were held in the quarries outside Syracuse, with no room to move or lie down so that those many who died remained wedged upright among the living, of their subsequent enslavement. Initially they were met with incredulity. The Athenians at home "thought that this total destruction was something that could not possibly be true." Next the citizens turned murderously on those who had advocated the expedition and on the prophets and soothsayers who had promised success. Happy for Alcibiades, perhaps, that he was absent then. But over the next months and years, as Alcibiades was seen to serve their enemies so effectively at Chios and Miletus, suborning colonies just as he had intended to do on Athens' behalf in Sicily, there must have been some of his fellow citizens who asked themselves what might have happened if only they had trusted him, if only he had been allowed to stand trial and clear his name, if only he had not been recalled. It is easier to admit to one's own errors than to believe oneself helpless in the hands of a malign providence. There were many in Athens who blamed themselves, collectively if not personally, who believed that in turning against Alcibiades they had brought about their own downfall.

In the winter of 412/411 BC, when Alcibiades was with the Persians, the Athenian fleet was based at Samos, less than a mile off the coast of Asia Minor. Somehow, without Tissaphernes' knowledge, Alcibiades communicated with the Athenian commanders there, first by letter and subsequently in secret meetings on the mainland. He intimated to them that if the democratic government in Athens could be replaced by an oligarchy he would be able to persuade Tissaphernes to alter his policy. He would talk the Persian into supporting Athens, into paying their men and calling on the Phoenician navy, then lying inactive to the south, to fight alongside them. All this, Alcibiades suggested, he would do, if they could secure his pardon and restore him to his lost command. Most of the commanders, at least, believed him. One of them, Pisander, was to tell the people of Athens that for the sake of a Persian alliance "we must bring Alcibiades back, because he is the only person now living who can arrange this for us." Once more Alcibiades had succeeded in presenting himself as one uniquely gifted, able, as no one else was, to alter destiny.

The Athenian commanders on Samos sent a delegation, led by Pisander, to Athens to advocate his recall and the change of constitution he demanded. With some difficulty they made their case. Devastated by the calamity in Sicily, Athens was no match for Sparta. Without Persian support it was in danger of extinction, not only as a colonial power but even as an independent city-state. The citizens were persuaded that the sacrifice of their cherished democratic rights, at least temporarily, was necessary for their very survival. The Assembly authorized Pisander and ten companions to negotiate with Alcibiades and Tissaphernes. They traveled back east to Sardis, where the satrap, with Alcibiades at his side, received them. Alcibiades spoke for his protector-cum-employer. To the Athenians' angry astonishment he made demands to which they could not possibly accede. Bitterly disappointed, Pisander—an ambitious man with no love for the democracy—resolved to forget Alcibiades and seize power on his own account. He returned to Athens, where he and his co-

conspirators staged a coup d'état. They established a savagely repressive oligarchic regime known as the Four Hundred. For three months they held power, imprisoning and murdering any who opposed them. In Samos, meanwhile, the Athenian navy, under Thrasybulus and Thrasyllus, both of whom were longtime associates of Alcibiades, swore to uphold the democracy, thus effectively splitting the Athenian polis into two opposed parts, one an unprotected city, the other a homeless armada. Thrasybulus, who had been from the first an enthusiastic advocate of Alcibiades' recall, with some difficulty persuaded the mass of soldiers and seamen to agree to it. At last, with their consent, he crossed to the mainland, and brought Alcibiades back with him to Samos. Four years after his life had been declared forfeit and his name had been cursed by every priest in the city Alcibiades was back among Athenians, albeit not actually in Athens. The troops elected him a general "and put everything into his hands."

There is much that is baffling about these events, not least Alcibiades' insistence on the overthrow of the Athenian democracy, which is inconsistent not only with his subsequent acceptance of Thrasybulus' invitation to become commander of the democratic forces, but also with his entire political history. But though the intricacies of his machinations during this tumultuous year will probably never be satisfactorily unraveled, his main strategy is clearly visible. It was that of the confidence trickster so audacious that he gets away with his sting precisely because of its enormity. By the time Pisander's delegation came to negotiate with him and Tissaphernes, he had lost what influence he had had over the satrap. The Spartan commander had contrived to let the Persian know that Alcibiades was communicating secretly with the Athenians. Tissaphernes may still have enjoyed Alcibiades' company but he no longer trusted him, or acted on his advice. Thrasybulus saved him just in time from a potentially lethal situation. (Tissaphernes might well soon have found it expedient, as another satrap was to do six years later, to trade Alcibiades' life for the Spartans' goodwill.) And yet, totally powerless as he was, dependent for his very survival on a foreign magnate who owed him nothing, he presented himself to the Athenians, oligarchs and democrats alike, as one who could dispose of the power of the greatest empire on earth. It is a measure of his astonishing nerve, of his indomitable charm, and of the potency of the glamour which had come to surround his name that they appear to have believed him.

On Samos he spoke to the assembled Athenian forces, giving them, as Thucydides remarks drily, "a very exaggerated idea of the strength of his influence with Tissaphernes" and assuring them that, thanks to him, the satrap was now their ally and would never let them go short of supplies "not even if he [Tissaphernes] ended up by having to sell his own bed." He, Alcibiades, he told them, had saved them. His speech was a pyrotechnical display of rabble-rousing optimism. He flattered and excited his hearers. He assured them of imminent victory. By the time he had finished speaking "there was not a man who for anything in the world would have parted with his present hopes of coming through safely and of taking vengeance on the Four Hundred." Intoxicated by the presence of their charismatic lost-and-found leader, the men were all for sailing on Athens directly. Alcibiades dissuaded them. Delegates arrived from Athens bearing placatory messages from the oligarchs. The troops would barely give them an audience and again, infuriated, cried out that they would sail on their own city and drive out the Four Hundred. Only Alcibiades' presence averted what would have been a catastrophe for Athens. Once again he refused, as he had done at the time of his recall from Sicily, to play the mutineer. Such was his ascendancy over the troops that his oratory prevailed. "There was not another man in existence," wrote Thucydides, "who could have controlled the mob at that time."

Just as he had used his supposed influence over Tissaphernes to win him authority over the Athenians, now he used his new authority over the Athenians to revive his influence over the Persian. His first action as an Athenian general was to revisit Sardis, making a display to Tissaphernes of his new status as the commander of an army, and to the Athenians of his supposedly close relationship with the satrap. (There is no record of Tissaphernes' having subsequently given the Athenians anything, and some historians have questioned whether the Phoenician fleet of which Alcibiades made so much ever even existed.) It was a game he continued to play until, in 410 BC, the emptiness of his hand was brutally exposed. The satrap happened to be in the neighborhood of the Athenian fleet. Alcibiades, still feeling the need to make a parade, for the Athenians' benefit, of his supposed friendship with him, visited him at the head of a princely retinue and brought splendid gifts, but Tissaphernes had received new orders from the Great King: he was to give the Spartans his unequivocal support. Alcibiades' pompous visit gave him a welcome opportunity to demonstrate his zeal. He had his visitor arrested and imprisoned in Sardis. Alcibiades got away after only a month, claiming that Tissaphernes was still sufficiently devoted to him to have connived at his escape, but he could no longer plausibly lay claim to any influence over Persian policy.

Fortunately for him, he no longer needed to. During the four years after his recall to Samos, he won, or helped to win, a series of brilliant victories for Athens in their struggle with the Peloponnesians for control of the Aegean and the Hellespont. By degrees, as one success followed another, his mystique became so potent that his followers felt themselves glorified by it. According to Plutarch, "the soldiers who had served under Alcibiades were so elated and confident that they disdained to mix any longer with the rest of the army: they boasted that the others had been defeated time and again, but that they were invincible." He was only one of several Athenian generals, of whom Thrasybulus at least was his equal in talent. But whether or not Alcibiades was the most able commander, he was certainly the most dazzling. It was he, not his peers, who addressed the troops before a battle, because it was he who had the gift of whipping up their excitement and securing their loyalty. And it was he to whom glory accrued. As Cornelius Nepos remarked, "Thrasybulus accomplished many victories without Alcibiades. The latter accomplished nothing without the former, and yet he [Alcibiades] by some gift of his nature, gained the credit for everything."

For Athens, as for Sparta, he was swift, astonishing. At the battle of Abydos his arrival with eighteen ships after racing north from Samos proved decisive. As he came into view "the Spartans turned and ran for shelter," records Xenophon. A year later, before the battle of Cyzicus, he gained a crucial lead by galloping overland across the Gallipoli peninsula. At the battle itself he played the decoy, luring the Spartans out into open sea where his colleagues, Theramenes and Thrasybulus, could close in on their flank. When the Spartans saw the trap and attempted to retreat, Alcibiades nimbly turned his ships and pursued them back to the shore. Cyzicus, a great victory for Athens, was a cooperative action, but it was Alcibiades, the fleet, the daring, who won most of the acclaim.

His Puck-like propensity for appearing where he was not looked for was theatrical. So were his other gifts, for dazzling the eye and mind with his presence, for conspicuous courage and for subterfuge. At Selymbria in 408 BC his arrangement with the friendly factions within the city, who were to show a lighted torch at midnight to signal that they were ready to open the gates and rise in support of him, was botched. The signal was given early, before Alcibiades' army was prepared. Determined not to miss his opportunity Alcibiades dashed into the city, followed by only fifty men, to find himself surrounded by the entire Selymbrian army. He was trapped. At any moment he could have been killed or captured. Coolly he ordered one of his men to sound a trumpet and another to make a formal proclamation forbidding the Selymbrians to take up arms. The Selymbrians, bewildered by a performance so inappropriate to the reality of the situation, believed the performance and discounted the reality. Nervous and disoriented, afraid perhaps that the rest of the Athenians had already entered the city (impossible to be sure in the darkness), they failed to use their advantage. Stupefied by Alcibiades' effrontery, they parleyed with him until his army at last came up and their surrender was assured.

In the same year he won the greater prize of Byzantium by similar sleight of hand. Again he made contact with people within the city who were ready to betray their Spartan masters. The Athenians had been blockading the harbor, but on the appointed day their fleet sailed away, or seemed to do so. At the same time Alcibiades' army, which had been besieging the city on the landward side, withdrew far enough to be out of sight. When night fell the army silently returned, while the Athenian fleet sailed back into harbor and attacked the Spartan ships there "with a great deal of shouting, commotion and uproar." The Spartans and their supporters raced down to the waterfront. Meanwhile Alcibiades' Byzantine allies placed ladders against the walls, allowing his men to flood into the city and to overwhelm its defenders. The decisive moment of the battle came when Alcibiades, who understood the strategic value of magnanimity, had it proclaimed throughout the city that the Byzantines would not be harmed, and a decisive proportion of the population abruptly changed sides.

The Athenian troops adored him, but he had yet to test the temper of the Athenians at home. Pisander's oligarchy was short-lived. The politically moderate government of the Five Thousand which replaced it endorsed Alcibiades' command and invited him to return. But he waited another four years before he risked reentering the city from which he had been cast out, in which his name had been anathematized and he himself condemned to die. When he finally went back he did so as the victor in a war that had made the Hellespont, at least temporarily, an Athenian lake. As Plutarch explains: "He had thought it best not to meet [the Athenians] empty-handed, without any positive achievement to his credit and owing his recall to the pity and good-nature of the people, but rather to arrive in a blaze of glory."

Two hundred years later Duris of Samos, who claimed to be Alcibiades' descendant, wrote an excited description of his return to Athens, at the head of a great fleet of ships decorated from stem to stern with captured shields and trophies, with flute players and actors timing the oarsmen's strokes and with Alcibiades' own ship rigged with purple sails "as though he were leading a crowd of revellers after some drinking party." More reliable sources give a less festive but more dramatic account. Thrasyllus went ahead with the main body of the fleet while Alcibiades, with only twenty ships, delayed. Perhaps he calculated that it would be to his advantage to let the bulk of the fighting men, who adored him, arrive in the city before he did, and to give them time to spread tales of his prowess among the citizens. He stopped to raise money—conscious as ever of its usefulness in procuring popularity—and sailed for Athens only after he had received word that the Assembly had expressed its approval by electing him general once again. Even then he was apprehensive. It is unclear from the ancient sources whether the death sentence against him had ever been formally revoked: he still had many enemies in the city. Arriving at Piraeus he anchored close to the shore and scanned the waiting crowd. Only when he had picked out a group of friends, including one of his cousins, did he feel safe enough to land. He came ashore surrounded by a bodyguard ready to fight off any attempt at arresting him.

His caution must quickly have given way to triumph. His return was greeted with wild scenes of celebration. This homecoming was his apotheosis, the moment when the Athenians received him as though he were one of Plato's men of gold, a redeemer who could put an end to all their troubles, a quasi-divine hero who could lead them forward to a glittering future. A vast crowd, near-hysterical with joy, had gathered on the waterfront. According to Diodorus Siculus, "all men thronged to the harbour to catch sight of Alcibiades, the slaves vying with the free so that the city was entirely deserted." The entire crowd, alight with enthusiasm, escorted him back into the city, yelling out their exultation as they went. People struggled to get close enough to embrace him and to crown him with garlands. Many wept "for they reflected that they would never have suffered the Sicilian disaster or any of their terrible disappointments if only they had left Alcibiades in command," but their regrets were mingled with rejoicing, for according to Diodorus "practically all men believed" that with his return from exile "great fortune had come again to the city."

Carried on the wave of the jubilant throng, Alcibiades made his way to the Pnyx, where he spoke to the full Assembly. He was a magnificent figure, his beauty, according to Plutarch, being as great in the prime of his manhood as it had been when he was a boy, "lending him extraordinary grace and charm." He was also a brilliant player on others' emotions.

Shrewdly, he chose to be magnanimous, to blame no one for his exile. Instead, with tears in his eyes, he spoke of "ill-fortune" and the "evil genius that had dogged his career." Many listeners wept. Others cried out angrily, just as if, remarks Cornelius Nepos drily, "it had been other people, and not those who were then shedding tears, that had condemned him for impiety." He ended his speech with rousing optimism, promising Athens a splendid future. His audience applauded ecstatically. His confiscated property was restored to him. The stelae recording his disgrace were taken down from the Acropolis and thrown into the sea. The priests were commanded to solemnly revoke the curses they had once cast on him. He was crowned with a golden crown and appointed general with absolute authority by land and sea—a title which only his guardian Pericles had held before him. For years, in Sparta, in Sardis, in Samos, he had been claiming superhuman powers for himself. Now at last that claim, unreal as it still was, was believed by his compatriots. Alcibiades was acclaimed throughout the city as the man who could make Athens great once more.

The extravagant joy which attended his homecoming was followed by an even more impressive demonstration of his rehabilitation. The grandest spectacle of the Athenian religious calendar was the procession which escorted the sacred objects and the image of the god Iacchus from Athens to Eleusis, some fourteen miles away, for the annual celebration of the Mysteries. The marchers included young men about to be initiated, initiates wreathed with myrtle, and long-robed priests. Bands of flute players, dancers, and hymn-singing choirs accompanied the procession, which halted frequently along the route to make sacrifices and to perform sacred rites. Holiday and awe-inspiring spectacle at once, the ceremony held profound significance for all Athenians, but for several years it had not taken place. The presence of the Spartan garrison at Decelea, in the mountains overlooking the route, had rendered it too dangerous. Instead Iacchus had been carried by boat to Eleusis with a small escort and none of the usual attendant ceremony, a compromise sadly emblematic of Athens' reduced and endangered condition.

Alcibiades—the traitor who had advised the Spartans to fortify Decelea, the blasphemer who had repeatedly made a mock of the Eleusinian Mysteries and who had been condemned to death for doing so—seized the chance to demonstrate his reformation with an operation exactly designed to erase his past sins. Scrupulously devout now, he first consulted the priests before announcing, with their approval, that the procession would take place. He posted lookouts on the hilltops all along the route, sent out an advance guard at daybreak to clear the way, and then, surrounding the procession with his troops, escorted it to Eleusis and back. Had King Agis led out an attacking force from Decelea, Alcibiades would have been able to make a parade of his military skills and his loyalty, fighting, in sight of all Athens, to defend the sacred mysteries. As it was, the procession went and returned unmolested. The participants had walked, according to Plutarch, "in solemn order and complete silence." Throughout the thirty-mile round-trip journey they must have been in a state of mingled terror and exaltation. When they returned safely to the city, their relief, and that of the watching citizens, was expressed in further outbursts of rapturous acclaim for Alcibiades. The poorer classes especially were convulsed by an "extraordinary passion" for him. The troops were exultant, boasting once again that under his command they were invincible. The one-time blasphemer was hailed as "a high priest and an initiator into the Mysteries." It seemed there was nothing he could not do.

To live in a democracy is not easy. The freeborn adult male citizens of fifth-century Athens were obliged to accept responsibility for their own destinies. There was no tyrant whom they could reproach for their misfortunes or fatherly autocrat on whom they could rely for protection. They were expected to participate in the making of crucial policy decisions. If those decisions proved to have been bad ones, there was no person or institution outside of themselves that the citizens could blame for their ill consequences. Nor was there any all-powerful authority who could erase their mistakes and comfort them in their troubles. Many people, in Athens in Alcibiades' lifetime as well as in the numerous modern democracies where demagogues have become dictators, longed to be reduced once more to the condition of infancy, to be made free of the wearisome responsibilities of independent adulthood.

In Athens political debate was urgent, incessant, bafflingly inconclusive. The political process was obstructed and complicated at every turn by envy, by corruption, and by the blackmailers who made a living by threatening to expose it. The tenure of any office was brief. There was no certainty, no continuity, no easygoing reliance on precedent. Every principle, and every practical detail, was to be debated and voted upon. This edgy insistence on examining every question afresh each time it arose is one of the things that made Athens so exhilarating a society, which gave it its extraordinary intellectual and political vitality. But it imposed a burden on the citizens which exasperated or frightened many, and which others found simply too great to bear. In the summer of 408 BC, when Alcibiades descended on Athens surrounded by the golden aura of the conquering hero, as splendid as one of those godlike men whom Aristotle judged fully entitled to enslave their fellows, there were many who entertained the fantasy of surrendering their exhausting freedom to him. People came to him and begged him to "rid them of those loud-mouthed wind-bags who were the bane of the city," to silence the ceaseless, bewildering play of argument and counterargument for which the entire city was the stage by seizing absolute power. In an extraordinary frenzy of self-abasement people begged him to make himself dictator, to "sweep away decrees and laws as he thought fit," to overturn the constitution and wipe out all opposition so that "he would be free to handle affairs," thus relieving the demoralized and insecure citizens of the awful burden of their liberty.

Alcibiades did not respond to the invitation. He had work to do elsewhere. The Spartan fleet under its formidable new commander Lysander was lying at Ephesus, a menace to the Athenian colonies. The Assembly granted Alcibiades all the men and ships he required, even allowing him the unprecedented honor of choosing his own fellow generals. Their generosity was expressive of the people's adulation of their new commander in chief. Besides, the Assembly's more thoughtful members were probably anxious to speed him on his way. "We do not know what Alcibiades himself thought of a dictatorship," writes Plutarch, "but certainly the leading citizens at this time were frightened of it." They mistook their man. The insatiable ambition Socrates had seen in his disciple was not for stay-at-home executive power, but for world-bestriding glory. Soon after the Eleusinian festival, just four months after he had entered the city, Alcibiades left Athens forever.

He had seduced the people and alarmed the leading democrats, but he had not won over the gods. The day on which he landed in Athens to be so rapturously received was the unluckiest of the year, the day when the image of Athena on the Acropolis was veiled for secret purification rites. Perhaps those citizens hostile to Alcibiades pointed out the inauspicious circumstance at the time, to be ignored by the ecstatic majority. Perhaps it was only with hindsight that people were to remember it as a sign of what was to come. At the zenith of his popularity the city's patron goddess turned her face away from him. Only months later the city's people were, as though in imitation, to withdraw their favor.

"If ever a man was destroyed by his own high reputation," wrote Plutarch, "it was Alcibiades." He was now expected to work miracles, and when he failed to do so the lethally volatile democratic Assembly began to grumble and to doubt his loyalty, "for they were convinced that nothing which he seriously wanted to achieve was beyond him." He sailed to Andros, where he established a fort but failed to take the city. When he arrived at Notium in Asia Minor, across the bay from the Peloponnesian fleet at Ephesus, he was unable to lure Lysander out of the safety of the harbor. The oarsmen began to defect: the Spartans, now subsidized by the Persian Prince Cyrus, were able to offer them 25 percent more pay than the Athenians. Alcibiades, foreseeing a long and expensive wait before he could force a decisive engagement, sailed off to raise funds elsewhere, leaving the main fleet under the temporary command of Antiochus, the pilot of his ship. It was a controversial appointment. Antiochus was a professional sailor, not one of the aristocratic trierarchs or amateur ship's captains who, though probably less competent, were his social superiors and who would have seen themselves as outranking him. He had known and served Alcibiades for nearly twenty years, ever since that long ago occasion when he had caught his future commander's errant quail for him in the Assembly. Alcibiades' decision to place him in command was audacious, unconventional, and, as it turned out, calamitous. In Alcibiades' absence, in defiance of his explicit order, Antiochus provoked a battle for which he was totally unprepared. Lysander put the Athenians to flight, sinking twenty ships. Antiochus was killed. Alcibiades raced back to Notium and attempted, unsuccessfully, to induce Lysander to fight again. Only a brilliant victory could have saved him, and it was not forthcoming.

When the news reached Athens all the old accusations against him were revived. He was arrogant. He was depraved. He was untrustworthy. The people who only months before had been ready to give up their political rights for the privilege of being his subjects now turned on him with a fury as irrational as their adulation had been. It was alleged that he intended to make himself a tyrant. It was pointed out that he had built a castle in Thrace—why, asked his accusers, would a loyal Athenian need such a bolt-hole? His appointment of Antiochus, unquestionably a mistake, was presented as evidence of his wicked frivolity. "He had entrusted the command," said one of his accusers, "to men who had won his confidence simply through their capacity for drinking and spinning sailors' yarns, because he wanted to leave himself free to cruise about raising money and indulging in debauchery and drunken orgies with the courtesans of Abydos and Ionia." He was accused of accepting a bribe from the king of Cyme, a city he had failed to take. None of the charges against him were substantiated. They did not need to be. After all, in 417 BC, the Athenians had come close to banishing him by ostracism for no reason at all except that he had grown too great. Now new generals were elected, one of whom was ordered to sail east and relieve Alcibiades of his command. On hearing that his city, which he had so grossly betrayed but to which he had since done such great service, had once again rejected him, Alcibiades left the fleet, left the Greek world entirely, and, Coriolanus-like, sought a world elsewhere. Taking only one ship, he sailed away northward to Thrace, where he had indeed had the foresight to acquire not one but three castles.

There, among the lawless barbarians, he recruited a private army and embarked upon the life of a brigand chief, a robber baron, preying upon his neighbors and taking prisoners for ransom. Adaptable as ever, he assumed the habits of his new countrymen, winning the friendship of the tribal chieftains by matching them, according to Cornelius Nepos, "in drunkenness and lust." Perhaps, as the historian and novelist Peter Green has suggested, this was the debauchery attendant on despair, but perhaps it was the zestful beginning of yet another new life. We shall see how Rodrigo Díaz de Vivar, the Cid, another hero who grew too great for the state he served and was therefore outcast, was to begin again as a bandit in the badlands of eleventh-century Spain and ultimately to make himself prince of a great city. After two years in Thrace Alcibiades was to boast that he was treated there "like a king."

In Athens meanwhile, as disaster followed upon disaster, he gradually acquired the mystique of a king over the water, a once and perhaps future redeemer of his native city. A year after the beginning of his second exile Aristophanes had a character in *The Frogs* say of him that the Athenians "yearn for him, they hate him, but they want to have him back." Just once more his history touched theirs, in an encounter which yet again identified him as the man who could have saved Athens if only Athens had allowed him to do so. In 405 BC, on the eve of the disastrous battle of Aegospotami, he appeared, a troubling deus ex machina, in the Athenian camp. The Athenian and Spartan fleets were drawn up facing each other in the narrowest part of the Hellespont, the Athenians being on the Thracian shore, only a few miles from his stronghold. Alcibiades, uninvited and unexpected, came riding in and demanded a meeting with the generals. He pointed out to them that their position was dangerously exposed, and too far from their source of supplies. He advised them to move and he offered them the armies of two Thracian kings on whom he could rely. The Athenian generals would not so much as listen to his advice. Perhaps they remembered how he had once offered to deliver Persian money and Phoenician ships and failed to do so. Perhaps they thought of how Thrasybulus had been eclipsed, and, as Diodorus suggests, were jealously protecting their own reputations, fearing "that if they were defeated they themselves would get the blame, but that the credit for any success would go to Alcibiades." Whatever their motives, they turned him away rudely, saying, "We are in command now, not you." As he rode out of the camp Alcibiades told his companions that had he not been so outrageously insulted the Spartans would have lost all their ships. Some thought this boast mere bravado, but many, including some modern historians, have believed him. Rejected for the third time, he galloped away. At Aegospotami the Athenian fleet was utterly destroyed. The survivors, including all but one of the generals, were slaughtered. A few months later Athens fell.

For the last year of his life Alcibiades was a fugitive. The Spartans still wanted him dead. Their victory rendered coastal Thrace unsafe for him. He withdrew into the interior, leaving behind the bulk of his possessions, which the neighboring chieftains promptly looted. As he traveled inland he was set upon and robbed of his remaining belongings, but he managed to escape capture and made his way, armed now only with his reputation and his miracle-working charm, to the headquarters of the Persian satrap Pharnabazus. Once more, as when he arrived at Tissaphernes' court, "he so captivated Pharnabazus that he became the Persian's closest friend." Graciously the satrap granted him the Phrygian city of Grynium and all its revenues. He had found a refuge, a protector, and an income. But, characteristically, he wanted more. He was in his forties, his prime, and his ambitions were still inordinate, his conception of his own potential still as extravagant as the awe he inspired. He resolved to make the formidable journey eastward to visit the Great King Artaxerxes II at Susa. He would have had in mind the example of Themistocles, the victor of Salamis, another great Athenian who, half a century earlier, had been banished and condemned to death by the city for whom he had won great victories, and who had been received with honor by a Persian king. Besides he had information that Artaxerxes' brother Cyrus, who was closely associated with the Spartan Lysander, was plotting to usurp the

Persian throne. Perhaps he hoped to foment war between Persia and Sparta, a war in which he might play a glorious part as the liberator of Athens.

He asked Pharnabazus to arrange an audience for him with the Great King. Pharnabazus demurred. Alcibiades set out anyway. He halted one night in a small town in Phrygia. There, while he lay in bed with the courtesan Timandra (whose daughter Lais was later said to be the most beautiful woman of her generation), hired killers heaped fuel around the wooden house in which he was lodged and set fire to it. Waking, Alcibiades seized his sword, wrapped a cloak around his left arm for a shield, and charged out through the flames. His assassins backed off, but from a distance they hurled javelins and spears at him until he fell. Then they closed in and hacked off his head before departing. Timandra wrapped his decapitated body in her own robe and buried it, or, according to Nepos, burned the dead Alcibiades in the fire which had been set to burn him alive.

Even his death, wretched as it was, is evidence of Alcibiades' extraordinary charisma. One story goes that the killers were the brothers of a girl he had seduced, but most of the sources agree they had been hired by Pharnabazus. The satrap had been persuaded to violate the duties of the host, and his affection for the man who had so captivated him, by the urgings of the Spartan Lysander, who had threatened that if he did not hand over Alcibiades, alive or dead, Sparta would break off its alliance with Persia. Lysander, in turn, was responding to pressure from Critias—the man who long ago had sat with Alcibiades at Socrates' feet, and who was now the leader of the puppet government which the Spartans had installed in Athens. Such was the potency of Alcibiades' reputation, so widespread the hope that he might yet come to save his city, that while he lived, complained Critias, "none of the arrangements he made at Athens would be permanent." In those dark days for Athens it was not only the oppressed democrats who ascribed to Alcibiades the power to turn the course of history single-handed. His enemies feared him, or feared the legend he had become, ascribing to him, or to it, superhuman powers. He was a man without a state, without an army, without a fortune, without allies, but he was also a human phoenix, one who had repeatedly risen from the ashes of disaster in a flaming glory all of his own making.

Alcibiades' talents were never fully put to the test. His career was a sequence of lost opportunities. Perhaps, given the chance, he might have won the war for Athens. Certainly Thucydides, who was as judicious as he was well-informed, believed that the Athenians' failure to trust Alcibiades (for which Alcibiades, who had failed to win their trust, was partially to blame) brought about the city's undoing: "Although in a public capacity his conduct of the war was excellent, his way of life made him objectionable to everyone as a person; thus they entrusted their affairs to other hands, and before long ruined the city." But great reputations do not flourish, as Alcibiades' did in his lifetime and afterwards, on the foundation only of what might have been. It is possible that his career, thwarted, dangerous, and isolated as it was, was one precisely suited to his particular genius. He was an actor, a seducer, a legend in his own lifetime and of his own making, a true con artist, one whose self-invented myth was a creation of awesome grandeur and brilliance, a man who owed the large place he occupied in his contemporaries' imagination not to any tangible achievement, but simply to the magnitude of his presence.

Poets of the classical and medieval era imagined Achilles to be a giant. He was born different from others. Statius describes him as a baby lapping not milk but "the entrails of lions and the marrow of half-dead wolves." Pindar, who lived in Athens a generation before Alcibiades, imagined the six-year-old Achilles outrunning deer, fighting with lions, and dragging the vast corpses of slaughtered boars back to Chiron's cave. In fiction and myth, exorbitant size and prodigious strength were the tokens of the hero, the human being of superhuman attributes. In the real world Alcibiades, marked out from others by his aristocratic origins, his striking beauty, his intimidating capacity for violence, and his inordinate self-confidence, was received by his contemporaries as though he were another such prodigy, a being innately and intrinsically greater than his fellows.

Such a person is not easily assimilable within any community; in a democracy his very existence is a form of sedition. The dizzying reversals of Alcibiades' career reflect the constant interplay between his fellow citizens' adulation of him and their ineradicable distrust of the magic whereby he was able temporarily, but never for long enough, to dominate them. They ascribed to him the potential to be alternately their savior or their oppressor. They "were convinced," wrote Nepos, "that it was to him that all their disasters and their successes were due." They imagined superhuman power for him: they adored him for it, and they found it unforgivable. Like Achilles he was as terrifying as a god, or a beast. "Better not bring up a lion inside your city / but if you must then humour all his moods," wrote Aristophanes, referring to Alcibiades. "Most people became frightened at a quality in him that was beyond the normal," wrote Thucydides. That supranormal quality posed a temptation as alluring as it was insidious. Perhaps what the Athenians feared most in Alcibiades was not any ambition of his to seize absolute power but their own longing to hand it to him, to abase themselves before him as a superman capable not only of rescuing them from their enemies but also of freeing them from the burden of being free.

III

CATO

London 1713: the first night of Joseph Addison's tragedy *Cato*, which was to enjoy such a triumph that Alexander Pope, who wrote the prologue, declared that "Cato was not so much the wonder of Rome in his days as he is of Britain in ours." The curtain rises on the last act. The hero is discovered "Solus, sitting in a thoughtful posture: in his hand Plato's book on the Immortality of the Soul. A drawn sword on the table by him." The tableau—the sword, the book, the pensive hero—was repeated exactly in numerous neoclassical paintings. Its drama lies not in what is represented, but in what is still to come, the horror to which (as most male members of Addison's classically educated eighteenth-century audience would have known) this tranquil scene is prelude. Before the night is out Cato will read the book through three times, and then, still serene, still "thoughtful," drive the sword into his belly. When that first attempt to free himself from tyranny fails he will submit calmly while his friends bind up the dreadful wound and remove the weapon. Alone once more, he will tear open his body with his bare hands and resolutely disembowel himself.

Cato, true until death. Cato, so inflexible in his righteousness that he was ready to kill himself not once, but twice. Cato, who had no self-pity, but grieved only for Rome and its venerable institutions. Cato, who on the night of his death read of the death of Socrates and who, like the Athenian philosopher, chose not to save himself from a death made inevitable by the mismatch between his own integrity and the imperfection of the world he inhabited. This Cato was venerated alike by pagan Rome and Christian Europe. Addison describes him as "godlike," an epithet first applied to him by Lucan nearly seventeen hundred years earlier. Of his contemporaries only Julius Caesar, whose most inveterate opponent he was, denied his virtue. Cicero and Brutus both eulogized him. Horace praised his "fierce heart." Virgil imagined for him an illustrious afterlife as lawgiver to the virtuous dead. To later generations of Romans, especially to the Stoics who formed the opposition to Nero's tyranny, he was an exemplar, a philosopher (though he left no philosophical writings), and the embodiment of their ideal. The Christian Fathers saw him as the paragon of pagan virtue. To Lactantius he was "the prince of Roman wisdom." To Jerome he had a glory "which could neither be increased by praise nor diminished by censure." Dante placed Brutus, who was Cato's son-in-law and political heir, in the lowest circle of hell with Judas Iscariot, in the very mouth of Satan, to be eaten alive ceaselessly through all eternity, and he condemned others who had, like Cato, committed the sin of self-murder to an afterlife of unremitting mute agony in the form of trees whose twigs ooze blood. But Cato is exempt. Despite being a suicide and a pagan he is the custodian of Dante's Purgatory and is destined eventually for a place in Paradise. In *Il convivio* Dante goes even further. Cato divorced his wife Marcia so that she could be married to his political ally Hortensius. After Hortensius's death he remarried her. The story has proved troubling to most Christian moralists, but Dante treats the couple's reunion as an allegory of the noble soul's return to God: "And what man on earth is more worthy to signify God than Cato? Surely no one."

It was his intransigence which rendered Cato all but divine. Sophocles, Alcibiades' contemporary and fellow Athenian, had described the tragic hero as one who refuses to compromise or conform but remains, however beset by trouble, as immovable as a rock pounded by stormy seas, or as the one tree which, when all the others preserve themselves by bending before a river in flood, stays rigidly upright and is therefore destroyed root and branch. Cato was as steadfast as that rock, as self-destructively stubborn as that tree. An Achilles, not an Odysseus, he was the antithesis of Alcibiades, the infinitely adaptable, infinitely persuasive charmer. Cato never charmed, never changed.

He has been revered as a hero, but he put all his energies into thwarting the aspirations of the heroic great men among his contemporaries, and into attempting to save his fellow Romans from the folly of the hero worship he so passionately denounced. The defining drama of his life was his unshakable opposition to Julius Caesar. Friedrich Nietzsche considered Caesar to be one of the few people in human history to have rivaled Alcibiades' particular claims to supermanhood, the two of them being Nietzsche's prime examples of "those marvellously incomprehensible and unfathomable men, those enigmatic men predestined for victory and the seduction of others." Cato was their opposite. Obstinately tenacious of a lost cause, he was predestined for defeat and temperamentally incapable of seduction.

Caesar—adroit and charismatic politician, promiscuous lover, ruthless, brilliant conqueror—was a hero of an instantly recognizable type. Cato's claim to heroic status is of quite a different nature. He is the willing sacrifice, the patiently enduring victim. His glory is that not of the brilliant winner but of the loser doggedly pursuing a course which leads inevitably to his own downfall. Small wonder that Christian theologians found his character so admirable, his story so inspiring. He embodied the values of asceticism and self-denial which Jesus Christ and his followers borrowed from pagan philosophers, and, like Christ's, his life can be seen with hindsight as a steady progress towards a martyr's death.

That death retrospectively invested his career and character with a melancholy grandeur which compensated for the glamour which, alive, he notably lacked. Curmudgeonly in manner, awkward and disobliging in his political dealings and his private relationships alike, he sought neither his contemporaries' affection nor posterity's admiration. Yet he received both. Cicero, who knew him well, wrote that he "alone outweighs a hundred thousand in my eyes." "I crawl in earthly slime," wrote Michel de Montaigne, some sixteen hundred years after Cato's death, "but I do not fail to note way up in the clouds the matchless heights of certain heroic souls," the loftiest of them all being Cato, "that great man who was truly a model which Nature chose to show how far human virtue and fortitude can reach."

He had a personality of tremendous force. His contemporaries were awed and intimidated by him, not as the Athenians had feared the capricious bully Alcibiades, more nearly as the moneylenders in the temple feared the righteous and indignant Christ. His mind was precise and vigorous and he was an orator of furious talent. He was deferred to by the soldiers he commanded, by the crowds he stirred or subdued, by those of his peers who recognized and admired his selflessness and integrity. But he was also a troublemaker and an oddity. He was a well-known figure in Rome, but one who inspired irritation and ridicule as well as respect.

He was a nuisance. He embarrassed and annoyed his peers by loudly denouncing corrupt practices which everyone else had come to accept as normal. He had no discretion, no urbanity. He looked peculiar. He habitually appeared in the Forum with bare feet and wearing no tunic beneath his toga, an outfit which seemed to his contemporaries at best indecorous, at worst indecent. When challenged about it he pointed to the statue of

Romulus (represented similarly underdressed) and said that what was good enough for the founder of Rome was good enough for him, an answer typical of his willful insistence on ignoring the political realities as well as the sartorial conventions of his own time. When he became praetor (a senior magistrate) his judgments were acknowledged to be scrupulously correct, but there were those who muttered that he disgraced the office by hearing cases—even those solemn ones in which important men stood to incur the death penalty—looking so raffish, so uncouth.

He never laughed, seldom smiled, and had no small talk. He stayed up late, all night sometimes, drinking heavily, but his nightlife was not of the gracious and hospitable kind that his fellow aristocrats found congenial. Rather he would engage in vehement debate with philosophers who tended to encourage him in his eccentricities. Rigorously ascetic, he disdained to think of his own comfort, and had a way of undermining other people's. He never rode if he could walk. When he traveled with friends he would stalk along beside their horses on his bare and callused feet, his head uncovered, talking indefatigably in the harsh, powerful voice that was his most effective political weapon. Few people felt easy in his company; he was too judgmental and too much inclined to speak his mind. To his posthumous admirers his disturbing ability to search out others' imperfections was among his godlike attributes. Montaigne called him one "in whose sight the very madmen would hide their faults." But his contemporaries shunned him for it. He was his community's self-appointed conscience, and the voice of conscience is one to which most people prefer not to listen. His incorruptibility dismayed his rivals because "the more clearly they saw the rectitude of his practice," writes Plutarch, "the more distressed were they at the difficulty of imitating it." All the great men of Rome "were hostile to Cato, feeling that they were put to shame by him." Even the great Pompey was said to have been unnerved by him: "Pompey admired him when he was present but . . . as if he must render account of his command while Cato was there, he was glad to send him away."

His life (95–46 BC) coincided with the last half century of the Roman Republic, a time of chronic political instability and convulsive change. It was a time when the institutions of the state had ceased to reflect the real distribution of power within it. Rome and all its provinces were nominally ruled by the Senate and the people of Rome, but by the end of Cato's life Rome's dominions extended from the Euphrates to the Atlantic, from the Sahara to the North Sea. The constitution, evolved within a city-state, provided none of the machinery required to subdue,

police, and administer an international empire. The prosecution of foreign wars and the exploitation of the conquered provinces required great
armies and teams of officials—none of which Rome's institutions could
provide. The provinces were effectively autonomous states, far larger and
frequently richer than the metropolis, with their own separate adminis-
trations. The proconsuls who conquered and governed them at their own
expense and to their own profit were often absent from Rome for years on
end, acting as effectively independent rulers in their allotted territories.
When they returned at last, enormously wealthy and to the adulation of
the people, they had, in reality, infinitely more clout than the institutions
they were supposed to serve. When Pompey celebrated his triumph on
returning from Asia in 61 BC, his chariot was preceded by the captive families of three conquered kings. He boasted of having killed or subjected
over twelve million people and of increasing Rome's public revenues by
70 percent. There was no room in the republic for such a man, no legitimate channel for his influence or proper way in which he could exert his
power. The Athenians had been afraid when Alcibiades demonstrated his
prowess, his wealth, and his international connections at Olympia. Just so
were the Roman republicans apprehensive as first Pompey and subsequently Crassus and Caesar grew so great they loomed over the state like
unstable colossi.

Cato was the little man who dared oppose these giants, the Prome-
theus nobly defying the ruthless gods (one of whom Caesar would soon
become) for the sake of oppressed humanity. Armed only with his voice,
his knowledge of the law, and his unshakable certainty of his own rectitude, he resolutely obstructed their every attempt to have their actual
power acknowledged. Whether he was wise to do so is open to question.
Theodor Mommsen, the great nineteenth-century German historian,
called Cato an "unbending dogmatical fool." Even Cicero, who thought
so highly of him and whose political ally he was throughout most of their
contemporaneous careers, found him exasperating at times. Cicero was a
pragmatist, a sophisticated political operator, and a practitioner of the art
of the possible. Cato, by contrast, loudly and dogmatically insisting on
the letter of ancient and anachronistic laws, repeatedly damaged his own
cause, exposing his allies' misdemeanors and defending his opponents'
rights. To many commentators, ancient and modern alike, it has appeared
that had it not been for Cato's dogged refusal to compromise his political
principles, or to allow anyone else to do so without being publicly
shamed, the Senate might have been able to come to terms with Julius

Caesar in 49 BC, that Caesar need never have led his troops across the Rubicon, that thousands of lives might have been saved.

But Cato's failings are identical with his claims to heroic status. What in the man was awkward was transmuted by time and changing political circumstance to become, in the context of the legend that grew up around him, evidence of his superhuman fortitude. His obstinate refusal to take note of historical change or political expediency is a manifestation of his magnificent staunchness. His tactlessness and naïveté are the tokens of his integrity. His unpopularity proves his resolution. Even his downfall is a measure of his selfless nobility. He opposes Julius Caesar—by common consent one of Western history's great men—and is inevitably defeated by him, but his defeat makes him even greater than that great opponent. He dies as a flawed and vulnerable person, and rises again as a marmoreal ideal. Seneca, writing in the next century, imagined the king of the gods coming down among men in search of instances of human grandeur. "I do not know what nobler sight Jupiter could find on earth," he wrote, "than the spectacle of Cato . . . standing erect amid the ruins of the commonwealth."

Cato's life began and ended in times of civil war. When he was seven years old the Roman general Sulla marched on Rome at the head of his legions, demanding the leadership of the campaign against King Mithridates of Pontus. The Senate capitulated. Sulla then departed for the east, leaving his followers to be killed by his political enemies. Five years later, after having subdued all Asia Minor, he returned to Italy and fought his way to Rome, confronting and defeating the armies of the consuls. Once he had taken the city the people granted him absolute power. He set about putting to death anyone who had opposed him. His proscriptions, the terrible lists of those outlawed with a price on their heads that served as an incitement to mass murder, were posted in the Forum. Forty senators and at least sixteen hundred others (nine thousand according to one source) were named. Some were formally executed, some murdered by Sulla's paid killers, some torn part by the mob. Cato was thirteen at the time. His father, by then dead, had been favored by Sulla. Plutarch, who wrote his *Life of Cato* a century and a half after Cato's death but whose sources included accounts (subsequently lost) written by Cato's contemporaries, relates that the boy's tutor took him to pay court to the dictator. Sulla's house was an "Inferno," where his opponents were tortured and on whose walls their severed heads were displayed. Eyeing the ghastly trophies, hearing the groans of the crowd around the gate, the boy asked why no one acted to stop the killing. The tutor replied that they were all afraid. Early in his life Cato witnessed at first hand what befalls a state whose constitution has been overturned by a military dictator.

He bore an illustrious name. He was the great-grandson of Cato the Censor, a man who was remembered as an embodiment of the stern virtues ascribed by posterity to the Roman Republic in its prime. The Censor was a byword for his asceticism and his moral rigor. He traveled everywhere on foot, even when he came to hold high office. At home he worked alongside his farm laborers, bare-chested in summer and in winter wearing only a sleeveless smock, and was content with a cold breakfast, a frugal dinner, and a humble cottage to live in. Wastage was abhorrent to him. To his rigorous avoidance of it he sacrificed both beauty and kindness. He disliked gardens: land was for tilling and grazing. When his slaves became too old to work he sold them rather than feed useless mouths. In office he was as harsh on others as he was on himself. When he discovered that one of his subordinates had been buying prisoners of war as slaves (a form of insider trading which was improper but not illegal), the man hanged himself rather than suffer the Censor's rebuke. Grim, graceless, and incorruptible, the elder Cato was unpopular but generally revered. The younger Cato, or so several of his contemporaries believed, took him as a model.

His early career followed the conventional path for a young man of Rome's ruling class. When Crassus put down the revolt of the slaves under Spartacus, Cato served as a volunteer in his army, his zeal and self-discipline, according to Plutarch, providing a striking contrast with the "effeminacy and luxury" of his fellow officers. He was without self-indulgence. Like his virtuous ancestor, who "never embraced his wife except when a loud peel of thunder occurred," he was sexually abstemious, remaining a virgin until his first marriage (something unusual enough to arouse comment). Surly and forbidding in company, in private he drilled himself rigorously for the political career before him. He frequented philosophers, especially the Stoic Antipater, "and devoted himself especially to ethical and political doctrines." He trained his voice and disciplined his body not only by exercising hard but by a program of self-mortification involving exposure to all weathers.

When he was twenty-eight he stood for election as one of the twenty-four military tribunes chosen each year. In canvassing for support he shamed and irritated his fellow candidates by being the only one of them to obey the law forbidding the employment of nomenclators, useful people (usually slaves) whose job it was to murmur in the candidate's ear the name of the man whose vote he was soliciting. Despite this self-imposed handicap he won his place and was posted to Macedonia to command a legion. He proved himself an efficient and popular officer. When his year's term of office was up he made a grand tour of Asia Minor before returning home, stopping at Ephesus to pay his respects to Pompey. To the surprise of all observers Rome's greatest commander—Caesar's career was only just beginning—rose to greet the young man, advanced towards him and gave him his hand "as though to honour a superior."

Cato was still young, his political career had yet to begin, but he was already somebody to whom the mighty deferred. Exactly how he achieved that status is mysterious. He was not physically remarkable: none of the ancient authors considered his looks worth describing. A portrait bust shows him with a lean and bony face, a serviceable container for a mind but not a thing of beauty. He came of a distinguished family, but so did plenty of other hopeful young Romans. He had inherited some money; so did most men of his class. He had done decent service in the army, but he was never to prove a particularly gifted warrior. His distinguishing characteristics were those of inflexibility and outspokenness, scarcely the best qualifications for worldly success. He was more studious than most, but what was impressive about him seems to have had little to do with his intellectual attainments. Something marked him out, something very different from the dangerous brilliance of Achilles or Alcibiades' winning glamour, something which his contemporaries called "authority."

According to Plutarch he was already a known and respected figure in his early teens. When Sulla was appointing leaders for the two teams of boys who performed the Troy Game, a ritual mock battle, one team rejected the youth appointed and clamored for Cato. In adulthood his acknowledged incorruptibility gave him a kind of power which was independent of any formal rank. From his first entry into public life, the amount of influence he was able to exert and the deference he inspired were unprecedented for one so comparatively young. His ascendancy over the Roman political scene has been described by the German historian Christian Meier as "one of the strangest phenomena in the whole of history." Inexplicable in terms of his official or social status, it can only have derived from the extraordinary force of his personality.

By the time he returned to Rome from Asia he was thirty, and therefore eligible to stand for election as one of the twenty quaestors. The constitution of republican Rome was a complicated hybrid, evolved over centuries. The state was administered by annually elected officials—in ascending order of seniority, quaestors, aediles, praetors, and consuls. The consuls, of whom two were elected at a time, each for a year's term, had originally been military commanders and generally absent from the metropolis, but by Cato's day it had become normal for them to remain in Rome for their year of office, departing at the end of it, each to his own province, which he would govern for an additional year.

The consuls were the senior members of the Senate, but they were not prime ministers. Each officeholder held power independently of all the rest. There might be alliances between them but there was no unified government, no cabinet of ministers working in concert. Anyone who had ever held office became a lifelong member of the Senate. Theoretically any free adult male could present himself for election to office once he attained the prescribed age. In practice only the rich could afford to do so. Election campaigns were expensive. Bribery was commonplace. And if it cost a lot of money to gain office, it cost far more to hold it. Officials were expected to provide their own staff, to lay on public games and maintain public buildings, all at their own expense. And not only were officeholders obliged to spend money copiously: they were debarred, for the rest of their lives, from earning it. It was forbidden for a senator to engage in business. Besides, to win elections it was necessary to have the right connections. Inevitably the majority of senators were drawn from a small pool of families, of which Cato's was one, of substantial wealth and long-established influence.

But Rome was nonetheless a democracy. The Senate was not a legislative body. Its members could propose laws, but those laws were passed or rejected by the people of Rome—the male, adult, unenslaved people—voting in person. And the people's interests were protected by the tribunes of the people, elected officials (ten a year) who shared with the consuls and praetors the right to propose laws to the voters, who had the devastating power of the veto—a single tribune could block any measure—and whose persons were sacrosanct.

In Cato's lifetime this ramshackle and mutually inconvenient assemblage of institutions began to self-destruct. The upholders of the ancient constitution—of whom Cato was to become the most passionately committed—struggled to enforce the elaborate rules which were designed, above all, to ensure that no one man should ever achieve too much power. They failed. Defying the Senate, making use of the tribunes and appealing direct to the people, first Pompey, then Crassus, and at last, and most conclusively, Julius Caesar demanded and obtained powers which vastly exceeded any that the constitution allowed. It was Cato's life's work to oppose them.

From his first entry into public life Cato signaled his punctilious regard for the workings of the constitution. To most candidates the post of quaestor, the most junior magistracy, was primarily the portal whereby a man entered the Senate, not so much a job as a rite of passage. In 65 BC Cato astonished all observers by qualifying himself for the position before applying for it. The quaestors were responsible for the administration of public funds. According to Plutarch, Cato "read the law relating to the quaestorships, learned all the details of the office from those who had had experience in it, and formed a general idea of its power and scope." Once elected he assumed control of the treasury and instituted a purge of the clerks who had been accepting bribes and embezzling money with impunity. Next he set about paying those, however insignificant, to whom the state was indebted, and "rigorously and inexorably" demanding payment from those, however influential, who were its debtors, a policy whose simple rectitude appeared to his contemporaries breathtakingly novel.

The society in which Cato lived was described by his contemporary Sallust (who was himself convicted of extortion) as one where "instead of modesty, incorruptibility and honesty, shamelessness, bribery and rapacity held sway." Sulla's coup, the ensuing civil wars, and his reign of terror had left the state punch-drunk and reeling. More recently and insidiously a series of constitutional reforms and counterreforms had undermined the perceived legitimacy of established institutions. Meanwhile wealth flooded into Rome from the conquered provinces, but there was no mechanism whereby the state could put it to good use and few channels for its redistribution among the populace. Rome had no revenue service. Romans paid no tax, but the inhabitants of the overseas provinces did. The money was collected by tax farmers, who paid dearly for the right to do the job and who set the level of tribute high enough to ensure themselves handsome profits. The Roman provincial governors who oversaw their operations took their cut as well. Corruption was endemic throughout the system. The records of Rome's law courts are full of cases of returning governors facing charges of extortion. It was a time when the best lacked all conviction: Sallust denounced those magnates who squandered their wealth shamefully on fantastically grandiose projects for beautifying their private grounds—"they levelled mountains and built upon the seas"—instead of spending it honorably for the public's good, and Cicero inveighed against aristocrats who chose to retire to their country estates and breed rare goldfish rather than wrestle with the intractable problems besetting the state.

In such a society Cato, scrupulously balancing his books, shone out. Heroes of a flashier sort disdain accountancy. In Alcibiades' youth, when his guardian Pericles was accused of using public money for his own private ends, Alcibiades told him "you should be seeking not how to render, but how not to render an accounting" and advised him to divert attention from his alleged embezzlements by provoking a major war. But Cato was a man who believed that right and wrong were absolute and nonnegotiable, that ethics was a discipline as clear and exact as arithmetic. In paintings of his death it is conventional for the artist to include, along with the sword and the book, an abacus, the tool of the accountant and token of his absolute integrity.

Under his administration the treasury became an instrument of justice. There were still at large several men known to have been used as assassins by Sulla at the time of his murderous proscriptions. "All men hated them as accursed and polluted wretches," says Plutarch, "but no one had the courage to punish them." No one, that is, except Cato. He demanded that they repay the large sums with which they had been rewarded for their killings, and publicly denounced them. Shortly thereafter they finally came to trial.

Eccentric as Cato's straight dealing was perceived to be, it won him a degree of respect quite disproportionate to his actual achievements. His truth telling became a byword. "When speaking of matters that were strange and incredible, people would say, as though using a proverb, 'This is not to be believed even though Cato says it.' " Any defendant who attempted to have him removed from a jury was immediately assumed to be guilty. His evident probity gave him a degree of power out of all proportion to his official rank. It was said that he had given the relatively lowly office of quaestor the dignity normally attached to that of consul.

He had become a notable player in the political game. That game, as played in the last years of the Roman Republic, was a rough one. Rome had no police force. Prominent people never went out alone. In good times they were accompanied wherever they went by an entourage of clients and servants. In bad times they had their own bodyguards, troops of armed slaves and gladiators in some cases so numerous as to amount to private armies. Political dispute developed, rapidly and often, into physical conflict. To read the ancient historians' account of the period is to be repeatedly astonished by the contrast between the grandeur and efficacy of Rome's rule over its expanding empire and the rowdiness and violence at the very heart of it. The Forum was not only parliament, law court, sports arena, theater, and place of worship. It was also, frequently, a battlefield. The temples which surrounded it, which were used on occasion as debating chambers or polling stations, could and frequently did serve as fortresses occupied and defended by fighting men. During his career Cato was spat upon, stripped of his toga, pelted with dung, dragged from the rostrum (the platform in the Forum from which orators addressed the people), beaten up, and hauled off to prison. He escaped with his life, but he was present on occasions when others did not. The making of a political speech, in his lifetime, was an act which called for considerable courage.

His quaestorship over, he was an assiduous senator, always first to arrive in the morning at the Senate house and last to leave, attending every session to ensure no corrupt measure could be debated without his being there to oppose it. But in 63 BC he resolved to take a reading holiday. He set off for his country estate, accompanied by a group of his favorite philosophers and several donkeys loaded down with books. The projected idyll—quiet reading and high-minded discussion in a bucolic setting—was aborted. On the road Cato met Metellus Nepos, brother-in-law and loyal supporter of Pompey. Learning that Nepos was on his way to Rome to stand for election as a tribune of the people, Cato decided that it was his duty to return forthwith and oppose him.

The republic, he thought, was in imminent danger. Two years previously, during Cato's quaestorship, a group of influential men had plotted a coup d'état. The plot was aborted, but those suspected of instigating it were all still at liberty, all highly visible on the political scene. The ancient historians differ as to who they were. Sallust identifies the ringleader as Catiline, a charismatic, dangerous man whom Cicero credited with a phenomenal gift for corrupting others and a corresponding one for "stimulating his associates into vigorous activity." Catiline was a glamorous figure: nineteen hundred years later Charles Baudelaire was to identify him, along with Alcibiades and Julius Caesar, as being one of the first and most brilliant of the dandies. Scandals clung to his name. He was said to have seduced a vestal virgin, even to have murdered his own stepson to please a mistress. His sulfurous reputation hadn't prevented him achieving the rank of praetor, but his first attempt to win the consulship was thwarted when he was accused of extortion. Sallust maintains that, blocked from attaining power by legitimate means, Catiline plotted to assassinate the successful candidates and make himself consul by force.

Suetonius, on the other hand, asserts that the chief conspirators were Crassus and Caesar. Crassus was a man some seventeen years older than Cato who had grown fabulously rich by profiting from others' misfortunes. He had laid the foundations of his wealth at the time of Sulla's proscriptions, buying up the confiscated property of murdered men at rock-bottom prices. He had multiplied it by acquiring burned-out houses for next to nothing—in Rome, a cramped and largely wooden city, fires were frequent and widespread—and rebuilding them with his workforce of hundreds of specially trained slaves until he was said to own most of Rome. A genial host, a generous dispenser of loans, and a shrewd patron of the potentially useful, he ensured that his money brought him immense influence. No one, he is reported to have said, could call himself rich until he was able to support an army on his income. He was one who could.

Julius Caesar was one of Crassus's many debtors. Five years older than Cato and politically and temperamentally his opposite, he was already noted for his military successes, his sexual promiscuity, and his fabulous munificence, all of which endeared him to the populace. As aedile in 65 BC, the year of the alleged conspiracy, he staged at his own expense a series of wild-beast hunts and games of unprecedented magnificence, filling the Forum with temporary colonnades and covering the Capitol hill with sideshows. In Alcibiades' lifetime Plato had warned that "any politician who seeks to please the people excessively . . . is doing so only in order to establish himself as a tyrant." Whether or not he was actually plotting sedition, Caesar was already one of the handful of men who threatened to destabilize the Roman state—as Alcibiades had once undermined the stability of Athens—simply by being too glittering, too popular, too great.

But though Catiline, Crassus, and Caesar were all present in Rome when Cato returned in 63 BC to stand for election, it was Pompey whom the guardians of republican principles were watching most apprehensively. It was because Metellus Nepos was Pompey's man that Cato had felt it so imperative to oppose him. Pompey had treated Cato graciously in Ephesus, but Cato was not the man to be won over by a display of good manners, however flattering. Cato was a legalist. His political philosophy was based on the premise that only by a strict and absolute adherence to the letter of the law could the republic be preserved. Pompey's entire career had been conducted in the law's defiance.

When only twenty-three Pompey had raised an army of his own and appointed himself its commander. When he returned triumphant from Spain in 71 BC he had insisted on being allowed to stand for consul—the highest office in the state—despite the fact that he was ten years too young and had not previously held an elected office, and he had backed up his demand by bringing his legions menacingly close to the city. Sulla had drastically reduced the powers of the tribunes, and enhanced those of the Senate. As consul in 70 BC, Pompey had reversed the balance. In subsequent years he had seen to it that a fair number of the tribunes were his supporters and he worked through them, as Caesar was to do later, to bypass the increasingly unhappy Senate, and appeal directly to the electorate for consent to the expansion of his privileges and power.

In 66 BC a tribune had proposed and seen to the passage of a law granting Pompey extraordinary and unprecedented powers to rid the eastern Mediterranean of pirates. In the following year another tribune had proposed he be granted command of the campaign against Mithridates of Pontus—Sulla's old adversary, who had risen against Rome again. Military commands brought glory, which in turn brought popularity. They brought tribute money and ransoms and loot which could be used to buy power. Besides, military commanders had armies, as the Senate did not. Pompey had been spectacularly successful, both against the pirates and against Mithridates. There were plenty who remembered that he had begun his career as one of Sulla's commanders, that it was Sulla who had named him "Pompey the Great." And Sulla, who had returned from defeating Mithridates to make war on Rome itself, had set a terrible precedent. In 63 BC the senators awaited the return of their victorious general with mounting fear.

Cato and Metellus Nepos were both among those elected to hold office as tribunes in the following year. At once Cato resumed his role as self-appointed guardian of public morality, while simultaneously demonstrating how unable, and indeed unwilling, he was to act the wily politician. He accused one of his own political allies, the consul Murena, of bribery. He was almost certainly correct in doing so. The bribing of voters was so commonplace that Cato's own refusal to practice it made him highly unpopular. But those who had assumed that Cato was their ally were exasperated. Cicero, the celebrated advocate who was the other great luminary of the constitutionalist party, defended Murena (and got him off), remarking acidly in court that Cato had acted "as if he were living in Plato's Republic, rather than among the dregs of Romulus's descendants," a remark designed less to lament the imperfection of modern life than to reproach the incorruptible Cato for his political ineptitude.

Later that year, though, Cato got the chance to demonstrate that what he lacked in adroitness he made up for in passion and persuasiveness. For years he had been developing his powers of oratory, rigorously preparing himself for his calling, and he had, besides, two gifts worth more than any acquired rhetorical skill. One was an exceptionally powerful voice. It was loud and penetrating enough for him to be able to speak, without any form of amplification, to enormous crowds, and he had trained and exercised it until he had the stamina and the lung power to speak all day at full volume. The other was ferocity. He is reported to have believed that political oratory was a discipline as warlike as the defense of a city, and he put his theory into practice. His speeches were performances of thunderous belligerence, full of devastating energy, of aggression and righteous rage. He was soon to have occasion to employ his talent.

Catiline had once more stood for election as consul and lost. Whether or not he had conspired against the state two years earlier, this time he certainly did. According to Sallust he bound his followers to him with a solemn ritual during which they were all required to drink from a cup full of human blood, and he prepared to lead an armed revolt.

Cicero was consul. He heard—from his wife, who had heard it from a female friend who had heard it from her lover who was one of Catiline's fellow conspirators—that Catiline's coup was imminent. Unable to act on such hearsay evidence, Cicero provided himself with a bodyguard of hired thugs and ostentatiously wore a breastplate in public, as though to announce that he knew he and his fellow officeholders were under threat and that he was ready to defend himself. Catiline, too, had his personal guard, made up, according to a contemporary, of "troops of criminals and reprobates of every kind." The situation was doubly dangerous. The prospect of an uprising was alarming in itself. Even worse, to Cato and like-minded senators, was the probability that Pompey would use it as a pretext for bringing his legions back to Italy and marching on Rome, ostensibly to suppress the revolt, but in fact to seize power for himself. It was among the most essential provisions of the Roman constitution that no army should ever be brought into Rome, and that a military leader must lay aside his command—and the legal immunity it gave him—before entering the city. When in Rome, all Romans were civilians and subject to the law. Sulla had breached that rule, with terrible consequences for the republic. There was a real prospect that Pompey, Sulla's protégé, might follow his lead.

In October there was an uprising in Etruria. In November an armed gang attempted to force its way into Cicero's house before dawn, apparently to assassinate him, but were driven off by his guards. In an atmosphere of mounting panic, rumors circulated that the conspirators intended to burn the city to the ground. The Senate declared a state of emergency, but still there was no concrete evidence against anyone. Catiline defiantly took his seat in the Senate. No one would sit next to him. Shortly afterwards he left to join the rebels in the countryside. At last a letter was intercepted naming the leading conspirators. On December 3 the five who were still in Rome were arrested.

What was to be done with them? Two days later the Senate met in a temple on the edge of the Forum. Outside were crowds whose shouts and murmurs could be heard from within the chamber, crowds which included many of Catiline's supporters. Around the building, and in all the other temples in the Forum, were stationed Cicero's armed guard. It was a dangerous and solemn occasion. The first speakers all demanded "the extreme penalty," clearly meaning death. Then came the turn of Julius Caesar.

Caesar's speech on that momentous December day was elegant, tightly argued, and—given that he himself was widely suspected of having instigated the earlier plot and of complicity in the current one—coolly audacious. Summary execution was illegal, he argued. The conspirators deserved punishment but to kill them without legal sanction would be to set a dangerous precedent. He advocated life imprisonment "under the severest terms" instead. So persuasive was he (and so intimidating) that all the following speakers endorsed his opinion, and of those who had spoken earlier several abjectly claimed that by "extreme penalty" they had meant not execution, but precisely the kind of sentence Caesar was now recommending. The outcome of the debate seemed certain. At this point, very late in the proceedings because senators spoke in order of seniority and he was one of the youngest and lowest-ranking, Cato intervened.

His speech was electrifying. Caesar had been suave; Cato was enraged. With the furious probity of a Saint-Just he denounced the pusillanimous senators. Sarcastic and passionate by turn, he sneered at them— "You, who have always valued your houses, villas, statues and paintings more highly than our country"—and fiercely drove them on. "Now in the name of the immortal gods I call upon you. . . . Wake up at last and lay hold of the reins of the state!" He mocked, he ranted, he painted a luridly dramatic picture of the dangers besetting the commonwealth. Finally, with awful solemnity, he demanded that the conspirators be put to death. The potency of his performance was demonstrated by its effect. When he had finished the senators, one after another, rose and went to stand beside him to signal their agreement. Caesar, who only minutes before had held the assembly in his hand, was left isolated. For once losing his famous imperturbability, Caesar protested furiously. There was a fracas, during which (according to some sources) Cato accused Caesar of complicity with the conspirators. Cicero's guard intervened, drawing their swords. Caesar was nearly killed in the ensuing mêlée. Some kind of order was restored. Caesar left. The Senate stood firm behind Cato. The conspirators were led, one by one, across the Forum, through the agitated crowd, which included some of their confederates, to the place of punishment. There, in an underground chamber "hideous and fearsome to behold," they were strangled. A few weeks later Catiline himself was killed in battle.

So began the essential drama of Cato's life. "For a long time," wrote Sallust, "no one at all appeared in Rome who was great. But within my own memory there have been two men of towering merit, Cato and Caesar." Two thousand years on Caesar is by far the more celebrated of the two, thanks in part to his skillful fostering of his own fame, in part to our culture's infatuation with military conquest. But to those who knew them the two looked evenly matched: a comparable pair of brilliantly gifted men. They clashed for the first time in the debate over the conspirators' sentence. From that day until his death seventeen years later Cato was to remain Caesar's most inveterate political opponent.

Each of them was the prime representative of one of two tendencies in Roman political life. (To call them parties would be to suggest a degree of cohesiveness notably absent from the political scene.) Cato was to become the most eloquent spokesman of the *optimates*, Caesar the most successful of the *populares*. *Optimates* and *populares* alike were oligarchs drawn from the same exclusive group of rich and well-descended Romans, but they differed in the ways in which they played the complicated political system of the republic. The *populares* were soldiers and empire builders, or their clients and admirers, who tended to bypass the Senate, to enlist the support of tribunes and through them of the electorate at large. Like Alcibiades, they were aristocratic populists, distrusted by their peers but adored by an electorate to whom they offered the violent excitements and huge potential profits of warfare. The *optimates*—civilians at heart—were the defenders of the power of the Senate, sticklers for the rules designed to uphold the senators' dignity and, most importantly, to ensure that military commanders were prevented from using their armies to seize personal power.

Within a week of the executions of Catilinarian conspirators the new tribunes, Cato and Metellus Nepos among them, took office, and so did Caesar as praetor. At once Nepos fulfilled Cato's worst fears by proposing that Pompey, his patron, be recalled to Rome with his legions "to restore order." When Nepos's proposal was discussed in the Senate, Caesar supported it, but Cato raged against it with such vehemence that some observers thought he was out of his mind. As a tribune he had the right to veto the measure and he announced that he would do so, swearing passionately "that while he lived Pompey should not enter the city with an armed force."

This was no empty piece of rhetoric. It was widely believed that the *populares* would prevent Cato by whatever means were necessary, up to and including murder, from blocking their way. He would have to declare his veto formally the following day when the people were asked to vote on the measure in the Forum. That night he slept deeply, but he was alone in his household in doing so. According to Plutarch "great dejection and fear reigned, his friends took no food and watched all night with one another in futile discussion on his behalf, while his wife and sisters wailed and wept."

It was customary for friends and political allies to call for an officeholder at his house in the morning and escort him down to the Forum as a public demonstration of support. But on the day of the vote, so effectively had Nepos and Caesar cowed their opponents, Cato had only one companion of note, another tribune by the name of Thermus. As the two of them, attended only by a handful of servants, made their way towards the place of assembly they met well-wishers who exhorted them to be on their guard but who fearfully declined to accompany them. Arriving, they found the Forum packed with people whom Nepos had succeeded in rousing to his cause and surrounded by his and Caesar's armed slaves. (Caesar owned several gladiatorial training schools and had brought a unprecedented number of gladiators to Rome for the games he staged in 65 BC. The games over, he kept the surviving slaves around him as an armed guard.)

Nepos and Caesar were already seated in a commanding position on the exceptionally high and steep podium of the Temple of Castor. On the temple steps a troop of gladiators were massed. Seeing them, Cato exclaimed, "What a bold man, and what a coward, to levy such an army against a single unarmed and defenceless person!" Accompanied only by Thermus he pushed through the hostile crowd. The gladiators, disconcerted by his courage, made way for him. Climbing onto the podium, he brusquely positioned himself between Nepos and Caesar.

A law upon which the people were to vote had first to be read out loud to them. A herald prepared to declaim Nepos's proposed measure. Cato, announcing his veto, stopped him. Nepos, in defiance of law and custom, attempted to override the veto. Snatching the document from the herald he began to read it himself. Cato ripped it from him. Nepos continued to recite it from memory. Thermus, Cato's sole supporter, clapped a hand over his mouth.

The tussle was taking place in full view of an excited and increasingly volatile crowd. People were yelling out encouragement for one side or another as though watching a gladiatorial show, and increasing numbers were shouting for Cato. "They urged one another to stay and band themselves together and not betray their liberty and the man who was striving to defend it." Furious at being so thwarted Nepos signaled to his guards, who charged into the mob with fearsome yells, precipitating a riot which lasted for several hours. It was a day of brutal mayhem. At one point Nepos, having temporarily regained control of the Forum, attempted to force what would have been an entirely illegal vote. At another, Cato, standing dangerously exposed on the tribunal, was stoned by the crowd and only saved from perhaps fatal injury by the intervention of the consul Murena (the man he had accused of bribery), who wrapped him in his own toga and dragged him into the shelter of a temple.

Nepos's followers were eventually driven out. Cato addressed the people and, battered and exhausted as he must have been, he spoke with such fervor he managed to win them over entirely. The Senate assembled again and rallied behind him, condemning Nepos's law. Nepos, according to Plutarch, saw "that his followers were completely terrified before Cato and thought him utterly invincible." In defiance of the rule that no tribune might leave the city during his term of office, he fled, "crying out that he was fleeing from Cato's tyranny," and made his way to Pompey's camp in Asia. Caesar's praetorship was temporarily suspended. The episode was a great political victory for Cato. Characteristically he contrived to make it a moral one as well when he opposed a motion to deprive Nepos of his office: the tribunate must remain inviolable, however flawed the tribune might be.

In 61 BC Pompey returned from the east and celebrated his triumph. He had conquered fifteen countries and taken nine hundred cities, eight hundred ships, and a thousand fortresses. For two whole days the celebrations engulfed Rome as the entire populace turned out to see the show. Captured monarchs and their children were led in procession along with manacled pirate chiefs. Huge placards proclaimed Pompey's victories. There were bands playing; there were military trophies; there were wagonloads of weaponry and precious metal. Finally there came Pompey himself wreathed with bay, his face painted to resemble Jupiter, his purple toga spangled with gold stars. He wore a cloak which had purportedly belonged to Alexander the Great. Beside him in his gem-encrusted chariot rode a slave whose task it was to whisper ceaselessly "Remember you are human" in his ear while all about the noisy, gaudy, amazing spectacle proclaimed the opposite. Behind the godlike victor marched lines of soldiers, all hymning his glory.

It was a spectacle which boded ill for republican liberty, but for the time being Cato's dark forebodings of civil war and dictatorship were not realized. Pompey, for all his magnificence, was still a republican. In Asia he had repudiated Nepos. Now he dismissed his army and reentered Rome as a private citizen, apparently intent on seeking a legitimate channel for his power. It was not his ambition but Cato's absolute refusal to allow any compromise or concession to be made to him that rendered that impossible.

Doggedly disobliging, implacably opposed to the slightest modification of a political system which, like Sophocles' tree, looked doomed to break if it would not bend, Cato watched and obstructed Pompey's every maneuver. It was Cato who persuaded the Senate not to grant Pompey's request that the consular elections be postponed so that he might stand for office. It was Cato who vociferously opposed the ratification of Pompey's settlements in the east. And it was Cato who spoke loudest against the bill whereby Pompey sought to reward his veterans for their

victories with plots carved out of the publicly owned land controlled by
the Senate. Pompey patiently endured Cato's relentless obstructiveness.
He attempted to dissolve this thorn in his flesh by proposing a double
marriage, with himself and his son as bridegrooms to Cato's nieces (or
perhaps his daughters), further evidence of the astonishingly high regard
in which this still comparatively junior politician was held. Cato refused,
saying, "Tell Pompey that Cato is not to be captured by way of the women's apartments." Once again, in rejecting an opportunity to bind
Pompey to the constitutionalist faction, he had done his own cause a
grave disservice.

He did it another one when he antagonized Crassus. A consortium of
tax farmers had paid too high for the right to raise money in Asia Minor.
Unable to make a profit, they attempted to renegotiate their contract
with the Senate. Crassus backed them. Cato opposed them with manic
obduracy. Talking indefatigably for day after day he succeeded in blocking the measure for months on end, effectively paralyzing the Senate by
the sheer power of his obstinate will.

In 60 BC Julius Caesar, who had been campaigning in Spain, also
returned to Rome. He had been granted a triumph for his Iberian conquests. In order to celebrate it he was obliged to remain outside the sacrosanct bounds of the city, but he wished (as Pompey had) to be elected
consul for the following year, and in order to declare his candidacy he had
to be in Rome. He asked the Senate's permission to stand for office in
absentia. Cato opposed him. A decision had to be reached before nightfall
on a certain day. Once more Cato filibustered, haranguing his colleagues
in his powerful, rasping voice until the sun went down. The next morning
Caesar laid aside his command, thus giving up his triumph, and entered
the city to seek election.

Rome's three most powerful men had each found that, thanks to
Cato's intransigence, they were unable to impose their will on the Senate.
They resolved instead to ignore it. In 60 BC Pompey, Caesar, and Crassus
arrived at a secret agreement. Their alliance (known as the First
Triumvirate) made them the effective though unacknowledged rulers of
Rome, their combined wealth, manpower, and political influence allow-
ing them to bypass or overrule all the institutions of government.

Cato was outraged. Over the next four years, in the face of political
intimidation that frequently escalated into violence, he unswervingly
opposed the incremental growth of the power of Rome's inordinately
great men. Every time a rule was bent, a precedent ignored, an extraordinary privilege granted, he was there to oppose the innovation. Tireless

and tiresome in equal measure, "always ready," as Theodor Mommsen wrote, "to throw himself into the breach whether it was necessary to do so or not," he let nothing pass. Caesar was consul in 59 BC. Cato obstructed and opposed his every move. Caesar proposed another bill making grants of land to Pompey's soldiers. Pompey brought his veterans, the very men who would benefit from the measure, into the city, a tacit threat to anyone inclined to oppose its passage. A time limit was set for the Senate's discussion. Nervously aware of the armed men thronging the streets around them, few dared speak at all, but when it came to Cato's turn he rose and, employing his favorite tactic, attempted to block the measure by speaking for hours on end. This time, though, he had an opponent with scant respect for senatorial procedure. Caesar set his gang of gladiators to drag him from the rostrum and haul him off to the prison cells where Catiline's co-conspirators had been done to death. As Cato was hustled away he continued to harangue the senators. Several followed him "with downcast looks." Caesar called them back, demanding they finish the business in hand. One bravely replied, "I prefer to be with Cato in prison rather than here with you." Cato was marched across the Forum, still talking at the top of his powerful voice to the shocked and fearful crowd. He was released almost immediately, but his imprisonment was a crucial turning point in the history of the republic, the moment when Caesar demonstrated that he would have his way, with or without the law.

There was little Cato could do in the face of such intimidation. Pompey, who had wished to be Cato's son-in-law, became Caesar's instead, marrying Caesar's daughter Julia, who was thirty years his junior. Increasingly confident, Caesar proposed a second land law. It was passed, for all Cato's protests, the people seeming as entranced by Caesar's glamour as the Athenians had been by Alcibiades' (or perhaps they were just afraid of his enforcers). So was the one granting Caesar Gaul and Illyria for his provinces, not for the usual one-year term, but for five years. A few years later Horace was to advise a poet wishing to represent Achilles, "Let him deny that the law was made for him." Caesar, bending every rule, ignoring every precedent, was acting with an Achillean disdain for legality. As the people gathered in the Forum to vote, Cato addressed them with desperate vehemence, warning "that they themselves were establishing a tyrant in their citadel." They voted for the measure regardless.

Caesar boasted at the end of his consulate that he had got everything he wanted to the accompaniment of his opponents' groans; now he was free to dance on their heads. He departed for Gaul, having first contrived the election as tribune of his protégé Clodius, the man who was to plunge Rome into a state of such anarchy that in Cicero's words "the blood that streamed from the Forum had to be mopped up with sponges."

Clodius, whose personal name was Pulcher, "Beautiful," dominated the circle of young aristocrats against whom Sallust railed for their "lewdness" and "luxury," their total lack of reverence for gods or manmade institutions. A blasphemer and sexual transgressor like Alcibiades, Clodius was also, as the events of the next six years were to show, a brilliant political organizer, a charismatic demagogue, and a man of dangerously unpredictable allegiance who was capable of turning savagely on magnates who had complacently imagined themselves to be manipulating him.

Immediately after taking office he legalized the previously outlawed *collegia*, institutions which were part trade union, part neighborhood self-defense group, and part political club, and set about transforming them into units of street-fighting men. Owing their new legitimacy to him, the *collegia* became Clodius's own instruments, making him, whether in or out of office, the warlord of the streets. First, though, he had to rid himself of those few public figures with the nerve and integrity to oppose him. He had Cicero sent into exile on the pretext that the executions of the Catilinarian conspirators had been illegal. Cato (without whom those executions would not have taken place) was treated less rudely. He was given the task of annexing Cyprus.

It was a prestigious and potentially lucrative assignment, but Cato saw it only as a means of getting rid of him. It was one of the fundamental differences between the constitutionalists like Cato and the *populares* that the former clung to the anachronistic sense that nowhere outside Rome mattered. When Cicero was appointed governor of Cilicia in Asia Minor, he was to tell his friend Atticus that the task was "a colossal bore." To others it might have seemed a way of seeing the world. But he was pining for "the world, the Forum," which to him seemed one and same. Likewise to Cato, that cramped and teeming rectangular space at the center of Rome was the hub of the universe, the only place were words and actions had consequences. He accepted overseas postings grudgingly, and dispatched them without enthusiasm. After his term of office as praetor came to an end he actually turned down the provincial governorship to which he was entitled. Pompey and Caesar, by contrast, made the provinces—the armies they were entitled to levy in order to subdue them and the fortunes they amassed there—the foundations of their power.

Cato's role in Cyprus turned out to be one to which he was exactly suited, that of inventory clerk. The island's ruler was a Ptolemy, brother of the king of Egypt, who was to be ousted ostensibly because he had supported the pirates against Pompey but also so that his personal wealth and the revenue from his prosperous island could be added to the magnificence of Rome. Cato was not required to act the conqueror. On receiving his letter calling upon him to abdicate, Ptolemy poisoned himself. All Cato had to do was take possession of his realm and convert his treasure into currency. This he did virtually single-handed, to the annoyance of his followers. Refusing to delegate any responsibility he personally negotiated with merchants and with private buyers, ensuring he got the highest possible price for all the jewels and golden cups and purple robes and other "furnishing of the princely sort" poor Ptolemy had left. "For this reason," reports Plutarch, "he gave offence to most of his friends, who thought that he distrusted them." (They were probably right.) The task was an immense one—the sum he brought back from Cyprus was so great that when it was carried through Rome to the treasury the crowds stood amazed at the quantity of it—but Cato insisted on making himself personally responsible for every detail of its collection and transport. He decided how the money was to be shipped and designed special coffers for the purpose, each one trailing a long rope with a cork float attached so they could be retrieved in the case of shipwreck. He had the accounts written out in duplicate. He had called the assignment an insult, but the people of Rome had voted that he must do it, so—punctilious and dutiful as ever—do it he did, with the driven thoroughness he brought to all his appointed tasks.

While he did so, the Roman Republic staggered under Clodius's assault. "District by district," records Cicero, "men were being conscripted and enrolled into units and were being incited to violence, to blows, to murder, to looting." The *collegia*'s fighting bands were swelled by slaves. Gangs of swordsmen controlled the city's public spaces. The Temple of Castor and Pollux, the building whose high podium dominated the Forum and where Cato had twice suffered violence at Caesar's hands, was converted from a place of worship and public assembly into a fortress. Clodius had its steps demolished, rendering access to it hard and defense of it easy, and made it his arsenal and military headquarters. The political meetings, trials, and plebiscites for which the Forum was the venue—all the public business of the state—now took place under the intimidating gaze of Clodius's enforcers. Meetings of the Senate were interrupted by yelling crowds. A debate on Cicero's possible recall from exile was broken up by rioters throwing stones and wielding clubs and swords. Some of the tribunes were injured (shockingly, since they were supposed to be inviolate) and several other people killed. When one of Clodius's associates was put on trial a mob of his supporters invaded the court, overturning benches, dragging the judge from his place, knocking over the urns which served as ballot boxes, and driving the prosecutors and jury in terror from the place. No one was exempt. Clodius had appeared originally to be the triumvirs' tool but now he turned viciously on one of them. When Pompey attempted to speak in the Forum, Clodius led a mob in heckling him cruelly. A fight broke out between Pompey's men and Clodius's: several people were killed and a man was caught apparently in the act of attempting to assassinate Pompey himself. Baffled and afraid, Pompey withdrew to his villa, where he lived virtually besieged.

By the time Cato returned from Cyprus in 56 BC with his haul of scrupulously catalogued treasure, some kind of balance of power had been established, but at great cost to the cause of the constitutionalists and to the stability of the state. One of the new year's tribunes, Milo, with Pompey's encouragement and sponsorship, had assembled his own private army of slaves and hired thugs and emerged as a rival to Clodius. For weeks the two gangs fought for control of the city. "The Tiber was full of citizens' corpses," wrote Cicero; "the public sewers were choked with them." Clodius was at least temporarily contained. Pompey, recovering his nerve, reasserted himself and saw to it that Cicero was recalled, amid scenes of public rejoicing all over Italy. Bread was scarce; the people were rioting for food. Cicero, returning a favor, advocated a measure granting Pompey control of the corn supply for the next five years, a commission which gave him ill-defined but enormous power both domestically and (since most of Rome's corn was imported) throughout the Mediterranean.

Endemic violence, a near-total collapse of the rule of law, disastrous food shortages, the acceptance even by a moderate like Cicero that only an armed potentate could save the disordered state: the situation to which Cato returned was the fulfillment of his direst predictions. At once he resumed his old task, that of preventing the great men from becoming greater, with ever-decreasing hopefulness but never-failing obduracy.

Caesar, Pompey, and Crassus renewed their pact. Pompey and Crassus were standing together for election as the next year's consuls. The constitutionalists in the Senate went into mourning, as though for the death of the republic, but no one dared stand in opposition to the two magnates until Cato, who was not yet old enough to be eligible himself, persuaded his brother-in-law Domitius Ahenobarbus to do so and to declare that, if elected, he would terminate Caesar's unprecedentedly long command in Gaul. Before dawn on the morning of the election Cato and Domitius went together to the Field of Mars, where voting was to take place. They were set upon in the darkness. Their torchbearer was killed. Cato was wounded in the arm. With furious resolution he tried to persuade Domitius to stand his ground. His eloquence was futile. Ahenobarbus, less principled, less courageous, or perhaps just more realistic, abandoned his candidacy and took to his heels.

Cato, determined that the triumvirs should not be unopposed, stood for election as praetor. Pompey and Crassus put up a candidate of their own and set about bribing the electorate in a vote-buying exercise of unprecedented scale and blatancy. On the day of the election Pompey had the Field of Mars surrounded by Milo's thugs. Those who voted the wrong way could expect to suffer for it. Even so, Cato's prestige was so great that the first votes declared were for him. Bribery and intimidation having both failed, Pompey invoked the gods. He declared he had heard thunder (no one else had). Thunder being a sign of divine displeasure, he canceled the ballot. His supporters went to work on the voters again (whether with their money or their swords is not recorded). By the time a second vote was held, those who had initially voted for Cato had changed their minds.

Measure by measure the triumvirs consolidated their power. As consuls, Pompey and Crassus saw to it that they were assigned, as their proconsular commands, Spain and Syria respectively. They introduced bills allowing them to wage war as and when they saw fit and to levy as many troops as they wished. In addition, Pompey had it agreed that he could delegate the government of Spain to his officials while he himself remained near Rome. Each time the people voted in their favor while all but one of the senators, listless in their impotence, allowed the legislation to pass without questioning or comment. The exception, of course, was Cato.

A man whose greatest skill was that of making a nuisance of himself, he let none of these measures pass without a hurly-burly. Over and over again he forced his way onto the rostrum to harangue the people. Over and over again he was manhandled down. He was briefly imprisoned again. Nothing could silence him. Denied the rostrum he would mount his supporters' shoulders instead. There was rioting. People were killed. But Pompey and Crassus, unperturbed, proceeded to their most controversial move. They proposed that Caesar's command in Gaul be extended for a further five years. This called from Cato a speech of uttermost passion and solemnity. He told Pompey that he had taken Caesar upon his

own shoulders "and that when he began to feel the burden and to be overcome by it he would neither have the power to put it away nor the
strength to bear it longer, and would therefore precipitate himself, burden and all, upon the city." The prophecy, with its strange and awful
image of the two giants, one weighing down upon the other, crushing the
state beneath them as they toppled, was remembered by the historians,
but in the short term it was as futile as all of Cato's efforts. Caesar got his
extended command.

Cato kept up his attack. He argued in the Senate that Caesar's
aggression against the German and Gallic tribes was not only wicked but
illegal: the Senate, which supposedly determined Rome's foreign policy,
had not authorized it. The Gallic war, on which Caesar's enormous (and
still extant) fame was based, constituted a monstrous atrocity, a genocidal
war-crime carried out in full view of all the world over a period of nearly
a decade. Caesar had taken prisoner the leaders of two German tribes
when they came to him under terms of truce, and then massacred some
four hundred thousand of their people. This, fulminated Cato, was an
outrage for which the gods would exact retribution. Caesar should be put
in chains and handed over to the enemy for just punishment. Until his
guilt was expiated all Rome would be accursed. Legally speaking Cato
was correct, but the people of Rome preferred conquests, however
achieved, to a clear conscience. Caesar fought on.

Over the next two years Cato struggled ever more desperately for the
cause of legitimacy. It was like building card houses in a hurricane. In
Gaul Caesar, conquering tribe after tribe and carting their treasure away
with him, grew ever richer and more powerful. At the end of each campaigning season he returned to the Italian peninsula, bringing some of
his legions with him, and established himself in winter quarters near
Ravenna, which was within his province of Cisalpine Gaul. There he
received visitors from Rome, clients and suitors to whom he dispensed
largesse, agents who watched over his interest in the metropolis, candidates begging him to use his power to help them to office. Officially
absent, he was nonetheless a drastically destabilizing offstage presence in
the drama of Rome's politics.

While Caesar's power grew insidiously, Pompey's was paraded with
superb ostentation. For five years he had been building a theater of
unprecedented size and grandeur on the Field of Mars. In 55 BC he inau-
gurated it with a series of spectacular shows. There were plays, extravagantly staged. ("What pleasure is there in having a Clytemnestra with six

hundred mules?" wrote Cicero, who found the display vulgar.) There was a bloody series of games in which five hundred lions and untold numbers of gladiators were killed. There was an elephant fight—"indeed a most horrifying spectacle," says Plutarch—which astonished the crowd. At the end of his consulate Pompey, invested now with the authority and the legal immunity of a proconsul but declining to leave Rome, withdrew to his villa near the city. There he bided his time while the republic tore itself to pieces.

Milo's and Clodius's gangs (the former apparently sponsored by Pompey, the latter by Caesar, but both in fact running way out of any sponsor's control) bullied the citizens and battled each other for control of the streets. Meetings of the Senate were cut short for fear of violent interruptions by the mobs that gathered outside the chamber. Gangs of armed slaves burst into the arena and put a stop to the sacred games. Elections took place, if at all, in an atmosphere of terror. It was apparent that the situation was untenable. "The city," wrote Suetonius, "began to roll and heave like the sea before a storm."

Yet Cato persisted. Mommsen called him a "pedantically stiff and half witless . . . cloud-walker," and certainly, viewed with hindsight, his dogged efforts to reform a political system on the eve of its extinction look absurd. But Cato, and most of his contemporaries, still assumed that the republic would last for generations to come. To like-minded Romans his resolute campaign to restore it to rectitude looked not stupid but saintly. Cato "stood alone against the vices of a degenerate state," wrote Seneca. "He stayed the fall of the republic to the utmost that one man's hand could do."

It didn't make him popular. Repeatedly, when he spoke in the Forum, he was jeered by hostile agitators. "He fared," says Plutarch, "as fruits do which make their appearance out of season. For as we look upon these with delight and admiration, but do not use them, so the old-fashioned character of Cato . . . among lives that were corrupted and customs that were debased, enjoyed great repute and fame, but was not suited to the needs of men." He was elected praetor on the second attempt and brought in a law banning bribery and requiring all candidates for office to submit full accounts of their election expenses. That year's candidates acquiesced on condition that Cato himself (the only man who could be trusted with the job) would act as their umpire, but the electors, accustomed to being paid for their votes, were outraged by the notion that they should give them free. A riot broke out. Cato was set upon by an angry mob. He was knocked down and would have been lynched had he not succeeded in hauling himself upright long enough to harangue the crowd into docility. As soon as he was eligible he stood for consul but, for all his prestige, he was roundly defeated. When Alcibiades returned to his native city (as Pompey had done and Caesar was shortly to do) in the golden nimbus of victory, the citizens had begged him to make himself their absolute ruler, while only a handful of dissenters wished him on his way. So Cato was one of very few of his contemporaries unsusceptible to the glamour of the conquering generals who rode triumphant into Rome, apparently as superhuman in their swaggering magnificence as Plato's men of gold. Compared with their splendor, Cato's virtue seemed a dull and unappealing thing. While he clung to republicanism, Lucan was to write, "all Rome clamoured to be enslaved."

In January 52 BC the first of the storms that had been so long gathering broke. The two urban warlords Clodius and Milo met, apparently by chance, some miles from Rome on the Appian Way. Clodius was attended by thirty slaves carrying swords, Milo by three hundred armed men, including several gladiators. A brawl began. Clodius was injured. He was carried into a tavern. Milo's men broke in and killed him. As soon as the news reached Rome the city exploded into violence. Clodius the beautiful, Clodius the insolent, was gone and the common people of Rome, to whom he had granted an intoxicating taste of their own power, ran wild. His associates, including two tribunes, displayed his corpse, naked and battered as it was, in the Forum. There were hysterical scenes of rage and grief. Prompted by the tribunes, the mob took over the Senate house, built a pyre of all the furniture and the senatorial records, hoisted Clodius's corpse on top and set fire to the building. The seat of government, the repository of centuries of tradition, the brain controlling all the vast body of the Roman world, was reduced to charred ruins. The rioting spread as fast as the flames.

For a month the chaos continued. A hostile mob attacked Milo's house, to be driven back by the archers of his personal guard. "Every day," according to Plutarch, "the Forum was occupied by three armies, and the evil had well-nigh become past checking." The Senate declared a state of emergency, but the previous year's consular elections had not taken place. There was no one to take control. "The city was left with no government at all, like a ship adrift with no one to steer her." A mob invaded the sacred grove where the fasces were kept and seized them. Then, as though craving someone who could save them from their own license, they swept on to Pompey's villa outside the city and clamored for him to make himself dictator. Pompey demurred. He was waiting for the more official invitation that he sensed could not be much longer withheld.

It came soon enough. Twelve years previously Cato had declared that "while he lived" he would never consent to Pompey's entering the city at the head of an army. Now, hopeless, he concluded that "any government was better than no government at all." To the astonishment of his peers he spoke in favor of a motion offering Pompey the post of sole consul.

Diplomatic and subtle as ever, Pompey invited Cato to work alongside him. Cato, his living opposite, stubbornly refused. He would be of no man's party. He would give his advice when asked for it, he said, but he would also give his candid opinion whether asked for it or not.

Pompey ordered his legions into the city. Gradually order was restored, but while the emergency lasted Rome was effectively a military dictatorship. When Milo was put on trial for the murder of Clodius, Pompey's troops ringing the place of judgment were so numerous and so menacing that even Cicero, who had undertaken Milo's defense, lost his nerve, failed to deliver the speech he had planned, and saw his client convicted.

The crisis over, Pompey stepped down, once more amazing the constitutionalists by the propriety of his behavior. But a second storm was imminent. Caesar's command in Gaul would lapse in the winter of 50 BC. Cato publicly swore that as soon as it did and Caesar therefore became once more subject to the law, he, Cato, would bring charges against him for the illegal acts he had perpetrated as consul in 59 BC, and for his unjustified and unsanctioned assaults on the people of Gaul.

Caesar had many clients and supporters in the city. Repeatedly tribunes of his party vetoed attempts to rescind his command and appoint a successor to him in Gaul. It looked increasingly probable that he would refuse to surrender his legions. In December the Senate voted by an overwhelming majority that both he and Pompey should give up their commands. Again one of the tribunes vetoed the measure, at which the Senate once more went into mourning. Caesar was in winter quarters at Ravenna. By this time the danger he posed, which Cato had been railing against, largely unheard, for years, had served to greatly enhance the latter's authority. In the general hysteria Cato was being acclaimed as a prophet, one whose vision was being proved true. Terrified that at any moment Caesar might launch a coup d'état, three senior senators visited Pompey, handed him a sword, and asked him to assume command of all the troops in Italy. Pompey accepted.

There was still a chance of peace. Caesar wanted power, but so long as he was permitted to attain it he was prepared to observe at least the outward forms of republican legitimacy. It was not he but Cato, by his strenuous insistence on refusing any compromise, who made war inevitable. A second Odysseus might have come to some kind of face-saving arrangement, might have bent rules and reinterpreted precedents, remodeling the anachronistic constitution to accommodate modern reality, but Cato was not Odysseus, and it was because he was incapable of Odyssean diplomacy that he has been remembered and revered for millennia. "I would rather have noise and thunder and storm-curses than a cautious, uncertain feline repose," wrote Nietzsche, meditating on the superman nearly two thousand years after Cato's death. There was nothing uncertain about Cato. He was neither beautiful, nor especially valorous, nor—so far as we know—fleet of foot, but he was all the same a true successor to Achilles in his abhorrence of anything less than absolute truthfulness, his immovable insistence on every article of his creed, his willingness to see his own cause defeated if the only alternative was a dilution of its purity, his preference for death over dishonor. Caesar offered to hand over Gaul to a governor of the Senate's choosing and to disband all but one of his legions if he could only be granted the right to stand for election as consul in his absence (and so return to Rome already protected by the privileges of office). It was not an unprecedented proposal, but Cato fulminated furiously against its acceptance. He would rather die, he said, than allow a citizen to dictate conditions to the republic.

The senators were persuaded. The offer was refused. A measure was proposed declaring Caesar a public enemy. One of the tribunes (Caesar's creature) vetoed it, whereupon the Senate declared a state of emergency. None of the ancient sources suggest that the two tribunes friendly to Caesar were physically threatened, but they acted as though they had been. Disguised as slaves, they slipped out of Rome, took one of the carriages-for-hire which waited at the city gates, and fled to Caesar's camp. Their flight provided a pretext for war. Caesar had once dreamed of raping his mother. On January 10, 49 BC, after another troubled night, he led his legions across the Rubicon and marched on his mother city.

His advance was inexorable and swift. Pompey had boasted that he had only to stamp his foot and all Italy would rise in his support. He was wrong: the people, apparently indifferent to the threat to senatorial rights and their own liberties, let Caesar pass. Despairing of holding the city against him, Pompey, most of the officeholders, and many senators abandoned Rome. After that day Cato never again cut his hair, trimmed his beard, wore a garland, or lay on a couch to eat. In deep mourning for the republic he had tried so hard to maintain, he followed Pompey, who was at least the Senate's appointed representative, into war.

His was not a warlike nature. As a young military tribune he had been popular with his soldiers for his refusal to make a show of his dignity and for his readiness to share their work and their hardships. When the time had come for him to leave, his legionaries wept and crowded round to embrace him, kissing his hands and laying down their cloaks in his path. Now, when he joined Pompey at his base in Dyrrhachium, in northern Greece, he again proved his talents as a leader. Before a battle the generals were addressing their troops, who listened to them "sluggishly and in silence." Then Cato spoke with his usual fervor and a great shout went up. But though he could generate enthusiasm for the fight in others, he himself felt none. A civilian by nature, he once wrote to Cicero, "it is a much more splendid thing . . . that a province should be held and preserved by the mercy and incorruptibility of its commander than by the strength of a military force." He loved neither fighting nor the cause for which he fought. When the Pompeians won a battle they all rejoiced except Cato, who "was weeping for his country . . . as he saw that many brave citizens had fallen by one another's hands." He had rejected Pompey's repeated attempts to annex him to his party. Now he privately told his friends that if Caesar triumphed he would kill himself: if Pompey did he would at least continue living but he would go into exile rather than submit to the dictatorship that he assumed was inevitable.

He was not to be trusted with any command which would empower him to turn on his commander. Pompey considered making him admiral of his fleet, but changed his mind, reflecting that "the very day of Caesar's defeat would find Cato demanding that he also lay down his arms and obey the laws." When Pompey marched on Pharsalus to suffer his devastating defeat at Caesar's hands, he left Cato at Dyrrhachium to mind the camp and guard the stores.

At Pharsalus Pompey's army, though twice as large as Caesar's, was routed. Pompey escaped by sea, but few of his supporters knew in the aftermath of the battle whether he was dead or alive, let alone where he had gone. Cato found himself the commander of those troops which had straggled back into camp after the battle. He led them out to join up with the still intact Pompeian fleet. A stickler for propriety even in this moment of calamity, he offered to surrender his command to Cicero, who was with the ships and who, as a former consul, outranked him. Cicero was appalled; an altogether more flexible and pragmatic character, he was in a hurry to return to Italy and find himself a place on the winning side. Cato helped him get away and set sail for Africa with the remnant of the Pompeian army. He had guessed, correctly, that Pompey would seek refuge in Egypt. In Libya he learned that he was right, and that in Egypt the great man had been murdered. He also heard that another Pompeian army, commanded by Scipio (a sadly inferior descendant of the Scipio who defeated Hannibal), was in Numidia and had the backing of the Numidian King Juba. Cato, who was proving himself a resourceful and efficient if not a bellicose commander, led his troops on an arduous march across the Sahara to join them. When they met, Cato, as scrupulous as ever in his observance of proper form, ceded overall command to Scipio—technically his superior—despite the fact that everyone, including Scipio himself, recognized that Cato would have been the better man to lead.

It took Caesar nearly two years to follow him into Numidia. The new ruler of Rome had business to attend to and battles to fight in Asia Minor, in Egypt, and back in Italy. Meanwhile Cato and his colleagues marched into the Phoenician port city of Utica and made it their base.

Enclosed on one side by the desert, on the other by the sea, Utica was an isolated place. Under occupation by Cato and his colleagues its political nature was complicated and volatile. There were some three hundred Roman citizens of no particular allegiance living there, most of them moneylenders or merchants of one kind or another. These people would no doubt be ready to adapt to whatever political situation they found themselves in. But there were also a number of Roman senators who had left Italy with Pompey and then, unlike Cicero and those numerous others who had thrown themselves on Caesar's mercy after Pharsalus, had come with Cato from Dyrrhachium. There was good reason to suppose that should they fall into Caesar's hands they would all be killed for their obstinate opposition. The African people of Utica were thought to favor Caesar. Scipio and Juba both wished to protect themselves and their followers against possible treachery by slaughtering the entire population. Cato dissuaded them from this atrocity and took upon himself the responsibility of keeping the city secure and its diverse inhabitants safe from each other. To do so he employed harsh measures. He forced all the indigenous young men of Utica to give up their arms and interned them in palisaded concentration camps outside the city walls. The rest of the population—women, children, and old men—were allowed to remain inside, living uneasily alongside the Roman occupiers while the latter fortified the city and stocked it with grain.

It was a tense and unhappy situation. The commanders bickered. Scipio accused Cato of cowardice. Cato, so observers believed, came profoundly to regret having handed over the command to a man he trusted neither to act competently in battle nor to be wise after it. Yet fractious and deeply divided as the Pompeian force at Utica might be, it seemed to contemporary observers and later Roman historians to have a tragic grandeur. To those who rejected Caesar's rule, whether still fighting for the scattered Pompeian resistance abroad or living resentfully under the new regime, the Senate Cato established in Utica was the one true Senate, and Utica itself, because Cato was there, was the one true Rome. Cut off with his fugitive army in what to a Roman was the back of beyond, he loomed up in the Romans' collective imagination, doomed but resolute, superbly alone, calmly awaiting Caesar's arrival and his own surely inevitable defeat and death with what Seneca called "the unflinching steadiness of a hero who did not totter when the whole state was in ruins."

At last Caesar, who in the previous year had visited the supposed site of Achilles' tomb, making a show, as Alexander had done, of his claim to be a successor to that paragon of warriors, got around to tackling the man whose claim to Achilles-like integrity was generally and annoyingly perceived to be so very much stronger than his own. He landed in Africa. Cato stayed in Utica to safeguard the supplies and keep the road to the sea open while Scipio led out the army. On April 6, 46 BC, at Thapsus the Pompeians were crushingly defeated, many of them trampled to death by their own stampeding elephants, and the majority of them were slaughtered.

The news reached Utica late at night, brought by a messenger who had been three days on the road. At once the Romans in the city panicked. There were tumultuous scenes in the unlit streets as people dashed from their houses, shouting in terror, only to run back again, unsure where to seek safety. They had no troops to defend them. They were horribly aware of the men of Utica, penned into the prison camp alongside the city and no doubt exulting in the news of their oppressors' defeat. They could see those men's relatives all around them. They were crazy with fear, and they had good cause to be. Only one man remained calm: Cato himself. Once more, as he had so often done in the Roman Forum, he made use of his stentorian voice and his powers of self-assertion to still a frenzied crowd.

Striding through the darkened streets, shouting out in his harsh

voice, grabbing hold of his compatriots as they ran past babbling in terror, he arrested the stampede. As soon as it was light he summoned all the
Romans present in Utica to assemble before the temple of Jupiter, he
himself making his appearance among them with characteristic sangfroid,
apparently immersed in a book (it was an inventory of the food supplies
and weaponry stockpiled in the city). He spoke serenely, asking them to
make up their minds whether they wished to fight or surrender to Caesar.
He would not despise them, he said, if they chose the latter, but if they
decided to fight—and here his tone became more fervent—their reward
would be a happy life, or a most glorious death. The immediate effect
of his oratory was impressive. "The majority, in view of his fearlessness, nobility and generosity, almost forgot their present troubles in the
conviction that he alone was an invincible leader and superior to every
fortune."

All too soon, though the mood of exaltation passed. Someone suggested that all present should be required to free their slaves, thereby providing the city with a defense force. Cato, correct as ever even in this
desperate moment, refused to infringe private property rights by making
such an action compulsory, but asked those who would give up their
slaves of their own free will to do so. The Roman merchants—slave owners all and probably slave traders too, for whom business counted for
more than politics—began to see the advantages of surrender. The situation was terrifyingly precarious. The merchants began talking about
overpowering and interning their fellow Romans, the senators, ready to
hand them over as a peace offering to the victorious Caesar.

A troop of horsemen, survivors from Scipio's defeated army,
appeared out of the desert. At last Cato had the manpower that he needed
so urgently. Accompanied by the senators, leaving the Roman merchants
in the city, he hurried out through the city's gates to welcome the new-
comers and enlist their help in defending the city. But the soldiers had
already endured a traumatic battle; they were demoralized and exhausted.
They could not be persuaded to make a stand against Caesar, who was
now perhaps only hours away. There were angry scenes both in the city,
where the merchants were working themselves into a state of self-
justifying indignation against anyone who might suggest they should risk
opposing Caesar, and outside, where the senators and their families, now
doubly threatened, wept and wailed. Eventually the horsemen issued
their ultimatum. They would stay and help defend Utica against Caesar
but only on condition that they first be permitted to slaughter all the
Uticans. Cato refused. They began to ride away, taking with them any

remaining hope of survival, let alone of saving the republic. Cato went after them. For once showing emotion, he wept as he grasped at their horses' bridles in a futile attempt to drag them back. For all his passion, the most he could get them to agree to was that they would guard the landward gates for one day while the senators made their escape by sea. Cato accepted.

They took up their positions. The Roman merchants meanwhile announced their intention of surrendering forthwith. They were not Cato, they said, "and could not carry the large thoughts of Cato." Petty as most mortals, they had resolved to take the safest and probably most profitable course. They offered to intercede with Caesar for Cato. He told them to do no such thing. "Prayer belonged to the conquered and the craving of grace to those who had done wrong." It was Caesar who was defeated, because since he had made war on his own country his guilt was exposed for all to see. He, Cato, was the true victor. It was as though he was already leaving this world: mundane definitions of success and failure no longer held any validity for him. Simply to be right was to prevail.

Throughout the last hours of his life he was fiercely active. His one outburst of emotion done with, he accepted his doom, and proceeded to do all that remained to be done with the scrupulous thoroughness with which, all his life, he had discharged his public duties. He was everywhere. He was in the city, urging the merchants not to betray the remaining senators. He was interviewing the emissary chosen by the merchants to go on their behalf to Caesar. He was disdainfully ignoring a message from another Pompeian commander who had escaped from Thapsus and wished to claim the leadership. He was patiently attempting to persuade those most at risk of Caesar's anger to get away. He was at the city's seaward gates controlling the rush to escape. He was down at the docks overseeing the embarkations and ensuring that each boat was properly provisioned. Most characteristically, he was handing over to the Uticans the detailed accounts of his administration, and returning the surplus funds to the public treasurer. While all around him others were prostrated by anxiety or brutalized by greed and fear he alone was imperturbably competent. The horsemen became uncontrollable and attacked the Uticans in the concentration camps, looting and killing. Having so passionately begged them to stay, Cato had eventually to bribe them to leave in order to stop the massacre.

At last, on the evening of the second day since the terrible news had arrived from Thapsus, he judged that the evacuation of those at risk was all but completed: his work was almost done. He retired to his quarters to

take a bath. Afterwards he dined. He ate sitting upright (the acme of dis-
comfort for a Roman), as he had ever since he left Rome, but afterwards,
over the wine, he joined in the high-minded conversation. His household, as usual, included at least two philosophers. The talk turned to the
Stoic definition of freedom. Cato "broke in with vehemence, and in loud
and harsh tones maintained his argument at greatest length and with
astonishing earnestness." His companions, understanding, fell silent. It
was a tenet of Stoicism that, as Lucan was to put it, "the happiest men are
those who chose freely to die at the right time."

After supper he walked for a while, gave orders to the officers of the
watch, embraced his son and close friends with especial affection, and
withdrew to his bedchamber. There he began to read Plato's *Phaedo*, in
which Socrates comforts his companions by offering them proofs of the
immortality of the soul before serenely, even joyfully, drinking the hem-
lock which will heal his soul of the flaws inherent in bodily life. While still
in the midst of his reading, Cato noticed that his sword was not hanging
in its usual place by his bed (his son had removed it). He called a servant
and asked where it was. The servant had no answer. Cato returned to his
book but a little later, without any evident anxiety or urgency, asked again
for the sword. Still it was not brought. He finished his reading and called
the servants again. This time he became angry and struck one over the
mouth, hurting his own hand. (This incident, in which the great man
gives evidence of irascibility, even nervousness, is omitted from some
accounts.)

He cried out that his friends had betrayed him, by so arranging that
he would fall unarmed into his enemy's hands. At that his son and several
companions rushed into the room sobbing and imploring him to save
himself. Cato addressed them sternly, asking if they considered him an
imbecile, reminding them that if deprived of the sword he had only to
hold his breath or dash his head against the wall when he chose to die, and
asking why, in this crisis, they wished him to "cast away those good old
opinions and arguments which have been part of our lives." All who heard
him wept, and, ashamed, left him alone once more. A child was sent with
his sword. He received it impassively, saying, "Now I am my own master."
Laying it aside, he returned to his reading (it was said that he read *Phaedo*
through three times in the course of that night) before lying down and
sleeping so deeply that those in the next room could hear his snores.

Around midnight he woke, asked the doctor to bandage his hand,
and sent a servant down to the harbor to report on the evacuation. When
the servant returned with the news that there were heavy seas and high

winds Cato, mindless of his own trouble, groaned with pity for those at sea, then briefly slept again, having sent the servant back down to the waterfront to ensure nothing further could be done to help the fugitives. When the servant returned for the second time, reporting that all was quiet, Cato, satisfied that his earthly responsibilities were fully discharged, dismissed him.

Alone, he drove his sword into his midriff and fell heavily, knocking over the abacus that stood in his chamber. His servants and his son ran in and found him alive but all besmeared with blood, his bowels protruding from the ghastly wound. His doctor sewed up the gash but Cato pushed him away (or perhaps waited until he and the other attendants had left) and tore his belly open once more. This time he accomplished his purpose. "He drew forth by his hand that holiest spirit," wrote Seneca, "too noble to be defiled by steel."

At once his reputation, released from the confines of his human reality, began to swell like a genie freed from a bottle. Alive he was a pugnacious politician, an obstructionist and filibusterer, a man of unquestionable probity and great courage but also a bit of an oddball, one who courted trouble to the detriment of his own cause, a prig, an embarrassment, a pedant, perhaps even a bore. His hostility to Caesar has been compared to the kind of bitter envy a dull schoolboy, a dutiful plodder and keeper of the rules, might feel for a charismatic, carelessly successful fellow student who defies authority and gets away with it by virtue of his cheek and charm. It is a cruelly reductive characterization (several of their contemporaries attest that Cato had a kind of personal magnetism different from but almost equal to Caesar's) but, all the same, it has the ring of partial truth to it.

Even judged by Cato's own standards he was not quite perfect. He was to be remembered as the one and only incorruptible Roman. "No man of that day," wrote Dio Cassius two centuries later, "took part in public life from pure motives and free from any desire of personal gain except Cato." But there were various episodes in his political career which suggest that his righteousness was not absolute. When he opposed the ratification of Pompey's arrangements in Asia Minor he was not only checking the growth of Pompey's inordinate power, he was also doing a favor to his own brother-in-law Lucullus, whom Pompey had supplanted.

As a tribune, just after the suppression of Catiline's rebellion, he had authorized the free distribution of grain to the populace, a crowd-pleasing measure which he furiously condemned as tending to demoralize and corrupt the people when Caesar did the same. When Caesar was elected consul in 55 BC Cato condoned the use of bribery, which he otherwise so rigorously condemned, to get the constitutionalist Bibulus elected as his colleague. He allowed Cicero to persuade him that he should swear to uphold a land law of Caesar's, on the grounds that otherwise he was likely to be exiled and "even if Cato did not need Rome, still Rome needed Cato." He would not declare Clodius's legislation as tribune invalid, though there was good reason for doing so, because then his own work in Cyprus would be annulled. Clodius had boasted at the time that in giving Cato the commission he had "torn out his tongue," and it was true: Cato had been embarrassingly compromised. But once he was dead all such lapses were forgotten. The noisy, obstreperous troublemaker was magnified into a figure of marmoreal grandeur and serenity. The inveterate opponent of great men was himself accorded greatness.

The process of his exaltation began within minutes of his death. The news of his suicide spread through the town. The people of Utica, whom he had twice saved from massacre, assembled outside his house, along with the remaining Romans. Caesar was fast approaching but, uncowed, they gave his adversary an honorable funeral. Cato's body, splendidly dressed (as it had never been in life), was carried at the head of a solemn procession to the seashore, where it was buried. When Caesar arrived to accept the Uticans' surrender, he exclaimed, "O Cato, I begrudge you your death; for you begrudged me the sparing of your life." Perhaps he meant that he would have been proud to act rightly towards such a paragon of righteousness; more likely he felt, as Cato did, that Cato's submission would have been an abject defeat, and his mercy the cruelest and most satisfying of victories. But Cato had eluded him. As Seneca triumphantly declared, "All the world has fallen under one man's sway, yet Cato has a way of escape: with one single hand he opens a wide path to freedom."

Dead, he would prove every bit as troublesome to Caesar as he had been when living. A painted placard depicting him tearing himself apart "like a wild animal" was carried in the triumph Caesar celebrated on returning to Rome. The gruesome image's effect was the opposite of that intended: instead of exulting in the death of Caesar's most inflexible opponent, the crowd groaned and muttered as it passed. Brutus wrote and published a eulogy to Cato. So, showing a degree of political courage unusual for him, did Cicero. Caesar commissioned his loyal historian Hirtius to reply to them in a text, now lost, which belittled Cato's virtues and catalogued his failings. This literary controversy over a dead man's reputation masked a more dangerous debate over his living enemy's claim to power: Caesar clearly considered it absolutely necessary to his own security that Cato be discredited. Unsatisfied with Hirtius's effort he wrote his own *Anti-Cato*, a pamphlet so extravagantly vitriolic that it defeated its own object. The allegations he made in it were luridly exaggerated. He accused Cato of financial greed and dishonesty, of sexual depravity and of laziness. He wrote that Cato had sieved the ashes from the funeral pyre of his much-loved brother in a search for gold, that he came drunk to the courts, and that he had an incestuous relationship with his sister Servilia (a particularly self-damaging accusation this—Servilia was actually Caesar's mistress). He was not believed. Cicero thought the pamphlet had greatly enhanced Cato's posthumous reputation, presumably by making manifest the hatred and fear he had inspired in his great opponent.

Cato's influence persisted, and grew deadly. Plutarch relates that when Cato was taken as a boy to the house of the dictator Sulla he asked his tutor, "Why didst thou not give me a sword, that I might slay this man and set my country free from slavery?" Whether or not Cato the child ever said such a thing, Cato the man never advocated or condoned the use of violence as a political tool. But though in life he had staunchly defended the forms of law against the summary use of force, in his afterlife he became the presiding genius of a political movement aimed at an act of lethal violence. Cato had initiated the opposition to Caesar, and that opposition achieved its end on the Ides of March, brought to a murderous conclusion by Brutus, Cato's nephew and son-in-law who, according to Plutarch, admired Cato "more than any other Roman."

Caesar was killed, but the Caesarean dynasty survived and flourished and Cato, who had made his name in opposition, flourished with it, growing ever greater in the Romans' collective memory. Cicero, who in his lifetime had found him an awkward colleague, paid tribute to him after his death in reverential terms as a "god-like and unique man" who had "remained ever true to his purpose and fixed resolve." To Horace, who was nineteen when Cato died, he was the model of the just man, even of manhood itself.

His posthumous exaltation had a philosophical basis. He became the exemplar of the increasingly influential ideal of Stoic virtue. In the fifth century BC Socrates had taught that nothing can harm the good man. To one whose mind is on eternal verities, no material loss, not even the loss of life itself, is of any consequence. In Plato's *Phaedo*, the book Cato chose to read three times on the last night of his life, Socrates explains that since a wise man's ultimate goal must be to free himself from his body, which "fills us with loves, desires and all sorts of fancies and a great deal of nonsense, with the result that we literally never get an opportunity to think at all about anything," he need dread no bodily harm. Death, which will free him to apprehend more clearly the ideas of which the things of this world are merely dim reflections, is actually desirable. When Cato rebuked his friends for hiding his sword and thus seeking to make him "cast away those good old opinions and arguments which have been part of our lives," these are the sort of arguments to which he referred.

The wise man had no fear. Indeed, the wisest had few emotions of any kind. Plato, synthesizing in *The Republic* the teachings of Socrates with the example of Sparta, promulgated an ideal of the impassive hero. Homer's heroes raged and wept, mourning each other's deaths and openly declaring the terror they felt at the prospect of their own. To Plato, the admirer of Spartan discipline and self-repression, they seemed contemptible. His decision to ban poets from his ideal republic was motivated partly by his revulsion from Homer's extended description of Achilles' lamentation for Patroclus. No hero (even Plato could not deny Achilles that status) should be seen to express himself with so little restraint, such a lack of the self-mastery which to Plato was the essential prerequisite not only of dignity but also of virtue.

Drawing on Socrates and Plato and on the mystic traditions of the Orphics and Pythagoreans, the Stoics, whose philosophy first evolved under that name in Athens in the second century BC, elaborated their vision of the wise man. The wise man hopes for nothing and therefore is delivered from all fear of disappointment. Desire, ambition, even human love are to be shunned. To ask for nothing is to render oneself invulnerable. That was the condition which Cato was judged to have achieved. When Seneca, writing some fifty years after his death, wished to answer the objection that the Stoic "wise man" was a chimera, he had only to point to Cato. "I almost think he surpasses our ideal."

In life Cato was a student of philosophy. Cicero reports that he had "a voracious appetite for reading." An early riser, he would always bring a book with him to the Senate and sit studying it until his fellow senators were assembled. In late Roman and medieval texts he is referred to as "Cato the philosopher," meaning not that he left behind him a body of written work (he didn't) but that he liked to ponder the profound and difficult questions with which philosophy is concerned. When he was granted leave of absence during his term as military tribune he took ship to Pergamum expressly in order to meet the celebrated philosopher Athenodorus and invite the old man to live with him thereafter. Back in Rome he sought out teachers and readers of philosophy, several of whom received his patronage. Even in Utica, in the last two terrible days of his life, he found time to confer with the two sages, one a Stoic, one a Peripatetic, who were attached to his household there.

What he learned he practiced. He went barefoot and inadequately dressed in all weathers not only to harden his body but also in order to train his spirit, "accustoming himself to be ashamed only of what was really shameful." What seemed to most of his contemporaries to be a lack of dignity and decorum in his appearance was a self-imposed penance, a spiritual exercise. He was, wrote Cicero, "endowed by nature with an austerity beyond belief."

He controlled his emotions as severely as he disciplined his body. For the Stoic a man, to be truly admirable, truly heroic, must appear to be totally insensible. Seneca, the great Roman exponent of Stoicism, was full of admiration for Socrates because neither prison nor poison could "even affect the expression on his face." Cato, likewise, was never seen to laugh (although Plutarch, who may have seen the humorous side of the paragon's humorlessness, reports that "once in a while he relaxed his features so far as to smile"). His wonderful impassivity became proverbial. When, in 62 BC, he was the only senator who dared oppose Pompey's recall to Rome, the people of his household kept watch the night before the crucial vote as though awaiting an execution, but Cato himself ate a hearty supper and slept soundly. When, in 52 BC, he was defeated in the election for consul he showed no sign of disappointment or humiliation. It was customary for unsuccessful candidates to retire at least temporarily from public view, but Cato passed the rest of the day playing ball in the Field of Mars and strolling with his friends in the Forum, barefoot and bizarrely underdressed as usual. Seneca wrote indignantly, about those who had dared abuse him, "He had to endure the vile language and spittle and all the other insults of a maddened crowd," but noted that Cato himself was oblivious to petty indignities. "He is a great and noble man who acts as does the lordly wild beast that listens unconcernedly to the baying of tiny dogs." Horace described him as being so sure of his righteousness and so tenacious of his purpose that "were the sky itself to fracture and collapse / the wreckage would immolate him unafraid."

The emotional frigidity which seemed so marvelous to his Stoic admirers affected even Cato's most intimate relationships. His first wife bore him two children before he divorced her on grounds of adultery. His second, Marcia, was the occasion of his most controversial act of self-denial. Their marriage appears to have been a satisfactory one. But while Marcia was pregnant with their third child a brilliant advocate named Hortensius, who was Cicero's only rival in the courts and who, as a fellow supporter of senatorial authority, was a valuable political ally of Cato's, expressed a desire to be more nearly related to him. Specifically he wished his heirs to be of Cato's family. He asked Cato to give him his daughter Portia "as noble soil for the production of children." Cato demurred: Portia was already married. Hortensius persevered. He would give Portia back to her original husband, he said, once she had borne him a child. Still Cato refused. Hortensius then asked for Marcia, "since she was still young enough to bear children and Cato had heirs enough." Cato, having conferred with his father-in-law (but not, as far as is recorded, with Marcia herself), consented, attended the wedding, and gave away the bride.

The story has shocked the majority of subsequent commentators. After Hortensius's death Cato remarried Marcia, who had been left an extremely rich widow, thus laying himself open to Julius Caesar's accusation of fortune hunting: "The woman was set as a bait for Hortensius, and lent by Cato when she was young that he might take her back when she was rich." To most of his contemporaries though, it was obvious that to accuse Cato of financial greed was as absurd as accusing Hercules of cowardice. Other charges are less easy to refute. Tertullian, writing in the third century, thought the transaction "vile," as emotionally repellent as it was morally reprehensible. Seneca wrote approvingly that Cato once expressed a regret at having been so weak as to have kissed his wife. To later generations it was the regret, not the kiss, that seemed reprehensible. Robert Graves (who translated Lucan) accurately pointed out that both Cato and Hortensius were treating Marcia as though she were no more worthy of consideration than a brood mare. But distasteful though the story may be, alike to a Father of the Church or to a post-Romantic, postfeminist modern reader, it is consistent with the rest of Cato's ethical code.

In *The Republic* Plato proposes that there should be no exclusive marriage among the elite. Instead "all the women are to be shared among all the men," and sexual intercourse is to be carefully controlled (as it was in Sparta) to ensure that only the fittest breed. Even Plato's Socrates is aware that this proposal is likely to cause an uproar, but it was consistent with the Platonic rejection of the worldly, physical love of one individual for another, in favor of the transcendental rapture Socrates describes in the *Symposium*. The Stoic philosophers elaborate the point. To the Stoic all human relationships, as well as the possession of worldly things, were temporary and provisional, not be invested with too much emotional intensity. A beloved person or object should be "taken care of as a thing that is not your own, as travellers treat their inn." Love is a weakness, and an expectation of sexual fidelity a form of avarice. In so coolly giving up Marcia, Cato was acting, according to his lights, with admirable detachment, as a number of subsequent commentators have understood. The Alexandrian historian Appian, writing in the second century AD, praised Cato for the "high-souled philosophy" of which he gave evidence when he gave away his wife, despite being extremely fond of her. Even the early-twentieth-century historian Sir Charles Oman, who found the story illustrative of "Roman morals in the aspect which appears most unlovely to us," conceded that it was also "surely the most extraordinary instance of altruism known."

A man unswayed by any emotion is as unalterable as a god. Socrates identifies consistency as the primary attribute of the deity. Among Plato's complaints against the poets was the charge that they represent the gods as sometimes mourning, sometimes rejoicing, whereas it was his belief that "whether acting or speaking, God is entirely uniform and truthful." Similarly to the Stoics it was the mark of the godlike wise man that, because his actions are determined by absolute moral principles, his behavior never varied. Cato, who never courted favor nor showed fear, awed his contemporaries by knowing his own mind and never changing it. As a boy he had been slow to learn, or, rather, slow to accept received ideas until he had thoroughly examined them and persuaded himself of their truth, "but what he once comprehended he held fast." As an adult he was equally dogged in his adherence to his notions of rectitude. At a dinner party once he diced for the first choice among the dishes. When he lost his host urged him to help himself anyway, but he refused. Even such a trivial and frivolous piece of cheating was repugnant to him. For Cato, everything was serious. He was slow to anger but "once angered he was inexorable." "No-one," wrote Seneca, "ever saw a change in Cato."

Paragon of Stoic virtue, the dead Cato was also a potent and usefully malleable political figurehead. He became the posthumous patron of numerous causes which the living Cato might well have found dubious. The process began early. The emperor Augustus, Caesar's heir, attempted to lay claim to some of the glory of Caesar's adversary. He wrote a biography of Cato, which he read aloud to friends, in which he suggested that his rival for power, Marcus Antonius, was as dangerously ambitious as Caesar had been while he himself, like Cato before him, represented legitimacy and good government. According to Macrobius, Augustus once visited Cato's house and, when one of his companions made a disparaging remark about the dead republican hero, reproved him saying, "Whoever wishes to preserve the state in its present form is a good citizen and a good man." Cato's virtue was thus co-opted into the service of the Caesarean revolution he had died opposing.

More appropriately Caesar's adversary became the model for those (many of them Stoics) who resisted Caesar's tyrannical successors. Pliny reports that prominent Romans critical of the emperors identified themselves by displaying busts of Cato in their houses. In death Cato not only grew, he changed as well, his iconic significance shifting until it became almost the direct opposite of what it had once been. In his lifetime, a period of political disorder so extreme as to foster a widespread yearning for stability, he had been revered as one who stood for legitimacy, tradition, and the scrupulous preservation of established institutions against the rampant individualism of his ambitious contemporaries. Afterwards, under emperors whose authority was all too brutally well established, he was idealized as the champion of an abstraction of which—legalist and conservative that he was—he would have heartily disapproved: that of liberty.

In the middle of the first century AD, when the emperor Nero turned cruelly on his opponents, one of his most outspoken critics was Thrasea Paetus. Thrasea wrote a biography of Cato, which the persecuted read to gain courage from Cato's example, rather as Cato himself had fortified himself for his own death by reading of Socrates'. Thrasea's story parallels Cato's. He too was a comparatively junior senator who became the most influential advocate of senatorial authority. His "grim and gloomy manner" was a tacit rebuke to Nero's self-indulgence, just as Cato by his austere example once shamed his frivolous fellow aristocrats. The informer who brought about his death told the emperor, "As this faction-loving country once talked of Caesar versus Cato, so now, Nero, it talks of you versus Thrasea." On the night of his death Thrasea was in his garden, engaging, like Cato, in a philosophical discussion. When a quaestor arrived with his death warrant, he calmly dismissed his friends and invited the quaestor to watch while he slit his wrists, saying, "Look, young man! For you have been born into an age when examples of fortitude may be a useful support." Just such an example was that of Cato: Haterius, another of Nero's victims, described him as "a model for living and for dying."

The two authors who did most to ensure Cato's immortality also lost their lives under Nero. Seneca, who so venerated Cato, was Nero's tutor and chief minister until, appalled by the emperor's despotism, he conspired to kill him. One of his fellow conspirators was his nephew, the poet Lucan, in whose epic account of the civil war, *Pharsalia*, Cato is celebrated as a figure of somber grandeur and sublime goodness. When their plot was discovered both Seneca and Lucan were compelled to kill themselves. Their works lived on, Seneca's essays especially being among the Latin texts most widely read and admired in medieval and Renaissance Europe, and Cato's image lived on in them, stern, selfless, incorruptible, superhuman. To Seneca, Cato was the epitome of republican virtue and the incarnation of the utopian ideal which the republic became in the imagination of those who lived after its ending. "The two whom heaven willed should never part were blotted out together," wrote Seneca. "For Cato did not survive freedom, nor freedom Cato." To Lucan, Cato was an even more exalted figure. "One day," he wrote, "when we are finally freed from slavery, if ever that should be, Cato will be deified, and Rome will have a god by whose name it need not be ashamed to swear."

The Cato Lucan describes in *Pharsalia* is a man of sorrows, but one whom no amount of grief or suffering can daunt. The most vivid and fantastical part of the poem's narrative is that describing the march on which Cato led his troops through the North African desert to rendezvous with Scipio and King Juba. As Plutarch tells it, the journey was not so terribly difficult: Cato, always the conscientious manager, had prepared prudently by bringing along herds of cattle and a great number of asses to carry water. Strabo, writing only three decades after the event and knowing North Africa, believed the march to have taken four weeks. But Lucan extends the ordeal for months during which the sun never ceases to beat cruelly down, there is nothing to eat but sand, and the desert is swarming with deadly serpents whose shapes are bizarre and whose venom causes men to die macabre and terrible deaths. One soldier swells up until he is no longer recognizable as a human being. Another dissolves, leaving only a puddle of stinking slime. Through all these terrors Lucan's Cato—austere, great-hearted, of adamantine resolution—remains unafraid. Every night he keeps watch, sitting on the bare ground. He endures sandstorms, heat, and thirst without complaining. He is an inspirational example of courage and self-control: "With Cato's eye on him no soldier dared utter a groan." When at last his army reaches a water hole and a soldier hands him a helmet full of water he is furious at the supposition that he might be so weak as to accept. "How dare you insult me," he roars. The only occasion on which he is the first to drink is one when the well is infested with serpents. Each time a soldier succumbs to snakebite Cato is beside him as he dies, "conferring on the victim a greater gift than life, the courage to die nobly."

Achilles was prepared to give his life to buy himself such praise from posterity. The pursuit of glory seemed to most of the thinkers of pagan antiquity proper and praiseworthy, and that glory was inseparable from fame. "It behoves all men," wrote Sallust, Cato's contemporary, "not to pass through life unheralded, like the beasts which Nature has fashioned grovelling and slave to the belly." Only ambition, a craving for celebrity which Sallust called "a fault not so far removed from being a virtue," could impel a man to transcend his degraded, animal nature, to live a life which amounted to something more than a ceaseless round of consumption and excretion, of futile exercise and sleep. For a Roman as for a Greek, fame offered the best hope of immortality. Plato's Socrates argued for the existence of an undying soul and Cato comforted himself with his theory but to most Romans, as to most Athenians, the afterlife was shadowy and uncertain. Only a great name was certain to endure. "The span of life which we enjoy is short," wrote Sallust. "It is fitting we may make the memory of our lives as long as possible." It was a token of Cato's oddity, one repeatedly remarked upon by his contemporaries, that he seemed careless of his reputation, that he actually rejected honors and memorials which would have assured him a place in posterity's life-preserving consciousness.

After he returned from Cyprus in 57 BC he declined the right to wear a purple-bordered robe in the theater. Throughout his career he avoided any kind of show of his status, a self-denial for which, in his lifetime, he was as often mocked as admired. He repeatedly refused presents—valuable gifts which were offered partly as bribes but also as acknowledgments of the receiver's status. When he assumed responsibility for the management of theatrical spectacles he used to give the actors not crowns of gold, as was customary, but wreaths of wild olive, and he presented them with figs and lettuces and bundles of firewood rather than the usual ostentatious gifts. ("One trusts," remarked Sir Charles Oman dryly, "that he remembered the difference when settling their salaries.") His reputation was tremendous but it grew without his fostering it. "That to which

Cato gave least thought was his in greatest measure, namely esteem, favour, surpassing honour," wrote Plutarch.

This carelessness of his seemed, to all the ancient commentators, remarkable. Dio Cassius, in summarizing his career, marveled that what he did he did "not with a view to power or glory or any honour, but solely for the sake of a life of independence, free from the dictation of tyrants." He was free as well from the need to please either the public or posterity. Achilles' glory existed only in the minds of the "men who come after." Julius Caesar's greatness was determined by his popularity. But Cato, indifferent to the opinion of others, guided only by the requirement of his self-respect, was in need of nobody's endorsement. "He preferred rather to be than to seem virtuous," wrote Sallust. "Hence the less he sought fame, the more it pursued him."

Frugality seems to have come naturally to him, and his distaste for pompous ostentation was something he shared with other members of the grand old republican families contemptuous of the vulgar new tycoons who came back from the colonies to make a spectacle of their wealth in Rome. But his deliberate underdressing, his exaggerated displays of modesty were not only the expression of his personality and his class-determined preferences, it was also a political performance, a kind of theater of poverty, a humble act with a proud subtext. By disdaining to parade his wealth as others did he, like his great-grandfather, was laying claim to something more illustrious, the high virtues of the fathers of the republic. His parsimony was pointed: "Cato did all this in disparagement of the usual practice," writes Plutarch. This was the period when all Gaul was bleeding to pay for the building program with which Caesar hoped to rival Pompey, and when at Caesar's games every gladiator wore armor of solid silver. In the short term Cato's indifference to fame and refusal of magnificence had a specific political significance.

In the longer term, after his death, they acquired a spiritual one, rendering Cato easily assimilable to the newfangled Christian valorization of self-denial and unworldliness. To Velleius Paterculus, Cato "resembled Virtue herself, and in all his acts he revealed a character nearer to that of gods than men." The gods whom Cato resembles are no longer the high-handed amoral deities of the Homeric cosmos but beings of unsullied righteousness, beings not unlike the Jewish prophet of whose crucifixion Pontius Pilate had washed his hands only a few years before Velleius Paterculus wrote his history.

In several of the key scenes in the drama of his life Cato plays a role which with hindsight was found to be rich in Christian associations. His opponents are conquerors and plutocrats, their greatness in the eyes of the world based on acts of aggression and self-aggrandizement. They cherish their honor, which they measure in terms of public recognition. They are proud of it and fiery in its defense: it was to protect his *dignitas*, wrote Caesar, that he crossed the Rubicon and plunged Rome into war. They display their wealth as though there were a virtue in the accumulation of gold. Cato is—or at least appears to be—their opposite.

Cato was a rich man and a member of Rome's ruling class, but he acted poor and he conducted himself like an outsider. He is the little man, vulnerable but unafraid, who dares oppose the great ones of the earth. Dressed in clothes humble to the point of unseemliness he enters the Forum poorly attended. Unarmed and unprotected he confronts gangs of sword-wielding gladiators. He is mocked and manhandled. He is spat upon and hauled off to prison. He bears his persecution patiently. His way is the way of nonviolent resistance: bullied and threatened he stands his ground, not fighting back but speaking out, shaming his persecutors with his tenacity and his courage, opposing their might with his righteousness. He is David to Caesar's Goliath, and like David he is easily understood to be a forerunner of Christ. Whatever Cato would have thought of Christianity, there were many reasons why Christians found his story congenial, and why they agreed that he was among the best of the pagans. His disdain for fame won their approval. As St. Augustine pointed out, most Romans burned to possess a glory which was defined by the "favourable judgement of men." How much better, how much more Christian, to aspire to virtue, as Cato apparently did, for its own sake! Even the equanimity with which he handed over his wife could be reconciled with Christian doctrine. Had not Christ taught that the love of one's family must cede first place to one's love for God?

Best of all, he died. St. Augustine compared him with Regulus, another admirable pagan. A Roman general of the third century BC, Regulus was taken prisoner by the Carthaginians and then sent back to Rome on parole to negotiate peace terms on his captors' behalf. Ever loyal to Rome, he advised the Senate to reject the Carthaginian terms. Then, although he knew that he was going back to certain torture and death, he insisted on keeping his word and returning to Carthage. Just so had Cato refused to save himself from the death that was coming to him. And just so had Jesus ridden into Jerusalem, and into the hands of his enemies, on Palm Sunday. "People commit suicide," wrote Lucretius in Cato's lifetime, "because they are afraid of dying." Cato was afraid of nothing, but in taking his life he assured himself of a life to come. When Manlius Boethius, the fifth-century Roman interpreter of Plato's philosophy who was posthumously revered as a Christian saint, wrote of "undefeated, death-defeating Cato," he was conflating two concepts derived from opposed ethical cultures. As an ancient pagan Cato was undefeated. He refused to ask for Caesar's clemency because his pride as a Roman forbade him to adopt the posture of the conquered. But it was as a proto-Christian that he was death-defeating because in dying he attained immortality, as Christ did and as his followers believed they would.

There was, though, a problem. Cato was not executed as Jesus was. He was not even, like Socrates, compelled to kill himself. He committed suicide of his own free will, and suicide was a sin. It was not only Christians who thought so. In the *Phaedo* Socrates reviews the case against taking one's own life. He rejects the Orphic concepts of earthly life as a punishment which we do not have the right to dodge, or a prison from which it is cowardly to escape, but he endorses the idea that we are the possessions of the gods, and that to do away with ourselves is to steal from our masters. In general, therefore, Socrates concludes that suicide is to be condemned. But when God sends "some necessary circumstance"—like the death sentence facing Socrates himself—then the philosopher will welcome his release for "if a man has trained himself throughout his life to live in a state as close as possible to death, would it not be ridiculous for him to be distressed when death comes to him?"

The Stoic thinkers whom Cato studied so assiduously went much further. Aristotle had declared that suicide was an unmanly act, but Diogenes, the first Cynic, formulated the maxim "Either reason or the rope"—if a man could not live a life which reason could approve, then he might as well hang himself. The Stoics, who adapted and developed Diogenes' ideas, maintained that happiness and wisdom alike depended on one's readiness to give up anything—life included—without regret. To die, wrote Epictetus, would afford the wise man the same joyful relief as walking out of a smoke-filled room. It was not a great step from that position to the idea, most vigorously expressed by Seneca, Cato's fervent admirer, that suicide is not only justifiable, it is the most perfectly dignified act a person can perform, the only way a mortal can be free, not only of human tyranny but of the caprices of fate. "Do you ask what is the highway to liberty? Any vein in your body . . . See you that precipice? Down that is the way to liberty. See you that sea, that river, that well? There sits liberty at the bottom." Cato, wrote Seneca admiringly, when he held the sword to his midriff, had "the wide road of freedom before him."

The Christian Fathers disagreed. Suicide was a form of murder. More subtly, it gave evidence of pride. Those who died rather than bear "the enslavement of their own body or the stupid opinion of the mob," wrote St. Augustine, betrayed their lack of Christian humility. The high Roman fashion for falling on one's sword rather than submit to another's authority implies an overvaluation of one's own dignity, an aristocratic flinching from degradation incompatible with the Christian imperative that all men should humble themselves before God. To a good Christian there need be no shame in defeat and humiliation. Augustine ascribed Cato's death "not to self-respect guarding against dishonour, but to weakness unable to bear adversity."

Most subsequent Christian thinkers endorsed his judgment, but Western culture is a curious amalgam in which the values of pagan antiquity have coexisted for centuries with those of Christian orthodoxy, however mutually contradictory they may be. Throughout most of the last two thousand years suicide has been condemned in actuality as a sin and a crime, suicides' bodies have been refused Christian burial and interred in the public highway, while secular authority, unable to punish the dead, has punished their heirs instead by confiscating their property. But meanwhile in poetry, paintings, ballads, and plays (including Seneca's, which enjoyed a tremendous vogue in the early Renaissance), those courageous and uncompromising enough to take their own lives have been wept over and venerated in blithe defiance of church and state alike.

Suicide is an eloquent admission of defeat, but defeat can be as heroic as victory. Homer's Hector hoped that "the men to come" would speak of him admiringly as one who had killed a prodigious number of other people, but Achilles, with a more sophisticated or more prescient understanding of the human psyche, looked for glory on the grounds that he himself was to be killed.

To most of the Romans of Cato's generation greatness was something which, like wealth and military preeminence, was accorded to a winner. Pompey and Caesar were, in their respective heydays, splendid successes, superb conquerors who celebrated their achievements with days-long processions and monumental marble buildings and heaps of dead gladiators in massive silver. Cato was a failure, and a foredoomed one, a man whose whole life was dedicated to a cause already lost, yet Lucan could write (inaccurately but fervently), "None of our ancestors, by the slaughter of foreign armies, won such fame as Cato."

The inception of the Christian era saw the arrival of a new kind of hero, the loser. Those ancient pagans who had been killed or killed themselves were revered anew as sacrificial victims: their suicides, though overtly condemned, won them the kind of pitying adoration accorded to the Christian martyrs. Cato, whose life's project had failed and who had died defeated, was all the more readily admired for the grimness of his story's end. On the frescoed walls of the fifteenth-century Sala dei Giganti in Padua he stands serenely holding the sword with which he ripped himself open, posed as the Christian martyrs are on church walls all over Europe, proudly displaying their mutilations and the instruments of their torment.

Christ crucified, the tortured martyrs, despairing pagans falling resolutely on their swords—these edifying spectacles of suffering all satisfy an apparently almost universal appetite for others' pain. The greater the suffering, the nobler the man who endures it: the more gruesome Cato's end, the brighter his glory. To Seneca it seemed that the gods had deliberately made it necessary for him to tear out his own innards in order that his full heroism might be made manifest; "to seek death needs not so great a soul as to re-seek it." From Olympus they looked down with "exceeding joy . . . as he made his escape by so glorious and memorable an end." Fifteen hundred years later Michel de Montaigne wrote that if he were asked to portray Cato "in his most exalted posture" he would paint him "all covered with blood and ripping out his entrails." Plenty of artists have done precisely that. In half a dozen Renaissance paintings Cato dies hideously, his torso contorted and bloody, his face gaping in pain. Physical horror is the corollary of spiritual glory. Agony is commuted into ecstasy. Montaigne asserted that "Virtue reaches such a pinnacle that she not only despises pain but delights in it. Witness the Younger Cato." He endured his death as a Stoic should, but "there was in the virtue of that man too much panache and green sap for it to stop there. I am convinced that he felt voluptuous pleasure in so noble a deed . . . some unutterable joy in his soul, an access of delight and a manly pleasure."

Honorary saint and enraptured martyr, Cato proved as useful an ideological totem in subsequent centuries as he had been in imperial Rome. To Dante he was that rare thing, a "free" man, because he was free of sin—a concept Cato would probably have found acceptably close to the Stoic ideal—but he was posthumously enlisted in the cause of other freedoms which he would surely have found at best alien, at worst deplorable. Lucan had imagined Cato in Egypt refusing to consult the oracle of Jupiter Amon on the grounds that he carried the god in his own heart. In retrospect, the story seems to carry a proto-Protestant message: Cato was accordingly a favorite of reforming sixteenth-century theologians. In his life Cato, a conservative and an oligarch whose first public service had been the suppression of a slave revolt, had struggled to defend the privileges of the ruling class and to prevent the rise of the people's chosen great men, but after his death he was venerated by those who would give power to the people. As the scourge of a would-be king he was admired by seventeenth-century English revolutionaries, and by the Hapsburgs' opponents in the Protestant states of Germany and the Netherlands. The English, who liked to congratulate themselves after 1688 on being the guardians of liberty, were especially partial to him: Jonathan Swift's Gulliver converses with the spirit of Brutus, who tells him that his companions in the underworld, who include Cato, are a fellowship "to which all ages of the world cannot add." In revolutionary France he was one of the idols of the new godless religion: his bust was on display in the Jacobin club, and for the 1797 Prix de Rome contending artists painted a powerfully muscled Cato displaying his gruesome wounds to a traumatized assembly of friends and servants. Paragon of integrity and fortitude, Cato was a hero of such unquestionable virtue that any movement claiming to value liberty—however that word might be defined—wanted him for its own.

In London in 1713, when Addison's tragedy was first performed, each of the political parties jostled the other to lay claim to its hero. On the first night the theater was packed with grandees of each persuasion. Addison was a Whig, but the Tory Lord Harley took the box next to him and occupied it ostentatiously; once the play began the applause from the competing factions was so loud the actors could hardly make themselves heard. The War of the Spanish Succession had recently ended after a string of British victories. To the Whigs, Cato was the stalwart defender of liberty, as admirably progressive and aggressive as their own nation. Digby Cotes, in a poem inspired by Addison's play, called him a "patriot, obstinately good" and compared him with Britannia, who "when her conquering sword she draws / Resolves to perish, or defend her cause." To a Tory, his story's significance lay elsewhere, in the fact that he did his utmost to obstruct Caesar's rise. The Tory Viscount Bolingbroke presented fifty guineas to the actor playing Cato, congratulating him on "defending the cause of liberty so well against a perpetual dictator," a transparent reference to eighteenth-century England's new Caesar, the victorious Duke of Marlborough, whose ambitions the Tories were determined to thwart.

The play was a prodigious success. "The town is so fond of it," wrote

Pope, "that the orange wenches and fruit women in the park offer the books at the side of coaches." Even Plato benefited: the *Phaedo* was republished as "the work mentioned in the tragedy of Cato." The play's first run was only ended by the pregnancy of the leading lady (who played Cato's daughter, a character inserted for love interest). The manager insisted she continue appearing for as long as was humanly possible: during the last few performances a midwife was waiting backstage. Numerous revivals and parodies followed. The play, and its protagonist, enjoyed an international vogue. Addison's Cato is "stern and awful as a god." He has no human weaknesses. "His towering soul / Midst all the shock and injuries of fortune / Rises superior." He is impervious to love and grief alike. He weeps for Rome, but hearing that his son, "obstinately brave and bent on death," has died in battle he says only, "I am satisfied." Voltaire thought him "one of the most beautiful characters the theatre can show." He dies serenely, illumined by a beam of heavenly light. "There fled the greatest soul that ever warm'd / A Roman breast."

"One's way of dying," wrote the samurai Daidōji Shigesuke in seventeenth-century Japan, "can validate one's whole life." Cato's botched and appalling suicide (which accidentally resembled the samurai death rite of hara-kiri) confirmed his heroic status. The Japanese veneration for the "nobility of failure"—for the uncompromised warrior who, defeated by overwhelming odds, is killed, or kills himself, by taking a sword to his own belly, as Cato did—is paralleled by the Western predilection for tragedy. As Alcibiades, the dazzling, arrogant darling of fortune, boarded his ship to sail to Sicily the effigy of the Adonis, the beloved victim whose myth is centered solely on his death and whose worship is all mourning, was being carried through the streets of Athens. Pathos has a glamour as potent as triumph's. Adonis is one of a long line of dying heroes and gods (Christ among them) whose legends transparently mirror the natural cycle of decay and renewal, while also appealing powerfully to a widespread sense that stories of downfall and death are more serious, more truthful, than those of victory and splendor. It was from the rites of another such divine victim, Dionysus, that tragedy evolved, and Cato's willingness to die for his principles elevated him to the status of tragic hero. Alexander Pope encapsulated his character in terms which exactly meet Aristotle's requirements for the form: "A brave man struggling in the storms of fate / And greatly falling with a falling state."

"You choose to cringe and fawn," Sophocles' Electra, whose resolve was as inexorable as Cato's, tells those who urge her to compromise her principles for her own safety. "Those are not my ways . . . You choose to live but I to die." Life is a process of ceaseless adaptation and change, but, choosing death, Cato achieved fixity, ensuring that he need never alter or dwindle. "His resolution defeated Mother Nature," wrote Lucan. He escaped the flux of life, attaining instead a glorious rigor mortis. Freed from his mortal flesh, transformed into an idea as unalterable as Plato's gods, or as the Stoics' ideal wise man, he escapes the decay which is the inevitable end of all physical creation.

More, he offers his admirers a kind of immortality by association. In his lifetime Cato had proposed handing Caesar over to the Germans to be killed in order that the pollution of his war crimes might not fall upon Rome: he understood the function of the scapegoat. After his death the related concept of the immaculate sacrifice became attached to his own story. In *Pharsalia* Lucan gives him an "oracular" speech in which he declares his longing to be "a national sin-offering," another Decius dying that his people might be saved. The story goes that Decius, who commanded the Romans in the Samnite wars of the fourth century BC, was told by the gods in a dream that in the next day's battle one army must lose its commander; the other would lose its entire force. He resolved to die that his country might be victorious. Ordering his men to remain in their places, he rode out all alone, charging into the enemy's ranks, where he was hacked to pieces. Lucan's Cato sees his own self-sacrifice in even grander terms. He will ensure not just his compatriots' victory but their redemption. "My blood would purge all the nations in our empire of the guilt incurred by this civil war. Let them strike at no one but myself, so be it only that my sacrificial blood may redeem all Italians." He aspires, in other words, to be a heroic victim like Jesus Christ, whose followers' souls are washed clean by his most precious blood.

Achilles died in pursuit of eternal glory for himself. Christ died, so his followers believe, to achieve everlasting life for all humanity. Cato had no such high hope. He killed himself simply because his probable future life seemed to him not worth living. But in the eyes of his posthumous admirers he achieved both glory and a transcendental victory akin to Christ's. Unaffected by cold or heat, by sexual passion or a greed for power, unsmiling, unafraid of despot or mob, godlike Cato is a paragon of freedom and fearlessness. And when he proves himself uncowed even by the inexorable sentence of mortality, he embodies the most poignant and intoxicating fantasy there is, that death has no call to be proud, that a mortal can conquer mortality. "The dying Roman," wrote Addison, "shames the pomp of death."

IV

EL CID

When Rodrigo Díaz de Vivar, known as the Cid, died in 1099 all Christendom, according to a French chronicler, lamented, and the "paynims" of Islamic Spain rejoiced. Rodrigo seemed to all his contemporaries, even those of his enemies who most heartily hated him, like one singled out for greatness. His tremendous successes, the ascendancy he established over his peers, even over the kings he intermittently served, awed those around him. He was a never-defeated warrior who rose by his own efforts from ordinary knight to fabulously wealthy ruler of a great city, the hero in his own lifetime of songs and fantastic tales. What Homer would have explained by ascribing divine ancestry to him, what Plato expressed by his metaphor of an admixture of gold in the clay of which the great man was made, the Cid's contemporaries put down variously to prodigious luck or to the will of God. To Christians he was fortune's favorite, the beneficiary of a felicitous astrological accident; the author of the *Poema de Mío Cid*, the epic poem honoring him which was first written down a century after his death, refers to him throughout as "he who was born in a happy hour." Muslims, who in eleventh-century Spain were on the whole both more devout and more intellectually sophisticated than the Christians with whom they unwillingly shared the peninsula, saw his genius as being a divine gift. Ibn Bassam, the Arab historian and biographer who was his contemporary and the voice of his enemies, who referred to him routinely as "that tyrant the Campeador— may God tear him to pieces," paid reluctantly generous tribute to the qualities in him which set him above other mere mortals: "This man was the scourge of his times, yet must he also be accounted, by virtue of his appetite for glory, of the prudent steadfastness of his character, and of his heroic courage, one of the greatest of God's miracles."

His story has been repeatedly rewritten to fit the political agenda of subsequent generations. He has been celebrated as the visionary warrior who initiated the Christian "reconquest" of Spain, as the saintly figurehead of the Counter-Reformation, and as Spain's national hero. He has been identified as the plainspoken commoner whose dauntless courage put the effete and haughty aristocracy to shame. He has been credited with loyally subduing rebellions on behalf of his royal master, King Alfonso VI, and laying the basis of a strong centralizing monarchy. He has been seen as the first patriot of a newly unified nation. Above all he has been revered as a crusader, a red-cross knight, a splendid fighter for the cause of Christ's church militant here on earth. The truth is somewhat cruder. Achilles fought for eternal glory, Alcibiades for worldly fame, Cato for the republic and his own self-respect. Rodrigo Díaz fought for money.

As a feudal vassal he served his lord, and subsequently his king, in observance of the contract obtaining between all medieval warriors and their liege lords, and he enriched himself in the process. When midway through his adult life he was banished from Castile, he turned mercenary, and for his service as the hired commander of the armies of the Muslim kings of Zaragoza he was rewarded with a great fortune. Finally, exiled for a second time, he campaigned on his own account, carving out a kingdom for himself in eastern Spain and making himself and all his followers rich on the proceeds of his looting and pillaging, his extortion and ransom taking, his slave trading and cattle rustling, his systematic despoliation of the cities he conquered and his opportunistic robbery of whatever undefended property fell in his way. For all this he was universally and heartily admired. The legendary English hero Robin Hood who lived (if he lived at all) in the next century, was said to rob the rich in order to give to the poor. The Cid was less discriminating. He robbed others, any others, in order to secure the loyalty of his own, and his own loved him for it.

> How well he rewarded each of his vassals!
> He has made his knights rich and his foot-soldiers,
> In all his company you would not find a needy man.
> Who serves a good lord lives always in delight.

Among the mixed motives which took the Greeks to Troy was the alluring prospect of looting the city's famous wealth. The Homeric warriors are shameless in their appetite for the spoils of war. In the *Iliad*, whenever a warrior falls where his friends cannot protect him, his valuable armor is immediately stripped from his corpse. The tales that Nestor tells of the glorious exploits of exemplary heroes describe the rustling of cattle and the plundering of settlements. One of Odysseus' laudatory epithets is "Sacker of Cities." He describes without the least compunction his unprovoked attack on a coastal city of inoffensive strangers, which he sacked, killing all its male inhabitants, abducting and enslaving its women, and dragging off all its portable treasure, and his son proudly boasts of the wealth that he "won by force." Homeric hosts inquire of strangers appearing on their shores whether they are "roving the waves like pirates, / sea wolves raiding at will, who risk their lives / to plunder other men." The inquiry is morally neutral: no insult is intended. As Thucydides noted, "This occupation was held to be honourable rather than disgraceful." Combat and robbery were closely allied, and both were fit occupations for the best of men. Production was work for peasants or slaves; men of the warrior caste helped themselves to the fruits of others' labors. In conservative Sparta boys were still in Alcibiades' lifetime half starved to ensure they would learn not to balk at theft, which was inseparable from warfare. "It is according to nature," wrote Aristotle, "that the art of war . . . should in a sense be a way of acquiring property."

But though it might be according to nature it was diametrically opposed to the code of aristocratic honor which had already, by the time Aristotle was writing, begun to complicate people's relationship with money. To the later ancients the greed for gold seemed a sordid thing. Plato sternly repudiated Odysseus' advice to Achilles, that he should accept Agamemnon's gifts, on the grounds that a true hero should have no desire for payment. When it was muttered in Athens that Alcibiades' enthusiasm for the Sicilian expedition arose from his hope of profiting financially by it, the suggestion was intentionally pejorative. By the time Cato lived an indifference to the profit motive had come to be the defining characteristic of a superior person. No one who was seen to busy himself in making money could sit in the Roman Senate, Sallust considered freedom from mercenary motives to be the defining characteristic of a noble mind, and Virgil despised Achilles on the ground that he had sold Hector's corpse for gold. The true aristocrat had no interest in accumulating wealth (not least because he already had plenty). It is a code which has persisted down to the present: few modern heads of state would dare acknowledge that a wish to seize another nation's oil revenues might be a motive for war. But it has coexisted, in most periods, with its antithesis. Beowulf, hero of the Anglo-Saxon epic of which the earliest surviving manuscript dates from the century before Rodrigo Díaz's lifetime, measures the glory he wins by the quantity of gold he gains. "I hope you will amass a shining hoard of treasure," says the Swedish Queen Wealtheow kindly to him as he sets out on his adventures. Sallust would have thought shameful, but Homer and the Beowulf poet would both readily have recognized and applauded, the robustly candid greed for gain which the poets and balladeers ascribe to the Cid.

To an eleventh-century knight the acquisition of wealth seemed in itself praiseworthy, in no way incompatible with honor or even with piety. It was a lord's duty to provide for his vassals. They risked their lives on his orders in exchange for a share in his plunder. The greater the plunder, the more his vassals loved him, the more highly he was honored for his largesse. In the *Poema de Mío Cid* Rodrigo Díaz leads his wife, Jimena, and daughters to the top of a high tower to show them the terrifying hordes of the invading Almoravids. Jimena is aghast: "In Heaven's name, Cid, what is this?" Her husband reassures her: "Be not alarmed. This is great and wonderful wealth that is coming to us." To Rodrigo Díaz, and to most of his contemporaries, a hostile army was not only a menace, a trial of strength, and an opportunity to prove one's honor by displaying one's courage; it was also, and this was paramount, an opportunity to make one's fortune.

Few perceived any contradiction between cupidity and Christianity, the faith which exalts the poor in heart. In 1097, two years before the Cid's death, when the forces of the First Crusade met the Turks at Dorylaeum, the watchword passed along the Christian lines ended with the ringing promise "Today you will all (God willing) be made rich men." When in the *Poema de Mío Cid* Rodrigo calls for reinforcements he is joined by thousands of recruits motivated, like the crusaders, by devoutness and rapacity at once. "All who scented plunder . . . crowds of good Christians" join his forces. After his victory he rejoices with them "God and His Holy Mother be praised! . . . We are rich now and in the future we shall be richer still." The *Carmen Campi Doctoris*, a poem written in praise of him in his lifetime, celebrates his marvelous exploits, and exultantly proclaims (no shred of criticism is intended), "He captures with his sword the wealth of kings."

. . .

The eleventh century in Spain was a fine time for soldiers of fortune. The Umayyad caliphate, which had ruled all Islamic Spain from Córdoba since 756, collapsed at the beginning of the century and its dominions split up into over a dozen petty kingdoms collectively known as Al-Andalus. At the courts of these Muslim kings the arts of poetry, of architecture, of gardening and textile design reached dazzling heights. Creative talent and scientific learning were equally honored. A poet was likely to be rewarded for his gift with high political office. Astronomers and mathematicians, who drew on ancient knowledge entirely lost in northern Europe at this period, were honored by rulers who were, in an impressively large number of cases, scholars themselves. The atmosphere was sophisticated, luxurious, intellectually and aesthetically refined, but it was not peaceful. In the words of 'Abd Allah, who was king of Granada and the Cid's contemporary, after the fall of the caliphate "every commander rose up in his own town and entrenched himself behind the walls of his own fortress. . . . These persons vied with one another for worldly power, and each sought to subdue the other." Their rivalrous wars provided a plethora of jobs for those whose stock in trade was their fighting skills.

When Rodrigo Díaz was born, around 1043, the Christians were confined to a relatively small area in the north of the peninsula. During the eighth century the Arab invaders had swept northwards as far as the Bay of Biscay, the Christians retreating before them, but gradually, over the next three hundred years, they withdrew again, allowing a handful of independent Christian principalities to emerge in their wake. These were frequently at odds with one another as well as with their Moorish neighbors. It was a literally fratricidal war of Christian with Christian which formed the background to Rodrigo Díaz's childhood. He was born at Vivar, in northern Castile, near the border with Navarre. The two kingdoms, ruled by brothers, were at war until, in 1054, the king of Navarre died in a pitched battle against King Ferdinand of Castile. Ferdinand, who had already conquered the neighboring states of León and Galicia, thus became the ruler of the largest Christian kingdom in Spain since the Arab invasion.

Castile was a raw new country, a pioneer state with the insecure, exhilarating character of a place where danger and opportunity were equally abundant. It was a land of wild beasts and outlaws, of cattle raids and blood feuds and summary justice. The landscape was harsh, the climate unforgiving. The people were a polyglot assortment of incomers from elsewhere: Basques from the north, Mozarabic Christians from the

Muslim kingdoms to the south, settlers from other Christian territories. There was plenty of land for the taking, and any landowner who could afford a horse counted in Castile as a nobleman, exempt from taxation, but bound to serve the king in his wars.

Rodrigo Díaz was one such. In several of the poems and ballads about him he is described as being a common man, the son of a miller like Robin Hood's companion Much. In the *Poema de Mío Cid* he is presented as a plainspeaking man of action who has made his own way. His toughness, his self-reliance, and his independence are sharply contrasted with the decadence and pusillanimity of lordlings stupidly vain of their pedigrees. This is pure fantasy, an attempt to make of his disputes with king and court a politicized class conflict and to recast him in the mold of the populist heroes of folklore. In fact he was a well-connected member of the Castilian nobility. His father, Diego Laínez, was a knight who did King Ferdinand good service in the war with Navarre, winning at least one battle and capturing for Castile three settlements along the border. His standing was sufficiently high to ensure that when he died his son should be taken into the household of Ferdinand's heir, Sancho.

The boys of ancient Sparta were taken from their parents to be trained for their future careers as dedicated killers. Similarly all over feudal Europe the sons of the warrior caste, the knights, were sent as soon as they were judged old enough to live with their fellows in the households of their liege lords. Rodrigo was about fourteen when he entered the household of Prince Sancho. There he was prepared for his knightly career.

A Christian nobleman's education was not aimed primarily at developing his intellect, but at priming his body as a lethal weapon. Rodrigo Díaz may have been literate. His autograph has survived to prove that he could at least sign his name. He probably studied the law: as an adult he was several times employed to adjudicate in disputes over property rights. But most of his time and energy would have been absorbed by arduous physical training. Like any young man who aspired to knighthood he had to master the highly demanding skills of swordsmanship, of fighting on horseback, and of charging with couched lance—the technique, new at the period, which transformed metal-clad man and galloping horse together into a missile terrible in its velocity and the weight of its impact. He was soon an adept. The legends describe the adult Rodrigo as a marvelous horseman, a wily tactician, and a fighting man of great prowess. The historical records confirm that he was a skilled and successful warrior. When Rodrigo attained adulthood Prince Sancho himself, according to the contemporary *Historia Roderici*, "girded him with the belt of knighthood." (Other versions of his story have Sancho's sister, Princess Urraca, performing the ceremony while gazing yearningly at the handsome new knight.) From that time on Sancho was his liege lord, and he was Sancho's vassal.

A great lord in feudal Europe provided for his vassals. Those closest to him slept under his roof and were fed and armed at his expense. Others lived on his land and followed in his train when he went campaigning. He distributed among them all a proportion of his wealth and of the spoils of war. His patronage was expected to be generous but its price was steep. According to the *Song of Roland*, which achieved the form in which we know it in Rodrigo Díaz's lifetime, "Men must endure much hardship for their liege . . . Suffer sharp wounds and let their bodies bleed." A knight was obliged to fight for his lord, whether in wars arising from affairs of state or in private disputes with rival grandees, and to bring to battle a retinue of those who in their turn owed allegiance to him, for the vassals of a prince like Sancho might themselves be great men, each with a train of vassals of his own. The relationship between vassal and lord was not indissoluble, as the Cid's story repeatedly demonstrates, but while it lasted its requirements were absolute. A vassal who failed to discharge his duties to his lord was dishonored and destitute. A lord who failed to provide for his vassals would lose them, and along with them all the power and status they conferred on him. "Without my men," the Cid was to tell the people of Valencia, "I am like a man who has lost his right arm, a bird with but a single wing or a warrior without lance or sword." In the late Middle Ages a knight's loyalty to his lord, his fealty, was idealized as a virtue equivalent to a Christian's devotion to his God, but to Rodrigo Díaz and his contemporaries the relationship was one based on urgent mutual need. To honor it was to keep one's place in the world. To betray it was not so much sin as folly.

In 1065 King Ferdinand died, splitting the domain he had fought so hard to unify by leaving a kingdom to each of his three sons. Rodrigo's master became King Sancho II of Castile, and promptly appointed his young vassal chief of his military staff.

According to legend Rodrigo Díaz was already, though still in his early twenties, known as the Cid. From fourteenth-century chronicles, from a long poem, the *Mocedades de Rodrigo*, probably also composed in the fourteenth century, and from the ballads come a wealth of stories about his youthful exploits. He is said to have defeated a French army on the other side of the Pyrenees, to have traveled to Rome and defied the Pope, kicking over a chair in the Vatican and threatening to use the Holy Father's robe as a saddlecloth. These stories are certainly untrue. Only slightly less fantastic is the legend that he captured five Moorish kings who agreed to pay him tribute and who were so impressed by his prowess and his courtesy that they gave him the name "al Sayeed" (the Lord), by which he was subsequently always known. But other exploits ascribed to him are perfectly credible. This was a time when there were plenty of opportunities for a young man to prove himself by fighting. The feudal system, whereby a lord was obliged to support a body of fighting men who could only contribute to their own keep by fighting for it, ensured that conflict was perpetual and endemic.

Rodrigo Díaz rose splendidly to the opportunities that came his way. He defeated and killed a "Saracen." He was victor in single combat with a celebrated Christian champion from Navarre. A song probably written about five years later celebrates the victory: "Then Rodrigo was acclaimed el Campeador [the Champion] and his exploit blazoned as an omen of the triumphs he was to achieve, of how he would lay low the counts and trample underfoot the power of Kings."

The Cid in his prime is an imposing character, a hero of a different stripe from the youthful, mother-dependent Achilles or from Alcibiades, the self-absorbed seducer. He more nearly resembles Odysseus, the captain who wished to protect his crew and bring them home. He is a father to his people, a commander who can be depended upon to lead them to victory, no flashy boy but a model of adult virility. In visual representations he appears most frequently in weighty armor, a figure of massive consequence mounted upon a warhorse, more thunderbolt than lightning. The historians of the eleventh century were frustratingly uninterested in physical description, so we know little of what he looked like, but from the poets at least we learn one thing: that he had a marvelous beard. According to the *Poema de Mío Cid* the king, on meeting with him after a long separation, could not take his eyes off the torrent of hair flowing down his chest. This wonderful growth is indicative of the Cid's manly vigor, his mature sagacity, his sexual potency, and his status as one on whom fortune always smiled. When he parleys with his enemies his awe-inspiring beard is cunningly plaited and knotted and sheathed in a sort of snood to save him from the intolerable insult of a tweaking. But when he rides out to war, then his beard is displayed in all its astonishing splendor, advertising that, being as lionhearted as he is lion-chinned, he is and will remain invincible. "Oh God!" exclaims the poet. "See what a beard he had!"

As Sancho's chief commander he played a leading part in a sequence of small wars. From 1068 until 1072 he was occupied in a power struggle between King Sancho and his two brothers—García, who had inherited the kingdom of Galicia, and Alfonso, to whom Ferdinand had bequeathed the largest and grandest of his dominions, León. García was driven out of his inheritance and went into exile in Seville. Alfonso was defeated first at Llantada and then again at the battle of Golpejera in the summer of 1072. In the latter engagement, according to legend, the Cid signally distinguished himself. King Sancho was captured and was being led from the field guarded by fourteen knights of León. The dauntless Rodrigo challenged them, slew thirteen, put the last one to flight, and rescued his king.

The Cid's story belongs to a period when poets, unhampered by the guilt or the horror which the subject evokes in the modern mind, wrote candidly about the intense happiness men could find in battle. The *Song of Roland* describes its young hero riding jubilantly out to the fight: "Well it becomes him to go equipped in arms / Bravely he goes and tosses up his lance . . . Nobly he bears him, with open face he laughs." The same zestful enthusiasm glows out of the *Poema de Mío Cid.* "My God, how great was the joy they felt that morning," exclaims the poet as he describes a battle during which the Cid and his men killed three hundred adversaries with "pitiless blows." For Rodrigo Díaz and his peers a battle was the setting in which they could experience the most absolute personal fulfillment. All their years of arduous training, all the pain and exhaustion they had suffered to perfect themselves, all the emotional sacrifices involved in making of themselves single-minded warriors were rewarded with this ecstatic moment, when, like the long-haired Spartan youths who beautified and ornamented themselves for battle and, horselike, "pranced and neighed for the contest," they rode out, high on adrenaline and self-love, to kill their fellow men. The Rodrigo Díaz of reality may have taken a soberer view of the grim business of warfare, but the Rodrigo Díaz of legend, the debonair Campeador galloping into battle on his marvelous warhorse and effortlessly disposing of fourteen opponents, vividly embodies the terrifying gaiety of the easy-conscienced killer.

The old stories tell that at Golpejera he also gave evidence of his subtlety as a tactician, or, depending on the interpreter's point of view, his treacherous cunning. The chronicles relate that the two kings agreed before the battle that whoever was victorious would win the other's kingdom outright. In the first day's fighting Alfonso's troops drove Sancho's from the field. Alfonso, believing himself the clear victor and wishing to avoid unnecessary slaughter of the men who would henceforth be his vassals, called off the pursuit and ordered his army back to camp, where they celebrated far into the night. At dawn the next day, on the Cid's advice, Sancho fell on them while they still slept and routed them. Alfonso took refuge in the sanctuary of a nearby church, from which he was ruthlessly and impiously dragged. As the nineteenth-century historian Reinhart Dozy sternly remarks: "That which Rodrigo advised his prince to do was nothing but treachery." Be that as it may, Sancho, the Cid's master, was briefly king of all his father's lands. He made a triumphal tour of León, parading his defeated and captive brother Alfonso through the cities of what had once been his own kingdom.

What Rodrigo thought of his master's predatory and unfraternal attacks on his brother-kings, history does not relate. In the stories preserved in the medieval ballads and chronicles his character varies startlingly. Sometimes he is a wily trickster, sometimes he is savage and proud. But there are several stories in which he appears as a wise arbiter, a latter-day Cato, the guardian of moral and legal rectitude. Legend has it that when old King Ferdinand was dying he demanded that each of his children swear to abide by the judgment of the Cid—then in his very early twenties—in any dispute which might arise between them. In several romances he acts impeccably, at least according to the feudal code which decreed that a vassal's loyalty to his lord must take precedence over the dictates of his own conscience. In one of the ballads King Sancho calls together his knights to tell them that he is rightfully the sole heir to all his father's realms. The knights, aghast at the lie and at a loss how to respond, turn to the foremost among them for a lead: "All eyes were fixed upon the Cid." He speaks out boldly. He reminds Sancho of the solemn vow he made to his father on his deathbed to honor the terms of his will. He warns him that if he breaks that oath he will have neither the protection of the law nor the blessing of God, but he concludes that, come what may, Sancho can count on his support: "As vassals true, we're bound to do / Whate'er thou dost require." The Rodrigo Díaz of the historical record was repeatedly to challenge his master, but the Cid of this story is obeying the rules of his caste, subordinating himself and his superb talents to the service of his king, taking fealty, the vassal's duty of loyal obedience to his liege lord, as his guiding principle.

Nine months after he had made himself ruler of his brother's kingdoms King Sancho was killed. Some form of treachery was involved in his death. Within weeks Alfonso was back in León, restored to his throne by his brother's death and king now of Castile as well. A month later Rodrigo Díaz reenters the historical record as a trusted and privileged servant of King Alfonso. He had transferred his allegiance to the prince who could not then and cannot now be cleared of the suspicion that he had contrived the murder of his brother, the Cid's former lord.

King Alfonso is the most important subsidiary character in the story of the Cid. He is Agamemnon to Rodrigo's Achilles, Caesar to his Cato—or viewed another way, Cato to his Caesar. Any estimation of the Cid's claims to virtue hinges on an interpretation of the relationship between the two of them.

Over the coming years Alfonso was to banish Rodrigo, and then twice recall him only to banish him again. The Cid, remembered as the quintessence of Castilian (and latterly—by extension, Spanish) virtue, spent nearly half of his adult life in exile from Castile. He offended his monarch so grievously that his property was confiscated, his wife put in chains, and he himself threatened with imprisonment and driven from the land. Only if the king was grossly at fault in casting him out can the Cid be entitled to his position as national hero.

The Cid's apologists ascribe these repeated fallings-out to Alfonso's reprehensible, even pathological, envy of his vassal's great talents and dazzling successes. The *Poema de Mío Cid*, which was first written down in the century after Díaz's death, represents him as a nobly selfless servant of his royal master, patiently enduring Alfonso's ingratitude and never for a moment thinking to challenge the authority of the inferior being whom God's will had made his overlord. This vision of him as the scrupulously loyal and forbearing vassal was taken up and developed by subsequent romance writers and historians. In the fifteenth century, when Spain was finally united under Ferdinand and Isabella, chroniclers began to ascribe to the Cid a prescient vision of a centralized monarchy holding sway over all the numerous states which, in his lifetime, shared the Iberian Peninsula. He was acclaimed as the true instigator of the Reconquest. The devoted loyalty the poet had ascribed to him qualified him to become the totemic hero of a nation-state—Spain—which first came into existence nearly four hundred years after his death.

There is, however, a contrary tradition, given poetic expression in some of the numerous ballads first collected in the sixteenth century but in many cases probably dating back to his lifetime, in which Rodrigo Díaz appears as a defiant outlaw, a ferocious taunter of established authority, a rebellious individualist who went gladly into exile to conquer other lands, not for his king's sake but for his own. The one reliable account of his life, the *Historia Roderici*, a precious brief biography written in Latin not long after his death by a monk who may have been an eyewitness to, or even a participant in, some of his campaigns, suggests that this latter tradition is closer to the truth. Rodrigo Díaz probably provoked, may even have desired, the repeated quarrels between himself and his king.

Such insubordination doesn't fit with the saintly role posthumously assigned to him. Nor does his switching allegiance with such alacrity to the man who had probably murdered his liege lord. A story evolved to deal with this awkwardness. The romances relate that Rodrigo refused to pay homage to Alfonso until the new king had sworn, publicly and solemnly, that he was innocent of Sancho's death. The scene is dramatic. The king and twelve of his gentlemen assemble in the church of San Gadea in Burgos. There Rodrigo orders Alfonso to lay his hand upon an iron door bolt, symbol of inviolability (a bolt purporting to be the very one is still proudly displayed in the church). The king submits but he is pale with anger, and he warns Rodrigo that he will not forget this public humiliation. "Thou swearest me, where doubt is none, / Rodrigo to thy sorrow; / The hand that takes the oath today / Thou hast to kiss tomorrow!"

The story fits with the conception of Alfonso as a relatively unimpressive figure, one who allowed himself to be coerced and humiliated by his superb subject and whose resentment of the other's dominance and anxiety about his own guilt was to poison the entire course of their subsequent relationship—a conception which is the necessary complement to that of Díaz as unjustly persecuted patriot, but which is hard to reconcile with Alfonso's strikingly successful record as ruler. It presents the Cid as a sage judge of unimpeachable probity and such natural personal authority that he could bend a king to his will. It casts him as the custodian of his culture's moral values, as the hero who challenges the illegal authority of a presumptuous lord, as Achilles challenged Agamemnon, or as Cato challenged Caesar. It cannot, however, be substantiated. The *Historia Roderici* tells a simpler story: "After the death of his lord King Sancho, who had maintained and loved him well, King Alfonso received him with honour as his vassal and kept him in his entourage with very respectful attention." In other words, Rodrigo, whose subsequent career can be most easily understood as that of an opportunist ready to serve any master who would reward him, transferred his allegiance without any apparent qualms of conscience to his dead lord's brother and enemy.

He served Alfonso for nine years, no longer commander in chief but still a man of high standing and steadily increasing wealth. He married Jimena, daughter of the count of Oviedo. His position seemed secure and promising. Alfonso's power was expanding and Rodrigo could look forward to sharing in the wealth flowing into the court. But something went wrong. In 1081, at the age of thirty-eight, Rodrigo Díaz was banished from Castile.

The Greeks who followed Agamemnon to Troy, as Homer tells it, left behind homes which, though prosperous enough, were austere by comparison with the city to which they laid siege. So the knights of eleventh-century Spain's comparatively penurious Christian principalities regarded with predatory envy the Islamic states of Moorish Spain. Like Troy, the great cities of Al-Andalus—Zaragoza, Valencia, Seville, Granada, Toledo—were famously, ostentatiously wealthy. Their sumptuous palaces, their inhabitants' gorgeous silks, their gold were irresistible to their northern neighbors. And though the Islamic kings were far from pacific, they were less wholeheartedly bellicose than their Christian rivals. The Trojan Prince Paris refused to be ashamed of preferring his chamber, with its scented furniture and rich hangings, its promise of erotic bliss, to the battlefield. So kings like al-Muqtadir of Zaragoza, who was described by a contemporary as "a real prodigy of nature in astrology, geometry and natural philosophy," who built two famously beautiful palaces, one named "the Abode of Pleasure," and extemporized verses in praise of them, had other values, other priorities, than those of the Christian noblemen whose entire education and social conditioning were designed to make fighters of them. The warriors of Castile, Aragon, and Navarre sensed that softness, that fatal lack of attention to the essential business of self-defense in a violent world, and exploited it ruthlessly, repeatedly, and with awful success.

The numerous aggressive raids by Christian against Muslim which form the background to Rodrigo Díaz's early life were not part of a crusade, or even of a reconquest: they were a protracted series of robberies by extortion. A city might be besieged, land ravaged, crops and buildings destroyed, storehouses plundered. In order to get rid of the invaders and end the destruction the victims would agree to the payment of vast sums in "tribute," in exchange for which they would be assured of their attackers' "protection" against any other aggressors.

It was as the leader of such a predatory raid that in 1067 Rodrigo Díaz confronted the king of Zaragoza, the man who was subsequently to be his master. And it was in the course of another that he was first to find himself fighting against the forces of his own king. In 1079 Alfonso dispatched two parties of knights, one to Granada and one, led by Rodrigo, to Seville, to collect tribute. Both groups became embroiled in an ongoing petty war between the two Muslim kings. Rodrigo, according to the *Historia Roderici*, wrote to those of his compatriots who had gone to Granada, imploring them to abstain "for the love of their lord King Alfonso" from taking up arms against the king of Seville. The other Castilians, of whom the most prominent was Alfonso's commander in chief Count García Ordóñez, took no notice, and advanced into Sevillian territory, laying waste to the countryside. Rodrigo led out an army to confront them at Cabra, where he won a decisive victory. He captured Count García Ordóñez and many other knights, appropriated their arms and their other baggage, and held them for three days before releasing them against promises of ransom.

His triumph, in which he had humiliated and impoverished the subjects of his own king, was the indirect cause of his downfall. Count García Ordóñez would remain his sworn enemy. In the *Poema de Mío Cid* Rodrigo boasts that at Cabra he had plucked the count's beard, which, if it were true, would constitute an unforgivable insult. Even if the phrase is to be understood metaphorically García Ordóñez had been grievously offended. He had lost face and he had probably also lost a lot of money. García Ordóñez was one of the king's favorites; he was married to Urraca, the king's sister. He was not a good man to antagonize.

Back at King Alfonso's court "many men," García Ordóñez surely among them, "became jealous and accused [Rodrigo] before the King of many false and untrue things." It was alleged that he had appropriated some of the tribute from Seville. His position at court was becoming precarious. Then in the following year he took it upon himself to launch reprisals against a troop of bandits who came over the border from the Muslim kingdom of Toledo. Alfonso had lent his assistance, at a fantastically high price, to the ineffectual king of Toledo, al-Qadir, who was now under his protection. Ignoring or perhaps not realizing this, Rodrigo undertook an ostensibly punitive but actually rapacious raid deep into Toledan territory. "He pillaged and laid waste the land of the Saracens" and took a vast number of captives (the *Historia Roderici* says seven thousand) "ruthlessly laying hold of all their wealth and possessions, and brought them back home with him."

This unauthorized assault on an ally, apparently undertaken primarily for Rodrigo's personal gain, was a grave offense. If the king's complex and delicate relations with the numerous neighboring rulers were not to be disrupted, such maverick actions could not be tolerated. In 1081 the Cid was banished from Castile.

There are two ways of reading the story of his banishment. The legends say that the blameless Cid lost the king's favor only because Alfonso listened to his enemies' malicious lies. The *Poema de Mío Cid* describes the people of Burgos standing at their windows to watch the exiled Rodrigo ride away. With one accord they weep and exclaim, "What a good vassal. If only he had a good lord!" Like Cato, the Cid of this version of his story is one whose loyalty to the institutions and laws of his homeland is unfailing, one who in exile more truly represents its values than does corrupt authority. He is betrayed, but never a betrayer. Like Cato, he abjures hairdressing as a token of his mourning, allowing his prodigious beard to grow unchecked. He is the nobly uncomplaining victim of an unworthy master. "The Cid though exiled, remained true to his King."

The contrary tradition, though, presents a Rodrigo who more closely resembles Achilles than Cato, a proud aristocrat who values his own dignity higher than that of any king, one whose violent rejection of any curb on his will makes him dangerous and, in the eyes of the poets who celebrate him, superb. There is a ballad in which the young Rodrigo and his father ride to the court of old King Ferdinand in order to ask pardon for killing another nobleman. Diego Laínez and the knights accompanying them are all peaceably disposed, but Rodrigo is "proud and free." Arriving before the king, old Don Diego kneels to kiss the royal hand. Rodrigo draws back. His father calls him to make his obeisance in turn. Abruptly furious, he draws his sword and threatens the king, who cries out: "Avaunt! Thou devil's child! / Thou hast the face and form of man, / the glare of lion wild." Still glaring Rodrigo leaps on his horse and cries out, "To kiss a kingly hand at all / Doth not beseem my race," before galloping away. In another ballad King Alfonso and the Cid quarrel violently after the oath-taking in San Gadea. Alfonso, incensed by his new subject's overweening behavior, banishes him (thus erasing eight years of history) and Rodrigo, jeering and outrageous, takes his leave declaring that he is glad to go. Neither of these stories has any known historical basis, but the facts of Rodrigo Díaz's career suggest that he may have resembled this turbulent, touchily proud fictional hero rather more closely than he did the alternative image of a servant impeccably obedient to a master right or wrong.

On going into exile, the Cid of historical fact was anyway less concerned with brooding on his relationship with his old master than he was with finding a new one. He had to eat, and so did his followers. Idealized heroes tend to have no bodily needs. To Homer the biological necessity of eating reduced a man's status at the same time as it proclaimed him a full member of the human race. Achilles on his rampage abjures all food. The moment in the *Iliad* when he urges Priam to eat is the turning point in his story, the demonstration that he has become once more fully human. In the later chivalric tradition, a true knight displayed his aristocratic calling by living like a lily of the field, taking no thought for food and drink. When, in Thomas Malory's version of the Arthurian legends, Sir Gareth comes disguised to King Arthur's court and asks to be fed for a year, he incurs the contempt of the whole Round Table. Such sordidly carnal matters were the business of lesser, ignoble folk. In Cervantes's brilliantly knowing send-up of the medieval romances an innkeeper asks Don Quixote for money. "Don Quixote replied that he had not a penny, since he had never read in histories concerning knights errant of any knight that had." It is for the plebeian Sancho Panza to negotiate for lodgings and put supper on the table, not for the likes of him.

But Rodrigo Díaz was neither a demigod nor a romantic hero. Rather he was an adventurer like the down-to-earth hero of the Welsh epic the *Mabinogion*, the object of whose quest is a highly useful object, a supernatural cauldron capable of magically generating enough food to feed an army. To Díaz and his followers, and to the early medieval poets and minstrels who first told his story, food was all-important, and their need of it nothing of which to be ashamed. It was a sufficient motive for warfare. "How can we earn our bread save by warring against the Moors?" he asks in the *Poema de Mío Cid.* Thrust out from Castile, he urgently needed to find a new master in whose service he and his men could fill their bellies.

In the fifth century BC a man who, like Alcibiades, had transgressed against the laws of his country simply went elsewhere for employment. So in the eleventh century AD Rodrigo Díaz was one of many who, having offended their lords, were sent into exile, and thus virtually compelled, since a nobleman's only business was warfare, to fight for another.

"Strong men / Should seek fame in far-off lands," wrote the *Beowulf* poet. In legends from all over Europe youthful heroes leave home to make their name fighting dragons and monsters. In the warrior societies described in epic literature a community's stock of wealth could only be increased by those who went outside it in order to win rewards for their prowess. Jason brought home the Golden Fleece. Beowulf sailed home after slaying two monsters, his ship laden with armor, horses, and jewelry. In reality as well young men went abroad to replenish the wealth of their homelands by earning fortunes fighting not monsters, but other people's enemies.

The armies of early medieval Europe were full of mercenaries, of knights-errant whose pursuit of adventure, of fame and fortune carried them from one end of the continent to the other. Harald Sigurdsson, who was king of Norway in the Cid's lifetime, had fought against the Poles for Russia and against the Bulgarians and the Muslims of Sicily for Byzantium before returning home laden, according to the saga, with "an immense hoard of money," enough to finance the coup which made him king. There were Norman knights fighting for pay and plunder everywhere from Barcelona to Constantinople even before the First Crusade took them into the Near East in their thousands. There were Italian condottieri fighting for England against France and vice versa, while Italy was overrun with soldiers of fortune from Germany and England. In 1849 the great Dutch Orientalist Reinhart Dozy, the first European historian to draw on Arabic sources in writing about Rodrigo Díaz, shocked Spaniards by describing their national hero as "a man without faith or law . . . who fought as a mercenary now for Christ, now for Mahomet, solely concerned with the money he could earn and the loot he could capture." Dozy's facts were right, but his disapproving tone was anachronistic. To a nineteenth-century scholar it seemed proper to slaughter one's fellow men in the service of king, country, or Christ, but not otherwise. But to Rodrigo Díaz and his contemporaries fighting was an intrinsically honorable occupation, one which did not need to be justified by reference to a good cause. "Those who are not noble by lineage," wrote the French knight Jean de Breuil, "are so by the exercise and profession of arms, which is noble in itself." A vassal fought for his lord, but if his lord cast him off he would seek his livelihood elsewhere, fighting for anyone who would requite his services well.

The *Poema de Mío Cid* (which conflates the circumstances of Rodrigo's two banishments) relates that he left his wife and infant daughters in the Castilian monastery of San Pedro de Cardeña, parting from Jimena in an agony of grief "as the fingernail from the flesh." His admirers have liked to dwell on the image of the Cid as the loving husband, the devoted family man. But this is the most explicit reference in all the medieval versions of his story to his love for Jimena, and it shows him leaving her, as Odysseus left Penelope, as Cato serenely gave up Marcia, turning his back on the feminine sphere of sex and family in order to embark upon his great adventure in proper heroic fashion, unencumbered and alone. Most of the ballads ascribe to him a contempt of domesticity fitting to a warrior and homeless hunter after fortune. In one Rodrigo boasts of his own toughness. He is a hard man, one who is always in arms, who sleeps only twice a week and then sleeps rough, who eats not at table but on the cold ground—"[a]nd for dessert I have assaults, / The fruits that please me best!" In another ballad Jimena writes to the king bewailing the fact that her beloved husband has become "a lion wild" who visits her only once a year and then comes to her drenched in gore, "bloodstained down to his horse's feet, / I cannot look for fright." The Cid of this vision is as antidomestic as the blood-boltered Achilles was when he rode into battle against the family men of Troy. According to legend the last words he spoke on his deathbed were addressed not to Jimena, but to his horse.

However regretful Rodrigo Díaz may have been to leave his homeland, his family, and his property (an exile's estates were automatically confiscated by the crown), his prospects were not bad. He was in his late thirties, a seasoned fighting man with a splendid reputation and a following large enough to constitute a formidable private army. The Latin poem *Carmen Campi Doctoris*, probably composed two years after his banishment, acclaims him as one who defeated counts and trampled kings beneath his feet. He could embark with some confidence on his second career, that of warlord for hire.

He traveled first to Barcelona to offer his services to its Christian ruler. He did not stay long: according to the *Poema de Mío Cid* he quarreled publicly and violently with the count's nephew. He went on to Zaragoza and there he found employment in the service of the Muslim King al-Muqtadir.

To Spaniards from the Counter-Reformation onward Spain has seemed to be above all a Christian country, one which owes its very existence to the expulsion of the infidel. The nineteenth-century historian Menéndez y Pelayo apostrophized his country: "Spain, the evangeliser of half the globe: Spain the hammer of the heretics: Spain, the sword of the Pope. This is our greatness and our glory: we have no other." It was only fitting that the totemic hero of a nation whose self-definition is to such extent a sacred one should be presented as a man not only of God, but of the right variety of god.

The old ballads told the robustly anticlerical story of the Cid kicking over the Pope's chair and threatening to use sacred vestments as saddlecloths, but that aspect of his legendary character was rapidly suppressed and he was subsequently idealized as a loyal son of the Church. His exceptional prowess and his unbroken string of successes came to be seen as a sign of divine election. Many stories were told of the miracles associated with him. Straight after his wedding, according to the *Romancero*, he set off on a pilgrimage to Santiago. Along the way he encountered a leper floundering in a bog. He rescued the wretched man, took him to an inn, gave him food and drink, and even invited him to share his bed. At midnight he was woken by the strangely thrilling sensation of one breathing on his back. The leper had vanished and in his place stood St. Lazarus, who told him, "Rodrigo, God doth love thee well, Thy fame shall aye increase; . . . thou shalt be victor to the last, And Heaven crown thy life." In the *Poema de Mío Cid* the angel Gabriel appears to him in a dream with an equally encouraging message: "Ride out, good Cid Campeador, for no man ever set forth at so fortunate a moment. All your life you will meet with success." Throughout the *Poema* he is presented as a Christian warrior, one who triumphed "with God's help" because "the creator was on his side," whose battle cry begins "In the name of the Creator and of St. James" and who longs to "besiege Valencia and restore it to the Christians."

The monks at Cardeña, where the Cid and Jimena were eventually buried, wrote a chronicle of his life in which St. Peter appears to him when he is mortally ill and says, "God so loves you that He will grant you victory in battle even after your death." The Cid rejoices and prepares himself to meet his end. Once he is dead his lieutenant Alvar Fanes (an historical figure, but one who was not present at Valencia at the time of Rodrigo Díaz's death) leads an assault on the Almoravid army which is besieging the city. "At that moment the prophecy of St. Peter was accomplished." The Christian forces, in reality few in number, are mysteriously augmented until they are "full seventy thousand strong," all clad in white and commanded by a spectral warrior of gigantic size "riding a white charger and carrying in one hand a standard of the same colour and in the other a flaming sword." The two hundred female warriors with shaven heads in the Almoravid vanguard are slaughtered, and the rest of the Moorish army is driven back into the sea, where ten thousand of them are drowned. The ballads and romances repeat the story.

Rodrigo Díaz became the focus of a religious cult, the first hero of the Christian Reconquest. His relics were venerated. In the fourteenth century King Alfonso XI borrowed from Cardeña a crucifix which was said to have been his and carried it with him into battle in an attempt to annex to himself the divinely sanctioned good fortune of the Cid Campeador. When Jaime I of Aragon reconquered Valencia he carried with him the marvelous sword Tizon, which, according to legend, the Cid had taken from the Moroccan king. In 1541 his coffin was opened in the course of being moved to a new and more grandiose tomb. A marvelous fragrance reportedly filled the church and the drought from which Castile had been suffering was relieved by a miraculous fall of rain. In 1554 King Philip II sought to have the Cid canonized; the Pope (a better, or anyway less partial, historian than the king of Spain) refused his request.

Rodrigo Díaz was certainly a Christian born and bred, but his piety is highly questionable. Like Homer's warriors, he looked for omens in the natural world. Ibn 'Alqama wrote that "he took auguries from the flight of birds and placed faith in these stories and other lies." In Valencia and in Murviedro he converted mosques into churches—perhaps in a spirit of pious dedication, perhaps as a way of humiliating the defeated while advertising his victory—but he was also plausibly accused of sacking and looting churches. He probably killed as many Christians as Muslims in his time, and he appears to have served his employers impartially, regardless of their faith. In the words of Reinhart Dozy: "It is remarkable that it should have been the gloomy, ferocious Philip II who demanded that the Cid should be placed in the catalogue of saints; the Cid who was more Muslim than catholic . . . the Cid, whom Philip, had he lived in his reign, would have had burned alive by his inquisitors as a heretic and a blasphemer." It is also remarkable that in none of the numerous ballads celebrating his exploits, in neither of the epic poems narrating his career, is any mention made of the fact that for five years, years when he was in his prime and which saw some of his most notable victories, the Cid was the faithful servant of a Muslim ruler.

The arts of war, so assiduously cultivated by the Christian knights of northern Europe, were less highly regarded by the Islamic kings of Al-Andalus, whose people were as exquisitely appreciative of beauty and the more delicate luxuries as their contemporaries, the courtiers of Heian Japan. King al-Ma'mun of Toledo commissioned a noted astronomer to construct a wonderful water-clock, celebrated throughout Al-Andalus. Al-Muzaffar, who was king of Badajoz during Rodrigo Díaz's childhood, wrote a fifty-volume book of "universal knowledge." His successor, al-Mutawakkil, was a poet and patron of poets. At his parties guests reclined by a stream of running water sunk in the floor along which dishes of fine food came floating by. In these kings' palaces, whose few surviving remains are still breathtaking for the intricacy and grace of their decoration and the splendor of their proportions, the grandees of Islamic Spain led a life which made their Christian contemporaries' ceaseless round of military exercises and aggressive campaigns seem boorish and primitive. They did not abjure warfare, but they delegated most of the gross and ugly work of fighting to others. They swelled their armies by buying troops of slaves from eastern Europe and promoting the ablest among them to positions of high command, or they hired Christian knights. The counts of Barcelona, who figured largely in Rodrigo Díaz's life, were among the many Christian noblemen who owed their positions to gold earned fighting for Muslim masters. Another was the Cid himself.

For five years Rodrigo served the kings of Zaragoza, first al-Muqtadir then, after his death, his son al-Mu'tamin and, when he died in his turn, his son al-Musta'in. In Sparta and at the Persian Tissaphernes' court, Alcibiades adapted his manners to the culture of his hosts. Rodrigo Díaz must have done the same. Ibn Bassam records that he liked to have the tales of Arab heroes read aloud to him—presumably in Arabic—while he ate. When his tomb was opened in 1541 he was found to have been buried wrapped in a piece of silk of Moorish design, and with a finely figured scimitar alongside him.

For the bulk of his time in the service of Zaragoza he was engaged once more in a dispute between rival siblings. Al-Muqtadir, like King Ferdinand, divided his kingdoms between his sons. Rodrigo's master, al-Mu'tamin, was at war throughout most of his reign with his brother al-Hayib, king of Denia, and al-Hayib's Christian allies the king of Aragon and the count of Barcelona. In this protracted and ignoble war Rodrigo did splendid service. His reputation had already stood high among his fellow Castilians before his banishment, but to Ibn Bassam, a Moor from Seville, it was the rulers of Zaragoza "who brought him out of his obscurity." During his years in their service his fame spread throughout Spain. In 1082 he won a series of battles, culminating in one near Almenar. With a small force he took on the much larger united army of his opponents and won a decisive victory, capturing the enemy's valuable baggage train and, better still, making prisoners of the count of Barcelona and all his retinue of knights. The sum demanded in ransom for such illustrious prisoners would have been enormous. The grateful king "showered him with innumerable rich presents and many gifts of gold and silver." Two years later he won another great victory, again taking captive a large number of ransomable opponents, including sixteen noblemen of Aragon. When he returned to Zaragoza with his plunder, al-Mu'tamin and his sons did him the signal honor of riding out to meet him "accompanied by a crowd of men and women who made the air ring with their cries of joy."

His position was now a splendid one, and when the king died and was succeeded by his son al-Musta'in, Rodrigo retained his high place, being treated by the new ruler with "the greatest honour and respect." The warrior who was to be remembered for centuries as the scourge of the paynim looked set to enjoy a protracted and glorious career as the first servant of a Muslim king.

In 1086 his past life and his new one came into dramatic confrontation. King Alfonso, who had been steadily extending the number of his tributaries and the area of his "protectorate," arrived before the walls of Zaragoza at the head of a large army, and settled down to besiege the city. The Cid's apologists have asserted that he would never have taken up arms on behalf of the infidel against the Castilian king, that he must have been elsewhere at the time, but there is no real reason to doubt that, as the king of Zaragoza's chief commander, he would have been responsible for the defense of the city against his former master's aggression. In any case the confrontation never became a conflict. Alfonso received news so alarming that he immediately lifted the siege and marched his army southward. The Almoravids from Africa had invaded Spain.

Half a century earlier the Almoravids had been a tiny sect of fundamentalist Muslims based near the mouth of the river Senegal on the west coast of Africa. Devout, ascetic, and ferociously militant, by 1079 they had overthrown the venerable kingdom of Ghana and conquered for themselves and for Islam a vast empire, extending from Africa's Atlantic coast halfway cross the Sahara and from the Niger all the way northwards to the Straits of Gibraltar. Their armies, at once disciplined and fanatical, seemed unstoppable. Their leader, Abu Bakr, had delegated control of the northern part of their territory to his cousin Yusuf, who had based himself in Marrakesh. Throughout the 1080s, as Alfonso's Castile became ever more menacingly aggressive, and ever more successful, the rulers of Islamic Spain repeatedly asked Yusuf, their co-religionist, to cross the straits from Africa and help them to defend themselves. In 1086 he at last complied.

The Almoravids' arrival in Spain coincided with a radical alteration in relations between Christians and Muslims in the peninsula. In 1085 Alfonso had conquered Toledo after a long siege. According to 'Abd Allah of Granada the city's fall "sent a great tremor through all Al-Andalus and filled the inhabitants with fear and despair." Alfonso was no mere marauder: he wanted kingdoms, not just kings' ransoms. And there were signs that he wished to impose his culture and his religion on those whose territories he annexed. In Toledo, in contravention of the terms of surrender and to the dismay of the inhabitants, the principal mosque was desecrated (or consecrated, depending on the observer's religious viewpoint) by its conversion into a Christian church. The Christians, once only a nuisance—frightening and expensive but bearable—to the Muslim states, had become a threat to their continued existence.

In Yusuf, with his revivalist fervor and his already immense new African empire, Alfonso faced a formidable rival. The cultured, luxury-loving kings of Al-Andalus initially patronized their new ally. They lived in exquisite palaces at the heart of stone-built cities. Yusuf's Marrakesh was a camp surrounded by a stockade of thorn. They sent him verses in classical Arabic which he did not understand. They laughed at his lack of refinement, but, though it took them some time to appreciate it, he had assets they lacked and desperately needed, assets which, in the crude scales of history would prove to weigh more than all the loveliness of their gardens or the erudition of their scholars. He had a huge, well-trained army which had never yet been defeated, he had empire-building ambition, and he had the charisma of the single-minded. 'Abd Allah, the king of Granada whom he was later to deprive of his kingdom, was to write of him, "Had I been able to give him my flesh and blood, I would have done so."

The confrontation between the Almoravids and Alfonso's newly expansionist Castile was profoundly different in kind from the venally motivated, easily resolved Christian-Muslim disputes of previous decades. It was a conflict not between rival communities within a heterodox society, but between two diverse and mutually intolerant cultures. Over the next decade both parties were accused of acts of savage cruelty. The Almoravids were said to decapitate the corpses of the Christians slain in battle and heap them into towers upon which the muezzin stood to call the faithful to morning prayers. The Christians (Rodrigo Díaz among them) were accused of burning their prisoners alive and of having them torn to pieces by dogs. Whether or not these stories are true (and they may be), the very fact they were told demonstrates the fear and horror in which each party was beginning to hold the other. Rodrigo Díaz had grown up in a more inclusive Spain and had fought alongside Muslims against Christians as well as vice versa. But the polarization of the two Spains which was to lead eventually to the Christian Reconquest, in the mythology of which he was to become—however incongruously—the first hero, had its beginning in his lifetime.

Alfonso's armies met Yusuf's at Sagrajas. The Christian knights fought as a loose association of individuals; the battles to which they were accustomed were agglomerations of numerous single combats. For the first time, facing the Almoravids, they encountered an army fighting with a single purpose and trained to maneuver as a unified force. The Africans were well disciplined and well equipped. They carried long shields of hippopotamus hide and, most terrible of all, they marched to the beat of huge drums, whose appalling reverberations were being heard for the first time ever in Europe. They were terrifying, and soon victorious. Alfonso was comprehensively, humiliatingly defeated.

Yusuf returned to Africa, but his intervention in Spanish affairs had redrawn the political map of Spain. He had urged the Islamic kings to "co-operate with one another and close ranks." Alfonso and the lesser Christian rulers were facing the possibility that their Muslim rivals might once again overrun the entire peninsula as they had done three centuries before. It was a moment of crisis as grave as that in which the Athenians had welcomed back Alcibiades. In his hour of need Alfonso turned to the man whose splendid reputation made him look, as Alcibiades had, like "the only man alive" who could save from calamity the state which had rejected him. He called upon the Cid. A month or two after the battle at Sagrajas the king and his celebrated former vassal were reconciled.

The *Poema de Mío Cid* describes their meeting (albeit placing it, in defiance of the historical record, some six years later). Rodrigo has sent Alfonso a rich present, two hundred horses, each equipped with a saddle and a sword. Alfonso, well pleased, accepts them and sends word that he is ready to take Rodrigo back into his favor. A rendezvous is arranged on neutral territory—an honor to the Cid, it being usual for a vassal to attend the king wherever he was holding his court. Each of the principals arrives attended by a great retinue. "Many were the sturdy mules, fine palfreys and swift chargers. Great was the display of splendid armour, rich capes and fur tunics; all men high and low were dressed in gay colours." When the Cid approaches, the king rides out to meet him, but Rodrigo orders his men to halt and then, dismounting, "he knelt down on his hands and knees on the ground and with his teeth he pulled up a mouthful of grass. With tears of joy streaming from his eyes he showed in this way his complete submission to his liege lord."

The ancient gesture of self-abasement, the ecstatic tears: this is the blissful reunion of a devoted servant with his master. The Rodrigo of the

Poema de Mío Cid repeatedly sends Alfonso a share of his captured booty, assures him that "he would always serve him as long as he lived," and declares, "I should not like to fight against my lord King Alfonso." Those interpreters who have chosen to see him as unswervingly loyal to Castile and his king have believed the poet, representing the Cid as accepting Alfonso's overtures after Sagrajas with rapturous relief. But there is a ballad which tells a different story about their reunion. Rodrigo, to Alfonso's fury, agrees to serve him, but only for a handsome fee: "whose vassal I consent to be / Must pay me like the rest." Once again the tough-talking ballad comes closer to the historical facts than the idealizing epic. Rodrigo persuaded his old master to reward him handsomely and in advance for the services he would be rendering. His sentence of banishment was lifted. He was granted overlordship of half a dozen castles with their lands and inhabitants, and according to the *Historia Roderici* Alfonso made the extraordinary concession that "all the lands or castles which he might acquire from the Saracens in the land of the Saracens should be absolutely his in full ownership." Normally one-fifth of any plundered property was due to the king, and he would rule as overlord over any territory his vassals might annex in his name. Not so for Rodrigo Díaz. Under the deal he struck with Alfonso he was to have the right to conquer a kingdom for himself.

For three years after their reconciliation Rodrigo served his king well enough for there to have been no further recorded fallings-out between them. In 1089 he was in the Levant, the east of Spain, collecting tribute and clashing once more with the coalition of al-Hayib and the count of Barcelona, when he received an urgent message from Alfonso: the Almoravids had returned to Spain and laid siege to Alfonso's southern outpost at Aledo. Alfonso himself was on the march with all the troops he could muster. Rodrigo was to join him with all speed. Rodrigo duly set off southward with his army, heading, so he afterwards claimed, for the place where Alfonso had proposed they should join forces. Their meeting never took place.

Rodrigo claimed that Alfonso had altered his route without informing him, that he had been waiting obediently at the appointed rendezvous while the king's army passed by, unknown to him, miles to the west. But García Ordóñez, the grandee whom he had humiliated ten years before, and others accused him of treacherously and deliberately contriving that the king should go into battle undermanned. Alfonso was convinced. Rodrigo offered to swear to his innocence, drafting four versions of the oath that he would take. In case that was not enough he offered to submit to the judicial process of trial by combat, declaring himself ready "to do battle in your court against any man of all those who have accused Rodrigo of some treachery or guile, alleging that he would thereby have the Moors slay you and your army . . . These charges are lies, wicked, and false, and utterly untrue." The king was not persuaded. Rodrigo's property was confiscated, his wife and children imprisoned and kept for a while in chains, and he himself was banished once more.

This time he did not seek a new master. In the Levant, during the previous year, he had exacted tribute on Alfonso's behalf. Now, as an independent warlord owing allegiance to no one, he returned to the same territory, intent this time on making a fortune not for his master but for himself. With his estates once more forfeit, he urgently needed money to buy the loyalty of the fighting men on whom his personal power depended.

When Alcibiades, like Rodrigo Díaz, was exiled for a second time, Plutarch relates that he "recruited a force of mercenaries and campaigned on his own account against the Thracian tribes. . . . He collected plenty of money from the prisoners he captured." In the same way Rodrigo, denied the possibility of further advancement within the hierarchy of the community into which he had been born, fought thenceforward for no cause but his own gain and personal aggrandizement, using means that in later periods would brand him a land pirate, an armed robber, a gangster chief. Historians anxious to protect his reputation have performed extraordinary feats of intellectual contortionism in their attempts to defend him against the charge of cupidity; to his contemporaries no defense would have seemed necessary. The Rodrigo of the *Poema de Mío Cid* succinctly explains his way of life to the count of Barcelona:

> We keep alive by taking from you and from others:
> And while it pleases our Heavenly Father we shall continue
> thus.

In the *Poema* he attacks towns full of noncombatants without any kind of provocation, solely for the sake of enriching himself and his followers. He appropriates gold and silver and rich garments. He rounds up and drives off sheep and cattle. He captures people and exchanges them for money, making "a great gain" sometimes by taking ransom from their relatives, sometimes by selling them to slave traders. At Alcocer he slaughters so many of the inhabitants that not enough are left alive and at liberty to ransom those captured, and since cutting off the prisoners' heads would be unprofitable he simply appropriates their houses and uses them as household slaves. He is not a crusader, not a chivalrous knight. He is a bandit, one who makes no pretense that his actions are in any way sanctioned by association with some higher good, be it the propagation of Christianity or the expansion of Castile. When the people of a city he is besieging march out against him he frankly recognizes that he has given them provocation. "We have settled in their land and are doing them all kinds of harm, drinking their wine and eating their bread, and they have every right to come and attack us. This cannot be decided without a fight."

Legends relate that he practiced fraud as well as robbery with violence. Like Odysseus, he is trickster and marauder at once. At the battle of Golpejera he had won a great victory for King Sancho by subterfuge and by violating the terms of an agreement. A story which appears in the *Poema de Mío Cid* and in several ballads tells how, on going into exile, he provides himself with cash with which to equip and feed his vassals by cheating a pair of Jewish moneylenders. He asks for a huge loan, offering as surety two chests which he claims contain golden treasure too heavy and too precious to be taken with him; in reality they are filled with nothing but sand. The moneylenders agree, and swear not to look into the chests for at least a year. The money is handed over. The man who acts as go-between in the deal accepts an agent's fee of thirty silver coins (the traditional price of treachery), enough to buy a rich fur coat and a good cloak. Later in the poem the moneylenders reappear, asking rather plaintively when they are to be repaid. The Cid's representative breezily promises them that they will be satisfied, but the poet does not bother to tell us whether they ever were. An iron-bound chest purporting to be one of the ones used in the scam is still shown to tourists in the Burgos cathedral. The story identifies the Cid as one of the cheating heroes of folklore. According to Ibn Bassam his favorites among the Arabic tales in which he delighted were those featuring Mohallab the Liar.

The fourteenth-century monk Alvaro Pelayo inveighed against knights "because they fight not for God but for booty, for their private interest and not for the common one," but for those who sang of the Cid's exploits in his lifetime his lack of concern for the "common interest" seemed normal and acceptable, while his growing wealth, regardless of the violent and dishonest means whereby he had got it, constituted his glory. Largesse, the generosity with which a great lord shared his booty with his followers, was the virtue to be cultivated above all others. And since largesse is practicable only for the rich man, and riches, for the knight, were to be acquired only by force, it is no wonder that, as a twelfth-century Provençal troubadour noted, "Now honour lies in steal-ing cattle, sheep and oxen, or pillaging churches and travellers."

Jesus Christ and Cato may each have taken pride in their poverty (genuine in Jesus' case, assumed in Cato's), but there's a commoner kind of greatness which is made manifest by the wealth the grandee squanders. In fifth-century BC Athens Alcibiades demonstrated his standing and made his bid for power by spending lavishly on horse breeding and cho-ruses. In Cato's lifetime Pompey and Caesar vied with each other as to which could be seen to spend the most on the entertainment of the peo-ple; Crassus spent a tenth of his enormous fortune on a feast for the entire population of Rome, and Cato's brother-in-law Lucullus gave another which made "Lucullan" a byword for extravagance two millennia later. In the *Poema de Mío Cid* Rodrigo Díaz is similarly munificent. He gives a great banquet: "one and all declared that for fully three years they had had no such meal." His followers and friends, even the guests at his daughters' wedding, all become rich men thanks to his fabulous generos-ity. He gives gold away almost as fast and in as tremendous quantities as he gets it. Even his appearance speaks eloquently of money. Warfare in the eleventh century was seriously bloody, but it was also spectacular. A knight advertised his prowess and his resulting wealth by equipping him-self with the most glittering armor, the most gorgeous harness he could afford. A Latin song describes the Cid arming before a battle: his match-less coat of mail, his sword inlaid with gold, his shield worked with a golden dragon, his African charger, the fabulous warhorse Babieca, who flew like the wind and leapt like a deer. In the *Poema de Mío Cid* he wears wonderful clothes: fine stockings, elaborately worked shoes, a shirt as bright as the sun with clasps of silver and gold, cuff links of precious metal made to his own design, a brocade tunic worked with gold, a fur-lined crimson coat with gold buckles.

In feudal society, material wealth—gold, silver, silks, horses, slaves, fine armor and weaponry—were not just the outward show of power. They were, or at least were capable of generating, the thing itself. The more a man got, the more he was seen to have, the greater he became. Beowulf, having slain two monsters and been appropriately rewarded, returns to his ships "proudly adorned in gold" and "exulting in his trea-sure," not because of any ignoble greed but because a "treasure-giver" and "gold-guardian" could attract other adventurous young men to his fol-lowing, and provided that he dispensed his gold hoard liberally he would be well served. For men's loyalty had to be bought, their services in battle paid for. A man's perceived stature depended on the number of his follow-ers, and the size of his following depended on his ability to dispense gold.

Besides, money could be used to buy everlasting life. Rodrigo's con-temporary Gonzalo Salvadórez bequeathed land to the monastery at Oña "in order that I may be remembered there for evermore." In the *Poema* the Cid sends a boot full of gold to the monastery of Cardeña to pay for masses for the saving of his soul. Immortality, for which Achilles had had to lay down his life, could, in early medieval Europe, be bought for cash.

Banished once more, with no liege lord to provide for him, Rodrigo Díaz urgently needed to demonstrate his ability to acquire riches. "Certain of his knights whom he had brought with him from Castile . . . returned to their homes," notes the *Historia Roderici*. They must have doubted his ability to continue dispensing largesse. He soon proved their doubts ill founded. In the spring of 1090 he led his war band into the ter-ritory of King al-Hayib of Denia. He besieged and took a castle which was also al-Hayib's treasury. In a cave within the walls Rodrigo found "much gold and silver and silk and innumerable precious stuffs." His funds thus replenished, he moved on to settle menacingly close to Denia itself. Cowed, the king "agreed a peace" with him, presumably by paying him to leave. He then marched into the district of Valencia, demanding tribute from King al-Qadir, but also accepting "many and innumerable tributes and gifts" from other dignitaries. He was proving as efficient at intimidating his prey on his own account as he had been when acting on behalf of Castile or Zaragoza.

In demanding tribute from other men's tributaries, though, he had challenged his victims' established overlords. Al-Hayib turned for help to his "protector," Count Berenguer of Barcelona. Once again the Cid, whose campaign in the east has been represented as an attempt to Christianize the area and make it impregnable to Almoravid attack, found himself confronting a Christian opponent.

They met in the mountains. Rodrigo was encamped high up. Berenguer took some of his troops even higher and attacked him from both sides at once. A desperate battle ensued. Rodrigo fell from his horse and was badly wounded, but he fought on and by the end of the day he had won what the *Historia Roderici* calls "a victory ever to be extolled and remembered." The enemy's camp was plundered and Count Berenguer taken captive, along with "many other most noble men," all of whom were ransomed. Al-Musta'in of Zaragoza, Rodrigo's former employer, who had remained neutral in this dispute, negotiated a settlement which resulted in Berenguer not only paying a vast sum of money to Rodrigo but also ceding to him the "protection" of the Muslim territories of the Levant over which he had previously considered himself overlord. It was less than a year since Rodrigo had been cast out from Alfonso's favor. Already he had not only made himself a fabulously rich man, he had established a power base for himself which assured him further enormous revenues in tribute. "I am Ruy Díaz de Vivar, the Cid Campeador!" cries Rodrigo as he hurtles into battle in the *Poema de Mío Cid*. His war cry proudly calls attention to himself, not as commander of an army, certainly not as a citizen of a state or the subject of a monarch, but as a superb and self-sufficient individual. By 1091 he had no further need of a king.

A king, however, had need of him. The Almoravids were becoming increasingly aggressive and expansionist. They had entered Spain initially to defend the Islamic kingdoms in the south from Christian intimidation. Now they began to devour those very kingdoms. As Yusuf's devoted admirer Ibn Bassam records, he "drove those petty kings off their thrones as the sun drives off the stars." One after another Granada, Seville, Córdoba, Málaga, and Almería fell to him. Their kings were imprisoned or sent into exile in Morocco, their treasures were plundered, their people subjected to the African conquerors. This invasion, presented both by its perpetrators and their opponents as a kind of holy war, had as its first victims the invaders' co-religionists.

In 1091 Alfonso resolved to halt Yusuf's advance. Rodrigo's remaining friends in Castile urged him to join forces with his former king. The queen herself wrote to him—although it appears that the king did not. Like Alcibiades the Cid was twice-banished, and like Alcibiades he was still, all the same, the man his compatriots looked to to save them and secure them victory. Rodrigo allowed himself to be persuaded. He joined Alfonso near Granada. Almost at once there was trouble between the king and his supposed subject. Their combined armies encamped within sight of the city, Rodrigo taking his troops further forward than the king's in order, according to his apologists, to protect his royal master from a surprise attack. To Alfonso it appeared that in positioning himself in advance Rodrigo was claiming precedence over his former lord. The chronicles describe his calling on his courtiers to "see how Rodrigo insults and affronts us!" The Almoravids refused to come out and fight. After a few days the Christian armies withdrew and marched north. They stopped en route at Ubeda. Rodrigo's choice of campsite again seemed like a mute assertion of superiority. This time the king could not, or rather had no further need to, contain his anger. When Rodrigo came to visit his tent he abused him violently and accused him, in the words of the *Historia Roderici*, of "many and various things."

Rodrigo Díaz and the king of Castile could no longer meet without challenging each other. As Agamemnon is infuriated by Achilles' assertion that he, the charismatic warrior, is as great as or greater than the acknowledged king, so Alfonso was provoked by the magnificence of this former vassal, whose standing as a self-made grandee called into question the inviolability of his own inherited supremacy. Alcibiades, even before his first banishment, had grown too great to be easily and safely accommodated within the state of which he was supposed to form part. By the time he returned to Athens in 406 BC the grandeur of his reputation threatened the stability of the democracy. It was against similarly outsize individuals that Cato had spoken so passionately, foreseeing any state obliged to include them would inevitably capsize under the weight of their inordinate greatness. The author of the *Historia Roderici* alleges that King Alfonso was so envious of the Cid's prestige that he lost control of his senses. That "envy" must have been reinforced by an awareness that Rodrigo, by now effective overlord of much of eastern Spain and backed, as Caesar and Pompey had each been, by a large army flushed with its successes and owing loyalty only to him, was a force too volatile and too potent to be readmitted to Castile. The Cid was a useful ally in extremity. The crisis past, he was best kept at arm's length.

There were, besides, indeed "many and various things" of which Alfonso might accuse him. In demanding tribute from al-Qadir, previously Alfonso's client, he was trespassing on his king's claims. Some of the chronicles and ballads suggest that in the last years of his life the Cid was still working on Alfonso's behalf, albeit building an independent principality for himself in Muslim territory (as Alfonso, desperately wooing him after the battle of Sagrajas, had specifically decreed he might). He is reported to have annexed cities in the king's name and to have dutifully shared all his takings with his royal master. So he is exonerated; even Alvaro Pelayo, the acerbic critic of knights-errant, was ready to forgive their acts of violence and robbery so long as they were undertaken in the service of a superior lord. The historical Rodrigo Díaz sometimes helped, sometimes hindered Alfonso in the enlargement of his kingdom, but the legendary Cid was remembered as his right-hand man, a subordinate as loyal as he was effective, the instrument whereby the monarch consolidated his rule. Even as late as 1992 a Spanish historian could write about "the Cid's mission to put an end to the fragmentation of feudal power in mediaeval Spanish society and make wars for the establishment of a centralised monarchy." The man three times banished for failing to abase himself as a subject, whose personal power was such a menace to his king's that the monarchical state could only preserve itself by ejecting him, is remembered as the creator of the very institution he threatened to destroy from within.

Perhaps Rodrigo Díaz did send Alfonso gifts, but if he did so his motives were not exactly those of a loyal servant. The *Poema* reports that he sent Alfonso the king of Morocco's richly decorated tent supported on two golden poles "so the King may believe the rumours he hears of the Cid's great wealth": the offering is not a token of obeisance but a display of his own independent grandeur. At Ubeda neither king nor Campeador acted towards each other in a way proper to allies, let alone to those bound to each other as lord and vassal. Alfonso, furious, ordered Rodrigo's arrest. Before the order could be carried out the Cid had marched away. The two were never to meet again.

At the center of Rodrigo Díaz's chosen field of operations in eastern Spain was the Muslim kingdom of Valencia. A seaport set in a fertile plain, Valencia was a rich prize. Alfonso had installed al-Qadir, the former king of Toledo, as its ruler, and extorted punitive levels of tribute from him in exchange for the favor, but the year after his quarrel with Rodrigo at Ubeda Alfonso set out to conquer it for himself, thus challenging Rodrigo on his own territory. Rodrigo responded promptly and with shocking ferocity.

In the ballads and legends the image of the Cid as a wise arbiter alternates with another, that of a man capable of extreme violence. There is a story about his early life which forms the theme of numerous medieval ballads. In it the aged Diego Laínez quarrels with a neighboring nobleman, the count of Gormaz. Laínez is too infirm to fight for himself. He needs a champion. Calling his sons, he puts them each to the test. According to one version of the story he bites their fingers until they scream with pain; according to another he ties their hands and pulls the cords so cruelly tight it causes them agony. One by one his elder sons beg him to release them but the youngest, Rodrigo, reacts with the ferocity of a tiger. His eyes burn and fill with blood. His cheeks flush. If Diego were not his father, he says, he would use his finger as a dagger to rip the old man's belly open and tear out his entrails with his bare hands. Diego

Laínez weeps with joy to find his child so savage. Rodrigo kills the count of Gormaz and brings his father, who is sitting down to dinner, the count's severed head, brandishing it before him with the words "the bitter herb will make thy banquet sweet."

Rodrigo Díaz had at least some of the cruelty and the capacity for ruthless destruction ascribed to him by the balladeers; the count of Barcelona, who frequently encountered him as an enemy, accused him of gross brutality. After Alfonso's attempt on Valencia he invaded Castile as a reprisal, choosing as his point of entry territory belonging to his old enemy García Ordóñez. The *Historia Roderici* describes his raid. At the head of a "very great and innumerable army, most savagely and mercilessly throughout these regions did he lay waste with relentless, destructive, irreligious fire. He took huge booty, yet it was saddening even to tears. With harsh and impious devastation did he lay waste and destroy all the land aforesaid. He altogether stripped it of all its goods and wealth and riches, and took these for himself." This is the man who is credited with having, with saintly forbearance and loyalty, refused all his life long to make war on Castile or Castile's king.

Alfonso, diverted by Rodrigo's assault, retreated from Valencia. Within months another threat appeared. An Almoravid army, commanded by Yusuf's son Aisa, was advancing steadily northward up the east coast towards Valencia. In October 1092 a small party of them entered the city at the invitation of the chief magistrate, the *qadi*, Ibn Jahhaf, to lend him support in a coup d'état. With their help he seized power from the wretched King al-Qadir, who attempted to escape disguised as a woman but was captured and decapitated. His head was paraded through the streets on a pole. His body was thrown in a pond. If Rodrigo Díaz could not swiftly make the city his own he was likely to lose control of the region altogether.

In the summer of 1093, presenting himself as the avenger of King al-Qadir—many of whose followers had joined his army—and the defender of legitimate authority, he began his siege of Valencia. He established strongholds to the north and south of the city and laid waste the surrounding countryside, burning crops and driving off cattle. He sent word to Ibn Jahhaf, demanding the release of a large quantity of grain he had earlier left in storage in the city, and when the *qadi* replied that the grain was now his and that he answered only to the Almoravid king, Rodrigo wrote again. "He swore by great oaths that he would not move from before Valencia until he had had his rights and had avenged the murder of al-Qadir upon Ibn Jahhaf's person." He provisioned his troops by terror-

izing the governors of Valencia's outlying fortresses into handing over all
they had. He sent out armed horsemen to raid the suburbs of the town
and intimidate the citizens. He burned the ships in the river, the wind-
mills, the surrounding villages.

The Valencians implored the Almoravids to send an army to relieve
them. In the words of Ibn 'Alqama, who was an eyewitness to the siege,
they longed for it to come, "as the sick man longs for health," but when it
arrived "by God's will," it withdrew without giving battle, presumably
because Yusuf had underestimated the Cid's strength and sent an insuffi-
cient force. When the people of Valencia saw it marching away, according
to a chronicle, "they counted themselves as already dead. They were as
though drunk. They no longer understood what was said to them. Their
faces became as black as pitch."

The siege became more rigorous. In the words of Ibn Bassam: "That
tyrant Rodrigo, whom God curse . . . fastened on that city as a creditor
fastens on a debtor, he loved it as a lover loves the place where he has
tasted the joys of love. . . . He deprived [Valencia] of the necessities of life,
killed its defenders, brought all kinds of evil upon it and rose up against it
on every surrounding hill." No one went in or out. Those who attempted
to leave the surrounding villages were captured on Rodrigo Díaz's orders
and they and their families sold to slavers. Within the city, the people
slowly starved. The rich ate horsemeat or "foul beasts" when they could
get them and when they could not chewed on leather. The poor, according to Ibn 'Alqama, resorted to cannibalism. "They ate rats, cats and
human corpses. They fell upon a Christian who fell in the ditch encir-
cling the city, dragged him up by the arm and shared out his flesh." Ibn
'Alqama reports that fugitives were mutilated on Rodrigo's orders, their
eyes put out, their hands cut off, their legs broken. Others were torn to
pieces by dogs, or burned to death in sight of those watching from the
city wall. At last Ibn Jahhaf, seeing that there was no further help to be
hoped for from the Almoravids, capitulated. Nearly a year after Rodrigo
Díaz's army had first sat down before the walls of the city its gates were
opened and the people of Valencia, those who were left alive, came out,
desperate to find food. "By the look of them," says the chronicler, "one
might have thought these wretches were issuing from the grave."

Rodrigo's terms were lenient. Ibn Jahhaf would continue to govern
the city. He himself would not enter it, but establish his quarters in a
nearby suburb. His Christian followers were under orders to respect the
Valencian Muslims and the Valencians were given permission to kill anyone of the conquering force who molested them within the city. The

walls would be guarded not by Castilians but by Mozarabic Christians. All estates would be restored to their rightful owners. "The moors," says the chronicler, "said that they had never seen so excellent or so honourable a man, nor one whose army was better disciplined."

"I hate that man like death itself who says one thing and means another," says Achilles. It was Cato's unswerving integrity, his absolute inability to seem anything other than what he was, that made him godlike. Honesty is an heroic virtue, especially honesty of the kind which manifests itself in absolute self-consistency, in a perfect match between what is said and what is done. The *Poema de Mío Cid* describes Rodrigo as one who would not change his mind for anything in the world, who never in his life went back on his word. But in the words of Ibn Bassam, when Rodrigo took Valencia he did so "using fraud, as was his custom." The terms of the peace treaty, so generous and conciliatory, were broken, one by one.

On June 15, 1094, Rodrigo Díaz entered Valencia (as he had promised he would not) and took for his own use its royal palace. According to the fourteenth-century chronicles he summoned the noblemen of the city to a garden and addressed them from a dais adorned with rich rugs in words which made explicit the fact that he had taken their city not for Castile or Christ, but for himself. "I am a man who has never possessed a kingdom, nor has any of my lineage. But from the day I came to this city I set my heart on it, I coveted its possession, and prayed God to grant it to me. See how great is the power of God!" Not great enough, however, to grant the second prayer Rodrigo is said to have uttered on this occasion: "God shield me from doing violence to anyone that I might have that which does not belong to me."

It was almost immediately evident that his promise to restore all Valencian property to its previous owners was not compatible with his other promise, that he would make all of his retainers rich men. "When my Cid took Valencia and entered the city," writes the author of the *Poema de Mío Cid*, "those who had gone on foot became knights on horses; / and who could count the gold and the silver? / All were rich, as many as were there." The besiegers made their fortunes only by the city's inhabitants losing theirs. In order to maintain his own greatness Rodrigo Díaz promptly and shamelessly broke the promises he had made.

"He began to extort enormous sums in tribute from Muslims, and to raid their estates," writes Ibn 'Alqama. He summoned all the richest men in the city to his palace and then held them prisoner there until they paid over vast sums in ransom. He told them: "You are mine to do with as I

will . . . I could take your possessions, your children, wives, everything."
Ibn 'Alqama reports that Rodrigo appointed Jewish tax gatherers to
harass the well-to-do citizens with demands which they dared not deny.
"Each Muslim had at his heels a police agent who accompanied him every
morning to ensure that he contribute something to the treasure chest of
the master of Valencia. If he failed to do this he was killed or tortured."
The Cid seemed determined to make all the wealth of Valencia his.

Relations between the Muslim inhabitants of Valencia and the
Christian conquerors were at best edgily suspicious, at worst downright
murderous. Eventually Rodrigo decided, as Cato had at Utica, that he
had to get rid of the city's men of fighting age. One day the citizens were
required to hand over all their weapons and metal implements, right
down to their needles and nails, and on the next the entire population was
ordered down to the waterfront. There they were herded into two
groups. Women, children, and the older and weaker men were allowed to
return home. Those young men who were physically fit and had a com-
bative air were banished—or perhaps worse. It was rumored they were all
killed. More probably Rodrigo sold them to the slave merchants who had
gathered like vultures around the troubled city. "If you could see Valencia
now," wrote Ibn Tahir, the former king of Murcia, who was living in
retirement in Valencia

> you would lament for her, you would weep at her
>   misfortune,
> For her sufferings have robbed her of her beauty,
> yes, even to the last trace of her moon and stars!

Rodrigo had yet to lay his hands upon the treasure of the murdered
King al-Qadir. That, or so he believed, was in the hands of the *qadi*, Ibn
Jahhaf. Under the terms of the surrender the *qadi* was to continue as the
city's governor, with the Cid's assurance that he had nothing to fear:
another promise made only to be broken. Within weeks the *qadi* had been
imprisoned, along with all of his family. Rodrigo had him repeatedly
interrogated and tortured. According to Ibn Bassam he made him swear,
formally and before witnesses, that he had retained none of the treasure,
with the penalty that if he were subsequently found to have been concealing any of it the Cid would have the right to spill his blood. Shortly thereafter he found some of the dead king's valuables in the *qadi*'s possession.
"Or at least," writes Ibn Bassam, "he claimed he had." Ibn Jahhaf was
tried for the crime of killing his king, and on being declared guilty he was
burned alive. According to an eyewitness, he was buried up to his armpits

in a ditch and a fire was built around him. "Once the fire had been lit he pulled the burning brands closer to his body, in order to hasten his death and cut short his sufferings." Rodrigo's own men were appalled by the cruelty of the execution. One of them succeeded with difficulty in dissuading the Cid from executing Ibn Jahhaf's women and children by the same method.

Besieged and starving, the Valencians had watched in vain for an Almoravid army. At last, in October 1094, four months after the city had capitulated to the Cid, that army arrived and the besieger found himself besieged. The Almoravid force far outnumbered Rodrigo's troops. Yusuf had dispatched troops from Morocco as well as levying reinforcements from the conquered kingdoms of southern Spain. His nephew Muhammad was in command and had orders to take the Cid alive and bring him back in chains. The Mozarabic Christians of Valencia, convinced that an Almoravid victory was imminent, hastened to befriend their Muslim neighbors. For ten days the Almoravids circled the city, firing arrows over the walls, "shrieking and shouting with a motley clamour of voices, filling the air with their bellowing" and beating their terrible drums.

It is at this moment in his career that the Cid appeared to posterity to be at his grandest and most tragic. He is surrounded on all sides by his enemies. He has no allies to call upon. Like Cato in Utica he prepares to hold out alone against an aggressor who threatens not only to kill him and all his followers but also to destroy the culture he is fighting to protect. "He stands out in majestic isolation before the immense Almoravide empire," writes Ramón Menéndez Pidal, the hugely influential early twentieth century nationalist historian who was largely responsible for synthesizing the legend of the Cid as the champion of Christendom and of the Spanish monarchy. Superbly alone, the Cid takes his place in the legendary pantheon of Christian warriors alongside Roland, whose opponents at Roncesvalles were actually Christian Basque separatists but whose legend tells how he was outnumbered and cut down with all his companions by a vast and ferocious army of alien, godless Moors. Christian Westerners tend to narrate this part of his story as though the Cid and his men stand in a small circle of light surrounded by a vast darkness which threatens at any moment to engulf them. Like numerous sacrificial heroes of imperialism, from Cato's contemporary Crassus, who was slaughtered with all his legions in the Parthian desert, to the nineteenth-century hero-victims, America's Colonel Custer and Britain's General Gordon, he prepares for a last stand against forces terrifying in their unfamiliarity. He is set to become a hero like Cato, one whose claim to greatness rests on the sorrow and the pity of his failure. In the 1961 film *El Cid*, from which most people nowadays derive their knowledge of him (on which Menéndez Pidal, by then in his nineties, was a consultant), he appears in the melancholy but exalted character of one who holds a beleaguered outpost of Christian civilization against the frightful hordes of the infidel, and who dies a noble and pathetic death in defense of his culture and in the service of his God.

To Rodrigo Díaz's contemporaries, though, his opponents were not aliens or savages but neighbors and competitors familiar from centuries of coexistence, and his story was not one of sacrifice and tragic failure but of splendid success. He was not killed in battle. He held Valencia against all comers until he died in his bed. In 1094 he led his troops out of the city and fell upon the Almoravids on the plain of Cuarte. "By God's clemency" (according to the *Historia Roderici*), or thanks to the Cid's wily tactics of splitting his forces and using one half as decoy while falling upon the enemy's rear with the other, he won a resounding victory. The Almoravids retreated in panic, leaving behind a fabulous quantity of plunder, "much gold and silver, most precious textiles, chargers, palfreys and mules and various sorts of weaponry . . . provisions and treasures untold." Rodrigo's own share of the spoils included the fabulous sword called Tizon, Muhammad's tent complete with golden tent posts, and hundreds, perhaps thousands, of prisoners, whom he sold off as slaves. The Christians, avid for this glittering loot, neglected to pursue the retreating enemy, but there was no need. The enemy—that part of it which had not been captured—was gone. It was the first time an Almoravid army had been defeated: it was a famous victory. In Aragon a scribe dated a charter "the year when the Almoravides came to Valencia and Rodrigo Díaz defeated them and took captive all their troops." Amid the ceaseless petty wars of the period, the Cid's victory at Cuarte marked an epoch.

He never ceased fighting. The poet Ibn Khafaja voiced the people's unhappiness under their conqueror's rule in his lament for Valencia:

> Swords have brought ruin on you, oh dwellings . . .
> One's thoughts are stirred, one weeps and weeps.

Rodrigo ruled not by the consent of his new subjects but by constant vigilance and the frequent employment of force. He was never secure. 'Abd Allah of Granada, writing his memoirs shortly after the Cid's great victory at Cuarte, left a gap in the text for recording the Muslim reconquest of Valencia that he was confident could not be far off.

Repeatedly Rodrigo succeeded in postponing it. In 1097 he once again confronted a Almoravid army led against him by Muhammad and once again he was victorious. Ibn Bassam paid furious tribute: "Victory always followed the banner of Rodrigo (God curse him!)." Later in that year he besieged and captured Almenara. In the spring of 1098 he laid siege to the grimly magnificent mountain fortress of Murviedro. Desperate, the inhabitants appealed for help to a number of grandees (including Alfonso, Rodrigo's erstwhile king), but no help came. By this time the Cid's reputation was so formidable that it did his fighting for him. Al-Musta'in of Zaragoza, his one-time employer, told the envoys from Murviedro, "Rodrigo is full of guile and a most mighty and invincible warrior," and refused to take him on. The count of Barcelona sent a similar message but offered to cause a diversion by besieging Oropesa. But as soon as the count heard a report (unfounded) that the Cid was marching towards him he lifted his siege and withdrew. A reputation for invincibility is often self-fulfilling. Not only could no one defeat the Cid, by this stage in his life no one wished to try. The people of Murviedro surrendered. Rodrigo ordered them to evacuate the citadel. They did so trusting, foolishly, to his clemency. Ruthless and rapacious as ever, he entered the city, celebrated a mass, and then rounded up the citizens, confiscated all of their possessions, and sent them back to Valencia in chains.

It was his last victory. In 1099 he died at Valencia. He was in his late fifties. "While he lived in this world," wrote the author of the *Historia Roderici*, "he always won a noble triumph over his enemies: never was he defeated by any man." Three years later his wife Jimena, who had assumed command of his troops and held out against a besieging Almoravid army for nearly a year, abandoned Valencia, taking with her the Cid's treasure, the spoils of so many battles, and the Cid's corpse. According to one of the chronicles the Almoravids did not dare to take possession of the undefended city until they found an inscription confirming that the invincible Rodrigo Díaz was truly dead.

When they did they were appalled by what they found. On leaving, Jimena had set fire to the city. "The plight in which they have left Valencia is enough to daze all who have set eyes on her, and plunge them into silent and gloomy thought," wrote Ibn Tāhir. "She is still clad in the dark mourning in which they left her. A veil still shrouds her face. Her heart yet beats beneath the burning embers, and it is shaken with sobs."

Rodrigo's body was taken back to Castile and buried at the monastery of Cardeña. There it spawned stories. When, nearly two centuries later, King Alfonso X paid a visit to Cardeña he was presented with a book in which the monks summarized for their royal master the pious legends which had grown up around the corpse of Rodrigo Díaz. The Cid, they related, was forewarned of his death by St. Peter, who appeared to him in a dream. When he had only seven more days to live he renounced all food, taking nothing each day but a spoonful each of some myrrh and balm which had been given him by the shah of Persia "until his flesh became fair and fresh as his strength slowly ebbed." Thus embalmed premortem, he died. Following his directions Jimena and his lieutenants kept his death secret so that no word might reach the Almoravids to embolden them, and so that his body might safely be taken back to Castile. They strapped the Cid's embalmed body, dressed as though for battle in full armor, helmet, and boots, upright in the saddle of his marvelous horse Babieca. His eyes were open, as though in life. Escorted by Jimena and a troop of a hundred knights, the dead Cid made his last ride back to Castile, the country from which he was three times exiled but which claimed him, once he was no longer alive to assert his independence, as its national hero, and back, semipagan that he was, into the keeping of the Church.

In 1095, four years before Rodrigo Díaz's death, Pope Urban had called upon all Christendom to join the First Crusade, using terms which made plain that he, at least, was under no illusions about the nature of the medieval knight: "You oppressors of orphans, you robbers of widows. You hope for the rewards of brigands for the shedding of Christian blood. As vultures nose out corpses you watch and follow wars." He was offering them the opportunity to redeem themselves. "Let those who have been robbers now be soldiers of Christ. . . . Let those who have been hirelings for a few pieces of silver now attain an eternal reward."

The crusade was, among other things, a way of sending into voluntary exile thousands of fighting men. The mercenaries—warriors who in supplying a demand created it, generating an endless sequence of petty wars between lords rich enough to hire them—and the knightly robbers who lived like Rodrigo Díaz by "taking from others what we need to live," were alike intolerably disruptive of civil society. "In our own time," wrote Guibert de Nogent, "God has instituted a Holy War, so that the order of knights and the unstable multitude who used to engage in mutual slaughter in the manner of ancient paganism may find a new way of winning salvation, so that now they may seek God's grace in their wonted habit." The "habit" of violence, so long as it was directed towards the enemies of Christendom, could be redeemed and valorized. The caste of warriors, long looked at askance by the clergy of an essentially pacifist religion, were at last to be allowed to have it both ways. "Behold," wrote the crusader poet Aymer de Pegulham, jubilantly celebrating the new militant theology of the crusader, "[w]ithout renouncing our rich garments, our station in life, all that pleases and charms, we can obtain both honour down here and joy in paradise." The Cid's posthumous transformation from mercenary warlord into the legendary champion of the Christian faith parallels the reclamation of the thousands of knights-errant throughout Europe who were, in actual fact and in their own lifetimes, being appropriated for the services of the Church. It was not only Rodrigo Díaz whose reputation was laundered and whose life reinterpreted in the generation after his death, but the whole of his caste.

The Spanish settlement of Santiago, Cuba, November 1518, nearly half a millennium after the lifetime of the Cid. Hernán Cortés, aged thirty-three, was assembling men, ships, and provisions for an expedition to the unexplored American mainland. At the same time he was preparing himself for the role of leader. "He began to polish and adorn his person," writes Bernal Díaz, who was one of his recruits. "He donned a plumed hat with a gold medal and chain, and a coat of velvet sown all over with gold knots." The governor of Cuba, Diego Velázquez de Cuéllar, had instructed him to explore the coast, to make contact with the natives, and, if possible, to barter with them. Cortés had more ambitious plans. He had it defiantly proclaimed to the sound of drums and trumpets that he was seeking men to come with him to discover, conquer, and settle new lands. Governor Velázquez kept a jester named Mad Cervantes, who was at least sane enough to see what was observable by all: "Have a care, master Velázquez," he taunted his master, "or we shall have to go a-hunting; some day or other, after this same captain of ours." Cortés learned that the governor was about to revoke his commission. He resolved to leave first. His fleet was not yet properly provisioned but he bribed the official in charge of the town's meat supply to hand over his entire stock and he ordered his men aboard. They sailed under cover of darkness. Next morning, when the ships were well out to sea, Cortés had himself rowed back in a boat full of heavily armed men to within shouting distance of the shore. Velázquez was on the waterfront. Cortés yelled, "Forgive me sir, but such things must be done rather than thought." Then he was rowed away, leaving Velázquez to issue futile orders for his arrest. The history of the conquest of Mexico begins with an act of revolt.

For the next four years Cortés was repeatedly obliged to fight, buy off, or suborn parties of Spaniards sent out in pursuit of him in the name of the Holy Roman Emperor Charles V. When the conquistador and his men invaded the empire of the Aztecs they were (although Cortés took care that not many of them should fully comprehend it) outcasts from their own community, operating outside the law. For a few months after Cortés marched into the city of Mexico, leveling its houses and killing its people until the silence hanging over the ruins was so sinister and so absolute that his men felt as if they had all suddenly gone deaf, he lorded it over all the vast territories he had conquered. But within months he had lost the character of master, in which he had been so successful, and reacquired that of vassal against which he had so audaciously rebelled. Ships began to arrive from Spain, carrying His Majesty's notaries, His Majesty's Treasurer and Accountant, His Majesty's Factor and Overseer.

Cortés once compared himself, with some justice, to Julius Caesar, but he neither could nor would cross the Rubicon and defy established authority. Instead, in an abject attempt to reinsert himself into the hierarchy from which he had broken away, he strove to present himself as one fit not to command, but to serve; one who would never, like Rodrigo Díaz, pitch his camp where it seemed to take precedence over his sovereign's, or like Alcibiades parade his personal splendor in such a way as to make the state to which he was subject appear shabby by comparison. "What I have desired above all else in the world is to make my fidelity and obedience known to your Majesty," he wrote. His professed meekness did him little good. He found himself demoted from conqueror to civil servant. He lost his authority, his army, even eventually his house, and ended his life wretchedly, tagging around Europe after the emperor pleading for money and honors, and above all for the recognition that Mexico was his. Cruelly but consistently, Charles withheld that recognition.

It was customary among the sixteenth-century Spanish colonists to mark their first arrival in the Americas by dedicating a mass to the memory of the Cid. As they made their way into the brand-new American world, Cortés's men used to hearten themselves at night by singing or reciting snatches from the ballads celebrating the exploits of that other outcast, Rodrigo Díaz, who, half a millennium before had defied his monarch and ridden off into the badlands to conquer a country for himself. But the world had changed and shrunk in those five hundred years. Even a newly discovered continent was not far enough from the Hapsburg emperor's court to permit a subject to grow into a king. No conquest undertaken for him would ever belong to the conquistador, not in the sense that Valencia had belonged to the Cid.

Rodrigo Díaz has been remembered in many ways—quintessential Spaniard, Christian champion, battle-winning corpse—but the nub of his legendary story is always the brightness of his wonderful luck. Born in a happy hour, he is blessed with all the attributes he needs to achieve—as Cortés could not—the fulfillment of his every ambition. The *Poema de Mío Cid* describes him sleeping one day on a couch at the center of his great hall when a caged lion gets loose. Two princes panic and hide, one behind a winepress or in the latrine, the other under the Cid's couch. The Cid wakes, rises coolly, and "with his cloak on his shoulders" (a sign of his courage this—everyone else present has wrapped his cloak about his arm to make a shield) walks over to the lion, who immediately acknowledges his mastery. The implication is clear. In one of the ballads the watching people cry out, "We see two lions here . . . and the bravest is the Cid." The Cid is by nature a king among men as the lion is a king among animals. Torrentially bearded, savage and haughty as a predatory beast, outcast from his homeland, he is as free of social constraints as a human can be, as free as Achilles on his rampage. He is beholden to no patron. He defers to no master. He kicks over the Pope's chair. He plucks the proud count's beard. He quarrels with his king. He drives his enemies before him. He is unrestrained by law or morality. Born in a happy hour, he epitomizes the felicity of perfect freedom. "Franchise," exemption from any form of servitude or obligation, was, according to the feudal and later the chivalric code, one of the attributes of the nobleman, but in a world where almost everyone owed allegiance to someone else the independence without which it was unattainable was a rare and wonderful thing. The Cid, self-created lord of his own city, achieved it, escaping the constraints of the normal human condition to become a godlike beast. "Oh God!" exclaims one of the ballads. "How the hearts of the lion and the eagle are united in this beautiful man!"

V

FRANCIS DRAKE

In 1581 Queen Elizabeth of England went down to Deptford and boarded Francis Drake's ship, the *Golden Hind*, recently returned from sailing all around the world. After a banquet described by one of the guests as "finer than has ever been seen in England since the time of King Henry," the queen produced a gilded sword. She had brought it, she told Drake, "to strike off his head."

It was a joke—the sword was used instead to dub Drake knight—but it was a deliberately menacing one. Drake had come home with a shipload of stolen treasure. Queen and sea captain were equally well aware that she might have, could have, and in many influential people's opinion should have had him put to death. The man who had just become, and has remained, one of England's favorite heroes was a barefaced criminal. Rodrigo Díaz robbed others in accordance with a code of conduct accepted in his time and place. Drake's thefts were more outrageous, unsanctioned, even in his own day, either by international law or conventional morality. Yet not only did he get away with them, they won him the admiration of all Europe.

His stealing was done openly and with a swagger. The English authorities seldom censured him for it (although Elizabeth's chief minister, Lord Burghley, refused to shake his hand), and the majority of his fellow countrymen enjoyed it lustily, acclaiming him "the master-thief of the unknown world." Versions of his story written when England was again under threat of invasion, first by Napoleon and later by Hitler, have redefined him against the grain of historical fact as his country's protector, saving England, liberty, true religion, and good Queen Bess by repelling the Armada, but to his contemporaries he was not a guardian but a predator, one celebrated for outrages against other people's property rights.

Another joke. A hatch door from the *Golden Hind* has been preserved in London's Inns of Court. All British lawyers, on being admitted to the bar, make their oaths over it. In treating a piece of salvage from his ship as a secular relic the upholders of legality are honoring a hostage taker and slave trader, a contrabandist, a burner of towns and kidnapper of persons, a hijacker of ships and stealer of bullion, one who in his later years served his country as a naval commander but who won his fame and made his fortune in his first, and generally more successful, career as a self-employed pirate. This time the joker is not Drake himself but time, which has distorted and prettified his image until the legal profession is ready to accept as a saint a man who once said, "I have not to do with you crafty lawyers—neither care I for the law, but I know what I will do." What he did on that occasion was to put to death a man who had once been his closest friend. What he went on to do was to steal enough gold, jewels, silks, and silver to pay off the national debt, equip an army, and make himself rich.

He was not interested in death and destruction. Achilles' glamour is at its most intense when it is most lethal, when he is vaunting his tally of victims, howling out his war cry as he drives his chariot over the bloody corpses of his prey. Drake would not have wasted his time so unprofitably. He was responsible for the death of thousands of men, but they were nearly all of them men under his command, the wretched soldiers and sailors who succumbed to disease on his voyages. His enemies he seldom killed. Why should he? A corpse was valueless; a ransomable prisoner was a source of income. Nor did he have much appetite for the wholesale destruction commonplace in warfare. He might set a ship adrift; he would certainly strip it of every movable and salable object it carried, but he seldom and only reluctantly destroyed one, even when his queen had expressly commanded him to do so, even when his country's security depended on the disabling of an enemy fleet. He was adopted retrospectively as a patriotic hero, but repeatedly, throughout his career, he neglected or deliberately turned away from actions which would have been of benefit to his country in order to pursue a profit. He was neither an ancient warrior avid for glory, nor a munificent liege lord like the Cid. He was a commercial adventurer, fit hero for a nation of shopkeepers.

"Drake is a man of medium stature, blonde, rather heavy than slender, merry, careful . . . He punishes resolutely. Sharp, restless, well-spoken, inclined to liberality and to ambition, vainglorious, boastful, not very cruel." So he was described by a Spanish official in Santo Domingo who had abundant opportunity to observe him in the course of their protracted haggling over the sum of money (what Rodrigo Díaz would have called "tribute") Drake had demanded for doing the Spanish colonists the favor of refraining from demolishing their town. The annalist John Stow, who also knew him personally, confirms several points of the description, notably the merriment: "He was low of stature, of strong limbs, broad breasted, round headed . . . fair and of a cheerful countenance." Drake's special brand of humor is the keynote of his legendary character and his most seductive characteristic. Cato was admired for his impassivity and rigid self-control. In Drake's famous jokes the godlike imperturbability of the Stoic hero is employed as a teasing strategy. He is one of the prime exemplars of a personal style which has seldom been out of fashion from his day to ours. Four centuries later Charles Baudelaire dubbed it dandyism and described it: "It is the delight in causing astonishment, and the proud satisfaction of never oneself being astonished. A dandy may be indifferent, or he may be unhappy; but in the latter case he will smile like the Spartan under the teeth of the fox." That was Drake's way. Jocular, laconic, bragging by understatement, never letting on to being intimidated by his enemy's might or astonished by his own good fortune, Francis Drake was cool.

In the Pacific he robbed Spanish ships of tons and tons of silver and joked afterwards that he had done their captains a favor by lightening their load. In Cádiz he risked his own and scores of his seamen's lives, gambling on a wind, and fired on some thirty Spanish ships. Afterward, making much of his achievement by making little, he said he had "singed the King of Spain's beard." Just before the Armada was launched he interrogated a Spanish prisoner about the size of the force in preparation. The man, whether ignorant or loyally intent on misleading the enemy, doubled the number of ships—which was in truth enough to make it, in John Hawkins's opinion, "the greatest and strongest combination . . . that ever was gathered in Christendom." Drake, nonchalant as ever, remarked absurdly—thrillingly—"That's not much." So he aggrandized himself by understatement, his insouciance a kind of braggadocio, implying that galleons and tempests were all one to him, that the death he repeatedly risked was nothing but an awfully big adventure, that, superhuman in his courage, his wiliness, and his fantastic self-confidence, he could master them all.

Achilles wasn't cool. Homeric heroes weep and rage and preen, boasting of their tremendous physiques and fabulous exploits, grieving over their comrades' deaths, anticipating with horror the possibility of their own. But Drake's sangfroid has venerable antecedents. It contains within it some of the insolence of Alcibiades playing at debauchery, so sure of his own glamour he wouldn't deign to sue for favor by conducting himself as a good citizen or a great commander was expected to do. And it resembles too the outlaw boldness that the Cid of the ballads shares with the English folk hero Robin Hood, the subversive, liberating humor of those who, by their audacity and the successful practice of violence, make a mockery of unpopular authority. The Cid, so the story goes, having captured the count of Barcelona, held him prisoner for three days, during which the count refused to take food. On the last day the noble prisoner relented and broke his hunger strike. The Cid sat laughing and cheering him on while he ate ravenously, and then, having accomplished his humiliation, magnanimously released him. Just so, according to the legends, did Robin Hood feast the abbots and barons he waylaid in Sherwood Forest, treating them to hearty meals of stolen venison before robbing them of all they possessed. And so Drake, having captured a Spanish ship, would entertain its owner and aristocratic passengers in his own cabin, feeding them well while the musicians who went around the world with him played for their pleasure. Then, having stolen all their assets, their ships and their precious cargoes, he would send them each away with a gewgaw as a present, a bowl engraved with his name or a handful of English coins, gifts insulting in their inadequacy but received with gratitude by grandees astonished to have escaped with their lives.

He was a great seaman, by common consent of his friends and enemies alike, and fantastically courageous. "He is one of the most skilled mariners in England," wrote a Spanish agent to Philip II. "No one else in England" would dare to do what he had done. In 1625 Sir Robert Mansell, who had served with him, said that "in his deep judgement in sea causes he did far exceed all others whomsoever," and the seventeenth-century historian Edmund Howes confirmed that he was "more skilful in all points of navigation than any that ever was before his time, in his time, or since his death." The Spaniards came to believe that he was a sorcerer or a devil, capable of doing things impossible for the common run of mortals. For Thucydides, Alcibiades was the only man alive in his time who could have saved Athens. Drake too made others believe that he was unique, free of the natural laws which limit most humans' capability, and free, by extension, of human law as well. He told his men as they prepared to embark on the most perilous part of their voyage around the world that the queen believed him to be "the only man that might do this exploit," and that if they mutinied they would be lost forever, drinking each other's blood in horrible anarchy on an alien shore, for he, and he alone, could master them, lead them on to great riches, and bring them safely home. He was probably right.

Some of Drake's feats were, and remain, amazing. On his voyage of circumnavigation he sailed nonstop for 9,700 miles, finding his way without reliable maps from Java, across the Indian Ocean, around the Cape of Good Hope and northward through the Atlantic, not to touch land until he reached Sierra Leone four months later, a piece of seamanship which his (generally very hostile) eighteenth-century biographer George Anderson called "a thing hardly to be credited, and which was never performed by any mariner before his time or since." His geographical discoveries were momentous. His successes as a raider of ships, whether on his own account or his country's, were fabulous both for the daring he displayed in them and the profits they yielded. But, for all that, he is chiefly remembered not for his exploits but for his image (which he himself helped to create), the image of an unflappable, invincible joker, a man who might inspire others to the pursuit of glory but who himself made mock of sublimity, an insulter (like Rodrigo Díaz) of other men's beards, a cocky adventurer uncowed by grandeur and untrammeled by morality, a laughing thief.

He was born in 1540, or thereabouts. According to one version of his early life he served his apprenticeship on board a coaster trading up and down the English Channel, inheriting the boat when his master died. According to another he grew up in Plymouth, as an apprentice in the household of the Hawkins family, to whom he was related. In Henry VIII's reign William Hawkins had been the first English mariner to make the triangular voyage to Africa and then across the Atlantic to trade with the Spanish settlers in America before bringing the profits home. Such a trade was in contravention of papal decree and therefore, in the eyes of most Europeans, of international law. In 1493, in response to Columbus's discoveries, the pope had granted the Spanish a monopoly of all trade with the still-mysterious lands to the west of the Atlantic; Africa and the East Indies were allotted to the Portuguese. The English never fully accepted the ruling, and William Hawkins was anyway careless of legality: in 1544 he served a prison sentence for taking a Spanish ship. In the next generation his son John Hawkins, whose career was to run parallel with Drake's for thirty years, made several similar voyages. In 1566 and again in 1567 Drake was in his fleet.

The cargo John Hawkins collected in Africa and sold in America was human. He was the first English slave trader, and not ashamed of it. He was to choose for his crest a "demi-Moor, bound and captive." Slave trading was seen as dirty work. Queen Elizabeth called it "detestable" and prophesied after Hawkins's first expedition that it "would call down the vengeance of Heaven." But the profits were enormous enough to quiet even the royal conscience: Elizabeth was one of Hawkins's backers for his 1567 voyage.

Sixteenth-century adventurers who sought their fortunes beyond the seas generally expected not to produce wealth but, like the Cid, to steal it. Christopher Columbus complained of those who followed him to the Caribbean that "they came simply believing that the gold was there to be shovelled and the spices already bound and at the water's edge . . . so blinded were they by greed." One such was Cortés, who told the colonial official who was urging him to settle on Santo Domingo, "I came to get gold, not to till the soil like a peasant." Walter Raleigh took no mining equipment, not a single sieve or spade, when traveling in search of the gold of El Dorado. Hawkins's practice was to assault any ship he encountered on the African coast and steal its cargo. Most of his slaves were acquired by this means, grabbed from the Portuguese who had had the labor of rounding them up. Others were abducted in raids on coastal villages, or captured with the connivance of their tribal enemies. On one occasion, in which Drake participated, Hawkins loaned his men as mercenaries to one of the rival chieftains of Sierra Leone. They assaulted, took, and burned to the ground a town which had been home to eight thousand people. Hawkins was rewarded with several hundred of the prisoners of war, who joined the rest of the "negroes and other cargo" (his words) below the decks of his ships.

Hawkins's customers were Spanish colonists in the Caribbean who, having virtually depopulated the regions in which they had settled, urgently required an alternative labor force. They had the need and Hawkins had the supply. But there was an obstacle: the settlers were forbidden to trade with any but their own compatriots. Local Spanish officials who permitted Hawkins to land were likely to lose their jobs, or perhaps worse. Hawkins's strategy for circumventing this problem was to save the local governors' face by the use of violence. He would attack a town, sometimes bombarding it from his ships, sometimes actually landing an assault force. The governor would agree to pay a "ransom" if he would only go away. Once the money was handed over, Hawkins would set ashore some slaves, the governor noting for the official record that they had been abandoned. Thus a trade would be done without being seen to be done.

These assaults on Caribbean towns were not charades. People died. Houses were destroyed. One of the first actions that can with any certainty be credited to Drake is the bombardment of the governor's house at Rio de la Hacha on the northern coast of what is now Colombia. The governor, an unusually law-abiding official, had steadfastly refused to have anything to do with the Englishmen. When Drake's cannonball failed to intimidate him, Hawkins landed with two hundred men and drove the Spanish out of the town. Still the governor resisted. Only when Hawkins had captured hostages, seized the contents of the treasury, and begun to burn houses a deal finally made. Their Whig apologists have celebrated the sixteenth-century English contrabandists in the Caribbean as defenders of the principles of free trade against the jealousy and greed of Spain, but "free" seems a curious epithet for trade made under such brutal duress.

The voyage of 1567–69, on which Drake for the first time commanded his own ship, ended in disaster. As Hawkins turned for home his ships were caught in furious storms and one was badly damaged. No safe port appeared. For nearly a month the little fleet was battered in unfamiliar waters until eventually they reached the Mexican port of San Juan de Ulúa, having first—in order to persuade the people there to sell them provisions and allow them time to repair their ships—attacked three Spanish ships and taken their passengers hostage.

They were permitted to enter the harbor but the very next day a fleet arrived from Spain, bringing the new viceroy, Don Martín Enríquez. Hawkins threatened to keep the Spaniards out of the port. Enríquez temporized, promising not to molest the English if they would just refit their ships and leave quietly. He had no intention of keeping that promise. To him Drake and Hawkins were pirates whom it was his clear duty to apprehend. As soon as reinforcements came up he ordered an attack. Three of the English ships were sunk. The two that got away were the *Minion*, with Hawkins on board, and the *Judith*, captained by Francis Drake. The *Minion* was grossly overmanned with sailors who had managed to escape from the lost ships and she carried almost no supplies. Hawkins had to put a hundred men ashore in Florida to take their chances (only two are known to have made it back to England). Forty-five more died on the journey home. After four months Drake brought the *Judith* safely in to Plymouth. Five days later the *Minion* came home, with only fifteen men left alive, scarcely enough to keep the ship on course. Drake's failure to help those on the *Minion* was much censured. One of the mariners later reported that Drake did everything Hawkins commanded him to do, another that he blamelessly "lost us." But Hawkins, in his published account of the voyage, wrote with unmistakable bitterness that the *Judith* "forsook us in our great misery." Drake was not named, but his reputation was stained ineradicably.

Never again, except in the pursuit of the Armada, during which he once again disobeyed orders and deserted his post, did Drake serve under another commander. Like Achilles, like Rodrigo Díaz, he fit uneasily into any community or chain of command. He didn't take orders well, nor did he find it easy to trust those to whom he gave them. Repeatedly in later years he rounded on his deputies and associates, accusing them of disloyalty, and in 1587 one of them, William Borough, turned the accusation back on him. When Drake had him tried for mutiny Borough spoke up, referring to what must have been the well-known story about Drake's conduct at San Juan de Ulúa, "when contrary to his admiral's command he came away and left his said Master in great extremity." He was an unreliable deputy, a tactlessly overweening commander. His greatest successes were achieved when he was completely autonomous, over the seas and far away, beyond the reach of any law except his own, absolute master of his own little ship.

The debacle at San Juan de Ulúa was the beginning of the story of his life as he liked to tell it. In the 1590s, after the abysmal failure of the counter-armada he led out against Spain, Drake set his chaplain, Philip Nichols, to saving his face by narrating the story of his wonderful adventures in the Caribbean twenty years earlier. In the resulting book, *Sir Francis Drake Revived,* all his raids on Spanish ships and territory in the West Indies are characterized as attempts to seek redress for the "wrongs received" on his voyage with Hawkins, for the viceroy's broken promise, and for his lost property. According to Nichols, it was the righteous "indignation engrafted in the bosom of all that are wronged" which made Drake a pirate. Drake himself probably genuinely believed this. As soon as he returned from San Juan de Ulúa he went to London to ask the Privy Council to grant him and Hawkins "commissions of reprisal" which would have allowed them to attack Spanish shipping and seize goods to the value of those they had lost. He was refused. Having failed to obtain authorization for his projected piracies from man, he sought it from God.

He told the contemporary historian William Camden that he had consulted a priest, who "had easily persuaded him" that it would be lawful to rob representatives of the nation that had cheated and robbed him. There is no need to question his sincerity in this: God's approval was important to him, and he felt he had a real grievance.

Only a quarter of the men who set out on Hawkins's voyage returned alive, but a substantial amount of the takings were saved. A hostile and probably unreliable Spanish source relates that Drake tried to claim all the booty, alleging that he had seen Hawkins's ship go down, and that when Hawkins gave him the lie by reappearing he was imprisoned for the attempted swindle. What is certain is that when he told Camden that at San Juan de Ulúa he had suffered the "loss of all his means" he was lying. His share of the profits was sufficient to allow him to take a wife and to return to the Caribbean in 1570 and again in 1571, his own master now, in ships paid for by himself.

The wealth flowing into Spain from the New World took the form of silver and gold mined in Chile and Peru and brought by ship up the Pacific coast of South America to Panama. From there it was transported across the isthmus to the Caribbean port of Nombre de Dios to be loaded onto the ships in which it was carried in a heavily guarded convoy to Europe. Those convoys were virtually impregnable: in a century and a half only three successful raids were made on the treasure fleets. But while it was still on land the bullion was harder to protect. The isthmus was about sixty miles across at that point, mountainous, pestilential, and swelteringly hot, with open grassland on the Pacific side, dense jungle along the northern Caribbean coast. The bullion was carried from coast to coast by mules in trains of forty or more animals apiece. Drake was one of a number of pirates, English and French, who preyed on the Spanish settlers around Nombre de Dios during the 1570s. All of them dreamed of capturing some of that precious metal.

Drake came of criminal stock. His father, Edmund Drake, a Protestant preacher, had been charged in 1548 with two robberies. He and an accomplice, armed with staves and swords, had on one occasion stolen a horse and on another waylaid a traveler, assaulted him so violently "that he feared for his life," and made off with his purse. Like father, like son. Francis Drake was genuinely devout. He was said to spend three hours a day on his knees, as many as his great opponent, King Philip II of Spain. But he, like Edmund, found his religious faith no bar to the repeated breach of the eighth commandment. He took to piracy with gusto.

The pirates waylaid and plundered the trading ships which passed up and down the Caribbean coastline of Central America and raided the poorly protected Spanish towns and storage depots. They used small open boats, pinnaces, which could go close inshore, rowing into the shallows to avoid pursuing frigates, dodging into creeks, darting up rivers. Drake was fast, ferocious, and bold. On his second trip he captured two Spanish frigates and a dozen or so small trading vessels, stripping them of all their valuable cargo (velvets and taffeta, gold and silver, wine and slaves). He and his men carried swords and arquebuses, painted their faces with red, white, and black warpaint, and sounded trumpets to announce their presence and intimidate their (usually unarmed) victims. They were young (only one of the men who went with Drake in 1572 had turned thirty), cocksure, and violent. They rowed up the Chagres River into the interior of the isthmus and snatched a stack of valuable merchandise from the wharf of the little riverside depot of Venta Cruces (which was guarded by only one man). They stripped a friar naked, and marooned captives on an uninhabited island. They killed seven men and wounded at least twice as many more. They left a letter full of swaggering menace on board a frigate which they had looted and smashed up after the terrified passengers, one of them a woman, leapt overboard into chest-deep water: "We are surprised that you ran from us in that fashion . . . And since you will not come courteously to talk with us, without evil or damage, you will find your frigate spoiled by your own fault; . . . if there be cause we will be devils rather than men." They stole so much booty they were puzzled how to take it home. Drake began to acquire the fearsome reputation which would soon make him the terror of all Spanish colonial officialdom. "This coast and the town . . . are in the greatest danger," wrote the governor of Nombre de Dios to his king. "It is plain we are going to suffer from this corsair."

In 1572, when he was in his early thirties, Drake fitted out two ships and set sail once more for the Caribbean. This was the voyage that was to make his first fortune and to establish his legend. It is described in detail in *Sir Francis Drake Revived*. Flagrantly self-congratulatory and imbued throughout with jocular triumphalism, the book reads like fiction but, exaggerated though it may be in detail, its main story is confirmed by soberer sources, both English and Spanish. It makes a thrilling tale.

He landed in the Caribbean in a harbor he had discovered the previous year. There he found a lead plate nailed to a tree with a warning message from one of his fellow pirates. "Captain Drake! If you fortune to come to this place, make haste away!" His refuge had been discovered. He moved swiftly on to Nombre de Dios, where he led his men ashore by night. There, so he claimed, they peered into a storeroom where they saw a scene to haunt them for the rest of their lives: a lighted candle, a saddled horse, and "a pile of bars of silver of, as near as we could guess, seventy feet in length, of ten feet in breadth, and twelve feet in height, piled up against the wall." A fabulous trove, but they failed to get their hands on it. There was a skirmish with the Spanish settlers, a sudden rainstorm; worst of all, Drake was wounded in the leg, and his men, declaring that though they would have risked all else to get the booty they "would in no case hazard their Captain's life," dragged him protesting through the shallows back to the boats.

It was a bitter disappointment. But at Nombre de Dios Drake had gained an invaluable ally, an African named Diego who had begged the English to take him with them and who told them "how we might have gold and silver enough, if we would, by means of the cimarrones."

The cimarrones were Africans—escaped slaves or the children of slaves. As the bishop of Panama reported in 1570, "of a thousand negroes who arrive annually, three hundred or more escape to the wilds." By 1572 these fugitives constituted a large and well-organized rebel community living deep in the forests under two kings of their own. Many of them had reached adulthood in African villages, so they were far better qualified for life in the tropical rain forest than their European abductors. Drake and his fellow Englishmen were to be greatly impressed not only by their physical strength and powers of endurance, but also by their skill in hunting and pathfinding and constructing shelters and by the orderliness and prosperity of their towns. They hated the Spanish (with good cause). According to a report written by the governor of Nombre de Dios in 1571, they "entered daily into the towns" to free their compatriots. They also stalked the mule trains from Panama and had several times ambushed them, killing men and making off with gold and silver, just as Drake himself intended to do.

Drake had been a slave trader in his time. On the Guinea coast with

Hawkins he saw black people as valuable commodities up for grabbing. In Panama in 1572 he found them useful allies in his project of grabbing gold. During his subsequent voyages he was to take a number of black slaves from Spanish ships, including a four-year-old "negrito." What became of most of them is unrecorded. He has been praised for being, by the standards of his day, unusually free of racism, but it is probably more accurate to say that he was an open-minded opportunist, one boldly unconventional enough to consider any strategy that might bring him nearer his end. It is telling that Diego, to whom he was to owe a fortune, became, not a sharer in that fortune, but his servant.

The alliance between Drake and the cimarrones, which Diego brokered, terrified the Spaniards. Like all slave owners, the Spanish colonists lived in fear of those they oppressed. The cimarrones, supplied with European weapons and stirred up to action by European greed, raised a specter which haunted them for the rest of Drake's life. When in 1585 Drake was once again in the Caribbean the rumor ran up and down the coast, and was reported in all the courts of Europe, that he was organizing a slave rebellion, that thousands of black warriors had risen at his call. It was pure fantasy—after 1572 Drake never again worked with black allies—but it goes partway towards explaining why the Spanish found him so uniquely menacing.

The cimarrones told Drake that nothing of value would be taken across the isthmus until the next Spanish fleet arrived in the new year. Leaving some of his party under the command of his brother John to build a stronghold which he named Fort Diego, Drake sailed off in one of the pinnaces to use the intervening time in hunting for booty.

There is something dreamlike about the impunity with which, according to the account in *Sir Francis Drake Revived*, Drake cruised up and down the Caribbean coast that year, helping himself to whatever he wanted. There were "above two hundred" Spanish frigates in the area at the time, "the most of which, during our abode in those parts, we took; and some of them twice or thrice each." He boarded ships unopposed and helped himself to their contents. He encountered Indians who cheerfully gave him information about the Spaniards' movements and "many sorts of dainty fruits and roots." He found five storehouses crammed with provisions intended for the Spanish treasure fleet. At his approach the solitary guard ran off to hide in the jungle, leaving Drake's men to help themselves to enough food for them "if we had been two thousand, yea three thousand persons." The Spanish officials and traders who were his prey—fully aware of his presence, fully aware of his thieving intentions—

seemed impotent to defend themselves against him. He took so many ships he had no use for them and set them adrift, or scuttled them, or burned them. At last, after he had encountered some unprecedentedly determined opposition from the Spaniards at Cartagena, and after his men had begun to weaken after weeks at sea in an open pinnace, he returned to Fort Diego to lie low.

In the only poem he is known to have written Drake invited all brave men to follow him along "the way to purchase gold." At Fort Diego he learned, if he did not already know it, in what currency that purchase was to be made. His brother John had been killed, along with another man, in an attempt to board a Spanish frigate. There was worse to follow. In January twenty-eight men out of the seventy-three he had brought with him died of disease, probably yellow fever; one of them was another of his brothers, Joseph Drake. The mariners renamed their camp Slaughter Island.

At last came the news that the Spanish fleet had landed at Nombre de Dios. The mule trains would be on the move. Leaving a few men to guard the ship and his ransomable Spanish prisoners, Drake set off with a party of eighteen Englishmen and twenty cimarrones, the latter, led by a remarkable man called Pedro, acting as guides, porters (the English, exhausted by the heat, were barely able to carry their own gear), providers of game, camp builders, and protectors.

For ten days they traveled in dead silence through the equatorial jungle, some of the cimarrones going ahead to hack a way through vegetation so dense that one of Drake's men later compared it to an English hedge. At last they found themselves on grassland overlooking Panama and the Pacific. Later, when they had come to believe him capable of almost any feat of cunning and courage, the Spaniards related that Drake disguised himself and went into the town, spending several days there gathering information. Had he done so it is unlikely he would have got away with it; even eight years later his Spanish was not good enough to dispense with an interpreter. In fact it was one of the cimarrones, risking recapture and certain death, who went into Panama. He returned after a few hours with the news that a mule train carrying at least eight loads of gold would set out as soon as darkness fell.

Drake's party concealed themselves. The mules came so close that as they lay in ambush the Englishmen could hear their bells sounding through the stillness of the night. For the second time fabulous wealth was so close they could all but touch it. For the second time they lost it. Drake had given strict orders that his men were to remain hidden until the mule trains were right upon them. But one of them, drunk on brandy, broke cover and was seen by a Spanish horseman traveling from the inland settlement of Venta Cruces towards Panama. One of the cimarrones pulled him back and sat on him to keep him quiet, but it was too late. The horseman galloped on and gave the alarm; the mule train turned back. Drake's party, disappointed and now in extreme danger, had to fight their way past a Spanish garrison at Venta Cruces before vanishing once more into the jungle. Their return to the coast was even harder than the outward journey. Drake would not permit any delay for hunting, so for days they traveled on nearly empty stomachs. When the exhausted, half-starved party reached the shore they seemed to their fellows "strangely changed," not only because "our long fasting and sore travail might somewhat forepine and waste us" but also because "the grief we drew inwardly, for that we returned without that gold and treasure we hoped for, did no doubt show her footprint in our faces."

Two months later, by which time their number had dwindled to thirty-one—which meant that of the men who had sailed from Plymouth with Drake more were now dead than alive—they tried again. At the end of March they came across a shipload of French pirates led by Captain Nicholas le Testu. It was a frightening encounter. Le Testu's men outnumbered Drake's and his ship was much larger, but amity was established. The two captains exchanged gifts. Le Testu gave Drake a scimitar which had belonged, so he said, to a king of France. Drake responded with a gold chain and medallion. They agreed to join forces and attack the mule trains together, sharing the profits equally between them. The ships were left in a deepwater harbor. Le Testu with twenty of his men and Drake with fifteen of his, along with a group of cimarrones under Pedro—who was, as before, the true leader of the expedition—set off in the pinnaces. This time, instead of crossing the isthmus, they were to ambush the mule trains on the road just short of Nombre de Dios. They landed at the mouth of the river Francisca. Some of the men were ordered to return to the ships, some twenty miles from the Francisca, and to bring the pinnaces back to the same spot in four days. The attacking force stealthily made their way through the jungle, the Frenchmen anxiously and correctly complaining that if the cimarrones were to abandon them they would never find their way back. By evening they had reached the road at a point so close to Nombre de Dios that as they lay hidden in the darkness they could hear the shipwrights working through the cool of the night on the ships of the Spanish fleet.

In *Sir Francis Drake Revived* the rest of the tale is told in a tone of

ever-increasing exultation, a gloriously self-satisfied paean to Drake's triumphant audacity and luck. In the morning they heard once again the
deep-toned mule bells approaching. There were so many that the cimarrones told them they would soon have more treasure than they could
carry. It was absolutely true. Three mule trains, totaling some hundred
and seventy mules, came into sight. Each train was guarded by fifteen
Spanish soldiers. They were carrying nearly thirty tons of silver in all, as
well as 100,000 pesos in gold. The pirates broke cover and seized the first
and last mule in each train. As they had been trained to do, the other animals instantly halted and lay down. There was a brief battle, during which
one of the cimarrones was killed and le Testu was shot in the stomach, but
then the Spanish troops, seeing themselves outnumbered, ran for the
town, leaving Drake's men to "ease some of the mules which were heavi-
est loaden" of their burdens. The black slaves who were acting as drovers
helped the robbers "through hatred of the Spaniard" by pointing out
where the gold was packed. They took it all, but the silver was too much
for them. They buried some of it, hid more in land crabs' burrows, and
sank the rest in a shallow stream, and then, according to the rueful
Spanish report, "they made off, rapidly and in military order, this realm
being powerless to prevent or hinder."

By the time the Spanish had raised a troop of soldiers to pursue
them, Drake's gang had vanished into the jungle. All, that is, except for le
Testu, who, badly wounded as he was, had been unable to keep up with
the rest. Once more Drake proved himself a bad colleague: he abandoned
his ally. Le Testu was captured. His head was cut off and displayed in the
marketplace of Nombre de Dios. The Spaniards found and retrieved
some, but not all, of the hidden silver, and then, with a fearsome storm
coming on, they returned to Nombre de Dios. But Drake was not yet
safe. Two of his party went astray in the jungle and were caught by the
Spaniards. Under torture, one of them told where Drake had arranged
to rendezvous with his pinnaces. After two days of struggling through
the jungle heavily laden with precious metal, and having weathered the
storm without shelter, Drake's men arrived at the river Francisca to find
lying offshore, not their own two boats, but seven Spanish ones full of
armed men.

It was a dreadful moment. They naturally assumed their pinnaces
had been found and captured. And if the pinnaces were taken, it could not
be long before one of the men on board them revealed under torture
where the ships were hidden. Pedro, taking in the hopelessness of the situation, suggested the Europeans abandon all thought of returning home

and join the cimarrones in their outcast life. But Drake was not ready to give up. He rallied the men with a speech of desperate enthusiasm. They had not yet been seen. There might yet be time to reach the ships, he said, not by land (the cimarrones estimated that would take sixteen days) but by water. Declaring that "we should venture no farther than he did," he called upon them to build a raft and volunteered to sail in it himself to fetch the ships.

Some sort of a craft was patched together from trees felled by the recent storm. The sail was a biscuit sack, the rudder a sapling. Drake and three other men, two French, one English, set off on their desperate mission. The raft rode so low that the water came up to their waists, rising to their armpits at each swell. Another storm, or even a high wind, and they would have foundered. Drenched in salt water and completely exposed beneath the tropical sun they rapidly became so sunburned that their skin peeled off in strips. Somehow they clung on, and for six hours they sailed like this through shark-haunted waters. Then, miraculously, they sighted their pinnaces, which had not been captured after all but had missed the rendezvous after the storm blew them miles to westward.

It was getting dark. They had no way of making contact. The pinnaces, oblivious to the totally submerged raft, sailed straight past it. Then, as the men on the raft watched in despair, came a second miracle: the pinnaces turned into a cove. Drake managed to bring his ramshackle vessel onto a beach just around a point from them. And then, close to physical prostration as he and his three companions must have been, half crazy from the strain of the last four days and the terror of their desperate raft ride and wild with the sudden relief, he staged a joke, what must for him have been one of his best ever. He ordered his companions to run frantically with him up to the pinnaces, as though they were being pursued by an enemy. Those aboard, evidently believing the four men to be the last survivors of some ghastly catastrophe, anxiously helped them into the boats and asked "how all his company did." Drake, keeping a straight face, grimly answered, "Well," his tone so somber that "his hearers all doubted that all went scarce Well." Then, when he had fully fooled them, with a flourish he was still gloating over when he edited Nichols's account twenty years later, he pulled a great disk of gold out of his shirt and told them, as they gaped at it, that "the voyage was made."

The rest was easy. By the time the pinnaces reached the Francisca the Spanish boats had called off the search and left. All the surviving men were safely brought aboard with their gold and taken back to the ships. Two weeks later Drake sent a party back to the scene of the holdup. The

Spaniards had dug up all the ground for a mile around, but his men were able to retrieve thirteen bars of silver that had not been found. The cimarrones were rewarded for their part in the adventure with presents of silks and linen and scrap iron. Pedro set his heart on the king's scimitar which le Testu had given Drake, and Drake, reluctantly but gracefully, gave it him. The Frenchmen sailed for Europe with half of the booty and so did the English, but not before Drake had indulged in one last act of outrageous insolence. The Spanish fleet, now fully laden and on the point of setting out for Spain, was assembled at Cartagena. Drake sailed past in full sight, his ship decorated with silk streamers and banners so long they swept the water, and flying the flag of St. George. No one opened fire. No one pursued him. That night he provisioned for the Atlantic crossing by stealing another shipload of food. On August 9, 1573, he reached home. It was a Sunday morning. When the news was whispered in the church the people of Plymouth streamed down to the waterfront, leaving the preacher speaking to vacant pews. Some went to welcome home their sons and lovers; others—more than forty families—to receive the grim news that their young men were dead. The rest went simply to see Francis Drake bring home his gold.

Drake was now, in Camden's words, "abundantly rich," but as far as his own countrymen were concerned he was still obscure. Two years after his return from the Caribbean the Earl of Essex, writing to the Privy Council, referred to "one Drake," whose ships might be for sale—clearly not a person of whom the earl or any of his peers had yet heard. To the Spanish, though—especially the Spanish officials in the Caribbean—he was already "El Corsario," *the* pirate, the quintessence of criminal predation, the adversary whose quasi-supernatural prowess would serve to explain and excuse their own failure to defend themselves against him. As the councillors of Panama wrote to Philip II: "This realm is at the present moment so terrified, and the spirits of all so disturbed, that we know not in what words to emphasise to Your Majesty our solicitude . . . Disaster is imminent."

The Spaniards also called Drake "El Draque," the dragon, a simple pun which vividly conveys the role he came to play in their collective imagination. A dragon is a solitary predator, the enemy of all settlements, all civil communities. To Drake's contemporaries dragons had until quite recently been real. One was sighted in Suffolk in 1405, "vast in body with a crested head, teeth like a saw and tail extending to an enormous length." It slunk off back into the marshes from which it had come after devouring "very many" sheep. Dragons represented the wild. They emerged from horrid meres or sinister caves or dark, mysterious forests. They were embodiments of disorder and untamed bestial energy. To the Spaniards in America, in their little settlements encompassed by vast tracts of frighteningly alien, unmapped landscapes, by towering mountains and impenetrable rain forests, and looking out over seas aswarm with pirates, their communities must have felt as vulnerable as the city St. George saved when he speared his dragon. And then came El Draque, swooping down, swift, fierce, and greedy, on the terrified settlers of Nombre de Dios, of Cartagena, of Rio de la Hacha, and on the inadequately defended ships which plied between then. He was only a well-armed sea bandit with rather more skill and courage than his victims were accustomed to, but he seemed to them superhuman.

By the time Drake returned from the Caribbean in 1572 Queen Elizabeth was in the process of coming to terms with Spain, and had undertaken to prohibit English seamen's raids on Spanish targets. Drake does not appear to have been censured for his robberies, but he was not praised either.

Three years later he went to Ireland as a member of an English invasion force under the Earl of Essex. In Ireland Drake was for the first time serving his country. Not that he was a salaried public servant. In Elizabethan England the defense of the realm was performed by private investors. According to Edmund Howes, Drake equipped three frigates at his own expense, and another contemporary source records that he lost all his money by doing so. He may have felt he had no option: it was later alleged that he had gone to Ireland "for fear of my lord admiral and the rest of the Council, because of his Indies voyages." Those three frigates may have been the price of his pardon for his past piracies.

The Irish expedition offered little opportunity to get rich but Drake was ambitious for more than mere property. He wanted social position, something which, as a horse thief's son who had made a fortune from piracy, he still lacked. In Ireland he formed what may have been the closest friendship of his life, one which as a self-avowed social climber he would have found most gratifying. Sir Thomas Doughty was a gentleman with important connections at court, "a sweet orator, a pregnant philosopher," an educated man with a knowledge of the ancient languages and the law, and "an approved soldier." We know very little of Drake's emotional life, beyond the bare facts that he was twice married, had no children, and loyally gave employment to his brothers. But by all accounts, including one sanctioned by Drake himself, he and Doughty loved each other with "great goodwill and inward affection, more than brotherly."

In Ireland Drake also made some powerful contacts. According to his own account, Essex subsequently recommended him to Walsingham, Elizabeth's spymaster and primary leader of the prowar party, as "a fit man to serve against the Spaniards." Or maybe it was Doughty who mentioned Drake to the influential courtier Christopher Hatton, and Hatton who introduced him to Walsingham. Either way Walsingham recommended him to the queen, and so was conceived the voyage that became Drake's circumnavigation of the world.

In 1572, crossing the isthmus of Panama, Drake had been taken by his cimarron guides to a tall tree growing on a ridge, from the top of which it was possible to see both the Atlantic and the Pacific oceans. The cimarrones, who used it as a lookout, had cut footholds all the way up, and had constructed a "bower" near the top where a dozen men could comfortably sit. Drake ascended, and had his first glimpse of the "Southern sea," the Pacific. He was greatly moved. Camden elaborates: Drake "became so inflamed with affectations of glory and wealth, and burnt with so vehement a desire to navigate that sea, that falling down there upon his knee" he prayed that he might do so "and thereunto he bound himself by a vow." Though it clearly displays the remodeling of hindsight, the story could be essentially true. As Drake prepared to intercept the flow of treasure from South America's Pacific coast, he may well have conceived a desire to follow it to its source.

When the *Pelican*, subsequently to be renamed the *Golden Hind*, and four other ships under Drake's overall command set sail from Plymouth in November 1577, no one, probably including Drake himself, knew quite how far it was going. The sailors, some 160 of them, had signed on for a cotton-buying trip to Alexandria, and continued to believe that that was where they were bound until the fleet was well out to sea. The "gentlemen" on board, who included Drake's beloved friend Thomas Doughty and John Winter, whose father William was the surveyor to the queen's ships, were probably all aware of the plan which had been first formulated by Walsingham and which had attracted a distinguished list of investors, including the queen herself. This ordained that Drake was to lead his fleet across the Atlantic, southward down the coast of South America and through the Magellan Strait to the Pacific. There he was to investigate the possibilities of trade with those of the natives "not under the obedience of princes" (in other words, those independent of Spain) and attempt to buy spices, drugs, and cochineal, before returning "the same way . . . homewards, as he went out."

This was a confidential plan, secret from Spain (or so it was hoped) and secret in England from all but those most closely involved. Drake believed that it had been kept even from Lord Burghley, the queen's chief minister, who would have thought it recklessly provocative given that in Spanish eyes the Americas in their entirety were "under the obedience" of Spain. But even this secret was a blind, a decent veil covering the naked- ness of the outrageous plan which many must have guessed at—if peace- ful trade was intended, why were there no trade goods on board?—but perhaps only the queen, Walsingham, and Drake himself had discussed. That plan, the secret within the secret, was that Drake's expedition was an aggressive one, its object plunder, and that it was sanctioned by the queen.

In midvoyage, at a time when he badly needed to reinforce his authority, Drake told his men that Walsingham had taken him late one night to the queen's apartments. It was a momentous meeting, the first between two canny and unscrupulous people who were to come to under- stand each other well. Elizabeth told Drake, or so he later claimed, that she wished to avenge herself upon the king of Spain for "diverse injuries" and asked his advice. Drake told her Philip could most easily and effec- tively be hurt by a voyage to "annoy him by his Indies," to prey upon his settlements in South America. This plan, to raid the colonies of a nation with which England was not at war, was too brazenly criminal to be set down in writing. The queen gave Drake a silk scarf on which she had embroidered the words "The Lord Guide and preserve thee," but she gave him no letter of commission for his projected terrorism. She was later to say of him that "the gentleman careth not if I should disavow him," and, as Drake well knew, she would have done so if necessary with- out compunction. He was as cautious as his monarch. When Walsingham asked him to write a proposal detailing where and how he hoped to "annoy" the Spaniards, he refused, "affirming that her Majesty was mor- tal, and that if it should please God to take her Majesty away, it might be that some prince might reign that might be in league with the Kings of Spain, and then will mine own hand be a witness against myself." But the nature of the voyage, and the source of its projected profits, are abundantly clear. Drake claimed that the queen had chosen him for "my practice and experience I had in that trade." The only "trade" in which he could boast much experience, as both Walsingham and Elizabeth knew well, was that of piracy.

Drake led his fleet southwards to the coast of Morocco, where one of the men was carried off by hostile Moors, and where they captured three Spanish fishing boats and three Portuguese ships. Later Drake's deputy John Winter was to say in court, "I did never give my consent or allowance any way to the taking of any ship or goods unlawfully." His conception of lawfulness seems to have been hazy: he was in the pinnace which captured the fishing boats. Before they had even crossed the Atlantic it was clear how this voyage was to be provisioned and how its investors were to make their profit: not by trade but by the seizure of others' goods.

The little fleet turned west. Off the Cape Verde Islands they encountered and captured a Portuguese ship. They set her crew and passengers adrift in a small pinnace but kept the ship, her cargo of wine and linen, and, most importantly, her pilot, Nuño de Silva, "a man well travelled both in Brasilia and most parts of India [i.e., South America] on this side of the land." Prodigious navigator as Drake was generally acknowledged to be, he knew his own limitations. In the absence of accurate maps and of any way of calculating longitude and therefore of fixing an exact position, a sixteenth-century seaman who knew his way was at a huge advantage over one with no firsthand knowledge. Throughout the next two years Drake was to seize, wherever he could, Spanish charts and Spanish pilots with almost as much avidity as he seized Spanish gold. Nuño de Silva, under what duress we do not know, led them across the Atlantic.

"And so we take our farewell from the ancient known parts of the world or earth to travel into the new discovered parts." So wrote Drake's chaplain, Francis Fletcher, in his journal of the voyage. Drake and many of his crew had seen the New World already, but for those back home who were to read accounts of his voyage it seemed that as his fleet turned westward they entered a world of marvels. On the Cape Verde Islands they saw and tasted strange and wonderful fruit—coconuts and bananas. They saw trees bearing blossoms and fruit together in what in England was the dead of winter. In the open ocean dolphins played around them. Flying fish landed on their decks, as though by the generosity of

Providence, providing them with fresh food. Their expedition was taking on the character of a fabulous voyage.

When Christopher Columbus sailed westward he carried with him a fantastic portfolio of illusions as to what he was going to find. Cuba to him was Cathay, an outlying region of the realms of the great khan. Hispaniola was Ophir, the fabulous land where King Solomon's emissaries used to buy pearls, precious stones, and gold mined by griffons. Jamaica was Sheba, whose queen was legendary and from "whence departed the three Kings who went to worship Christ," and Venezuela was, quite literally, Paradise. The Europeans who followed Columbus to America did not have to strive so feverishly to fill its great and unknown mass with images drawn from their own cultural store but still they expected, and frequently found, marvels. Some were real, strange beasts like llamas and armadillos, strange substances like tobacco and cocaine. Some were exaggerations of reality: Magellan and his men encountered giants in Patagonia where subsequent travelers found the people barely above ordinary height. Some, like the tantalizing myth of El Dorado, were almost entirely fantastic. But anyone going on such an expedition went in the tremulous expectation of being amazed.

For all the strange and frightening novelties they were to encounter, though, the problem which was to preoccupy Drake and all his party as they crossed the Atlantic and made their way southward along the South American seaboard was one they had brought along with them. Before he passed through the Strait of Magellan and into the Great Southern Sea, Drake quarreled with Sir Thomas Doughty and put him to death.

Long after the event Drake let it be known that he had been informed, even before they left Plymouth, that Doughty was plotting treachery. The relationship between the two men whose mutual affection was compared by one observer to that of Damon and Pythias, the exemplary friends of classical mythology, festered rapidly. The first recorded sign of trouble came just before they began the Atlantic crossing. According to one account Doughty accused Drake's brother Thomas of pilfering. Drake defended Thomas furiously, accusing Doughty of trying to undermine his authority by casting slurs on his kin. Another account suggests it was Doughty whom some of the sailors suspected of theft. Drake confronted him and he explained indignantly that the trifles found on him—

gloves, a ring, a few coins—had been given him by the Portuguese prisoners. According to one of the seamen, "From this time forth grudges did seem to grow between them from day to day."

The crossing was arduous. For over two months they traveled out of sight of land, reliant on rain to supplement their dangerously inadequate water supply. For three weeks they were becalmed near the equator. Sweltering in their increasingly noisome little ships (the *Pelican*, by far the biggest, was barely seventy feet long), they were tormented by "the effects of sultring heat, not without the affrights of flashing lightnings, and terrifyings of often claps of thunder." They were going into unknown regions full of terrors both real and imaginary. It was not only in order to baffle the Spaniards that a false destination for the voyage had been advertised. Crossing the Atlantic for the first time, Columbus had falsified his log, deliberately underestimating the distance his ships had traveled lest his seamen, terrified at the idea of the vast expanse of ocean separating them from their homes, might refuse to go on. The master of one of Drake's ships was to say later that if he had known he was bound for the Pacific he "would have been hanged in England rather than have come on this voyage."

The distance they were traveling was in itself giddying. Even more daunting was the idea of what they might encounter along the way. Fletcher, an educated man, approached the equator with trepidation, recollecting the opinions of "Aristotle, Pythagoras, Thales, and many others" that the sun burned so fiercely there that nothing could live beneath it. They were headed for an alien continent inhabited by giants and cannibals. And even without these extravagant causes for anxieties they had others, all too well attested. Many of them must have remembered that of the men who embarked on Drake's previous, far less ambitious voyage, less than half had returned.

Fear and fatigue may have stoked Drake's quarrel with Doughty. Robert Mansell, who knew and admired Drake, was to number among his imperfections "aptness to anger, and bitterness in disgracing." His quarrel with Doughty bears out the description. Drake and those around him came to believe, perhaps correctly, that Doughty was trying to foment mutiny. There was an incident involving Drake's trumpeter which ended with Drake summarily removing Doughty from his command on the *Pelican* and sending him, without even giving him a hearing, to the small supply boat, the *Swan*, where he complained he was in effect a prisoner. Not long afterwards Doughty confronted Drake himself, apparently accusing him of breaking his oath, an unforgivable insult. Drake struck him, and had him lashed to the mast.

When the fleet anchored at last on the coast of Argentina Drake destroyed the *Swan* and ordered Doughty and his brother John aboard another ship. When Doughty refused to go Drake had him lifted aboard with the ship's tackle, a brutal humiliation. Before they moved on, a seaman waded out into waist-deep water and shouted out that he would rather give himself up to the cannibals (whom they believed to be all around them) than make false accusations against a gentleman, a suggestion that Drake was trying to fabricate a case against Doughty. Not long afterward Drake warned his crew that the Doughtys were a "very bad couple of men" and that their presence jeopardized the outcome of the voyage.

They sailed southwards, keeping together with difficulty as their ships were repeatedly swept apart by storms. Magellan's men had called the South Atlantic the "sea of graves." For Drake and his men it was scarcely less fearsome. At last, some two months after they had first sighted South America, they reached Port San Julian in southern Patagonia, the last safe anchorage before the Magellan Strait, where Drake intended to wait out the worst of the southern winter. It was an ominous place, walled with towering black rock, and it had a dismal history. It was there that Magellan, fifty-eight years before, had suppressed a mutiny and had two of his officers hung, drawn, and quartered. One of the gibbets on which the remains had been displayed was still standing. With a kind of ghoulish piety Drake's men cut it down and used the timber to make tankards.

It was bitterly cold, with long hours of darkness. Magellan's ships, at the same latitude and in a milder season, became weighed down with ice. Food was scarce, and the men were growing weak. Drake ordered some of them to sleep ashore, a necessary measure because the ships needed to be cleaned after their months at sea, but those who did so had no shelter as they lay on the ground, wrapped only in their cloaks. To add to the party's unease, two days after their arrival, they had their first fight with the natives. Earlier encounters with native Americans further up the coast had been peaceable. They had exchanged knives and bells and bugles for feather headdresses, ornaments of carved bone, and plumed birds. On one occasion the English had played their trumpets and viols for a group of curious Indians and the Indians, delighted, had danced so merrily that Captain Winter joined them. One had snatched a red cap with a gold band off Drake's head, but he had smiled and "would suffer no man to hurt any of them."

In Port San Julian things did not go so well. Magellan, in the same place, had antagonized the initially friendly "giants" by abducting two of their number. Half a century later they had not forgotten that Europeans were not to be trusted. Drake, on shore with six men, was attacked by a group of natives with bows and arrows. Two Englishmen were shot dead. Drake then shot one of the natives at point-blank range with an arquebus. The man died horribly with "so hideous and horrible a roar as if ten bulls had joined together in roaring" and the rest of the natives, of whom a number had appeared out of the woods on all sides, retreated. They were not seen again during the weeks Drake remained in the anchorage, but, as the Englishmen must have been uneasily aware, they were presumably there, watching their unwelcome visitors from the cover of the cliffs and woods.

It was in that hostile and frightening place that Drake put Thomas Doughty on trial and had him killed. The proceedings took place on the beach. A detailed report has survived, that of a mariner named John Cooke. Drake appointed a jury, which included several men known to be Doughty's friends, and witnesses were called. Doughty demanded to see the queen's commission which would have given Drake the authority to conduct such a trial. Drake, who had no such commission, responded brutally. He ordered that Doughty's arms should be bound "for I will be safe of my life."

The nature of the charges was hazy, the ensuing argument between Drake and Doughty acrimonious and incoherent. Eventually Drake asked the jury to decide on the truth of the allegations that Doughty had sought to "overthrow the voyage." Leonard Vicary, a friend of Doughty and a member of the jury, objected: "This is not law, nor agreeable to justice." He asked Drake, " 'There is I trust, no matter of death?' 'No, no, Master Vicary' quoth he."

The jury found the allegations to be true. Drake then left Doughty under guard and called the rest of the men around him down by the water's edge, and showed them a bundle of letters from important people, from Essex and Hatton and Walsingham, as though to demonstrate the basis of his authority. But still he couldn't produce a commission from the queen. With ludicrous effrontery he pretended to have forgotten to bring it out: "God's will! I have left in my cabin that I should especially have had." He then harangued the crowd, telling them that Doughty sought to kill him, and in doing so he would be the death of all of them, for without

Drake, their admiral and chief navigator, they would be lost for ever in this horrid place. He told them that while Doughty lived their voyage could not go forward, but that if it did each man would be made rich enough to live like a gentleman. Then, flagrantly going back on his assurance to Vicary, he called out, "Therefore my masters, they that think this man worthy to die let them with me hold up their hands." A majority did so.

Two days later Doughty, who had comported himself in the meanwhile with a dignity and serene courage which impressed everyone, made his confession to Francis Fletcher (admitting to nothing which would have justified his execution), took the sacrament with Drake, dined with him, spoke with him alone for fifteen minutes, embraced him, bade him farewell, and then laid his head on the block. The execution accomplished, Drake lifted the decapitated head with the words "Lo, this is the end of traitors," and ordered that the corpse be buried on an island which he named the Island of True Justice. (John Cooke designated it differently, as "that place where will was law and reason put in exile.")

The episode left a permanent stain on Drake's reputation. Despotic and irascible as he was, he repeatedly, later in life, quarreled with his deputies, questioning their loyalty or accusing them of cowardice. Each time his killing of Thomas Doughty was brought up against him. Once they returned to England John Doughty charged him with murder. Queen Elizabeth didn't immediately disallow the case but she contrived to have it thrown out of court on a technicality. Drake was not found guilty, but neither was he exonerated.

The story remains enigmatic. Malicious gossip suggested a sexual motive for the killing: Doughty was said to have been having an affair with Drake's wife. Camden had heard variously that Drake was jealous of Doughty's popularity and "cut him off as an emulator of his glory," and that he had received secret instructions from Lord Leicester to "make away Doughty by any colour whatsoever." Perhaps Doughty really was trying to usurp Drake's command or perhaps, like John Winter, he was nervous about Drake's piracies. If so, Drake may well have felt he had to silence him before he began on the massive robberies he had come to perpetrate: in killing Doughty, he killed his own conscience.

Or maybe Drake's anxiety was of quite a different kind. Dante consigned his Ulysses to Hell because he had run out on his responsibilities as father, son, and husband, driven by his culpable "longing to explore the world, to know the vices and virtues of all people," and sailed, like Drake, far out to the west, past the Pillars of Hercules, "beyond which men were not to sail." Two and a half centuries later exploration no longer seemed sinful in itself, but there was still something transgressive about adventures which led people so far from home and family and pitted their puny intelligence against the tremendous forces of the unmapped natural world. Sailors have always, notoriously, been prone to superstition and on Drake's voyage there was especial cause for fear. John Doughty was a self-proclaimed sorcerer. He told the seamen that he knew how to poison a man with a diamond, inducing a secret malady which took a year to kill, and that he and his brother could raise the devil in the form of a bear, or lion, or an armed man. These were dangerous claims. As their quarrel accelerated Drake repeatedly accused both the Doughty brothers of conjuring up storms. "At any time when we had any foul weather, he would say that Thomas Doughty was the occasioner thereof."

In Elizabethan England even the most sophisticated of intellectuals took magic seriously. Drake himself was believed to be a wizard. His Spanish enemies thought him one, and in several stories which were still being told in Devon at the beginning of the nineteenth century he is credited with magical powers and with having a devil at his beck and call. According to one fable his wife, despairing of his ever returning from his circumnavigation, resolved to marry again. As she approached the altar to celebrate her second wedding, Drake, on the other side of the world, divined what she was about and fired a cannonball clean through the earth, so that it erupted suddenly through the Devonian church floor, an awful warning to his faithless wife and a stunning way of getting rid of her suitor. Robert Southey, collecting folk tales in the 1820s, was told that the missile could still be seen.

Whatever the nature of the threat Doughty posed, Drake had to confront and overcome it before he attempted the passage through the Magellan Strait. In retrospect, Doughty's execution, performed beneath Magellan's gibbet, takes on the nature of a sacrificial ritual, a purge of Drake's personal trepidation and the excision of a point of weakness in his troop of men. Before the Greek ships could sail for Troy, before Achilles and his fellows could begin their grim quest for glory, Agamemnon sacrificed his daughter Iphigenia at Aulis. In Patagonia Drake, putting to death the man who had been, by all accounts, his closest friend, hardened himself and his fleet for the ordeal ahead of them by the spilling of human blood.

That ordeal was indeed awful. With surprising candor Drake told his men, "I have taken that in hand that I know not in the world how to go through withal; it passeth my capacity, it hath even bereaved me of my wits to think on it." Two and a half centuries later, Southey found West Country people still boasting of Drake's fabulous exploit in "shooting the gulf" and, on further questioning them, realized that the "gulf" they envisioned was not simply a geographical one, a stretch of navigable water, but a fabulous chasm dividing the ends of the earth one from another. According to their cosmography the earth was not a perfect globe. East and West curved round toward each other, but the twain did not quite meet, and Drake's ships, in passing from the known world to the unknown, would have to leap over a horrid abyss, bottomless and dreadful, before reaching the questionable safety of the ocean beyond.

Drake knew better, but even he, a master navigator, was at the limits of the known. He was heading for the Strait of Magellan because, like all other Europeans at the time, he believed the land to the south, the archipelago of islands including Tierra del Fuego which constitute the triangular tip of South America, was the outlying region of a vast unexplored continent, Terra Australis, which stretched southward unbroken across the Antarctic to the South Pole. It is a misconception which may have made little difference to his plans—later sailors often chose to pass through the strait, where they could take on water and trap penguins, rather than expose themselves to the ferocious seas around Cape Horn— but it is a measure of the darkness into which he was going. At Port San Julian he was a man afraid, not because he was a coward but because he was about to attempt something which as far as he knew had been achieved only once before in human history. And of Magellan's crews only one man in fifteen came back alive; Magellan himself was among the dead.

First Drake reestablished his authority on a new basis. Hernán Cortés, on landing in Mexico, proclaimed the foundation of the city of Vera Cruz (this foundation was a purely conceptual act, the city had as yet no material existence) and appointed a council to govern it. The councillors declared all preexisting orders and appointments (including Cortés's generalship) invalid. They then instantly reappointed Cortés, who from this time on owed his authority not to the Spanish colonial government but to his own initiative and his men's consent. Similarly Drake, before embarking on his voyage into the unknown, claimed absolute control over his little fleet.

On the Sunday after Doughty's execution Drake ordered every man in his company to make his confession to Francis Fletcher and to receive the sacrament, presumably with the intention of putting the fear of God into any would-be mutineer. Throughout the time they remained at Port

San Julian he issued a stream of threats, declaring at one time that anyone who was even an eighth as guilty as Doughty should die for it, at another going aboard John Winter's ship, the *Elizabeth*, and threatening to hang thirty of her crew. Then, on August 11, when he was almost ready to sail on, he called the entire company ashore again for a great assembly on the beach. Fletcher appeared ready to deliver a sermon, but Drake forestalled him: "Nay, soft, Master Fletcher," he said, "I must preach this day myself." He began by reminding his men how far they were from home and friends and how compassed about with enemies; he exhorted them to work together. He then offered one of the ships, the *Marigold*, to any who wished to turn for home, but he made sure it was an offer they couldn't accept: "Take heed they that go homeward, for if I find them in my way I will surely sink them." The men all agreed to stay. He then asked them from whom they wished to receive their pay. From him, they replied. He asked them further whether they would have wages "or stand to my courtesy." They chose the latter. In other words, rather than accept the regular pay (presumably for the short trip to Alexandria for which they had originally signed up) they would settle for a share of whatever spoils the voyage might yield, to be paid not by the syndicate of investors who had got up the expedition, but by Drake himself, at his "courtesy." They were henceforth to be his men, and his alone. He had dissolved their allegiance to the modern state of Tudor England and reformed the company on the archaic lines of a feudal war band, with himself as liege lord.

They were probably a fit crew for the task before them. It was by no means unusual for half or more of the men on a long voyage to die in the course of it: only those with very little to lose went to sea. Richard Hakluyt described the men on a typical voyage of discovery as being drawn from prisons and "dark corners." Sailors were decayed merchants, debtors, escaped convicts, and "others that hide their heads." Walter Raleigh called them the "scum of men," and Drake himself said they were "unruly without government" and "the most envious [in the archaic sense of surly and begrudging] people of the world." According to John Cooke, who was one of them, the men who went around the world with him were "a company of desperate bankrupts that could not live in their country without the spoil of that as others had gotten by the sweat of their brows."

There were yet the officers and gentlemen to be dealt with. Rodrigo Díaz, whose father was a nobleman and who grew up at court, was romanticized by the balladeers as a man of the people, one whose hard-headed, hardworking, hard-fighting persona put the silk-clad courtiers to shame. To those who sang of his exploits in the centuries after his death it was an important part of his legend that the Cid was a self-made man, neither an obsequious courtier dependent for his fortune on his lord's grace nor an effete aristocrat who owed his status to an accident of birth. One ballad has him defiantly asserting that his brocaded tents are finer than the king's and, what is more, they are evidence of wealth not passively come by but hard-earned: "I gained them on the battle field / With this good lance of mine." Another, in which he refuses to abase himself before the king, pointedly contrasts his bluntness of manner and plainness of dress with the fancy clothes and propitiating ways of highborn courtiers: "They all bestrode their prancing mules, / A steed of war rode he." They have scented gloves and plumed hats; he has gauntlets and a steel casque. While their swords hang idle from their belts, Rodrigo carries his in his hand, ready for any challenge.

What the Cid was imagined to be, Francis Drake really was. He was not wholly uneducated. He was literate and a fine draftsman and he had learned enough astronomy and mathematics to become a superlative navigator. He had made himself rich. But his origins were obscure to the point of shadiness. Back home, where social advantage and political clout might rate as high as actual achievement, where charm counted for as much as courage, Drake (no Alcibiades) was at a disadvantage. But at Port San Julian he decreed into existence a classless society in which all (other) men were equal, and equally subordinate to him. "Here is such controversy between the sailors and the gentlemen, and such stomaching between the gentlemen and sailors, that it doth even make me mad to hear it," he said. "But my masters, I must have it left, for I must have the gentleman to hale and draw with the mariner, and the mariner with the gentleman." His speech has been quoted over and over again as a statement of egalitarianism and a sturdy refusal of social injustice, and so it can be read, but it is worth bearing in mind that the man who wrote it down, John Cooke, said of Drake that "he in tyranny excelled all men."

Still standing in the freezing cold and louring semidarkness of that dismal beach Drake turned to the most important of the gentlemen, his captains, and one by one he publicly dismissed them from their commands. This was no rehearsed charade. John Winter, Drake's vice admiral, and John Thomas, captain of the *Marigold*, both protested vehemently, asking him to give his reasons for sacking them. He responded by asking brusquely "whether they could make any reason why he should not do so." The killing of Doughty had given him an awful power over his subordinates. Back in England John Winter was to say that as Drake's officer he went in fear of his life. There was no further protest. Drake harangued the company a while longer, describing the genesis of the voyage in terms which stressed his own paramount authority and his closeness to the queen, and then he declared all the officers reappointed. Like the crew, they were now, willy-nilly, Drake's men.

Four days later the little fleet, now reduced to only three ships, the *Pelican* (soon to be renamed the *Golden Hind*—Drake gave it its new name soon after entering the strait), the *Elizabeth*, and the *Marigold*, moved on southwards.

The Magellan Strait is not a channel but a maze. The Atlantic entrance is framed, in Francis Fletcher's account, by "high and steep grey cliffs full of black stars, against which the sea beating, sheweth as it were the spouting of whales." The passage is tortuous, sometimes a narrow channel between awesome cliffs, sometimes opening out into lakes immeasurably deep. Fierce and erratic currents race from east to west. As Drake's men entered they saw a volcano, "burning aloft in the air, in a wonderful sort, without intermission." All around towered mountains whitened by ice and snow but made gloomy by their own monstrous shadows. Surrounded by this awful grandeur the little ships battled against the elements. Fletcher describes whirlpools that "would pierce into the very bowels of the sea." Winds roared through the chasms, sometimes sweeping them back in an hour over distances it had taken them days to cover, at others meeting with contrary winds in terrifying welters of howling air and water. On an island they found a human skeleton, which in the written accounts of the voyage takes on a portentous weight as the sentinel over a pass as terrible as the Valley of the Shadow itself. De Silva, the kidnapped Portuguese pilot, reported that in passing the strait "many of Drake's men died of cold."

After sixteen days they reached the Pacific Ocean, but their ordeals were not over. A series of storms engulfed the ships and for some six weeks they struggled desperately with ferocious winds and wild seas. The darkness of the southern winter was compounded by an eclipse of the sun. The men, already enfeebled by the bitter cold, began to succumb to scurvy. Of the fifty men on the *Elizabeth* only five escaped the sickness. At times they were close enough to shore to hear the waves crashing against rocks invisible to them in the darkness and fog. At others they were driven far out into the uncharted oceans. Those who survived came to believe they were being subjected to a fearful test through which only those marked out for hero status could pass while others perished or turned back dismayed.

One of the ships, the *Marigold*, was lost. Fletcher recorded seeing her go down "swallowed up with horrible and unmerciful waves, or rather mountains of the sea" and hearing the anguished cries of the twenty-eight men on board her. Then the *Elizabeth*, captained by Winter, became separated from Drake's *Golden Hind* as they both struggled to avoid being dashed to pieces among rocks. Winter managed to find his way back into the strait and to anchor there. A few weeks later he turned for home— because the master and mariners refused to go further, according to his account; because he himself had despaired, according to one of theirs.

The *Golden Hind* was left alone. Driven before winds "such as if the bowels of the earth had been set all at liberty," buffeted by seas "rolled up from the depths, even from the roots of the rocks, as if it had been a scroll of parchment," scudding onwards in great clouds of spray, carried "by the violence of the winds to water the exceeding tops of high and lofty mountains," Drake and his men, now only 60 or so remaining of the 160 (or thereabouts) who had left Plymouth eleven months before, were driven farther and farther south until at last they were able to anchor by an island. There Drake, or so he later told Richard Hawkins, made the most momentous of his geographical discoveries: that beyond him there was nothing but water, that "both the seas [the Atlantic and the Pacific] are one." Some of his contemporaries were skeptical. Richard Madox, who sailed to the strait in 1582, believed that Drake had cribbed the astounding information from stolen Spanish charts and claimed it for his own discovery like "a man who has cast off all shame." But Drake's account is perfectly plausible. He told Hawkins that he went ashore carrying a compass with him and at the southernmost point of the southernmost island of the archipelago he "cast himself down upon the uttermost point, grovelling, and so reached out his body over it." Like a figurehead on the prow of the American continent, he breasted the tumultuous ocean that no other European had seen before him. Returning to his ship he declared he had been on the "southernmost known land in the world."

More tempests, more vast waves heaving through the icy murk, more hunger, sickness, fear, and confusion. Then, at last "our troubles did make an end, the storm ceased, and all our calamities (only the absence of our friends excepted) were removed." Drake had penetrated the strait, a passage narrow, intricate, and as fraught with danger as the mythical vagina dentata, and having passed through it into the great ocean of pleasure he attained a marvelous consummation. That this part of his story constituted a potent sexual image was not lost on Renaissance commentators. A contemporary poet, writing after Drake's return, specifically likened the Strait of Magellan to a woman's genitals:

That world-dividing gulf where he that venters
With swelling sails and ravished senses enters
To a new world of bliss.

It was late October, the southern spring. The weather brightened. The days lengthened. Drake turned northward again, and like the heroes of folklore who have been tried by fantastic ordeals and come through unscathed, he was rewarded with his heart's desire.

The whole vast Pacific Ocean was the Spaniards', by papal decree and therefore, in Catholic eyes, by divine appointment. Before the arrival of the *Golden Hind* there were no pirates there, no alien craft larger than the Indians' bark canoes, no human predators to be feared and therefore no need for any but the most rudimentary defenses. As the viceroy was later to explain to King Philip in an attempt to excuse his failure to halt Drake's depredations: "In many places there are no more than four Spaniards. . . . the ports are all without artillery . . . there is no mode of defence." Drake and his men, making their way up the coast of Chile and Peru, ransacking unarmed ships and pillaging unguarded townships, came perhaps as close as anyone ever would to discovering El Dorado, that fabulous realm where precious metal was left lying around for the taking, where a man could, almost without effort, grow rich.

In 1628 Drake's nephew, another Francis, published an account of this voyage, *The World Encompassed by Sir Francis Drake*, claiming to have written it himself. In fact the book was probably written to Drake's order by Philip Nichols (using Fletcher's narrative) in the 1590s, around the same time as *Sir Francis Drake Revived*, but suppressed by order of Queen Elizabeth: she was most unwilling, even so long after the event, that the rival powers should know in detail exactly where Drake had been. The two books share a shamelessly evident purpose, being written, as the epigraph to *The World Encompassed* candidly states, "for the honour of the actor," and they have in common the tone of laconic but swaggering glee which is the hallmark of Drake's perceived character and which is what distinguishes his amazing journey from all the other fabled Renaissance voyages into the unknown. Columbus's expedition was piously undertaken and fraught with sacred significance and imperialist ambitions. Magellan's was desperately brave and ultimately tragic. Raleigh's ventures were shaped by intellectual ambition and undermined by a privileging of poetic vision over practical preparation. Drake's, by contrast, were (or at least were so presented by him and imagined by the public) the adventures of a scallywag, a wonderful sequence of tricks which, by a combination of cool audacity and inspired mischief, he was able to play. His approved version of his adventures on the western coast of South America is jocular throughout. This run of luck is just too good to be serious.

At Valparaíso an unsuspecting crew of Spanish sailors, assuming Drake's men to be compatriots, welcomed them aboard with the beating of a drum and the offer of wine. They responded by punching the pilot in the face before abducting him, putting the rest of the crew ashore, and making off with the ship and its cargo of Chilean wine and four hundred pounds of gold. At Tarapacá they went ashore to take on water and found a man asleep with thirteen bars of silver beside him. They didn't like to interrupt his nap, or so Nichol's chortlingly triumphant account runs, but since they had inadvertently done so they relieved him of the silver, a responsibility "which otherwise perhaps would have kept him waking." On another occasion they encountered a Spaniard and an Indian boy driving eight llamas, each carrying some hundred pounds of silver. "We could not endure to see a gentleman Spaniard turned carrier," so they "became drovers, only his directions were not so perfect that we could keep the way which he intended." They stopped ship after ship and "made somewhat bold to bid ourselves welcome," boarding them, stripping them of their fabulous cargoes of bullion and jewels, and sending them on their way "somewhat lighter than before." The jokes express a rising elation. On one ship which they captured without opposition they found eighty pounds of gold, a great gold crucifix, and "certain emeralds near as long as a man's finger." The ancients believed that west of the sunset lay the fabulous realm of the Hesperides, where a dragon guarded trees bearing apples of pure gold. Drake, sailing westward, seemed to have reached it. The dragon, dozy and fangless, did nothing while bars of silver as numerous as the apples of legend fell into the Englishman's outstretched hand.

There is no sign Drake felt any compunction about his piracies. He had persuaded himself that the Spaniards, because of their treacherous treatment of him at San Juan de Ulúa, owed him a fortune. Besides, to a Protestant Englishman the Spaniards had no more right to their property in America than he did: they were unprincipled conquerors who had enslaved the native Americans and stolen their gold. Drake's men, sailing up the coast of Chile, were indignant but not surprised to see mounted Spaniards with Indians "running as dogs at their heels, all naked, and in most miserable bondage." They heard stories of the Spanish torturing their Indian slaves, spattering them with hot bacon fat or whipping them for their own sadistic pleasure. Ali Baba helped himself freely to the treasure he found and nobody blamed him because the victims of his theft were themselves thieves. So Drake robbed the Spaniards and because they were, in his eyes anyway, robbers themselves he did so without scruple.

To take what was theirs was not only permissible, it might even be an act of piety. The dispossession of the English monasteries formed the background to Drake's childhood. He grew up in a society where the seizing of property from Catholic institutions was something condoned and enthusiastically perpetrated by established authority. By the standards of his time, he was not a bigot: he once told a Welsh Catholic seaman that "God would receive the good work that he might perform in either law, that of Rome or that of England." But his Protestantism was an essential part of his identity. The Spaniards called him "el Luterano." He was *the* Lutheran (a word the Spaniards used as a catch-all term for Protestants) just as he was *the* corsair. When at sea he would spend two to three hours of every day praying or leading his men in prayer, and when he had Spanish prisoners on board he made a point of making them attend the services, at which he himself sometimes preached; of demonstrating his freedom from "superstition" by eating meat on Fridays; and of displaying his copy of John Foxe's *Book of Martyrs*. Drake corresponded on friendly terms with Foxe, whose book, a gruesome and savagely anti-Catholic account of the executions of Protestants under Queen Mary, was hugely influential. It probably helped persuade Drake that those he stripped of their possessions were fully deserving of any punishment he might mete out to them. So, as he cruised northwards through the Pacific enriching himself he was avenging the wronged native Americans, serving his country, and doing the work of the Protestant God. He had entered a kind of moral limbo, a never-never land in which theft was no longer a crime, so long as its victims were Spanish, and where an Englishman could do no wrong.

There were setbacks. On one occasion Drake's men were surprised ashore by a party of around a hundred Spaniards and their Indian auxiliaries. One Englishman was killed, and while his fellows watched from their boat the Spaniards mutilated his corpse, hacking off his head and right hand and cutting out his heart. But this was an isolated incident. In Drake's legend, as it subsequently took shape, the *Golden Hind* is poignantly small and vulnerably isolated, all alone and unsupported on the wrong side of the world, but to those defending the little ports into which she sailed she was fearsome. Unlike the Spanish ships in the region, which carried no heavy artillery, she had eighteen cannon, three of bronze and the rest of cast iron: there wasn't a warship to match her in all the Pacific. When Drake sailed into port Spanish officials took to the woods. When he boarded a ship its crew would stand meekly by while his men searched for valuables. In Mormorena he terrorized the only two Spanish officials into allowing him to obtain provisions from the natives. In Callao he found a large number (somewhere between nine and thirty— contemporary sources disagree) of undefended Spanish ships at anchor. He searched each vessel in turn, cut their cables, and in some cases chopped down their masts before the alarm was raised. When word of his depredations reached Lima, the viceroy sent out two hundred horsemen to repel his attack but Drake was already back at sea. Three hundred men in two ships gave chase but the *Golden Hind* easily outpaced them and the Spaniards turned back, discouraged and dreadfully seasick.

Later, back in England, a nobleman who evidently saw Drake as a braggart and a bore, as many courtiers did, was to remark acidly that it was no great accomplishment to capture a defenseless vessel with a well-armed ship. The sneer is largely justified, but it is precisely the dreamlike ease with which Drake achieved his ends which gives this expedition and its commander their mystique. Only upon the exceptional, the divinely favored, does fortune smile so broadly. The Red Sea parted before the people of Israel because they were God's chosen ones. Achilles was able to slaughter so many of his opponents because he had god-given invulnerability, god-given armor, god-given status as a supreme warrior. The Cid, "born in a happy hour," took cities and kings' ransoms with ease, and his apparently effortless success was itself a demonstration of his greatness. Insouciance is the mark of the natural-born winner, easy victory the prerogative of the superman. So Drake, laughingly disabling the Spaniards' ships, robbing their towns, and stealing their treasure, has the magical irresistibility which is the sure sign, in myth, fairy tale, and popular history, of the happy hero.

Between October and the following April he sailed easily northward, becoming ever more confident, more audacious, and more rich. He was to boast to one of his prisoners that during that time "he took forty vessels, large and small, and that only four of those he met have escaped him." His investors and his queen were on the other side of the world. Doughty was dead, Winter had turned for home. He was answerable to no one. He was having the time of his life.

He lived in style, insofar as it was possible on his cramped little ship.

His own quarters were fitted up for "ornament and delight." Like Alcibiades he acted on the principle that his own ostentation redounded to his country's credit: he had taken with him from England "rich furniture . . . whereby the civility and magnificence of his native country might, amongst all nations whithersoever he should come, be the more admired." Musicians played to him while he dined off gold and silver dishes, eating, as one of his Spanish prisoners observed, "all possible dainties" and enjoying the fragrance of "perfumed waters" that he claimed had been given to him by the queen.

His authority was absolute. The "gentlemen" dined with him, and according to Don Francisco de Zárate, who was held prisoner on the *Golden Hind* for two days, he treated them as a council "which he calls together for even the most trivial matter." This council existed rather to provide Drake with company than to aid him in decision making. "He takes advice from no one . . . but he enjoys hearing what they say." As for the rest of the men, Zárate reported that "he treats them with affection and they treat him with respect" and "all said that they adored him." But that adoration was tempered with awe. The men were kept on a tight rein. Zárate was impressed by the pirates' discipline: "When our ship was sacked, no man dared take anything without his orders." Another witness, a pilot whom Drake captured and kept in chains, reported that "all his men trembled before him, bowing to the ground."

As his run of luck lengthened, and his success came to amaze even him, he boasted of it with naked glee. He showed off his booty to his captives "like a shameless robber who fears neither God nor man." He was the terror of his enemies, the undisputed ruler of his own people, the owner of a growing hoard of treasure, and he was high on the wonder of his own cleverness and courage and cheek.

He preferred robbery with menaces to robbery with violence. He was a frightening man. When he suspected the steward of a captured ship of concealing gold from him, he subjected the man to a false hanging, putting the noose around his neck and dropping him from a makeshift gallows over the side of the ship, but with a rope long enough to allow him to fall into the sea and survive. He used the same terrifying trick on a Spanish pilot, Alonso Sánchez Colchero, who courageously refused to work for him, and when Colchero still held out shut him in an iron cage at the bottom of the ship. Other captives were terrorized into collaborating, acting as his pilots, guides, or informers; he threatened to have their heads cut off if they didn't do so, and even boasted to them of how he had had Doughty killed for disobeying him. He talked of throwing two thousand Spanish heads into the harbor at Callao. But though his words were murderous his actions were not.

In 1572 in the Caribbean he had restrained his cimarron allies when they wanted to cut Spanish throats. After he returned from his circumnavigation, when the Spaniards were alleging all sorts of atrocities against him, his entire crew signed a document testifying that during the whole voyage he had been responsible for the death of only one Spanish sailor, and had never sunk a ship with men on board. What seemed to his contemporaries the cruelest act perpetrated in the course of the voyage was his abandoning the kidnapped pilot Nuño de Silva on Spanish territory. De Silva had guided him and his fleet across the Atlantic and had been on board the *Golden Hind*, by all accounts cooperating freely, for fifteen months. Drake put him ashore in Guatulco where, predictably, he fell into the hands of the Inquisition and was hideously punished for his collaboration. It was ruthless of Drake—shockingly so—but it was an act of callous negligence rather than of violent aggression.

With his prisoners on the *Golden Hind* he was mockingly polite. Don San Juan de Antón, from whom he stole a shipload of bullion, was given breakfast at his own table and eventually dismissed with presents, a German musket and a basin of gilded silver with Drake's name engraved on it. He fed Don Francisco de Zárate with tidbits from his own platter while they dined together to the sound of trumpets and viols. He allowed the hidalgo to keep his rich clothes, a favor for which Zárate was pitifully grateful, on condition he handed over a gold falcon with an emerald set in its breast. Some black captives remained on the *Golden Hind* (perhaps by their own choice), but all of his Spanish prisoners were eventually released, either put ashore or set adrift in their own vessels. He was punctiliously gracious with his victims. After robbing San Juan de Antón of a fortune, he gave him a letter of safe conduct in case he should meet John Winter, ordering Winter not to do him any injury and to pay him for any of his stores he felt obliged to grab. He was playing the tease, the joker, the cat who suddenly lifts its paw and lets the mouse run, demonstrating his power not by exercising it but by refraining from doing so.

At Callao he boarded a ship which he had been informed was carrying a great load of silver. He was disappointed: the bullion had been unloaded. But his disappointment was mitigated by the news of another ship, the *Nuestra Señora de la Concepción*, which had sailed northward for Panama only a few days earlier laden with silver and gold. For the next two weeks he chased her, offering a gold chain to the first man to sight her sail.

He encountered and robbed four other ships, taking wine and more gold. At last, at noon on March 1, John Drake, the admiral's nephew, won the chain. Drake slowed down so as not to alarm his prey. Some nine hours later, when darkness was beginning to fall, the two ships finally met. Before the Spanish captain, San Juan de Antón, could work out what was happening, the Englishmen had grappled his ship and someone was shouting "Englishmen! Strike sail!" By his own account de Antón yelled back, "Come on board to strike the sails yourselves!" It was a foolhardy challenge. A shrill whistle and then a trumpet sounded on the *Golden Hind*. The English opened fire with arquebuses, bows and arrows, and cannon. A piece of chain shot carried away one of the Spaniard's masts. There was no answering fire: the Spanish ship carried no big guns. The Englishmen swarmed aboard. De Antón surrendered and was taken to Drake, whom he found insouciantly removing his helmet and coat of mail. His glee translated into genial magnanimity, Drake embraced his captive saying, "Have patience, for such is the usage of war," before locking him in his own cabin.

In happier days the *Nuestra Señora de la Concepción* had been nicknamed the *Cacafuego* (shit-fire). This time she hadn't fired at all. As Drake's men methodically removed her entire cargo and restowed it in their own hold, one of her men ruefully suggested she should be rechristened the *Cacaplata* (shit-silver). The takings were fantastic. As the narrator of the *The World Encompassed* puts it, with the jubilantly affected nonchalance of one who knows his news is so astounding that he can be sure it will have its effect even if he throws it away, "We found in her some fruit, conserves, sugar, meal and other victuals, and (that which was the especiallest cause of her heavy and slow sailing) a certain quantity of jewels and precious stones, thirteen chest of rials of plate, eighty pound weight in gold, twenty-six tons of uncoined silver, two very fair gilt silver drinking bowls, and the like trifles."

For six days a pinnace went back and forth between the two ships "to do John de Anton a kindness, in freeing him of the care of those things with which his ship was loaden." The rocks carried as ballast in the hold of the *Golden Hind* were thrown out to make way for the precious loot; Drake gave San Juan de Antón six hundredweight of iron and some tar, presumably for the same reason. At last "we bade farewell and parted, he hastening somewhat lighter than before to Panama, we plying off to sea." Their voyage was made.

Drake had traveled further from home than any of his countrymen before him. Among the tales Southey found being told about him in the early nineteenth century was a scrap of dialogue in which he asks his men, when the *Golden Hind* is in the South Pacific, whether they know where they are and a boy nonplusses Drake and proves his own quickness by replying that yes, he knows very well he is "just under London Bridge."

In this topsy-turvy underworld, home's antithesis, Drake had got himself a fortune. Now he had to find a way of bringing it back. After careening his ship on an island off the coast of Nicaragua, then taking and looting two more Spanish ships, he proceeded northwards. He raided the little settlement of Guatulco. As soon as they heard his guns most of the inhabitants ran for the woods, leaving their homes to be ransacked, their church to be desecrated and their food stores stolen. Thus provisioned, Drake sailed out of the Spaniards' ken.

He left behind him a colonial government in uproar and the making of a tremendous legend. The English Dragon, arriving suddenly, his eighteen guns blazing, where no European enemy of Spain had ever ventured before, was an apparition so terrifying neither his victims nor their posterity could ever get over it. Over four centuries later in Peru and Chile children are still being warned that if they don't behave themselves El Draque will come and carry them off.

Traveling northward Drake assumed a new character, no longer the piratical tormentor of the king of Spain and avenger of the private insult inflicted on him at San Juan de Ulúa, but empire-building discoverer. According to *The World Encompassed* and to the account in Hakluyt's *Voyages* (also largely based on Francis Fletcher's notes), he sailed as far north as the latitude where Seattle now stands searching for the elusive Gulf of Anian, the northwest passage, until the unexpected configuration of the coastline exploded his faith in the gulf's existence and the cold became too extreme to endure. The ropes were stiff with ice, meat froze solid as soon as it was removed from the fire, and the men, famished though they were, preferred to go hungry rather than take their hands out from under their clothes to eat. Drake turned south, and anchored somewhere in the region of what is now San Francisco. There he and his men became the objects of worship to the local people, who showered them with gifts and begged Drake "that he would take the province and kingdom into his hand, and become their king and patron." Drake graciously agreed (on behalf of Queen Elizabeth), named the country Nova Albion, and in token of its annexation he set up a post to which he nailed an inscribed brass plate and a silver sixpence engraved with the queen's head before sailing off, ever westward-ho, to the "excessive sorrow" of his new subjects.

This part of the voyage has been much disputed. The observations—meteorological, zoological, topographical, and anthropological—of *The World Encompassed* are so wildly inaccurate that they have persuaded some critics that Drake never visited northern California at all. But the tales of Renaissance travelers are generally a mixture of fact with fiction. Magellan's men reported that the Patagonians were giants. Drake's men used to mock this exaggeration. "This people which they call Giants . . . indeed be not at all," testified John Winter. But as they sailed up the Pacific coast Drake was entertaining his Spanish prisoners with tall tales of preternaturally tall savages. Travelers tell the lies expected of them; their travels may be genuine nonetheless.

Drake's original orders from Walsingham and the queen were to make contact with any native Americans he might come across who were still independent of Spain and open trading relations with them. His attempts to do so while still south of the equator had been perfunctory and markedly unsuccessful. Near Lima he and his men had been attacked by a troop of some five hundred Indians and several men had been wounded, Drake—who got an arrow in his face just below his right eye—among them. For the most part, though, his relations with native Americans had been distant but friendly. He paid, if only in trinkets, for the supplies with which the Indians provided him. It was an Indian who acted as pilot and led him to Valparaíso, and Drake recompensed him honorably, putting him ashore again "bountifully rewarded and enriched with many good things." Just as he had been ready to make common cause with the cimarrones in Panama, so in South America he was ready to profit by the Indians' hostility to the Spanish, and to treat them decently as potential helpers. He showed no sign, though, of wishing to establish more enduring relationships with them, whether as overlord or trading partner. In the Strait of Magellan he declared that he had annexed a group of islands and named them the Elizabethides, but there is no record of his having informed the inhabitants of their change of status. In Nova Albion, though, he played a new role.

In his lifetime a novel idea had become current, one so far viewed as marginal, eccentric, and tinged with suspect spiritual fervor, the idea of a "British Empire." It was first promulgated by John Dee, the astronomer, mathematician, and magician whose book *The Perfect Art of Navigation* Drake would have known, and whose acquaintance he made soon after his return in 1580. Both terms of the phrase were studiedly arcane. The word "British" was an obsolete one which Dee used because it conjured up associations with King Arthur (defender of ancient Britain against the Saxon invasions), and it embraced the Welshness of the Tudor dynasty. The concept of empire, in the sixteenth century, was essentially religious. The Roman Empire had been sanctified in its last phases as the vehicle of the Christian faith; its successor, the loose association of central European states fancifully named the Holy Roman Empire, owed its numinous authority to the same idea. To Dee and to his friend Edmund Spenser, who drew extensively on Dee's occult theories in evolving the allegory of *The Faerie Queene*, the "British Empire" was not only a dreamed-of geopolitical entity, it was also a new Golden Age characterized by freedom, purity, and the union of all nations in the radiance of true (Protestant) faith. In its original form it was, like all the concepts of the occult philosophy in which Dee was an adept, extremely complex and probably untranslatable into actual worldly experience. But to Dee himself as well as to simpler minds it was also a realizable project. Dee was an enthusiastic advocate for the expansion of the navy, on the grounds that an empire whose influence was to be felt all around the world needed its ships and its brave admirals. Drake's journey about the earth, and especially his annexation of Nova Albion, could happily be fitted into Dee's vision. Nailing his sixpence to a wooden post in California he was making (or was understood by others to have been making) a modest beginning towards realizing that tremendous dream.

How the people whose king he claimed to have become understood the action can only be guessed at. According to *The World Encompassed*, they received Drake and his men with wonder "as men ravished in their minds with the sight of such things as they never had seen or heard of." They made long speeches, which the Englishmen found totally incomprehensible. They brought gifts of feathers and tobacco. They "began among themselves a kind of most lamentable weeping and crying out which they continued a great while together." The women shrieked and clawed at their cheeks until the blood ran, and flung themselves violently and repeatedly to the ground, dashing themselves on "hard stones, knobby hillocks, stocks of wood and pricking bushes." The Englishmen supposed that this was some kind of "bloody sacrifice" and that it indicated that they all, and Drake in particular, had been taken for gods. Five days after their landing—by which time Drake's men had built for themselves a walled camp—the entire population of the surrounding country descended upon them, led by their "king." There followed much parading and singing and dancing, more incomprehensible orations and more frenzied acts of self-mutilation. At last Drake bravely invited the king and his entourage, which included an honor guard of one hundred "tall and warlike men," to enter the English camp. There "the king and divers other made several orations, or rather, if we had understood them, supplications, that he [Drake] would take the province and kingdom into his hand, and become their king and patron: making signs that they would resign unto him their right and title in the whole land, and become his vassals in themselves and their posterities."

"If we had understood them" indeed. When Christopher Columbus met a young chieftain and his entourage on what is now Haiti, they attempted to communicate but, by Columbus's own account, "they did not understand me nor I them." Yet only a few lines down from that admission Columbus writes "he told me the whole island was at my command." In a situation where real communication is impossible the hearer can place any words he wishes in the speaker's mouth. The Californian Indians, having finished their orations, gave Drake a headdress and some bone necklaces. What they meant these gifts to signify we will never know, but *The World Encompassed* describes them as a crown and chains of office, and goes on: "he took the sceptre, crown and dignity of the said country into his hand." In Port San Julian he had abolished all considerations of social rank or extraneous loyalty, making himself sole ruler of his ship's company. In California he extended his sovereignty. Briefly he appeared in the role of one who, like the Cid, leaves his homeland behind and founds a new realm in which he can reign supreme. But his sojourn in his new land was brief. Three weeks later he left Nova Albion forever, while the subjects he had claimed for himself and Queen Elizabeth moaned and wrung their hands and lit fires (perhaps in token of mourning, perhaps in celebratory relief) along the white cliffs which had reminded their visitors of home. In his little, storm-battered, silver-ballasted ship, Drake sailed westward across the Pacific.

He had no other option. The Spanish were on the watch for him all down the South American coast, and it was generally accepted at the time (wrongly, as Winter, unbeknown to Drake, had just proved) that the prevailing winds and currents make the Strait of Magellan impassable west to east. He could have tried to carry his treasure overland across the isthmus of Panama and capture a Spanish ship on the Atlantic side for his voyage home, but the risks would have been enormous. Vast as the Pacific was, and totally unknown to English seamen, it was no longer the *mare incognita* Magellan had traversed half a century before: the Spanish crossed regularly to the Philippines, bringing back silk and porcelain. Drake had stolen Spanish charts, perhaps including one which could have shown him his way. He resolved to go home by going on.

For sixty-eight days he and his men saw nothing but air and water. When they finally made a landfall it was an unhappy one. The inhabitants of the Micronesian island where they had anchored swarmed out in canoes to meet the strangers, but attempts to barter with them collapsed when the islanders began to grab at the Englishmen's clothes and knives, refusing to return or pay for what they seized. (Magellan's men had had an almost identical experience.) Drake fired off one of his big guns. In his authorized account this was done "not to hurt them, but to affright them," but according to John Drake twenty of the islanders were killed.

They landed again in the Philippines, after which the Spanish charts were no use to them. Recruiting (or abducting) two fishermen as pilots Drake threaded his way southward through the Celebes until at last he reached the Moluccas, the fabled Spice Islands, those pinpricks on the map which were the object of so much fantasy, covetousness, and courageous endeavor in Renaissance Europe. It was to reach these islands that Prince Henry the Navigator had sent his adventurers south and east, that Frobisher had gone north, that Magellan had sailed west. Long before Europeans even knew that America existed, before El Dorado was so much as a rumor, the Spice Islands had featured in the European imagination as the ultimate goal for the bold adventurer, a place were fortunes grew literally on trees.

Drake anchored off the island of Ternate, where the sultan, whose father had been murdered by the Portuguese, gave him a splendid welcome. For the first time Drake and his men were encountering a highly developed non-European culture. The court was cosmopolitan: among the people Drake's men met there were two Turks and an Italian, all merchants with official positions at court, a gentleman in exile from China who begged Drake to return there with him, and a Spaniard employed as a military officer. The sultan, a Muslim, received them with "royal and kingly state . . . very strange and marvellous." He was delighted with Drake's musicians but in every other form of display he outshone and dazzled his visitors. His great galleys, each rowed by eighty men, were splendid. His robes of cloth of gold, his large and numerous jewels, his ranks of solemn, gorgeously dressed courtiers, his gold-embossed canopies, his carpets, his great fans set with sapphires, his council chamber all hung about with embroideries were awe-inspiring. Drake himself, suspicious of the sultan's intentions, did not go ashore, but those of his men who did were sharp-eyed and potentially aggressive enough to notice that the palace was guarded with only two cannon "and those at present untraversable because unmounted," but the country's recent history—the Sultan had successfully expelled the Portuguese from all of his dominions (said to extend to a hundred islands)—was not such as to encourage any presumptuous ideas of conquest. Instead Drake entered into a treaty with him, whereby the sultan promised to trade exclusively with England on condition that the English should undertake, so soon as was practicable, "to decorate that sea" with English ships and help him drive out the Portuguese.

In Ternate Drake traded some linen for several tons of cloves, a commodity not much less precious than gold, then sailed on to an uninhabited island where he stopped to careen and reprovision his ship. When he moved on he left three Africans, two men and one woman, behind. According to John Drake they were to "found a settlement," and Drake gave them "rice and seeds and means of making fire." What they felt about this is unrecorded. Whether they had stayed voluntarily to make their own paradise or whether they experienced their marooning as the fearful fate most European seamen would have considered it we will never know: none of Drake's compatriots cared enough to record their feelings. It is the sexual dimension of this story which interested contemporaries: the woman, Maria, was pregnant, and according to an anonymous contemporary account she was "a proper . . . wench" and had been "gotten with child between the captain and his men pirates." This was to arouse much disapproval. William Camden includes "a fair negress given unto him for a present by a Spaniard whose ship he had spared" among those things he "purposely omits" from his account of Drake's voyage (a weaselly way of saying and unsaying at one and the same time). The Elizabethans' prurient interest in Maria contrasts with their total indifference to the two men abandoned with her, and indeed to all the other black people Drake captured from Spanish ships, and whose ultimate fate is unrecorded.

Drake picked his way gingerly on southward through the islands of the East Indies with no charts to guide him. Abruptly, just as darkness fell one night, the ship drove with all sails spread onto a submerged reef. Captain and crew alike abandoned hope, "there being no probability how anything could be saved, or any person escape alive." As the wind wedged them ever more inextricably onto the reef and the waves thudded against the damaged timbers, Drake led the terrified crew in prayer and preached them an extempore sermon on the "joys of that other life." Against all likelihood, the ship stayed above water. Drake had himself let down in a boat to take soundings, hoping to be able to drop anchor and haul the ship off by its cable, but the reef rose sheer from a great depth. Nowhere could he touch bottom. The whole night was passed in "prayers and tears." With first light Drake tried again to find an anchor hold and was again unsuccessful. He gave orders that some of the artillery and three tons of cloves be thrown overboard to lighten the ship—to no avail. The *Golden Hind*, pounded by surf, could not hold together much longer. "Every thief reconciled himself to his fellow thief and so yielded themselves to death." In this moment of despair Francis Fletcher preached a sermon and administered the sacrament. Then, wonderfully, the wind dropped. The ship heeled over and fell back into deep water. They were saved.

Afterwards, presumably in a mood of nearly hysterical euphoria, Drake conducted a curious and unpleasant charade. Francis Fletcher was chained to a hatch and forced to wear a label declaring him "the falsest knave that liveth" while Drake, sitting cross-legged on a chest and waving his slippers in his hand, "excommunicated" him and sent him to the Devil. It's a bizarre and opaque episode, but there is a plausible explanation. Fletcher had liked and admired Doughty. In his sermon preached at a moment when he expected shortly to be facing not Drake's judgment but God's he must surely have suggested that the shipwreck was a just punishment for Doughty's unlawful killing.

The remaining two months of Drake's sojourn in the East Indies were happier. He stopped at two more islands at each of which his men were impressed by the prosperity and sophistication of their hosts. They rounded the south coast of Java, becoming the first Europeans to realize that it was an island, not a part of the imaginary Terra Australis. Then, from Java, apparently without maps, Drake sailed nonstop across the Indian Ocean, around the Cape of Good Hope and northward through the Atlantic, not touching land until he reached Sierra Leone over four months later, by which time the water supplies were down to the last half pint per man. In September 1580, with just one of his original five ships, with 58 men of the 160 with whom he had set sail two years and ten months previously, and with enough stolen goods in his hold to restore his country's fortunes and make him one of the richest men in it, Francis Drake came home.

. . .

This homecoming is the pivot on which his life's story swings round. Before the voyage began Sir Thomas Doughty had allegedly said that "if we brought home gold we should be the better welcome," a remark which was interpreted at his summary trial as a slur on the integrity of the queen and her councillors, and became one of the pretexts for his execution. But it was precisely on the hope that gold could procure him a welcome, and on the monarch's corruptibility, that Drake was now gambling for his fortune, his glory, and his life.

In September 1580 a fishing boat in the waters off Plymouth was hailed by a returning ship with the question "How was the Queen?" The ship was the *Golden Hind*, and Drake's motive for asking the question was more pressing than any sentimental concern he might feel about Elizabeth's health. It was over a year since he had last heard news (false, as it happened) from Europe. His ship was crammed full of plunder stolen either from Spanish citizens or from Spain itself, a country with whom England was not at war. If the queen were dead and had been succeeded by the Catholic Mary, Queen of Scots, England would not be safe for him. Even if Elizabeth was still on the throne his position was uncertain. The crimes he had committed—the theft of property, the abduction of persons, the hijacking of ships—he had committed, or so he claimed, with the queen's connivance, but he could produce no written orders to prove it and, as he very well knew, the queen, if it suited her, would lie without scruple and without mercy to disassociate herself and her government from his offenses. When he embarked on his voyage Elizabeth's policy had been hostile to Spain and her position strong enough to risk exasperating Philip II by encouraging Drake's terrorist attacks on Spanish colonies. If now she felt weaker or more placatory she might decide to appease her powerful enemy and return Drake's plunder to its rightful owners. She might charge him with the piracy of which he was incontrovertibly guilty. She might do what international and local law alike required her to do, and have him put to death.

Someone who had offended as outrageously as Drake had done had to be either wholly repudiated or wholeheartedly endorsed, to be accorded either death or glory. Elizabeth chose the latter, for a mixture of motives of which the paramount one was undoubtedly that which poor Doughty had so rashly made explicit. She wanted Drake's loot, and she could only lay her hands on it by claiming it had been acquired in her service. She allowed Drake to become a national hero, but she didn't let him forget that he did so at her sufferance; hence the lethally jocular business with the gilded sword at the celebratory banquet at Deptford. But having issued her warning the queen was indulgent. That day, having ordered the French envoy to knight her new hero, she watched smilingly while Drake's crew, dressed as "red Indians," danced for her. Then Drake himself regaled her with his traveler's tales for four hours while the jealous courtiers yawned and muttered and the crowd on shore of the "vulgar sort"—a crowd so numerous that earlier in the day a bridge had collapsed under their weight, tumbling a hundred of them into the river—raucously celebrated the honoring of the public favorite, the new-made "golden knight."

Drake's celebrity was immediate and enormous. "The commons . . . applauded him with all praise and admiration," wrote Camden. He was compared to Jason, to Hercules, to the Sun itself. "His name and fame became admirable in all places," wrote another contemporary, John Stow, "the people swarming daily in the streets to behold him. . . . Books, pictures and ballads were published in his praise."

The story of his voyage was satisfying on many levels. The mismatch of that small solitary ship with the immensity of the oceans over which it had sailed was fabulous, and so was the booty Drake had brought home. The quantity of his loot was thrilling. A year before his return some Spanish merchants had brought the news of his captures in the Pacific to London. "The adventurers who provided money and ships for the voyage are beside themselves with joy," reported Bernardino de Mendoza, the Spanish ambassador in England. Drake was a worthy successor to the archetypal heroes of epic literature, the great individualists who leave home to go to the ends of the earth and come back bringing untold riches. Rodrigo Díaz, banished from Castile, rode off into the badlands with a band of followers loyal to him and him alone and won fortunes for them and himself. Drake, shooting the gulf to the other side of the world and returning laden with gold and silver, was a hero after the same exhilarating pattern.

No one ever knew for certain how much Drake's haul amounted to. All the accounts are deliberate underestimates. The Spaniards habitually undervalued their cargoes by as much as half in order to evade customs duties. Drake and his queen consistently lied about how much he had got so that if he were ever obliged to make restitution he would be able to hold most of his booty back. But even if he had taken only what he owned up to, his success would have been sensational. The treasure taken off the

Nuestra Señora de la Concepción alone was equivalent to half the queen of England's total annual revenue.

Elizabeth hung on to it. She authorized a report (which nobody believed) that Drake had brought home next to nothing. She publicly ordered Drake to lodge all of his treasure in the Tower of London while its ultimate fate remained undecided, but she gave secret permission for him to remove £10,000 worth (a huge fortune) for himself before any of it was registered. Other even larger amounts somehow escaped the notice of the tactfully negligent official receiver, who referred in a later report to "the portion that was landed secretly" and confirmed that he had only "taken notice of so much as he [Drake] has revealed." Later Mendoza complained that Drake had given Elizabeth at least £100,000 more than had ever reached the Tower. None of the loot, whether secret or declared, was ever returned to its Spanish owners. For years Elizabeth quibbled and temporized about it, refusing to discuss the matter until the Spanish had justified their intervention in Ireland, suggesting (preposterously) that the Spanish crews of the ships Drake captured might have stolen the treasure themselves, demanding that Drake's victims—the owners of the ships he had seized, robbed, and set adrift—should come to London to present their case. Meanwhile the treasure was allowed to seep discreetly away. The queen retained enough to pay off the national debt and invest £42,000 in the Levant Company. The other investors all received, according to a seventeenth-century source, a staggering 4,700 percent return on their stakes.

Beowulf tackled monsters. Rodrigo Díaz took on the might of the Almoravid armies who seemed to their Christian opponents as alien and terrifying, with their drums and rhinoceros-hide shields, as any fabulous beast. So Drake, who to the Spanish was the dragon, was to his fellow Englishmen the dragon slayer, the brave little man who stands up to a gigantic foe. This was an image of himself that he liked. He boasted that he would make war single-handed against the king of Spain and all his forces, and he approved the preamble to *Sir Francis Drake Revived* in which his defiance, that of "a mean subject of Her Majesty's" who dared to take on "the mightiest monarch of all the world," is likened to that of the ant who in a popular fable contrives to revenge himself upon an eagle. Drake was physically small, politically impotent, a social outsider with no army at his command and no constitutional authority. Like Jack the Giant-Killer, like David who slew the giant Goliath with a pebble and sling, he entered legend as one of those vulnerable individuals who take on stupendous opponents and, by virtue of their cheek and cunning and the righteousness of their cause, triumph over impossible odds.

His struggle with the might of Spain was understood by his contemporaries to be the core of his story. And so it has remained. To reach one of the Spice Islands and establish a trading agreement with its potentate was, potentially at least, as substantial an achievement as any of Drake's hit-and-run American piracies. But this part of his great adventure has been all but forgotten. To the English and Spanish alike, Drake's story is essentially a story about Spain, and Spain in the sixteenth century was an opponent fit for a hero.

It was an empire set on world domination, and one which in Drake's lifetime looked near to achieving that aim. In 1526 Gonzalo Fernández de Oviedo addressed the king of Spain as "universal and sole monarch of the world." He was speaking figuratively, but also prescriptively. The "discovery" and colonization of Central and South America had not only made Spain rich, it had also made the Spanish king the overall ruler of an empire commensurate with Rome's, one on which, in Ariosto's line (later impudently annexed by British propagandists), "the sun never sets." And as the Spanish in general and King Philip II in particular considered themselves to be the arm of the church, they had a sacred mission, as well as a secular ambition, to extend that empire to include all the nations of the earth.

To the English Protestants, that growing empire was the enemy of true religion and the oppressor of all free peoples. Pride, luxury, and horrific cruelty were its characteristics. Wrote the Victorian poet W. H. Smith:

> How brilliant with delusive glow
> Glamour above and death below
> Spain's glories past have been

Smith was drawing on a vision first elaborated by the sixteenth-century Protestant propagandists who drew a picture of Spanish power in which the torture chambers of the Inquisition, immense galleys rowed by wretched slaves, and South American gold mines worked by Indians whipped on until they dropped dead at their tasks (images drawn from reality) all featured prominently. The Spanish missionary Las Casas's devastating indictment of his compatriots' behavior in the new world, *A Brief Relation of the Destruction of the Indies*, was read avidly, diffusing a horrifying vision of the Spanish colonists as rapaciously cruel conquerors.

The story of a plucky sea captain in one little ship, daring to "annoy" a power so titanic and so darkly dreadful and getting away with it, was to the English mind exhilarating in its promise that the evil empire could be outfaced and even outdone.

The giant-killer was also a kind of crusader, for in sixteenth-century Europe the enemies of true religion were not infidels, but fellow Christians. Drake's piety has been questioned, but only by those simple-minded enough to imagine a sincerely held religious faith to be incompatible with violent or immoral behavior. There is no reason to doubt that he really believed, along with most of his Protestant contemporaries, that in robbing Catholic Spain to enrich Protestant England, he was engaged on a holy mission. Drake lived in an age when doctrinal difference led swiftly to violence. There is no reliable account of his having personally desecrated any place of Catholic worship, but he did not restrain his men from doing so. In South America they sacked Spanish churches. They stamped on communion wafers and smashed crucifixes and other images. They used altar cloths to wipe the sweat from their faces. They made off with chalices and monstrances and embroidered vestments. Back on board ship they taunted their prisoners with being "idolators," grabbed their rosaries and holy medals and crucifixes and broke them or threw them into the sea.

The ugly reality of such acts of hooliganism could be veiled by graceful theory. Soon after Drake returned from his circumnavigation Edmund Spenser began work on *The Faerie Queene*, in which he elaborated a new Protestant and patriotic mythology. He conflated the two archaic idealisms of crusading Christianity and of chivalry, casting the Anglican church as a maiden, Una, in need of protection by gallant knights. Drake, for all his plebeian origins, fit neatly into this elegant schema. His reputation for chivalric *courtoisie* was already established. Entertaining his noble prisoners at his table, offering them good food and music and civil conversation and then sending them away with gifts, he was acting like a good knight and true, one who fought only within the rules of the tournament—which restricted violence but allowed the demanding of stupendous ransoms—and who didn't hit a man when he was down. At large in the Pacific, he could be imagined as being both knight-errant in pursuit of adventure for the exercise of his own noble spirit, and also as the champion of Queen Elizabeth and of Una, the one true faith.

He could, more realistically, have been applauded for his discoveries. Drake's voyage had taken him into many seas totally unknown to his compatriots, and some into which he was the first European to venture. In

Ariosto's *Orlando Furioso*, written half a century earlier, a prophetess fore-tells an imminent golden age when "New mariners and masters new shall rise . . . / To find new lands, new stars, new seas, new skies." Ariosto intended the prophecy to refer to the reign of the Holy Roman Emperor Charles V, but his Elizabethan English translator, Sir John Harington, was able, by some judicious mistranslation, to make the whole vision applicable to Elizabethan England, and Harington's own marginal notes make it plain he intended this passage to be read as a tribute to Francis Drake.

Drake's discoveries mattered to him. He took pains to record them. As he sailed up the coast of South America, he and his nephew John spent a large part of their time drawing and painting pictures of the lands they were seeing, of their flora and fauna and topography. Nuño de Silva reports that both men were talented draftsmen, and as Don Francisco de Zárate divined, Drake's pictures had a practical purpose: "No one who guides himself according to these paintings can possibly go astray." On his return Drake gave the queen a map six feet long showing his route around the world and his logbook, probably illustrated with the paintings he had made.

Neither map nor logbook was ever seen again. Elizabeth wanted the Spanish to know as little as possible about where Drake had been and what he had been doing: all information about his voyage was to be sup-pressed. A few weeks after his return the great German geographer Gerardus Mercator complained that it was impossible to find out his route: the English authorities were either deliberately concealing it, or "putting out different accounts." Wildly inaccurate rumors about his amazing journey proliferated. The scholars of Winchester School com-posed an ode on the occasion of his knighthood in which they congratu-lated him on having visited both the poles. But hard information was closely guarded. Nine years later, when Hakluyt began to publish his *Principal Navigations, Voyages, and Discoveries of the English Nation*, the embargo was still in place. Hakluyt initially omitted Drake's circumnavi-gation—surely the most obvious of all candidates for inclusion—and he subsequently revealed that he had been "seriously dealt withal" by those who wished to prevent publication of any account of it. Later still, in 1592, Drake wrote to the queen reminding her reproachfully that all reports of his journey "hitherto have been silenced."

But though he never in his lifetime got due acknowledgment for his discoveries, his success was splendid. During the months after his return he was constantly at court, "squandering," according to Mendoza, "more

money than any man in England." He was not much liked in the socially
exalted circles in which he now found himself. He was a stocky little man
with small eyes and sandy hair: he had no physical graces to mitigate his
lack of courtly manners. He was brash, boastful, pugnacious, and a bit of
a bore. He made himself insufferable to the snobbish and the fastidious.
Lord Sussex snubbed him when he bragged of the ships he had taken, and
when Drake responded angrily Lord Arundel told him he was impudent
and shameless. With the insecurity of the newly risen he insisted too
loudly on his claims to respect. "In Sir Francis," wrote Robert Mansell,
who knew him, "was an insatiable desire of honour indeed beyond reason." He was also "too much pleased with open flattery."

Others had more serious objections. The people fondly called him
"the master thief of the unknown world." There were those who didn't
care to associate with such a person, especially one so crassly eager to buy
favor with his dirty money. Drake, like the Cid, was a throwback to an
ancient type of robber-hero. As such he was an anomaly at a Renaissance
court where new values prevailed and new ideals emphasized public
responsibility and the protection of the commonwealth by means of the
law. "Nothing angered worse Sir Francis Drake," wrote Camden, "than
to see the nobles and chiefest of the court refuse that gold and silver
which he presented them withal, as if he had not lawfully come by it."
That "as if" is lenient. Two hundred years later George Anderson, whose
tartly hostile biography of Drake was published in 1784, wrote: "The
actions which gave rise to Drake's popularity are such as a courageous
leader with a band of armed followers might easily perform by entering
the cities or towns on the coast of Britain, cutting the throats of the watch
and all who happen to be awake in the streets, breaking open and plundering houses and churches and making their escape with their
booty . . . Would the man who should undertake and execute an enterprise of such a horrid nature, be justly entitled to the name of Hero?"
There were plenty of people at the Elizabethan court, whether jealous,
snobbish, or morally scrupulous, ready to ask the same question.

Aristocrats held aloof, but nothing could dent Drake's fame. The
"commons applauded him with all praise and admiration." Better still, he
had the queen's favor. She wore the five enormous emeralds he had given
her in a new crown and flaunted it before the Spanish ambassador. She
granted him extended audiences; she sent him gifts of jewels and scarves
and cups. She spoke with him at length whenever she saw him, which was
often: once he visited her nine times in one day. She gave him lands and
manors. She decreed that the *Golden Hind* should be kept at Deptford "in

perpetual memory" of his amazing voyage. He was now an international celebrity. John Stow reports that "many princes of Italy, Germany and other, as well enemies as friends . . . desired his picture." In Italy his portrait, exhibited in Ferrara, drew a great crowd of sightseers. In France King Henri III had copies given to all his leading courtiers. "In brief," wrote John Stow, "he was as famous in Europe and America as Tamburlane in Asia."

He had nothing left to prove. Withdrawing to the West Country, where he was better appreciated than he was at court, he shrewdly invested some of his money in rentable property in Plymouth. He bought a country estate, Buckland Abbey in Devonshire, designed himself a coat of arms, and settled down to enjoy his success. He became mayor of Plymouth and a member of Parliament. When his first wife died, he married again, this time into the gentry. He grew fat, and had himself painted by Nicholas Hilliard and Marcus Gheeraerts. He was to describe himself in verse as one "who seeks by gain and wealth to advance his house and blood." He had achieved his objective.

He was not left to enjoy his retirement. In 1585 Philip II ordered that all English ships in Spanish ports should be seized. Elizabeth retaliated by giving Drake a commission—that seal of royal approval he had so signally lacked for his circumnavigation—as admiral of a wide-ranging aggressive raid on Spanish ports in Europe and America. With an army of some 2,300 men to be commanded on land by Walsingham's son-in-law, Christopher Carleill, with Martin Frobisher as his vice admiral and with over twenty-five ships, he appeared in a new role, no longer the quick-witted pirate and adventurer making a mock of the forces massed against him, but now himself master of an imposing fleet.

It was not a role in which he was entirely happy. In each of his subsequent campaigns he was to have serious disputes with one or more of his senior officers. As he had told the jury trying Sir Thomas Doughty on the beach at Port San Julian, "I know what I will do," and he didn't like to be hampered in the doing of it by doubts and questions. "Sir Francis was a willing hearer of every man's opinion, but commonly a follower of his own," wrote Robert Mansell. Some of his colleagues and subordinate officers found that hard to bear. He wanted them to be his own men, as the men on the *Golden Hind*—officers and crew alike—had been after

Port San Julian. In 1585 he demanded that all the officers take an oath of loyalty to him, an unnecessary measure which by offending their pride came close to provoking a mutiny.

In Santiago, in the Cape Verde Islands, and in the Caribbean though, Carleill and Drake worked well together, assaulting, sacking, and looting towns, raising money as the Cid had done, by burning houses and destroying crops until paid to go away. Financially the expedition was a failure. The Spanish settlers were terrorized into giving Drake all they had, but it wasn't as much as he had hoped. The investors got back only 75 percent of their stakes. Drake himself lost all the money he had put up. In human terms the losses were terrible: nearly a third of the men in the English fleet died of yellow fever. But the effect on morale, both English and Spanish, was electric. As Drake rampaged through the Caribbean rumors spread throughout Europe: he had released 12,000 black slaves, he had captured twenty-six ships, he had laid waste every city on the Spanish Main. The truth was less impressive, but the fictions had their effect. The legend of Drake's astonishing audacity and luck spread far and wide, high and low. While Spanish seamen began to believe him a wizard, perhaps even a devil, and told stories about the familiar spirit with whom he communed, the pope himself wrote, "God alone knows what he may succeed in doing!" "Truly," wrote Burghley, "Sir Francis Drake is a fearful man to the King of Spain."

It was partly in response to this outrageous terrorism that King Philip resolved to order an assault on England, and to assemble the Armada that was to accomplish it. Elizabeth responded. Early in 1587 Mary, Queen of Scots, focus over the previous years of numerous Spanish-sponsored plots, was beheaded. In March Drake was commissioned to attack the Spanish fleet in the ports where it was gathering. In both cases Elizabeth, either really vacillating or deviously covering herself, subsequently disowned her own decisions. She signed Mary's death warrant but afterwards claimed it had been acted upon too precipitately and against her wishes. Just after Drake's fleet left Plymouth a pinnace was sent after him carrying new orders from the queen forbidding him "to enter forcibly into any of the said King's [Philip's] ports or havens, or to offer violence to any of his towns or shipping within harbour." Of all his actions the one for which England's other favorite sailor, Horatio Nelson, is most widely remembered is the apocryphal one of his holding his telescope to his blind eye so that he would not see the signal to withdraw from battle. Drake, too, made sure an unwelcome order should not reach him. Perhaps he set sail early deliberately in order to avoid receiving it. Or perhaps (for she was as wily as he) the queen never intended that it should reach him in time.

Late one afternoon just over two weeks later Drake arrived off Cádiz, his fleet trailing behind him. Sir Robert Mansell, writing in 1625, described him as "being of a lively spirit, resolute, quick and sufficiently valiant." In this raid he was at his happy best. The wind was with him. Ignoring the anxiety of his vice admiral, William Borough, who wanted to wait until the stragglers had caught them up and to call a captain's conference before undertaking any action, Drake sailed straight into the harbor "with more speed and arrogance," according to a Spanish customs officer who was there, "than any pirate has ever shown." There were at least sixty ships in the harbor, and the place was virtually undefended, the Spanish, according to one of them, having such "confidence that no enemy would dare to enter the bay . . . nor had it been heard in many centuries previous of any having such daring to break through the entrances of their port." Like the fast runner Achilles, like Alcibiades in the Hellespont, like the devil that the Spanish were beginning to believe that he was, Drake appeared where no one had ever dreamed he might possibly be. Two galleys rowed out to meet him, but fled as soon as the English ships fired at them. Onshore the terrified townspeople stampeded into the castle; twenty-two of them were killed in the crush. All that night and all the next day Drake was in the harbor, looting and burning ship after ship. The pitch and tar with which the ships were coated burned tremendously: "smoke and flames rose up so that it seemed like a huge volcano, or something out of Hell," wrote a Spanish eyewitness. The city filled up with Spanish troops, but there was nothing they dared to do. The English ships were out of reach of the guns onshore. Somewhere between twenty-five and thirty-nine ships (Spanish estimates tend to be lower than English ones) were destroyed or captured while the Spaniards watched helplessly from the shore. All the while Borough kept begging Drake to withdraw, pointing out that without a favorable wind they might all find themselves trapped. Eventually, without Drake's permission, he sailed his own ship back out to sea. But Drake continued implacable, unflappable, serenely relying on his luck to get him out when he had finished his work of destruction.

On the evening of the second day, with a great noise of trumpets, Drake prepared to leave. That was when the wind dropped, just as the timorous Borough had predicted it might. Drake hung on, and so did his luck. In the small hours of the following morning he found enough breeze to lead his ships out through the narrow mouth of the harbor "as well," according to a Spanish witness, "as the most experienced local pilot."

The Spaniards tried valiantly to spin the story into the appearance of a Spanish victory. They celebrated a great mass to thank God for having saved the city and "humbled the pride of the enemy," and Fray Pedro Simon wrote a triumphant report claiming that the English had lost many ships and men. "Thus were the thresholds of the gate of Spain watered with the blood of these wolves, in order that the scent might keep their fellows away from our doors." As propaganda for domestic consumption it may have worked, but the international community was not duped. "Just look at Drake!" exclaimed the Pope. "Who is he? What forces does he have? And yet he burned twenty five of the king's ships! . . . We are sorry to say it, but we have a poor opinion of this Spanish Armada, and fear some disaster." Before it had even fully come into existence, the Armada's credibility was already being undermined by the potency of Drake's ever-increasing fame.

Sailing southward to Cape St. Vincent Drake stormed and took the castle at Sagres and permitted his men to ransack the monastery there, destroying images and burning the buildings. A Spanish official reported that they "committed their usual feasts and drunkenness, their diabolical rampages and obscenities." Using Sagres as his base he proceeded to harass all the supply ships passing along the southern coast of Spain, bringing provisions for the nascent Armada. Queen Elizabeth's agent reported that he seized and burnt forty-seven supply ships and between fifty and sixty fishing boats. The operation was not only brilliant but useful. Drake deprived the Armada of vast quantities of essential materials, some of which, most importantly the timber staves for making water barrels, they were never able to replace. Soldiers on their way to join the army assembling in Lisbon had to make their way overland. "The English are masters of the sea," wrote the Venetian ambassador to Madrid. "Lisbon and the whole coast is, as it were, blockaded." Strategically Drake's expedition was a triumph, but financially it was disappointing. Tuna fish and barrel staves do not constitute valuable plunder, and even in this time of national emergency the expedition's backers, including not only Drake himself but also the queen, wanted a profit. When news came that there were treasure ships approaching the Azores, Drake abandoned his blockade and set off in search of a prize.

In the Azores he encountered a Portuguese carrack, a huge and hugely valuable ship. Her crew put up a more determined defense than any of Drake's previous prey, but she was outnumbered; eventually the English took possession of her and of her fabulous cargo of spices, silk, ebony, jewels, gold, and silver. She was almost as great a prize as the *Cacafuego* had been, although, since it had taken a fleet rather than a single little ship to capture her, the profits this time were not so prodigious. The expedition's commercial success was assured. So, as it happened, was the temporary frustration of Spanish war plans. King Philip, alarmed by Drake's disappearance and fearful of what he might be doing out in the Atlantic, ordered the Spanish fleet to pursue him. For three wasted months they hunted him in vain, returning with men so exhausted and sick and ships so weatherbeaten that the planned attack on England had to be postponed until the following year.

Drake returned to honor and riches. There was no question this time of returning the plunder. It took seventeen ships to carry the *San Felipe*'s fabulous cargo from Plymouth to London, Drake having first personally delivered to the queen a chest packed full of priceless golden trinkets—knives, forks, pomanders, rings, and every kind of jewel. It appears that, despite what Burghley was telling the Spanish ambassador about his queen's grave displeasure at Drake's aggressive actions, she accepted the gifts with enthusiasm. Drake himself was permitted to keep £20,000, an even greater fortune than the one he already had.

His reputation was at its zenith. He was bold and brilliant and, best of all, he was successful. It seemed to his countrymen that there was nothing he couldn't do. He was just the champion England needed, and the need was urgent. England was about to face a danger as appalling as those which had persuaded the Athenians to recall Alcibiades and the king of Castile to plead for the services of the banished Cid. The Spanish assault on England had been hampered and hindered, but it had not been stopped. In July of 1588 the great Armada finally set sail, some 125 ships carrying 30,000 men. John Hawkins called it "the greatest and strongest combination, to my understanding, that ever was gathered in Christendom," and it was advancing on England with the manifest intention of invading the country and subjecting the English people to the kind of horrors, the whip, the torture, the stake, which—as every English person had had dinned into them by the Protestant authorities—had already been inflicted upon the peoples of Spanish America.

The story of the defeat of the Spanish Armada, as it took shape almost immediately in the English popular imagination, is the story of a mighty empire defeated by a tiny island; of the representatives of authoritarianism mocked by the defenders of liberty; of an archaic, conservative power, throttled by its own pride, outpaced by a creative, energetic, progressive race of unconventional improvisers. It is at the heart of this story that Francis Drake, the daylight robber, the irreverent captain who singed a king's beard, appears to best effect, as the personification of all that was bold and dashing about Elizabethan England. The image which encapsulates that story, an image which is almost entirely false, is that of the huge, lumbering, incongruously magnificent Armada taunted and goaded by a gnat-swarm of tiny nimble ships.

That image began to circulate almost immediately. Thomas Nash wrote about the Spanish fleet "like a high wood, that overshadowed the shrubs of our low ships," and Camden, who had access to several participants in the campaign, described the Spanish ships as being so huge "the winds grew tired of carrying them" and the ocean groaned under their weight, while the English ships were "far the lesser." The image of this unequal conflict took firm root in the popular imagination. In one of the folk stories Southey collected in the 1820s, Drake, on receiving news of the Armada's approach, took a piece of wood and insouciantly began to whittle it. His wood shavings, flying off, fell into the sea and each one became a ship. Drake with his wood chips nicely confounds expectation by defeating an opponent much larger, much better equipped, and far more pompous than himself. And Drake the wizard, conjuring ships from nowhere, is a reminder of the widespread belief that the English success against the Armada was a kind of miracle, given the odds against it, something which could only have been contrived by magic, or the extraordinary pluck and audacity of hero born, like Rodrigo Díaz, in a happy hour.

In fact the English had the technological advantage. The stupendous strength and mass of the Armada is a part of legend as well as of history. What is less well-known is that the English fleet assembled to meet it was half as large again. If any single Englishman can claim credit for the Armada's failure, it was Drake's old employer John Hawkins. Like Drake, Hawkins had exchanged piracy for public service and had been since 1578 treasurer of the queen's navy, in which capacity he had overseen the construction of what were, by general agreement, the best fighting ships in the world. The Spanish ships were transporting an invading army, and were designed as troop-carriers-cum-fortresses. The English ships, built for action, had none of the massive superstructures which made the

Spanish galleons loom so tall. But though they were lower they were not smaller. The average tonnage of the English ships was rather greater than that of the Spanish and there was not a single vessel in the Armada as big as Martin Frobisher's 1,100-ton *Triumph*. The English were also ferociously well armed: when the *Revenge*, which was Drake's ship for the Armada campaign, was captured at Flores in the Azores three years later it was carrying 70 tons of artillery. The English ships were narrower and far more responsive than those of the Spanish. Medina-Sidonia, the Spanish admiral, described them enviously as "so fast and so nimble they can do anything they like with them." But they were not wood chips: they were massive, lethal instruments of war.

Drake was not the commander in chief, although nearly all the Spaniards, up to and including Philip II, seem to have believed that he was and the English populace saw him as their prime protector. The English legend of the Armada stresses the rigidly hierarchical nature of Spanish society and contrasts it with the meritocratic openness of Elizabethan England, where a man of the people, like Drake, could rise to the top. In fact both fleets were led (ably as it happens) by noblemen with little seagoing experience who owed their high commands primarily to their social rank, the Spanish Duke of Medina-Sidonia and the English Lord Howard of Effingham. Drake was not a good manager of men. There were people, Elizabeth among them, who remembered Thomas Doughty, and the memory was revived on each of the several occasions when Drake's high-handedness opened a breach between himself and his associates. In 1585 he had come close to provoking a mutiny by crassly insisting that his officers take an oath of loyalty. In 1587 his vice admiral, Borough, had argued furiously with him at Cádiz, and subsequently allowed himself to be carried home by a mutinous crew. It was not the kind of record to inspire anyone to offer him overall command of the English fleet.

Before the Armada ever left harbor it was clear to all of its senior commanders that it was bound to fail of its purpose. King Philip's orders were that it should pass through the Channel in close formation, avoiding battle if possible, and make contact with the Spanish army in the Netherlands under the command of the prince of Parma. It would then, in some way which was never properly defined, help and protect Parma's troops as they somehow crossed the Straits of Dover to invade England in concert with the soldiers carried on the Armada's ships. Both Medina-Sidonia and Parma had plainly told Philip that this plan could not possibly be carried out. The Armada's big ships could not go into the shallow waters off Dunkirk to take off Parma's men, so the entire Spanish army would have to embark in barges and small boats. In any but the calmest seas they would all be drowned if they managed (as was unlikely) to get past the Dutch, who were patrolling the coastline in shallow-draft vessels and from whom the Armada, standing out to sea, would be unable to protect them.

No solution to these difficulties had been suggested or even, apparently, seriously looked for. Parma wrote gloomily that the success of the Armada "must depend on the holy and mighty will of God, for the zeal and industry of men cannot suffice." To King Philip that situation appeared, if not exactly ideal, satisfactory enough. He had asked that the invasion attempt should be granted the status of a crusade. The Pope, whose relations with the Spanish king were by no means as harmonious as Spanish propaganda suggested—Philip, in his view, "had no more care for the Catholic religion than a dog"—refused. But there were few in the Spanish fleet who doubted that God was on their side. Catholic Spaniards (and Catholic Englishmen, of whom there were two hundred with the Armada) read of the Catholics martyred under the Protestant Tudor monarchs and deduced that English Protestants were wicked persecutors of the staunch and godly. Medina-Sidonia's exhortation to his men on setting out declared that "the saints in heaven will go in company with us," among them Thomas More, Mary, Queen of Scots, and others whom "Elizabeth has torn in pieces with ferocious cruelty and nicely calculated tortures." They were sailing to England, he told his men, in order to rescue weeping virgins and "tender children, suckled in the poison of heresy, who are doomed to perdition unless deliverance reaches them betimes." This being so, King Philip felt confident of heavenly assistance. "Since it is all for his cause, God will send good weather," he told Parma. To Medina-Sidonia he wrote: "This is a matter guided by His Hand and He will help you." The Armada was launched, as one of its despairing commanders noted, "in the confident hope of a miracle," a hope which proved forlorn.

The English were as certain of divine favor as the Spanish. Protestant Englishmen like Drake read Foxe's account of the Protestant martyrdoms under the Catholic Queen Mary, Philip's wife, and adumbrated an idea of Spain as persecutor of true religion which exactly mirrored the Spanish vision of England. More generally Spain was envisioned as an outpost of Hell, a place of bloody magnificence, its grandeur based on the sufferings of thousands upon thousands of African and American slaves and illumined by the ghastly fires of the auto-da-fé.

In 1587 Drake told Walsingham he and his men stood "as one body . . . for our gracious Queen and country against Antichrist and his members." "God will help us," wrote Hawkins to Walsingham, "for we defend . . . our religion, God's own cause." Both fleets were well provided with priests; in both, services were held on every ship daily, and the crews were obliged to attend not only for their own spiritual welfare but to bring luck to their side. Philip II gave orders that all the Armada troops should avoid oaths and blasphemies because God would reward the virtuous and punish the sinful. And so, in the opinion of the English, he did.

For six days the Armada sailed eastward through the English Channel, at first in a crescent-shaped line two miles long, later in a tight circle. The English fleet followed behind. The Spanish ships were crammed with armed men ready to grapple and fight, ship to ship, hand to hand. The English were equipped for the newer style of naval warfare, one in which the work was done by big guns. Accordingly they kept their distance.

The Spanish were powerless to inflict any harm on the English. Juan Martínez de Recalde explained their problem with prescient accuracy before they even set sail: "If we can come to close quarters, Spanish valour and Spanish steel and the great masses of soldiers we shall have on board will make our victory certain. But unless God helps us by a miracle, the English, who have faster and handier ships than ours, and who know their advantage just as well as we do, will never close with us at all, but lay off and batter us with their culverins, without our being able to do them any serious hurt." The English were equally incapable of harming their opponents. They could run rings around the Spanish ships, but their guns were not powerful enough at long range to do any serious damage. During the six days the two fleets took to pass through the Channel the English fired "a terrible value of great shot," but not a single Spanish ship was sunk; few were even disabled. "We pluck their feathers by little and little," wrote Howard optimistically, but in truth he was not able even to do that.

At last, on the seventh day of the pursuit, the Armada came to rest near Calais. There Medina-Sidonia received the shattering news that Parma had never received any of the messengers sent to inform him of the Armada's approach. His army would not be ready to set out to sea for six days. That night the English sent fireships into the Armada. They did little harm but the Spaniards panicked. Nearly all of them cut their cables, leaving behind the anchors whose loss would cost so many of them their lives on the return journey, and retreated in disorder. The next morning, off Gravelines, before they could properly reform, the two fleets finally joined battle.

This was the fight which would enter English history books as "the defeat of the Spanish Armada," but to those who took part in it the engagement appeared inconclusive. By the end of it the Armada was battered but still battleworthy, while the English were almost entirely out of ammunition. Parma's men were still being embarked. But the next day—as the medal struck in England to celebrate the occasion has it—"FLAVIT," "HE BREATHED." A wind came up, threatening to force the Armada onto the shoals off the Flemish coast. The English stood safely out to sea and prayed. God's allegiance seemed to waver: the wind dropped. But then, next morning, HE breathed again, and this time what the deity exhaled was recognized by all concerned as a Protestant wind. Before it the Armada, still battleworthy, was swept helplessly away northward to meet the terrible sequence of storms, including one of the only two typhoons to have hit the North Atlantic in the last five hundred years, which reduced it by the time its remnant returned home to Spain to barely more than half its original strength.

Warfare, wrote the great medievalist Johan Huizinga, is a form of divination. When Rodrigo Díaz volunteered to clear his name by submitting to a judicial duel, he was following the very ancient belief that to come through mortal combat alive and victorious is to demonstrate one's virtue and one's status as God's (or the gods') chosen one. All duels, most drunken fistfights, and a great many wars have derived at least part of their motivation from the notion that the winner of a fight proves conclusively that he is the "better man." In a holy war especially the outcome both proves and is determined by the partisanship of the deity. The result of the Armada campaign was decided, as both parties had expected it would be, by divine intervention. It was read by the English as a clear indication that God was a Protestant, by the Spanish as a terrible signal that he considered them unworthy to represent his holy Catholic Church. King Philip sank into a depression from which he never fully recovered. Queen Elizabeth wrote a verse celebrating her victory and the divine favor of which it was evidence:

> He made the winds and water rise
> To scatter all mine enemies

. . .

What part Drake played in all this is a matter of dispute. Howard seldom mentions him in his reports. To the Spaniards, however, he was the paramount Englishman. He was their bugbear, the man they wished to make scapegoat for all Protestant Europe. A young Spanish woman whose dreams were recorded by her priest between 1587 and 1590 sees him repeatedly in her nightmares as a clever, bold, and utterly ruthless persecutor of all Catholics. In ballads circulating at the time he appears as the sole representative of England:

> My brother Bartolo
> Is sailing for England
> To kill el Draque

The whole great Armada had been assembled, according to the testimony of a Spanish prisoner who may not have been privy to the complexities of his king's foreign policy but who was unquestionably voicing what many of his compatriots believed, because "it was not convenient that one Drake, with two or three rotten ships, should come always, and at his pleasure, to spoil the havens of Spain." One Spanish gentleman became so excited in demonstrating to his friends what he would do to Drake, were he ever to lay hands on him, that he shot a bystander dead.

Alcibiades' glittering reputation led the Athenians to assume that their navy's successes in the Hellespont were all his, because among the admirals he, rather than the superbly competent but less flashy Thrasybulus, was the one of whom great things were expected. So Drake, being already a popular celebrity, was given the credit for all his colleagues' achievements, for the use of fireships (actually the initiative of William Winter), for Howard's strategy, even for the ultimate dispersal of the Armada, for which the better informed of his contemporaries gave most of the credit to God and which modern historians, saying the same thing in a different idiom, ascribe to luck and the weather. Drake, always a braggart, helped to magnify his contribution. "He reporteth that no man hath done so good service as he," said Frobisher furiously afterwards, "but he lyeth in his teeth." But fame is a self-propagating phenomenon. No amount of swaggering by Drake could have made him as celebrated as he was. Only rumor could do that, and the almost universal tendency to believe a good story regardless of its claims to authenticity. "Have you heard how Drake with his fleet has offered battle to the Armada?" exclaimed the Pope, whose agents must certainly have informed him of Howard's existence, but who preferred to ignore it. "With what courage! . . . He is a great captain."

In fact he was Howard's vice admiral. Howard treated his charismatic deputy with great generosity and tact, and Drake, as second in command, was sufficiently high placed to have his own way with impunity while remaining free of cramping responsibility.

When the Armada was first sighted off the coast of Cornwall, an awful wall of ships two miles long sailing steadily eastward with a following wind, the English fleet was at Plymouth. One of the best-known legends about Drake relates that he was playing bowls when the news of the Armada's imminent approach reached him and that he insisted on playing out the game. Stow, writing in 1600, has it that the English "officers and others kept revels on the shore . . . at the instant of the foe's approach," but the story of Drake's bowls dates from over a hundred years after the event and his famous words, "There is time to win the game and beat the Spaniards too," were first published in 1835. The story is in many ways implausible. The playing of bowls in a public place was illegal under Puritan legislation which Drake himself would probably have endorsed: one of his few actions as a member of Parliament had been to introduce a bill forbidding bearbaiting, hunting, and hawking on the Sabbath. (The queen, who enjoyed bearbaiting, vetoed it.) But true or not, it's a story Drake would probably have liked, and it neatly conflates the Drake his contemporaries knew, the impudently irreverent rule-breaker with a penchant for self-congratulation, with the marmorial calm of the Stoic hero. (Cato, on the day of his defeat in the consular elections, gave evidence of his sublime imperturbability by playing a ballgame on the Field of Mars.)

In fact the English had twenty-four hours' notice, thanks to a patriotic pirate who had raced to Plymouth to report sighting the Spanish off the Lizard—more than enough time for a game of bowls. But if Drake played until the tide turned, as soon as it did he set to work. If the Spanish chose to blockade the entrance to Plymouth Sound, the English fleet could be trapped inside. With contrary winds pinning them ashore the English ships had to be towed out by rowing boats, or hauled out on their anchors. It was a desperately slow and laborious process, but by the following morning the entire fleet was at sea. For twenty-four hours, in dreadful weather, they struggled against the wind. Half the ships sailed, hidden by the rain, straight across the front of the Armada and back around its southern wing. Another group, probably led by Drake, traveled perilously close inshore with the wind almost dead against them to pass the Armada's northern tip. At dawn on July 21, as the Spaniards approached Plymouth, they sighted the English fleet for the first time, not ahead of them, boxed into harbor, but chivvying them from behind with the advantage of the wind. The entire exhausting, perilous maneuver had been—as it happens—unnecessary. Medina-Sidonia, under orders to avoid battle, would almost certainly have sailed straight past Plymouth, leaving the English fleet to issue out unmolested and follow in his wake. But neither Howard nor Drake knew that. For fighting sailing ships the "weather gauge," the windward position, was a decisive advantage. The English had made sure they had it by thirty-six hours of ceaseless, back-breaking, and frightening work by the sailors, and by a combination of enormously skilled seamanship, local knowledge, and imaginative energy that can surely be credited to Drake.

Two days later, off Portland Bill, the ships under Drake's command played a crucial part in a ferocious battle. "There was never seen a more hot fight than this was," wrote Howard. On another occasion a Spanish supply ship was isolated and set upon by a group of English ships, almost certainly led by Drake. As the Armada passed the Isle of Wight it was he who led an attack on its southern flank which very nearly succeeded in driving the Spanish onto some shoals. Medina-Sidonia saw the danger and changed course in time, but Drake had at least ensured that, even had they wished, the Spanish would not be able to enter the Solent, a possible starting point for the immediate invasion on which the English generally imagined them to be intent.

The fireship attack off Calais which broke up the Armada's formation and its morale has often been credited to Drake. In fact it was William Winter who proposed it, but Drake did give two of his own ships to be burned. In the battle at Gravelines the following day, the last engagement of the campaign, he led the English into battle but at some point in the day he sailed on, apparently in pursuit of those Spanish ships which were escaping into the North Sea. Martin Frobisher later asserted that he had done so either because his nerve for battle gave out, or because he preferred chasing prizes to fighting for his country—"I know not whether he be a cowardly knave or a traitor, but the one I will swear"—but Frobisher by this time was so angry with Drake that his opinion cannot count for very much. According to the narrative by Pietro Ubaldino, Drake stayed so close to the thick of the fighting that twice cannonballs came crashing into his own cabin, the first breaking the bed, the second taking off a gentleman's toes.

Frobisher's fury relates to the only one of Drake's actions during that momentous week which has been widely recorded. Off Plymouth two Spanish ships collided. The *Nuestra Señora del Rosario*, commanded by Don Pedro Valdés, was so disabled that Medina-Sidonia, judging it impossible to take her in tow, ordered the fleet to abandon her and sail on. It was a tough decision, not only because Valdés was one of the Armada's most distinguished commanders and his ship large and well armed, but also because she was one of the Armada's pay ships. Her cargo included 52,000 ducats, about a third of the Armada's money.

Howard, too, wanted to keep his fleet together. Recognizing the temptation she presented, he gave explicit instructions that the *Nuestra Señora del Rosario* was to be left where she was. That night, as the English followed the Armada up the Channel, he ordered Drake to lead the way displaying a lantern on his stern for the rest of the fleet to follow. There are two versions of what happened next. According to Drake his lookout reported ships traveling in the opposite direction to the south. Thinking that the Spaniards might be trying to do what he and Howard had done before, creeping back around the enemy under cover of darkness in order to get the advantage of the wind before morning, he resolved to investigate. Not wanting to lead the entire fleet off course, he extinguished his lantern, turned back, overtook the mysterious ships, discovered them to be harmless German freighters, and set off the rejoin the fleet. The story is just about plausible, but only Drake's most unflinching supporters have believed it, because while the English fleet wandered without a guide in the dark—Howard finding himself at dawn dangerously close to the Armada's rear—Drake took possession of the *Nuestra Señora del Rosario*.

He had deliberately disobeyed orders and imperiled the whole fleet in order to sneak back and grab a prize, but his action was almost universally applauded. When news of the capture reached London bonfires were lit. The incident presented the spectacle of a Spanish ship overpowered by an English one, a spectacle otherwise sadly missing from the story of the Armada. Besides, the *Nuestra Señora del Rosario* was the richest prize of the whole campaign and Drake was not the only person in the Channel that week to be motivated by cupidity.

Both parties to this latest holy war hoped for plunder as fervently as the crusaders of old. Medina-Sidonia promised his men the glory of doing God's work but assured them as well that the expedition would be "profitable also because of the plunder and endless riches we shall gather in England." The English were equally greedy for loot. Lord Admiral Howard missed most of the climactic battle at Gravelines: he wasted that crucial morning attempting to take possession of a Spanish ship which had gone aground off Calais. (Eventually the French, who wanted the takings for themselves, succeeded in seeing him off, bombarding his ship from the shore.) Even Martin Frobisher, who fulminated so furiously against Drake afterwards, was not making a principled protest. What enraged him was not that Drake was a deserter who had preferred loot to duty, but that he, Frobisher, might not get his cut. "I will make him spend the best blood in his belly," he declared, because he "thinketh to cozen us of our share of fifteen thousand ducats."

Discreditable as the episode may seem, it did nothing to dim Drake's reputation. Gold-greed, lawlessness, and a preference for going his own way were, after all, among the qualities for which he was celebrated. And the circumstances under which the *Nuestra Señora del Rosario* was taken were designed to heighten his renown even further, not because it was so hard, but because, like so many of his most splendid successes, it was so easy. Towards the end of Rodrigo Díaz's life King Musta'in of Zaragoza, who had once been his employer, declared, "I would not myself dare to engage him in battle." By 1588 Drake's reputation, like the Cid's, was so formidable that it did his fighting for him. The *Nuestra Señora del Rosario* had fifty-two guns and a crew of 450 men, all of whose duty it surely should have been to keep her and her treasure out of English hands, but when Drake called upon him to surrender, Valdés did so without firing a shot. He afterwards declared that it was no shame to surrender to a commander of "valour and felicity so great that Mars and Neptune seemed to attend him." Drake's fame was now so tremendous that, like Achilles showing himself on the ramparts around the Greek camp, he had only to be present to put the fear of death into his opponents. He came, he was seen, and he conquered.

It was the last of Drake's glory days. The aftermath of the Armada campaign was bitter for those Englishmen who had fought in it. The English fleet began to pursue the Spanish northwards but storms and disease soon halted the hunt. Drake put in at Margate with typhus on his ship. The men could not be discharged because there was no money with which to pay them. Their food was turning rotten; soon as many men were dying of food poisoning as of disease. There were not enough clothes. The English ships and soon the streets of Margate, Harwich, and Broadstairs filled up with corpses. Howard and Drake went to London to report on the situation but were given inadequate funds and no sympathy. In Spain the survivors of the Armada returned to find hospitals set up to receive them in every port, and they were all paid. In England the government economized by deliberately lethal procrastination. "By death, by discharging of sick men and such like . . . there may be spared something in the general pay," wrote Burghley—the later the money was given, the fewer seamen there would be left alive to demand it. While Elizabeth rode her white horse at Tilbury, posed for her portrait, and struck her medals, the sailors who had, according to the triumphalist rhetoric of the time, won such an audacious victory for her in repulsing the invincible Armada, were left to die, naked, filthy, starving, and unpaid.

Drake himself was handsomely rewarded for his share in the battles, not least by being allowed to keep Don Pedro Valdés and, ultimately, his ransom. "I wish you joy of your prisoner," said the queen graciously, meeting him in St. James's Park. Besides, a lot of the money carried on the *Nuestra Señora del Rosario* went missing before Drake handed it over to Howard. Hakluyt believed "the soldiers [Spanish and English] merrily shared the treasure amongst themselves," but Drake's heirs alleged he had kept a good portion of it over and above what he was due.

He had done well financially but his popularity was running out. His baiting of Spain seemed exciting so long as it was carried on over the seas and far away, but once its consequences were felt in England itself the public turned against him. A Spanish prisoner reported that Drake was "much disliked as the cause of the wars." Nor was he loved by the seamen on whom his success depended. Ever since he returned from his circumnavigation stories had circulated about his meanness in paying the sailors who risked their lives on his expeditions. Ambassador Mendoza reported to Philip II that the crew of the *Golden Hind* had never received their share of his booty, a nasty aspersion which is lent credence by the fact that when Drake was trying to recruit men for a further voyage in 1581 the captains refused to sign on unless someone other than Drake would guarantee their pay. In the Caribbean in 1585 his men were hard to control. In Santo Domingo, according to a Spanish witness, they perpetrated "endless atrocities," using the churches as abattoirs and latrines, breaking open tombs and smashing holy effigies. Drake had to resort to extreme measures to maintain discipline. "This Francis treats his people harshly and hangs many," wrote one Spanish observer (in fact he hanged two). "With the seamen he is harsh," wrote another. On returning home and finding they were to be given only half pay, the men rioted. Carleill and the other land captains voluntarily divided their share of the spoils among the soldiers and sailors to make up the shortfall; Drake did not. He did not give money when he ought to have done, and he frequently kept it when he ought not to have done. He had learned from his queen's example on his return from his circumnavigation how to hide his profits. For the rest of his life his reputation was to be clouded by rumors of false accounting, embezzlement, and, especially, a chariness in providing for his men. He had assumed for himself the autocratic status and the predatory practices of a feudal liege lord, but he was signally lacking in *largesse*.

In England his perceived status dwindled, but in Spain, as the traumatic news of the Armada's failure spread, Drake's reputation grew ever more tremendous. Defeat could be more easily borne if it was inflicted by a superhuman adversary. In contemporary sources he appears as a sorcerer helped by a familiar spirit. He is demonic, the arch-opponent, the anti-Christ, the "untameable wolf." But he is also a great man. Spanish poets described him as a "noble English gentleman . . . skilled in navigation, . . . shrewd and astute . . . No one ever equalled him"; as "famous Drake, and yet most infamous"; as "[a] captain . . . whose glittering memory / will last undimmed through future centuries." In the eyes of his enemies Drake achieved a wicked grandeur which for his countrymen he never possessed.

Of the 130 ships which made up the Armada 70 returned to Spain— from the Spanish point of view, devastatingly few; from the English, dangerously many. Immediately Drake began to beg the queen for her commission to harry them at home. Eventually she consented. In April of the following year Drake and Sir John Norris, with whom he had served in Ireland fourteen years before, led out a counter-armada. It consisted of 180 ships crowded with armed men, for this, like the slightly smaller Spanish Armada of the previous year, was an invasion force. Like its predecessor, it was a catastrophic failure.

The expedition's aims were diverse and mutually contradictory. Poorly provisioned, poorly planned, and poorly motivated, the fleet began to fall apart almost immediately: over thirty ships turned back without even seeing Spain. The queen wanted the Spanish ships at harbor along Spain's northern coastline destroyed. Drake led his men first to Corunna, where they landed and overran the unfortified lower portion of the town. They ransacked houses, broke open wine cellars, and went on a drunken rampage which lasted for days. They burned the countryside for three miles around and pursued and slaughtered any Spaniards they could catch. But their assault on the fortified upper town failed. Worse, at Corunna many of the men fell ill with what they first imagined to be a colossal mass hangover, but which seems in fact to have been typhus compounded by dysentery.

Had they gone on to Santander, wrote an English agent a month later, Drake would have "done such service as never subject had done." Dozens of the returned Armada ships were in harbor there. "With twelve sail of his ships he might have destroyed all the forces which the Spaniards had." But he had little stomach for sinking warships: there was no money in it. Instead, disregarding the queen's instructions, he and Norris resolved on an assault on Lisbon. They had with them a pretender to the throne of Portugal, Dom António, who had been hanging around the English court for years and who, were they to install him as king, could be relied upon to be generous to the English in general, and to Drake in particular. Norris and a small army went ashore to march on Lisbon overland, Drake promising to sail up the Tagus to meet them. For reasons he never satisfactorily explained he failed to do so. The Portuguese declined to rise in support of Dom António. Norris was obliged to retreat ignominiously, harried by Spanish troops. More and more of the men were falling ill. On the march back to the coast nearly a third of Norris's soldiers died of disease.

Somewhat desperately Drake and Norris turned towards the Azores in the hope of at least covering their expenses by capturing some treasure. The men were dying by hundreds now. Twice they turned back, beaten by storms. Drake gave up. The counter-armada returned to England having achieved very little and lost much, including the lives of nearly two-thirds of its men and its admiral's charismatic reputation.

One of the expedition's officers reported to Walsingham that in failing to meet Norris at Lisbon, Drake had been either incompetent or cowardly or both. Norris's soldiers, according to Camden, "spoke disgracefully" of Drake, "as if through his cowardice they had failed of their hoped-for victory." On the voyage out he had supplemented the inadequate provisions the fleet had been carrying by hijacking French, Danish, and Hanseatic ships and stealing their cargoes. Once the Privy Council began to look into the expedition's finances, much of the loot, whether legitimately seized from Spain or illegitimately from neutrals, turned out to have unaccountably disappeared. Drake was ordered to return a French ship and both he and Norris were reprimanded for their mismanagement. The queen wrote sourly that Drake had taken more care of his profit than of her service. He was no longer England's "Golden Knight." "The leaders were craven," wrote a pamphleteer in the Netherlands, adding, "The proud Drake was mobbed on his return to Plymouth by the women whom he had made widows." The soldiers and sailors, unpaid once more, rioted in London. "Drake," reports a contemporary, "was much blamed by the common consent of all men."

A hero is both more and less than human. In this Renaissance depiction of his education, Achilles' ambivalent nature—half bestial, half divine—is mirrored by that of his mentor, the centaur Chiron.

Male sex and a readiness for violent action are among a hero's essential attributes. In this medieval illumination, Achilles, having apparently taken refuge in a convent, inadvertently displays his masculinity by showing an interest in armor.

Achilles fighting Memnon on a red-figure krater dating from approximately 490 BC.

The climax of Achilles' rampage, depicted by Peter Paul Rubens. Killing Hector, Achilles knows that his own death must follow shortly.

In this painting by the 18th-century artist Hubert Robert, Alexander the Great, who kept a copy of the *Iliad* beneath his pillow, pays homage at Achilles' tomb before embarking on his Asian conquests.

Opposite This image of Achilles, dating from Alcibiades' lifetime, shows how the latter would have dressed for battle.

Above The exquisite Alcibiades, whom Baudelaire identified as the first of the dandies, depicted by François-André Vincent.

Above A detail from Raphael's *School of Athens*. Alcibiades stands in the center with Socrates, who taught him, saved his life in battle, and loved him more than anything but philosophy.

Below The Death of Socrates by Jacques-Louis David. On trial for his life, Socrates invoked Achilles, who, like him, preferred death to compromise. Three and a half centuries later, Cato read through Plato's account of Socrates' suicide three times before killing himself.

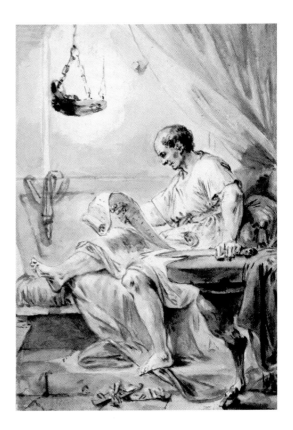

Above Bernhard Rode's *Cato Unwilling to Survive the Freedom of his Fatherland.* Cato, the model of Stoic virtue, serenely prepares himself for death with a sword in one hand and a scroll in the other.

Right A portrait bust of Cato found in Morocco and dating from 1ˢᵗ–3ʳᵈ century AD.

Above The Leave-taking of Cato Uticensis by Ercole Gennari. Selfless to the last, Cato takes time to console and advise his son before taking his own life.

Left The Death of Cato by Giambattista Langetti, one of the less gruesome of numerous Renaissance paintings of Cato in what Michel de Montaigne called his "most excellent posture"—the act of disemboweling himself.

The Mocking of Christ by Fra Angelico. Cato was praised for the impassive calm with which he endured abuse, and was latterly admired by Christians as the most virtuous of pagans. Here Christ—derided, beaten, and spat upon as Cato had been—suffers with Stoic dignity.

Contrary models of greatness:
Cato and his great opponent, Julius Caesar, were both revered in medieval Europe.

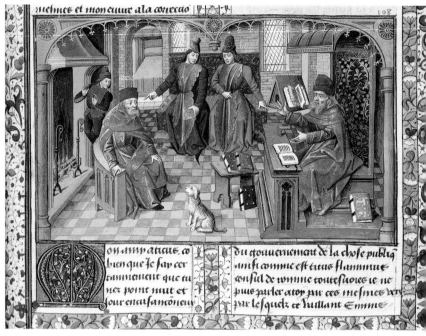

on mup aticus. co
bien que Je far cer
tumnement que tu
ner point mut et
Jour enarfaronenn

du gouuernement de la chose publiq
unfi comme est titus flaminue
conful de romme toutesuotee ie ne
puie parler ator pur ces mesmes ver
pur lesquelz ce huitlant Emme

Above Cato, who considered
the just administration of a
province far more glorious
than its conquest, con-
verses with three fellow-
philosophers.

Right Julius Caesar leads his
armies into Gaul at the outset of the campaign that
Cato denounced as criminal
genocide, but which won
Caesar undying fame.

Cid ruydiaz.

Above El Cid, in an image based on his monument in Burgos. His beard, token of his masculine vigor, was said to be the wonder of all beholders.

Left Rodrigo Díaz, the Cid, goes into battle.

Counter-Reformation propagandists reinvented the Cid as a Christian warrior making holy war on the alien infidels. But in the Spain in which Rodrigo Díaz grew up, Muslim and Christian had coexisted for centuries, the former being in general the better-versed in classical culture. This image of Socrates with students comes from Islamic Turkey.

The Cid triumphant on a monument in Seville. Mounted on his fabulous war-horse Babieca, the Cid is the personification of martial energy, the "force" Simone Weil was later to associate with Achilles.

Drake's voyage around the world. Drake claimed to be the first European to have seen that there was open sea to the south of Cape Horn: most of his contemporaries believed Tierra del Fuego to be a part of a continent extending all the way to the South Pole.

Sir Francis Drake by Nicholas Hilliard. When he returned from his circumnavigation of the world, Drake became an international celebrity. A portrait of him exhibited in Italy drew great crowds and the King of France distributed copies to all his leading courtiers, while in England a bridge collapsed under the weight of people who turned out to see him.

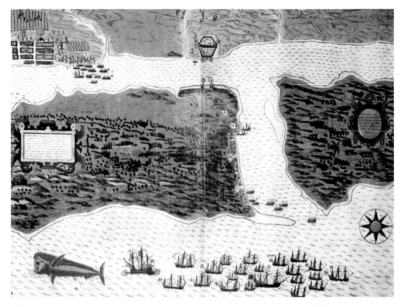

Above A 16th-century chart showing Drake's raid on St. Augustine, Florida, in 1585.

Below Drake encounters the native inhabitants of northern California. Drake's chaplain alleged that they begged Drake to make himself their king.

It was six years before he went to sea again. Meanwhile he worked with Philip Nichols on the chaplain's account of his two great successes, *Sir Francis Drake Revived* and *The World Encompassed by Sir Francis Drake*, compensating for his contemporaries' loss of faith in him by burnishing his legend for posterity. In 1592 he wrote the queen a dedicatory letter presenting the former book as a "remembrance" of "service done to Your Majesty by your poor vassal against your great enemy." The hint was eventually taken. In 1595 he received Elizabeth's commission to embark on a voyage to the Caribbean.

He had colleagues: by this time, reported one of his officers, he was considered too "self-willed and peremptory" to be entrusted with sole command. He and his old acquaintance Sir John Hawkins were joint admirals at sea, with Sir Thomas Baskerville in command of the thousand soldiers they carried. Their objectives were the capture of a galleon in Puerto Rico and an assault on Panama. Neither was accomplished. The expedition was dangerously underprovisioned. The officers accused Drake of keeping for himself money that should have been spent on supplies. The two commanders quarreled, a sad end to their long association. Hawkins died, worn out, off Puerto Rico. Drake carried on, but he had lost his confidence, his luck, and his grip on actuality.

In the quarter century that had elapsed since his first piratical raids on Caribbean ports the Spaniards had learned to defend themselves. They easily repelled his attack on Puerto Rico. Afterwards he boasted to the younger and less experienced men, "I will bring thee to twenty places far more wealthy and easier to be gotten," but it was an empty boast. Throughout the voyage he was slow and indecisive, allowing news of his coming to precede him to each of his targeted ports. He extorted some pearls from the inhabitants of Rio de la Hacha then burned the place to the ground. He landed at Nombre de Dios, which he had once called "the mouth of the treasure of the world," but found little worth taking. He set Baskerville's troops to march across the isthmus to Panama, as he had once done himself, but the Spanish were ready for them, and they were unable to force their way through. After this repulse Drake, according to Thomas Maynarde, who was with him, "never carried mirth nor joy in his face."

He, who had never taken anyone's advice, asked his officers what they wanted to do next. He was at a loss. He had returned to the scene of his first great triumph, where he had come as a young man among young men and helped himself to what he wanted from every ship in the Caribbean, and he found himself impotent. He was only fifty or so, but he talked with the fretful nostalgia of an old man. The Caribbean was not what it was, he told Maynarde pathetically, "he never thought a place would be so changed." Even the weather was not as good as he remembered it. There were no ships worth plundering, no vulnerable ports into which he could burst with a handful of men and help himself to stacks of silver. He had returned to his own personal paradise and found it altered, "as it were from a delicious and pleasant arbour into a waste and desert wilderness."

The fleet wandered, effectively leaderless. Drake contracted dysentery. While he lay helpless and wretched, his brother Thomas and his wife's nephew were both in his cabin (or so they later alleged against one another), the one rifling through his possessions, the other pressing him to sign amendments to his will. There was gossip later that one or the other of them tried to poison him, but most agreed that it was sickness that "did untie his clothes" and sorrow that "did rend at once the robe of his mortality asunder." Late one night he became delirious, jabbering words (presumably either obscene or blasphemous) which those present decided it best not to record, and calling his servant to help him put on his armor so that he might meet his death like a warrior. His wish was not granted. He was forced back into bed, where he died soon after, to be buried at sea, "the trumpets in doleful manner echoing their lamentation for so great a loss." On returning to England Thomas, his brother and heir, proved himself a true Drake by refusing to pay the seamen's wages. It was a miserable end.

"It is good news," said King Philip II when he was told on his sickbed of Drake's death. "Now I will get well." He was wrong—he never recovered—but he was not the only Spaniard to greet the news with exaggerated emotion. All Seville was illuminated and solemn thanksgivings said for the passing of Spain's great opponent. Lope de Vega celebrated the death of the man who most Spaniards still believed to be responsible for the rout of the Armada (with which de Vega had sailed) with the composition of an epic poem, *La Dragontea*. In it Drake is a damned monster as magnificent as he is wicked. He is "great-hearted" and all but invincible and the poem climaxes with a coruscating picture of him in his dragonish form; black and green and glittering, his eyes shining like the dawn, his fiery breath lighting up the heavens, "his steely sides impregnable / to all the darts, and all the spears of Spain." In Hispanic legend Drake was to remain for centuries the marauding Dragon. As late as 1898 a Puerto Rican author wrote that "this new Attila left pain and sorrow behind him; his ships left a red wake of freshly spilled blood." Seen through Spanish eyes he was a figure of colossal stature and dark splendor, a brilliant evildoer, the supreme opponent of Catholic virtue and good colonial government.

To his compatriots he was a smaller, more playful character, alternately the impudent trickster who steals the dragon's hoard and the plucky fellow who dares to fight the dragon and cut him down. In England, for at least two generations after his death, his fame rested on his marvelous success in getting wealth. While the Spanish poet Mira de Amescua was writing a tirade against "This pirate blind in his greed . . . / This impious glutton for gold and for silver," Robert Hayman eulogized him as one who "brought back heaps of gold into his nest." The *Golden Hind*, which had been kept as a curiosity at Deptford until it became so decayed that its remnants reminded a Venetian diplomat of "the bleached ribs and bare skull of a dead horse," was broken up in 1662 and its timbers carved into highly prized mementoes. One of them inspired Abraham Cowley's ode on "Sitting and drinking in the Chair made out of the relics of Sir Francis Drake's ship," in which the poet re-created the jubilant wonder Drake's captured wealth still aroused:

> With gold there our vessel we'll store;
> And never, and never be poor
> No never be poor any more

Gradually, though, Drake's remembered character evolved from that of brilliantly successful fortune-hunter to immortal defender of his people. Wrote Charles Fitzgeffrey in 1596:

> He who alive to them a dragon was
> Shall be a dragon until them again

In 1620 Henry Holland included Drake in his *Heroeologia*, his book on great men, and promised that he would one day rise from his watery grave to repel England's enemies. He had joined the pantheon of dead but death-defeating heroes, the saviors who (like Jesus Christ, King Arthur, and Charlemagne) will one day rise again.

In 1800, when England was once again under threat of invasion by a European autocrat with his sights set on world domination, an opera called *Francis Drake and the Iron Arm* was presented to great applause in

London. By that time England had a new maritime hero. Horatio Nelson was a man of a very different stamp from Francis Drake, more of a Cato than a bold corsair. Physically frail and morally persnickety, he came close to scuttling his own career at its outset by overzealous adherence to the laws against trading with foreign powers in the Caribbean, the same waters where Drake, with Hawkins, had used cannon shot to persuade reluctant Spaniards to break the rules and buy their slaves. But heartily though they would surely have disliked each other, Drake and Nelson had much in common.

Nelson was another small man with an inordinate regard for titles and the trappings of success and an appetite for Hispanic treasure. It was not in defending his country against Napoleon's aggression that he lost his arm but in a raid on a Spanish ship laden with American silver from which, as he wrote his sister, he hoped to "laughing come back rich." Like Drake he was a man on the make and, like Drake, he was fully aware of the value of celebrity and active in promoting his own image. Drake oversaw the writing of two books about himself explicitly designed to present him as an exemplary hero "for the stirring up of heroic spirits, to benefit their country and eternise their names by like noble attempts." Nelson wrote self-congratulatory accounts of each of his major battles and an autobiographical memoir ending with the words "Without having any inheritance . . . I have received all the honours of my profession, been created a peer of Great Britain, etc. And I may say to the Reader, 'GO THOU AND DO LIKEWISE.' "

Also like Drake, Nelson was an individualist who irritated his peers and exasperated his superiors (eighteen of the admirals invited to his funeral declined to attend) and who was never entrusted with supreme command. To the public he was the man who had held off Napoleon, just as Drake was the man who had repelled the Armada, but in fact, like Drake in 1588, Nelson was one of several officers under an extremely able commander in chief. That commander, Earl St. Vincent, wrote after Nelson's death: "Animal courage was the sole merit of Lord Nelson, his private character most disgraceful, in every sense of the word." But disgraceful or not, he was loved and venerated, as Drake had been in his heyday, as the only man alive who could have saved his country. After his victory at the Battle of the Nile emperors and kings loaded him with decorations and diamond-studded gifts, highborn ladies inundated him with embroidered sashes, and when he finally returned to England he was mobbed by rapturous crowds who insisted on taking his horses from their traces and dragging his carriage through the streets themselves.

Nelson considered himself punctiliously loyal. He longed for acceptance into the ranks of the establishment. But the public loved him, as their forebears had loved Drake, for his brilliant acts of insubordination. The telescope-to-the-blind-eye story is mere fable, but it is true that Nelson ignored the signal to withdraw at Copenhagen, and that he broke the line at Cape St. Vincent in direct contravention of all the principles of contemporary naval warfare and of his superior's orders. He was a prig who said of himself that "conscious rectitude" bore him though all difficulties, but he was adored as a wayward and audacious original after the model of Sir Francis Drake. By the end of the Victorian era the two had become so inseparable in the English popular imagination that Nelson was understood to be Drake's avatar. In 1908 the poet Alfred Noyes described Drake as "first upon the deep that rolls to Trafalgar." In 1916, in the middle of the First World War, a letter to *The Times* reported a rumor current in Devon to the effect that Drake's spirit was abroad again, as it had been "about a hundred years ago, when a little man, under the pseudonym of Nelson (for all Devonshire knows that Nelson was a reincarnation of Sir Francis), went sailing by to Trafalgar."

It was not only incarnate in the body of Horatio Nelson that Drake returned to earth. In 1897 Sir Henry Newbolt published his poem *Drake's Drum*, a stirring piece of patriotic mythmaking which combines a compellingly rhythmic beat with the potent figure of the once-and-future national redeemer:

> Drake he's in his hammock till the great Armadas come
> (Capten art tha sleepin' there below?)

The poem alludes to a legend which Newbolt apparently invented: it appears in no earlier source, although it does echo a story from the fifteenth-century Hussite wars. In this tale an earlier Protestant hero, blind General Zizka, asks as he lies dying that his skin be used to cover a drum that will beat for the continuance of the heroic struggle for religious reform. A drum which Drake purportedly took with him on his circumnavigation has been on show to visitors in his house at Buckland Abbey since 1799, but it was Newbolt who imagined the dying Drake telling his men (in a fanciful version of the Devon accent):

> Take my drum to England, hang et by the shore,
> Strike et when your powder's runnin' low;
> If the Dons sight Devon, I'll quit the port of Heaven,
> An' drum them up the Channel as we drummed
> them long ago.

When the German fleet surrendered at Scapa Flow in 1918 several English officers claimed to have heard a mysterious drumbeat emanating from none knew whence. (Newbolt was much read in the public schools where the evidently suggestible young men of the officer class were educated.)

The Second World War found England's immortal savior "ware and wakin' " again, as Newbolt had promised he would be. As the Armada sailed up the Channel in 1588, the youth of England, according to William Camden, "out of their entire love to their country, hired ships from all parts at their own private expense and joined with the fleet in great number." (Camden omits to mention that Lord Admiral Howard refused the services of these volunteers, for whom he had no arms or provisions.) When, after the fall of France in 1940, the routed British army was taken off the beaches of Dunkirk with the help of a host of privately owned boats crewed by their civilian owners every British newspaper carried references to the Armada, and to the myriad loyal Englishmen who had cheerfully and voluntarily set out to sea to stop it. The supposed "littleness" of the English ships which confronted the Armada was repeatedly likened to the genuine smallness of some of the vessels involved in the evacuation, and Robert Nathan wrote a splendidly tear-jerking and phenomenally popular ballad about two plucky children sailing over to Dunkirk to rescue the brave soldiers in their dinghy. The poem ends with the lines "There at his side sat Francis Drake / And held him true, and steered him home." In the months after Dunkirk, as the British braced themselves to repel or endure the apparently inevitable German invasion, several army officers reported hearing an insistent drumming along England's south coast. The "capten sleepin' there below" was getting ready to bestir himself again.

Drake as immortal savior, as England's fatherly guardian and guide, has become so reputable as to be almost unrecognizable as the man daubed with red and black warpaint who once robbed every ship in the Caribbean two or three times over. In the era when John Dee's mystic vision of a British Empire became a reality Drake assumed a new retroactive glory as one of its pioneers and a founder of the navy whereby Britannia ruled the waves. By the mid–nineteenth century his robberies had been varnished over with a layer of plausible justifications so thick as to render them almost invisible and his role in the frustration of the Armada vastly inflated. In 1892 Sir Julian Corbett published an exhaustive biography presenting him as the wise and prescient initiator of Britain's naval greatness. He became a patriot. "When Drake went down to the Horn, / England was crowned thereby," wrote Rudyard Kipling. When (and if) Drake reached Cape Horn he was not working for England's glory but for his own and his investors' profit, but that did not prevent him becoming a totemic figure to sentimental nationalists. "The soul of Francis Drake was England," wrote Noyes; he was "England to all English hearts."

Castile (latterly Spain) had the Cid: England (latterly Britain) had Drake. Two great imperial powers adopted as their heroes men who in their lifetimes were shameless bandits. It is no coincidence. To his contemporaries and to most of his posterity the Cid's errantry, his independence of any established authority, and his freedom to go where he pleased and make of himself what he willed is the most exhilarating aspect of his story. So Drake's carelessness of law and convention is the essence of his appeal. He is the presiding genius of Charles Kingsley's *Westward Ho!*, a novel disgraceful for its xenophobia, its rabid anti-Catholicism, and the startlingly perverse treatment of the female characters, but which earned the enormous popularity it enjoyed in the 1850s and in most of the succeeding century with its seductive idealization of the Elizabethan adventures and of their "mighty conquests achieved with the laughing recklessness of boys at play." Kingsley presents them as the precursors of the nineteenth-century empire-builders, and Drake in particular is held up for admiration. Over the famous game of bowls he mutters to Hawkins that he intends to "let Orlando-Furioso-punctilio-fire-eaters go and get their knuckles rapped" while he lags behind the fleet in the hope of prizes. He is a scavenger. ("Where the carcass is, is our place, eh?" agrees Hawkins.) He has a deplorable lack of public spirit, but he is a hero for all that. "Of such captains as Franky Drake Heaven never makes but one at a time; and if we lose him, goodbye to England's luck." He is another of the heroes defined by their uniqueness, the "only man alive" who can do what he can do.

Like Cato, and much more fittingly, Drake stands for freedom. Many imperialists have sincerely believed that by subjecting other peoples to their rule they were setting them free, of other oppressors or of their own ignorance and backwardness. Drake, the pirate, unreachable by any law as he sailed around the world, autonomous and uncontrollable in the little ship of which he was absolute master, is a potent figure of liberty, and as it happens a not inapposite patron for imperialists devoted to the taking of that which did not belong to them. In his legend Spain and its dominions are, first and foremost, a domain of unfreedom where a rigid religious orthodoxy and an autocratic monarch punish anyone who lays claim to independence with gruesome tortures and with death. England—contrasted with this somber, oppressive enemy—becomes in its own self-congratulatory literature the epitome of all that is creative and permissive of individual liberty. With its little island territory and its little ships, it is an outlaw state like Robin Hood's greenwood, a hideaway for free spirits, and Drake is its personification. Defiantly he refuses an unjust law. Boldly he confronts the mighty oppressor. As he raids the ports of the Spanish Main in Noyes's poem, "There came sounds across the heaving sea / of rending chains."

To point out that what he was actually doing in the Caribbean was liberating not slaves or oppressed native Americans but other people's property is correct but does nothing to undermine his allure. In reality criminality and freedom seldom go together: lawlessness opens the way to oppression. But in the imaginary world of popular legend and national myth the criminal is a free spirit. Like the legendary thief and murderer Robin Hood, like the corsairs and highwaymen of Romantic fiction and poetry, like the gangsters and gunmen of twentieth-century cinema, Drake was and has remained an object of affection and admiration because of, not despite, the fact that the actions for which he is known were socially disruptive, violent, and illegal, excusable only on the shaky grounds that his victims were foreigners, and Catholics to boot.

VI

WALLENSTEIN

When Achilles showed himself, flame-capped and awful, his enemies panicked and died; when he drove into battle, filthy with his victims' blood, the Trojans scattered and fled. Homer's hero was terror incarnate. So was Albrecht Wenzel Eusebius von Wallenstein, Duke of Friedland, the commander in chief of the Holy Roman Emperor's armies during the Thirty Years' War. On the frescoed ceiling of the great audience chamber of his palace in Prague a grim-faced, splendidly accoutred warrior drives a four-horse chariot hurtling through the skies. He is the god of war, or Wallenstein himself, or more likely both, for in the minds of his contemporaries Wallenstein was the war's genius, the personification of the devastating conflict by which Europe was racked. Storm, fire, and horror were reputed to be his accomplices. An eighteenth-century historian wrote: "When all around him fell in ruins, when smoke and dust filled the air, and the moans of mortal agony beat upon the ear, when all grovelled with terror shriekingly on their knees before him and he tore aside his hand from mothers and children who, clinging to him, implored their lives, then speechless satisfaction gleamed upon his face." To his enemies and allies alike he seemed as ruthless as fate. In the words of the great Romantic historian and dramatist Friedrich Schiller, who wrote about him repeatedly: "In the night only, Friedland's star can beam." Darkness was his element, terror his instrument. Observers noted the fearful omens by which the epochs of his life were marked. On the day he assumed command of the emperor's armies Vesuvius erupted; on the night he died, according to witnesses' reports, the town in which he was killed was shaken by a storm so violent no one present could remember ever having seen the like.

It's an unhappy land that needs heroes, wrote Brecht, and seventeenth-century Germany was a land in which unhappiness was endemic, in which the kind of desperation which had led the Athenians to see in the treacherous Alcibiades an omnipotent savior gripped peasants and princes alike. An English preacher named Edmund Calamy described it as "a Golgotha, a place of dead men's skulls . . . a field of blood." From 1618 until 1648 central Europe was a battlefield, convulsed by the sequence of conflicts—nationalist uprisings, foreign invasions, peasant revolts, sectarian killings, power struggles between princes—known collectively as the Thirty Years' War. "Some nations are chastised with the sword," wrote Calamy, "others with famine, others with the man-destroying plague. But poor Germany hath been sorely whipped with all these three iron whips at the same time, and for above twenty years space."

Half-starved armies of uncertain allegiance traversed the territories of the Holy Roman Empire, alternately dodging and pursuing each other through the brief summer campaigning season and in winter descending on the towns or roaming across the countryside in search of food, shelter, and loot. In their wake they left burned-out villages, ruined crops, and, where there had once been viable communities, isolated groups of destitute civilians. Peasants, preferring looting to being looted, abandoned their smallholdings and turned soldier. "One may travel ten miles without seeing man or beast," wrote a contemporary observer. "In all the villages the houses are filled with corpses, carcasses intermingled, slain by pest and hunger and partially devoured by wolves, dogs and carrion-crows, because there is no one left to bury them." It was the worst of times, a period when the Four Horsemen of the Apocalypse stalked the land, an era of violent action so chaotic and futile that it felt like stasis.

Hans Jakob von Grimmelshausen, author of the novel *Simplicissimus the Vagabond*, the one masterpiece to emerge from the war, has Jupiter (not the king of Olympus but a deranged, flea-tormented tramp of the same name) prophesy the coming of "such a great hero that he will need no soldiers, and yet will reform the world." The advent of such a redeemer was yearned for. As the years dragged by it came to seem that only a superman could do what battles and diplomacy seemed equally impotent to achieve and effect the transition from a war which generated nothing but more war to a productive peace. Several candidates for the role presented themselves. "Numerous were the dark hero forms that loomed out of the chaos of blood and fire," wrote a nineteenth-century German historian of the war. Darkest and most imposing of them all was Wallenstein, who rose from comparative obscurity to become generalissimo over all the imperial troops, who was stripped of his office when his power grew so great that even the emperor he served came to fear him, who was recalled when those who had conspired to get rid of him became persuaded that he was the only man alive capable of saving the empire, and who was eventually murdered in his nightshirt, deserted by all but a handful of the tens of thousands of men he had commanded, so ill he could barely stand but still so menacingly charismatic that the emperor felt it needful to have prayers read in all the churches in Vienna invoking divine assistance for the work of assassinating him.

Heroes are not necessarily amiable. Fear is an emotion as overwhelming as love, and a man capable of inspiring it may be accorded as much respect, as much devotion even, as a hero of a milder sort. Alcibiades had beauty and charm, Cato integrity, the Cid munificence, and Drake a saucy wit, but they all shared a further quality, a menacing edge that made others, friends as well as enemies, uneasy. In Wallenstein that quality was paramount. It was the danger he apparently embodied that impressed his contemporaries, moving them first to accord him power unprecedented within his society for a man of his origins, and eventually to kill him. The Greeks valued Achilles for his awesome capacity for violence, not only because it was useful to them when turned against their enemies, but also because it was so intrinsically impressive. They described it as being a divine attribute. In the seventeenth century Wallenstein's contemporaries were more apt to see his fearsomeness as diabolical, but they were still awed by it, and ready to depend on it for the safekeeping of their state.

Wallenstein was a truly frightening man. He was not—no mere mortal could have been—the omnipotent fury that his admirers and detractors alike imagined him, but he sometimes came near it. As a teenage student he was nicknamed "Mad Wallenstein." He stabbed a fellow student in the leg. He thrashed a servant so brutally the university authorities stepped in and ordered him to pay compensation to the boy's family. He terrorized a professor, yelling outside his house at dead of night, smashing his windows, and attempting to break down his door. He was one of a group who set upon a local man in the street and killed him.

As an adult he used his rage, holding himself tightly in check until such times as it suited him to be terrible. He was not a sacker of cities. He was responsible for no notorious massacre. He always preferred exhausting or outmaneuvering a hostile army to slaughtering it. In an age when what would now be considered war crimes or atrocities were commonplace, he was probably less guilty than most of his peers. Count

Khevenhüller, the courtier and annalist who observed his career at first hand, praised the discipline in his armies: "he maintained exemplary order, so that the land was not wasted or burned, nor the people driven from hut and house." Yet to his contemporaries and to posterity alike an aura of suppressed violence, of potentially devastating destructiveness seemed to hang about him. Stories circulated demonstrating his ruthlessness. A soldier accused of looting was to be hanged. The man protested his innocence. "Let him be hanged guiltless then," said Wallenstein. "The guilty will tremble so much the more."

In private he was fiercely irritable. He is said to have stabbed a page who disturbed him against his orders, and to have had a man executed for waking him too early. When, on the last night of his life, his assassins came clattering up the stairs to kill him they were met by a servant terrified not by their grim faces and clashing weapons but by the thought of how angry his master would be at the intrusion. A nineteenth-century scholar, contemplating his portrait, thought that he bore "the dark and sinister aspect of a man whose hands have been imbrued in blood, whose seared conscience hesitates at no means, however base, cruel, or unholy, for the attainment of his purpose." That idea of Wallenstein was already current in his lifetime. In attempting to justify his murder his rivals in the imperial court were to accuse him of conspiring to butcher not only the emperor but the entire imperial family, and to burn Vienna to the ground. Such was his supposed cruelty, the capacity for destruction ascribed to him, and the enormity of his imagined ambition.

He was born into a noble but impoverished Bohemian family. Orphaned while still a child, he was brought up by guardians. Bohemia was a part of the Holy Roman Empire but it had its own separate history and venerable culture. Wallenstein's first language was Czech, his second Italian. After his death he was likened to Arminius, the tribal chieftain who dared to challenge Rome and who, Germanized as Hermann, was the totemic hero of German nationalism, but in his lifetime the German princes saw him as an untrustworthy foreigner, an alien whose interests might well conflict with their own. In fact, as a man with several far-flung homes in none of which he spent much time, he seems to have felt few sentimental ties to any place or nation.

He was born a Protestant, but in his late teens he converted to Catholicism. According to Count Khevenhüller his conversion was occasioned by a miracle. He was dozing over a book when he toppled out of an upstairs window and was saved from certain death by the Virgin Mary, who caught him in her arms and wafted him gently down to earth. The story may have been developed to confound critics who doubted his commitment to the Church. It strikingly resembles those told about another, more celebrated defenestration, the incident commonly identified as the beginning of the Thirty Years' War, when Bohemian nationalists threw two imperial agents from the windows of Hradcany Castle in Prague. On that occasion, according to a contemporary account "several devout and trustworthy people . . . saw the most serene Virgin Mary catch [the imperial delegate Count Martinic] in the air with her cloak" and set him down so gently "it was as if he was merely sitting down . . . despite his corpulent body." (Protestant Bohemian sources, by contrast, reported that Martinic and his fellow victim Slavata owed their soft landing to a handy dungheap.) Wallenstein, later a notorious skeptic, responded to his own miraculous escape with a markedly un-Christian blend of pride and solipsism. His first biographer, Gualdo Priorato (who served under him and whose *Life* was first published in 1643) saw it as inspiring his faith, not in the Almighty, but in his own status as one of the elect: "He believed himself reserved for extraordinary achievements; and from that moment made it the study of his life to penetrate the future and discover the high destiny that waited him."

Wallenstein was one of many Bohemian noblemen who returned to the old faith in the first two decades of the century and thereby greatly improved their secular career prospects. At the height of his power as generalissimo to a zealously Catholic emperor Wallenstein was to come to be seen as the sword bearer of the Counter-Reformation, the protector of the Holy Roman Church as well as of the Holy Roman Empire, but he himself consistently denied that he was fighting a religious war. Some of his contemporaries doubted whether he was a Christian at all.

The Emperor Ferdinand II, whom he served for most of his adult life, was a sectarian zealot. As a nineteen-year-old, Archduke Ferdinand had made a pilgrimage to Loreto, and there vowed to drive all heretics from his realm. On his return to his duchy of Styria he expelled all Lutheran preachers. He prohibited Protestant worship on pain of death. He ordered the burning of ten thousand books, and gave the citizens three weeks to either go to mass or leave the country. His councillors, foreseeing economic disaster and probable civil war, begged him to reconsider but his resolution, according to a contemporary chronicle, was "as a block of marble." "Better a desert than a country full of heretics," he said. Thousands went into exile, the great astronomer Johannes Kepler (later Wallenstein's protégé) among them. Some forty thousand, less stalwart or less devout, converted. Lesser lords took their cue from their ruler. Protestants told horror stories of Catholic masters using hounds to drive their vassals to mass, or holding down those who still refused to swallow the host and forcing their jaws open with pincers.

That was not Wallenstein's way. Protestants were always welcome in his armies and were trusted with high commands. He went through the forms of attending mass and of ascribing his successes to God's favor, but an imperial councillor alleged that he "reeks of atheism and troubles not about God." He "often utters the most horrendous blasphemies and oaths," reported another associate, and the Duke of Weimar rejected his offer of an alliance on the grounds that "he who does not trust in God can never be trusted by men." He was fascinated by, and credulous of, astrology, building observatories on his estates and commissioning horoscopes which he scrutinized for clues to the future. When driven from office in 1630 he told the emperor's messengers he had expected nothing better: he had seen that his downfall was foretold by the stars. Towards the end of his life he began (like Drake) to acquire the sinister reputation of a wizard, a dabbler in black arts. Kepler, who was one of the several astrologers who formed part of his household over the years, wrote that he was inclined "to alchemy, sorcery, incantation, communion with spirits." Like Rodrigo Díaz, another figurehead of the Counter-Reformation, he was one whose faith in signs and omens is well attested but whose claim to be considered a good Christian is doubtful.

Religion was one of the numerous causes at issue in the Thirty Years' War. Sectarian hostility pervaded the empire, in which each petty state had its established religion and its religious minorities, and it was complicated at every point by secular politics. The world through which Wallenstein moved was one, like Cato's Rome, whose political institutions failed to match the actual distribution of power. The Holy Roman Emperor was nominally the ruler of all central Europe from the Baltic southward to the Alps, from the French border eastwards to the domains of the Turkish sultan. The emperor did not, supposedly, inherit his title— he was chosen by the seven electors, four of them secular rulers of states within the empire, three of them archbishops—but for nearly two centuries every emperor had been a Hapsburg. Under the wavering control of these emperors a multitude of lesser rulers held sway in states whose constitutions and whose political and religious histories were bewilderingly diverse. There were free cities administered by elected councils. There were hereditary principalities. There were archbishoprics and bishoprics, duchies, margravates, kingdoms. Each of these multifarious states had its own governmental institutions, estates or diets, oligarchic councils or autocratic ministers. Each jealously insisted on preserving its own right of self-determination (collectively known as the German liberties) from any encroachment by the centralizing power of the emperor.

A state's religious policy was often ambivalent. In several places a Catholic prince had to tussle with a predominantly Protestant diet. And sectarian differences tangled with class conflict: the nobility was predominantly Catholic, the bourgeoisie Protestant. Each small polity was linked to others within larger, looser institutions. In the circles of the empire, established in the early sixteenth century, geographically contiguous states banded together for purposes of defense. More recently the Catholic princes had formed a league to defend their interests, and the Protestants a union to promote theirs. It would have been a bewilderingly complex situation, even had it been a fixed and self-consistent one, and it was not. Seventeenth-century states were not closed systems. Ties of kinship cut across and contradicted local political loyalties; so did religious affiliations. One man might hold several offices and contrary identities. When King Christian of Denmark led an army into the imperial territory of Pomerania, he did so, or so he claimed, not as a foreign invader but as the Duke of Schleswig-Holstein, a member of the Lower Saxon Circle with a legitimate interest in events in the region. There were states, the empire itself among them, without armies. More disruptively, there were armies without states, like that of the formidably successful mercenary Count Mansfeld, armies which functioned like landless states with their own hierarchies, their own economies, their vast populations; lacking only *lebensraum*, they would settle on others' territory like monstrous parasites. The empire was a labyrinth (a word which recurs in Wallenstein's correspondence). It was a world where chronic instability lapsed repeatedly into violence on a massive scale. It was also a world which presented unlimited opportunities for a man of sufficient energy and ruthlessness, talent and luck.

It wasn't until he was nearly forty that Wallenstein began to attract the world's notice. In his twenties he served the emperor with modest distinction in campaigns against the Turks and the Venetians, and he married. His first wife was a widow with a large fortune and estates in Moravia (now, like Bohemia, part of the Czech Republic). Legend has it that she was old and ugly, and that she nearly killed him by secretly administering too strong a dose of a love potion, an aphrodisiac rendered necessary by her unseemly lust and lack of charms. The story sounds like misogynist tosh: she was only three years older than Wallenstein. She died five years after their marriage. A decade later he was to found a monastery in her honor, and to have her coffin reburied there, a gesture which suggests that he was at least properly appreciative of the part her fortune played in procuring him a place in the world.

He was cautious and canny and he had a sharp eye for the main chance. He attended the imperial court in Vienna, as was necessary for an ambitious man. There he conducted himself in the style of a great nobleman, dispensing bribes and rewards with notable munificence; it was recorded with respect that he never gave less than a thousand gulden. But according to Khevenhüller "when he had exhausted his store he returned home and remained there until he had amassed enough to come to court again." So he bided his time and nurtured both his fortune and his reputation until, in 1618, heralded by the ominous appearance of a comet, the long war began.

When the representatives of the Bohemian Estates initiated hostilities by tossing Counts Martinic and Slavata into either a dungheap or the cloak of the Serene Virgin Mary, Wallenstein showed no sympathy for his compatriots' struggle to establish their political independence and religious freedom. He was by then attached to the court of Ferdinand of Styria, who shortly thereafter became emperor. A Protestant Bohemian by birth, Wallenstein had become a Catholic Imperialist by choice. Achilles, Alcibiades, and Rodrigo Díaz all threatened to shatter the political structures within which they had grown too great. So too, much later, did Wallenstein (or so his killers believed), but for most of his active career he was to work with prodigious energy and success to build up the state he served, to make the empire the great power it was designed to be. His detractors were to say that he did so only for his own aggrandizement, but even if Wallenstein ever did aspire to make the great political and military engine he created his own, that would not, in itself, have been monstrous. The office of emperor, after all, was an elective one. Military men, from Julius Caesar to Wallenstein's contemporary Oliver Cromwell, have achieved ultimate power often enough. Napoleon Bonaparte, the self-made emperor who married a daughter of the imperial house of Austria, asked on St. Helena to be sent histories of the Thirty Years' War. He must have found much to interest him in the story of Wallenstein.

In November 1618 Ferdinand, Wallenstein's master, sent troops into

Bohemia to put down the uprising. Wallenstein was at home on his wife's estates in the adjoining state of Moravia. When the fighting spread into Moravia the following year he found himself obliged to make a hard choice. Wallenstein held a colonel's commission in the Moravian militia. The Moravian diet sympathized with the Bohemian rebels. He did not. He contemplated mounting an imperialist coup d'état in Moravia. That proving impracticable, he resolved to defect. At the head of forty muske-teers he forced his way into the treasury for the district where he was stationed and demanded its entire contents, threatening to hang the treasurer. The money was carried out and loaded onto wagons, along with all the ammunition he could seize. Wallenstein led his men through Hungary to the imperial court at Vienna. Like Drake before him he com-mitted what its victims would see as a felonious act; and like Drake he brought enough money with him to ensure that he would be well received. Ferdinand was more scrupulous and politically less secure than Drake's queen. He felt obliged to hand back to the Moravian authorities the wagonloads of iron-hinged chests full of coinage that Wallenstein had stolen, but he wrote privately that Wallenstein had done well.

It was Wallenstein's first betrayal, or, viewed from the other side, his first act of distinguished loyalty. In 1619 it was impossible to be a Bohemian or Moravian subject of the Holy Roman Empire without being, from at least one point of view, a traitor. In Moravia, his country by marriage and his home for the previous ten years, and his native Bohemia alike Wallenstein was vilified. He was tried in his absence by the Moravian diet and found guilty of "vicious treason, unmindful of the dic-tates of honour." He was banished, and all his estates were confiscated. Count Thurn, leader of the Bohemian rebels, called him a turncoat and a pirate: "There sits the proud beast, hath lost his honour, goods and chat-tels, besides his soul, and doth he not do penance is like to go to Purgatory." To Czech patriots his offense was unforgivable. Two cen-turies later Frantisek Palacky, the nationalist historian, was shown a statue of Wallenstein. He gazed at it for a few moments and then turned away, muttering, "Scoundrel!"

In 1620, at the invitation of the rebellious nobility, the Protestant elector of the Palatinate, Frederick, accepted the title of king of Bohemia in defi-ance of the emperor. Accompanied by his wife, Elizabeth (daughter of

James I of England), he established his court in Prague. His reign lasted only a few months. In November 1620 the combined armies of the emperor and the Catholic elector of Bavaria defeated the Bohemians at the battle of the White Mountain, Frederick and his family fled ignominiously, and Hapsburg rule was reestablished.

Wallenstein was not at the White Mountain but he was in Prague only days after Frederick's defeat, ready to participate in the carve-up of Bohemia. All who had taken part in the rebellion were tried and punished. Twenty-seven were executed, their heads cut off one after another by a single swordsman in a sickening four-and-a-half-hour ceremony outside Prague's town hall, during which Wallenstein was responsible for keeping order. Twelve of the heads were displayed above the Charles Bridge; they were to rot there for ten years. But what the emperor and his servants wanted more even than the satisfaction afforded by such gruesome spectacles was the Bohemian aristocracy's property. A Saxon agent in Prague reported that "all they crave is money and blood." Wallenstein was one of those responsible for wringing the maximum possible quantity of both commodities (especially money) out of the defeated rebels.

By the middle of the 1620s Wallenstein was an enormously rich man. He was an industrious and energetic manager of his own estates. When he turned his back on Moravia he temporarily lost his properties there, but he later recovered and promptly sold them. Meanwhile he had evidently found a safer place to deposit some of his valuables: in 1620 he paid for a large tract of land by selling some silver tableware he had stored in Vienna. He was not above engaging in trade: he sold quantities of Moravian wine in Prague. But there were quicker, less laborious ways of making a fortune. Wallenstein began with some assets, and Bohemia after the rebels' defeat was a place where assets could be made to breed fast. "He often speculated," wrote Khevenhüller, and his speculations were neither reckless nor impulsive. "He was very active and discreet and had spies everywhere."

He also made money by literally making money. He was a member of a syndicate granted a monopoly over the purchase of silver and the right to mint coin. Under the syndicate's control, and to its members' handsome profit, the number of gulden made from half a pound of silver rose from nineteen to seventy-nine. The results were, predictably, disastrous. In an ever-accelerating cycle of devaluation and inflation the Bohemian economy was effectively destroyed. Savings were rendered worthless. Wage earners became destitute. Schools and universities closed. Craftsmen and tradesmen subsisted by barter. "We will not sell good meat for bad coin," proclaimed the butchers. "It was then, for the first time," wrote the Czech Pavel Stransky in 1633, "that we learned from experience that neither plague nor war, nor hostile foreign incursions into our land, neither pillage nor fire, could do so much harm to good people as frequent changes in the value of money." Wallenstein, unperturbed, made his profit and established some useful contacts. One of his fellow members of the syndicate was the brilliant Belgian financier Hans de Witte, whose moneylending, banking, and dealing had brought him contacts all over Europe. De Witte soon became closely associated with Wallenstein, so closely that when Wallenstein fell from power he killed himself.

Crassus, Cato's adversary, laid the foundations of his fortune by buying up at rock-bottom prices the confiscated property of Sulla's victims and then converted his wealth into power by lending unrepayably vast sums of money to the most influential men in Rome. Some seventeen hundred years later in Bohemia Wallenstein followed his lead. After their victory the imperialists confiscated all the land and money of the leading Bohemian rebels. Those whose guilt was judged to be of a lesser degree were required to hand over half, a third, or a quarter of what they owned. Not, however, that they were allowed to keep the remainder. The imperial officers "bought" the rest of their possessions at prices decided by those same officers, and paid for it all in the new devalued coinage. All of these estates were then available for sale to those whom the emperor deemed worthy.

The suppression of the Bohemian rebellion had been catastrophically expensive. In 1620 Wallenstein, probably backed by de Witte, offered the emperor the loan of the colossal sum of 60,000 gulden. As security he asked for the estate of Gitschin, which comprised three towns, sixty-seven villages, four manors, thirteen farms, and numerous breweries and workshops. The emperor first demurred, then agreed. Again and again the process was repeated. As security for "loans" to the emperor, which would never be repaid, Wallenstein acquired one after another of the rebels' confiscated estates. In February 1621 he volunteered to provide a garrison, at his own expense, for the fortress of Friedland, whose owner had fled to Poland. In June, after advancing a further 58,000 gulden to the emperor, he became Friedland's proprietor. By 1623, whether by purchase or by accepting land as security against loans, he had made himself the owner of a quarter of all Bohemia.

As Wallenstein's property increased so did his status. In 1622, he was appointed military governor of Prague, which made him, after the imperial viceroy, the most important man in Bohemia. He began to build his vast and somber palace in the city, flattening twenty-six houses, four gardens, and a lime kiln to make way for it. He used troops to evict those who refused to move. Some of the houses were demolished with their inhabitants still inside. The palace's public aspect is a handsome Italianate façade, boasting thirty-six high arched windows and a grand portal. Imposing as it is, this front gives no indication of the scale of the grounds and additional buildings which stretch away behind it. A complex of courtyards and enclosed gardens with stabling for three hundred horses, a walled park, and a covered way to the nearby monastery of St. Thomas, the palace was another labyrinth, at the heart of which Wallenstein lurked, insulated by the spacious grandeur with which he had surrounded himself from the clamor of the world outside.

He was forty years old. As the last and most momentous decade of his life began he was well past his physical prime. Contemporary portraits show a stern, pale, strongly sculpted face: hair receding from a high, furrowed brow, a long straight nose, high cheekbones, full red lips, a look of dour watchfulness. He is described as being exceptionally tall. The delinquent "Mad Wallenstein" had matured into a man who intimidated not so much by his rages (though they were still notorious) as by his reserve. He had no confidants, no advisers. He was famously unreadable. "None but God delves to the bottom of his heart," wrote one who knew him. Kepler had noted that the gloomy planet Saturn had been in the ascendant at his birth, inducing a tendency to "melancholy, always vigilant thinking," and indicating that he would be "harsh to those beneath him . . . usually silent . . . of an assiduous, restless temper."

He had an intelligence so incisive, so vigorous that the shilly-shallying of others irritated him almost beyond bearing. He abhorred futile words, his own or others'. Once, when a delegate visited him with an unwelcome proposal when he was ill in bed, he hid his face in his pillow and stopped his ears with both hands. He had no time to fritter way, no taste for frivolity. "He had a marked aversion to regular court jesters, as well as to buffoons of every kind," noted Gualdo Priorato. In an era when even the highest-ranking grandees in Europe opened their letters to each other with paragraph upon paragraph of courteous salutation, he addressed all his correspondents, up to and including the emperor, with a brusqueness close to lèse-majesté. "The Duke of Friedland doth incline in thoughts and manners to be somewhat rough," commented the emperor.

He was not a committee man. He disdained to justify himself, to explain himself, to listen to others' arguments. "When he commanded," according to a French tract published shortly after his death, "no man must open his mouth but execute his order without reply." One of his most frequent rejoinders (in Italian, his second language, and his favorite for expressions of emotion) was "*non si può*"—it can't be done. He seldom deigned to explain to those whose requests he thus brushed aside why it couldn't, even if the inquirer was his imperial master. When the representatives of the city of Magdeburg came to implore him to reduce the levy he had imposed upon them, he interrupted their petition rudely: "I cannot haggle. I am no trader." "I have no longer any use for the dean," he wrote of a cleric who had balked at some too-summary order. "He wants to be supplicated. That I neither care nor am accustomed to do." In 1619, when one of his officers rode up alongside his horse to remonstrate against his astonishing order to lead the Moravian militia out of Moravia, Wallenstein silenced the man with a single barked-out word, drew his sword and killed him.

He was not incommunicative. At home in Gitschin he would write ten or twelve letters a day in his own hand, over and above the far greater number dictated to secretaries. On campaign his output was no less; his inexhaustible energies were never fully occupied by what was happening in the here and now, even when the business to hand was a battle on which the fate of all Europe might hang. As indefatigable and as attentive to detail as Cato had been, he controlled, even at long distance and when absent for months or even years on end, every facet of his property's management. As he drove the emperor's enemies out of Silesia he took the time to write to his agent ordering that silkworks be established on his estate and Italian weavers brought to work there. One the eve of his conclusive campaign against King Christian of Denmark he sent orders that a hundred lime trees be procured for an avenue in his garden. Shortly before his momentous encounter with King Gustavus II Adolphus at Lützen he wrote to the supervisor of buildings on his estates urging him to have tiles baked so that an entire town could be reroofed: "It is our desire that nowhere shall shingle roofs obtain." But, voluminous though they are, his letters are essentially functional. To his subordinates he issues orders. To his political masters he reports his movements. With

Count Karl von Harrach, the eminent courtier who was his second father-in-law and who probably came closer than anyone else ever did to being his friend, he exchanged information.

As a young man he had frequented the court, as was necessary for a man on the make. But once he was in position of power he stayed away for longer and longer intervals. Like the Cid of the *Poema*, a man of action contemptuous of effete silk-slippered lordlings, he was riled by the airs and graces of those of superior hereditary rank but inferior achievements. He was impatient of the rigmarole by which the gradations of social and political hierarchy were marked, even when it was designed to honor him. He disliked being bowed to or flattered or fawned upon. "He was not pleased that anyone should stand to salute him, nor that anybody should behold or look on him as he passed," wrote a contemporary. If someone addressed him overceremoniously he would abruptly turn away. And if he was irked by deference to himself, he abhorred being required to defer to others. He avoided having to humble himself before those who could claim to be his superiors by refusing to see them. On his way to court in 1626 he fell ill, and was obliged to stay for nearly a month in a wretched inn in an out-of-the-way village. The illness, whether psychosomatic or assumed, certainly seems to have been connected with his reluctance to expose himself to courtiers' games. "I have a harder fight with certain ministers than with the enemy," he wrote. At the time he died it was seven years since he had last been in Vienna, the imperial capital, six years since he had laid eyes on the emperor whose commander in chief he was.

Immured in his palace he awed the public not by spectacular appearances, but by his absence and invisibility. He wanted neither to see nor be seen by hoi polloi. It was not easy to gain access to him. Where possible he liked to observe a man covertly before granting him an audience. The tribulations of the elector of Brandenburg's envoy, Count Bertram von Pfuel, were typical. In his desperate attempts to obtain a few minutes' conversation with Wallenstein, von Pfuel lay in wait for his carriage on Prague's Charles Bridge and thrust a letter through the window as it passed. He joined the press of noblemen who stood all day by the entrance gate to Wallenstein's palace, hoping to catch the great man's attention as he returned home. He sweated for hours and hours in anterooms. At last he received an invitation to dinner, but was seated nowhere near Wallenstein. He was granted, or so he thought, an appointment, only to see Wallenstein's carriage roll away from the gate just as he arrived. Another appointment. Again von Pfuel arrived to see his quarry in the act of escaping him. With reckless temerity he asked to be allowed to join Wallenstein in his carriage for the brief journey up to the Castle. Wallenstein consented, but when von Pfuel brought out some notes he declared that he could not abide anything in writing (he, who wrote or dictated dozens of letters a day) and that he had too much on his mind to attend von Pfuel's requests. Those with whom Wallenstein wished to communicate would hear from him in his own time. To force oneself into his presence was to incur his displeasure.

He was as fastidious about what he touched as he was about whom he met. In his household the tablecloths and napkins were only used once. He bathed regularly—to his contemporaries' astonishment—in a silver bath made especially for him in Genoa, or in a tub constructed by a gold-smith from Prague. His dress was magnificent. Tradition has it that he invariably wore black, with just a sash of blood red, an outfit consonant with his fabulous reputation as a sabled prince of darkness, but his tailors' bills reveal his taste for more variety in his sumptuous ostentation: "eigh-teen ells long carmine fringes for His Princely Grace's gloves," "a robe of scarlet thickly edged in carmine and a doublet of red satin." Red—clearly visible across a battlefield—was useful. "In the field," wrote Priorato, who had fought under his command, "his usual dress was a buff or elk-skin coat, red hose, a red scarf, a scarlet cloak and a grey castor hat, adorned with red feathers." He loved blue as well: blue leather tooled in gold to line the walls of his palace in Prague, powder-blue liveries for his scores of pages. It was said that he painted his lips.

He was a harsh but scrupulous employer of servants and commander of soldiers, one who paid promptly and demanded punctilious obedience. According to Schiller he issued an order that all his men were to wear red sashes. "A captain of horse no sooner heard the order than pulling off his gold-embroidered sash, he trampled it under foot. Wallenstein promoted him on the spot." A contemporary writer reports that he preferred his officers to be "men of mean condition" who, owing their elevation to him alone, would therefore be the more devoted to him. But "whosoever sought to enrol in his service was to take very good heed for he dismissed none unless it came of his own accord." His people were to be his absolutely, and preferably forever.

He was already suffering from gout, brought on—or so he be-lieved—by drinking too much wine. Several of his most prominent con-temporaries were sots. King Christian of Denmark was sometimes too

inebriated to deal with matters of state for weeks on end. Elector John
George of Saxony, the most powerful of the German Protestant princes,
was another drunk. "He is a mere brute," said Wallenstein; "see how he
lives." It was an era when what passed for moderate consumption might
well have been enough to damage a person's health. By the time
Wallenstein entered middle age he ate and drank abstemiously, preferring
beer brewed on his own estates to wine and avoiding red meat. But it was
too late to save him from the gout, which was a constant and ever-
worsening trial. Towards the end of his life he had to be carried into battle in a litter. Already, in the early 1620s, he wore fur-lined boots designed
to mitigate the pain in his feet, and he rode with stirrups made of velvet.
Suffering made him irascible. "Our General is in the grip of his gout,"
wrote one of the councillors most friendly towards him, "Hardly one in
the town durst other than whisper in his neighbour's ear lest he disturb
the Prince by the clamour of his speech." He detested noise. In Prague,
and wherever he stayed on his travels, he ordered that all the streets
adjoining his residence be covered with straw to muffle the sound of passing footsteps and closed off with chains to exclude wheeled traffic. No
cock might be permitted to crow in his neighborhood. When he felt
unwell, as he often did, he forbade the ringing of church bells. His officers removed their spurs before entering his presence lest their jingling
irritate him. In his vicinity his attendants crept and murmured. His court
was populous—at the height of his power his household numbered nine
hundred people—but it was not animated. He kept a lavish table for
guests and dependents, but he himself dined meagerly and alone.

Landownership was for him both a business, at which he worked
assiduously, and a pleasure. He disliked dogs—presumptuous, fawning,
noisy creatures—and it is said that when he entered a town he would have
all the strays rounded up and killed. But he took pleasure in animals who
kept to their proper place. In the palace grounds in Prague he had an
aviary built to resemble a marvelous grotto for his collection of exotic
birds, and at Gitschin he kept a zoo, where he liked to admire the red
deer. He was no huntsman, unlike the emperor, and unlike the elector of
Saxony, who claimed to have killed over 150,000 animals. But he was, like
Alcibiades, an enthusiastic breeder of horses, of which he kept hundreds
and on which he spent thousands of gulden. An Irish adventurer describes
his stables, where the mangers were of marble "and by each manger a
spring of clear water to give drink." The warhorse shot under him at the
battle of Lützen he had stuffed and mounted and displayed in his palace
in Prague.

On his vast Bohemian estates he was de facto an independent ruler. At Gitschin he conjured up a brand-new city built to an orderly plan incorporating handsome squares and parks and grand avenues and a massive palace for Wallenstein himself. A contemporary biographer, watching five thousand men at work on the project, compared the scene with the construction of Carthage as described by Virgil. He had his own court, his own executioner, his own councillors and chancellery, and his own governor, Gerhard von Taxis, who stood in for him when he was absent. He might be a warrior but he was always, first and foremost, an administrator. He had farms, mines, industries, and a subject population who were both his labor force and his captive market. No one in his land might drink any but his beer except "if they travel, when now and then a draught must at need be quaffed, though otherwise positively not." Cheese makers were brought from Italy and a tailor from Paris so that Wallenstein could eat Parmesan and wear French fashion without spending cash outside his own domain. He decreed how much butter and cheese his cows should yield; he gave orders that every house was to have a store of water, that by every chimney a ladder was to be kept. He required the burghers of his towns to build their houses "of stone or brick, executed finely and neatly" (order and seemliness were as important to his fastidious mind as productivity). Everything in the realm he had acquired was to be efficient, prosperous, and subservient to him. Golo Mann, a recent biographer, has remarked how often, in his correspondence, the phrase "*für mich*" (for me) recurs. Von Taxis wrote to him once that deposits of a mineral "red in colour," called cinnabar, had been found on his land. Wallenstein responded acidly: "Take me not for such a fool. I know very well what cinnabar is. Let it work for me."

He married his second wife, Isabella von Harrach, in 1623. He was often away from her on campaign but he spoke kindly of her. Letters she wrote to him have survived, and seem genuinely affectionate. Of all the many allegations made against him, none has to do with his sexual conduct, which can probably therefore be assumed (given how many watchers there were eager to discredit him) to have been irreproachable. Kepler had said that Wallenstein would "lack brotherly or marital love" and perhaps he was too dourly self-contained to be other than a little frigid emotionally but he was always solicitous for Isabella's safety and conscious of what was due to her. She bore him a son, who died in infancy, and a daughter.

. . .

Wallenstein had become a great man in Bohemia. It was not enough. Soon after his wedding he made the move which eventually led to him becoming, in his own person, a great European power. The Holy Roman Emperor had no standing army. Ferdinand's realm was geographically enormous, politically ramshackle, threatened by invaders without and dissenters within, and yet he had no regular troops of his own for its defense. In each crisis ad hoc armies were pieced together from local levies and militias (like the Moravian force with which Wallenstein had served), augmented by units recruited at their own expense by ambitious private gentlemen. In 1617, for instance, when the Venetians were besieging Gradisca, Wallenstein had raised a regiment and led it to help relieve the city on the emperor's behalf. These piecemeal and unreliable forces were never enough. The emperor had to depend on the military support of the princes of the empire, who were under no constitutional obligation to use their armies on his behalf and who expected to be well rewarded when they did so. In order to subdue the rebellious Bohemians he had had to call upon the aid of the Elector Maximilian of Bavaria, to whom, by the time the uprising had been put down, he was massively in debt. Without a sufficient army or the money to raise one Ferdinand was dangerously dependent on his subject rulers, and that dependence made nonsense of his supposed authority over them.

Wallenstein saw his need. He must also have seen how tremendous might be the reward to anyone who could supply it. In the spring of 1623 he made the emperor an astounding offer. He, Wallenstein, a private individual albeit a rich one, a nobleman but not from one of the empire's great families, would do what no one else, not even the mighty Hapsburg himself, seemed capable of doing. He would provide the emperor with an army. He had to repeat his offer several times. So unprecedented, so extraordinary was it that the emperor and his ministers were initially suspicious, even afraid.

Schiller was to liken Wallenstein's political opponents to ignorant conjurors who invoke a mighty spirit, "and when he comes, / straight their flesh creeps and quivers, and they dread him / more than the ills 'gainst which they called him up." In Wallenstein's lifetime there were still, supposedly, conjurors abroad in Europe. Half a century earlier John Doughty had told members of Drake's crew that he could summon up spirits, and later in his life Wallenstein was rumored to have the same skill. It was a dangerous gift. A conjuror summoned spirits at his or her peril: in several medieval legends a magician is punished for his impious breaching of the divide between nature and the supernatural when a spirit he has called up proves too potent for him to master, defies him, torments him, and eventually drags him down to Hell. During the sixteenth century a version of those legends began to be told about a Doctor Faustus of Wurttemberg. In the 1580s *The History of the Damnable life and deserved death of Doctor John Faustus* was published first in German and soon thereafter in French and English. Faustus summons up a devil, Mephistopheles, who promises to gratify his every wish for a period of years on condition that at the end of that time he will surrender his soul in payment. It was a compelling story. In England Christopher Marlowe made of it a beautiful and terrible warning of the worthlessness of all pleasure, knowledge, and power in the face of eternal damnation. But the story could be read not only as a parable about an individual's spiritual ordeal, but also as a political allegory. The Athenians, having made Alcibiades commander of the most splendid fighting force ever mustered by a Greek city, immediately recoiled aghast at the danger he constituted—thus empowered—to themselves as well as to their enemies. Alfonso of Castile twice summoned Rodrigo Díaz to his rescue and, having done so, hastened to be rid of him. Wallenstein, a new Mephistopheles, offered his imperial master a superb temptation: the military power to make himself ruler of the best part of Europe in fact as well as in name. Ferdinand hesitated because he and his councillors could all sense the infernal danger of the deal. So far Wallenstein had been a loyal servant of the empire, but Wallenstein at the head of an army on the scale he proposed would be a servant with terrifying powers, and there was no knowing what diabolical price he might eventually exact for his service.

The promised army, which Wallenstein grandly called his "armada," was to be no piffling and ephemeral task force. There was the question of how it was to be financed. "Actions which are great in themselves," Niccolò Machiavelli had written, "always seem to bring more glory than blame, of whatever kind they are." Acting accordingly, Wallenstein told Ferdinand and his councillors that though he could not provide for an army of twenty thousand men, one of fifty thousand would sustain itself. The stench of sulfur was growing unmistakable. Some of the expenses Wallenstein would pay, thus placing the emperor even further in his debt, but he could not possibly pay them all. Crassus had said that no man was rich until he could afford his own army, but though Wallenstein was very rich indeed, even by Crassus's standards, neither he, nor probably any private individual in Europe at the time, was rich enough to pay and provision fifty thousand men. What he meant by his gnomic claim was that the larger the army, the more effective an instrument of terror it would be, and the more efficiently it would be able to extort the cash and food and material it needed from the civilian populations of the emperor's enemies and, if necessary, from the emperor's subjects. "War," says a character in the great dramatic trilogy Schiller based on Wallenstein's story, "must nourish war."

Ferdinand wavered; Wallenstein, peremptory as ever, threatened to withdraw. "I have made the offer of myself, to serve his Majesty, and this I will most loyally carry out. But if I see that time is wilfully thrown away . . . then I will enter no such labyrinth where my honour must be sacrificed." His impatience was effective. In June 1625 he was appointed overall commander of all the imperial troops and given a title appropriate to his new power, that of the Duke of Friedland (the name by which he was thenceforward normally known to his contemporaries). The vision painted on the ceiling of the great hall in Prague was to be realized. Wallenstein's apotheosis from mortal magnate to divine (or diabolical) warlord was begun.

He was ready. His offer had not been made impetuously or without forethought. Within a week his army numbered over twenty thousand. By summer's end he had his fifty thousand men. It was a time when dragon's teeth sprouted faster than wheat, when it was easier to call up an army than it was to bring in a harvest. The empire was full of unemployed foreign fighters, men from England, Scotland, and Ireland, from the plains of northern Italy, from Croatia and Hungary, men who for a variety of reasons had been unable to find a livelihood at home. There were those who descended on warring Germany in search of adventure, like the English gentleman Sir James Turner, who wrote that "a restless desire entered my mind to be if not an actor, at least a spectator of these wars." And for each of these Hotspurs there was a host of the kind of riffraff Falstaff might have recruited, men like those in Francis Drake's crew, the "company of desperate bankrupts that could not live in their country without the spoil of that as others had gotten by the sweat of their brows." They changed sides frequently. Turner, who fought for Denmark and Sweden, "swallowed without chewing, in Germany, a very dangerous maxim, which military men there too much follow, which was that so we serve our master honestly, it is no matter what master we serve." After a battle it was usual for the survivors of the defeated army to join the victor's and fight on alongside their former adversaries. They were not idealists serving a cause, or patriots doing their duty: they were hired killers trying to save their skins and scrape together a living under any master they could find.

The living they found in Germany was insecure. Soldiers went hungry as often as the civilian populace did. Wallenstein's proposal, to create and keep in being—year in, year out—an army substantial enough to deter or otherwise to meet any uprising or attack was startlingly novel. The usual practice was to demobilize an army as soon as the immediate danger was past, or at the end of the summer's campaigning season, whichever was the sooner, leaving the countryside aswarm with men, all of them violent by profession and by practice and with no legitimate way of getting a livelihood. A soldier's life was a harsh one, and likely to be short. There were no medical corps, no field hospitals. When he fought the Swedes before Nuremberg Wallenstein rode through the lines tossing gold coins to the wounded so that they might buy themselves food once they had been, as they inevitably would be, abandoned. King Gustavus II Adolphus, marching back over the battlefield weeks later, was sickened to see those who had survived so long "famished and untended, crawling among the bodies of dead men and beasts." But, grim though the soldiers' life might be, it offered at least a chance of survival. As the wars lasted longer and spread wider, eroding the structures of civilian life, the indigenous population joined the ranks of the homeless mercenaries. A peasant who had lost his crops, his hut, his horse to looters had little choice but to try fighting himself. Throughout the Thirty Years' War, whatever else may have been in short supply—whether hard cash or horses, bread or iron—there was never any scarcity of food for powder.

Five years later those who clamored for Wallenstein's dismissal were to accuse him of having burdened the empire with an army of monstrous magnitude, and at a time, moreover, when the emperor had no need of it. But although there was not exactly a war on, there were enemies to confront. The Protestant princes of the Lower Saxon Circle, restive under their Catholic emperor, had called upon King Christian of Denmark to act as their commander in chief. Other powers—England, Sweden, Holland, and France—had encouraged him to accept and to play the part aggressively. By the time Wallenstein was ready to march the northern reaches of the empire were full of Danish troops. There was an ever-present possibility that Bethlen Gabor, the prince of Transylvania, might strike towards Vienna from the southeast. There was also an army led by Ernst von Mansfeld moving eastward into the empire from the Netherlands. Count Mansfeld was a mercenary warlord, a latter-day Cid, who was accustomed to place his army at the disposal of the highest bidder. On this occasion his sponsors were the Dutch and the English, each of whom had reasons for wishing to undermine Hapsburg power.

Wallenstein was the imperial general, but he was not operating alone.

He was working in alliance with Maximilian, elector of Bavaria, who had subdued Bohemia for the emperor. For the rest of Wallenstein's life Maximilian was to be a major character in his story, as colleague and rival, political ally and private enemy. A nobleman and hereditary ruler, he was one who, unlike the new general, had been born great. He was the Emperor Ferdinand's brother-in-law and senior by five years and, like Ferdinand, he was a fervid Catholic. He wore a hair shirt beneath his robes of state and had made a vow, written in his own blood, to dedicate his life to the service of the Virgin Mary. But besides being the most potent of the Catholic imperialists he was also, and always primarily, archduke of Bavaria, more concerned to protect his own territory than the Hapsburg hereditary lands around Vienna, and more interested in the aggrandizement of his own dynasty than the protection of Ferdinand's. His interests did not exactly coincide with those of the emperor; they were often directly in conflict with those of the emperor's new commander in chief, who was in the process of usurping Maximilian's own role—one fruitful in both wealth and honor—as the emperor's military protector.

It was an age when crowned kings still led their armies into battle, but Maximilian, like Ferdinand, preferred to delegate. His commander in chief was General Johann Tserclaes von Tilly, sixty-six years old in 1625 and as full of battle honors as he was of years. Tilly and Wallenstein cooperated tolerably well, though Tilly knew and resented the fact that his junior associate outshone and outmaneuvered him. Thrasybulus to Wallenstein's Alcibiades, he bitterly observed how the other was celebrated for victories he himself had made possible: "No matter how hard I labour they let me gnaw a few bones while others [meaning Wallenstein] pass through the door pushed open by me and enjoy the meat." Wallenstein, blithely condescending, habitually referred to Tilly as "the good old man."

In October 1625 the two generals met, only to separate again in search of territory in which their armies could wait for spring. As Wallenstein's troops—followed, as all contemporary armies were, by a train of women and children and sutlers and servants which doubled its size— moved northward, the chief magistrate of a town they passed wrote, "God help the place where they should lay their winter quarters!"

A seventeenth-century army on the march was a terrifying phenomenon, and not only to its ostensible enemies. Armies carried disease with them—typhus, bubonic plague, something deadly known as "the Hungarian sickness." Pursuing Count Mansfeld once, in three weeks Wallenstein lost three-quarters of the twenty thousand men with whom he set out to exposure or sickness. How many of the civilian population perished infected by them we will never know. And not all of the killing of civilians was done involuntarily. The official documents, as well as the pamphlets and news sheets of the time, are full of accounts of violent robberies perpetrated by soldiery. An Englishman who served Mansfeld recorded starkly, after taking a town, "we entered killing man, woman and child: the execution continued the space of two hours, the pillaging two days." In 1632 a Scottish mercenary gave a graphic account of relations between the armies and the peasants over whose land they marched: "The boors cruelly used our soldiers that went aside to plunder in cutting off their noses and ears, hands and feet, pulling out their eyes, with sundry other cruelties which they used, being justly repaid by the soldiers in the burning of many dorps [villages] on the march, also leaving the boors dead where they were found."

Wallenstein, ever pragmatic, did his best to prevent his men destroying the civilian economy on which he depended for their sustenance. But harsh as his discipline was—on his first long march in 1625 he had fifteen men hanged in his presence one morning for looting—he couldn't alter the habitual behavior of the troops. And though indiscriminate pillage was a wasteful stupidity he attempted to control, organized extortion was his usual practice. This much was normal: in the past those noblemen who had raised troops for the emperor had been permitted to cover their expenses by plundering their enemies. But the size of Wallenstein's army meant that the emperor's loyal subjects, as well as his vanquished enemies, had to help house, feed, and pay for it. The levies Wallenstein exacted from the inhabitants of the districts in which he quartered his troops on occasion rose as high as 24 percent of all their assets, with ferocious penalties for nonpayment.

In 1625 he marched into the archbishoprics of Halberstadt and Magdeburg, declaring that he would harm neither the people nor their rulers so long as his men could be provided with food and shelter. The threat was effective. His men accommodated, Wallenstein established his court in the castle at Halberstadt, protected by the two hundred lancers of his private bodyguard, and prepared for spring.

There, as everywhere he went, he worked. He was a warrior but he was also, always, an administrator. A Bavarian agent who observed him closely (he was always surrounded by spies) called him "*il grand economo.*" In his own person he combined the roles of commander in chief, quartermaster, and supplier. He had brought to the war all the backup provided by his enormous, prodigiously well-run estates. The army needed beer, flour, boots, muskets: at Gitschin he had breweries, farms, mills, tanneries, mines, and foundries ready to provide them. His detractors, from his day to this, have accused him of corruption, but those who suspect him of making money on the side overlook the fact that, so absolute was his monopoly, there was no "side" that was outside its compass. As general, he was paying himself, as supplier, to equip and provision his own army (the cost, at some notional future date, to be refunded by the emperor). He had made of himself a one-man military-industrial complex.

In 1626 he defeated Count Mansfeld at Dessau and chased his surviving troops through Hungary into Croatia, but it was Tilly who had the more glorious victory, slaughtering the armies of King Christian of Denmark and his allies at Lutter. An agent reported to the elector of Bavaria, Tilly's master, that Wallenstein, on receiving the news of his colleague's triumph, had thrown a wineglass across the room in rage. True or not, the story reflects the popular impression that the allied generals were in competition, and that Tilly was winning. Wallenstein answered carping criticism bluntly—"Had I served God as well, I would assuredly be the foremost saint in Heaven"—but at the imperial court there were voices asking whether the comparatively modest achievements of the Duke of Friedland had been worth the honors heaped upon him—not to mention the expense of his monstrous armada.

It was too late, though, to think of getting rid of him. A spirit may be conjured up but it cannot so readily be persuaded to return to the hellish regions from which it came, for it could not render the extraordinary service for which it has been summoned if it didn't have powers far exceeding those of its mortal master. No one, not even the Emperor Ferdinand, would ever again feel safely able to deny Wallenstein his will. He was not yet suspected of planning to use his soldiers against his empire, but they were nonetheless a constant and appalling threat to the community they ostensibly served.

An army of mercenaries could never be trusted not to turn on its own masters. In the first year of Wallenstein's command the Venetian ambassador in Vienna reported that the army's "loyalty is in doubt . . . there is fear of mutiny and joinder with the enemy." These were fears which Wallenstein deliberately fostered. Over the next few years he was repeatedly to proffer his resignation when crossed—perhaps sincerely, but also as a reminder of how irreplaceable he was—and in doing so he was apt to hint darkly at how his removal would increase the danger posed by his troops. "One must avoid casting the men deliberately into despair, for by the God to whom I pray, they will grow mutinous."

Nominally the emperor's officers and men alike were, in fact, Wallenstein's. "They are as strangers on the soil they tread," says an officer in Schiller's *Wallenstein*, making the valid point that mercenary troops, many of them foreigners, with no sentimental or political motive for devotion to emperor or empire, owed their loyalty only to the commander in chief. Wallenstein's officers were bound to him financially. The army was held together not only by chains of command but by a great web of financial credit at the center of which sat the commander in chief. Each colonel had raised troops at his own expense on the understanding that he would eventually be recompensed; the guarantor of that debt was Wallenstein. Besides he had a knack of binding them to him emotionally by alternately intimidating and indulging them. He could be munificent. After a successful raid he rewarded one of his colonels with four thousand crowns and a horse. The colonel, a reckless gambler, promptly lost it all at cards. Before he could rise from the table Wallenstein's page handed him a purse containing another small fortune. But he could also be terrible. From time to time he would let loose his fury and rage at his officers in front of their men. Once, when he rode into a town at the head of troops to find that the provisions he ordered had not been delivered, he yelled abuse at the quartermasters responsible while all his officers stood by and the townspeople ran up to find out what the commotion was about. Exonerating documents were timidly offered him; he tore them up. He raved; he was beside himself. According to one of the shocked and humiliated quartermasters he called them "mean curs, sluggards, brutes and rascals, and continued so until at last he himself wearied." Afterwards one of his highest-ranking officers contacted the offended men, not exactly to apologize, but to advise them to forget the incident. Those around him accepted that Wallenstein's fury was like a rocket's exhaust, and enduring it was the price allies and associates had to pay for the privilege of proximity to his stupendous energy.

Backed by his tens of thousands of armed men, his position assured by the fear that without him they might prove uncontrollable, Wallenstein's position seemed unassailable. "His armies flourished," wrote Schiller, "while all the states through which they passed withered. What cared he for the detestation of the people and the complaints of princes? His army adored him, and the very enormity of his guilt enabled him to bid defiance to its consequences." He was the lion tamer who cannot be dispensed with for fear of the lion. When, pursuing Mansfeld southward, he had sent to the emperor demanding pay for his troops, warning ominously that without it they might "take a different direction of their own," the Venetian envoy observed: "These are demands which would cost any other prince his head, but Wallenstein is feared because he commands a large army."

In the next year those voices grumbling against him were stilled, at least for a time. 1627 was Wallenstein's annus mirabilis, the year when he marched from victory to victory, sweeping northwards through the empire, driving the emperor's enemies before him. His confidence was superb, his strategy audacious, his will adamantine. Triumphantly he vindicated the claims he had made to Ferdinand and his councillors and the demands he had made on the exchequer. He was inexorable, tremendous. It was this year's campaign which won him the reputation for invincibility, omnipotence even, which led his contemporaries to believe that he, and he alone, could defeat the empire's most formidable attacker. At the head of an army forty thousand strong he drove the Danes and their allies out of Silesia. He joined forces once again with Tilly but, the latter having been wounded, Wallenstein was left in undisputed command. He drove on northward, cities and fortresses falling like overripe fruit to him and his lieutenants, through Mecklenburg, Pomerania, Holstein, Jutland. Finally he overran the Danish peninsula itself. Christian, a king without a country now, fled to the islands. The abbot of Kremsmünster spoke for the majority when he wrote that Wallenstein's "martial progress, amazing in so short a time, is so great that all are taken aback and say '*Quid est hoc?*' What is this?"

He was given his reward. The Emperor Ferdinand offered the crown of Denmark to his victorious general. Wallenstein judiciously refused the honor "for I would not be able to maintain myself," but he accepted the duchies of Mecklenburg and Sagan, with all their lands and palaces, and the Order of the Golden Fleece.

He had declined a kingdom, but he was now richer and more powerful than many kings were. He had achieved the kind of eminence that attracts lethal envy and arouses the suspicions of any latter-day Catos wary of new-made military grandees. In England in the previous year Parliament had moved to impeach George Villiers, the first Duke of Buckingham. Buckingham had been the homosexual King James I's adored favorite. (The king called him "Steenie"—after St. Stephen, whose "face was as the face of an angel"—and "my sweet child and wife.") An exceptionally beautiful and brilliantly manipulative young man who

Left Albrecht von Wallenstein in a version of his portrait by Anthony Van Dyck. His "dark and sinister aspect," wrote a 19th-century commentator, was that of a man "whose hands have been imbrued in blood."

Below A caricature of 1629 shows Wallenstein riding on a peasant. His warmaking was seen to impose an intolerable burden on the people of the Holy Roman Empire.

This contemporary engraving narrates the story of Wallenstein's assassination in strip-cartoon style.

Jordan 3u Eger ift erftochen worden Anno 1634.

Ob. Lei Butler

Ob. Jordan

General Friedlandt.

Friedlanders triumphwagen ift ein mift furch.

4

Giuseppe Garibaldi
a Roma 1849

Above A contemporary lithograph of the Battle of San Antonio. This is one of the numerous popular images of Garibaldi's exploits in South America that enhanced his celebrity in Europe.

Opposite Garbaldi in 1849, at the time of the siege of Rome. "You have only to look into his face," wrote one of his admirers, "and you feel that here is, perhaps, the one man in the world you would follow blindfold to death."

Opposite Garibaldi in his prime. With his wide-set eyes, long nose, and tawny whiskers he seemed to his admirers to resemble a lion.

Above Garibaldi arrives in Southampton. When he visited England in 1864 he was welcomed by enormous, ecstatic crowds.

Garibaldi's name and image were widely used for merchandizing. There were Garibaldi shirts, Garibaldi hats, Garibaldi cigars, Garibaldi biscuits, and (right) a Garibaldi Elixir.

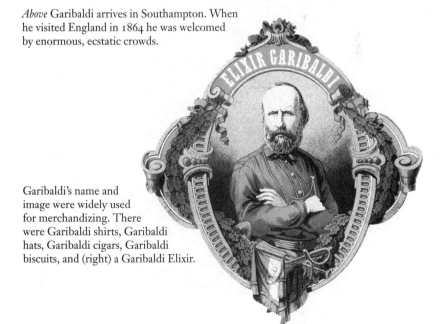

Garibaldi in the poncho and fez he habitually wore in his later years. "He looked," wrote a French minister, "like a prophet, or an old comedian."

was hailed by his admirers as a "second Alcibiades," Buckingham had used his personal glamour to acquire both political power and vast wealth. At the zenith of his career he was as rich as the king and, as first minister, second only to him in authority. He put his magnificence at the service of the state, strutting on diplomatic missions in pearl-encrusted suits whose cost would have provisioned a sizable army, but like Alcibiades he outshone the institution he supposedly represented, angering as many as he dazzled. When his royal patron died he cast his spell over the new king: Charles I was as entranced by him as his father had been. But when Buckingham made an ill-judged and expensive attempt to intervene in the German wars Parliament turned on him, identifying him as the "chief cause of all these evils and mischiefs with which the country is afflicted." The king saved him from impeachment by dissolving Parliament, but two years later, after another disastrous military adventure, he was stabbed to death in a crowded tavern. His rise to power had been meteoric, but it had made him so much hated that when his body was carried through the streets of London to Westminster Abbey the guards lining the route defiantly held their weapons erect instead of trailing them (as was customary at a funeral) and crowds gathered outside the Tower to pray for his murderer. His was a story which Wallenstein, another upstart potentate whose position depended on a monarch's favor, would have done well to mark.

In December 1627 Wallenstein waited on the emperor, who was hunting not far from Prague. Ferdinand received him early and bade him cover his head. Wallenstein hesitated. He was a military hero, the savior of the empire and by now three times over a duke, but only the hereditary princes of the empire were privileged to keep their hats on in the imperial presence. For one who, like Wallenstein, had been born into the lesser nobility to be granted the status of a prince would be all but unprecedented. Twice the emperor repeated the order before Wallenstein, understanding the stupendous honor being done to him, presumed to obey. A little later the same morning the court gathered for the ceremony of the emperor's breakfast. Ferdinand dipped his hands in a silver bowl. It was for a prince of the empire to hand him a towel. Wallenstein, bareheaded again, fulfilled that function. Once more, in public acknowledgment of his new status, Ferdinand invited him to put on his hat. He did so, "whereby," observed the papal nuncio who was present, "he perhaps drew upon himself more the silent envy of the Court than its whispered censure."

Envy, whispered censure, mummery with hats and towels and wash-

basins—this was the kind of thing Wallenstein detested. But its significance must have pleased him. Achilles, in revolt, declared himself independent of all authority save that of the gods. Wallenstein, now an
imperial prince, need defer to no one except the Holy Roman Emperor,
God's secular deputy. The greater the master, the less the humiliation of
serving him. Later, when asked to place some of his troops under Tilly's
command, Wallenstein refused, saying haughtily, "I am wont to serve the
House of Austria, not to let myself be bullied by a Bavarian slave." That
spring Ferdinand appointed him generalissimo, with authority to "ordain
and command" in the emperor's absence, as though he were the emperor
himself.

Ferdinand also pronounced him Admiral of the German Ocean and
the Baltic Sea. The title preempted reality, for the emperor had no ships,
but Wallenstein intended that he soon should have. His first biographer
relates that in the previous year, when he found himself unable to pursue
the Danes into the offshore islands where they took refuge, "he ordered
red-hot shot to be fired into the rebellious waves which had dared to limit
his conquests." Any let to the extent of his power made him angry beyond
reason. Now he planned to have a canal dug across the neck of the Danish
peninsula, allowing ships to pass from the North Sea into the Baltic. With
the cooperation of the port cities of the Hanseatic League, and with ships
loaned by the Spanish, he would extend the imperial dominion northward, ruling the waves and thus gaining control of all northern Europe's
seaborn trade. He had made the imperial power paramount on land, its
foreign enemies defeated, its internal critics cowed. Now he promulgated
a grandiose vision of an expanded empire. He talked of attacking the
Turk, of seizing control of the sea. The nineteenth-century historian Sir
Adolphus Ward opined that no one except Napoleon had ever evolved a
plan for European domination "so daring in outline and systematic in
detail."

It was not for Wallenstein to realize that vision. Three centuries elapsed
before Adolf Hitler, who admired him immensely, succeeded in creating a
newly efficient and ruthlessly predatory German Reich. Meanwhile, that
spring of 1628, the season of Wallenstein's apogee, his luck changed. In
January his first and only son, a seven-week-old baby, died (he had already

decreed that his other child, a girl, would not be his heir). And there was irritating news from the north.

While he wintered in Bohemia, visiting court and attending to his own estates, he had left his army under the command of Hans Georg von Arnim. Arnim's career, which to the modern mind looks like a sequence of betrayals, vividly illustrates how much the concept of loyalty has shifted since the seventeenth century, for he was generally acknowledged by his contemporaries to be a man of unusual probity. A Lutheran, he was noted for his sobriety, for his strict discipline, and for his practice of leading his men in prayer before a battle. He had served the king of Sweden, the king of Sweden's inveterate enemy the king of Poland, and Count Mansfeld (and therefore whomever Count Mansfeld was serving at the time). In 1627 he had been offered employment by both the king of Denmark and Denmark's scourge, Wallenstein. Somewhat surprisingly, given his religious allegiance, he had chosen the latter. Wallenstein respected his judgment and his professionalism, appointed him his deputy, and wrote to him up to seven times a day.

In Wallenstein's absence Arnim attempted to install a garrison in the semiautonomous Baltic harbor city of Stralsund. The Stralsunders resisted. The kings of Denmark and Sweden both offered them their support. By the time Wallenstein made his way back northward that summer the situation was escalating at an alarming rate. En route Wallenstein was taken ill. From his sickbed he wrote to Arnim: "I see that they of Stralsund persist in their mulishness, wherefore I am resolved to deal seriously with them." It was a bad-tempered decision taken without enough knowledge of the circumstances. The Danes sent Stralsund a regiment of Scottish mercenaries. The Swedes followed suit with eight ships full of fighting men and ammunition. A local dispute about quartering had become an international incident.

Wallenstein arrived at the beginning of July and, as though exasperated beyond all caution by the city's defiance, exclaimed (or so it was reported), "Stralsund must down, were it hung with chains to Heaven." A hubristic blasphemy, and a stupidly conceded hostage to fortune. Stralsund was all but an island, protected on its landward side by marshes and accessible only along five easily defended causeways. For forty-eight hours Wallenstein bombarded the city by day, while by night his foot soldiers advanced along the narrow approach routes in the darkness, stumbling over each other into the Stralsunders' direct fire, and the cavalry floundered through the marshes alongside. Twelve thousand imperial troops were killed in the mud. This petty conflict was costing way too much. Wallenstein offered lenient terms. He wanted now only "to come out with honour and soon depart." But Stralsund's allies did not want to let him go so easily. Negotiations dragged on. More Danish troops arrived, and another thousand Scots. Wallenstein had made the elementary mistake of attempting to blockade a seaport with only a land army. The city council refused to accept any terms whatsoever until he had withdrawn his troops. It had been raining for days. Wallenstein's men, in order to protect their forward positions, had to stand up to their waists in water. On July 24, barely three weeks after he had arrived on the scene, he gave the order to retreat.

To Protestant pamphleteers of the time and Protestant historians thereafter the resistance of Stralsund, the staunch little city which withstood the dual might of the Catholic Church and the Holy Roman Emperor as represented by the cruel and saturnine Duke of Friedland, became an heroic legend. To Wallenstein's detractors at court it was a useful instance of his vincibility. In the short term, though, he was quickly able to efface the unfortunate impression it made. He had been waiting for the opportunity to finish off the Danish challenge. As long as the imperial fleet remained a figment of Wallenstein's imagination, King Christian was safe until he dared venture back onto the mainland. Wallenstein taunted him: "He is soused full every day and I hope to Heaven that in his cups he will one day venture something and creep out of his watery holes, when he will assuredly be ours." Sure enough, less than a month after Wallenstein withdrew from Stralsund, Christian, with seven thousand men, took the coastal town and fortress of Wolgast. Wallenstein moved immediately. The ensuing battle was bloody and conclusive. The Danish forces were trapped between the imperial army and the sea and slaughtered, all but the handful of survivors whom Christian managed to take off with him in his ships. The war with Denmark was effectively over, the peace treaty was formally signed the following June. Wallenstein's critics were silenced. He was once more the victorious generalissimo.

The war ebbed southward. Wallenstein let it go. There was a dispute over the succession of the dukedom of Mantua in which the French and Spanish and eventually the emperor became involved, but Wallenstein held himself aloof from it. In typically uncompromising fashion he told a Spanish envoy that "the thought of procuring a single soldier from him should not enter their minds, even though the Emperor in person were to give him the order." Instead he occupied himself with his new duchy of Mecklenburg.

The former rulers, a pair of brothers who had sided with Denmark and been exiled for it, had left their palace empty. Wallenstein moved in, along with the eight hundred or so people who made up his court (but without his duchess), and set about refurnishing it to his usual taste. Tapestries, gold-embossed leather wall-hangings, fine table linen, damask, carpets in his favorite blue from Venice and Lucca, thirty thousand talers' worth of silver from Genoa. A Calvinist church was demolished to provide space and stone for a new wing. He was simultaneously building a brand-new palace in his third duchy, Sagan. According to the Irishman Thomas Carew the plans for it were so marvelous that it would have proved the eighth wonder of the world. It was never completed. In the whole of the rest of his life Wallenstein was to spend only nine days in Sagan.

As he stripped and redecorated the palace, so he revised and improved Mecklenburg's government. "I see what impertinences and protractions have been indulged by the Estates," he wrote. "They shall not deal with me as they used to deal with the former Dukes, for I shall assuredly not suffer it." He rewrote the constitution. He established a postal service. He introduced uniform weights and measures. He built almshouses. He drastically reduced the number of legal cases awaiting resolution. He installed garrisons and built citadels. He exacted large quantities of money in rent, in license fees, in excise duties, and in "contributions." When the hereditary owners of all these assets, the former dukes, sent an envoy naïvely asking that their successor might intercede with the emperor on their behalf, Wallenstein told him brutally, "Come again on such a mission and I shall lay your head before your feet." The man began to remonstrate. Wallenstein cut him short: "You have heard."

While he ordered his new estates, the second decade of the wars began. Wallenstein's own territories were havens of peace and prosperity in what was beginning to seem to contemporary observers a howling wilderness. An imperial official compared the generalissimo's Bohemian estates around Gitschin and Friedland to a "*terra felix.*" "A general state of peace, delectable and beneficial, predominates." How lamentable the contrast afforded by the "*terra deserta*" that was the rest of Bohemia. There "towns, precious castles, markets, villages all tumble down and the cherished fruitful soil is overgrown with thistles and thorns." Throughout most of the enormous empire it was the same, and the damage had been done not by the fighting but by the simple passage of armies over the land. The contrast between Wallenstein's *terra felix* and the surrounding desert was easily explained. As commander in chief he was enabled to ensure, as the official remarked, that "the military is not in the least allowed passage, and still less billeting." As a result, "everything is to be found in a condition of greatest prosperity."

Wallenstein, *il grand economo* who abhorred waste, used to argue fiercely against his political masters when they suggested he march across arable country when the corn was still green, but few military commanders and none of the common soldiers had his foresight. Foreign mercenaries and dispossessed peasants-turned-soldiers were careless how much destruction they caused, and they were all hungry. It was mercenaries returning from the German battlefields who introduced the word "plunder" into the English language.

Historians are still arguing about the exact extent of the devastation wrought by the war. Certainly many of the atrocious tales and shocking statistics contained in contemporary documents are exaggerated (because the authors wished either to maximize the amount of compensation they could claim or to blacken their opponents' reputation), but the stark truth was bad enough to appall foreign travelers and to reduce the emperor's wretched subjects to despair. A Silesian mystic announced that the end of the world was at hand: the death and destruction all around was a prelude to the Last Judgment. It was all but impossible to imagine life ever resuming its normal patterns. A shoemaker's diary of the war years records thirty separate occasions when he and his family had to flee from their village to hide from marauding armies. An English traveler's journal for 1636 describes "castles battered, pillaged and burnt," villages deserted by people fleeing from the plague, houses left to burn, plundered churches, cities pillaged and apparently deserted but for starving children watching from doorways, broken bridges, woods full of scavenging mercenaries, and roads lined with gallows from which corpses swung. *The Lamentations of Germany*, published in London in 1638, is a horrific illustrated anthology of refugees' testimonies. The picture captions include "Priests slain at the altar," "Snails and frogs eagerly eaten," "Mother lamenting over six dead children." Contemporary broadsheets show pictures of parents eating their own children, of graves gaping open while the desperate gnaw exhumed corpses. Unverifiable as such images are, they indicate that the peoples of the empire felt themselves to be living through a time of unspeakable horror, when suffering was endemic and when the structures of everyday life had been so fatally undermined as to leave them no shelter against chaos and old night.

In such a situation people look around for a culprit. And by this time, for many people, Wallenstein had come to personify the war. It was one of the functions of the commander in chief to take upon himself the guilt and the odium of warfare. When it was suggested that the emperor's heir, the young king of Hungary, should be the supreme commander, councillors objected that were he to play such a part it would inevitably and irreparably damage his relations with the people he would one day rule, for the generalissimo could not but be a "scourge" and an "oppressor." No matter that Wallenstein had not started the ghastly chain of conflicts, no matter that he was (or was supposed to be) a mere servant and instrument of the emperor. It was Wallenstein who had called into being the army which lay like a malign and ravenous parasite on the empire. It was Wallenstein whose harsh motto was "Better a ruined land than a lost land." It was Wallenstein whose armies, as envisioned by the contemporary English playwright Henry Glapthorne, stained all the fields crimson and swam "through rising seas of blood" to victory. It was Wallenstein whose agents came to town after town demanding "contributions" so extortionate that all trade, all husbandry was rendered futile, and whose soldiers tramped back and forth through the empire, eating the land empty and spreading disease. It was Wallenstein whose ambition (whether for himself or his imperial master) seemed the most obvious cause of the prolongation of the war. People punned on his name: Wallenstein—*allen ein Stein*—a (tomb)stone for all.

As Drake had entered the visions and nightmares of the Spanish people, so Wallenstein entered those of his own. A mystic, one Christina Poniatowska, arrived at Gitschin in search of "the raving dog, him of Wallenstein." Finding him absent, she gave the duchess a letter enjoining him to repent, then fell into a trance in which she saw Wallenstein, his clothes drenched in blood, attempting to climb a ladder to Heaven but being thrown down. Even the less ecstatic credited him with supernatural powers of destruction. At the time of his last visit to Vienna a fire broke out, destroying the bishop's palace and 148 other houses. "The arrival of the Duke of Friedland has brought us nothing but storm, fire and terror," wrote a courtier. "When he came to Prague in January his own house took fire. What else is to be concluded but that he will burn and spoil much else and at length himself be consumed?" In the public mind, he took on the character of Mars or of Thanatos, the embodiment of devastation and of death.

Such fantasies need not have bothered him. It was not an era when public opinion had much influence over the actions of the mighty. But there were plenty among the powerful, too, who feared and hated him. His huge army had fundamentally altered the balance of power. The electors, whose puppet the emperor had formerly been, were now the emperor's intimidated subjects. His exorbitant demands for "contributions" had damaged the interests not only of the common people but of their masters as well. At a meeting of the electors in 1627 there were unanimous complaints that "territorial rulers are at the mercy of Colonels and Captains, who are uninvited war profiteers and criminals, breaking the laws of the Empire." The army's very existence was a menace. Pompey and Caesar once loomed over Rome, threatening to crush the life out of the state if they chose to fall upon it: Wallenstein and his army, similarly inordinate, lay upon the Holy Roman Empire, an insupportable weight, crushing the life out of it by slow degrees. "The Duke of Friedland," declared the elector of Mainz, "has disgusted and offended to the utmost nearly each and every territorial ruler in the empire." Wallenstein was fully aware of how much he was resented. "All Electors and Princes, yea a multitude of others must I make my enemies for the sake of the Emperor," he wrote. While he had Ferdinand's protection there was little anyone could do to harm him. But in 1628, the very year in whose beginning he had been so loaded with honors, that protection began to fail.

"Had Wallenstein been a greater diplomatist," wrote Oswald Spengler, "and had he in particular taken the trouble, as Richelieu did, to bring the person of the monarch under his influence, then probably it would have been all up with princedom within the Empire." But Wallenstein served a master with a strong will and a sacred mission. As archduke of Styria Ferdinand had terrorized or tortured his Protestant subjects until they recanted or went into exile. As emperor he had been more circumspect, but with the Danes and their Protestant allies defeated and his personal power assured by Wallenstein's troops he finally felt secure enough to recommence his persecutions. In 1629 he introduced the Edict of Restitution, a measure requiring that all the property of the Catholic Church which had fallen into secular hands since 1552 should be restored. It was an incendiary act. (Ten years later a similar proposal would provoke the Scottish Covenanters into rebellion against Charles I of England and Scotland, the first link in the chain of events which led eventually to his decapitation and the temporary overthrow of the monarchy.) All Protestants, and many moderate Catholics, were appalled.

One of the surviving printed copies of the original edict bears the comment, scrawled by a contemporary Catholic hand, *"Radix Omnium Malorum"*—"the root of all evil."

It was not a measure that Wallenstein could happily enforce. He had maintained from the outset of his command that he was not fighting a religious war. His aims were not sectarian but political, the establishment and preservation of strong, centralized imperial government. His army was a secular, cosmopolitan organization into which men of all denominations were welcomed. Arnim, his second in command, was Lutheran. What he himself believed no one knew for certain. Allusions to the Lord God displeased him. When the master of his mint issued coins bearing a pious legend, he wrote brusquely, "I know not who put into your head the *'Dominus Protector Meus.'* " As duke of Mecklenburg his only interference in his subjects' habits of worship had been his order that they pray for him, *"für mich."*

He saw the Edict of Restitution as an act of political self-destruction, bound to alienate the empire's Protestants and incline them to welcome any foreign invader bold enough to challenge the Hapsburgs. But Ferdinand had once exclaimed, "Better a desert than a country full of heretics!" and his priorities had not changed. His confessor, the Jesuit Father Lamormaini, told the elector of Bavaria: "The Edict must stand firm, whatever evil might finally come from it. It matters little that the Emperor, because of it, lose not only Austria but all of his kingdoms . . . provided he save his soul." No wonder Wallenstein, whose task it was to protect the emperor's secular interests, came to see the Jesuits as his chief enemies at court. His agenda was a radically different one. "The Edict," he unguardedly told the people of Magdeburg, "cannot stand."

As the aims of the emperor and his commander in chief diverged there were plenty of whisperers and insinuators standing ready to widen the gap between them. Like Alcibiades and the Cid before him Wallenstein had grown too great to be a subject, as observers, both foreign ambassadors and imperial nobles, repeatedly observed. "He holds the entire court in contempt and quarrels openly with ministers . . . He insults ruling sovereigns," wrote one. Another reported "that Friedland has so far divested the Emperor of his power as only to leave him with the name." In a confidential report prepared for Maximilian of Bavaria he is compared to Attila, Theodoric, and Berengar, "those ancients, amazing to history, who as simple leaders of armies attained to kingdoms and"—a pointed addition this—"strove after the Imperial dignity."

Count Khevenhüller records that when Wallenstein was made duke of Mecklenburg a group of conservative princes (jealous of their own hereditary privileges and unsettled by the spectacle of two of their number being dispossessed in favor of the upstart from Bohemia) protested. Latter-day Catos indignant at the prospect of a second Caesar's taking to himself the power that had long been vested in their own aristocratic oligarchy, they warned the emperor that "when sovereigns have granted their servants more authority than is meet, they have often regretted it, with all too belated remorse." The emperor took note. In 1628, even as he was conferring new honors on Wallenstein, Ferdinand had seemed to the Spanish ambassador "extremely apprehensive on account of the Duke of Friedland's capricious disposition." The ambassador asked why in that case he had not "dared" to relieve the duke of his command. "He opines that this would have for its consequence greater evils than if for the while a good mien is shown him." For all the gracious business with the hat and the hand towel, for all the dukedoms and high titles he granted him, what the emperor felt for his generalissimo was not favor but fear.

Wallenstein knew that his prodigious success was a provocation, but he did nothing to mollify those outraged by it. The splendor in which he lived was a kind of insolence: he had taken for his motto *Invita Invidia*—"defying (or inviting) envy." The prince of Hohenzollern marveled at his personal guard, six hundred men "whose clothes were thickly sewn with gold thread, their bandoleers stuck with embossed silver and the iron points silvered on their pikes, in such sort that no Emperor ever had a like bodyguard." The electors complained that "not one of them, neither King nor Emperor, had ever had a court to compare."

Had he taken the trouble to do so Wallenstein could perhaps have stopped the growing faction determined to bring about his dismissal. When he was in Vienna the Venetian ambassador noted, "Before Wallenstein arrived at court everyone spoke ill of him. Today none lets his voice be heard." But he never deigned to defend himself. He was too arrogant to dance attendance on those he despised, too contemptuous of others' ill-informed opinions to bother trying to change them. In holding aloof from the court he allowed rumors and irrational fears to flourish. One of his own generals said of him, "The common false repute of this lord is so imbued into folk that I can often only with difficulty prevent myself from believing all tidings of the like . . . although I was by him at the very time and hour as that which is narrated was happening." Absent and invisible to the eye, he grew to monstrous size in the minds of those who feared him.

A majority of the electors, led by Maximilian of Bavaria, resolved to be rid of him. Their objection to him, and his army, was not based simply on envy of his inordinate power. It was a part of a long-running political debate about monarchy in general, and the nature of the empire in particular. In 1619 Professor Reinking of the University of Geissen had published a thesis drawing on the *Institutes* of the Roman Emperor Justinian to demonstrate the emperor to be "the greatest authority in the Christian world" and an absolute monarch whose wishes had the power of law, a doctrine which unsurprisingly found favor with Ferdinand. But other theoreticians differed. In 1608 a Dr. Horleder had written that the empire (an abstraction represented by the electors and princes) was superior to the emperor who was its servant, and in 1603 Althusias declared that the emperor was the steward, not the possessor, of supreme power. Most dangerous of all, the half-Swedish political philosopher Chemnitz expressed the opinion that if the emperor were to threaten the sovereignty and liberty of the empire, then the empire's representatives would be duty-bound to combat him, and if necessary depose him by force. Ferdinand had Chemnitz's book burned.

To the electors and princes it appeared that Wallenstein had handed Ferdinand the power to make himself a tyrant. As long as the emperor was still dependent for his military security on the cooperation of his princely subjects his power was limited by his incapacity to enforce his will. By 1630, with Wallenstein's army at his disposal, he could defy them. Besides, it was Wallenstein who had benefited when the emperor, against all precedent, had stripped the hereditary dukes of Mecklenburg of their titles. It was Wallenstein who was now, so improperly, a prince and duke himself, having been granted those titles by an emperor whose disregard for venerable tradition showed him reprehensibly careless of ancient rights. And it was Wallenstein who was to be held responsible for the empire's agony. Maximilian and the other electors had identified him as the scapegoat onto whom all responsibility for the war could be loaded, and the imperial representative against whom they could vent their hostility to the emperor without overt treason.

In July 1630 there was to be a session of the Electoral Diet, the most august and influential of the empire's governmental institutions. The diet was a great occasion, politically, diplomatically, and socially. The emperor with all his court, the electors with theirs and legions of observers, courtiers, spies, and hangers-on all came to Regensburg for it. The city was packed. The emperor's retinue alone numbered over three thousand people. There were banquets, tournaments, wolf hunts. People traveled across Europe on the flimsiest pretext to be there.

Wallenstein was not present. A month earlier he had taken up residence in Memmingen, four days' journey from Regensburg. Like Julius Caesar receiving envoys and agents in Ravenna in the months before he finally led an army against Rome, he was a menacing offstage presence. Maximilian had written that to displace him from his command would be "intensely hazardous." There were plenty of people in Regensburg who imagined him to be ready to follow Caesar's lead and stage a coup d'état rather than yield up his command.

That hot and anxious summer Wallenstein's reputation grew ever more diabolical. The potentate whose power he was thought to envy was not entitled "Holy" as an empty courtesy: Ferdinand saw himself, and was seen by many Catholics, as the true Church's secular guardian. To defy or, worse, to usurp his power would be not only a political crime but also a mortal sin. A generation later John Milton, having participated in a prolonged and successful rebellion against divine monarchy, was to write the story of the ruined archangel, "who durst defy the Omnipotent to arms." Wallenstein, whose piety was so questionable, who held court in such insolent grandeur at Memmingen, resembled the Miltonic fiend whom "transcendent glory raised / Above his fellows, with Monarchal pride / Conscious of highest worth." He was suspected of disloyalty, and disloyalty to Heaven's anointed representative was tantamount to Satanic revolt.

The diet opened and the emperor invited his electors' advice on a wide range of matters of policy. Led by Maximilian of Bavaria they answered as though there were only one issue to be resolved. Wallenstein and his army, they said, had become a curse. They asserted that "the soldiery, now become unspeakably numerous, served no other purpose than to lay waste the common fatherland." They rehearsed in gruesome and heartbreaking detail the sufferings of their subjects. They talked of "cruel and unnecessary exactions," of churches despoiled, of the starving reduced to eating grass, of food and property "wrung from the people in barbarous ways," and they asserted that "the whole blame for the misery, disgrace, and infamy . . . rested with the new Duke in Mecklenburg who as commander of the imperial forces had been invested, without the consent of the states, with such powers as no one before him had ever exercised." Wallenstein's army must be reduced to a third of its size and Wallenstein himself, "a man of restless and ferocious spirit," one who "sickens and is abominated by the entire human race" and, not only that, a foreigner, a Czech, must be replaced with "such a captain-general as is indigenous to the Empire and an eminent representative of it" (someone, in fact, just like Maximilian).

The emperor hesitated and equivocated. There were long hot days of talk, of petitions and evasive answers, of proposals and counterproposals. For the emperor to sacrifice his military commander on the electors' say-so would be humiliating for him, but he wanted them to acknowledge his son, the king of Hungary, as his successor and he needed their support for the Edict of Restitution. In exchange he might be prevailed upon to make this concession. Perhaps, too, though he never acknowledged it, he would be glad to be rid of his generalissimo. If he were to divest himself of Wallenstein, perhaps he could simultaneously divest himself of the odium Wallenstein's great success in his service had brought upon them both. His contemporary, King Charles I of England, would soon agree to the impeachment and execution of his right-hand man, the Earl of Strafford, in a futile attempt to restore his own popularity. Charles sacrificed Strafford even though he had loved and trusted him. There is no evidence to suggest that Ferdinand felt any affection for Wallenstein, the high-handed, unbiddable subject who addressed him so "roughly," to whom by now he owed sums so vast there was no prospect of his ever being rid of the debt, whose ultimate ambitions could not be read.

On August 13 the emperor told the electors that he had resolved on "a change in the direction of his armed forces." His capitulation, his abject failure to stand by his own commander, was muffled up in euphemism. He composed a letter assuring Wallenstein of his "abiding favour" and "high esteem" and concern for his "safety, honour and good name" and entrusted it to the two of his councillors who had always been on best terms with the generalissimo. They were to carry it to Wallenstein in Memmingen and "persuade him to resign, at the same time assuring him of the Imperial favour." To ask Wallenstein—a man notorious for his hauteur and for the violence of his rage—to abjure his power struck all who contemplated it as a task of dangerous presumption. A chronicler records that the two emissaries made their four-day journey with fear knocking at their hearts. To their amazement Wallenstein received them calmly. According to one account he told them, "Gladder tidings could not have been brought me. I thank God that I am out of the meshes." According to another he produced an astrological chart. He had known what was to be, he said, for it was written in the stars that the elector of Bavaria was bound to dominate the emperor at this period and so, "though it grieves me that his Majesty has shown me so little grace, yet will I obey."

The electors were incredulous. The man they had so feared, from whose baleful power they had despaired of ever ridding themselves, had gone quietly, for no apparent reason other than that he had been asked to go. It was the first of the three bathetic surprises Wallenstein's story was to afford those who participated in it, surprises which derived their power to shock from the superhuman status he had acquired in the imaginations of those around him. He was only a man, but they thought him an evil genius, Mephistopheles to Ferdinand's Faust. Had Wallenstein really been an unholy spirit he would have imposed an awful punishment upon his pusillanimous employer. He would have ignited the heavens, scorched the earth, and dragged Ferdinand off to perdition. He would never have done what in fact he did, which was to send word to von Taxis, his governor at Gitschin, that he would soon be home. "Make provision of all things against my coming." He ordered that the stables, the riding school, and the tennis court should be made ready and supplies of wine and vermouth laid in. Making no attempt to appeal his dismissal or even to reproach the emperor, he withdrew with quiet dignity to his estates in Bohemia and settled down to the life of a wealthy landowner, serenely detached from affairs of state.

After Wallenstein's death imperial propagandists asserted that his calm was a mask, that, furious, he at once began to plot his revenge. Many people, then and later, believed it. The theory is psychologically plausible. Wallenstein had done great things for Ferdinand. In *The Tragedy of Albertus Wallenstein*, written by the English dramatist Henry Glapthorne and first performed only five years after Wallenstein's death, Glapthorne's Wallenstein boasts of being the emperor's eagle, who "snatched up his crown, that lay despised on earth / And heaved it up to heaven," and the architect of his power: "I took the reeling pillars of his state and pitched them fair and even." All the boasts the playwright puts in Wallenstein's mouth are well founded in fact. Wallenstein had made Ferdinand secure and greatly extended his power at the cost of his own popularity. As he himself remarked: "That I am hated in the Empire results from this: that I have served the Emperor far too well, against the will of many persons." He had good cause to feel betrayed, and to betray a betrayer is easily justified. No wonder so many people, including eventually Ferdinand himself, were to believe that he determined to avenge himself on his "insulting" and ungrateful master. But there are other, more convincing ways of explaining Wallenstein's stoic acceptance of his fall from power.

One is that he was so exhausted and depressed that he truly welcomed it. At Memmingen a groom reported that he "displays excessive melancholy, admits no one to his presence, treats his servants and attendants badly beyond bounds." Throughout the first years of his command his letters to his father-in-law, Count Harrach, are full of complaints. He is so tired, so overworked. He is ill and in pain. There has been a radical misunderstanding: what he offered to do was to bring an army into being, not to support it at his own expense; now he is in trouble, "for I perceive the court thinks I should both wage this war and furnish its funds." He can see no feasible way to continue the war, and no hope of ending it. In what was surely a piece of despairing hyperbole but has been taken for prophecy, he wrote that the fighting might "perchance continue for Thirty Years before something salutary may ensue." Again and again he employs the image of the labyrinth: he feels that he is lost in it and that before he finds a way out he will, in every sense of the word, be ruined. He longs to "take my quittance, for by the God whom I worship I am no longer able to remain while I see myself scurvily used."

He knew how much he was hated. A year earlier one of the emperor's counselors had written warning him that Tilly had secret orders from Ferdinand to imprison him or to "send you out of the world in a shorter and more summary manner." Wallenstein dismissed the warning: "I wonder how you can give ear to such childish tales. The Emperor is a just and grateful sovereign who rewards faithful service in a different way from what you suppose." But he didn't doubt that there were many people who wanted him dead: in March 1630 he asked a trusted apothecary to procure for him an antidote to poison. His financial situation was also alarming. The fantastically complex system of credit whereby the war was financed was in the process of collapsing around him. The very day after Ferdinand agreed to his dismissal, before anyone outside Regensburg could have known of it, Hans de Witte, on whose financial wizardry so much of Wallenstein's magnificence had been based, wrote telling him he would be unable to raise the money for the next of the monthly payments he had been sending him. The banker's credit had been undermined by the uncertainty of his client's situation. A month later de Witte drowned himself in the well in his garden. Wallenstein's response to the despair of his longtime associate was chilling. "The tale passes current here that Hans de Witte has hanged himself," he wrote to von Taxis. "See what things of mine there are with him and fetch them as speedily as may be, in particular tapestries, gilded leather and other things. . . . We are in no wise indebted to him." But heartless as he may have been, he was not invulnerable. About the time of the Regensburg diet he laid off a large number of his servants without pay. The failure of de Witte's credit might well have made it impossible for him to continue as commander even had the emperor not required his resignation.

There is yet another way of reading the story. Wallenstein's rivals had timed their move against him preposterously badly. Two years earlier Wallenstein had commissioned an astrologer to cast the horoscope of Gustavus Adolphus, the king of Sweden, and written that "in the Swedes we shall find a worse enemy than the Turks." He had perceived that the king, vigorous, bellicose, and so far enormously successful, was potentially the most formidable enemy the Hapsburg emperor faced. Throughout the period of Wallenstein's first command Gustavus Adolphus was engaged in a protracted conflict with his cousin, the king of Poland, but as soon as he extricated himself from it he turned his attentions southward. A devout Lutheran, he was ready to take on the role of champion of the German Protestants. On July 6, 1630, the third day of the Regensburg diet, he landed with an advance guard of thirteen thousand men at the mouth of the Oder. By the time Wallenstein had been persuaded to resign the Swedes had overrun Pomerania. Without any protest or appeal the former generalissimo withdrew to Bohemia knowing that the emperor had agreed to render himself militarily impotent at the very moment that his realm was undergoing a major foreign invasion. Dividing his time between Gitschin and Prague, Wallenstein waited for the emperor, for Germany, for all Catholic Europe, to discover that they could not do without him, that he, like Alcibiades two millennia before him, was "the only man alive" who could do what had to be done.

Achilles, having fallen out with his royal master, fumed and raged in his tent. Wallenstein awaited his recall with apparent equanimity. He laid on boar hunts, not so much for himself as for his ever-growing retinue. He was reunited with his duchess. He began work on extending his gardens in Prague and building a second palace at Gitschin. He spent his days among his papers and his nights with his favorite resident astrologer, Battista Senno. It has been plausibly suggested that this was the happiest period of his life. Meanwhile the Swedes swept southward. Wallenstein's duchy of Mecklenburg was among their conquests; he accepted its loss with surprising sangfroid. The emperor continued to write to him, courteously addressing him by all his titles.

His army had been partly dispersed, the remnant being united with the Bavarian troops under General Tilly. Officers unwilling to serve under any other commander followed Wallenstein into Bohemia and attached themselves to his court (so did several of the emperor's chamberlains). Others sought service elsewhere. Arnim switched sides again, to become commander in chief to Gustavus Adolphus's most important ally among the German princes, the Lutheran elector of Saxony. It was a job which better suited his religious affiliation than his role as Wallenstein's second in command had done. When the two men met again it was as opponents.

There were those who asked themselves whether Wallenstein himself might be willing to serve a new and more appreciative master. While he busied himself with embellishing his garden (thirty statues commissioned from the Dutch sculptor Adrien de Vries, a great bronze basin surmounted by a statue of Venus, an aviary built to resemble a fantastic grotto containing four hundred singing birds), all Europe waited, wondering and apprehensive, to see what he would do next. In November 1630 Gustavus Adolphus wrote to him in the friendliest terms promising that he, unlike the ungrateful emperor, would be ready to show him every favor and offering to make him viceroy of Bohemia (once the country had been won from the imperialists). But when General Tilly wrote to inquire whether it was true, as a French gazetteer had reported, that Wallenstein had repaid the courtesy by sending the king a gold chain, Wallenstein retorted curtly that he was preparing a chain of very different kind for Gustavus Adolphus's neck. Gustavus Adolphus's messenger had been Count Thurn, erstwhile leader of the Bohemian rebels, now an exile and in service with the Swedes but still dreaming of an independent Bohemia. In the summer of 1631 a Bohemian agent, whose testimony would later be crucial in making the imperial case against Wallenstein, brought him a proposal, probably also originating with Gustavus Adolphus, offering him fourteen thousand Swedish troops under Count Thurn for an unspecified purpose—perhaps the reconquest of Bohemia?

Wallenstein responded evasively to all these overtures. His accusers were later to allege that for the rest of his life he was secretly working for Sweden and its German Protestant allies, and perhaps for France as well, against the interests of those he pretended to serve, but they could never prove it incontrovertibly. It is hard to imagine why he should have wished to do so. He knew very soon after he had been obliged to resign his command that, should he want to go to war again, he would have no need of a new master.

By March 1631, less than half a year after his dismissal, Ferdinand was begging him to come to Vienna and advise on how the crisis could be met. He did not stir. The empire was fragmenting as one after another of the Protestant princes allied themselves with Sweden. The imperial cause looked hopeless. Wallenstein's former officers wrote to him, deploring the muddle and lack of strategy in the imperial and Bavarian armies, now united under the command of General Tilly. Tilly himself wrote: "Your Princely Grace can account yourself fortunate that you have riddance of this heavy toil and great burden." He probably meant it sincerely. In September he was crushingly defeated by Gustavus Adolphus at Breitenfeld. A caricature in a contemporary broadsheet shows Wallenstein at ease in a grandly regal chair, laughing uproariously at the news of his former colleague's discomfiture and the rout of the army that had been his own. The caption says that he laughed nonstop, "shaking belly and chair," for fourteen days. Wallenstein was not much given to belly laughs. It was more plausibly reported that, hearing the news, he remarked that had he been Tilly he would have killed himself.

In November Sweden's allies, the Saxons under Arnim, invaded Bohemia. Wallenstein, a private citizen now, left his palace in Prague, the exodus of his enormous household triggering a citywide panic. The imperial garrison withdrew without a battle, leaving the Saxons to occupy the capital. Arnim, who was said to have chosen his route through Bohemia to cause minimum damage to his former commander's estates, posted guards in front of Wallenstein's palace to protect it from looters. Rumor circulated to the effect that he would not have had the effrontery to march on Prague at all had Wallenstein not invited him to do so. The former generalissimo now commanded no fighting force but it was still assured, such was the magnitude of his reputation, that the kingdom of Bohemia lay in his gift.

Gustavus Adolphus was celebrated by English and other Protestant commentators as the glittering champion of religious and political freedom, a second Gideon who tackled oppressors as bravely as the biblical hero had challenged the Midianites. Seen from the viewpoint of the Holy Roman Emperor and his Catholic subjects, though, he was a sinister predator from the land of outer darkness. The "Lion of Midnight" they called him, the "Midnight King." As he swept through Germany at the head of his "hunger-wolves" he laid waste the land. A far more belligerent commander than Wallenstein, he seldom withdrew when he could fight. "It was his maxim," wrote Schiller, "never to decline a battle, so long as it cost him nothing but men." Those who attempted to deflect his aggression by diplomatic means received short shrift. Rulers of the territories standing in his way begged him to pass them by, honoring their "neutrality." He scoffed at them: "What is 'neutrality'? I do not understand it . . . It is nothing but rubbish which the wind raises and carries away." No one could withstand him. "We cry 'Help, Help' but there is nobody to hear," wrote one of Ferdinand's councillors as the imperial capital came under threat. General Tilly was seventy-three years old and, after Breitenfeld, according to a Bavarian councillor, "wholly perplexed and seemingly cast down." None of his lieutenants seemed a plausible successor. There was, by common consent, only one man in all Europe who could save the situation. In December 1631, only a year and a quarter after he had so brusquely dismissed him, the emperor—by pleading, by imploring, by granting him this time such extraordinary powers and privileges that it seemed to contemporary observers that he had effectively handed over to his subject his imperial authority—prevailed upon Wallenstein to resume his command.

The generalissimo took up his old position not with jubilation but cautiously and by grudging degrees. Initially he agreed to serve for three months only, to raise an army but not to lead it. He was proud, said his detractors then and later. He wished to humble the emperor who had cast him off, to make his master beg. Perhaps he did, but he was also wary of finding himself once more saddled with the costs of an extended campaign. This time the army was to be financed in a more orderly fashion, with each district of the empire required to pay a levy. That established, Wallenstein began his recruiting.

Schiller's Wallenstein boasts:

> I did it. Like a god of war, my name
> went throughout the world. The drum was beat; and, lo;
> The plough, the workshop, is forsaken, all
> Swarm to the old familiar long-loved banners

It was true. Wallenstein was accounted one born in a happy hour, like Rodrigo Díaz, and believed, moreover, to have supernatural powers. Most of the participants in the Thirty Years' War had encountered witches and believed in magic. The Duke of Brunswick issued his troops bullets made of glass, the only kind which would not be stopped by the spell which, so he understood, had rendered the entire imperial army invulnerable. Wallenstein's reputation for wizardry greatly enhanced his standing as a military commander. It was popularly believed that he had made a pact with the powers of darkness which rendered him invincible, that he had "enchained victory to his banner." He had, besides, a reputation for paying his men promptly. By the end of March he had nearly a hundred thousand men assembled, one of the biggest armies Europe had ever seen, and once more the farms and mines and factories of his Bohemian estates were supplying him with food, clothes, and weapons.

The three months elapsed. It was unthinkable that anyone other than Wallenstein could lead the army he had created. The emperor entreated him to assume command. He remained immovable. The emperor begged him at least to come to Vienna for talks. He refused to go. (Already he had not seen Ferdinand for four years—they would not meet again.) At last, in the middle of April, when the huge army had already been notionally without a commander in chief for weeks, he agreed to meet the imperial minister Prince Eggenberg at Gollersdorf. There he laid out the conditions on which he would consent to assume the command. Whatever they were, they were accepted.

When, after the invasion of the Almoravids, Rodrigo Díaz consented to fight again for the king of Castile who had once driven him out, he insisted on terms of service so extraordinary as to render him effectively his master's equal. So, in a similar situation, did Wallenstein. According to contemporary but unreliable sources, he demanded that he be generalissimo in "*assolutissima forma*" of all Hapsburg armies, Spanish as well as Austrian. There had been talk of Ferdinand's heir, the king of Hungary, acting as his joint commander: Wallenstein not only rejected the suggestion, but required an assurance that neither the young king nor his father the emperor would ever come near the army. He would have unrestricted authority to confiscate and award property, a power which gave him unlimited opportunities to win allies and castigate rivals. Neither the emperor nor any of his ministers would have any power to reverse his decisions. He, and he alone, would grant pardons; a pardon granted by the emperor would be valid only if he, Wallenstein, had endorsed it. The emperor would guarantee the costs of the war, and would immediately grant Wallenstein a large sum of money for his personal use. On top of all this he was granted the license, as the Cid had been, to build a kingdom for himself. He would have the right to keep and rule over any territory that he conquered. At the war's conclusion he would receive compensation for any property he had lost (Mecklenburg, for instance, which was already in the hands of the Swedes) and he would be rewarded for his services with a part of the Hapsburgs' hereditary lands.

Cardinal Richelieu, ignoring the fact that he himself was another example of a subject who had overtopped his ruler, described the agreement as "an outrage perpetrated by the servant against his master." Schiller, in the next century, saw it as a clear prelude to rebellion: by it the emperor was deprived of his authority, and placed at the mercy of his general. Wallenstein, who had been dismissed—as Alcibiades and the Cid had been in their time—because he had grown too great, was now returned, with new, officially sanctioned powers which made him greater still.

His army was multiethnic, polyglot, a horde as menacing as any that ever swept in off the steppes. Thomas Carlyle was to describe them as "all the wild lawless spirits of Europe assembled within the circuit of a single trench . . . Ishmaelites, their hands against every man, and every man's hand against them; the instruments of rapine; tarnished with almost every vice and knowing scarcely any virtue but those of reckless bravery and uncalculating obedience to their leader." Carlyle, writing in the mid-nineteenth century, was referring to Schiller's drama, but Schiller accurately reproduced firsthand impressions of Wallenstein's army. Its leaders were exotic, frightening. There was General Ottavio Piccolomini, of whom much more later, whom the German historian Wolfgang Menzel called "a venal Italian mercenary, the most depraved wretch that appeared on the scene during the war," who was generally held responsible for the disgraceful murder of a Danish prince under the flag of truce and whose use of violence in exacting "contributions" struck even Wallenstein himself as culpably extreme. There was Count Isolani, crazy gambler and leader of the Croats. There was General von Pappenheim, a byword for courage and for bellicosity who bore on his brow a birthmark in the shape of crossed swords and who had been Tilly's lieutenant when their armies sacked and burned the great city of Magdeburg, the worst atrocity of that atrocious war.

The troops these generals led seemed, to the civilian eye, outlandish and savage. Isolani's Croats, horsemen who operated as scouts and skirmishers, wore Turkish armor which gave them the look, to the devout peasant, of the infidel, Christendom's enemy. The Scots, English, Irish, and Italian mercenaries were no less alien, jabbering in their incomprehensible languages, all too evidently gathered on the bleeding empire like flies on a carcass, greedy, vicious, and predatory. Alongside the strangers were known enemies, men who had fought for Denmark or Sweden or for Count Mansfeld until the misfortunes of war had swept them onto the other side, and, curiously enough for an imperial army, there were thousands of refugees from imperial persecution. Ferdinand was still energetically attempting to impose Catholicism on all his Austrian subjects. As a contemporary news sheet reported: "Peasants do not want to be reformed and are going to war in large numbers—there being nine to ten thousand of them in Friedland's army." When Rodrigo Díaz took Valencia, a triumph which was to be represented in the centuries to come as a victory for the Cross, he did so at the head of a partially Muslim army, the supporters of the deposed King al-Qadir having joined his forces. So Wallenstein, military representative of the Catholic Church, was followed by hordes of persecuted Protestants. Driven from their homes and deprived of their land and livelihoods by the emperor's religious policies, they could find no other way of supporting themselves but by killing and dying for the emperor.

These warriors conducted themselves as savagely as those of any other contemporary army. A pamphlet entitled *The Dreadful but Truthful Narration of the Exceedingly Barbarous, Verily Satanic Devastation by the Imperialists of the Town of Goldberg* describes an occasion when some of Wallenstein's troops axed the gates and overran a town, raping the women, stealing all movable goods, and then torturing the men in a variety of horrific ways to induce them to reveal where more treasure might be concealed. Homeless and inimical to homeless and civility alike, the soldiers seemed to those they supposedly defended to be beasts of prey, feeding on flocks the peasant fattened, as wild and wolfish as Achilles and his Myrmidons must have looked to those who watched them, terrified, from the walls of Troy. And Wallenstein, their leader, whom Carlyle imagined as "the object of universal reverence where nothing else is revered," epitomized the dread they inspired. "Leaving a hundred villages in flames," wrote the nineteenth-century historian Wolfgang Menzel, "he marched with terror in his van."

The war was by now hydra-headed. While Wallenstein negotiated the terms of his recall, Gustavus Adolphus once again defeated Tilly, this time actually in Bavaria. The "good old man" was wounded in the thigh. Two weeks later he died. His employer, the Elector Maximilian, was driven from Munich, his capital, and "crept with a stick around the church like a shadow on its wall, so cast down that he could scarce be recognised." Gustavus Adolphus took up residence in Maximilian's palace and ordered his men, as he bluntly informed the French ambassador, to "scorch and ravage the land." The elector, who had so recently brought about Wallenstein's fall from office, wrote to him beseeching him "that in accordance with the kind affection and care ever displayed by you for me . . . you will at this present most dire pass and need not leave me defenceless." Wallenstein ignored the cant about kind affection. Bavaria was lost. Before attending to it he proposed to drive the emperor's Saxon enemies, led by Arnim, out of Bohemia.

He did so promptly. Gustavus Adolphus, alarmed, turned back northwards. The Bavarian army, now led by the elector in person, marched to join the imperial one. The once-haughty Maximilian, thoroughly humbled, was obliged to place himself and his army under the restored generalissimo's command. The two men met on July 1. "All eyes," writes Count Khevenhüller, "were on them." Personal antagonists but political and military allies, they greeted each other with decorum, but observers noted that "His Electoral Highness has learnt the art of dissimulation better than the Duke" and fancied that they could read Wallenstein's hatred and fierce triumphant joy in the flashing of his eyes.

Gustavus Adolphus found his way barred by their combined forces. He fell back on Nuremberg and set twenty thousand soldiers and as many more peasants to work surrounding the town with ditches and ramparts. Wallenstein encamped his armies to the southwest of the town, cutting off its lines of supply, and set himself to wait. His camp extended for miles. It contained villages, woods, a river, and a hill surmounted by a ruined castle, the Alte Veste, and it was as grimly defended as Nuremberg now was. For two months he waited while Maximilian, his unwilling assistant, fretted and chivvied him, longing for action. The Swedish chancellor Oxenstierna was approaching with a second army to reinforce Gustavus Adolphus's. Neither the Swedes nor Wallenstein's allies could understand why the generalissimo did not move to prevent its coming. But he had foreseen that Oxenstierna brought disaster, not salvation, to the Swedish king. He was showing them all, as he curtly told Maximilian, a new way to make war.

It was high summer. Inside Nuremberg food was running out, and so was water. The horses died first. Their carcasses rotted in the streets. Then came disease. A contemporary chronicler records that over twenty-nine thousand people died inside the city. In Wallenstein's camp men were dying too, but not so fast. There was no way that Gustavus Adolphus could accommodate another thirty thousand men. As soon as his reinforcements arrived he was obliged to come out from behind his ramparts and fight. For two days he bombarded the imperial camp but

Wallenstein did not respond. On the third day Gustavus Adolphus ordered a general assault, and this time Wallenstein fought back. "The combat started right early," he reported to the emperor, "and lasted most hotly all day. Many officers and men of Your Majesty's army are dead and wounded . . . but in this encounter the King of Sweden hath mightily blunted his antlers." He himself had been commanding the troops from the Alte Veste, visible from all sides in his scarlet cloak.

There was a pause. It was August. The Swedish army melted away ever faster in the disease-fostering sun. Wallenstein still had food. In the two weeks after the battle Gustavus Adolphus lost another fifteen thousand men, many of whom simply crossed over to the imperial camp to save themselves from starvation. He sent an emissary proposing to Wallenstein that they should meet to discuss terms for peace. Wallenstein sent word back that he (the generalissimo *in assolutissima forma*) was not authorized to do any such thing. At last Gustavus Adolphus led his surviving troops out of Nuremberg and marched away. Wallenstein sent scouts after them, but he let them go. The Elector Maximilian, beside himself with frustration, stormed at him: Why this endless waiting? Why not more fighting? Why had he not pursued the Swedes? "'Twas all to no avail," he reported bitterly. "We had to experience how the Duke gibed at us, as though we had not experience enough in these matters." Wallenstein was perfectly satisfied with his own performance. Thirty years earlier William Shakespeare had written his *Troilus and Cressida*, in which Achilles, paragon of warrior-heroes, is reimagined as a vain, delinquent bullyboy and in which the foul-mouthed truth teller Thersites mocks him as one of the "oxen" with whom the clever men, Ulysses and Nestor, "plough up the wars." Wallenstein was no ox. It was not his way to fight needless battles. What traditional commanders achieved with dash and bravado and violent action, he achieved by more modern methods, by patience and foresight, and by letting the awful weight of his army lie like an incubus on the Swedes, as it had for so long lain on the empire's own people.

Gustavus Adolphus marched south. Wallenstein went north, headed for Saxony. Gustavus Adolphus turned around and followed him. In November the opponents closed on each other again near Lützen. "We expect tomorrow already to meet the king," wrote Wallenstein on the 10th. But four days later, when the king of Sweden continued to evade a battle, he resolved to disperse his troops for the winter. It was a disastrous mistake. On the morning of the 15th his invaluable General von Pappenheim left with eight thousand men, and so did other smaller divisions. Around midday one of them found itself riding into the entire Swedish army, on its way to Lützen to fall upon Wallenstein's depleted forces. Cannon were fired as a signal to all who could hear to race back and rejoin Wallenstein. Messengers galloped after Pappenheim. At about four o'clock, mercifully too late on a November day to do battle, the Swedes marched into view and took up their positions across a stream from the imperial army. All through the night Wallenstein's men came straggling back in to be led to their battle stations while the generalissimo, whose gout, by this stage of his life, caused him almost perpetual pain, was carried up and down the torchlit lines in a crimson litter borne by mules. Pappenheim and his men would not return until the next day. By his own error Wallenstein found himself outnumbered.

When morning came both armies were shrouded in fog, but by eleven the fighting had begun, by Wallenstein's own account "with such a fury as no man hath ever seen or heard." Overcoming the pain in his legs and feet, he led his men on horseback. The battle lasted all day and deep into the night. "Whole regiments of the enemy were slain," wrote Wallenstein, "whilst on our side sundry thousand men too were left upon the field." Hour by hour the lines fluctuated as positions were taken and retaken, and all the time the killing went on until, according to an eyewitness, the entire plain was covered with piles of the dead. Among them was King Gustavus Adolphus, the Lion of Midnight, the second Gideon. Unable to control his great white horse after a shot in the arm, too nearsighted to be sure in which direction safety lay, he blundered into a group of imperial soldiers who shot and stabbed him repeatedly, dragged him from his horse, made off with his gold watch and silver spurs, stripped him naked, and left his corpse among the thousands on the battlefield.

Afterwards the imperial generalissimo received letters of hyperbolical congratulation. "Beloved Son and Noble gentleman," wrote the Pope. "Thy bravery has liberated not only Germany, nay the whole of the Christian globe from its most dangerous enemy." Te Deums were sung in thanksgiving in all the Catholic capitals of Europe, and in Madrid a twenty-four-act drama representing the battle was staged to great applause. Wallenstein expressed himself glad of his formidable rival's death. "It is well for him and me that he is gone: there was not enough room in Germany for both our heads." But the day itself was a triumph for no one. Most historians account it a Swedish victory, despite the king's death, because at nightfall Wallenstein withdrew, leaving his artillery on the field and (as usual) abandoning his wounded, but neither side gained any lasting advantage from the slaughter. The day's action is best summed up in the bald, exhausted words of the imperial army's Colonel Holk (who, like thousands of the other combatants, was disinclined from partisan heroics by the fact that he had, in his time, served on both sides): "The blood-bath lasted seven hours and, after both sides had suffered unheard-of ravage, the one withdrew along the one route, the other along the other route." Wallenstein never fought such a battle again.

He led his army into Bohemia. Khevenhüller is one of several of his contemporaries who attest to the munificence with which he rewarded good service, but remarks as well that he was "cruel, and famous for saying 'Let the beast hang!' " In Prague that winter those of his officers who had performed well were lavishly paid. Ottavio Piccolomini, who had had three horses killed under him at Lützen, received a fortune in ready money. Holk, a Dane who had fought against Wallenstein at Stralsund but was now his trusted deputy, was granted four great Bohemian estates, each including eighteen villages. But the punishments Wallenstein meted out were as great as the rewards. A scaffold was erected on the same spot where the Bohemian rebels had been executed twelve years before, in a deliberate echo of that grisly performance. Seven officers accused of cowardice had to stand by and watch their swords broken on the scaffold in a public ritual of disgrace. Fourteen more were beheaded. Wallenstein was not present. Holk was in charge. The last man to die seemed to all observers especially pitiful. Even Holk, who was noted for his icy-heartedness and who had seen thousands upon thousands of young men killed for no good reason, was moved, noting the condemned was a mere "child." He changed the order of execution so as to give him every hope of a last-minute reprieve. When none came Holk halted the killing, to the crowd's vociferous approval. While the condemned remained kneeling on the scaffold Holk rode over the bridge to Wallenstein's palace to ask if an exception could be made. The answer came that it could not: "*Non si può.*" The young man's head was hacked off. It was his twentieth birthday.

That winter Wallenstein was more aloof, more choleric than ever. He shut himself up in the recesses of his palace in Prague. Few people had access to him. "His Princely Grace keeps himself very rare," reported a Bavarian agent. Even senior officers had to wait weeks for an audience. He had long felt himself to be immured in a labyrinth. Now he was taking on the characteristics of the Minotaur, a fabulous monster, seldom seen, pathetic but greatly to be feared. Those who did gain admittance were shocked by how ill he looked. He was emaciated. His face, ineffectually half-hidden by a silk scarf, was yellowish green and blotched with black. Something—gout, arthritis, or perhaps tertiary syphilis—was progressively crippling him. He never mounted a horse again after Lützen. There were weeks when he could not even sign his name.

As he declined physically his political stature grew ever greater. Ambassadors traveled from all over Europe to court his favor. Imperial ministers came to seek his advice. Letters passed between him and all his potential opponents and allies. He was functioning now as an all-but-independent potentate, almost as far from the emperor in Vienna as Rodrigo Díaz in Valencia had been from Alfonso in Castile. Nearly twenty years earlier Kepler had seen in the stars that his independence of mind would predispose him to insubordination and a "contempt and disregard for human precepts and practices." After his death his chief secretary testified that in Prague that winter he received letters from Ferdinand with apparent distaste. He pushed them aside, left them unread for days, and frequently failed to reply.

That February the last year of his life began. Later, after he had been killed, the imperial commissioners published a "*Detailed and Thorough Report of the Abominable Treason Planned by Friedland and his Adherents,*" a retrospective justification of his murder in which it was alleged that he had been the instigator and chief intended beneficiary of a treacherous conspiracy against the emperor. But try as they might, and urgently though they needed to do so in order to clear their master of the charge of having unlawfully murdered his loyal servant, the emperor's officials were unable to find conclusive proof of Wallenstein's guilt. Unquestionably, during the winter and spring of 1632–33 a plan was formed by others—notably by Richelieu and by those among the Bohemian émigrés who still hoped for an independent homeland—that Wallenstein should use the imperial army against the emperor, make himself king of Bohemia, and ally himself with the French, the Swedes, the Saxons, or a combination of all three. Whether or not Wallenstein ever assented to the scheme is a question on which historians are still unable to agree, not because there is any lack of documentation, but because what there is is so contradictory. Wallenstein's motives were at the time, and are therefore likely perpetually to remain, obscure. He said one thing to this emissary, another to that. He listened to proposals, he read letters, but he responded only equivocally and seldom in writing. It was in this last phase of his life that he acquired his reputation for inscrutability. "One of the maxims of the Duke of Friedland," wrote Priorato, "was to give out one thing and to perform the other." Even Arnim, his one-time deputy who knew him as well as anyone, was baffled. He who had always been so brusque, so shockingly careless of the niceties of diplomatic speech, so prone to ungovernable rage, began to be talked of as an enigma, a master of deception.

Schiller, the most brilliant author yet to have told his story, produced two almost diametrically opposed interpretations of the last phase of Wallenstein's life. In his *History of the Thirty Years' War*, completed in 1797, he followed the imperialist line. He described Wallenstein as a man with an insatiable appetite for power who "concealed under a glittering and theatrical pomp the dark designs of a restless genius." He imagined that the unforgivable insult of Wallenstein's dismissal at Regensburg must have been welcome to him "as it seemed to tear in pieces the record of past favours, to absolve him from every obligation towards his former benefactor." Thenceforward everything he did was done for vengeance's sake. He accepted the command for the second time so that he could call up an army to use against the emperor, and for the rest of his life he was planning his treachery.

So Schiller wrote, but he could only make the facts fit the theory by some strenuously tortuous reasoning. He alleged that the good service Wallenstein had done during his first generalship had been done with the wicked intent of alienating the German princes from the emperor in order to make the emperor dependent solely upon Wallenstein himself—but it is much easier to suppose that he gave good service because he was a good servant. To reconcile the contradictions between Wallenstein's actual behavior in his last year and his supposed motives, Schiller fell back on the conventional solution of proposing that Wallenstein was indeed a man of almost unfathomable mystery. "Torn by burning passions within, while all without bespoke calmness and indifference, he brooded over projects of ambition and revenge and slowly but surely advanced towards his end." But even as he was writing it, honest historian that he was, Schiller had to acknowledge he could not believe what he wrote. In his final summing-up of Wallenstein's career he admitted that he had been able to find no definitive evidence of his treachery (nor, despite exhaustive archival searches, has any subsequent historian), and he concluded: "Wallenstein fell not because he was a rebel, but he became a rebel because he fell." Two years later Schiller embarked on his tripartite tragedy, *Wallenstein's Camp*, *The Piccolomini*, and *Wallenstein's Death*, taking that conclusion as his cue. The Wallenstein of Schiller's plays is far from being one who "slowly but surely advanced towards his end." Rather he is one who, entangled in a web of intrigue and counterintrigue, finds himself obliged, willy-nilly, to play for real a role he had only assumed as a stratagem; one who, like most of Schiller's heroes, is a helpless and ultimately blameless victim of historical forces far beyond his control.

Among Wallenstein's closest associates were two families of the Czech nobility, the Trckas and the Kinskys, who still dreamed of reversing the defeat of the White Mountain and of installing a native-born, non-Hapsburg king in Bohemia. These powerless people had powerful connections. Encouraged by what he heard from them, Cardinal Richelieu sent his ambassador to Wallenstein proposing an alliance and assuring him the king of France was prepared to afford him armed support "in mounting to the throne of Bohemia, or even higher." Wallenstein heard the proposals, read personal letters from the great cardinal and from his adviser Father Joseph, but made no reply. What he thought of the proposition we do not know. Nor did his contemporaries. The French ambassador, baffled and frustrated, eventually gave up trying to guess. "The Duke of Friedland's game is too subtle for me," he reported. The Swedish chancellor Oxenstierna, also prompted by Czech émigrés, made a similar offer. He would welcome Wallenstein as an ally and would give him every support, but only if he would unequivocally declare himself, by word or deed, to be no longer the emperor's man. Once more, Wallenstein made no reply. He was associating with politically compromising people, but they were people with whom, as the emperor's representative, he had legitimate cause to negotiate. As he had written to Arnim years before, when the latter was his deputy, "those to whom we entrust the command of armies may surely be allowed to hold conversation with an adversary." He was listening to proposals which it would have been safer not to have heard, but as far as anyone has ever been able to discover he did not give them his assent. In May he went forth to war once more as the imperial generalissimo.

He rode out in state. "All the court attendants were clad in uniforms of blue and scarlet, and ten trumpeters, sounding their silver gilt trumpets, opened the way." There were fourteen coaches each drawn by six horses and a train of baggage wagons covered with gilded leather. "The train announced the man who, in power and splendour vied even with the emperor himself," wrote an observer. Wallenstein is said to have remarked that it was "a pretty train, a brave sight, but our return shall be with one far comelier." The promise was remembered (or invented) for its piquancy. That return never took place.

Arnim, still the elector of Saxony's commander, was in Silesia along with the forces of the elector of Brandenburg, another of Sweden's allies, and Swedish troops under the command of the Bohemian nationalist Count Thurn. Wallenstein's forces easily outnumbered their combined armies. But instead of attacking them, he proposed an armistice.

He had seen at Lützen how little advantage could be gained from how much killing. His contemporary the Spanish ambassador wrote: "The wars of mankind today are not limited to a trial of natural strength, like a bull-fight, nor even to mere battles. Rather they depend on losing or gaining friends or allies, and it is to this end that good statesmen must turn all their attention and energy." It was a lesson Wallenstein already knew by heart.

He apparently sought to isolate the Swedes by making a separate peace with their allies within the empire. It was a sound policy, and one for which he believed himself to have Ferdinand's sanction. The Elector John George of Saxony, Arnim's employer, the most powerful of the German Protestant princes, was one whose alliance he particularly sought. Back in 1626, when Christian of Denmark launched his foray into the empire, John George had urged his fellow members of the Lower Saxon Circle to remain loyal to the emperor rather than support their foreign coreligionist. Like Wallenstein, the elector was in favor of a strong, centralized imperial government, so long as it was perceived to be just and reasonable, and so long as it permitted religious freedom. After the Edict of Restitution and after the appalling sack of the Protestant city of Magdeburg by Tilly's army, John George had entered into an alliance with the Swedes, but Wallenstein had good cause to see him as a natural ally. To a more amenable, less doctrinaire emperor than Ferdinand he could have been a loyal and vitally important subject, one whose allegiance would have secured that of many smaller powers. Wallenstein and Arnim met at Heidersdorf for extended talks. Arnim took Wallenstein's proposed terms back to the electors of Saxony and Brandenburg, who rejected them. The armistice was nominally over, but still Wallenstein did not attack.

This pacific dithering was not what most imperialists wanted of the man whose attendant spirits were supposed to be "storm, fire and terror." Back in Vienna a pamphlet appeared, expressing grave doubts about Wallenstein's health and his general competence and asking sarcastically,

"Would it be better to bring down in ruin the House of Austria and shortly the whole of Christendom rather than to hurt the Generalissimo's susceptibilities?"

At the end of August Wallenstein and Arnim—those old comrades—agreed to a second armistice. Emissaries galloped off to all interested parties to discuss a peace plan so vaguely formulated that no one seemed able to agree on what its main points were. Oxenstierna and Thurn both understood that Wallenstein had finally agreed to turn on his emperor. If they were right Wallenstein was indeed, at least ostensibly, contemplating treachery. But, if he was, when he and Arnim met again in September he had changed his mind. "With great vehemence," he insisted that what he wanted was for the Protestant electors and their Bohemian allies to unite with him and his emperor in driving all the foreigners—Swedish, Spanish, and French alike—out of the empire. When Arnim's representative protested that the Swedes were Saxony's allies, Wallenstein was "seized by an ague" and broke off negotiations.

What he was thinking of in that last year is as hard to plumb now as it was for his contemporaries. His killers were to ascribe to him a will as unconquerable and courage as dauntless as those of Milton's Satan, who boasted of the "fixed mind / and high disdain . . . That with the mightiest raised me to contend," but a fixed mind was precisely what Wallenstein, towards the end of his life, most signally lacked. "Certain it is that no safe treaty can be concluded with the man," wrote Arnim, exasperated, "for there is no steadiness in him." Some saw in his apparent inconsistencies the devious machinations of a conspirator cunning past men's thought; others saw the vacillations of one sick, or superstitious, or desperate.

Contemporaries, including Count Adam Trcka, his brother-in-law, who was at this period one of his most favored associates, and Arnim, who had been both his trusted lieutenant and his opponent, deplored the inordinate influence his astrologers had over him. At the end of the second armistice, when his policy seemed to have changed so abruptly and inexplicably, one of his colonels put it about that the alteration could be ascribed to an astrologer's prediction that he would win a great battle in November. "Since he is so superstitious as to heed the influence of the stars and mostly to govern his actions by astrological reports," he had therefore decided he could gain more by confrontation than by peace talks. He had always sought guidance from the stars. Kepler (who was more skeptical than his patron) once wrote irritably that Wallenstein had kept him for three weeks at work on updating his horoscope, "a waste of time for him and for me." Kepler had repeatedly and sternly refused

Wallenstein's requests for precise predictions of terrestrial events. But Battista Senno was more obliging, and it is possible Wallenstein's physical deterioration had rendered him at once less decisive and more credulous.

Certainly he was not well. When obliged to leave his couch he was carried everywhere in a litter. He was taking quantities of powders and potions to alleviate his suffering, drugs whose effect on his state of mind were probably little understood by contemporary physicians and are impossible to gauge in retrospect. He was seized by seismic rages over which he no longer seemed to have control. Besides, the decay of his body may have been accompanied by more than the inevitable exhaustion and irascibility of one in constant pain. One scholar, after studying his apothecary's bills, has concluded that he may have been subject to a form of urine poisoning likely to induce hallucinations and other delusions. Those who spoke with him during these months refer repeatedly to his being taken ill in the middle of important conferences, suggesting that he was subject to some form of dementia.

He wanted peace. That much seems clear. He was not one to fight to the last man for a lost cause. He was no dogmatic, incorruptible Cato. There was no principle he would not concede, no alliance or concession he would not contemplate. He once said, "When all the land is in ruins, then we will have to make peace." The words have been quoted by those who would make a desperate warrior of him as though they signified an indomitable resolve. But they were written in bitter irritation against the intriguing diplomats whose machinations threatened to prolong the war ad infinitum and the bigots whose intolerance made any agreement so hard.

He wanted, as he had always wanted, a unified empire and the expulsion of foreign meddlers. Everything he worked for would have benefited the emperor, but the emperor himself was a major obstacle to its accomplishment. In the course of his negotiations with Arnim that last summer, Wallenstein was several times to express his frustration with Ferdinand, and his hostility to the Jesuits and Spaniards who encouraged him in his militant Catholicism. Wallenstein worked for political unity, not religious uniformity. Ferdinand's Edict of Restitution, the "root of all evil," had riven apart the empire he was trying to weld into a whole. Before setting out in May he had said to two emissaries from Oxenstierna, "Are we not arch-fools to be knocking our heads for the sake of others when, since we have the armies in our power, we could arrange a peace to our liking?" There is no clear evidence that he ever thought of ousting the emperor, but there are plenty of indications that he did aspire to the role of independent arbiter, what Schiller calls "the man of destiny," one with the authority to propose a peace settlement and force it on the emperor and his enemies alike.

Another cause of contention arose between emperor and generalissimo. The Spanish Hapsburg prince, the cardinal infante, was proceeding through the western empire towards the Netherlands. He asked for the loan of the imperial troops under Colonel Aldringen, which were stationed in Austria but under Wallenstein's overall command. Wallenstein forbade Aldringen to move. At the beginning of August Ferdinand wrote to Wallenstein with a "request" that he should hand over the troops. Before the letter was sealed he changed the word "request" to "command." So much for Wallenstein's supremacy "*in assolutissima forma.*" Two weeks later an imperial minister came to Silesia with secret instructions to sound out some of Wallenstein's senior officers "that his Imperial Majesty shall be assured of their steadfast loyalty and devotion in the case of a change pertaining to the Duke of Friedland by reason of his illness or otherwise." The author of a contemporary French tract wrote that Wallenstein "was much honoured by his own and foreign soldiers by whom, once known, he was almost adored," but perhaps his charisma was dwindling along with his health. Subsequent events suggest that the assurances given the emperor's representative by at least two of those approached, Octavio Piccolomini and Matthias Gallas, were eminently satisfactory. Already Wallenstein's second downfall was being encompassed.

When the second round of his talks with Arnim broke down, Wallenstein told the Saxon emissary darkly that when the armistice expired "I shall know what it is that thereafter I have to do!" He did. He marched on Steinau, a stronghold held by Count Thurn's Swedes. So swift and surprising was Wallenstein's aggressive move that the Swedes did not even attempt to defend themselves. Within half an hour they surrendered. Five thousand of them joined Wallenstein's army. Thurn was captured (but subsequently released). Wallenstein swept on, the Swedish army fleeing before him from fortress after fortress.

It was good service, but it was not enough. In August, what purported to be word-for-word accounts of the meeting at Heidersdorf between Wallenstein and Arnim reached the emperor in Vienna. According to this secret, unverifiable account Wallenstein had promised independence for Bohemia and a pardon for all the exiled rebels, while hinting that he might make himself king of Bohemia and margrave of Moravia. He had railed against the elector of Bavaria and against the Jesuits. About Maximilian Wallenstein was quoted as saying, "The

Bavarian started this game. No assistance shall I render him . . . Would that his land were already ruined. Would that he were long dead. If he make not peace I shall myself wage war against him." About Ferdinand he is alleged to have said, "If the Emperor will not make peace and keep the agreement I shall force him to it." As the report circulated even those ministers who had previously been considered part of the "Friedland faction" hastened to distance themselves from him. That autumn a courtier reported that in Vienna, despite his brilliant successes in the field, Wallenstein was spoken of "publicly and without shame . . . with incredible contempt and malice."

While he chased the Swedes northwards their ally Bernard of Weimar was threatening Regensburg on the Bavarian border. Maximilian implored the emperor to send Wallenstein and his army to his aid. The emperor would gladly have complied but it was becoming exasperatingly, humiliatingly, even alarmingly obvious that he could not command his commander. Wallenstein refused to take the threat to Regensburg seriously, declared that he was unable to send troops there, then gave himself the lie by setting out in force but too late. Before he could reach the scene Regensburg had been taken by the Protestants. He had achieved nothing by his belated move except a demonstration of his own failing judgment. The emperor urged him to attempt to retake the city. But Wallenstein never deliberately engaged in a battle he could not win. It was getting cold, time to search for winter quarters. Ignoring the imperial orders Wallenstein led his army back into Bohemia to camp at Pilsen.

By the time he marched back into Pilsen he had no friends left at court. In 408 BC, after the defeat of his fleet at Notium, the Athenians drastically revised their estimation of Alcibiades. A few months before they had adored him and offered him unprecedented powers, but at his first failure they recalled all their grievances against him. So now Wallenstein's whole career was being reviewed and reinterpreted as that of a traitor. It is a part of the price heroes pay for their heroic status that no allowance is made, by those who adore or fear them for their imagined superhuman capacities, for the fallibility inherent in their merely human nature. When Alcibiades took command of the Athenian fleet for the second time it was generally believed that he was omnipotent and invincible; therefore, if he lost a battle it must have been because he had deliberately and treacherously refrained from winning it. So too it was assumed of Wallenstein that nothing but treason could have prevented his career from being one long parade of victories.

His ambition, maintained his detractors, had always been insatiable, and since his dismissal at Regensburg it had been reinforced by his festering anger and his craving for revenge. It was said that in the period of his retirement he had sabotaged Tilly's campaign by refusing to sell food and other material from Friedland to the army. A pamphlet revived the allegation that he had treacherously invited Arnim and his Saxons into Prague in 1631. It was suggested yet again that he had agreed to reassume his command only in order to undo the empire from within. People whispered that he had held back, deliberately and treacherously, from attacking the Swedish army in Nuremberg because a conclusive victory would not have been in his own personal interests. An imperial committee found that his withdrawal from Lützen was an act of cowardice. His recent release of Count Thurn constituted collusion with the enemy. Even his dislike for the noise of crowing cocks was adduced against him: like St. Peter he was a betrayer of his master. His failure to save Regensburg was deliberate and malicious, motivated by his hatred of Elector Maximilian. And his subsequent disobedience and withdrawal to Pilsen was—even in the opinion of Prince Eggenburg, who, among all the imperial councillors, had been the one most sympathetic to him—"the most pernicious, the most perilous, the most heedless thing that the Duke has ever done." His entire course of action since his recall was shown to be a slow, devious, diabolically wicked progress towards the moment when he could avenge himself on his imperial master.

The emperor was afraid. Following the advice of his councillors and the urgings of Maximilian of Bavaria, he determined to test his authority. Wallenstein had announced his intention to settle his army in winter quarters in Bohemia. Ferdinand sent word that he was to do no such thing. He was to turn around and return to Bavaria, there to attack Bernard of Weimar, and afterwards to quarter his troops in Saxony or Brandenburg (hostile territories which would have to be made to admit the imperial army at the point of the sword). "This," concluded the emperor, "is my definite decision on which I fully insist."

It was the first time he had ever issued so peremptory an order to his generalissimo. Perhaps by ill luck, perhaps by design of those who longed for Wallenstein's overthrow, the order on which he chose to "fully insist" was all but impossible to obey. It was December. Wallenstein had never attempted a military action so late in the year. It was bitterly cold. The ground was frozen hard. There was snow on the hills. To attempt to mount an aggressive campaign at such a season was to court mutiny, the rapid loss of men through desertion, illness, and exposure and—eventually—near-certain defeat.

It is at this point in Wallenstein's career that the action of Friedrich Schiller's great dramatic trilogy, *Wallenstein's Camp, The Piccolomini*, and *Wallenstein's Death*, begins. Schiller avails himself of poetic license to juggle a little with the actual course of events. Writing at the end of the eighteenth century, at a time of emergent German nationalism, he picks as the breaking point an earlier order of the emperor's, that requiring Wallenstein to place Aldringen and his troops under Spanish command, an adjustment which allows him to make the most of Wallenstein's "patriotic" opposition to Spanish and Jesuit factions at court. But the essential shape of the historical drama played out at Pilsen is recognizable in the plays. Schiller knew what he was writing about, and both the historian and the dramatist in him perceived that from the point when Wallenstein was placed in a position where he could not but defy his emperor his downfall was inevitable. The rest of his story has the nightmarish shapeliness of tragedy, a course of events racing ineluctably to its ghastly end.

At Pilsen Wallenstein was isolated. His contemporary Robert Burton wrote that among those most gnawed by melancholy were "the mighty when they grow old, they who neither loved nor were loved, who only exploited others, *sibi nati*, those born for themselves." Wallenstein was not old, but he was terribly aged: the description fits. Several of his officers had their wives with them at Pilsen, but his duchess stayed away. There was no one close to him who was not, in some measure, using him. Years earlier he had written to his father-in-law, "We must regard it as a maxim that we can trust absolutely no one." He was right. Even his astrologer Senno, with whom, it was said, he sat up through long sleepless nights in a vain attempt to foresee his future, was taking money from one of his assassins-to-be to disclose the nature of their conversations. In recounting the last weeks of his life the language of fidelity and treason is turned upside down. The "loyalists" were those of his officers who, while apparently still deferring to him, were secretly reporting his every questionable saying back to the court. The "traitors" were those who stood staunchly by their commander, and in some cases died with him. "Loyalists" and "traitors" contributed in approximately equal measure to the digging of the pit into which he fell.

In his darkened, silenced room overlooking the main square in Pilsen Wallenstein worked indefatigably, sending off messengers to the Protestant electors, still intent on making peace. And as he intrigued, others made him, willy-nilly, an actor in intrigues of their own. In the last weeks of his life he was simultaneously the ferocious warlord whom none dared affront and a helpless victim of others' scheming. His rivals at the imperial court sought to entrap him into overt treachery so as to be rid of him. His allies among the Protestants were anxious to lure him into committing himself unequivocally to their cause. To Catholic imperialists and Protestant rebels alike Wallenstein was a prey whom they were trying to drive into a trap. A Saxon general wrote jubilantly to Arnim in January, "He [Wallenstein] is now so far in that he can no longer escape."

Among his officers the treacherous "loyalists" were, as events would reveal, in the majority. The three most prominent among them, the triumvirate who would encompass his proscription and death, were Aldringen, Gallas, and Piccolomini. Aldringen, who was far away in Bavaria, had shown himself a less than wholehearted supporter of his generalissimo when he had obeyed (as how could he not?) the emperor's order to place his troops at the disposal of the cardinal infante. Already Wallenstein was unsure of him. But the other two, Gallas, who would replace him as commander in chief, and Piccolomini, on whose say-so he would be found guilty of the most heinous treason, were his most favored lieutenants. Piccolomini especially had been, since Holk died of bubonic plague, his preferred confidant. After his death it was said that Wallenstein had trusted Piccolomini "blinded by a conjunction in their stars." In December Wallenstein promoted him to the rank of field marshal. But his magnanimity was not enough to earn gratitude or forestall betrayal.

The faithful "traitors" served him hardly any better. A second, opposed triumvirate of the two Bohemians, Counts Trcka and Kinsky, and the Hungarian Christian von Ilow was to stand by him to the end, but it is arguable that without their machinations that end need never have come. Trcka and Kinsky, dreaming of an independent Bohemia and a Hapsburg-free empire, had been wooing the French, the Swedes, the Saxons with promises of Wallenstein's readiness to lead a revolt, while wooing Wallenstein with promises of French, Swedish, and Saxon support should he do so. Perhaps he knew and approved everything they were doing, but time and time again his actions belied their claims of his readiness to switch sides.

On receiving the emperor's "definite decision" Wallenstein attempted to protect himself. He knew how insecure he was. One of the imperial councillors was at Pilsen. Wallenstein told him, "I see well enough with what a bandage you would blindfold me, but I shall tear it from my eyes. I observe the efforts that are being made to snatch the army from under my fingers." But he no longer had the energy or the faith in his own authority that had once made him capable of intimidating an emperor and an empire alike. Samuel Taylor Coleridge, who translated Schiller's trilogy, saw his dominant characteristic as "weakness," an analysis which would have astonished any seventeenth-century observer but which fits with what we know of his last, sad days. Francis Drake, on his final voyage, for the first time sought his officers' advice. So Wallenstein, instead of returning the curt *"non si può"* that would have been characteristic of him in more confident times, called all the senior officers with him at Pilsen to a council of war. The emperor's orders were read out. Unanimously the officers agreed that it was impossible to execute them. Wallenstein wrote to his master, enclosing an account of their decision, and asking for the emperor's approval.

Ferdinand's fear was mounting. He complained that "this business is never out of my thoughts. It rises with me in the morning and goes to bed with me at night and completely deprives me of rest." Pamphlets denouncing Wallenstein were circulating in cities all over the empire. One of them warned the emperor that his general was vengeful, arrogant, ungodly, and stark raving mad and concluded: "Salvation lies but one way: Expel your commander . . . Thus speaks God through me, his angel. Perform it swiftly. Follow his counsel or perish." On New Year's Eve 1633 a Bavarian agent wrote to Maximilian to tell him that the emperor had at last resolved in secret to follow the angel's advice and dismiss his generalissimo.

Wallenstein was by now bedridden for all but a few hours each day and in unremitting pain. Ilow announced that no one might hope to see the duke unless he summoned them, and even those so privileged could not hope for a coherent discussion with him: he was in such agony that he "incessantly swore the most frightful curses." One of his officers allowed into his presence on January 10 found the generalissimo incoherent, writhing in his bed and moaning, "Oh, peace! Oh, peace! Peace! Oh, peace!" He told a priest that "were he not afraid of Hell's perpetual punishments he would swallow the most virulent poison so as finally to be released from all his misery." The Minotaur was stricken. Yet this pathetic figure was still, in the imagination of his enemies, monstrously formidable. Even the emperor, nominally the most powerful man in Europe, hesitated, afraid to move against him. "Why this delay?" asked the Spanish ambassador in Vienna, Count Oñate. "A dagger or a pistol will remove him." But Ferdinand had yet to nerve himself for murder.

On January 3, Ottavio Piccolomini had a private meeting with Gallas and another "loyalist" general, Colloredo. According to the report he wrote shortly after Wallenstein's death, Piccolomini revealed to his two colleagues that Wallenstein himself had told him that he intended to go over to the enemy, taking the imperial army with him. He had told Piccolomini, or so Piccolomini said, that he would capture the emperor, drive the Hapsburgs out of the empire, and divide up its territories among his adherents. Colloredo was shocked and furious. Wallenstein, he said, was a rascal who should be "swiftly strangled." Gallas was equally shocked but hesitant. He couldn't believe (and perhaps he was right not to) that Wallenstein would go so far. Within a week the Spanish ambassador had passed Piccolomini's allegations on to the emperor. (Wallenstein had been outspokenly critical of Spain's influence on the Empire's affairs—the Spaniards were impatient for his fall.) Ferdinand's New Year's resolution to rid himself of Wallenstein suddenly acquired new urgency.

While Wallenstein kept to his bed he was represented by Christian von Ilow. Eight years before Wallenstein had listed his reasons for disliking Ilow: "First he is a proud, puffed-up fellow. Secondly he enjoys stirring up intrigue among the commanders." The duke's feelings on this subject had altered, but Ilow's capacity for intrigue remained. The role he played during the last two months of Wallenstein's life was a crucial, and profoundly ambiguous, one. It is open to question whether he was loyally enacting his master's will or whether (as Schiller believed) he was a schemer working, with Trcka, to maneuver Wallenstein into making some gesture which the emperor could never forgive, so that thenceforward Wallenstein would have no choice but to commit himself to rebellion.

At the beginning of January Ilow summoned all forty-seven of the imperial army's generals and colonels to Pilsen. By January 11 they had gathered in the town. That day Ilow entertained them all in his house and held forth to them about the Jesuits and Spaniards who, he said, had such undue influence over the emperor. He then broke it to them that Wallenstein, having given his all to the imperial cause only to be rewarded with ingratitude and slander, intended to resign his command. The announcement was greeted with an outcry of dismay and anger. Financial self-interest, as well as personal loyalty and the professional soldier's furious rejection of the meddling of slippered courtiers, made them vehement for Wallenstein. Twice that afternoon a delegation of officers, each led by the inflammatory Ilow, invaded the generalissimo's crepuscular private quarters to implore him to reconsider. On the second occasion, gracious but exhausted, Wallenstein agreed to remain at his post. Afterwards Ilow suggested that it would be fitting that the officers make a reciprocal gesture, vowing to commit themselves to the commander in chief's service, just as he had so nobly and selflessly committed himself to theirs. All of them agreed.

The next evening Ilow held a banquet for all the assembled officers in the town hall. The generalissimo, in whose palace courtiers had once dared to speak only in whispers, kept to his room across the square within easy earshot of the long, rowdy party. There was music, a lot of wine, much shouting, many drunken, sentimental toasts, a great deal of furniture overturned and smashed. In the midst of the uproar a document was circulated. It was an oath of loyalty to Wallenstein for all to sign. It was a strange moment for such solemn business. Some hung back. (The arch-"loyalist" Piccolomini was later to claim that during this period he had approached at least eighteen officers to assure himself of their loyalty to the emperor—which might carry with it the corollary of disloyalty to the emperor's generalissimo.) The atmosphere grew violent. One shouted that anyone who refused to add his name was a scoundrel, a second threatened to throw the first out of the window, a third drew his sword on the second. Trcka, also sword in hand, declared himself ready to kill anyone who opposed the general, whereupon Piccolomini involuntarily exclaimed, "Traitor!" (for was not the emperor himself by now Wallenstein's opponent?), and then, as though to distract attention from this too-revealing exclamation, grabbed another officer and whirled him, madly capering, around the hall. Some signed but not all, and many of those who did scrawled their names so clumsily (perhaps because they were drunk, perhaps because they were sufficiently sober to foresee the danger the document represented) that they could not afterwards be identified.

The oath was designed to commit the officers firmly to Wallenstein's cause. The signatories—so Ilow argues in Schiller's play, and so he probably thought in real life—no longer had the option of going to Vienna, should Wallenstein rebel, and assuring the emperor that they had had no part in the rebellion. Their own handwriting would give them the lie. And as for the officers, so perhaps for the commander. Schiller's Ilow is a tempter, using the oath as a way of nerving Wallenstein to take the plunge into open rebellion. Certainly Ilow must have been able to foresee—it would not have been hard—how the oath-taking would look from Vienna. It could be taken to be the unequivocal gesture of defiance on Wallenstein's part for which so many people on both sides were waiting. Wallenstein was entrapped by it, as securely as those he or his lieutenants sought to entrap.

The following morning Wallenstein summoned all forty-seven of the officers to his rooms and received them, dressed and seated in an armchair. He had heard, he told them, that some among them were reluctant to sign the oath. That being so he could not continue in his office. "I would sooner be dead than see myself living so; I shall withdraw and nurse my health." One of his furious rages seized him. He ranted about money, about the Spaniards, about the iniquities of those about the emperor. His tirade was furious, despairing. He recalled a time when "we had flooded the whole empire with our army, held all fortresses and passes." If peace could not be made then, then when would it ever come? He said that his detractors at court were out to dishonor him, perhaps even to poison him. He raved on until, suddenly spent, he advised the officers to think again about the oath and with a nod dismissed them. Sheepish and hungover, the officers adjourned, drew up a petition begging the generalissimo to forgive them their drunkenness of the night before and then, every single one of them, signed the oath. The majority of those who thereby solemnly swore to defend and serve Wallenstein would shortly desert him. Six weeks later three of them were party to his death.

Shortly after the events at Pilsen it was being said that the wording of the oath had changed between its being read aloud to the officers and their being required to sign, that the first draft contained a redeeming clause making the officers' duty to serve Wallenstein conditional on Wallenstein's continuing to serve the emperor. Given the number of the signatories and the fact that, however drunk they were at Ilow's banquet, they all signed again on five separate copies the following day, it seems unlikely that anyone would have attempted, let alone got away with, such a deception. Count Oñate told another version of the story: the original draft had indeed contained such a clause but Wallenstein had edited it out. This may be disinformation designed as further evidence of Wallenstein's disloyalty, but it sounds consonant with Wallenstein's character. He had not wished that his coins should bear the slogan "The Lord is my protector"; no more did he wish his officers to swear loyalty to him only as his master's servant. He was nobody's protégé. He stood alone. At Pilsen, if Oñate's version is correct, he refused to solicit his men's loyalty in his official persona as the emperor's lieutenant. He wanted their allegiance to be for him alone, *"für mich."*

It was his undoing. The Pilsen oath, apparently designed to ensure his security, rendered his downfall inevitable. The news of it, arriving in Vienna so soon after Piccolomini's allegations, seemed to confirm them. If he was not bent on mutiny and rebellion, why ever should Wallenstein have needed such an assurance of his officers' support? The emperor bestirred himself. To summon Wallenstein, the Satanic genius of the war, to explain and defend himself was a prospect too frightening to contemplate. He would be tried in absentia. A panel of three judges, all of them eminent councillors who had formerly been on affable terms with Wallenstein, were appointed to determine his guilt. Docilely they did so.

He had always been aloof. His absences and hauteur, his refusal to participate in the life of the court and the state, had rendered him awesome. Now, so far from the capital, he loomed like a nightmare on the edge of the imperial world. Count Oñate, indefatigably fanning the hysteria, remarked to the Bavarian agent that as a captive Wallenstein would constitute a hideous danger to state security: it would be easier to kill him. Prince von Liechtenstein wrote a memorial to the emperor in which he said the same thing, but more guardedly, arguing that "extreme remedies are appropriate to extreme wickedness." To his contemporaries Wallenstein was not just a military commander whose politics were unreliable. Danger and ruin attended him. Perils mounted, wrote Oñate, "with every day that this man is still allowed to live."

A proclamation was drafted, dated January 24 but not to be made public until Ferdinand and his councillors judged the moment safe, in which the emperor addressed all of his officers, absolving them from any duty of obedience towards Wallenstein, pardoning those who had been misled into subscribing to the oath at Pilsen, and appointing Count Gallas as acting commander in chief. At the same time, so Ferdinand's confessor later revealed, "the Emperor furnished several of the loyalest—namely Gallas, Aldringen, Piccolomini, Colloredo—who pretended to be of Friedland's party, with plenary authority to take prisoner the leading members of the conspiracy and if at all possible, to bring them to Vienna or else to slay them as convicted felons." So, covertly and with no chance to defend himself, Wallenstein was sentenced to death.

For nearly three weeks nothing happened. Two years earlier the French jurist Cardin le Bret had addressed the question of "whether obedience is due to commands which, although they seem unjust, have the welfare of the state as their constant object, as if the prince would command the killing of someone who was notoriously rebellious, factious and seditious." Le Bret concluded with a quotation from Seneca: *"Necessitas omnem legem frangit"*—necessity breaks every law. But the fact remained that such an execution was "unjust." Aldringen, Piccolomini, and Gallas knew what was required of them, but they were all afraid to act. So, it seems, was the emperor, who continued to write graciously to Wallenstein for twenty days after he had authorized his murder, addressing him as "well-born beloved cousin."

Eventually Count Gallas broke the deadlock. On February 12 he left Pilsen, his coach and horses lent him by the unsuspecting Wallenstein, ostensibly to summon Aldringen and return with him. The next day Piccolomini also went. He told Wallenstein he was afraid that Aldringen might either suborn or imprison Gallas, and that he had better go after Gallas and bring him back. Wallenstein lent him, too, a coach. When in 1630 the news of his dismissal was brought to Wallenstein at Memmingen observers were struck by his lack of surprise. Then the all-powerful commander was imagined to be as omniscient as he was omnipotent, served certainly by silent squadrons of spies on earth, and probably by the stars as well. But now, clearly, he was unaware of what was being prepared against him. One does not oblige deserters or one's would-be assassins by providing them with transport.

In Vienna rumor and panic were spreading. The emperor ordered that prayers should be said in all the churches for a happy outcome to an unspecified "matter of the first importance." A fire near a munitions store terrified the populace. A suspect general was arrested, placed under a constant guard by fifty men, and accused of being under orders from Wallenstein to start fires at all four corners of the city. While Vienna burned, it was alleged, assassins hired by Wallenstein and already hiding in the city would have murdered the entire imperial family. On February 17 Aldringen arrived in the capital and was granted an audience with the emperor. What he said persuaded Ferdinand that the time had come at last to announce Wallenstein's proscription. The next morning the imperial proclamation drafted more than three weeks before was finally made public. Copies were sent to all senior military officers and nailed up in public places. A new proclamation was drafted "letting it be heard how he [Wallenstein] would utterly exterminate Us and Our worshipful House" and denouncing "his perjured disloyalty and barbaric tyranny which before has never been heard of nor is to be found in the histories." The Jesuits' superior-general ordered "one thousand masses weekly for the safety of the Emperor and the happiness of the Empire." As Alcibiades' disgrace was inscribed on the stones of the Parthenon and proclaimed by all the priests in Athens, so from every pulpit in Vienna Wallenstein, for so long the sword and buckler of the Catholic Church, was declared not only a traitor but a fiend.

Piccolomini's allegations, now backed up by Aldringen (who had not been at Pilsen or laid eyes on Wallenstein that winter) and so enthusiastically promoted by Count Oñate, had proved sufficient to persuade the emperor of Wallenstein's guilt, but the emperor's descendants were to continue to doubt it. Ferdinand's grandson, the Emperor Leopold, visiting Prague, asked the gentleman who pointed out Wallenstein's palace to him, "Do you know for certain that Wallenstein was a rebel?" For certain no one ever knew, or knows now. In the next century Frederick the Great of Prussia asked the Emperor Joseph II "how it really stood with that story of Wallenstein's death." The emperor replied, "I cannot possibly doubt the honour and integrity of my ancestor," an answer so evasive that it can only be understood to signify the exact opposite of what it ostensibly said. Ferdinand had plenty of motives other than a sincere belief in his commander in chief's treachery for wanting to be rid of him. Wallenstein had become increasingly insubordinate, more and more difficult to control. There was also the question of money. Only two days after his proscription was made public the emperor decreed that Wallenstein's estates were to be seized. The stupendous debt the empire owed him was annulled and the richest land in all Bohemia, the *terra felix*, was once more in Hapsburg hands.

Communications were slow. For two days after all Vienna had been apprised of his "perjured disloyalty and barbaric tyranny," Wallenstein continued to write on routine matters to imperial ministers. But gradually, insidiously, the news seeped into the camp. Gallas remained inexplicably absent. So did Aldringen and Piccolomini. More people leaked away. A colonel sent to see what had happened to Gallas did not return. Wallenstein's nephew, who had gone to Vienna taking a letter to Councillor Eggenberg (one of those supposed friends of Wallenstein who had pronounced him guilty), never came back either. One Colonel Diodati suddenly left the camp, without orders, taking his regiment with him. The officer sent after them was not seen in Pilsen again. These silent exits were eerie, disquieting. Ten years earlier Kepler had warned Wallenstein that the month of March 1634, now only a few days off, was one of immense but ominous significance for him. On February 19 Wallenstein—uneasy but still unaware of his own dismissal—invited the assembled officers into his quarters. This time he received them in bed.

Once more they were asked to swear their loyalty to him. They did so, each with their own private provisos. Colonel Walter Butler, an Irishman with plausible manners but no fortune as yet, was among those who bound themselves "to live and die at His Princely Grace's side." On the 20th Wallenstein sent another messenger to Vienna. The messenger, arrested by Gallas, vanished along with the rest.

The "traitors," Ilow, Trcka, and Kinsky, planned to march on Prague and to establish a base on the White Mountain, as though to raise an independent Bohemia, phoenixlike, from the battlefield where it had been immolated fourteen years before. There perhaps Wallenstein would have been proclaimed king in defiance of the Hapsburgs, as Piccolomini and the others claimed he intended. Whether in fact he had assented to the plan, whether he even knew about it, is unproven. A Saxon emissary who saw Wallenstein on February 19 reported that he looked "like a corpse." It is possible that Ilow and the Bohemians judged he was by now so ill he could be used as the Cid's corpse was in the 1961 film, as the inert but symbolically potent figurehead for a campaign over which he had no control. In any event, the plan was aborted. On the 21st Trcka set out towards Prague at the head of a column of troops. He had traveled only ten miles when he met an officer on the road who was able to tell him what was happening in the world. The revelation was devastating. Wallenstein was deposed. Prague was in the hands of troops who took their orders from Gallas and Piccolomini, Wallenstein's trusted deputies who had denounced him and usurped his place. The troops stationed in Austria had all renewed their oaths to the emperor, vowing to obey Wallenstein no more. Piccolomini was less than a day's march away with forces outnumbering those at Pilsen and with orders to overpower Wallenstein and carry him to Vienna.

So many had left the camp to disappear silently; Trcka came back to Pilsen with his dreadful news. At last Wallenstein awoke to what had happened to him. Alcibiades, when condemned in his own city, went over to the Spartans. So now, probably for the first time and with no other option available to him, Wallenstein resolved to effect the change of sides he had been suspected for years of contemplating. He decided to retreat immediately, that night, to the frontier fortress of Eger, there if possible to unite his troops with those of the Saxons under Arnim, or with the Swedes under the Duke of Weimar.

No one slept. Messengers were sent at the gallop to those of Wallenstein's officers stationed in the countryside round about on whom he thought he could still rely. One of them was Colonel Walter Butler.

Wallenstein's servants worked feverishly. His household in Pilsen, albeit greatly reduced from the splendor of his glory days, comprised two hundred people. There was gold plate to be stowed away, hangings and candlesticks, fur coverlets and tooled leather screens, washbowls of silver and porcelain and fine tablecloths to be laid in chests and loaded onto wagons. And while the servants packed, the soldiers looted. Trcka and Ilow, knowing that their estates would surely be confiscated, grabbed what they could before leaving Bohemia: they gave orders that the townspeople were to be forced at pistol point to hand over any cash or gold or jewelry they possessed. All through the night Wallenstein worked, sequestered with his secretaries, firing off letter after letter in a vain attempt to close the wound through which his power was bleeding. His efforts were unavailing. Around him in the darkness his army leaked away. Officers who three days earlier had signed an oath to serve him to the death scrambled to desert him, taking their regiments with them. At first light next morning, "in the greatest disorder" and "indescribable panic," the remnant got under way.

Wallenstein had once had a hundred thousand men under arms. Scarcely fourteen hundred followed him to Eger. Of all his senior officers only the three faithful "traitors," Kinsky, Trcka and Ilow, remained. The march was slow and wretched. The snow was turning to slush. Wallenstein was lifted repeatedly from his carriage into a litter slung between horses, and then back into his carriage; in neither conveyance could he escape from pain. En route Colonel Butler, who had obediently brought his regiment to join the forces of the commander in chief, fell into line. Wallenstein, to whom so few had proved true, was touched by his loyalty. He invited Butler to ride in his coach, an extraordinary favor from one who so disliked promiscuous friendliness, and assured the Irishman that henceforth he would command not one regiment but two, both financed by himself, Wallenstein, the munificent plutocrat and generalissimo. (As he spoke imperial officials were already in possession of Gitschin, of Sagan, and of his palace in Prague.) Butler expressed his gratitude politely, but somewhere along the way it struck him that there might be a surer way of growing rich. The journey took three days. In the darkness of the second night on the road Butler dispatched his chaplain to Piccolomini with a secret message. Before Wallenstein arrived in Eger, Gallas was able to tell Aldringen, "I hope, and I believe it to be certain, that Colonel Butler will deal the blow."

Eger lies in a bend of the river Elbe on Bohemia's northwest frontier. On a hill behind it rises a castle of black rock. Wallenstein and his train reached it on the evening of Friday, February 24. The commander of the imperial garrison there, Colonel Gordon, received them. The common soldiers were to encamp outside the town. The officers and their households were lodged within, Gordon giving up his own house in town to Wallenstein and settling for the night in the castle. That night Colonel Butler invited Gordon and his deputy, Major Leslie, another Scotsman, to dinner. At 11 p.m. a messenger arrived from Pilsen, bringing a copy of the imperial proclamation of January 24. Leslie escorted the messenger to Wallenstein, who now read the words of his dismissal for the first time. All but incoherent with exhaustion, pain, and fury, Wallenstein raved of what he had done for the emperor, of how churlishly he had been rewarded, of how bitterly he resented the injustice done him, of how he would make the emperor repent. Leslie listened meekly, and later wrote down what he heard. Then he returned to Butler's lodging. Some time that night he, Gordon, and Butler, "the three heroes" as they later termed themselves, agreed what must be done.

On Saturday morning the two triumvirates—Kinsky, Ilow, and Trcka, who would die with Wallenstein; and Gordon, Leslie, and Butler, who would kill him—were all summoned to Wallenstein's room. The latter three were persuaded by the former to swear that they would obey Wallenstein, and him alone. (Despite the events of the previous week Ilow seems to have clung to his faith in the efficacy of oaths.) They did so, and then withdrew. A little later Gordon sent to invite Kinsky, Ilow, and Trcka to dine with him in the castle above the town at six o'clock. They accepted. That afternoon one of Wallenstein's officials read out for his approval a draft order to all officers in the field in which the customary fiction that "we do naught other than to perform the service of his Imperial Majesty" was reiterated. The man had served Wallenstein long enough to know what the generalissimo's rage was like, but the one that ensued was the worst he had endured. "With the most frightful maledictions and fulminations. . . . Tormented by all the Furies, he ordered me to go to Hell." Wallenstein had crossed his Rubicon. The officers must know now that it was not for the emperor they fought, but for him alone, "*für mich.*"

Darkness fell. Kinsky, Ilow, Trcka, Trcka's adjutant, and a handful of attendants went up the hill to the castle to keep their dinner engagement. Gordon, Leslie, and Butler received them and escorted them to a wainscoted chamber with doors at either end, while their attendants were led to the kitchen to eat. There was good food on the table and plenty of wine. The guests relaxed. They did not know that after they were all seated, and their plates and glasses filled, the kitchen door was locked on the outside imprisoning their servants, seventy of Butler's Irish troops entered the castle and were stationed by the gates and the drawbridge was drawn up behind them. The wine was poured copiously. The party became noisy. Ilow was especially boisterous, bragging that within days Wallenstein would have an army greater than any he had commanded before. Then, at a signal from Leslie, the room's two doors were thrown open and seven swordsmen rushed in through each one shouting, "Who is a good Imperialist?" Gordon, Butler, and Leslie rose, overturning the table and yelling, "*Vivat Ferdinandus!*" Kinsky was killed almost at once. Ilow and Trcka managed to draw their swords. It was dark, all the lights having been knocked out. Plates and windows were smashed. Ilow and the hapless adjutant were slaughtered where they were. Trcka, a famed warrior (and one who, more prosaically, was protected by his leather coat), managed to force his way out of the mêlée and make his way to the gate, where Butler's seventy Irishmen brought him down with their spears.

No musket had been fired. No one in the town below had heard anything. Gordon remained in the castle to see to the disposal of the bodies. Leslie led a troop of men through the streets to forestall any disturbances. Butler, who had pledged himself anew that morning to be Wallenstein's obedient servant, led the swordsmen, already blooded that night, to the house where Wallenstein lay. They had no difficulty gaining entrance. No special guard had been placed, only the usual patrols to keep away noisy dogs and traffic, and Wallenstein, again as usual, had chosen the most secluded apartments in the house, out of earshot of most of his household. Butler waited by the gate. Seven men barged through the courtyard into the house and up the stairs, shouting, "Rebels!" They shoved aside Wallenstein's cupbearer who was coming down with a gold beaker. They killed the groom of the chamber who tried to hush them. They broke down the barred door to Wallenstein's bedroom. Wallenstein had dragged himself out of bed. When they crashed in, their torches flaring, he remained tottering upright and spread his arms wide. He said something, perhaps a plea for "quarter." The leader killed him with one hard thrust of his spear. Later the killers stressed what courage and resolution it had taken to accomplish the death of "so heinous, vengeful a man, feared by all the world." In the actual event the ease of it seemed to have made them giddy. One of them picked up the body and made to toss it out the window. Another stayed him. Wallenstein's corpse was wrapped in something red, not one of his famous scarlet cloaks but a bedspread or hanging, and dragged, thudding and jolting, down the stairs. Afterwards the killers stripped it naked, clothes being, in seventeenth-century Europe as in Jerusalem at the time of Jesus Christ's crucifixion, too expensive to waste on the dead.

In 1630, when Wallenstein accepted his dismissal and—instead of raising the insurrection so many had been dreading—went quietly into retirement, observers were nonplussed, their relief tinged with a kind of disappointment that the diabolical warlord of their imagination was as easily cast down as any other man. His mortality was the second shocking disillusionment his life's story afforded. It was a time when people readily believed that a man might be, if not actually immortal, at least invulnerable. Many of those who fought in the Thirty Years' War carried amulets for which they paid large sums on the understanding that these would ensure their survival. Few people were surprised to hear that it had taken spearmen to kill Count Trcka—it was well-known that he had magical protection from wounds by sword or musket. And of course Wallenstein himself, the genius of war, could not be killed like any other mere mortal. At Lützen he wore no armor, evidence, said his critics, that he had supernatural, probably infernal, protection. (Nor, as it happens, did Gustavus Adolphus, but in his case his preference for less cumbersome clothing was taken to demonstrate his courage and his pious trust in God.) During the battle every single one of Wallenstein's attendants was killed but he himself passed unscathed through the fighting. It was said that one of his spurs was shot away by a cannonball, and at the end of the day, when he removed his shirt, dozens of bullets fell from its folds but not one had so much as grazed his flesh. Volcanoes spat fire when he took the field. Cities burned as he rode into them. It seemed absolutely incredible that simply by shoving a piece of barbed and pointed metal into his chest one could kill such a man.

His death was hailed by those who had desired it as a miracle. When the news reached the Jesuits' superior general he jubilantly gave thanks to the Most High, noting that the "marvellous deed" had been effected in response to the thousands of masses said by members of the order all over Europe. That murdering Wallenstein had been God's own work was confirmed by a near-contemporary painting of the killing in which the assassins wear haloes. Several reports presented his death as a kind of exorcism. In 1628 the mystic Christina Poniatowska had had a premonitory vision of his end: "As he [Wallenstein] lay stretched upon the ground flames belched with a horrid roar from his mouth while poison and pitch were ejaculated from his heart until this was pierced by a bolt sent from Heaven"—a vision which closely corresponds with some of the murderers' own accounts of his actual death. One of them said that as he fell he belched prodigiously "so fearful a noise that hearers were amazed," emitting a terrible stink of tobacco. Tobacco was the devil's weed, and its ashes were associated with those of sacked and burning cities. Gallas was told that as the spear drove into him a great cloud of smoke erupted from his breast, with a noise of a musket firing. "Presumably it was the Devil who departed from him," said Gallas.

Many were excited by the drama of Wallenstein's end. Prints depicting the murders at Eger sold by the hundred. Plays and poems about Wallenstein were published all over Europe. The downfall of one so high and mighty afforded a nasty satisfaction to those low enough to have envied and feared him. A "Farewell to Wallenstein" circulating at the time is charged with the combination of pious disapproval and greedy schadenfreude with which the tribulations of the rich and famous have been greeted by hoi polloi from that day to this:

> That's what happens when
> a man is too ambitious.
> The Devil silently comes
> and trips him up.
> No tree grows up to Heaven.
> The axe is always ready to fell it to the ground.

The spin put upon the story in contemporary reports varied according to the reporter's politics. Loyalist broadsheets published grotesque caricatures of the fallen potentate, and a Zurich weekly news sheet carried a derisive epitaph on the "Admiral of ships and sailors short / General without open battle fought." With equal gusto oppositional voices, both internal and foreign, used the murder as an example of Hapsburg wickedness. The Swedes magnified Wallenstein, partly in order to foster anxiety and divisions in the imperial ranks, partly (as the Spanish had magnified Drake) in order to excuse themselves for having failed to defeat him. "Who but Wallenstein broke at Nuremberg that most victorious and great force drawn together by Our Most Gracious King and Master, now resting in God?" asked the author of a Swedish broadsheet. "I gladly laud the enemy's valour." Protestants acclaimed Wallenstein as a martyr, killed for his faith by scheming papists. Butler, Gordon, and Leslie were compared with Ravaillac, assassin of Henry IV of France, and demonized as "perjured, godless, disloyal, ignoble knaves." To nationalists he became the victim of the Spanish influence at court. "He was German!" exclaimed one pamphleteer inaccurately. "That was his crime. Thence flowed his affliction and all calamity."

His posthumous reputation, though, was too important a matter for its formation to be left to the spontaneous workings of popular prejudice. As the loyal Count Khevenhüller records, there were mischievous people ready to call "the prompt and noble execution at Eger a wicked and infamous murder." To correct such an impression the emperor needed to demonstrate that Wallenstein was indeed a traitor, and one so dangerous that he could not possibly have been allowed to survive long enough to stand trial.

It proved hard. Piccolomini drafted a report glorifying his own part in the affair but could not be persuaded to sign it. He had not been permitted to reveal that Wallenstein's murder had been authorized by the emperor: he must have realized the report could therefore be used to make a scapegoat of him. Six of Wallenstein's officers were accused of being his co-conspirators, but the charge was dropped for lack of evidence. All but one of them were released after a short term in prison. The unlucky one, Count Schaffgotsch, was tortured for three hours before his execution, but still he had nothing to tell his inquisitors that they could use.

A posthumous trial of Wallenstein himself was mooted but the plan was abandoned: to initiate a trial was to suggest that the accused just might be innocent, an idea too dangerous to entertain. When eventually the *Detailed and Thorough Report of the Abominable Treason Planned by Friedland and His Adherents* was published by the Imperial Chancellery, it contained only the same vague allegations that had long been circulating at court. The threat Wallenstein posed to the state was indefinable and unprovable. Like that of Alcibiades or of Rodrigo Díaz it lay not in anything he might or might not have done, but in what he had become. Cardinal Richelieu, most worldly wise of all contemporary observers, judged that such a man as Wallenstein must inevitably, eventually fall from favor, "whether it be that monarchs weary of a man to whom they have already granted so much that no more gifts are at their disposal, or that they look askance at those who have to such degree deserved well of them that all and everything which still remains for bestowal is their due." Hostile pamphleteers and lampoonists made much of Ferdinand's ingratitude in killing the man to whom he was so indebted, but the cardinal understood that it was precisely because the emperor owed Wallenstein everything that Wallenstein had to die.

The third and most dully bathetic of the three surprises afforded by the story of Wallenstein's downfall was the revelation that not only could Wallenstein be killed, he could be dispensed with. He, along with most of his contemporaries, had considered himself essential, not only the chief builder of imperial dominion but its foundation stone. In Glapthorne's play he boasts, "I have been the Atlas to [the emperor's] power." But Atlas died and the skies didn't fall. Ferdinand's heir, the young king of Hungary, took over as imperial commander in chief and proved both able and fortunate. The general mutiny of which the Ferdinand and his ministers had for so long lived in terror never took place. The French General Peblis reported that after the murder of Wallenstein the imperial army was apparently well disciplined and quiescent, "at which I marvel as I firmly believed after such a tragedy a great change would follow." He was one of many who noted with relief, disappointment, or simple amazement of how little consequence was the passing of so great a man. Schiller presents Wallenstein as a tragic hero after the Aristotelian model: "this great Monarch-spirit, if he fall / Will drag a world into ruin with him." But only the few men killed with him at Eger, and the further handful subsequently accused of conspiring with him, were dragged down. For the rest, the world just went on turning.

Nothing changed. Wallenstein believed he could have brought the war to an end. "I had peace in my hands," he told an officer shortly before leaving for Eger. He was wrong. He knew neither how profoundly the Protestant princes with whom he was negotiating distrusted him, nor how far his influence over the emperor had declined. Others had seen him as one of the war's instigators and prayed that with his removal peace might follow, but another fourteen grievous years were to pass before the Peace of Westphalia was concluded. Alive he had awed princes and intimidated an emperor. Dead he dwindled to nothing. His body, like the Cid's, was miraculously preserved. Two and a quarter years after his death it was transported to the Carthusian monastery he had founded near Gitschin and the monks demonstrated their gratitude to their benefactor by reporting that it showed no visible or odoriferous sign of decay. But his estates were broken up, his achievements belittled; his reputation shriveled away. The incarnation of terror had turned out to be nothing more than a man. His greatness and his danger proved, like Alcibiades' world-conquering charm, a stupendous illusion. Alcibiades, brilliant con man, had created his own charisma. Wallenstein's was the product of others' fear. But in each case, once the man was dead the vision of his greatness vanished like smoke.

Sir Thomas Browne, Wallenstein's contemporary, called mortality "the very disgrace and ignominy of our nature." Achilles and his fellows sought illustrious and memorable deaths to compensate for the shortness of their lives. But Wallenstein, who had been so famously grand and awful when alive, died ignominiously and "after his death," wrote Cardinal Richelieu, who shrewdly appreciated the minatory parallels between his own career and that of the emperor's overmighty servant, "he was reviled by whoever would have extolled him if he had remained alive. Let the tree fall and all will hurry to strip its foliage and hack it to pieces." Wallenstein's story offers no consolation. Coleridge found that the effort of working on it "wasted and depressed my spirits, and left a sense of wearisomeness and disgust which unfitted me for anything." Hegel was appalled by the pessimism of Schiller's version: "When the play ends it is all over. Night reigns. Death has won the war." In 1934 Wallenstein's descendants commissioned a marble plaque to mark his burial place. Its epitaph is desolate: *Quid lucidius sole? Et hic deficiet.* "What is brighter than the sun? Even that light must fail."

VII

GARIBALDI

Giuseppe Garibaldi was the best beloved hero of mid-nineteenth-century Europe. At the height of his fame Alexander Herzen described him, without undue hyperbole, as "the Uncrowned King of the Peoples, their enthusiastic hope, their living legend, their holy man—and this from the Ukraine and Serbia to Andalucia and Scotland, from South America to the northern of the United States." Locks of his hair, bandages from his wounds, even the soapsuds from his bath were bought and treasured as relics. He was believed to be invincible, and invulnerable as well. His enemies, on hearing of his approach, laid down their rifles and ran. Duchesses were besotted with him. Peasants fell to their knees and worshiped him. His ecstatic admirers went into fits of convulsions on seeing him pass by. "It seemed to me," wrote one of his officers, "as if God spoke to me from his mouth."

In his long and eventful life he was (or appeared to be), serially or simultaneously, many different kinds of hero. In his twenties he was a bold revolutionary and bolder lover, banished from his native Piedmont for attempting to raise a rebellion and succored as he went on the run by a sequence of adoring women. Exiled, he went to South America and acquired an aura of exoticism fighting for liberty in faraway places, dressed in the archaic costume which was to remain his hallmark and accompanied by Anita, the Amazonian wife whom he had met and married with deliciously romantic precipitancy. To Europeans feeling cramped in their increasingly tamed and industrialized landscapes he was idealized as a child of the wilderness, colorful and free. It was "his fortune never to take full part in the common prose life of civilised men," wrote G. M. Trevelyan, whose three-volume biography of him was written

when his exploits were still living memory, "though he moved it profoundly, like a great wind blowing off an unknown shore."

Back in Europe he was the figurehead of the Risorgimento, Italy's
nationalist liberation movement, maneuvering his guerrilla units to out-
wit and humiliate the armies of an oppressive great power as Drake had
once humbled Spain. After Rome fell to the French in 1849 he was a fugitive again, this time one with the heartbreaking allure of the defeated ide-
alist. As Cato had stood erect amid the ruins of the first republic of Rome,
so Garibaldi acquired a melancholy grandeur from his part in the failed
defense of the second one, a tragic character made doubly affecting by the
fact that he had lost not only his political dream but also the love of his
life: Anita died in his arms as four armies crisscrossed Italy, intent on
hunting him down. Ten years later that romantic loser, the doomed defender of a lost cause, underwent another metamorphosis to become an
unstoppable conqueror, one whose amazing victories can stand comparison even with the Cid's marvelous luck. At the head of a band of just over
a thousand untrained and ill-equipped volunteers he drove the Bourbons
out of southern Italy, an achievement which ensured that for the remaining two decades of his life he was the world's most fêted celebrity, venerated for his perceived saintliness, assiduously courted for his prodigious
popular influence, and—such was the potency of his reputation and the
volatility of his political passions—a source of unremitting anxiety to the
authorities of the Italian nation which he had brought into being. His
contemporary, the Japanese hero Saigō Takamori (whose life story in
many ways parallels his), once wrote, "He who cares neither about his life,
nor about his fame, nor about rank or money—such a man is hard to deal
with. Yet it is only such a man who will undergo every hardship with his
companions in order to carry out great work for the country." As "hard to
deal with" as Cato, as valiant as the Cid, Garibaldi was such a man.

For the second half of his life he lived on Caprera, a windswept island
off the northern coast of Sardinia, where, between campaigns, he followed the routine of a peasant smallholder. Three hotels were built on
the next island to accommodate the tourists who came from all over
Europe to peer across the straits in the hope of catching sight of him
chasing his goats or hoeing his beans. When her foreign secretary proposed she write to him, Queen Victoria demurred on the grounds that to
do so might constitute "a recognition of the General's position as a
European power." Her concern was justified. Garibaldi was the son of a
simple sailor. He never became rich. Although he was briefly the dictator
of half Italy he abdicated from that post and never afterwards held

another one anywhere near commensurate with his tremendous prestige, but, simple citizen though he was, he was a "power." As such he became a menace to the nation he had helped create, another person of seditionary greatness like Alcibiades, Wallenstein, or the Cid. King Victor Emmanuel, whom Garibaldi made the first monarch of all Italy, was repeatedly to use him only to cast him aside, to arrest and imprison him, to blockade him into his island home, to send out armies against him. When it was rumored that he was contemplating starting a new revolution the Italian government judged it necessary to send eight warships to prevent him from leaving Caprera, provoking him into yet another demonstration of his superiority—as a solitary individual—over the might of a kingdom. As the massive vessels cruised the straits he slipped past them, rowing himself alone in a little boat.

In 1840, when Garibaldi was still on the other side of the Atlantic fighting unsuccessfully for the independence of Rio Grande do Sul, Thomas Carlyle gave the series of lectures in London which were subsequently published under the title *On Heroes, Hero-worship, and the Heroic in History.* The lectures were sensationally successful—the fashionable and the high-minded alike scrambled for tickets—and the book was a best-seller. In them Carlyle deplored the skepticism of his age which "denies the existence and desirableness of Great Men" and enunciated his theory that "every advance which humanity had made was due to special individuals supremely gifted in mind and character, whom Providence sent among them at favoured epochs," that "the history of the world is but the biography of Great Men." Each of his lectures was on one such person. Collectively they add up to an image of the complete hero, a man (they are all male) of "deep, rude, earnest mind," splendidly free of worldly sophistication, inarticulate almost to the point of dumbness, driven by passionate conviction. When Garibaldi returned to Europe he was generally found to be the all-but-perfect incarnation of that ideal.

He was a plain man. Giuseppe Mazzini, the theorist of the Risorgimento, its head as Garibaldi was its heart and arm, was largely responsible for the creation of Garibaldi's public image but privately he scoffed at him. At the height of Garibaldi's fame it was commonplace to compare him, with his long tawny hair, his air of impassive nobility, his unswerving courage, to a lion, king among beasts. When the medieval poets made the same comparison with the Cid they did so with unreserved admiration, but nineteenth-century politicians, although happy to make use of a hero, were less impressed by godlike animals. "Have you ever noticed the face of a lion?" wrote Mazzini to a confidant. "Don't you think it is a very stupid face? Well, that is Garibaldi." Another contemporary thought he had "the heart of a child and the head of a buffalo." But Garibaldi's simplicity was that not of the simpleminded but of the single-minded. "Sincerity, a deep great genuine sincerity is the first characteristic of all men in any way heroic," said Carlyle. Garibaldi had it. He was a man without any kind of duplicity. He was as incapable of tact and diplomacy and political game playing as Cato had been. What he believed he believed entirely. He entertained no doubts, no second thoughts. He had not a scrap of deviousness or subtlety about him, no irony, no eye for the ridiculous, no sense of humor whatsoever. He was a man like Carlyle's Luther, a man of "rugged honesty, homeliness; a rugged sterling sense and strength" or Carlyle's Cromwell, who resembled the craggy Alps, "huge granite masses rooted in the Heart of the World." Athenian intellectuals of the fifth century BC saw the Spartans both as tongue-tied primitives and as repositories of archaic nobility; so Garibaldi, with his white horse, his billowing cloak, and his career as peripatetic as any knight-errant's, seemed to nineteenth-century Europeans like a throwback to a simpler and grander age. His valor, his unblemished probity, and his austerity, "though a little affected," reminded a French official who knew him in Uruguay of the ancient Romans. Alexandre Dumas, the creator of *The Three Musketeers* and an enthusiastic admirer of Garibaldi's, titled his book on the campaign Garibaldi fought in Uruguay *The New Troy*.

His revolutionary career began in his twenties when, as a seaman in the Piedmontese navy, he was recruited by Young Italy, the underground liberation movement Mazzini had founded in 1831. Italy at the time was what the Austrian Prince Metternich called it, a "geographical expression" corresponding to no political reality. The peninsula was divided into a number of distinct states, the majority of them governed—more or less oppressively—by foreigners. The Pope reigned over much of central Italy. Southern Italy and Sicily were ruled from Naples by a Bourbon king. Most of the north was under Austrian domination, the exception being the independent Kingdom of Piedmont, Garibaldi's native country, which also controlled Sardinia. Mazzini's aim was to dethrone the kings, oust the priests, expel the foreigners, and unite all of these disparate states in a brand-new sovereign republic of Italy. It was a cause to stir the blood of Romantics everywhere. "Only think," Byron had written. "A free Italy . . . It is a grand object—the very *poetry* of politics."

Garibaldi grew up in Nice, which was part of France at the time of his birth. His first language was Ligurian, his second French. He was no more an obvious candidate for the role of Italy's national hero than the Italian-speaking Corsican Bonaparte had been for that of France. Nor might he have seemed an eligible target for recruitment to an Italian nationalist organization. According to Risorgimento myth, and Garibaldi's own account, it was Mazzini himself who won him over to the cause. That meeting was later depicted on prints decorating homes all over Italy, showing the visionary Mazzini, with his long dark hair and burning eyes, gazing enraptured at Garibaldi, the leonine warrior who would translate his dream of a united Republican Italy into reality. In fact the meeting never took place. But be that as it may, by 1834 Garibaldi was a member of Young Italy, and one of a group of mutinous seamen in the Piedmontese navy plotting to seize their ships in the harbor at Genoa and put them to revolutionary use. The mutiny was aborted. Garibaldi, who had gone ashore to join the uprising which never happened, thus effectively deserting, went into hiding.

It was a time when a man could be shot dead simply for reading a republican journal: Garibaldi was in grave danger. He escaped, helped on his way by several women and, according to legend, making love to at least three of them in the course of one afternoon while the Piedmontese authorities searched the streets and cafés for him and his co-conspirators. (Decades later several dozen Genoese matrons wrote to him, each claiming to have been among the three. A man who, like the ideal chivalric knight, combined a zest for warfare with punctilious politeness—especially to ladies—Garibaldi replied to each one of them, offering courteous thanks and good wishes, while evading any questions as to his own memories of their alleged past intimacies.) He was tried in absentia and sentenced to death.

Making his way to Marseilles after some thrilling escapades (leaping from the upstairs windows of a customs house, singing revolutionary songs to placate an innkeeper who had threatened to turn him in, saving a boy from drowning), he found a ship bound for Rio de Janeiro—a popular destination for political refugees—and worked his passage there to begin the fourteen years of exile during which, in his absence and largely without his knowledge, he became a celebrity of the Italian liberation movement.

He had been found guilty of treason, but then every revolution, every independence movement, every rebellion against oppressive or unjust authority must begin with a similar offense. In 1560, six years before Drake first crossed the Atlantic, 370 Spanish conquistadors set out eastwards from Lima into the interior of South America in search of El Dorado. Four months later their leader was murdered by a gang of mutineers led by Lope de Aguirre, a psychotic killer and visionary who styled himself, in signing his declaration of the expedition's new purpose, "the Wrath of God, Prince of Freedom" and—most strikingly—"traitor." Aguirre was the subject of Drake's opponent Philip of Spain, the man who came closer than any other ruler since the fall of Rome to world domination. To declare oneself traitor against such an authority was insanely self-destructive, but it could be presented as a politically and morally heroic act, even perhaps a sacred duty. God's wrath had been aroused by Philip's hubristic annexation of greater power than it was proper for a mere mortal to wield. Aguirre, the Wrath of God, would establish a free state in his defiance. Aguirre's adventure ended in a frenzied orgy of killing. Nearly half of his companions were murdered by him or on his orders. He himself was eventually hunted down by the Spanish colonial authorities and trapped and killed near Caracas, but—crazy and dangerous as he was—he had won himself a place in history as one of the first heroes of the American independence movement and an unusually self-aware example of the principle that every act of rebellion is, seen the other way around, an act of treachery.

In Brazil Garibaldi scraped together a living as a coastal trader until he found himself a cause and a more congenial occupation. Nationalism was, in the age of Romantic revolutionaries, an international movement. "The man who defends his own country or attacks the country of others is no more than a soldier," wrote Garibaldi years later, "but the man who . . . goes to offer his sword and his blood to every people struggling against tyranny is more than a soldier; he is a hero." All over Europe and America men fought to liberate countries not their own. Frenchmen gave their lives to help the settlers of North America to throw off the English yoke. Byron was involved with the Carbonari, the precursors of Young Italy, and before finally deciding to go to Missolonghi to fight for the Greeks he had named his yacht the *Bolívar* and was contemplating going to South

America instead. Englishmen and Germans fought for the Greeks against the Turks. There were Irishmen fighting in Chile, Germans fighting in Hungary, Italians fighting in Poland, and Poles fighting everywhere.

When Garibaldi arrived there, Brazil was still ruled, albeit precariously, by a Portuguese emperor. In 1835 General Benito Gonçalves raised a rebellion in the southern district of Rio Grande do Sul with a view to establishing an independent republic. Garibaldi—who had recently written to a fellow exile, "My God, I am weary of dragging on this life of a trading sailor, so useless to our country. I long to plunge into it once again"—promptly plunged.

He loved to fight. When, years later, he came to write his memoirs he was to declare himself a pacifist and dwell on his own gentleness and distaste for unnecessary bloodshed, on how as a child he had wept for hours after inadvertently breaking the leg of a grasshopper, but warfare intoxicated him. He was more than once to be strongly criticized by his own allies for provoking an unnecessary battle. He was also lauded and adored for his quixotic insistence on fighting to the finish against overwhelming odds. Several of his most celebrated actions were ghastly defeats, virtual massacres which a commander more careful of his men's lives might have evaded or cut short by surrendering, but which won Garibaldi the glory of one prepared for martyrdom (his own or his men's).

For four years he fought for the cause of Rio Grande do Sul on land and sea, and for another six years he served the liberal government in a Uruguayan civil war. These were small wars fought in immense landscapes. The Rio Grandense navy, of which Garibaldi became commander, consisted of only two ships. With them Garibaldi, an audacious gadfly like Drake harassing an elephantine empire, took on the sixty-seven ships of the Brazilian navy, the biggest in South America. Rio Grande do Sul was the size of the British Isles; Brazil, from which it wished to secede, of all Europe including Russia. In these huge tracts of scantily populated land, covered by forests or pampas where the grass grew tall enough to conceal a man on horseback, the little armies and even littler guerrilla bands spent as much time searching for each other as they did fighting.

When they did make contact their engagements were brief (one of Garibaldi's most decisive battles lasted one and a half hours) and brutal. Later Garibaldi was idealized as a spotless paladin, but the record of his actual experience is as bloodstained as an irregular fighter's tends to be. No one, maneuvering as fast as their horses could carry them over those vast plains, wished to take prisoners. There is a story which was frequently retold in later years, of how in Brazil Garibaldi intervened (as Wallenstein had once refused to do) to stop the execution of a boy, saying that he might yet be of use to the community. The anecdote is supposed to illustrate Garibaldi's clemency, and so it does, but he had already had four men's throats cut that day.

His men were, as a rule, the same kind of "scum of the earth" that had crewed the *Golden Hind.* Garibaldi himself once described them as "unchained wild beasts." (According to one source every one of the sixty men who made up the Rio Grandense navy was a convicted murderer.) They were pirates, as Garibaldi candidly acknowledged, and, according to one of their opponents, they acted accordingly: "They sacked and destroyed every creature or valuable thing which had the misfortune to fall into their power." Discipline was hard to maintain. For decades Garibaldi was haunted by the memory of his troop, drunk and uncontrollable, using a corpse as a table, on which they set up candles and laid out their cards for a game. For some of the horrors he was directly responsible. After a defeat he blew up his ships with some of his men still on board. His detractors accused him of thus slaughtering his wounded. Garibaldi counterclaimed that the men who had remained on board were not wounded but drunk. Either way, they were helpless, and they died.

His adventures and tribulations were many. He was captured and tortured; the story goes that later, when he had his torturer in his power, he demonstrated his saintly forgiveness by bringing the man a cup of coffee made with his own hands. He was overtaken by a hurricane at sea and had to swim ashore, abandoning his sinking ship (although he was an experienced seaman he does not appear to have been a very lucky one). On one occasion he and fourteen (or perhaps eleven—his accounts vary) men held out for several hours against 150 attackers, singing the Rio Grandense national anthem all the while, and eventually put them to flight, "which proves," he wrote afterwards, "that one free man is worth twelve enslaved ones"—something he seems all his life to have truly believed.

He also fell in love. Photographs, which show him lean and beaky-faced, his famous tawny mane smoothed down, fail to capture it, but plenty of his contemporaries testify to Garibaldi's extraordinary sex appeal. His life was crowded with women, lovers and would-be lovers, wives and would-be wives, adoring fans, women who encountered him by chance when on the run and risked their lives to save him. Stories circulated about his sexual voracity and Garibaldi himself did nothing to dispel the rumors. As he explained, he had no patience with coy maidens, no time or relish for extended courtship. "When a woman takes my fancy I say, Do you love me? I love you! You don't love me? *Tant pis pour toi.*" But energetic womanizer as he undoubtedly was, he was also a romantic. In Rio Grande do Sul he met the love of his life, and laid claim to her with his normal abruptness.

He was half a world away from family and home. The last of the Italian comrades who had accompanied him across the Atlantic had been killed when his ship went down. "In the immense void made around me by the terrible catastrophe I felt the want of a human heart to love me; without this heart existence to me was insupportable." Sailing into a port he raised his telescope to scan the town and saw just what he was after, a young woman who, as one of the nineteenth century's most celebrated real-life romantic heroines, is conventionally portrayed as an exquisite beauty, but who was described by one who knew her as being tall and stout, with pendulous breasts and a face covered in freckles, this rather unprepossessing picture mitigated by the attractions of large black eyes and thick, flowing black hair. By the time Garibaldi had disembarked she was nowhere in sight. Despondent, he wandered around until he happened to encounter a man he knew who invited him home for coffee. There, in the dimness of the little house, he found the girl whom he had been pursuing. To continue the story in his own words: "We both remained enraptured and silent, gazing on each other like two people who had met before, and seeking in each other's faces something which makes it easier to recall the forgotten past. At last I greeted her and said to her 'You must be mine.'" Anita was already married, a fact at which Garibaldi hinted in his memoirs, speaking vaguely of having "sinned greatly" and of an "innocent existence shattered" by their elopement, but which his more prudish admirers, willfully ignoring these semiconfessions, did their utmost to deny or suppress for over a century. All the same, she went with him. "My impudence was magnetic. I had formed a tie, pronounced a decree, which only death could annul."

Anita made him a formidable mate. As a teenager she had horsewhipped a man who attempted to rape her. When she left town with Garibaldi she gave her sewing scissors to a girlfriend, as though in token that she was leaving feminine domesticity behind her. "She looked upon battles as a pleasure," he wrote, "and the hardships of camp life as a pastime." When, during a battle at sea, he saw her thrown to the deck by a cannonball which killed the two men who had been standing beside her, he begged her to go below. She agreed, but only so that she could tongue-lash the men who were skulking in safety belowdecks and chase them back up to rejoin the fight. She was Garibaldi's lieutenant by day, his lover by night. She was tireless, fearless, and absolutely devoted to her man. During one battle a bullet passed through her hat, her horse was shot from under her, and she was taken prisoner. Undaunted, she harangued the Brazilian officer before whom she was brought, passionately condemning him and all his fellow imperialists. That night, when her guards were asleep, she escaped. For four days she struggled through the dense forest, living on berries. When she finally arrived at a friendly homestead she paused only long enough to drink one cup of coffee before galloping off to rejoin Garibaldi.

The Cid had his Jimena, but the presence of Anita at Garibaldi's side, in actual fact and in the frequently retold stories associated with them, is a novel element in his heroic reputation. She is the personification of his tremendous sexual energy, her vigor and physical courage a measure of the fabulous virility of the man who could make her his own. Their first son, Menotti, was conceived, or so Garibaldi maintained, on the battlefield, after a hard and successful day's fighting.

Even for such a superman and superwoman, though, the life of a guerrilla fighter was incompatible with parenthood. After Menotti's birth Garibaldi abandoned the cause of Rio Grande do Sul and went south to Montevideo, the Uruguayan capital. There he attempted to make a living as a cattle trader, a merchant in macaroni, and a teacher of mathematics, proving himself lamentably incompetent in all three fields. It was probably with some relief that he welcomed the outbreak of a civil war between the liberal Uruguayan government and right-wing rebels backed by Argentina.

Montevideo was a polyglot city, a refuge for exiles from all over Europe and an outpost of liberalism. The president called on the foreign communities to organize themselves for warfare and he asked Garibaldi to create an Italian legion to assist in the defense of the liberal cause. In its first battle (when Garibaldi was not present) the legion disgraced itself. Two of the three battalions refused orders to advance and then ran away. Six days later Garibaldi harangued them and—demonstrating his magical power to infuse courage into even the most craven—led them in a swift, ferocious, and successful bayonet charge from which they returned with only three men wounded and over forty enemy prisoners. The following month they were awarded their colors, a banner bearing the symbol of

Young Italy, an erupting volcano on a black background. (The black sig-nified their mourning that Italy was not yet free, the volcano the sub-merged but explosive power of the revolutionary movement.) In company Garibaldi had long been given to singing patriotic Italian songs; not one for false modesty, he maintained that "if I had had no other voca-tion, I could have been a good singer." At last in Montevideo he found himself fighting alongside fellow devotees of the Italian nationalist cause, albeit on the wrong continent and in the wrong war.

For five years, as commander of the Italian legion and as commander in chief of the tiny Uruguayan navy, Garibaldi served his adopted country. Few of the actions he undertook on behalf of Montevideo were actually successful, but several were glorious. He was celebrated not for any capacity to secure strategic advantages but for his unflinching courage, his romantic gallantry, his readiness to tackle tremendous odds and to fight to the finish, and for what he himself described, with the simplicity of one alluding to a matter of acknowledged fact, "the boundless confi-dence that I in general inspire in those I command."

A guerrilla, not a regular soldier, he was not a disciplinarian, not a spit-and-polish man. He had learned the arts of warfare among men who lived rough and fought dirty. In Rio Grande his troops had lived off cap-tured cattle, or by robbing the country people. In Montevideo he enlisted criminals and deserters, to the disapproval of regular officers. His men desecrated churches. They broke down cattle fences. They stripped the towns in which they were quartered of valuables. On one occasion, when an Argentine couple offered their house for use as a hospital, Garibaldi's men abused their generosity to the extent of robbing the silver even while one of their own wounded comrades lay stretched out on the dining room table. "These men are coarse, cruel, and have acquired immoral habits through leading a life of adventure, and they respect no authority except that of their leader, Colonel Garibaldi," wrote a regular Uruguayan gen-eral, torn between disapproval and professional envy. Garibaldi permitted all kinds of unruliness. "He knows how to get his men killed, but not how to flog them," wrote another observer, but he was as unorthodox in his readiness to impose a supreme penalty as in his reluctance to make use of pettier ones. He was capable, said one of his officers years later, of ordering an execution without even laying down his cigar. In Montevideo he wore his pistols in his belt at all times, and when asked by a British emissary how he dealt with a troublemaker, he replied coolly, "I blow his brains out."

He had the toughness and the outlaw swagger of a Francis Drake and, unlike Drake, he was a beautiful man. He was short, only about five foot six, and a dispassionate observer records that he seemed to squint slightly, but he had the gift (more valuable than perfect features) of dazzling all who laid eyes on him. An English lady who met him years later noted in her dairy, "I have today seen the face of Garibaldi; and now all the devotion of his friends is made clear as day to me. You have only to look into his face, and you feel that here is, perhaps, the one man in the world you would follow blindfolded to death." Those who encountered him in Montevideo described the nobility and regularity of his face, his piercing eyes, his spellbinding voice, "low and veiled and almost tremulous with inner emotions." His personality was as compelling as his appearance. The future president of Argentina saw in him "a true hero in flesh and blood, with a sublime ideal."

Years later one of Queen Victoria's advisers was to tell her, Garibaldi "has achieved great things by 'dash.' " Dash he had aplenty. His principles were simple and absolute. His appearance was extravagantly theatrical. His hats were large, his threadbare clothes were covered with a swirling white poncho, his red-blond hair and beard were long. Male hair is potently symbolic stuff. Spartan boys signaled their virility and belligerence by growing theirs and went into battle with it all braided and bewreathed with flowers. The Cid's voluminous beard was the token of his strength and patriarchal dignity. For Garibaldi's contemporaries hair was, besides, the badge of the revolutionary. When the king of Naples saw a group of young gentlemen with loose unpowdered hair at the opera, he left immediately and ordered out the troops.

The Italian legionaries emulated their leader. Garibaldi addressed them as the "sons of heroism" and encouraged them to conduct themselves as a privileged elite. A contemporary Portuguese newspaper described their flowing locks and tremendous mustaches, their "Sicilian capotes" and plumed hats, their belts stuck with daggers and pistols. In 1843, at a loss for how, in a blockaded city, to obtain uniforms for its volunteer forces, the Montevidean government requisitioned a stock of bright red smocks due to have been shipped to Buenos Aires for the slaughterhouse workers. Belted around the waist they could pass for military tunics. So the look was complete. As the distinctive dress of Garibaldi's followers, the red shirts were to become famous all over the world, prized as relics long after their wearers were dead.

Garibaldi looked like a brigand, but though his men might loot and pillage he himself was scrupulously honest, more of a Cato than a Drake. Like Cato, he became a byword for the frugality of his style of living. He really had no taste for luxury. He later came close to marrying a rich English widow, but balked at committing himself to her, explaining that a way of life which involved spending three hours at the dinner table would be intolerable to him. In 1860, on his victorious progress through Sicily and southern Italy, he twice found himself in undisputed possession of a royal palace. On each occasion he chose a small, bare room in which to erect his own camp bed, leaving his staff to enjoy the ballrooms and grand saloons. In Uruguay, when there was prize money to be distributed he gave his portion to the poor. In 1845 he turned down the government's offer of land grants to the members of the Italian legion on the grounds that he and his men needed no recompense for performing "the duty of every free man, to fight for freedom wherever it is attacked by tyranny." (What his legionaries thought of this high-minded refusal we do not know.)

He lived austerely. In Montevideo he and Anita and their growing family lived in a single rented room, sharing a kitchen with the other occupants of the house. Garibaldi seldom drank anything other than water and ate very little; he subsisted chiefly on small quantities of bread, garlic, and fruit and on large quantities of cigars (the latter, in that time and place, being the dirt-cheap solace of the poor).

He was as upright as he was frugal. Even his opponents paid tribute to his integrity. When at the end of his sojourn in South America he resigned his Uruguayan command, his erstwhile enemies immediately tried to buy his services, offering to pay him any sum he asked. But Garibaldi was no Rodrigo Díaz to fight first on one side, then on the other. As the leader of his opponents in Uruguay wrote, "He cannot be won. He is a stubborn savage." All his life people whose honesty was less absolute than his were to belittle him in similar terms, equating his straight dealing with doltishness. Others, though, were impressed. The British envoy deputed to broker a peace in Uruguay was repeatedly frustrated in his mission by Garibaldi who, determined to refuse all compromises, persistently turned down the terms offered, but he came away with a profound respect for the man who had been so troublesome to him: "a disinterested individual among those who only sought their own personal advantage . . . a person of great courage and military skill."

Garibaldi arrived in Montevideo an unemployed vagrant. By the time he left he was the most influential man in the city, despite the fact that he had no money and never used his devoted legion to enforce his own power. He rose to become overall commander of all the Uruguayan forces, to the outrage of more orthodox officers who called it a "degradation" and "a humiliation and infamy" to be placed under the command of a "vile adventurer," the "Italian pirate José Garibaldi." In his memoirs he boasted that he was so loved by the people of Montevideo he might easily have made himself dictator had he wished. It was probably true.

In 1847 he fought the battle of Sant' Antonio, the most celebrated engagement of his South American career. It was a defeat, like so many of his triumphs, but the grateful Montevidean government declared it all the same a "glorious day" and "a brilliant feat of arms." Garibaldi and 186 of his men were attacked in open country by some fifteen hundred of the enemy. "The enemy are numerous, we are few; so much the better!" Garibaldi told his men. "The fewer we are, the more glorious will be the fight." They took cover behind a derelict building and, refusing all calls to surrender, held out for nine hours against repeated assaults, fending off their attackers with musket and bayonet while the fifteen-year-old bugler sounded his bugle and Garibaldi led them in singing the Uruguayan national anthem. By nightfall thirty of them were dead, including all the officers. Under cover of darkness those that were left retreated, fighting off further attacks all the way back to the safety of a town three miles off. Garibaldi was promoted to the rank of general. The date was inscribed in letters of gold on the Italian legion's banner while the legionaries were granted badges bearing the misleading but stirring legend "Invincible."

Sant' Antonio was for Garibaldi, like Achilles' immersion in the Styx, the close encounter with death which procured him immortal life. All the time he had been fighting in South America's local wars he had firmly believed himself, however irrationally, to be serving the cause of Italy's liberation, a cause to which he described his comrades who died in Rio Grande do Sul or Montevideo as martyrs. Mazzini, in exile in England, endorsed his interpretation, reporting his exploits with fervent enthusiasm in his journal *L'Apostolato Repubblicano* (published in London but clandestinely circulated in Italy), gradually building up his reputation, as the years went by, to heroic proportions.

A brilliant propagandist, Mazzini knew that a movement needs its totemic figure: Garibaldi seemed made for the part. Out of the muddled and politically ambiguous material provided by Garibaldi's South American adventures Mazzini manufactured a stirring epic. While at home Italian nationalists hardly dared identify themselves for fear of Metternich's omnipresent agents and the chains and dungeons of Austria, Garibaldi at large on the pampas and broad rivers of the southern hemisphere provided an exhilarating model of energy and daring. And as his reputation grew, others besides Mazzini were drawn to exploit it. In Germany Paul Harro Harring, who had met Garibaldi in 1842, published a fervently romantic novel with him as its brave and noble hero. Gradually not only the radical press but mainstream newspapers as well began to take note of him. The war in Uruguay was of intense interest to the European powers. On its outcome depended who would control the lucrative flow of trade in and out of the River Plate. It was widely reported, and journalists seized on Garibaldi as the most colorful and sympathetic character on the liberal side. Reports of the battle of Sant' Antonio were received with tremendous excitement in Italy. In Genoa Garibaldi's name was cheered by the congress. In Florence his admirers raised money to buy him a sword of honor. He was probably not aware of it himself, but in the years of his absence he had become a great man.

In Italy cracks were finally appearing in the political structures he dreamed of dismantling. In 1847 a new Pope, Pius IX, introduced some cautiously liberal reforms. Mazzini from London and Garibaldi from Montevideo—priest-haters though they both were—each wrote to him urging him to do more, and Garibaldi offered him the services of the entire Italian legion of Montevideo should he undertake to liberate and unify Italy. Pius did not respond. Meanwhile King Charles Albert of Piedmont (whose subject Garibaldi was) followed the Pope's lead with some minor constitutional reforms and the abolition of press censorship. In December a Piedmontese ship carrying copies of the newly uncensored and outspokenly revolutionary newspapers arrived in Montevideo and the entire Italian community turned out into the streets chanting patriotic songs for a torchlit parade, led by the legion with Garibaldi at its head. It was time for the Italian hero to see Italy again. A month later Garibaldi sent Anita and their children ahead to Europe. In April he followed, bringing just sixty-three legionaries with him. He did not know where he was going. He was still under sentence of death in Piedmont. But with those sixty-three men he intended to start a revolution.

He was just in time. It was 1848. In June Garibaldi made his first European landfall, putting into a port in Spain to buy supplies and to hear the amazing news that the French monarchy had been overthrown, Prince Metternich had fled from Vienna, there were uprisings in Sicily, Naples, Florence, Milan, Lombardy, Venice, Parma, and Modena. King Charles Albert had declared war on Austria. Garibaldi's sixty-three volunteers now had the entire Piedmontese army on their side.

All over Italy people were waiting for him. The hour had struck. The curtain had risen. All that was lacking was the hero, and Garibaldi had been assigned that role. "The future of Italy is in his hands; that is predestined," said one of his officers that year. Mazzini had seen to it that the stories of his do-or-die courage, his dashing band of red-shirted followers, his devotion to his country which remained true even when he was driven across the world by despotic authorities, had been disseminated all over Italy. When Anita disembarked with the children she was astonished to be met by huge crowds chanting "Long live Garibaldi! Long live the family of Garibaldi!" When the man himself finally arrived the harbor was full of small boats packed with waving enthusiasts, and a banquet for four hundred guests had been organized in his honor. It was a fine homecoming for one who had left the country as an insignificant seaman under sentence of death. The exile had returned, to be welcomed as a redeemer. His long absence had kept him free of the compromising entanglements of actual Italian politics. He swept in from the vast pampas, from across the vaster sea, pure, brave, and true-hearted as a knight of old, ready to take his place at the head of the great struggle about to begin.

He looked, and acted, the part to perfection. To his admirers he seemed as beautiful as Alcibiades, as masculine as the Cid, and in the great plumed hat and sweeping poncho that he was to continue to wear for the rest of his life he appeared both exotic and archaic. Alexander Herzen called him "a hero of antiquity, a figure out of the Aeneid." Victor Hugo agreed: "Virgil would have called him *vir*, a man." Against the background of the moral maze of nineteenth-century diplomacy and of the increasingly sordid and gruesome practice of modern warfare he stood out, pure and glittering. Half a century earlier Edmund Burke had written, "The age of chivalry is gone: that of sophisters, economists and calculators has succeeded: and the glory of Europe is extinguished for ever." Garibaldi seemed like the incarnation of that lost glory.

Young Italy was a republican movement. Mazzini, back on Italian soil at last, was calling vociferously for republican governments in the newly liberated or soon-to-be-liberated states and warning his supporters to beware of replacing the Austrian oppressor with a homegrown one. But Garibaldi was far more a nationalist than he was a republican. (This was to be the cause of bitter arguments between him and Mazzini throughout the rest of their lives.) To him what mattered was that Italy should be under Italian rule. Forget about politics, he told his admirers. "The great and only question of the moment is the expulsion of the foreigner. Men, arms, money, that is what we need, not idle arguments about political systems." He offered his services to Charles Albert, king of Piedmont, the monarch against whom, fourteen years before, he had attempted to raise a rebellion and whose government had condemned him to death.

The king was embarrassed. For all the rest of his life—regardless of his immense popularity—Garibaldi was to be undervalued, snubbed, and frustrated by those whom he served. One of Charles Albert's ministers told him that he might be more welcome in the newly proclaimed republic of Venice. "There you can ply your trade as a buccaneer. That's your place—there's none for you here." Garibaldi was undeterred. He demanded, and got, an audience with Charles Albert. It did him no good. As the king wrote to one of his ministers, it was absolutely impossible to employ the adventurer, with his questionable past and his known republicanism. The best course, he concluded (showing how little he knew his man), would be to pay Garibaldi to go away. Garibaldi went anyway. The Milanese had driven out their Austrian governors and proclaimed an independent state of Lombardy. They allowed Garibaldi to take command of a rabble of some fifteen hundred deserters and invalids, inadequately armed and dressed in the ousted Austrians' abandoned white uniforms.

Piedmont and its allies were rapidly defeated. Within weeks of Garibaldi's arrival Milan was reoccupied by the Austrians and Charles Albert surrendered. But Garibaldi refused to give up. He issued a proclamation, which was distributed all over Italy, confirming all that his admirers had heard about his dauntless courage, his patriotism, and his high-minded integrity. "The King [of Piedmont] has a crown which he wishes to save by guilt and cowardice," but he and his companions would never, he declared, "abandon, without sacrificing ourselves, our sacred soil to the mockery of those who oppress and ravage it." He liked to fight against impossible odds. In Rio Grande do Sul, as he afterwards boasted, "with a crew of sixteen men and a barque of thirty tons, I declared war on an empire." His unpromising band of Milanese had already dwindled to barely a thousand men but with them he would take on all Austria. "The war will continue," he wrote.

He led his men into the mountains around Lake Como where he embarked upon a guerrilla campaign. He commandeered two pleasure steamers and in these he cruised the lake, descending on Austrian positions while the local women (or so he recalled in his memoirs) waved to him from their flower-bedecked balconies, their faces alive with joy "as if they wished to fly to welcome the brave men." His successes were small. His soldiers kept defecting. "With what contempt," he wrote to Anita, "you must look on this generation of hermaphrodites in Italy, on these countrymen of mine that I have tried to make noble with such little result!" He himself was the acme of nobility and manliness. "The body keeps pace with the soul of that man," wrote one of his officers; "both are of iron."

After less than a month, with only seventy troops left, he gave up and retreated over the border into Switzerland. But he had greatly enhanced his personal myth. The man who dared to defy the might of an empire with his little band of poorly equipped men had proved himself worthy of the great role allotted him. When he arrived in Livorno a few weeks later, the streets were decorated in his honor, a huge crowd turned out to greet him, and when he went to the opera the entire audience rose cheering to its feet.

It was a doubly romantic age, and Garibaldi seemed a fit hero both by the standards of the old romances and of the new Romanticism. Two centuries earlier, in 1637, Rodrigo Díaz had been brought back to life as Don Rodrigue, the hero of Pierre Corneille's high-minded tragedy *Le Cid*. Corneille reimagined the mercenary warlord as a man prepared to sacrifice everything—love, happiness, and life itself—to satisfy the dictates of honor. When Byron was a schoolboy *Le Cid* was his favorite reading. The Romantic poet and brilliant self-mythologizer, whom Carlyle called "the noblest spirit in Europe," liked to present his own expatriate life as a kind of principled exile, the refusal of a great-hearted man of honor to acquiesce in the grubby littleness of modern life. No wonder he was especially moved by the story of Don Rodrigue, an aristocrat of unimpeachable integrity, unflinching pride. So were many of his French contemporaries. In 1811, when Napoleon's armies occupied Burgos, they paid markedly mixed homage at the tomb of the Cid. Some of the officers, according to Robert Southey "used to visit the church and spout passages of Corneille's tragedy." Meanwhile the less educated soldiery deliberately desecrated the shrine of Spain's national hero, using the tomb for target practice and leaving it badly knocked about by their bullets. The Cid, at the opening of the nineteenth century, was both a high-minded devotee of an archaic but stirring concept of honor and a modern patriot defined by his nationality. And so, two generations later, was Garibaldi, serving the modern cause of nationalism in a style which gave him the luster of a hero from medieval romance.

Throughout the autumn of 1848 Garibaldi was a rebel without a cause, crisscrossing northern Italy at the head of an irregular band of adoring volunteers—the few dozen who had followed him from South America, now supplemented by Italian recruits—in search of a people willing to be freed. Everywhere he went he was greeted by noisily ecstatic crowds, hailing him as the Hero of Montevideo and the Hope of Italy, and by embarrassed officials torn between their desire to claim a share in his popularity by being seen to welcome him and their anxiety to get rid of him and his ill-disciplined train as soon as possible.

Imperfectly liberated, imperfectly subdued, all Italy was in a state of political flux. The people were excitable, their rulers nervous. In the diplomatic intricacies of the moment Garibaldi's outspoken republicanism and hostility to all foreigners were potentially as destructive as stones flung through a spider web. Besides, the Garibaldini (as the General's followers were known) had no quartermaster. "Organising troops is the most tedious of occupations for me," wrote Garibaldi later. His genius was for inspiring his men; he never gave much thought to the dull business of feeding them. Since Wallenstein's day it had become commonplace for a state to support a standing army, financing it through tax revenues, but the Garibaldini were stateless volunteers. It was nobody's responsibility to pay or provide for them. They were modern knights-errant, and as Don Quixote remarked, a knight carries no purse. A regular officer who campaigned alongside them the following year described with shocked fascination their method of provisioning themselves. "Three or four threw themselves on the bare backs of their horses and, armed with long lassoes, set off at full speed in search of sheep or oxen. When they had collected a sufficient quantity they returned, driving their ill-gotten flocks before them . . . and then all indiscriminately, officers and men, fell to, killing, cutting up and roasting at enormous fires quarters of oxen, besides kids and young pigs, to say nothing of booty of smaller sort, such as poultry, geese, etc." When they needed a barracks Garibaldi liked to take over monasteries, both because their architecture was appropriate to the purpose and because, anticlerical as he was, he derived satisfaction from flouting the Church. (To him priests were "the very scourge of that Italy which, seven or seventy times, they have sold to the stranger," the "black brood, pestilent scum of humanity, caryatids of thrones still reeking with the scent of human burnt offerings where tyranny still reigns.") Any door closed to him he had blown open. To the Quixotes who followed Garibaldi it no doubt seemed that whatever the people on whom they preyed might lose in the way of livestock and other provisions would be amply repaid by the great gift of Freedom which he intended eventually to bestow upon them. To the Sancho Panzas of the regimes through whose territories they passed they seemed predatory, disruptive, and extremely expensive.

At last they found an adventure worthy of them. In Rome, in November 1848, the chief minister of the Papal States was stabbed to death on the steps of the government offices. Nine days later, after a revolutionary mob had invaded his palace and killed his confessor, the Pope, disguised as an ordinary priest and trembling so violently that he was unable to walk unaided, escaped down a secret staircase and through a back door and fled to the court of the Bourbon king Ferdinand of Naples. Reformists called an election for a new constituent assembly. Mazzini, exultant, arrived from London to become the dominant member of a triumvirate of chief ministers. The election was to be the most democratic in all preceding human history. All adult male Romans were eligible to vote.

It was wonderful. "Rome to me," wrote Garibaldi in his memoirs, was a "gigantic sublime ruin" haunted by a "luminous spectre"—that of republican liberty. He had been on his way to Venice. Promptly he turned around and marched his men towards Rome, establishing a base for them to the north of the city. He himself stood for election to the new assembly. He was, then and always, a disruptive parliamentarian. Incapacitated by rheumatism (an inconveniently unheroic disease which plagued him increasingly for the rest of his life), he had to be carried into the chamber on a stretcher, but to him it seemed that it was his fellows who were supine. At the first session he interrupted the lengthy process of swearing in the new deputies, crying out that to waste time on formalities was a crime. "Are the descendants of the ancient Romans, the Romans of today, incapable of being Republicans?" His interruption was ignored, his frustration soothed. It took the assembly another three days to reach the point to which he had been so impatient to leap. In February 1849, nearly nineteen centuries after Cato had killed himself in despair of saving it, the Roman Republic was revived.

It was not allowed to remain undisturbed for long. In April the new French president, Louis-Napoleon, sent an army to restore the Pope and to "liberate" Rome from the handful of dangerous radicals who, as he saw it, had forced themselves upon the unwilling citizens.

It was Garibaldi's moment. "It was then," wrote the republican officer Giacomo Medici, "the providential man appeared." On April 27 Garibaldi led his followers into Rome through streets packed with people shouting out his name. "It is impossible to describe the enthusiasm which took possession of the population at the sight of him," wrote Medici. Hats and handkerchiefs were thrown in the air. A young German artist who was one of the adoring multitude wrote: "I went after him; thousands did likewise. He only had to show himself. We all worshipped him. We could not help it." The hour had come, and so had the man. "This mysterious conqueror surrounded by such a brilliant halo of glory . . . was, in the minds of the Roman people, the only man capable of maintaining the decree of resistance," wrote an onlooker. To Medici "he might have been thought the protecting God of the republic who hastened to the defence of Rome."

He entered the city riding, as usual, on a white horse, his tawny hair and beard flowing beneath a broad black hat with long feathers, his white cloak flung back to show his inevitable red shirt. When Alcibiades returned to Athens the older men had pointed him out to their juniors; now the women of Rome held their babies up to see Garibaldi, calling out, "Oh isn't he beautiful! Beautiful!" Others, recognizing his resemblance to the bearded redeemer Jesus Christ, fell to their knees as he went by.

Behind him clattered the Garibaldini. They were not ranked neatly like regular soldiers, but slouching and swaggering like a band of brigands. Their hats were big, their hair was long. Garibaldi himself was the only officer among them to have a batman, a black Brazilian, Andrea Aguiar, who was his constant and—to European eyes—exotic companion. The rest carried all their belongings on their saddles, South American style, including a roll of cloth which, hoisted on a sword for a tent pole, became their shelter. As homeless and therefore invulnerable as the Scythians about whom Herodotus wrote, they seemed both noble and savage, magnificent and alarming in equal measure.

The battle which they had come to join had already, before the

French even arrived at the walls, the tragic glamour of one which could not possibly be won. "There is no religion without its martyrs," Mazzini had once said. "Let us found ours, even if it be by our blood." Soon after his arrival in Rome he concluded: "The foes are too many, too strong and too subtle." But if the republic could not stand, it could at least fall beautifully. For him, the defense of the city was to be an episode of noble self-sacrifice, a story of uplifting sadness. "For the sake of the future," he wrote later, "it was our duty to offer our *morituri te salutant* to Italy from Rome." And at the center of the sublime and sorrowful spectacle he was planning for the inspiration of all ages to come would stand the hero he had done so much to create, the noble warrior clad, like the spectral figure seen by Rodrigo Díaz's men after his death, in white and red, and riding upon a great white horse, the stainless champion whose archaic hair-style so fittingly resembled that of the Savior who had laid down his life for others. It is unlikely that many Romans foresaw their defeat as clearly as Mazzini did, but it was evident to all and sundry that they faced awful odds. If Garibaldi was Christ, then his entrance into Rome was his Palm Sunday, as the people ran through the streets avid for a glimpse of him, of the man who had come to save them and perhaps to lay down his life.

He is remembered as the defender of the Roman Republic, just as Francis Drake rather than Admiral Howard is remembered as the man who put the Spanish Armada to flight. In fact the Roman commander was General Avezzana. Of the nearly twenty thousand men under his command, the troops assigned to Garibaldi constituted only a fraction. But theirs was the battle that came to stand for the whole heartbreaking story of the failed defense of the new republic.

Just outside, and perched on a hill above, the city's western walls stood a private house set in gardens, the Villa Corsini. If the French were allowed to set up their cannon there they would be able to fire into the city. If Rome's defenders controlled it they might be able to prevent the French passing beneath them to attack the walls. On April 29, with Avezzana's approval, Garibaldi occupied the garden and set up his headquarters in the villa. The next day the French army approached. Garibaldi sent his men, seasoned Garibaldini and new recruits alike, racing down the hill to repulse them. The French held their ground through an hour's hand-to-hand fighting, but when Garibaldi led a second charge himself, "erect on horseback," as one of his officers described him, "his hair streaming to the winds like a statue of brass representing the god of battles," they turned and ran. It was an astounding victory. Ten thousand Frenchmen—the descendants of those who, under another Napoleon, had swept through Italy in still living memory—were turned back by barely four thousand Italians under the command of a maverick general who had managed to transform a rabble of irregulars and volunteers into a victorious army almost literally overnight.

Garibaldi was wounded in the stomach. He gave no sign that he was hurt and fought on, his saddle drenched with blood. That night he sent for a doctor. "Come to me after dark. I have been wounded but nobody must know." His stoic endurance, the secrecy and the secret's not-too-long-delayed revelation helped to render him not just a conquering hero but a suffering saint as well. Meanwhile to his enemies he was a bugbear. Had it not been for Garibaldi, Louis-Napoleon told the French Assembly, their army would have marched unopposed into Rome. As Drake seemed a greater man to the Spanish than he did to his own compatriots, so Garibaldi, an adored but subordinate commander in Rome, seemed in Paris to be sole guardian of his city.

A two-week armistice was agreed for negotiation. Meanwhile the army of the Bourbon king of Naples was menacing Rome from the south. Garibaldi went to meet it under the command of a General Roselli. There was a desperate, inconclusive battle at Velletri, where Garibaldi came close to being killed when he and his horse were thrown down and badly trampled by some of his own retreating cavalry. He survived thanks to some boys who dragged him clear of a tangled pile of fallen horses and men, and returned to Rome. On June 1 the French General Oudinot gave notice that he was ending the armistice. His letter was (probably deliberately) ambiguous. The Romans, understanding themselves to have three days to prepare, were taken unawares when, on June 2, French troops occupied the undefended Villa Corsini. Garibaldi was given the task of recapturing it.

The battle for the Villa Corsini which took place on June 3 was a terrible one, as stupid in its futile wasting of young men's lives as the charge of the Light Brigade at Balaclava six years later, and equally celebrated. For seventeen hours, from dawn to dusk on a sweltering hot day, Garibaldi sent wave after wave of men up the rising ground between the city and the villa, through its garden gate, which they could pass only five at a time, and up the steeply sloping drive toward the front of the four-story villa on top of the hill, from every window, balcony, and terrace of which the French were firing on them. Their chances of success were negligible, their chances of dying hideously high. That they obeyed him is evidence not only of their courage but also of the power of his hold over them.

He had a mesmerist's capacity to impose his will. One volunteer recalled: "He laid his hand on my shoulder and simply said, with that low strange smothered voice that seemed like a spirit speaking inside me 'Courage! Courage! We are going to fight for our country.' Do you think I could ever turn back after that?" An officer leading one of the assault parties described afterwards how, on receiving Garibaldi's order to "go, with twenty of your bravest men, and take the Villa Corsini at the point of the bayonet," he was at first "transfixed by astonishment," so preposterous and so terrible did it seem. He did it all the same. By the time he reached the steps below the villa only twelve of his twenty men were left alive. Seven made it back, two of them badly wounded. Another recalled how, as his men fell all around him, he imagined for a moment that they were tripping over the roots of vines—so inconceivable was the grim speed with which they were being killed. "Those hurrying past would try to drag away a fallen comrade, but the man who stretched out his hand to help would bring it suddenly back to clutch at his own death-wound." One in six of the men and boys (some of his soldiers were as young as twelve years old) under Garibaldi's command died. Twice the villa was captured, but each time the French, who could approach it safely under cover of trees to the rear, swiftly retook it. Throughout the day Garibaldi himself, an unmistakable target on his white horse, directed operations from beneath the villa, well within reach of the French marksmen. It was said of Wallenstein that after the battle of Lützen musket balls clattered out of his buff coat. He was one of those superhuman warriors whom gunshot, however well aimed, could not kill. So was Garibaldi. By nightfall, so the story goes, his white poncho and his wide plumed hat were both riddled with bullet holes.

It was a catastrophic defeat. With the French immovably entrenched in the villa the eventual fall of Rome was inevitable. Garibaldi was privately much criticized by his colleagues both for the pointless slaughter and for the failure. He was never one to spare his men: "Even with the certainty of defeat we had to fight," he declared once after an occasion when he had fought on pointlessly for two whole days, "at least for the honour of our arms." Now there were murmurs that he was not only gallant to the point of foolhardiness but perhaps incompetent as well. In the opinion of his fellow republican Pisacane he might have taken and held the villa if only he had concentrated his forces. Another officer judged that "he was utterly incapable of directing the manoeuvres of men by which alone the scale can be turned in a field of battle." Working with small guerrilla bands he could be innovative and astonishing, but he never found any other way of approaching a conventional battle than that of sending his men marching straight on the enemy (uphill if necessary) with swords drawn or bayonets fixed, a strategy productive of stirring spectacles but horribly wasteful of lives. But the glory of an engagement is not measured by its utility, or even by its outcome. His defeat at Sant' Antonio had made Garibaldi an international celebrity. His defeat at the Villa Corsini made him something greater. On the night after the battle Mazzini issued a proclamation: "Romans! This day is a day of heroes, a page of history. Yesterday we said to you, 'be great'; today we say to you 'you are great.'" June 3 is a solemn festival in the calendar of the Risorgimento, the day on which Italians had proved that they would give their lives to make their country their own. The men and boys shot down in the gardens of the Villa Corsini became the movement's martyrs, and Garibaldi, who sent them to their deaths, gained by association with them an aura of tragic numinosity, of one ready to give his life that others might be free.

For another month the republic held out. Garibaldi commanded the defense of the most desperately beleaguered section of the walls, taking hair-raising risks with his own life. His headquarters were in range of the French guns and shook under their bombardment as though suffering a perpetual earthquake. Every morning he climbed a watchtower and there, unhurriedly, he lit his first cigar of the morning while French sharpshooters filled the air around him with bullets. "I can safely say," he wrote later, reveling in his own bravado, "I never heard a tempest make such a hissing noise in my life." Every day he rode along the line of walls, unmistakable in his brilliant clothes and his broad plumed hat, with his black servant Aguiar, yet another badge of his identity, just behind him. To his enemies he was a clear target, to his followers a vision. One man told Trevelyan nearly half a century later how, sleeping on the ramparts early one morning, he had "opened his eyes, dreamily half aware that a horse was stepping tenderly across his body. He had a vision of the rider's face looking down at him out of masses of curling golden hair. It was imprinted on his brain as one of the noblest things in art or nature which he had ever seen." Garibaldi took his meals in the open while shells burst around him. It was said that those who dined with him were likely to be killed before they had time to digest their meal. Somehow, amazingly, he survived. Death was everywhere, and Garibaldi was supremely happy. He wrote to Anita, "Here they live, die and suffer amputation, all to the cry of 'Viva la Repubblica!' One hour of our life in Rome is worth a century of ordinary existence."

On the night of June 29 the French launched their final offensive. For two hours Garibaldi led the defenders as they struggled to hold back the attack. "Garibaldi was greater than I have ever seen him, greater than anybody has ever seen him. His sword was like lightning," wrote one of his officers. "At every moment I feared to see him fall, but no, there he remained, as immovable as destiny." At last, as a section of the wall collapsed under the French barrage and the invaders came pouring through the gap, he rode down the hill and over the Tiber to the Capitol, where the assembly was in session. The city was lost; the great political experiment had failed. But when Garibaldi walked into the chamber covered with blood, sweat, and dust, his sword filthy and dented at his side, the assembly rose as one man to cheer him.

The republican government surrendered. Garibaldi did not. The previous year he had refused to accept defeat when King Charles Albert did. Now, once again, he announced his attention of fighting on. While Mazzini and his fellow politicians scrambled for safety abroad he declared that he would lead any who would follow him out of Rome's eastern gates to continue the fight in the countryside.

For weeks he had been chafing against Mazzini's determination to defend the city. A guerrilla by experience and inclination, he favored relinquishing towns, which too easily turned into traps, and taking to open country where speed and cunning could be used to compensate for inferiority of numbers or weaponry. He had begged to be allowed to pursue the French after their initial defeat. He had wanted to lead his men out of Rome and circle round behind their lines. On the route to Velletri he had disguised himself as a peasant in order to spy out the Neapolitan positions with a view to harassing them with repeated raids. After the battle he had wanted to chase the Neopolitan army back into its own territory. All these plans had been thwarted by his political leaders, whose sole aim was to hang on tight to Rome. The ancient, sacred city was a potent symbol. Mazzini had declared: "Within those walls is the future of the nation."

Garibaldi disagreed. "Rome" was not brick and marble: it was a great idea. It stood for republican liberty and for a vague and luminous cluster of other concepts worth dying for. It was no longer enshrined in a place; it was incarnated in a man. In Utica, staunchly defending the defunct republic, Cato was Rome. Now Rome was Garibaldi. "Wherever we shall be," he ringingly proclaimed, "there will be Rome."

At five o'clock on the afternoon of July 2 Garibaldi rode his white horse into Bernini's grand piazza before St. Peter's. His appearance had been expected. The magnificent space was teeming with people. Very slowly he made his way through the crowd towards the obelisk in the piazza's center. "Women stormed him from all sides," wrote one who was there. The din was tremendous. People were cheering and yelling out his name. Others were weeping, and some were cursing him for taking away their sons, for it was already known what he intended to do. He waited. For all his much-lauded simplicity he was a superb orator, with a talent for crowd control to match Cato's and a great gift for stillness. When he had a speech to make he would hold silent, his face half hidden by his great black hat, until the crowd was awed into quietness, before he addressed them in his slow, resonant voice. (The French novelist and journalist Maxim du Camp thought it the most beautiful he had ever heard.) This time, when he gestured for the shouting to stop and that vast and hysterical crowd hushed to hear him, his words were harsh and noble. He asked for volunteers to march out of Rome with him and continue the fight.

Rodrigo Díaz had enticed men to follow him into exile with promises of the great fortunes they could win under his command; similarly, Drake had assured his men that he would make them as rich as gentlemen. Garibaldi held out no such inducements. He was offering not money or social status, but something even more headily intoxicating: the tragic glamour of defeat which had transfigured Cato, and the ennoblement of suffering. "They wrong man greatly," wrote Carlyle, "who say he can be seduced by ease. Difficulty, abnegation, martyrdom, *death* are the *allurements* that act on the heart of man." Eighty years later Winston Churchill told the British Parliament, "I have nothing to offer but blood, toil, tears and sweat." Garibaldi, anticipating him, issued a stirring challenge to his listeners. He told the people of Rome that those who came with him "will have no pay, no provisions, and no rest. I offer hunger, cold, forced marches, battles and death. Whoever is not satisfied with such a life must remain behind. He who has the name of Italy not only his lips but in his heart, let him follow me." Two hours later he led 4,700 volunteers eastward out of Rome, his heart, he afterwards recorded, "as sad as death." Anita was among them. She was six months pregnant but she had disregarded all his messages forbidding her to join him. Her hair cropped short, sitting astride her horse in men's clothes, she rode out with him to fight for a Rome of the mind.

At last Garibaldi was free and autonomous. Mazzini—with whom he was by then bitterly angry, blaming him for their defeat—could no longer thwart him. There were no superior officers anymore, no triumvirate, no assembly, no one whatsoever in authority over him.

He was never a willing subordinate. In South America once, when a senior general attempted to give him orders, he responded with a frigidly polite note: "I have decided to act myself . . . and I must ask your Excellency not to take any contrary action, and inform you that I shall take all steps to prevent this." The mutinous threat was followed by action. A month later he ordered the local chief of police to escort the unfortunate general onto a ship which would take him back to Montevideo: he had effectively deposed his superior, in what in a more orderly military situation would have amounted to an act of mutiny punishable by death. In 1848 he peremptorily cabled the leaders of the Tuscan government: "I ask will you take Garibaldi as commander of Tuscan forces to operate against Bourbons. Yes or No. Garibaldi." He would be commander or he would be nothing.

A few days before the Roman Republic capitulated, an agitator had ridden through the streets shouting out to anyone who would listen that only Garibaldi could save Rome, that Garibaldi should be made dictator. Garibaldi demurred, disowning his advocate, but only on the grounds that it was too late: the loss of the city was by then inevitable. He had already told Mazzini, "It is not possible for me to be of use to the Republic except in two ways; either as absolute dictator, or as a simple soldier." Since his time the word "dictatorship" has acquired overtones it did not yet have in the 1840s. In the ancient Roman Republic, upon which the constitution of the new republic was based, dictators were appointed for six-month periods in times of war or other emergency, an arrangement which Garibaldi was to describe as "propitious." Garibaldi was probably sincere when he later explained he had made the demand "as sometimes in my life I had demanded and seized the helm of a vessel which was being driven on the breakers." The fact remained that he wanted absolute power, and when Mazzini refused to hand it over to him, insisting that he continue to serve Rome as a subordinate general, he consistently defied the authority of those over him.

On the march to Velletri Roselli had found him uncontrollable, pushing ahead and eventually provoking a battle at a time the superior general had expressly forbidden him to do so. During the defense of Rome in June he had repeatedly disobeyed or ignored orders. When he wanted more men he took them from other units in defiance of the high command, and when ordered to lead his men in a counterattack he flatly refused to do so. Like Achilles, like Rodrigo Díaz, like Drake, he was a man who fit only uneasily, if at all, into a chain of command. Leading his volunteer army out of the gates of Rome he was at last coming into his own. Now he was indeed sole dictator of a republic which existed nowhere outside of his own imagination but which was at least entirely under his control.

Two months later the volunteer army was disbanded, most of its leaders had been captured and executed, Anita was dead, and Garibaldi himself was a solitary refugee. He had hoped and believed that he had only to "throw myself in the midst of an energetic population" to "kindle the flame of their patriotism," that his little band of volunteers would grow and grow as enthusiastic nationalists rallied to his cause. He was wrong. The educated urban middle class might care about their country, but the peasants Garibaldi counted on enlisting now disliked "liberals" even more than foreigners and looked upon those who had driven the Pope from Rome as impious heathen. They closed their doors to Garibaldi, refused him food and transport, and informed the French and Austrians of his movements, behavior which Garibaldi blamed on the fell influence of the priesthood, but which may have had as much to do with the Garibaldini's locustlike way of stripping the country bare. The London *Times* called them "brigands," and that is how they were received in the towns and villages where they looked for shelter. Garibaldi forbade looting; on one occasion he had a man shot for stealing a hen. But he could not always control his rabble of volunteers. Nor could he feed them by any means other than a kind of requisitioning which was barely more legitimate than straightforward pillage would have been. He paid for the provisions he demanded in the worthless currency of the defunct Roman republic, or he extorted "loans" to be repaid when Italy was free.

What had begun as an act of magnificent defiance became a hopeless flight, yet one of his biographers has claimed that the retreat from Rome was "a *tour de force* of astonishing and enduring brilliance," one which "triumphantly confirmed his reputation as one of the greatest of guerrilla leaders." It was certainly to become one of the most popular acts in the drama of his life, one in which he appears both as the fabulously skillful and audacious individual defying not one but four great powers and as the pathetic protagonist of a heartbreaking tale of love and death.

The French were behind him. To the south were the troops of the Bourbon king of Naples. To the west was an army of six thousand Spaniards, just landed to defend the interests of the Pope. To the north, lying between Garibaldi and the republic of Venice (the only one of the free states established in the previous year's flurry of revolutions that was still undefeated), lay the Austrians. Garibaldi could not afford to risk a pitched battle. Marching by night, resting only for a few hours by day, keeping always to the least frequented roads or to mule tracks generally regarded as impassable, he led his army in wild zigzags which their pursuers could not follow. They would set out at nightfall in one direction and then, while the peasants who had seen them go passed on information about their apparent destination to the French or Austrian spies behind them, they would wheel round in the dark and appear at dawn miles from where they were awaited. After the first few days they abandoned their carts, taking nothing more than they and their pack animals could carry and the cattle whom they drove in front of them for food. Garibaldi himself, galloping on ahead to reconnoiter, wheeling down his little army's flanks to watch for danger, was tireless. Naturally ascetic, he was at his most effective, his swiftest and surest when he had least. Some years later he was to write of how he dreamed of equipping a ship (this was after he had reverted to the seaman's life) and sailing the world in support of good causes everywhere, a kind of mobile revolution. He was a patriot who was never much at ease in his *patria*, one whose brilliance was most apparent when he was homeless and on the run.

It was not only the people of the countryside through which he passed that disappointed him by their lack of fervor for his cause. Every night some of his men slipped away under cover of darkness; in every town some few remained behind. Over and over again over the remaining years of his life he was to discover how hard it was to convert the adulation he inspired into those things he actually needed—money, armaments, manpower. He could call up an ecstatic crowd with ease, but he couldn't hold together an army. Many of those who had left Rome with him probably never intended to fight for his lost cause but, wanting to get away from the soon-to-be-occupied city, or eager to return to homes in the countryside, saw the Garibaldini as a convoy with which they could travel more safely. Others simply lost heart. His mobile revolution was melting away. To add to his unhappiness Anita was unwell. Contemporary sources are all too coy to specify her complaint, but it was presumably related to her pregnancy.

On July 31, a month after he had set out from Rome with such uplifting words, he led his remaining fifteen hundred men into the refuge of the tiny independent state of San Marino. Even as he was negotiating with the San Marinesi for their reception a party of Austrians was harrying his rearguard. His last order of the day read: "Soldiers, I release you from your duty to follow me, and leave you free to return to your homes. But remember that although the Roman war for the independence of Italy has ended Italy remains in shameful slavery." He himself, true to form, intended to fight on. In a café where his disconsolate staff had gathered he made another of his ringingly pessimistic offers. "Whoever wishes to follow me, I offer him fresh battles, suffering and exile—but treaties with foreigners, never!" He then mounted and rode off, without so much as turning his head to see who would follow him. Some 230 men did, and so did Anita.

The countryside was full of Austrian troops. Their only hope of escaping to a raise another revolution was to make their way to the Adriatic coast and thence by sea to Venice. With the help of a local guide, maintaining absolute silence, they passed by night through the Austrian lines. They reached the sea at a little harbor where Garibaldi gave his white horse to a local sympathizer with orders that it should be shot rather than allowed to fall into Austrian hands. They seized thirteen fishing boats and forced their owners to ready them for the trip to Venice. A high wind had come up, the fishermen protested it was impossible even to get out of port in such weather, but Garibaldi—a seaman before he was a general—leaped into the sea to fix the anchors on which the boats were to be hauled out. The fishermen, balking at risking the boats on which their livelihoods depended and perhaps their lives as well, "could be made to move at all—not to speak of doing the necessary work—only by mean of blows with the flat of our swords."

For the whole of the following day they sailed north but at night they ran into an Austrian naval squadron. The majority of the boats were captured (the fishermen making no effort to avoid it). The remaining three boats, carrying about ninety people in all (including Garibaldi and Anita), made it to the shore, with the Austrians in close pursuit. Anita was by now in such pain she couldn't walk. Garibaldi carried her through the breakers. As the others raced for the cover of the dunes the two of them and a wounded officer, Major Culiolo, were soon the only people left exposed on the beach. They had landed by ill chance on what was effectively an island, an area of marshland cut off by canals and lagoons from the mainland. They would unquestionably have been captured very shortly—Austrian troops were already advancing towards them—but a local landowner played deus ex machina. Giacomo Bonnet, two of whose brothers had fought in Rome with Garibaldi, had seen what was happening out at sea and had rushed down to the beach to offer his help if it was needed. Finding Garibaldi he hurried him, Anita, and Culiolo to a hut secluded in the marshes, and gave them clothes (both the men had been wearing the unmistakable red shirt). He then helped them carry Anita two miles across the marshes to a farmhouse, where she was put to bed. She was now so ill it was clear that any attempt to escape with her would be hopeless for all of them. Bonnet proposed that she should be left in another safe house where a trustworthy doctor could be called to attend her while Garibaldi and Culiolo made their escape. Garibaldi reluctantly agreed.

Again the little party moved, Anita this time lying in a cart. She was delirious and incoherent. When Garibaldi tried to explain that he must go on without her she clung to him, crying hysterically and saying, as she had often said before when he tried to persuade her not to follow him into battle, "You want to leave me!" This time it was her husband, not herself, whom she was endangering, but she was beyond understanding that.

Their ordeal continued. There were Austrian troops everywhere. A large reward had been offered for any information leading to Garibaldi's capture. Anyone helping him to escape put themselves in extreme danger. Bonnet was only the first of the dozens who were to take that risk in the month that followed. He found two boatmen and arranged, without telling them who their passengers were to be, for them to take Garibaldi and his companions over the lagoon to the mainland that night. They embarked, but halfway across the boatmen guessed who they were carrying and, terrified of the danger they had been tricked into incurring, landed them on a tiny island and rowed off. It was three in the morning. There was no shelter, no prospect of rescue. The two men lay beside Anita on the ground, trying to keep her warm as she muttered and raved.

Help came five hours later. The boatmen had been unable to keep their lethal secret to themselves and one of those they told had reported the news to the ever-reliable Bonnet. He found another boatman, a republican willing to risk his own life to rescue Garibaldi. He took them off the island, rowed with numerous delays across to the mainland, procured a cart in which they laid Anita, and then slowly escorted them to another farm twelve miles off. It was late in the afternoon by the time they arrived there. As they carried Anita into the house she died.

For the next month Garibaldi was under the protection of the impressively well organized and courageous republican resistance movement. He had been bitterly disappointed in the failure of Italians in general to offer their lives for the sake of independence, but he had cause to be deeply grateful to and respectful of the network of people who hid him in woods, in fields, in their homes or stables, who guided him by back roads and unmapped pathways right across Italy, who fed him and provided him with disguises, all risking their liberty and probably their lives to protect him.

While his followers were imprisoned, tortured, and, in many cases, shot, he evaded all the strenuous efforts of the Austrians to catch him. Once, riding in a hired cart, he drove past a whole troop of Austrian soldiers marching the other way in pursuit of him. On another occasion he was sleeping in a clump of bushes when he was awakened by the voices of a party of Austrians passing within feet of him. On yet another, when he was resting in an inn, a group of Croats serving in the Austrian army came in and he had to sit for hours, keeping to the room's dimmest corner, while they talked of what they would do to "the infamous Garibaldi" when they caught him. On that occasion (according to her own less-than-reliable story—Garibaldi himself does not appear to have remembered her) he was saved by the innkeeper's daughter, who led him to a safe house. When one of their guides failed to meet up with them, he and Culiolo were for several frightening days unprotected until Garibaldi, taking a necessary but potentially fatal risk, revealed his identity to a young man whom he had overheard talking sympathetically about him. He was lucky. The man kept the secret and found them a guide. On September 2 they reached the west coast and were taken by friendly fishermen northwards and put ashore over the border in the kingdom of Piedmont, where neither Austrians, French, Neapolitans, nor the papal authorities could harm them. There, in Garibaldi's homeland, reached after such tribulations, he was promptly put under arrest.

The new king, Victor Emmanuel, the man whom Garibaldi was later to be instrumental in making king of all Italy, held his throne on Austria's sufferance on the understanding he would tolerate neither radicalism in general nor Young Italy in particular. Garibaldi's return was intensely embarrassing for him. In Genoa, where Garibaldi was held prisoner, and in Nice, where he was allowed to go ashore on parole for a few hours to visit his mother and children, he was applauded by crowds full of enthusiasm for him and indignation at his detention. In both places the ship on which he was being transported was surrounded by little boats crammed with sightseers and supporters. In the Piedmontese parliament there were angry scenes so noisy that a Turin newspaper reported that two days later sessions were still preternaturally quiet, so many of the deputies having lost their voices shouting out their views on Garibaldi. One of them called upon his peers to "imitate his greatness if you can; if you are unable to do so respect it": Garibaldi, he said, was his country's glory. Eventually the opposition proposed a motion censuring the government for their treatment of him, and it was carried all but unanimously. Garibaldi was released, but on condition that he leave Italy forthwith.

Exiled for the second time, he was hard put to find a place of refuge. He was evicted from Tunisia, refused entry to Gibraltar. Eventually he settled in Tangier. He was only forty-two, but like an old man whose glory days are over and done he found himself a place in the sun and began to write his memoirs. He had already, for some years, been plagued by rheumatism and arthritis. The indifference of the Italian peasants who had failed to rally to his cause and the Italian troops who had deserted him had left him profoundly depressed: "I was ashamed to belong to these degenerate descendants of the greatest of nations, who were incapable of keeping the field a month without their three meals a day." He had lost the wife who seems to have been, in reality as well as in popular legend, the love of his life. He was separated from his children, whom he left behind in Nice under the care of their grandmother and family friends. Italy, "the only hope of my life" as he wrote that year, had "fallen back again into shame and prostitution." He had lost his cause.

Seven months later he traveled to New York. To Americans European republicans in exile were heroic figures. Lajos Kossuth, leader of the Hungarian revolution, was to be greeted in the following year by a thirty-one-gun salute as his ship docked, by reception committees, banquets, parades, and brass bands. He was invited to see in the new year at the White House and to address Congress. Similar levels of razzmatazz had been planned to welcome Garibaldi, but he rejected them. At Staten Island, where, under the rules of quarantine, he had to stay for several days, he was unable to avoid a stream of visitors, whom he received sitting on a sofa carried in for the purpose, his rheumatism being so severe he was unable to stand. But at the earliest opportunity he took the ferry on his own and slipped away to a friend's house. Three days later he wrote to the Italian Committee declining to attend the civic reception they had planned for him and declaring his intention to settle down and quietly earn a living.

His reluctance to receive applause has been ascribed to his admirable modesty, but at this period in his life he was so downcast that he was probably in no fit state to play the celebrity. "We love to associate with heroic persons," wrote Carlyle's American friend Ralph Waldo Emerson that year. "With the great our thoughts and manners easily become great." Garibaldi in exile had no energy to spare, no surplus greatness he would willingly allow others to siphon off. Besides, he knew precisely how useful, and how useless, public enthusiasm could be. In his year and a half in Italy he had all too often stood on balconies or sat his horse while rapturous crowds pressed around him, yelling his name in ecstasies of enthusiasm, only to find that when he was ready to leave town only two or three, or none, of those who seemed to adore him so had volunteered to join him. America would have given him parades and banquets, used him as entertainment and as a focus for vague and thrilling dreams of heroic rebellion against ill-defined tyranny, but America would not grant him citizenship. As an alien he was not permitted to captain a ship. He lived with an Italian friend, idle and wretched, and so miserably humiliated by his dependent status that he insisted on working as a porter in his hosts' candle factory. Once he went down to the waterfront and tried to sign on as an ordinary seaman but was rejected by both the ships he tried. In despair he applied for work as a docker, only to be told that he was too old. Only three years before he had been admiral in chief of the (admittedly small) Montevidean navy. Now, for all his celebrity, he was an unemployable, superannuated immigrant.

"Great natures," wrote Aristotle, "are especially prone to sorrow." It was Achilles' mournful awareness of his own imminent death that made him the most compelling character in the *Iliad*. Mid-nineteenth-century Europe (and America) had been, in the two generations before Garibaldi, first entranced by the *weltschmerz* of young Werther and subsequently enthralled by the melancholy exiles of Childe Harold and his creator. Garibaldi's pitifully fallen fortunes and his status as a wanderer hunted from his homeland by those too crass in their sensibilities or cruel in their pursuit of political advantage to appreciate the romance of his character did nothing to diminish his reputation in the short term and, subsequently, when he was once again the man of the hour, this second exile became a particularly affecting passage in the legend of his life. "A great heart that breaks," wrote Dumas about him, "is a spectacle which breaks all hearts."

For the time being, though, the man himself had more urgent priorities than the mythification of his life story. Garibaldi had a livelihood to get. He drifted for a year, but at last a kindly disposed Italian businessman offered him the command of a merchant ship. He became a seaman again, a modern Odysseus traveling ever farther from the homeland on which he claimed his heart was set. He had his share of adventures. He nearly died of a fever contracted in Panama. In Canton he was fired at by pirates. In Lima he was accused of embezzlement (probably actually just incompetent accounting—he really does seem to have been above financial greed), and, after he had beaten up a Frenchman who had insulted him and Italy, of murder. Also in Peru he went ashore to visit Manuela Saenz de Thorne, who had been Simon Bolívar's mistress. She was paralyzed. Garibaldi, whose rheumatism was bad again, lay down beside her and for several hours the two of them lay chastely together in the darkened room, talking over past struggles, past glories. Since leaving Italy, he wrote to a friend, "I have led an unhappy life, restless and embittered by memory." Visiting London with a cargo of coal in his ship's hold he dined with Mazzini, Kossuth, the French republican Ledru-Rollin, and Herzen, all of them, like Garibaldi, mourning a lost cause while eking out a living in an adopted land. He had joined the melancholy brotherhood of revolutionary refugees.

At last, in 1854, he received indirect word that the government of Piedmont, under the new prime minister Count Camillo Cavour, would not prevent him if he wished to return. He reclaimed his children and bought some land on Caprera, a rocky little island off the coast of Sardinia. There, with the help of his son Menotti, he built himself a simple one-story house and settled down to a kind of self-imposed internal exile. He hoed beans and milked goats. His great days appeared to be over.

The life of Garibaldi the man had dwindled to that of a retired seaman—he was to write in his memoirs that the five years after his return to Europe "present no points of interest." But the reputation of Garibaldi the hero was still flourishing. The *New York Tribune*, announcing his arrival in America, had described him as the "world-famed Italian." It was hardly an exaggeration. Garibaldi and Anita galloping across the pampas, their eyes alight with revolutionary fervor, their long hair streaming behind them; Garibaldi sitting his white horse impassive amid a storm of bullets while his men marched willingly to their deaths at his command;

Garibaldi pursued through Italy by four armies and eluding them all; Garibaldi weeping over Anita as she died in his arms: these were potent images and they were widely exploited for political, romantic, and commercial ends.

Already, on both sides of the Atlantic, people were collecting Garibaldiana. The story goes that Garibaldi gave his American host the red shirt he had worn during the defense of Rome, though skeptics have wondered how Garibaldi, who surely took no luggage with him when he carried the dying Anita through the marshes, could still have had it with him in New York. In Italy Robert and Elizabeth Barrett Browning hired one of the ex-Garibaldini as a manservant, a human souvenir. Sympathizers of all sorts and all nations found ways to honor him. Visiting Newcastle to pick up a load of coal he was presented with a ceremonial sword and scroll paid for by the subscribed pennies of over a thousand working men ready to honor "the glorious defender of the Roman Republic." When Garibaldi's mother died in 1852, Alexander Herzen, who had yet to meet him, attended her funeral as a tribute to his fellow fighter in the cause of freedom. Even Mazzini, with whom Garibaldi had frequently quarreled in Rome, was sufficiently devoted to their shared cause and sufficiently generous to be ready to blow on the coals of his glory. "There is around the name of Garibaldi a halo which nothing can extinguish," he wrote. "Garibaldi's name is all-powerful."

It was true. And that halo, that all-powerful name, made Garibaldi a political tool far too useful to be left to rust indefinitely. In December 1858, nine years after he had been deported from Piedmont, Piedmont's new chief minister summoned him to Turin. His premature retirement was over. The second act of his heroic drama was about to begin.

The man who recalled him, Count Camillo Cavour, Victor Emmanuel's chief minister, was to play a crucial if profoundly equivocal role in that drama. Cavour was Garibaldi's antithesis—Athens to his Sparta, Odysseus to his Achilles. Garibaldi's heart was always prominently, often unwisely, displayed on his sleeve. Cavour was a political games player whose machinations were so intricately tortuous that no one, either among his contemporaries or among modern historians, has ever been able to distinguish with absolute certainty between his genuine aims and those assumed for diplomacy's sake. Garibaldi compared himself with the heroes of romance and swaggered in archaic fancy dress. Cavour was a modern bureaucrat, a desk man and a diplomat, short-haired, neatly waistcoated and trousered. To the cartoonists of the European press Cavour's trademark was his little round spectacles—when the Empress Eugénie, playing charades at Fontainebleau in 1860, wanted one of her gentlemen to represent Cavour she suggested he do so simply by donning a pair. (Garibaldi, as it happened, was by this time almost equally near-sighted, but while Cavour's specs were perfectly of a piece with his publicly perceived character, those of Garibaldi's admirers who managed to contrive a meeting with him were dismayed to find him peering at them through pince-nez—haloed heroes were not supposed to wear eyeglasses.) Cavour was to exploit Garibaldi, to thwart him and betray him. Garibaldi later said of him and his king, "They use men like they use oranges. They suck the juice out to the last drop and throw the peel away in the corner," and it was true. But it was also true that without Cavour's enlightened decision to enlist him Garibaldi could not have achieved any of the miracles he was to perform over the next two years.

In 1858 Cavour and Louis-Napoleon, now the Emperor Napoleon III, secretly agreed to go to war together on the Austrians with the intention of sweeping them out of northern Italy. The Piedmontese commander in chief was General La Marmora, to whom had fallen the tricky task of arresting Garibaldi in 1849. He had noted then: "Garibaldi is not an ordinary man . . . It was a great mistake not to make use of him. If there is another war he will be a man to employ." Cavour was of the same opinion. At their December meeting he told Garibaldi that as soon as a pretext could be found the war would begin, and he asked for his assistance. A friend who saw Garibaldi soon afterward recalls: "His face was radiant, his voice was broken with emotion as, extending his arms, he exclaimed: 'This time we shall do it!' "

"The adherence of Garibaldi is an event of immense importance," wrote the Marquis of Pallavicino, another republican who had decided to support the Piedmontese monarchy. "It secures for us the sympathies and, when required, the active assistance of all the youth of Italy." But Cavour had to be careful how he used the man whose chiefest claim to glory was the resolution with which he had defended Rome against Piedmont's new allies, the French. While Garibaldi's name was given great prominence, Garibaldi the man was kept to the sidelines. He was ordered to set up camp forty miles from Turin. The thousands of young men who joined up expressly in order to serve under him were diverted to other regiments. "I was kept as a flag to attract recruits," he wrote later, "to summon volunteers in large numbers but to command only a small proportion of them, and those the least fit to bear arms." To his force were assigned the boys and the old men, the physically feeble and the disaffected—"We intend to give the deserters to Garibaldi," wrote Cavour to a fellow minister—and he was fobbed off with the scantiest of equipment, superannuated muskets, not enough boots, not enough cartridge belts, no artillery, no horses.

None of it mattered. The war, which lasted ten weeks, was only a limited success for Cavour: Piedmont gained only Lombardy, less than he had hoped. But for Garibaldi it was glorious. He was operating, as he had done eleven years before, in the mountainous regions around the Italian lakes, doing what he did best, appearing where he was least expected, swinging round in midmarch, leaving roads to scramble over mountain paths and arriving—swift, silent, and unexpected—miles from where he was looked for, leading his men as they dashed down a mountainside like a living torrent, sweeping unopposed into unguarded towns, helping himself to supplies and ammunition left behind by Austrian garrisons which fled precipitately when he appeared. He ordered his men to jettison even their knapsacks and stow all they needed into bread bags and pockets. He himself left his general's helmet behind and resumed his favorite broad-brimmed black hat, slinging his poncho over his uniform. His troop called themselves the Cacciatori delle Alpi. Ill trained and unfit at the beginning of the campaign, they were transfigured by their sense of participation in an adventure as romantic as it was successful. "*Sono nella poesia*," wrote Nino Bixio, one of his commanders. "I am living in poetry."

Everywhere Garibaldi was greeted with rapture. He seemed, wrote a local official, not so much a general as "the head of a new religion followed by a crowd of fanatics . . . it was delirium." The villages through which the Cacciatori passed were full of people cheering and throwing flowers. They brought their babies so Garibaldi could bless or even—to the scandal of the orthodox—baptize them. They made shrines to him, lighting candles before his picture. "The people were wild with delight," wrote one of the Cacciatori later. "Men with torches marched on either side of Garibaldi's horse and old and young rushed forward kissing his feet and clothes. Old men with tears streaming down their faces and young girls threw their arms round our necks and greeted us as deliverers." Bands played, bells pealed, crowds yelled "Viva l'Italia! Viva Garibaldi!" In every town they took, Garibaldi would speak to the people in his thrilling solemn voice, always holding himself aloof from rejoicing, always urging them on to sacrifice. "Come! He who stays at home is a coward. I promise you weariness, hardship and battles. We will conquer or die!" The Croats in the Austrian army told tales of bullets rebounding from Garibaldi's chest and called him the "Red Devil." To his Italian supporters he was something very like a messiah.

It was all very irritating for Cavour, and for the regular officers of the Piedmontese army who fought equally hard and never received anything like the adulation accorded Garibaldi. He was given a gold medal but soon afterwards he suffered his first defeat when his troops were attacked by a far larger Austrian force. The reinforcements he had been promised didn't reach him in time and he was obliged to retreat. Garibaldi believed for years afterwards that their nonappearance represented "a deliberate attempt to get rid of a man who had it in his power to become dangerous."

The war ended in July, but for Garibaldi—who had commissioned a song which became known as "the Garibaldi hymn" with the refrain "*Va fuori d'Italia, va fuori, O stranier*" ("Get out of Italy! Get out, foreigner!")—the struggle would never end until Italy was free. Until he set off for Sicily in April of the following year he was once again a warrior without a war, a hero without a plot.

Both publicly and privately he was living in an atmosphere of frantically heightened emotion. As he traveled through central Italy in the summer and autumn of 1859 he was received everywhere by crowds whose adulation now amounted to a kind of hysteria. They wept and cheered as he spoke to them from balconies. They took the horses out of his carriage and dragged it themselves through villages packed with ecstatic worshipers. When he revisited the territory through which he had fled in 1849 he was mobbed by people asking for his blessing and showing him relics—shirts and handkerchiefs supposedly his which they had treasured for ten years and which they now begged him to reconsecrate by his touch. He was entertained at a banquet in the house where Anita had died. Afterwards forty young men dressed in black carried her exhumed coffin, which he wished to have reburied in Nice, twenty miles on foot to Ravenna. Wherever he went bells rang, scarves waved, women swooned, cigars patriotically wrapped in red, green, and white ribbons were sold, bands played the Garibaldi hymn. And it was not only those around him who had succumbed to Garibaldi fever. Biographies of him were published that summer in Paris, Amsterdam, Weimar, and London. In London his exploits were enacted on the stage of Astley's Theatre, and as he lay in bed (throughout his life he slept little, waking shortly after midnight and reading in bed until dawn) he could, and did, read fervently admiring accounts of his exploits in the *Illustrated London News*.

He was also the object of a great deal of sexual attention. Even during the years of his exile, depressed and unresponsive as he was, he had been assiduously courted by numerous high-minded but impressionable ladies infatuated with the romance of his story and his tawny locks. He was briefly engaged to a rich English widow. She gave him a ship, but their marriage never took place. Failing a wife he got himself a housekeeper, a young woman from Nice named Battistina Ravello who cooked and cleaned for him on Caprera, shared his bed, and bore him a daughter. He considered marrying her but was deflected from doing so by two other women. The first was Baroness Speranza von Schwartz, a cosmopolitan writer of independent means and equally independent mind. She visited Garibaldi on Caprera and struck him as a possible mate. A year later he proposed to her. She temporized, perhaps because she suspected that he was sleeping with Battistina. But in the event it was neither the housekeeper nor the literary baroness who became his second wife.

When Garibaldi met Anita he had felt an urgent need for a woman. He seems to have been in the same state of mind in 1859. In the early summer, while campaigning near Lake Maggiore, he met a seventeen-year-old aristocrat, the Marchesina Giuseppina Raimondi, who appeared to him on the road, as he afterwards put it, "like a lovely vision." She was carrying a message from his supporters in Como. The Austrian lines were between his position and the town. Giuseppina, a young lady traveling by carriage escorted only by a priest, had passed through them unsuspected. Garibaldi was immediately smitten. "At the first sight of this dear creature . . . her features were indelibly engraved upon my heart." She went back with him to his headquarters and there, so he afterwards wrote, he went down on his knees to her exclaiming, "Oh that I might belong to you in some way or another." Still, he held back from committing himself, and a few weeks after their meeting he wrote to her confessing that he was "neither physically nor spiritually free." Two months later Speranza von Schwartz was traveling as part of his entourage through central Italy when she learned that the housekeeper, Battistina, had just given birth to his daughter. Speranza took her leave. Battistina waited in vain for Garibaldi to return to her. In October Garibaldi, who seems to have been being buffeted by some sort of erotic and emotional hurricane, met and promptly proposed to yet a fourth woman, the young widow Marchesa Paulina Zucchine, who wisely refused him. Finally, at the end of November, he became engaged to Giuseppina Raimondi, and in January, disastrously for both of them, they were married.

The episode is a pathetic one, discreditable to all concerned. Garibaldi may have figured in the erotic fantasies of women all over Europe (the twelve-year-old heroine of Elizabeth Anna Hart's novel *The Runaway* tells her father that Garibaldi is the only man in the world she will marry), but in prosaic reality people meeting him for the first time tended to be greatly disappointed. A French journalist who interviewed him that year arrived with a head full of pictures of "a felt hat, a ferocious countenance imbedded in a mass of dishevelled hair, a blouse and large waist-belt adorned with a dozen cavalry pistols, a naked sabre" and was nonplussed to meet instead a bespectacled and neatly brushed officer (Garibaldi was always fastidious—once in South America he had taken time off in the middle of a battle to wash a sweat-stained shirt), a rheumaticky middle-aged man whose leonine mane was beginning to recede. The spirited girl driving through enemy lines to serve the cause must have seemed to Garibaldi a second Anita, but he was no longer the kind of physically compelling man whom a young woman would follow on a word.

As the teenage bride and the fifty-three-year-old general (who was even less spry than usual—he had had to put off the wedding after falling from a horse and breaking his kneecap) came out of the church, a young Major Rovelli, Giuseppina's cousin, gave Garibaldi a note. Garibaldi read it and passed it on to Giuseppina, demanding to know whether its contents were true. She told him that they were. Furious, he picked up a chair and went as though to strike her with it, calling her a whore. She faced him coolly, saying she had thought him a hero but saw now he was just a brutal soldier. He handed her to her father and left, never to speak to her again.

Twenty years later the contents of the fatal note were made public in the course of their divorce proceedings. It had revealed that Giuseppina, with her father's knowledge and connivance, had had several lovers (including Rovelli himself) beginning when she was only eleven, that at the time she married Garibaldi she was in love with one of his officers, a Lieutenant Caroli, and that the very night before her wedding she had been in bed with someone other than her bridegroom (whether Caroli or Rovelli is unclear). It appears that she had reluctantly agreed to the marriage on the insistence of her father. It was pitiful; Garibaldi had been first infatuated and then humiliated by a seedily exploitative father and a damaged girl. But the year that had begun so cruelly was to be the year of his apotheosis.

In April there was an uprising in Sicily, partly engineered by Mazzini, against the regime of the Bourbon king Francis of Naples, of whose domains the island formed part. The insurrection was quickly contained, but there were many who believed that, with support, it could be revived. In Genoa a Sicilian Committee was formed, several of its members being long-term associates of Garibaldi's, and they proposed that he lead an expedition to the island to make common cause with the revolutionaries there. Three times before he had turned down similar suggestions from Mazzini but this time he was at least half persuaded. He established himself in a villa at Quarto, a few miles from Genoa, and for nearly a month he vacillated.

He made preparations. He ordered new red shirts for himself and his followers. During the previous winter he had instituted a "Million Rifles Fund," appealing for money so that the Risorgimento should not be short of weapons. Now he asked that two hundred of the rifles purchased with the fund be sent to him. The house in which he was staying was besieged by journalists, police agents, and foreign spies all agog to discover his intentions. Unable to go out, Garibaldi, who was in the habit of taking long walks every morning, expended his surplus physical energy in digging the garden. While he cultivated his borrowed plot his following was growing. He had two hundred volunteers in mid-April, five hundred ten days later, over a thousand by the beginning of May.

The status of the projected expedition to Sicily was uncertain. Garibaldi asked for Victor Emmanuel's sanction. The king hesitated for several days and then, probably persuaded by Cavour, refused. He couldn't overtly agree to an unprovoked attack on a neighboring kingdom with which Piedmont was not at war. It made no difference. In and around Rome eleven years earlier Garibaldi had been repeatedly restrained from taking initiatives, and he had never ceased to believe that he had been right and his more cautious commanding officers wrong. At the end of the previous year's war his birthplace—to his furious chagrin—had been ceded to France once more. Arriving in Quarto he characterized himself as a man without a country: "Now that Nice belongs to Italy no longer," he told his host, "I am like Jesus Christ—I have no longer a stone on which to lay my head." He was one of the long line of homeless heroes operating outside of any fixed community. He owed allegiance now only to Italy, a country not yet found on any map. He was not to be

Westmacott's statue of Achilles at Hyde Park Corner was erected in 1822 in honor of the Duke of Wellington. The female subscribers, embarrassed by its nudity, asked the sculptor to add a fig-leaf. Here spectators of the 1919 Trooping of the Colour use it as a viewing platform.

Gabriele D'Annunzio, would-be Superman, painted by Romaine Brooks, who was one of his numerous lovers.

Opposite El Cid proved his heroism by facing lions undaunted; Garibaldi looked like a lion; Benito Mussolini, self-appointed successor to a line of great men extending from Julius Caesar to Garibaldi, posed with a lion cub on his lap.

A scene from *Napoleon: The Hundred Days* by Benito Mussolini, staged in London in 1932. Mussolini, like Nietzsche, revered Napoleon.

By the middle of the 19th century, Drake, the self-serving pirate, had been reinvented as a dutiful public servant and protoimperialist. Here he kneels meekly to receive his knighthood.

The Cid's earthly remains, like the relics of saints, were too greatly venerated to be allowed to rest in peace. Here Baron Dominique Vivant Denon, traveler, connoisseur, and curator of Napoleon's collection, is depicted by Alexandre Fragonard *Replacing the Bones of Le Cid in His Tomb*. Some fragments of those bones, however, remained in Denon's possession.

Charlton Heston, as the hero of Anthony Mann's 1961 film *El Cid*, rides out to battle. In the film's climactic sequence the corpse of the Cid, strapped into the warhorse's saddle, leads his troops to a posthumous victory.

General Franco, hailed by his propagandists as the second Cid, gave every help to the film's makers. Here his waxwork image, as inert as Rodrigo Díaz's corpse, is moved by employees at Madame Tussaud's—the manipulator manipulated.

Opposite Adolf Hitler, a great admirer of Wallenstein's, photographed in 1925 by Heinrich Hoffman. Hitler, like Cato, took pains to perfect his oratorical style. This picture, preserved against his orders, shows him rehearsing gestures to a gramophone record of his own speeches.

Above The song the Sirens sing is of the exhilaration and glory of warfare. This Roman mosaic from the 3rd century AD shows Odysseus strapped to the mast, his ears stopped with wax, intent on resisting temptation and reaching home.

In his end is his beginning. In Giorgio di Chirico's *The Return of Ulysses* it seems that, for all the hero's adventures, his protracted wanderings, he has never really left his own front room.

held back from Sicily by his lack of an official order from the Kingdom of Piedmont.

Cavour's attitude towards the plan is hard to gauge. The British diplomat James Hudson, a perspicacious observer, reported a few weeks later that "at the outset nobody believed in the possibility of Garibaldi's success; and Cavour and *tutti quanti* thought the country well rid of him. . . . The argument was if he fails we are rid of a troublesome fellow, and if he succeeds Italy will derive some profit from his success." Once the expedition was launched beyond recall Cavour's attitude to it seems to have been not unlike Queen Elizabeth's to Drake's piracies, one of public disassociation and private satisfaction, and later he was to declare that he had always secretly admired Garibaldi and wished him well. But there is evidence to suggest that initially he wholeheartedly deplored the venture. A few days before the expedition departed he took a special train to Bologna, where the king was staying, and during the several hours the two men spent alone together the chief minister allegedly did his utmost to persuade the king to have Garibaldi arrested and the volunteers dispersed, and declared at last that if no one else would do it he would put his own hand on Garibaldi's collar. It may be true. As Garibaldi's ships steamed southwards they were followed or outdistanced by a series of messages from Cavour to the governor of Sardinia, the first ones ordering him to arrest the expedition if it entered a Sardinian port, the later ones to stop it "at all costs" (the underlining is Cavour's).

"The Great Man," wrote Carlyle, "was always a lightning out of Heaven; the rest of men waited for him like fuel, and then they too would flame." Mazzini had believed for years that if Garibaldi were to go to Sicily his presence would be encouragement enough to raise a host of revolutionaries. Garibaldi himself was not so sure. More cautious now than when he had crossed the Atlantic with sixty-three men to free Italy, he would not attempt to lead an insurrection in Sicily, or anywhere else, without reliable information that the local people were ready to give their enthusiastic support. He had, after all, only one thousand men. The Neapolitans had twenty-five times that number.

A classic catch: without Garibaldi there would be no popular uprising, without a popular uprising Garibaldi would not go. There was no straight way of getting past the obstacle. It was the Sicilian republican (and future prime minister of Italy) Francesco Crispi who found a crooked one. On April 27 he received a telegram with news from Sicily. It was in a code no one at Quarto beside himself understood. Sadly he told Garibaldi that it reported that a further attempted insurrection had failed and it ended "Do not start." Garibaldi accordingly summoned together the volunteers who were encamped all around the villa and on the beach and told them, with tears in his eyes, that they would not be going to Sicily. The announcement was received with furious disappointment. Some, bitterly let down, went home at once. Others, including Nino Bixio, who had long been one of his most trusted officers, accused Garibaldi of cowardice and declared their intention of going anyway. Crispi had been working towards the liberation of Sicily for years. He saw the expedition which was the cause's best hope flying to pieces. He made his intervention. On April 29 he told Garibaldi he had had another look at the encrypted telegram and he could see now that his first reading of it had been quite, quite wrong. This time, he alleged, he had deciphered its true meaning: "The insurrection suppressed in the city of Palermo maintains itself in the provinces." He produced other telegrams (forged, or so Nino Bixio said later) which confirmed his revised interpretation. On April 30 Garibaldi announced that he would take his volunteers to Sicily after all.

When Alcibiades led out his fleet to Sicily all Athens was afire with ambition, greed, and battle ardor. Garibaldi's expedition was a more modest affair: no gilded triremes, no massed warriors, no official endorsement, just a scruffy band of idealists and adventurers. "The Thousand" (the name under which they were remembered; actually they were 1,089) were untrained almost to a man. Victor Emmanuel had refused Garibaldi's request that he might enlist the Cacciatori delle Alpi. His new volunteers were of many sorts and conditions. There were a hundred doctors, a hundred and fifty lawyers. There were students, journalists, gentleman-adventurers, laborers, tramps, and artists. There was one woman. The youngest of the volunteers was eleven years old (Garibaldi had no scruples about asking children to kill and be killed), the oldest had fought half a century earlier under the first Napoleon. All of them, like Bixio the previous year, were "living in poetry" and about to enter legend. Their adventure was to become modern Italy's foundation myth. The most prominent among them are commemorated in street names all over the peninsula. Fifty-five years after their embarkation from Quarto G. M. Trevelyan talked to some of those who were still alive. "Those who remember the day," he wrote, "speak of it as something too sacred ever to return."

There was though, one aspect, besides their destination, in which Garibaldi's expedition resembled Alcibiades'. Both were led by outlaws. Subsequent histories, especially Fascist versions which sought to present the Risorgimento as a pan-Italian project in which all true patriots thought and fought as one, a prototype for the Fascist revolution, have tried to minimize the distance between Garibaldi and Victor Emmanuel's government, but there is no disguising it. He wasn't hindered: *The Times* of London pointed out there had rarely been so flagrant a toleration by a government of preparations for warlike operations against a friendly foreign state. But he was not helped either. His request for weapons from the Million Rifles Fund was refused by the governor of Milan. The muskets Garibaldi did manage to obtain were old and rusty. Nine out of ten of them, he complained, "would not even fire." He had no ships. No one, whether government authority or private backer, wanted to be seen to have provided him with transport until finally the manager of a Genoese shipping company agreed to turn a blind eye while he "stole" two steamers.

On May 5, under cover of darkness, the Thousand embarked. Their expedition had an awkward, flustered beginning. While the majority of them waited in little boats, seasick and anxious, throughout the night, Nino Bixio and a group of volunteers had had to fight for their ships after all, the crew being more careful of their employer's property than he was. Of the two vessels only one had a functioning engine and had to take the other one in tow. The boatmen who had been employed to bring out the ammunition failed to turn up, a more profitable venture in the smuggling line having presented itself. At last, just before dawn, the ships arrived. With obsolete guns, no ammunition, barely enough food to get them through the day (Garibaldi never could be bothered with provisions), and so little space on their ramshackle stolen transports they could barely sit, let alone lie down, the Thousand set off on their great adventure.

Garibaldi was calm, sure, magnificent. All his life he swung between two states of being. Frustration made him twitchy. "Poor Garibaldi," wrote one of his closest friends. "He ruins himself in times of inaction; he talks too much, writes too much, and listens too much to those who know nothing." In action, though, he became as strong, still, and silent as a hero should be. In the Alps the previous year his men had noticed that during a battle he spoke only when he had to and consulted no one. He would sit his horse for hours, silent, immobile, and intensely watchful, his wide-brimmed black hat pulled low over his eyes. His concentration was intense, almost trancelike, his self-confidence equally absolute. From the moment he left the beach at Quarto he was in a state of serene euphoria. Miracles were expected of him: he confidently expected them of himself.

They duly occurred. After a brief stop in a Tuscan port where they managed to bamboozle the governor into giving them supplies of food and ammunition, the Garibaldini arrived off Marsala, on Sicily's west coast, on May 11. By an astonishing coincidence of their luck and the Neapolitan commander's mismanagement the city was undefended. Two Neapolitan warships had sailed out of Marsala's harbor only hours before Garibaldi's decrepit steamers struggled into it: they were still visible in the distance. One turned back and fired on the Garibaldini as they disembarked but the shells fell short. Only two men and a dog were wounded. Safely onshore Garibaldi declared himself Dictator of Sicily. It was a preposterous title—there were still twenty-six thousand Neapolitan troops on the island—but with astonishing rapidity and ease Garibaldi gave it substance.

From Marsala, where the native populace were disappointingly wary of their new dictator, he led his men on toward Palermo. A few peasants joined them. "I hope we shall become an avalanche," wrote Garibaldi, but they were as yet a scarcely perceptible rockfall. Then, on May 15, they encountered some two thousand Neapolitan troops near the village of Calatafimi. When they first sighted each other the opposing armies were each on high ground, with a valley between them. The Neapolitans advanced across the valley first: the Thousand drove them back. The Neapolitans retreated to the crest of their hill: the Thousand followed them, advancing unprotected straight into the enemy's fire just as Garibaldi's men had done at the Villa Corsini a decade before. Garibaldi led, once more riding a white horse. Near the top of the punishingly steep slope they faltered, finding what shelter they could behind the low walls which broke up the terraced hillside. It was blazingly hot. They had no way of defending themselves against the enemy's cannon, no shelter from the sweltering sun, no provision for helping their wounded. Their ancient guns were little use against the Neapolitans' modern rifles. Surely they had no alternative but to retreat. "What shall we do, General?" someone asked Garibaldi. "Italians," he told them (or so one of them later reported), "here we shall make Italy—or die!" Thirty of them (including a thirteen-year-old boy) died. The rest made Italy.

They marched onto the enemy's guns, clambering and scrambling, bayonets fixed, Garibaldi leading the attack, on foot now and brandishing his sword. When they closed with the Neapolitans both sides fought ferociously, but it was the Neapolitans who eventually gave way. At midnight they withdrew from Calatafimi. But more important than any strategic advantage gained by the battle was its effect as spectacle. Throughout the day ever-growing groups of peasants gathered on the surrounding ridges to watch the fighting. What they saw impressed them profoundly.

Perhaps they identified Garibaldi as a saint, a representative of Christ's church militant. Perhaps they associated him with a legend current on the island about a supernatural warrior of olden times who would one day come again (like Arthur, like Christ, like Drake) to restore justice and redeem his people. When next day Garibaldi passed through a village the people all fell to their knees as he passed.

He had shown that the impossible could be done, if only by someone resolute, courageous, and unrealistic enough to attempt it. Carlyle elaborated his vision of the hero in passionate rejection of modern notions of biological, social, and economic determinism. In telling tales of great men he wanted to prove that "Man is heaven-born; not the thrall of circumstances, of Necessity, but the victorious subduer thereof." To his mind, his great exemplars asserted the value of human dignity and the freedom of the human will in the face of the apparently inexorable forces by which (according to newfangled theories he found repugnant) human character and human history are shaped. Darwin's *Origin of Species* was published the year before the Thousand invaded Sicily, the first volume of Marx's *Das Kapital* seven years later. But Garibaldi, winning his amazing victories in defiance of all statistical probability, seemed—to the enormous international audience who followed his exploits in the press—to be doing something that made nonsense of the ideas that humans were simply highly evolved mammals, and that historical change was effected by forces so large and generalized as to make any piffling individual actions futile. Here was one man challenging an entrenched political system and overcoming it! Here were battles won, not by big battalions and even bigger guns but by valor and devotion! It was a prospect immensely flattering and consoling to all who contemplated it, one which allowed people who had begun to be anxious about their status in the cosmos to feel once more proud to be human. (There is, of course, another way of reading the story—Garibaldi, in taking on the corrupt and demoralized Bourbon monarchy, was felling a tree already rotten and ready to topple at a touch—but that is not the way it was read.)

The miracles kept coming, thanks in large part to the incompetence and irresolution of the Neapolitan generals. Garibaldi led his band towards Palermo, dodging and weaving to the bafflement of those attempting to block or pursue him. The Neapolitans were too slow and cautious to catch him in a straight chase, too ill informed to find him once he began to play hide-and-seek. Their intelligence was almost incredibly scant: at a time when they were totally unable to find the Thousand in the thirty miles which separated Calatafimi from the capital, a journalist from

The Times made his way to Garibaldi's camp with no difficulty at all, simply by asking directions of the locals.

It is questionable to what extent the Sicilian peasantry who swelled the ranks of the Thousand cared about, or even understood, the cause of a united Italy. According to a skeptical joke current at the time, when they echoed Garibaldi's cry of "Viva l'Italia," most of them were under the impression they were honoring a mistress of the general's, "la Talia." But Mazzini had been at least partly right: there were plenty of people in Sicily who had been waiting, not specifically for Garibaldi perhaps, but for anyone capable of giving them a lead in turning on their masters from the mainland. In northern and central Italy the cause of Italian liberation was of interest only to the educated; there were no peasants among the Thousand, as Garibaldi recorded in sorrow. But in Sicily Garibaldi was fighting a cause with which the country people were ready to identify themselves with a degree of violent intensity which he found almost frightening. As the Neapolitans fled back down the road from Calatafimi those injured or unarmed or simply too exhausted to defend themselves were set upon by the local people. Garibaldi, a day later, was sickened to find the roadside lined with their mutilated bodies left out for the dogs. "A miserable sight!" he wrote. "The corpses of Italians . . . torn in pieces by their own brothers with a fury which would have horrified the hyenas." But whatever his qualms, he made good use of the Sicilians' hostility toward their Neapolitan "brothers." And he was enough of an opportunist to adapt himself to his new public's religious sensibilities. He was beginning to understand, with Carlyle, the link between religious devotion and hero worship. He saw that the Sicilian populace, pious if hardly orthodox, were ready to see in him a saint, an avenging angel, even perhaps a messiah, and he was careful not to alienate them by revealing his views on the clergy ("ministers of falsehood," "descendants of Torquemada"). He recruited a friar and in Sicily he kept him always with him as a sign to the watching peasantry that God was on his side. To the surprise of some of his officers, who had seen him blasting open the doors of monasteries and had never before known him to pray, he made a point of very publicly attending mass.

By May 26 Garibaldi was encamped within six miles of Palermo. Almost every Sicilian in the city seems to have known he was there, and so did the British whose ships were in the harbor. A delegation of revolutionaries came out to meet him and coordinate plans. Even the prisoners in the jail knew he was at hand. Only General Lanza, in command of the twenty thousand Neapolitan troops in and around the city, remained oblivious. Towards the end of the day, when an informer finally reached him with the news of Garibaldi's presence within striking distance of the walls, he dismissed the man, declaring the story preposterous.

That night the Thousand, joined now by some three thousand excitable Sicilian volunteers, broke through the gates, with Garibaldi leading the assault. He was greeted with tumultuous excitement. "One must know these Sicilians," wrote the Hungarian volunteer Fernand Eber, "to have an idea of the frenzy, screaming, shouting, crying and hugging; all would kiss Garibaldi's hands and embrace his knees." He quickly established control of the narrow, mazelike streets of the medieval center. The Neapolitans bombarded the city from their headquarters in the royal palace and from their ships in the harbor. The barrage reduced large areas of the city to rubble and set fire to more of it, but the Garibaldini, undaunted, retreated into inaccessible back streets and erected barricades. The Neapolitans seemed at a loss as to how to deal with them. General Lanza had all the advantages except for optimism. He seems to have believed as unquestioningly as any member of the Thousand in Garibaldi's ability to work miracles, and his faith was cripplingly demoralizing.

The fighting continued for three days during which the Palermitans, bitterly angry at the bombardment of their town and further alienated by the behavior of the Neapolitan troops—who tore through the ruins, destroying any structure left standing in their hunt for loot and setting fire to what remained—gave ever more enthusiastic support to the Thousand. Lanza had at least eighteen thousand troops concentrated around the royal palace but he was afraid to order them forward into the lethal trap which the old town, occupied by the Garibaldini, had become. Garibaldi, as usual on battlefield, was serene and fearless, whether leading assaults on the Neapolitan positions or directing operations from his headquarters. All around him men were being shot but he, as always, was invulnerable. The Palermitans, watching him sitting on the steps of a fountain eating the fruit or smelling the flowers that adoring women continually brought him, concluded he must be a sorcerer. People noticed he had a habit of fiddling with the strap of his whip, and told each other it was the amulet which was shielding him from danger.

It was the difference between his resolute self-confidence and Lanza's fear which decided the battle. By the third day Garibaldi's men were on the point of running out of ammunition altogether, but Lanza cracked first. He was effectually trapped in the palace, unable to get his wounded men out or provisions in. He asked for a ceasefire, to which Garibaldi agreed. The timing of the truce was yet another of Garibaldi's amazing strokes of luck (or miracles). While he and Lanza's representative were negotiating on board a British ship in the harbor, four fresh battalions of Neapolitan troops were marching into the city at the Garibaldini's rear. A lookout on the palace roof saw them come. Lanza's staff desperately tried to persuade him to start fighting again. With the reinforcements so well positioned Garibaldi could have been defeated within an hour. But Lanza, honorable, exhausted, or both, would not go back on his word. Garibaldi had twenty-four hours' grace. He returned from the harbor to find a vast and intensely excited crowd awaiting him. As moved by their enthusiasm as they were by his he urged them to work all night for "tomorrow will be a day of life or death."

All night long the city was brilliantly illuminated while women, children, and priests repaired the barricades and in workshops all over the city smiths, carpenters, anyone who had the appropriate skills struggled to convert what material they could find into weapons. When morning came General Lanza, listening to his officers' reports of the people's determination, asked for a further three days' armistice. Garibaldi demanded the entire contents of the mint as the price of his agreement. Lanza agreed. He had not been defeated, but already he was acting like a loser.

When they burst into Palermo the Garibaldini had been ragged, filthy, and exhausted after weeks of sleeping out in all weathers. Their newly recruited Sicilian allies were panicky and undisciplined. They had perilously little ammunition to start with. By the time the first truce was called they had next to none at all and only four hundred functioning muskets. During the armistice Garibaldi had managed to beg and buy some powder from American and Greek ships in the harbor, but there is no doubt that had the Neapolitans fought on they could have driven him out. But Lanza despaired. His report to his royal master was so pessimistic that it persuaded King Francis the situation was hopeless. On June 7 he capitulated to Garibaldi. The Neapolitan army marched sullenly out of Palermo while a squad of redshirts, fronted by Garibaldi's eighteen-year-old son Menotti on a big black horse, watched them go. The Thousand had put twenty thousand to flight.

· · ·

So amazing was the spectacle of an undefeated army fleeing before a tiny volunteer force supported by a mob of virtually unarmed civilians that almost immediately conspiracy theories began circulating. The observable facts were literally incredible—people were persuaded the truth must lie hidden. There must have been bribery or blackmail. Some sinister body—the Freemasons, the Mafia, the British—must have been in on it. But no historian has ever managed to find evidence for any of these theories. The truth is simply that Garibaldi achieved the apparently impossible in Sicily because it was, by this time, expected of him. His fantastic success in Sicily shows that he was one of those born in a happy hour, like the Cid, whose successes bred further and greater success until—like Valdés surrendering to Drake—his enemies, even those whose strength enormously overtopped his, simply abandoned all hope of defeating him. To Alexandre Dumas, who joined him in Sicily soon after the fall of Palermo, he seemed capable of absolutely anything. "If he were to say to me 'I am setting out tomorrow on an expedition to capture the moon' I should doubtless reply, 'All right, go on. Just write and tell me as soon as you have taken it, and add a little postscript saying what steps I must take to come and join you there.' "

The romance of his little band of rebels taking on a kingdom (and a notoriously oppressive one at that) was an international sensation. From Canada to Siberia, where the exiled anarchist Mikhail Bakunin found everyone hanging on the news from Sicily, from Bengal to Valparaíso, the exploits of the Thousand and their leonine leader were avidly read and retold. "This man, almost alone, becomes the man of prodigy," wrote Dumas. "He makes thrones tremble, he is the oriflamme of the new era. All Europe has her eyes upon him and awakes each morning asking where he is and what he has done." In Britain especially, where William Gladstone had been inveighing against the Bourbon monarchy's oppressions, Garibaldi fever was rife. Fashionable British women ate Garibaldi biscuits (a line so successful they are still in production) and wore red Garibaldi blouses and round Garibaldi hats. A fund was set up to raise money in his support. The second Duke of Wellington gave £50, Florence Nightingale £10, and Charles Dickens £5 while thousands of workingmen contributed their shillings to "liberate Italy from the Yoke of Tyranny." "Garibaldi is a demi-god," reported the Italian ambassador from London. "Lady John [Russell, the foreign secretary's wife] can no longer sleep because of him."

Hundreds of new volunteers from here, there, and everywhere descended on Palermo. Some came in search of adventure, some wanted a part in the most romantic real-life drama currently playing in Europe. Others seized the chance to strike a blow in the struggle for a somewhat hazily defined ideal in which liberty, national sovereignty, and revolution for revolution's sake all played their part. And there were those who simply enjoyed striking a blow. Dumas arrived accompanied by a nineteen-year-old mistress dressed in a velvet sailor suit, whom he used to introduce variously as his son or his nephew. The Countess de la Torre came, bringing a hussar tunic, a big plumed hat, and a sword way too large for her. There were British (not all of them welcome, as being unused to wine they tended to get quickly and violently drunk). There were five hundred Hungarians, numerous Frenchmen, some Germans, Americans, Poles. Some were high-minded idealists. Some had come, as one candidly explained to an English reporter, "at all costs to have a lark." The Englishman John Peard, who liked to go into battle in his tweed suit until persuaded that unless he donned something more recognizably military he risked being summarily executed as a spy, probably spoke for many when he replied to an inquiry about his motives for volunteering by saying that he had "the greatest respect" for Italian independence "but I am also very fond of shooting."

As well as the fighting men came sightseers—eccentrics and thrill seekers of both sexes and several nationalities anxious to watch from close-up the great adventure unfolding in Sicily, and to bring themselves close to the man a British enthusiast described as "THE THE THE man of action at the present." Their enthusiasm was matched by that of the Sicilians, to whom Garibaldi seemed all but godlike. Palermo was so hung with red banners that to Dumas it felt like a field of poppies. Every day the dictator (the man who had characterized priests as "black-robed cockroaches") was invited to little parties in the city's numerous convents. In one the nuns, exclaiming that he was the image of Our Lord, all swarmed around to kiss him on the lips. In others he was showered with gifts; sweets, flowers, handkerchiefs, and embroidered banners, of which a typical one bore the slogan "To thee Giuseppe: Saint and Hero! Mighty as St. George! Beautiful as the Seraphim!" A decade earlier Thomas Carlyle had lamented that the heroic age was over, that now "heroic action is paralysed" and the human capacity for hero worship had been dulled by the "iron ignoble circle of necessity." Garibaldi in Sicily gave him the lie.

His tremendous international celebrity was both a source of power and an unassailable protection. "We cannot struggle with him," Cavour told one of his confidants. "He is stronger than we are . . . There is only one thing to be done. Associate ourselves with him." It was quite an admission: the maverick freedom fighter was "stronger" than the established government and standing army of Piedmont. It was not a situation Cavour wished to see perpetuated. Just as Queen Elizabeth could only lay claim to Francis Drake's plunder if she acknowledged, after the fact, that he had acted on her behalf, so Victor Emmanuel would only be able to assume control of the dominions conquered by Garibaldi if he treated the conqueror as his representative. Accordingly, Cavour proceeded to act as though all the obstructions he had put in the way of the Thousand's embarkation had never been, as though Garibaldi had all along simply been carrying out his and the king's orders. He dispatched an emissary, Giuseppe La Farina, to Sicily with instructions to prepare the way for the annexation of the island to the Kingdom of Piedmont.

Garibaldi was not so easily bullied. Like Rodrigo Díaz in Valencia he was now master of his own territory. Quartered in Palermo's royal palace (he had, of course, chosen one of the smallest and barest rooms) he was briefly a real dictator, a ruler with absolute power over the little country which he, at the head of a troop owing loyalty to him alone, had liberated. When high mass was said in the cathedral he presided on the royal throne, claiming the right of "apostolic legateship." (No wonder he and Mazzini—the uncompromising republican—fell out so frequently.) While the Gospel was read he unsheathed his sword, token that he had by no means come to the end of his martial miracles. In 326 BC Alexander the Great, having conquered the Persian Empire and brought his army through Afghanistan and into India, summoned together his homesick, exhausted men and told them he intended to march on past the Ganges to the Eastern Ocean which he thought lay somewhere beyond. There was a long silence, until one of his officers at last had the temerity to say, "Sire, if there is one thing above all others a successful man like you should know, it is *when to stop.*" Like Alexander, Garibaldi was splendidly lacking in that knowledge. He had no intention of stopping until he had wrested all southern Italy from the Bourbons, and he knew Cavour could never consent to such a venture. He had to retain his autonomy. A month after La Farina's arrival Garibaldi had him arrested and banished from the island.

He still had fighting to do. The Neapolitan troops had retreated eastwards after the fall of Palermo but they had not yet left Sicily. A month later Garibaldi's men confronted a force of twenty-five hundred Neapolitan troops at Milazzo. Many of his troops were seeing action for the first time. Garibaldi outdid himself in his efforts to put heart into them. Before an assault he positioned himself so that a whole troop of untried men would file past him, then he murmured a few words of encouragement to each one. He himself went into battle armed only with a walking stick and a cigar. When his men balked before a wall from behind which came heavy rifle fire he walked straight up to it without pausing to look back to see if his men would follow. They did. The Neapolitan marksmen fled. "Garibaldi is here," a volunteer wrote home, "or all would be lost."

Milazzo surrendered on July 23, and the garrison marched out of the castle leaving the cannons and all their ammunition behind. There were another fifteen thousand Neapolitan troops in the region but they were never deployed. Five days later, on the orders of King Francis, the Neapolitan commander in Sicily capitulated and took all his troops off by sea. Garibaldi was now dictator of the island in fact as well as in name, and he had won his position not by fighting off his enemies, but by frightening them away.

He had thus given himself a job for which he had no aptitude whatsoever. The business of government bothered and bewildered him. According to one of his long-term associates, "Finance, taxation, police, law courts, bureaucratic machinery were alike for him artificial and oppressive accretions to the life of nature. . . . In his heart he despised and abhorred them." Having made Sicily his, he longed not to reform its institutions or reestablish its economy, but to leave it behind him. Even before he finally defeated the Neapolitans at Milazzo he was planning to cross the Strait of Messina to the Italian mainland and defeat them at home.

Cavour, with equal determination, was planning to prevent him. "We must stop Garibaldi from conquering Naples," he wrote early in July. He persuaded King Victor Emmanuel to write to Garibaldi forbidding him to move. He ordered the Piedmontese admiral who was stationed in Sicily to prevent Garibaldi crossing the Strait of Messina "at all costs." He urged the Neapolitans to "attack Garibaldi, catch him and execute him." The astounding success of the Sicilian adventure had presented Cavour with an irresolvable dilemma. As a Piedmontese politician he needed to assure Victor Emmanuel's subjects that he was as proud and glad of Garibaldi's triumphs as they were. But as a diplomat and statesman he had an equally imperative need to distance his administration from what most of the crowned heads of Europe saw as an act of aggression by dangerous radicals and seditionaries. (Prince Albert, on being shown a photograph of the queen of Naples in shooting costume, remarked that it was a pity she had not yet shot Garibaldi.) Later Cavour was to claim that all his efforts to obstruct the triumphant progress of the Risorgimento's golden warrior were deceptions designed to fool the enemy, but there seems no reason to believe it. For a republican revolutionary to topple a monarchy seemed to him an ineffably dangerous precedent: even if Victor Emmanuel were to gain a kingdom by it, it would be at an intolerable cost to his authority and prestige. "He will become, in the eyes of the majority of Italians, no more than the friend of Garibaldi."

King Victor Emmanuel, however, was far more susceptible than his chief minister to the excitement Garibaldi's great adventure was generating; he was genuinely of two minds. A few days after the battle of Milazzo an emissary arrived in Sicily from Turin carrying two letters from the king to Garibaldi. The official one, Cavour-approved, expressly forbade him to lead his troops onto the mainland. The second, secret one instructed him to disobey the orders contained in the first. Garibaldi would probably have done so anyway: he was a loose cannon whose onrush had by now gathered an unstoppable momentum. "Your Majesty knows the high esteem and love I bear you," he wrote. "But . . . if now I delayed any longer I should fail in my duty and imperil the sacred cause of Italy. Allow me then, Sire, this time to disobey you." Like Nelson, he was about to serve his country by breaking the line.

The main body of his troops were drawn up near the lighthouse on Cape Faro at the narrowest point of the Strait of Messina. For days on end Garibaldi stood in the lighthouse, scrutinizing the coast of the mainland through a telescope, silent, intent, waiting for the opportune moment. On August 18, he finally gave the order for half of his force to set out, not from Faro, as most of his supporters and all the Neapolitans expected, but from Taormina. He had two unarmed steamers to transport an army which now numbered 3,360 men. One of them sprang a leak. Garibaldi, seaman that he was, plugged it using a mound of manure. After a hair-raising thirty-hour journey he and his men landed safely at Italy's southernmost tip while the Neapolitan warships still waited for them, oblivious, forty miles to the north. Garibaldi marched on Reggio and took it after a sharp but swift battle. Meanwhile the Neapolitans, hearing he had dodged them, sailed south in pursuit. The fifteen hundred Garibaldini still waiting on the beaches of Faro promptly seized their opportunity to cross the strait in a flotilla of little fishing boats. By the time the warships returned the Garibaldini were ashore. The Neapolitans vented their frustration at being so outwitted by sinking the abandoned boats.

In Calabria, the southernmost and least governable region of Italy, Garibaldi's dream of a popular uprising at last came true. In 1849, in the Papal States, he had been asking a generally devout population to rise up against God's representative on earth. Now he had come to oust the oppressive secular regime of a foreign dynasty. In the countryside the peasants formed themselves into guerrilla bands to fight alongside the invaders. In the towns Garibaldi was acclaimed under his title of dictator, the people being so emboldened by his presence that in one place they poured out into the streets to give him an enthusiastic welcome even before the Neapolitan troops had pulled out of town.

"The population was frantic in their demonstrations of joy," wrote one of the English volunteers. Wherever Garibaldi appeared people crowded round him, reaching out to touch him, kissing his feet, kneeling to ask for his blessing for themselves and their babies. In town after town he proceeded to the main square, mounted a balcony, and spoke to the people. He was solemn and splendid. Speaking slowly and ringingly in his beautiful deep voice he would addresses them caressingly, flatteringly, as the liberators of their own land. Finally he would raise his right arm with forefinger extended in what was becoming his personal salute—"the Garibaldi sign," one finger for one Italy—while his auditors held up their fingers in turn and wept and roared.

Town after town fell to the advancing Garibaldini with hardly a blow fired. "The Great Man," wrote Carlyle, "is a Force of Nature." Garibaldi was sweeping through Calabria like a tempest or a forest fire: before him the opposing army simply melted away. Within less than a week of Garibaldi's landing, six thousand of the sixteen thousand Neapolitan troops in the province had deserted. When he identified himself to sentries stationed to prevent his entering a town they waved him through. His name worked like magic, even when he was not actually present. Six of the Garibaldini, accidentally separated from their unit, ran into a whole battalion of Neapolitan troops. They claimed to be Garibaldi's scouts, and announced that the dictator was a short ride behind them. The entire Neapolitan battalion promptly surrendered, dropped their rifles, and went home. At Soveria a force of over a thousand Neapolitan troops surrendered to Garibaldi, who had with him only one fifth that number, most of them Calabrian partisans armed with hoes and sticks. It was fantastic, dreamlike, thrilling. Like Drake in the Pacific Garibaldi seemed untouchable, unstoppable. The Neapolitan soldiers said of him, as his German detractors had said of Wallenstein and as the Spaniards had said of Drake, that he was (or was possessed by) a devil and they told the old story about the bullets which had no power to harm him tumbling from his shirt as he undressed. The people of Calabria, equally if differently persuaded of his superhuman character, knelt down and worshiped him.

Halfway to Naples he left his troops behind. He was intent upon claiming the capital before anyone (Cavour for instance) could forestall him. He had taken Sicily with a mere handful of men: why should he not take Naples alone? Traveling in a light carriage, attended only by a few of his staff, he raced northwards. Just in advance of him rode the English amateur of shooting John Peard who, tall, bearded, and sandy-haired, resembled him physically. In each town that either Garibaldi or Peard entered people would flock around them, kissing their hands, their feet, their knees. Peard demurred, protesting that he was not the general, but it made no difference to the people's enthusiasm: like Patroclus dressed in Achilles' armor, Peard, the hero's simulacrum, had the same effect that the hero himself would have done. People refused to believe that he was not the real thing. They understood, they said, that his arrival was to be kept secret from the Bourbon authorities but he must let them worship nonetheless. Garibaldi himself accepted the adoration as his due, mounting balconies and standing impassive and serene while brass bands played, people were seized by convulsive fits brought on by the intensity of their joy, or fell to their knees hailing him as a second Jesus Christ.

At Eboli, some sixty miles short of Naples, Peard marched into the telegraph station and ordered the terrified clerk to send a telegram to the Neopolitan minister of war, informing him that Garibaldi had arrived at the head of five thousand men, and that another five thousand would shortly be disembarking in the Bay of Naples, and advising an immediate withdrawal of the garrison at Salerno, the last line of defense south of the city. The minister was fooled. Eight hours later Salerno was evacuated.

Garibaldi raced on. In Wallenstein's lifetime, Grimmelshausen's *Simplicissimus* had elaborated the fantasy of a hero whose personal qualities were so extraordinary that he needed no army. Wallenstein, with his prodigious ability to conjure an army out of the ravaged earth, seemed like a figurative and approximate realization of that vision, but Garibaldi fulfilled it literally. His nearest troops were now a full forty-eight hours' march behind him. Not that he was alone. A gathering snowball of excited hangers-on had attached themselves to his retinue, eager to participate in his astonishing progress. Journalists, aristocratic Grand Tourists, adventurers of all descriptions, including several thrill-seeking

English ladies, galloped their carriages alongside his, pestering him for autographs, drinking in details for their memoirs.

The rumors of his imminent arrival were enough to topple the monarchy. Five times, as Garibaldi had progressed through Sicily and Calabria, King Francis II, despairing of repelling this invincible opponent by human means, had telegraphed the Pope to ask for a blessing. On September 4, while Garibaldi was still south of Eboli, Francis realized that even God couldn't save his throne for him. He and his queen drove down to the waterfront and steamed away. As their ship left the harbor its captain hoisted a signal ordering all the others in port to follow. Not one did so. The king's admirals, like the king's ministers, were all going over to Garibaldi. A few hours later Don Liborio Romana, who was not only the chief of police and commander of the National Guard but also chief of the Camorra (which is to Calabria what the Mafia is to Sicily), sent Garibaldi a telegram addressing him as "Dictator of the Two Sicilies" and offering to place in his hands "the power of the State and her destinies."

Garibaldi was ready. The mayor and the National Guard officer who had come out to greet him begged him to delay his entrance into Naples for twenty-four hours so that triumphal arches could be erected and, more importantly, so that the garrisons of the king's troops who were still holding the city's four formidably well-armed fortresses could be evicted. Garibaldi would not hear of it. There were others who might try to fill the vacuum the king's departure had left. "Naples is in danger," he said. "We must go there today, at once, this minute." He went straight to the railway terminus at Vietri and commandeered a train for the last few miles of his journey. Hundreds of people swarmed onto it with him, all singing, cheering, shouting, and waving muskets or tricolor flags. The heat was intense, the noise literally deafening, the mood ecstatic. The train crept along, impeded by the crowds alongside the tracks, by "demonstrations of welcome from all classes; from the fishermen who left their boats on the beach, from the swarthy fellows, naked to the waist, who were winnowing corn on the flat house roofs as well as from the National Guards."

At each station the cheering mobs brought the train to a lengthy standstill. At Portici a naval officer managed to force his way into Garibaldi's carriage, frantic with urgency, to warn him that the Bourbon troops in the city's fortresses had trained their cannon on the railway station. But nothing could stop Garibaldi now. He betrayed no emotion. He had written in his memoirs that, like Horatio Nelson, he could ask, "What is fear?" Now, as stubborn and as splendid as Nelson clamping his telescope to his blind eye, he asked, "What cannon? . . . When the people receive us like this there are no cannon."

He was right. When the train finally pulled into Naples station it was immediately engulfed by a crowd which knocked down the barriers, drowned out Don Liborio's speech of welcome, and swept Garibaldi away. His supporters managed to get him into an open carriage and attempted to steer it by a safe route into the city center. It couldn't be done. The movement of the crowd was irresistible. The carriage was carried helplessly towards the nearest of the fortresses. As it passed beneath the cannon Garibaldi, unmistakable in his black hat, his red shirt, his knotted silk kerchief, rose to his feet in the open carriage, folded his arms, and gazed steadfastly upward at the guns. None fired. It was a heart-stopping moment. ("If he were not Garibaldi he would be the greatest tragic actor known," remarked one of his officers.) Calmly sitting down again, he went on, serene and impassive in the midst of all the hysterical excitement his arrival had provoked, while around him the crowd, who adored him even though they were not yet sure of his name, yelled themselves into a frenzy of adoration of Garibaldo, Gallipot, Galliboard, the bringer of freedom, the champion of Italian unity, the second Jesus. He hadn't conquered Naples, any more than Alcibiades conquered Selymbria. He had simply arrived, and like Alcibiades on that long ago occasion, acted like a conqueror until the act became a reality. He had ousted a king, faced down an army, and taken a city, and he had done it armed only with his fame.

All that night and for several nights thereafter the people of Naples danced in the streets. "Not only was all business suspended but the people roused themselves into a state of frenzy bordering on madness," wrote one observer. The city was alive with flaring lights and waving banners and chanting people. "Here and there an excited orator addressed the crowd about him with wild declamations; little bands of enthusiasts . . . went dancing through the streets and burst into the cafes. . . . An unfortunate man who did not cry 'Viva Garibaldi!' when he was bidden was ripped open by enthusiasts and died on the spot." "The town was running mad with flags, daggers and red shirts," wrote the English minister. When Garibaldi attended the ballet the performance had to be halted because all the audience could do was shout "Viva!" and raise their arms as though in prayer to the box in which he sat.

He had won Naples, and by extension the Kingdom of the Two Sicilies of which it was capital, with amazing ease. Knowing what to do with it was far harder for him. Shakespeare's Thersites jeered at Achilles, calling him and the oafish Ajax Ulysses' oxen. In Naples, Garibaldi, was a conquering hero, but he was also an ox plowing a field whose harvest both Mazzini and Cavour hoped to make their own.

He was no statesman. Taciturn and self-reliant in battle, in the corridors of power he was hesitant and disastrously impressionable. Throughout the two months during which he personally ruled half Italy he dithered and vacillated. An English observer wrote at the time, "The stories told in Naples of his utter incapacity for civil Government are extraordinary. He signed almost anything which the Ministers gave him, and next day would sign a decree cancelling the former, because others got round him and told him to do so."

He had to decide whether to give in to Cavour's increasingly pressing demands that he allow his conquests to be annexed to the Kingdom of Piedmont, or to insist that they remain under his own independent dictatorship. Should he act as though he were the Cid of the *Poema*, the great servant laying the spoils of his conquests at the foot of the throne, or should he play the Cid of historical reality, an autonomous warlord ruling his own domain as he thought fit? He seemed incapable of making up his mind. The republicans wanted to call elections for an independent constituent assembly. Cavour's supporters, and most of the Neapolitan middle class, wanted a plebiscite to get public endorsement for an immediate annexation by Piedmont. Garibaldi, under intense pressure from both parties, gave in to both, ordering both the election and the referendum without apparently having any idea that the two were incompatible. "The weakness of the man is something fabulous!" wrote Mazzini, exasperated beyond measure to see how easy it was for rival plowmen to lead away his ox.

Mazzini had slipped secretly back into Italy just after the Thousand left from Quarto. He arrived in Naples ten days after Garibaldi made his triumphal entrance. Garibaldi shocked Cavour's agents and the Neapolitan aristocracy by receiving Mazzini cordially. Mazzini urged him to attack King Francis, who had joined his remaining troops near Capua, and, after routing them, to invade the Papal States. It was a plan with which Garibaldi was happy to concur.

He moved out of the city and established his headquarters at Caserta. Built in the previous century in direct imitation of Versailles, Caserta was the largest palace in Europe. Garibaldi characteristically chose one of the smallest rooms, but soon the rest of the apartments were packed with sightseers, suitors of all sorts, and more besotted English ladies. A lock of

Garibaldi's hair was considered an accessory more desirable and more charged with erotic symbolism than any jewel. Ever polite, he obligingly submitted to having his hair cut so that the expatriate English ladies of the city could each have some of the clippings. The locks of Garibaldi's hair in circulation were soon almost as numerous as fragments of the True Cross.

Shaking free of this time-wasting foolishness, on October 1 Garibaldi took on, and after a day and a half of fighting defeated, the armies of the king of Naples on the river Volturno. The original Thousand had been multiplied twentyfold by the volunteers that had flocked to Garibaldi over the previous weeks, giving him by far the largest army he had ever commanded, facing some twenty-eight thousand Bourbon troops. By nineteenth-century standards, this was large-scale warfare. Garibaldi was magnificent. "He was like thunder. He was beautiful in the battle, like Raphael's archangel Michael trampling on the demon," one of his soldiers recalled. "His eyes devoured the enemies, consumed them, laid them low." For the first time he had too many men to be able to inspire more than a small proportion by his own words or gestures, but throughout the battle he dashed from one point to another on horseback or in an open carriage, leaping down whenever he came into contact with the enemy to lead a charge, saber in hard, shouting, "Victory! Victory!" Skeptical veterans asked, "What victory?" but once more Garibaldi demonstrated his ability to translate hope into reality. The battle was won.

But it was not one of those amazing victories to which Garibaldi had become accustomed that summer. This time the opposing army had neither deserted en masse nor retreated in needless panic. Garibaldi, sobered by it, told Mazzini that he could not possibly annihilate King Francis's army, let alone conquer the Papal States. Instead he withdrew into Naples to wrestle with the increasingly intractable political problems by which he was beset.

He had declared his intention of proclaiming Victor Emmanuel king of all Italy in the Quirinale Palace in Rome. But Victor Emmanuel, under Cavour's influence, didn't want Rome—or not yet anyway, not until his ally Napoleon III was ready to relinquish it peaceably—and he had no desire to accept Italy from Garibaldi. He wanted to be seen to conquer it for himself.

Within days of Garibaldi's arrival in Naples Cavour dispatched the Piedmontese army to invade the Papal States and march through them into the Kingdom of Naples. While Garibaldi was confronting the Neapolitans at Volturno, the Piedmontese army was advancing on their rear.

Cavour was now determined to remove Garibaldi from whatever power he had. Garibaldi was well aware of his hostility, but he fondly believed that the king (who had after all deceived his chief minister in conniving at Garibaldi's crossing of the Strait of Messina) would stand by him. Increasingly he began to see all his setbacks as the products of Cavour's malevolence. He wrote to Victor Emmanuel demanding that he sack his chief minister. Victor Emmanuel replied that as a constitutional monarch he was not in a position to dismiss a member of an elected government; he was severely displeased. A few days later Cavour wrote with satisfaction that it was this "insolent ultimatum" which had finally decided the king "to march on Naples at the head of his army to bring Garibaldi to his senses, and to throw into the sea this nest of Red Republicans and Socialist demagogues."

The plebiscites took place. Both in Sicily and in Calabria Garibaldi had been greeted as something like a god, but the people's adoration of him, as it turned out, was no more constant than the ecstatic fervor with which the Athenians had welcomed Alcibiades home in 410 BC. They yearned for a hero to effect a regime change and to provide them with an occasion for tumultuous excitement, but once that excitement was over they had no further use for him. Both in Palermo and in Naples the people gave an overwhelming "yes" to annexation. Garibaldi, the adored liberator, had been voted out of office. Victor Emmanuel, having made himself master of the former Papal States of Umbria and the Marche, led his army towards Naples to claim the new adjunct to his kingdom. Garibaldi rode out to receive him.

On October 26, thirty miles north of the city, they met. Garibaldi and his men had waited since before dawn. Cavour had said privately that he would stop at nothing, not even civil war, to teach Garibaldi his place, but Garibaldi needed no such lesson. He had been slow to make up his mind to the annexation of his conquests by Piedmont, but he had always looked forward to this moment. For months he had been boasting of how with his "victorious sword" he would make all Italy his and then lay it at his monarch's feet. He had spoken of the occasion as one of glorious consummation, when a grateful king would acknowledge the great services of his loyal champion, embracing him and praising him and heaping him with honors. It wasn't like that at all. As the battalions of the royal army began to file by, their commanders saluted him correctly, but it was evident to Alberto Mario, one of Garibaldi's companions, that "all were alike averse to Garibaldi, this plebeian donor of a realm." When the royal party approached, Garibaldi rode up to the king, removed his hat, and said with a flourish, "I salute the first King of Italy." Victor Emmanuel, failing to take his cue, eschewed grand rhetoric to rejoin blandly "How are you, my dear Garibaldi?"

The two rode side by side for the next eight miles, redshirts and soldiers of the royal guard pairing off behind them. Mario strained his ears to hear what a king would say to a hero on such a momentous day: Victor Emmanuel talked about the weather and the state of the roads. At one point a group of peasants gathered around them, crying, "Viva Garibaldi!" Garibaldi, embarrassed, pulled his horse back, shouting out "This is your king! The King of Italy! *Viva il Re!*" but he was unable to deflect the crowd's attention away from himself. The shouts of "Viva Garibaldi" continued. Garibaldi did not, as Rodrigo Díaz had done, position his camp in such a way as to seem to claim preeminence, but he was, like the Cid, a hero whose reputation was so great that he could not help but outshine his king. Victor Emmanuel, accordingly, resolved to hustle him out of sight.

Before they reached Naples the king had informed Garibaldi that he himself, at the head of his regular troops, would finish off the Neapolitan army. The final conquest of the Bourbon kingdom was to be his show. The Garibaldini were to stay in the rear, out of the limelight, Garibaldi with them. On parting from him Garibaldi was silent. His "countenance was full of melancholic sweetness," wrote Mario. "Never did I feel drawn to him with such tenderness." He stopped to eat a breakfast of bread and cheese and water. Having tasted the water he spat it out, declaring there must have been a dead animal in the well.

Over the next two weeks he had to swallow bitterer things than bad water. Abruptly demoted from autocrat to not-quite-trustworthy, not-quite-respectable servant he had to bear the ungracious sneers of the courtiers and the commanders of the Piedmontese army. The senior minister in the king's entourage, the man who was there to supplant him as the governor of the Two Sicilies, declined to hold any discussions with him, and when they met refused to shake his hand. His personal anthem, the "Garibaldi hymn," was banned. Finally, on November 6, came a snub so hurtful that the pain of it stayed with Garibaldi for the rest of his life.

Victor Emmanuel had agreed to review the Garibaldini. It was to be a solemn and ceremonious occasion. The redshirts prepared themselves. Surely this was the moment when the king would publicly and generously express his gratitude to the surviving members of the Thousand and those later volunteers who with them had doubled the extent of his dominions, men who had left their homes and families to fight, unpaid and often unfed, risking their lives, seeing their comrades die, to make him the first king of Italy. It rained. The redshirts were drawn up, probably for the first time ever, in parade-ground order. Six hours passed, and then another six. Garibaldi, who had been bedridden with rheumatism since his first meeting with the king, waited out the downpour with his men. The king never came. Garibaldi, still brooding years later over the insult, blamed Cavour for persuading him to stay away. But the story going the rounds in Naples in 1860 was that Victor Emmanuel had spent the afternoon alone with a woman. It was not that he deliberately withheld public acclaim from Garibaldi and his brave band; it was simply that something more amusing had turned up.

The next day Victor Emmanuel entered Naples with Garibaldi beside him in his open carriage. Garibaldi had initially refused to join him, but had finally allowed himself to be persuaded. It was still raining. Neither man was seen to speak. The triumphal arches collapsed under the downpour. Rivulets of dark blue dye ran down from the king's beard, streaking his uniform. Garibaldi attended the king to the cathedral and stood beside him while he knelt to give thanks for his victory. At the reception afterwards he stood apart and, to the consternation of a court functionary, kept his hat on. One of his supporters pointed out that Spanish grandees had the right to keep their heads covered in the presence of their monarch (as princes of the Holy Roman Emperor had in Wallenstein's day); Garibaldi was a grandee of Italy "and perhaps something more." The following day he formally abdicated his dictatorship, acknowledging Victor Emmanuel as king of all the territories he had conquered that summer, but he asked the king to appoint him their governor. Victor Emmanuel refused, perhaps out of a jealous desire to exclude his dangerously popular servant from political power, perhaps also because he had concluded—along with everybody else with influence in Naples—that Garibaldi's two-month rule had been enough to demonstrate his administrative incompetence.

Denied the power he wanted, Garibaldi was offered only honors and rewards for which he (like Cato) had no use: the specially created rank of field marshal, money and estates for his son and himself, a dowry for his daughter, a castle, a steamship, a dukedom. He refused them all. He was known all over Italy and most of the Western world as "the General." Belatedly Victor Emmanuel granted him a commission as general in the Piedmontese army. Garibaldi screwed up the piece of paper and dropped it on the floor. He announced that he was going home to Caprera. That evening he visited the British Admiral Mundy, who had followed him north from Palermo. "His whole manner," noted Mundy, "was that of a man who was suffering a poignant grief." He left Naples as a solitary passenger on a steamship, slipping away before dawn. Since he set out from Quarto six months previously he had made himself absolute ruler of half Italy. All he took home to show for it was a sack of seedcorn.

He went back to Caprera to resume clearing stones and planting beans. Cavour, and his counterparts in office all over Europe, let out a collective sigh of relief. Ten years earlier Emerson had written, "Mankind have, in all ages, attached themselves to a few persons who, either by the quality of the idea they embodied or by the largeness of their reception, were entitled to the position of leaders and law-givers." The idea Garibaldi embodied—Byron's "grand object" and "poetry of politics"—was a luminous one. His reception could hardly have been larger. From comparable beginnings Bonaparte had become an emperor, Bolívar (whom Garibaldi revered) a president for life with the power to appoint his own successor. But Garibaldi, invincible on the battlefield, meek and manipulable off it, surrendered his power.

The modesty of his homecoming, the Christ-like self-abnegation it demonstrated, was immediately recognized as evidence of his noble nature. He was repeatedly, then and later, likened to Cincinnatus, the hero of the early days of Rome, a landowner who in time of crisis assumed command of the Roman armies, was elected dictator but then, when victory was assured, voluntarily laid down his power and—asking no reward for having saved the republic—went back to his farm. It was a comforting story, one designed to allay the tremor of anxiety aroused in conservative breasts by the figure of an individual whose popular following was so grossly incommensurate with his position in any political hierarchy. But it didn't fit the facts about Garibaldi, who had no intention of beating his sword into a plowshare.

His mission was not yet accomplished. The Bourbons had been driven from the Kingdom of the Two Sicilies, but Rome and Venice were still occupied by the French and Austrians respectively. Before he left Naples he addressed the Garibaldini in words startlingly inappropriate to the cessation of warfare: "To arms, all of you, all of you! If March 1861 does not see a million Italians in arms, alas for liberty! Alas for the Italian way of life!" He had told Admiral Mundy not to visit him in Caprera in the spring because by then he hoped to have returned to the fight.

For the next seven years he was to play an increasingly disruptive part in Italian affairs. He had a vision of himself as leader, not of a thousand volunteers but of a hundred thousand, or even perhaps a million, operating independently of any civil government. In the winter before he went to Sicily he had launched an appeal for a million men and the money to buy a million rifles, a project which terrified statesmen all over Europe. He had been elected president of the Italian National Society, a patriotic pressure group, dissolved it and proclaimed a new, more belligerently political association, the Armed Nation, with the avowed intention of raising an independent volunteer army—an idea which so alarmed the British minster in Turin that he talked Victor Emmanuel into ordering Garibaldi to disband it. Garibaldi, like Alcibiades, Caesar, and the Cid before him, was even then too influential and too reckless for the stability of the state.

A year later, his reputation newly burnished by the glory he had won in Sicily and Naples, his international prestige by now immense, he was an even more threatening and destabilizing presence. The American minister in Turin described him as one "who believed, quite rightly, that his achievements and prestige had placed him in a position in which he could negotiate as an equal with kings and governments." No wonder the king and government of the new Italy looked at him askance.

He was indignant at the treatment accorded his Garibaldini after he left Naples. Few of his officers had been granted commissions in the Piedmontese army. Many complained, correctly, that they were treated worse than the Neapolitan soldiers, who as members of a trained army were more easily assimilable than the undisciplined individualists who had conquered the Two Sicilies. Garibaldi wrote a letter which was read out in the Turinese parliament and widely quoted, complaining of the treatment accorded to the nation's heroes. He issued a press release calling for the creation of a corps of volunteers to complement the regular army, one which, it was understood, would be under his command.

In April 1861 the newly elected parliament of the enlarged Italy was sitting in Turin. Garibaldi, who was the member for Naples, arrived in the city amid scenes of great public excitement. For five days he kept to his hotel room, laid up by rheumatism. No one knew precisely what he had come to do or say, but some kind of high drama was expected. People traveled all the way across Italy to be in the parliament house when he took his seat. Veterans of Sicily and Calabria, wearing their red shirts, filled the public galleries while grand ladies struggled for standing room.

Twenty minutes after the session began Garibaldi arrived, hobbling between two supporters. The Garibaldini in the galleries rose and cheered nonstop for five minutes but the majority of the deputies sat silent. Garibaldi was dressed as usual in his red shirt and poncho. The costume which had once seemed so romantically exotic had outlived the fashion it had inspired: it struck several observers as undignified and embarrassing, as inappropriate to the occasion as Cato's bared chest had seemed when he officiated in the law courts. To the French minister Garibaldi looked like "a prophet, or, if you prefer, an old comedian."

An orator of genius when speaking extempore to massed crowds, Garibaldi lost his nerve when faced with a sophisticated audience of knowing politicians. He could whip up excitement like no one else alive, but he was nothing like so skilled at presenting an argument. "Politics were not his forte," wrote a British diplomat who once tried to help him write a speech. "He always seemed to miss the principal points." When he rose to speak in Turin he had a sheaf of notes in his hand which he had evident difficulty in reading, despite the fact that he was not only wearing his usual pince-nez but using a large magnifying glass as well. He meandered incoherently. It was turning out to be a sadly disappointing performance. But then, as though abruptly coming to himself, he laid aside his papers and began to speak as he had done from balconies all over southern Italy, from the heart. His voice was as resonant and beautiful as ever. Enunciating his words with majestic slowness, he accused Cavour of having been ready to order the Piedmontese army to open fire on the Garibaldini outside Naples the previous year. The charge, as many of those present must have known, was substantially correct.

"The effect was tremendous," according to a Prussian diplomat's wife. "All the deputies left their seats, crowding down to the centre, all talking, screaming and gesticulating at once." The redshirts in the gallery were roaring. Cavour was hammering on the dispatch box and shouting, "It's not true!" A fight broke out, a group of opposition deputies trying to set upon Cavour and being violently repulsed by his supporters. Only Garibaldi, immobilized by rheumatism, remained still until the noise subsided then implacably repeated his accusation: "You were planning to wage a fratricidal war!" The session was suspended.

When it resumed twenty minutes later Cavour, once more in control of himself, was suavely conciliatory. Garibaldi was not. He never said what he did not mean and, meaning it, he would not unsay it. For the third time he repeated his accusation. He reiterated his demand for a volunteer force to be placed under his command and stalked out of the chamber. Carlyle had praised Oliver Cromwell, whose inarticulacy seemed to him the mark of a truly great soul, for breaking through the glib subtleties of parliamentary debate with a "voice from the battle-whirlwind." Garibaldi seemed to his admirers equally splendid, both in his initial failure to display the weaselly talents of the professional politician and in his subsequent leonine roar. The galleries emptied as the redshirts poured out to escort their beloved leader in procession through the streets, followed by the sightseers who had come not to hear the debate but to gaze upon the hero.

"Arrogant toward the Government, insolent towards Parliament" was the verdict on his performance, according to the French attaché in Turin, who noted that in political circles Garibaldi was "very unpopular and regarded as a man dangerous for Italy." His request for a volunteer force was rejected out of hand. Italy's representatives had turned their backs on him. Back on Caprera he cast about for a new cause, as Cavour put it, "like a bear searching for prey to devour." After Wallenstein's dismissal at Regensburg all Europe was in suspense, wondering to whom he would next offer his services. So, in 1861, every foreign ministry was speculating anxiously about where Garibaldi would next raise a revolution. Montenegro? Mexico? Dalmatia? Spain? Hungary? Greece? Ionia? Russia? Or perhaps America? That summer, the first year of the U.S. Civil War, he received first a spate of letters and then a delegation from Abraham Lincoln's secretary of state. There was already a "Garibaldi guard" serving the Union, a legion of European volunteers who wore red shirts and "Garibaldi caps." Now Garibaldi himself was offered a major general's commission in the Union army. He replied that he would consider the post of commander in chief but nothing less—no mere modern major general he. Besides, he was not interested in fighting to protect the interests of one group of morally compromised American states against those of another group. If he wanted Garibaldi's services Abraham Lincoln must announce the abolition of slavery forthwith, something he was not ready to do. The negotiations foundered. Garibaldi stayed in Europe.

On Caprera he continued to live the ascetic, energetic life he preferred, rising at dawn every day to cultivate his vegetable patch, but his solitude now was frequently interrupted. His children, Menotti, Ricciotti, and Teresa, were with him. Old friends and comrades in arms came to stay, sometimes for long periods, and were pressed into service as laborers or secretaries. Sacks of mail arrived by every steamer, the great majority of the letters from women begging for Garibaldi's autograph or a lock of his hair. Politicians from Turin came and went—soliciting his support or just keeping an eye on him—and so did sightseers, or rather pilgrims come to worship at the shrine of the man one of them described as a "superhuman being . . . the fountain-head of all that is noble, generous and holy." Strangers who had an introduction, or whose rank was such as to make them sure of their welcome, would land uninvited on the island. Admirers insufficiently well connected or brazen to visit Caprera itself contented themselves with gazing at him across the water. The first hotel was opened on the previously unfrequented island of La Maddalena, separated from Caprera by a narrow strip of water, to accommodate the visitors who came to watch him through binoculars as he chased the wild goats, hoed his beans, and smoked his cigars.

Garibaldi played the celebrity game gracefully. He never altered his routine (one lady visitor was incredulous, privately asking whether the great man really did his own digging; she could not believe it, but it was true), but he readily handed out signed photographs and locks of his hair and red shirts to those who came to adore him. An English aristocrat arrived in his yacht and was served fried blackbirds for dinner, a meal which he declared was a dish for which most of his friends would have paid its weight in gold (not for gastronomic reasons, but because he had eaten it at the table of the great Garibaldi). Every celebrity hunter wanted a trophy, every pilgrim a relic. Garibaldi was amused when he found one visitor gathering pebbles to take home as mementoes of his visit to Caprera. Others picked the hairs from his comb or collected his nail clippings, and one especially fortunate souvenir hunter spotted a laborer wearing his old general's uniform and bought it for a splendid sum. Another asked for a pair of Garibaldi boots, to be told that he had only one pair and couldn't spare them since "the shoemaker lives on that shore on which it has pleased others to make me a foreigner." And while some took away, others gave. The officers of an American ship, stopping by to visit and observing that Garibaldi had only three chairs, presented him with a dozen more. A consortium of English admirers bought him a fifty-foot yacht. Others raised enough money to buy out the owner of the other half of Caprera for him, making him proprietor of the whole island.

A private island, however, was not enough to satisfy him: he wanted a nation. In the spring of 1863 he set out not to seek a liberation movement abroad but to foment one at home. The Piedmontese government continued to tolerate the French in Rome and the Austrians in Venice, but he could not. He had no army but he had a multitude of supporters. He traveled first through northern Italy and then through Sicily, everywhere he went addressing enormous and enthusiastic crowds and calling upon them to rise up and drive out the foreigners. His watchwords were "Rome and Venice!" "Rome or Death!"

To what extent he was defying Victor Emmanuel, whose overt policy was that of peaceable coexistence with France and passive acceptance of Austria, is a matter of dispute. Before he began his tour Garibaldi visited Turin and talked with Victor Emmanuel and with his new prime minister, Rattazzi (Cavour had died the previous year). What was said during these meetings was, and has remained, secret. It is possible that the king gave Garibaldi covert encouragement, hoping to profit by any success he might score as he had profited by his conquest of the Two Sicilies. People asked where Garibaldi's funding was coming from if not from the government in Turin, and it was rumored later that year that he carried with him a tin box containing secret orders from the king. But if those orders existed they were never produced, and if Victor Emmanuel ever thought it wise to make use of Garibaldi in such a way, by the end of the year he had emphatically changed his mind.

Everywhere Garibaldi went he whipped up storms of enthusiasm. Repeatedly in the past he had been furiously disappointed by his inability to convert worshipers into recruits, but this time he was received not only with adoration, but with action. Like the volcanic fire on the banner of Montevideo's Italian legion, his army was invisible and dormant, but he had only to set foot in Italy and speak from a few balconies for it to erupt into the light.

In the Turinese parliament, before a critical and politically sophisticated audience, he had fumbled his notes and tangled his arguments, but when speaking to a multitude he was, as he always had been, an electrifying orator. Fully aware of the excitement he could generate simply by presenting himself, he would stand silently while the adoring crowd roared and wept. Then, at the moment of maximum expectation, he would raise his thrilling voice and call out questions to which his hearers would bellow back the familiar answers—"Whose is the victory?" "Italy's!" "What are we fighting for?" "Rome or Death!"—a secular litany which, involving the crowd in the inflaming of their own emotions, led repeatedly to a collective rapture. This was not the canvassing of a politician: it was the advent of a messiah. A poster printed in Sicily is headed "In the name of the Father of the Nation," and contains versions of the

Ten Commandments ("Thou shalt not be a soldier of the General's in vain"), of the Lord's Prayer ("Give us this day our daily cartridges"), and of the catechism, in which Garibaldi is defined as a second Trinity, "The Father of the Nation, the Son of the People, and the Spirit of Liberty." To fight for Garibaldi had become a sacred duty.

In northern Italy in April Garibaldi called upon his followers to form "rifle clubs" with guns subsidized by the Million Rifles Fund. Thousands of young men took up the suggestion, the clubs constituting a kind of unofficial militia loyal to "the General." In May a group of about a hundred of them were arrested, apparently on their way to invade the Austrian Tyrol. The government, embarrassed and unwilling to be seen to oppose the people's idol, announced that the men were not true Garibaldini but agitators who had falsely used the General's name. Garibaldi exposed the lie by going to the prison where his men were being held, offering to stand security for them, and issuing a statement to the press confirming that they had been acting on his orders. No action was taken against him. Instead he received a visit from one of the king's ministers, with whom he talked alone in his room and then in a rowing boat on Lake Maggiore. Again it is impossible to know what passed between them, but it seems likely that the minister begged him to quiet down and go away, for shortly thereafter Garibaldi returned to Caprera, staying there for ten days before abruptly announcing he was setting off for Sicily.

The "second Jesus" was proving almost as troublesome to established authority as the first one had been. Had Garibaldi but known how to wait quietly Rome could have been Italy's that summer without a single death. Napoleon III was ready to withdraw his troops, but what he would have been willing to do in his own time he was too proud to do under pressure from a populist agitator: "A nation like France does not give way to the threats of a Garibaldi," he declared. "Death if they like, but Rome never," added the Empress Eugénie, a far more militant Catholic than her husband. Garibaldi's outspokenness and lack of finesse was as damaging to his own cause as Cato's had been to his. Garibaldi was an Achilles, not an Odysseus. He was never to understand that there were less romantic, less violent, more efficient ways of altering international relations than by running into the enemy's fire flourishing a saber. He was becoming a grave embarrassment to Victor Emmanuel, who wished neither to associate himself with his actions, nor to admit how far beyond the government's control he now was.

Volunteers from all over Italy and elsewhere, including some opposition MPs from Turin, joined him in Sicily. By the beginning of August he had assembled a force of some three thousand men near Palermo. The British foreign secretary, Lord John Russell, wrote to him reminding him that no "individual, however distinguished, has a right to determine for his country the momentous question of peace or war." Garibaldi ignored the warning. His speeches became increasingly incendiary, until at last Victor Emmanuel responded. He issued a proclamation declaring that no one but he, the king, was to decide if and when Rome or Venice were to be liberated, expressly forbidding any Italian, however eminent, to make war on a foreign state, and announcing that any individual who assembled an army without his authority would be guilty of high treason and of fomenting civil war.

Garibaldi ignored the proclamation. Perhaps he believed that, like the orders Victor Emmanuel had sent him three years before forbidding him to cross the Strait of Messina, it was a blind to placate foreign powers, not to be taken seriously. Three days after its publication he led his men eastward across Sicily. The governor of the island, an old friend of his, resigned rather than be obliged to restrain him. He reached Catania on Sicily's east coast. The troops of the royal Piedmontese army stationed in the town surrendered to him immediately and the townspeople lit all their lamps in a welcome which had them all cheering him until three in the morning. A week later he seized two vessels, one French and one Italian, and crossed to the mainland. There were ships of the Italian navy in the vicinity but they made no attempt to intercept him. (Their officers were later court-martialed for negligence but acquitted.) It appeared that Garibaldi had begun a second miracle-working progress through southern Italy. All over the Western world people watched enthralled. That week Ivan Turgenev wrote to Alexander Herzen from Baden-Baden, "But what of Garibaldi? One cannot help trembling as one follows every movement . . . Surely Brutus, who perishes not only *always* in history, but even in Shakespeare, cannot triumph? One cannot believe it—one's heart stops beating."

Garibaldi was bound for the Papal States to drive out the French. Before embarking at Catania he proclaimed: "I bow to the Majesty of Victor Emmanuel!" Like the Cid of the *Poema*, he was still claiming to make his conquests in his king's name. When the Piedmontese garrison at Reggio marched out against him he retreated. He had no intention of fighting his fellow Italians. He still imagined that a monarch would condone any defiance so long as it was profitable. Wallenstein had wished to impose a secularized and greatly strengthened empire on a reluctant emperor; so Garibaldi intended to force a kingdom on an unwilling king. But Victor Emmanuel was no longer prepared to accept gifts under duress. He ordered out an army to hunt down and stop Garibaldi.

The royal troops found Garibaldi in the mountains of Aspromonte. Garibaldi's men were drawn up on a plateau, their General standing before them. Their position was strong, but to defend it would be to initiate a civil war. Garibaldi gave orders that no one was to fire. For nearly an hour he watched the royal army approach until they were within gunshot. As they advanced uphill, they began to shoot the Garibaldini. Garibaldi stood still.

When Napoleon Bonaparte returned from exile in Elba in 1815, not a single one of the thousands of troops ordered out to stop him marching on Paris could find it in himself to fire a gun at the fallen emperor. Nearly half a century later Garibaldi appears to have believed it was as impossible for an Italian soldier to shoot him as it had been for a French one to shoot Napoleon. He was wrong. He must have hoped that the Italian troops would lay down their arms as so many of the Neapolitans had done three years before, that by the power of his oratory and his physical presence he could avert a battle and win over an army. Stranger and more marvelous things had happened. But at Aspromonte, instead of the demoralized Neapolitan army with its pusillanimous generals, Garibaldi was facing disciplined troops and determined officers. Finding themselves unopposed they advanced the faster and fired the more. Even the heroic drama of unresisting martyrdom was spoiled when some of the Garibaldini, understandably, lost their nerve and fired back. Garibaldi, of whom it was once said that he used to shake bullets by the hundred out of his shirt while remaining unscathed, was hit in the thigh and the foot. By the time a colonel came to accept his surrender, he was no longer grandly upright but in great pain on the ground. As a doctor investigated his foot he lit a cigar and told the man to amputate immediately if he judged it necessary. But he was felled, metaphorically as well as literally. The myth of his invincibility had been shattered.

As Wallenstein's murderers had congratulated themselves on their heroic courage in taking on a sick man in a nightshirt, so Victor Emmanuel rewarded his soldiers generously for having defeated an unresisting enemy: seventy-six medals for valor were awarded after the nonbattle of Aspromonte. Garibaldi was charged with treason and imprisoned, to the outrage of his admirers everywhere. There were demonstrations in his support all over Italy: Rattazzi was obliged to resign as prime minister. In

London a hundred thousand people attended a rally in Hyde Park protesting against his arrest. A Swiss poet composed an epic on the tragedy of Aspromonte.

Defeated and suffering, the second Jesus was now seen to be enduring his Passion. The wound to Garibaldi's foot became one of the stigmata. A print of the period shows him hanging from the cross while an angel flies down to crown him. The Redeemer had fallen foul of secular authority, as redeemers tend to: he had come among his people and his people had received him not. In prison he lay on a bed donated by Lady Palmerston and he was attended by no fewer than twelve of the most distinguished surgeons in Europe, their fees paid by his admirers. After one of the twelve eventually succeeded in extracting the bullet from his foot while he bit down hard on his cigar an English gentleman offered "a fabulous sum" for it. He was refused: Menotti Garibaldi wanted the horrid keepsake for himself. But thousands of bloodstained handkerchiefs, each one said to have been used to staunch the great man's wound, subsequently went on sale.

Within weeks Victor Emmanuel, anxious to shrug off as quickly as possible the opprobrium of being Garibaldi's oppressor, granted him and his men an amnesty. Garibaldi retired to Caprera, permanently lamed and even more fundamentally disabled by the shock of being treated—he, the people's hero!—as a public enemy. In 1866, when Victor Emmanuel, in partnership this time with Bismarck's Prussia, finally resolved to declare war on Austria again, he accepted with alacrity the king's invitation to serve, leaving the island on the very same day to take up his command, but he was not what he had once been. For the third time he was operating in the Alps, from a base on Lake Garda. But like Drake returning to the Caribbean for his last voyage he found the scenes of his early glory sadly changed. He was wounded early in the campaign. The Austrian Tyrolese who opposed him were as wise to the techniques of guerrilla warfare as he was. When peace was concluded the Tyrol, of which he had eventually succeeded in gaining control, was granted to Austria. All his efforts had been futile. In 1848 in similar circumstances he had refused to lay down his arms. But this time he acquiesced in a grim one-word telegram: "*Obbedisco*"—I obey.

That telegram was much quoted. Like the comparison with Cincinnatus it conjured up an image of Garibaldi as the great servant, one who willingly sacrificed his own ambitions and aspirations to subordinate himself to the state. It was an image designed to reassure all established authority, but it was a grossly misleading one. Garibaldi's obedience was short-lived. Alcibiades, after he defected to Sparta, declared, "None of you should think the worse of me. . . . The Athens I love is not the one that is wronging me now . . . The man who really loves his country is not the one who refuses to attack it when he has been unjustly driven from it, but the man whose desire of it is so strong that he will shrink from nothing in his efforts to get back there again." Garibaldi, bitterly disappointed in the Italy that had come into being, whose regime now seemed to him so compromised, so ignoble, longed to "get back" to the pure-hearted Italy he had once envisioned. When an uprising in Sicily was suppressed with what seemed to him unjustified brutality he resigned his parliamentary seat in disgust. In the following year he was once more traveling around the country, defying the government and calling wherever he went for volunteers for the liberation of Rome.

History was repeating itself. Once again Garibaldi was fomenting sedition in the name of patriotism. Once again Victor Emmanuel's government issued a proclamation calling on all Italians to respect the authority of Parliament and the frontiers of foreign states. Once again Garibaldi went ahead in defiance of the government's explicit veto. Once again he told his recruits that they would be marching against foreigners, and were to avoid fighting the Italian army. He traveled by rail. At every station the train was surrounded by huge crowds. At every station Garibaldi announced that he would lead his irregular army on Rome. He was flagrantly defying the government. At Sinalunga he, along with fifty of his followers, was arrested. Again there were demonstrations, many of them violent, all over Italy; even the soldiers on guard outside his prison window shouted, "Long live Garibaldi, free! Long live Rome, the capital!" Again Rattazzi feared for his political life. Again Garibaldi was rapidly released and shipped back to Caprera.

That autumn his son Menotti led a troop of volunteers across the border into the Papal States. Everyone concerned was certain that the outcome of the invasion would depend on whether or not Garibaldi himself could join it. The government could not keep him in prison, but they were determined to keep him at home, and they were prepared to tie up eight warships in order to blockade him on Caprera. It was useless. On October 2 Garibaldi was stopped by a salvo of cannon as he tried to row himself to a neighboring island and obliged to go back, but two weeks later, on a misty night, he made his escape. He was all alone. With his oars wrapped in rags to deaden the sound he passed so close to the ships that he could hear the seamen talking on board. He was sixty years old and barely able to walk, but he succeeded in making his way—hiding out in a cave for a day and a night, crossing Sardinia on horseback (a seventeen-hour ride), persuading a naval patrol that he was just a fisherman—onto the mainland. When the news of his escape got out Rattazzi again resigned.

Garibaldi went to Florence, by this time the capital. He spoke publicly, declaring, "We have the right to Rome! Rome is ours!" The government, leaderless after Rattazzi's resignation, made no move to arrest him; to have done so might well have provoked civil war. He joined Menotti's men inside the Papal States and defeated the papal garrison at Monte Rotondo, but on November 2, at Mentana, his force of some forty-five hundred men met an army of some eleven thousand French and papal troops. "It is Garibaldi's custom never to count either the enemy or his own men," one of his most devoted officers once wrote, but he had lost his ability to communicate his faith to his followers. Seeing the odds against them, at Mentana the invincible Garibaldini turned and fled.

Garibaldi was devastated. He appeared transformed, wrote an observer afterwards, "gloomy, hoarse, pale . . . I have never seen anyone age so quickly as he did at that moment." He led his men back over the frontier and took a train for Livorno, intending to go straight home, but he had defied the law and the government was determined, now that his charisma had failed him, to make a show of its recovered power to treat him as it would any other citizen. At Perugia he was arrested, taken off the train, and imprisoned for the third time. Once released, he went quietly back to Caprera under orders to stay there.

Three years later Victor Emmanuel finally took Rome, but Garibaldi had no part in his triumph. Instead he wrote novels, so badly that the first one was turned down by nineteen publishers, even though its author was one of the most famous people in the world. He revised and updated his autobiography, the bitterness of his added commentary reflecting his disenchantment with the new Italy he had helped bring into being. "Every hero becomes a bore at last," wrote Ralph Waldo Emerson, and Garibaldi in old age became, not boring exactly, but as cantankerous and complaining as he had every right to be. He married his housekeeper. He fought once more: when France became a republic again, and came under threat from Prussia, he cabled the French government: "What remains of me is at your service, dispose of me." His offer was accepted: the great Garibaldi would be an invaluable asset to any cause. A French radical managed to break the blockade of Caprera, whisking him off the island in a little sailing boat. He served loyally, even though he was so crippled by rheumatism and his old wounds that he had to be carried around the battlefields on a stretcher, but he had fought both Catholicism and France too often for Catholic Frenchmen to forgive him. To the majority of his new allies he was at best an enemy, at worst a criminal. When he was elected to the National Assembly he was shouted down, and so was Victor Hugo, who tried to defend him. He left the next day for Caprera, where he stayed, virtually imprisoned, for the rest of his life.

He had long outlasted his finest hours and had lived to make the degrading and disorientating transition from antique hero to modern celebrity. In 1864, a few months after his traumatic defeat by his own countrymen at Aspromonte, he visited London. Britain was hospitable to foreign revolutionaries in exile. Garibaldi had been kindly received here in 1854. Ten years later, wounded, depressed, and unwanted at home, he agreed to make another visit.

To Mazzini, who was living in England once again, and to his allies in the British radical movement, Garibaldi's visit represented an invaluable propagandist and fund-raising opportunity. They planned a whole series of mass open-air rallies in the north of England where he would speak, generating enthusiasm for radical causes and large sums of money. But he was not only a political totem and a salable spectacle: he was also a toy of fashion. The Duke and Duchess of Sutherland invited him to stay. Lord Shaftesbury planned a banquet in his honor. Everyone who was anyone wished to meet him. Even before he arrived he was being fought over. His itinerary was much disputed, and not only because his time might be limited. His visit would carry a very different symbolic significance if he appeared first at a workers' rally in the industrialized north than if his first stop in England were a ducal residence. What Garibaldi himself, who was never much interested in the niceties of politics and whose English was rudimentary, wanted from the visit is uncertain. As so often in peacetime, he seemed to be passive and infinitely suggestible—going where he was invited, politely allowing himself to be used.

The welcome he was accorded was astonishing. Alexander Herzen described it as a Shakespearean fantasy: "Prologue: Flourish of trumpets. The idol of the masses, the one grand popular figure of our age . . . enters in all the brilliance of its glory. Everything bows down before it, everything celebrates its triumph; this is Carlyle's hero-worship being performed before our eyes." As soon as the ship on which Garibaldi was traveling docked at Southampton the crowds who had been waiting on the waterfront swarmed up the ramps and besieged him in his cabin. "It was more boisterous than a battle," wrote one reporter. He went to the Isle of Wight, staying there as the guest of the Liberal MP. He visited Alfred, Lord Tennyson, who had already written poems in his praise and who was delighted by his "majestic meekness." "What a noble human being!" he wrote afterwards. "I expected to see a hero and was not disappointed. His manners have a certain divine simplicity in them such as I have never witnessed." The photographer Julia Margaret Cameron, another inhabitant of the island, went down on her knees to beg him to pose for a portrait. Lady Tennyson worried that he might think Cameron was begging for alms, but Garibaldi, who had seen whole villages full of Calabrian and Sicilian peasants kneeling to adore him, accepted her obeisance without fuss.

On April 11 he went to London, traveling in a special train draped with the Italian flag. There were reception committees, both official and unofficial, in each station through which he passed. As his train entered the suburbs it was engulfed by hordes of waving, cheering people. There were people on rooftops, people on railway wagons, people on bridges, people cramming the embankments. He got out at Nine Elms. On the platform a brass band was playing the Garibaldi hymn. He was escorted through the hubbub to the Duke of Sutherland's carriage, in which he was joined by the duke and by some pushy Italian businessmen who clambered aboard uninvited. His progress across the Thames and through the center of London to the Sutherlands' house in St. James's, a distance of about three miles, took six hours. Half a million people had come to see him, more even than had turned out for the Prince of Wales's wedding the previous year. There were banners. There were brass bands, their braying scarcely audible above the cheering voices. People pressed around the carriage so thickly it was repeatedly brought to a complete standstill. When it finally reached its destination it fell to pieces. The pressure of the crowds surging against it had lifted the sides off their hinges: the vehicle had been held together for the latter part of the journey only by the crush of bodies all around it.

For the next week Garibaldi was the toast of all London society. He could do no wrong: even when he lit up a cigar in the Duchess of Sutherland's boudoir he was excused. He met Palmerston and Gladstone, Lord John Russell, Florence Nightingale, and the Archbishop of Canterbury. He went to the opera (*Norma*). He twice addressed his adoring public in the Crystal Palace. The Prince of Wales visited him, slipping through the garden gate in a forlorn attempt to avoid the journalists who followed Garibaldi everywhere, and found him dignified, noble, and "un-charlatan-like." He drove through more enthusiastic crowds to the Guildhall where the mayor gave him the Freedom of the City. He lunched at the Reform Club, where Lord Ebury described him as an "instrument of God." He visited the House of Lords and was warmly welcomed by peers of all political persuasions. He attended a banquet at Fishmonger's Hall, shaking hands with every one of the 350 guests; his sons, Menotti and Ricciotti, who had reasonably assumed the occasion was a dinner for fishmongers and had accordingly dressed down, were denied admission. He spent a weekend at Cliveden. "The triumphant ovations increase with every day," wrote Herzen. "The people of England have gone really quite mad about Garibaldi," wrote Queen Victoria in her diary. Like Lord Byron before him, Garibaldi, the new corsair, had inflamed all London. Everywhere he went he was greeted with a feverish excitement fueled by an eroticism which was all the more hysterical for the fact that in Protestant Britain it could be less easily expressed, as it had been in Italy, as quasi-religious fervor. A musical based on his adventures played to packed theaters. Babies were named after him. Sales of Garibaldi biscuits rose again. The Sutherlands' servants were making small fortunes selling the hairs from his comb, the clippings from his toenails, even the scummy water from his bath.

This reception, so hectically rapturous, was almost unmitigatedly frivolous. Garibaldi's hostility towards the Pope and his priests agreed well with British anti-Catholicism, but otherwise neither the crowds of hoi polloi who mobbed him in streets nor the grandees who flirted with and condescended to him in their drawing rooms cared a whit about his politics. They approved in a general way the notion of "liberty," of which the British had for two centuries liked to consider themselves the protectors, and most of them had an idea that Garibaldi had done splendid things for the sake of that abstraction. Beyond that they did not inquire. The cause to which he had dedicated his life, that of Italy's unity and independence, was a matter of indifference to all but a few of them. They neither knew nor cared whether they adored him as Italy's hero or as the seditionary who was such an annoyance to Italy's legitimate government. They did not ask themselves what his passionate advocacy of the rights of nations to self-determination and independent sovereignty might lead him to think of British policy in Ireland, or in India. They did not bother themselves with the question of whether, as law-abiding citizens of a monarchical state, they should be so eager to salute a man who had so recently, and so inveterately, rebelled against his king.

They loved him for his looks. They acclaimed him as a focus of erotic excitement, a time traveler from an archaic world of epic adventure and romantic passion, and a tragic victim. "He came," remarked the Countess Martinengo Cesaresco astutely, "the prisoner of Aspromonte, not the conqueror of Sicily." He was a nationalist revolutionary but, wounded and impotent, he was a welcome guest even in the metropolis of an imperial power. He had all but died for his cause, and the pathos and grandeur of his sacrifice were affecting enough to obscure the nature of that cause from those who would otherwise most vehemently have disapproved of it, freeing them to luxuriate in a delirium of hero worship.

In the 1960s students all over the Western world pinned posters of Che Guevara to their walls, not because they took an informed interest in Latin American politics, but because he had a beautiful face and because as he glared bravely upwards and outwards beneath his beret he picturesquely embodied the stirring myth of the brave freedom fighter slain by oppressors. The fashion was not for a political program, but for a poster. Similarly Garibaldi in London became a sign which signified nothing, or nothing that the man himself would have recognized as having validity or weight. It seemed only three people in London that April Fools' week declined to be swept away by Garibaldi-mania, and what distinguished them from the crowd of their fellow Londoners was the fact that they did him the justice of taking his convictions seriously. One was the queen, another her prime minister, Benjamin Disraeli, and the third Karl Marx. To Queen Victoria, although her son and heir and several of the princesses had succumbed, it seemed evident that a monarch could not condone and should not meet a man of his political stamp: "Honest, disinterested and brave, Garibaldi certainly is," she noted in her diary. "But a revolutionist!" The extravagant adulation accorded him made her feel "half-ashamed of being the head of a nation capable of such follies." Marx was entirely of her mind. As one who deplored both nationalism and sentimentality he found the reception accorded to Garibaldi a "miserable spectacle of imbecility." He flatly refused to deliver a greeting from the German socialist association to the visiting hero.

While Garibaldi was gallivanting around the metropolis, fêted by the high and mighty, Mazzini and his British associates observed his appropriation by the establishment with growing dismay. Mazzini had visited him on the Isle of Wight. Garibaldi, to the disapproval of his aristocratic mentors, received him warmly, but Mazzini had failed to take control, as he had wished, of the hero's itinerary. Nearly fifty rallies had been planned in Newcastle, Glasgow, Birmingham, Manchester, and Salford, events which promised to be immensely beneficial to the self-confidence of the British radical movement and financially profitable to any cause for which Garibaldi could be persuaded to solicit donations. These rallies, in their organizers' eyes, were the real purpose of Garibaldi's visit. They never took place.

On Sunday, April 17, ignoring the attempts to dissuade him made by the Duke of Sutherland's coachman, Garibaldi went to lunch with Alexander Herzen. The occasion was a gathering of exiled revolutionaries from all over Europe, Mazzini among them. Garibaldi made a speech in which he acknowledged Mazzini to be his first teacher, "My friend, my master!" The following day he called on the exiled French republicans Ledru-Rollin and Louis Blanc. He had demonstrated that he was not just an aristocrat's plaything, but he was to do no more. One week to the day after he had arrived in London he issued a public statement to the effect that he would not be traveling to the provinces as planned, but would leave forthwith for home.

The circumstances surrounding his abrupt decision are ambiguous. His grand friends seemed anxious to put it about that he was too ill and exhausted to make the projected tour, but Garibaldi himself confided in a trusted friend that he was leaving "because I am not wanted," and when a radical organizer arrived posthaste from Newcastle to try to persuade him to change his mind Garibaldi told him that Gladstone had made it plain to him that if he persisted in acting the politician rather than the anodyne celebrity he would become an embarrassment to the British government.

It is unquestionably true that he was physically frail. It is also true that powerful people were determined to prevent him touring the north if they possibly could. His politics were those of nationality, but the British radicals had hoped to enlist his image to support their very different politics of class, and in doing so they had made him a threat to the country's rulers. Besides, he had unwittingly come athwart Britain's sectarian divisions. He was a friend to the common man and an enemy of the Pope, but a great many of the common men and women to whom he would be speaking in Liverpool and Glasgow were Irish Catholics who were likely to be infuriated by his anticlericalism. Foreseeing trouble, the forces of law and order resolved to head him off. But his sudden abandonment of his plans seem to owe as much to his own disenchantment as to either illness or political pressure. The wishes of ministers and monarchs had never before deterred him from doing what he wanted to do, but this time he meekly allowed himself to be turned away.

Mazzini was all for campaigning against his "expulsion," but Garibaldi himself forestalled any protest by publishing a declaration that no pressure had been put on him to leave. It seems that, acquiescent though he had been, he was tired of being used by others, whether as a political totem, a fund-raising device, or, above all, as the occasion for outbreaks of wildly enjoyable hysteria. He asked one of his radical contacts why the English people, who had accorded Kossuth a welcome almost as rapturous as the one they had granted him, had done nothing to help Hungary. Too often in his life Garibaldi had ridden into a town to be received with demonstrations of frantic adoration only to ride out of it again with no new recruits, no donated money, and no real political support. He would not be fooled that way again. "It is not with flowers, fêtes and illuminations that the warlike and disciplined soldiers of a despotism are fought, but with soldiers still more warlike and more disciplined than they are," he wrote. He was beginning to understand just how superficial was the British people's interest in him.

The powerful patronized him. Gladstone found his "simple nobility" and "naturalness" and, above all, his "perfect consciousness of his position" (his inferiority in other words) "very striking and very fine." Lord Granville told Queen Victoria, "Garibaldi has all the qualifications for making him a popular idol in this country," but added, "He is a goose." The gentlemen condescended; the ladies swooned. Both the dowager Duchess of Sutherland and her daughter-in-law, the young duchess, seem to have fallen in love with Garibaldi. Another of his hostesses wrote to him to tell him how she had gazed, her heart full of anguish, at the pillow where his head had rested, and how she treasured the handkerchief she had found beneath it. "Your visit is truly the greatest glory of my life!" It was not for this that Garibaldi had come to England, to provide fodder for the erotic fantasies of women to whom he was a picturesque curiosity, women who were enraptured by him while unconsciously looking down on him, adoring him precisely because he was so far from being socially acceptable, thrilled by his political fervor just because it seemed to them so outlandish and transgressive.

In 1997 a photograph was published in newspapers all around the world showing Nelson Mandela, by then president of South Africa, with the British girl band the Spice Girls. Mandela's image conforms more closely than that of almost any other public figure of the recent past to the ancient ideal of the hero. A rebel against unjust authority, he struggled courageously and suffered patiently in a cause of profound and deadly seriousness. During his years in prison his fame spread far beyond South Africa. He was internationally celebrated, pitied, and revered as one who had stood up against tyranny and staunchly borne his cruel punishment, and he was awaited as a messiah who would rise again from the living death of Robben Island and redeem his people. The Spice Girls, on the other hand, were an unpretentious group of pretty young women who never pretended to be anything other than a phenomenally well marketed show business act. In the photographs of the president's meeting with the pop singers, tragic history was juxtaposed with light entertainment; the two were presented with disturbing blandness as equivalent—just two different ways of being world famous. In London Garibaldi, who had been a Mandela, found himself being accorded the reception due to a Spice Girl. He pleaded illness, and he fled.

He could escape London, but he could not escape the process which was transforming him from free subject to helpless object available for use in others' propaganda. During his two-month dictatorship in Naples in 1860 he had introduced a raft of liberal legislation—children's homes, price controls on bread, free education, religious tolerance, savings banks to replace the lottery, freedom for the press. Cavour, determined to erase all trace of dangerous radicalism, instructed the new governor "mercilessly to sweep away all the shit left in that stable." After Garibaldi left, every single one of his measures was repealed. He had promised the people of southern Italy their liberty, but it soon seemed to him (and to many) that their compatriots of the north, into whose keeping he had delivered them, exploited them as callously as the ousted regime had done. In 1865 he wrote to Victor Emmanuel that "the government is now more hated there than the Bourbons." It was a sad admission from the man who had done so much, and with such good intentions, to impose that government. An aging Achilles, he condemned modern politicians as "the sons of Thersites." In his last years he felt himself living in "days of shame and misery," in a "mephitic atmosphere of robbery and intrigue." Modern Italians appeared to him merely the "degenerate descendants of the greatest of nations," a people to whom he was ashamed to belong, and their rulers were a "government of thieves."

He died in 1882. The Italian parliament, organ of the state which had condemned him to death, which had driven him into exile, which had three times imprisoned him, which had led out its armies against him and confined him to his little island for years, adjourned itself for two weeks in sign of mourning. He had wished his body to be burned, like Shelley's, on an open pyre by the sea. His wish was disregarded. It was decided that his corpse belonged not to him but to his country. He was buried with all due, and much undue, pomp.

"All whose brilliance has made them prominent are unpopular in their lifetimes," Alcibiades told the assembled Athenians in 416 BC. "But later you will find their countries boasting of them." Dead heroes are often more useful, and always more malleable, than living ones. In 1860, while Garibaldi was steaming towards Marsala to make Italy, Victor Emmanuel wrote: "Of course it would be a great misfortune, but if the Neapolitan cruisers were to capture and hang my poor Garibaldi . . . it would simplify things a good deal. And what a fine monument we should erect to him!" In the event Victor Emmanuel was disappointed of his hope. He predeceased "poor Garibaldi" by four years. It was he himself who was honored with a "fine monument," the grandiose structure of sugar-white marble which stands in the very center of Rome, upstaging Michelangelo's Piazza Capitolina, dwarfing the ruins of the ancient Forum. At the center of the huge edifice rises the equestrian statue of Victor Emmanuel, thirty-seven feet tall (in life he was a little man) and splendid in gilded bronze. Behind and below is the entrance to the Museum of the Risorgimento, where alongside copious Garibaldiana are displayed albums full of photographs of Garibaldi's Thousand. After Patroclus's death Achilles slaughtered twelve Trojan prisoners and immolated their bodies on his dead friend's pyre. Garibaldi and his Thousand, their memories entombed in the base of Victor Emmanuel's monument, are the sacrificial victims who, dead and no longer troublesome, fuel a glory which the majority of them—republicans like their leader—would surely have found abhorrent. Two years before he died, contemplating the country he had brought into being, Garibaldi was to own bleakly, "It was a different Italy that I had dreamed of all my life."

VIII

ODYSSEUS

Achilles was killed beneath the walls of Troy. The nine Muses sang his dirge. A host of nereids dressed his corpse in robes of supernatural beauty. For seventeen days the Greeks desisted from battle to mourn him and on the eighteenth they burned his body along with those of droves of sheep and cattle. They paraded in full battle armor around the pyre. They gathered up his charred bones, preserved them in wine and aromatic oils, and placed them in a golden urn and then they buried them beneath a splendid tomb on a high headland

> a landmark glimpsed from far out to sea
> by men of our day and men of days to come.

That was Achilles' end—solemn, public and conclusive, the end to which he had freely consented.

Achilles chooses death; Odysseus, his opposite, longs to go home and reclaim his life. But before he can regain Ithaca Odysseus must undergo the temporary death customarily imposed on semidivine men and incarnated gods. He goes down into the underworld where the "burnt-out wraiths" shrill and flitter like bats, the place of nonbeing which Homer evokes with such pathos and horror that Plato would have liked to ban the reading of his description for fear that it might prove demoralizing to fighting men. There Odysseus meets the shade of Achilles and compliments him on the godlike qualities which won him so much honor in his lifetime and which entitle him now to "lord it over the dead." Achilles' response is grim: "No winning words about death to me shining Odysseus!" The pact he made (irrevocable now) has proved more terrible than he could have imagined. The immortal fame he won was a piffling satisfaction, no compensation for the loss of precious life. These are the sentiments Plato wanted to keep from those "on whom freedom places the obligation to fear servitude more than death." They would be wrong to do so, says Achilles. He would prefer to be slave to a landless peasant, if he could only be alive again, than rule over all the "breathless dead." He paid for glory with his life, and glory wasn't worth the price. Paragon of heroes, he announces that the heroic code is founded on a misestimation.

In 1867 when Garibaldi—the dauntless warrior who held out the prospect of violent death as though it were a privilege, the diplomatic dunderhead who repeatedly alienated his allies because he couldn't tell a lie, the man as beautiful as a god, the nineteenth-century Achilles—had returned defeated from Mentana, Alexander Herzen apostrophized him: "Garibaldi, last of the Saints, last of the Mohicans, fold your hands and take your rest. . . . You have done your part. Make room now for madness, for the frenzy of blood . . . Now there will be lakes of blood, seas of blood, mountains of corpses." Herzen could not have foreseen the forms that madness would take, but he was right about the blood, and he was right to connect its spilling with the cult of a conquering hero. Achilles has always had critics alive to the terrible aspect of his glory. Homer's Agamemnon calls him "the most violent man alive." Euripides and Flavius Philostratus both represented him as a vengeful ghost. Plato found him contemptibly self-indulgent and disgracefully arrogant. To Cicero his rage seemed like a mental illness. Horace wrote of his anger and the damage he did to his own people. To Virgil and Catullus he appeared criminally destructive, a mass murderer and an agent of social collapse. Shakespeare characterized him as a preening bullyboy, a vain, unscrupulous thug.

Just to the northwest of London's Hyde Park Corner stands a monumental piece of sculpture erected in 1822 in honor of the Duke of Wellington, a man who, because he lived to a great old age and involved himself in the compromising business of government, is not now remembered with the degree of romantic adoration accorded Nelson (whom Wellington, at their only meeting, found "so vain and silly as to surprise and almost disgust me") but who was in his lifetime venerated as his nation's savior and champion. It is a statue of Achilles. It shows a sword-wielding warrior with furrowed brow, sneering lip, and stupendous musculature. Cast from the metal of captured Napoleonic cannon, it is a piece of hard lines and slabby masses, product of the exaggeratedly virile aesthetic tradition from which fascist and socialist-realist art would eventually evolve. One of Oscar Wilde's sophisticated young ladies, on receiving an unwelcome marriage proposal in front of it, exclaims, "Really . . . that dreadful Achilles!" The goings-on for which he has been the inspiration, in her opinion, "are quite appalling."

On May 5, 1915, eight months after the outbreak of the First World War and fifty-five years after Garibaldi and his Thousand scrambled aboard their clapped-out hijacked steamers and set off to make Italy, those few of the expeditionaries who were still living returned to Quarto. A monument commemorating their marvelous adventure was to be unveiled. Peppino Garibaldi, the great man's grandson, was there. And so were thousands upon thousands of other Italians, from all but the highest (the king himself stayed away for diplomatic reasons—Garibaldi's political legacy was as embarrassing to the monarchy he had served as the man himself had been) to the lowest. They had come to pay their respects to a dead hero whom time had all but deified. And they had come as well to applaud a living idol, Gabriele D'Annunzio, Italy's foremost poet and most flamboyant celebrity. A swindler and a spendthrift who seldom honored a contract or paid a debt, a fastidious aesthete who refused to occupy a hotel room until his servants had checked the linen and cluttered the place up with the silk damask cushions and precious knickknacks with which he always traveled, a seductive conversationalist and the author of reams of elaborately decadent verse—D'Annunzio was an incongruous disciple for the taciturn and frugal Garibaldi. But the two men had some traits in common. D'Annunzio was, as Garibaldi had been in his time, an energetic and prodigiously successful lover and the object of popular adulation approaching the intensity of worship. He had fought only in private duels (after one of which an overenthusiastic and injudicious second had dressed his head wound with an ointment which left him completely bald), but, like Garibaldi, he had an Achillean thirst for death and glory. He was also, like Garibaldi, an ardent nationalist who detested Austria and its allies.

Five years earlier, in flight from his creditors and in pursuit of a statuesque beauty who had modeled for Rodin, D'Annunzio had moved precipitately to France. Now, with German guns already audible in Paris, he had returned, in response to pleas from the French government and the urgent invitations of the Italian interventionist party, to inaugurate a campaign designed to persuade Italy's leaders to enter the war on the side of the Allies. Invited to give an address on the occasion of the unveiling of a monument at Quarto, he had accepted eagerly. Here was an occasion which would allow him to return home haloed with associations perfectly adjudged to flatter his sense of himself as Italy's new champion. He would stand where Garibaldi had stood and speak where Garibaldi had spoken. He too would have his legion: he was to be escorted by Peppino Garibaldi's Italian volunteers, who had been fighting for France. And like the dead hero he would urge his countrymen to kill and die for him and for glory. He pawned, not for the first time, the emerald ring the great actress Eleonora Duse had given him. He prevailed upon the couturier Paquin to donate a load of fine new red shirts for the Italian legion (the Garibaldini's outlaw style appealed to him as a romantic fantasy: in reality he preferred his own and his attendants' clothes well cut). He disposed of his dogs—he adored greyhounds—giving two of them to Marshal Pétain. He wrote his speech. Abandoning his mistresses and creditors and his rented home (whose contents, when he finally reclaimed them, made up eight truckloads), he turned his back on France as insouciantly as he had previously abandoned Italy and set off for Quarto to assume the glory of association with Garibaldi's great name.

Garibaldi had changed since the time of his death. Like Cato, who had died a human-size defender of tradition and political propriety only to rise again as a titanic advocate of liberty, so Garibaldi, in his grave, had both swelled and altered. The new nation of Italy had been energetic in generating its own foundation myth and that myth's hero was Garibaldi. In 1895 a colossal equestrian statue of him was erected on the Janiculum looking down, sorrowful and sublime, on the city he had failed to save. And as his image brooded in fact over Italy's capital, so the idea of him loomed enormous in Italians' imagination. The frustrations and trials of his later life had ensured the preservation of his reputed purity. Excluded from power, he had been exempted from guilt by association with a succession of increasingly corrupt and unpopular governments. He was Italy's creator, its patron saint, its conscience and its redeemer. His name was on street signs all over the peninsula. In Vienna in 1896 Sigmund Freud thought that his own father on his deathbed looked like Garibaldi. Afterwards he dreamed he saw his father alive again and leading a popular uprising and in his dream he was deeply gratified that his parent was showing himself worthy of his resemblance to such a marvelous man.

D'Annunzio had played his part in Garibaldi's posthumous inflation, composing a thousand-line poem recounting the adventure of the Thousand which he read aloud to a packed theater in 1901. The poem conjures up an image of Garibaldi as grand and marmoreal as Seneca's vision of Cato. He sits his white horse, his fair hair streaming, his white cloak billowing like the white wings of the Victory of Samothrace. On Caprera the wind howls around him, as once in Palermo the intoxicated population howled out their adoration of him, but neither the raging elements nor the storms of human emotion perturb him. He is silent and impassive, a "Lord of Fate" not to be cowed or elated by anything the world can show him.

D'Annunzio's younger English contemporary Alfred Noyes worshipfully described Francis Drake in similar terms as

> A Titan that had stood
> Thundering commands against the thundering heavens,
> On lightning-shattered, storm-swept decks, and quaffed
> Great draughts of glory from the untameable seas

These tremendous heroes riding out the tempests unmoved are recognizably descended from the stoic wise man, but they are descendants grown so colossal as to dwarf the rest of their race. In the millennium after the *Iliad* was first written down poets tried to account for Achilles' extraordinary prowess by making him monstrously large. Virgil called him the "huge Achilles." Quintus of Smyrna, writing in the fourth century AD, compared him to a Titan, and wrote of the vast bones, like those of a giant, lying in the ashes of his funeral pyre. So Noyes's Drake and D'Annunzio's Garibaldi had grown. They were not just great humans. They were supermen.

The superman had ancient antecedents, but in D'Annunzio's lifetime he was reborn from the head of Friedrich Nietzsche. The brilliant son of a Lutheran pastor, Nietzsche was elected to a prestigious professorship when only twenty-four and succumbed to madness twenty years later, having first produced a sequence of visionary texts which read more like prophetic books than philosophical treatises and which were to prove influential in ways more dreadful than even their author—whose lucid pessimism cost him his sanity—could ever have imagined. Twenty-five hundred years earlier Aristotle had imagined a godlike man so exceptional he would naturally, by right of his extraordinary gifts, transcend all moral judgment or constitutional control. Nietzsche went further. In 1883, the year after Garibaldi's death, he began writing *Thus Spake Zarathustra*, the work in which he prophesied the evolution of the superman, a being whose will and courage would be sufficient to transcend the "dirt and miserable ease" of mundane existence, who would be to humans as humans are to the apes, a hero compounded of lightning and madness, "to whom nothing is forbidden except weakness, whether that weakness be called vice or virtue."

Nietzsche poured contempt on the ideals of democracy and the cherishing of the greatest happiness of the greatest number. "Mankind in the mass sacrificed to the prosperity of a single stronger species of man—that would be an advance," he wrote. "I teach that there are higher and lower men, and that a single individual can under certain circumstances justify the existence of entire millennia." Such a "higher being" was worth a countless number of mere ordinary humans. The emergence of Napoleon seemed to him adequate compensation for the all the bloodshed attendant on the French Revolution (which he otherwise deplored). "For the sake of a similar prize one would have to desire the anarchic collapse of our entire civilisation."

To D'Annunzio—who unhesitatingly identified himself as one of Nietzsche's higher beings—these were entirely congenial ideas. Nietzsche's superman cared nothing for received opinion or conventional morality. One of the mottoes D'Annunzio had printed on his writing paper was "*Me ne frego*" (a obscene expression of indifference—*fregarsi* means to masturbate). He read Nietzsche in French translations during the 1890s and in his fiction thereafter he repeatedly describes a hero who is too exceptional to be constrained by any moral or legal code and too intent on realizing his own greatness to have any consideration for others.

Garibaldi was not the Christian saint he has sometimes been taken for, but he was not a Nietzschean superman either. At Quarto his name was used to lend credence to a cause with whose aims he would certainly have been sympathetic, but whose Nietzschean overtones might have repelled him. He was an avowed pacifist (admittedly rather incongruously, given that fighting had been most of his life's work). "It is a crime for men to be forced to butcher one another in order to come to an understanding," he wrote. Nietzsche celebrated "the desire to destroy, to change, to create something new . . . an exuberant force, pregnant with Future." That force was increasingly palpable in Italy's cultural and political life in the early years of the twentieth century. The most vocal of the younger generation were greedy for novelty, for violent transformation, for a holocaust. "So let them come, the gay incendiaries with charred fingers!" wrote Federico Marinetti, spokesman of the Futurists. The past was to be swept away, and if some gold was lost along with the dross—well, so be it. D'Annunzio, urging his countrymen to go to war, was bringing a message many of them were more than ready to hear. Marinetti called war "the world's only hygiene." As Nietzsche had declared, "One has renounced the *grand* life when one renounces war."

D'Annunzio was, by common consent even of those who detested him, a mesmerizing orator. His speech at Quarto was incoherent but intoxicating. He paid tribute to the heroism of the Thousand. He quoted Garibaldi's most famous line, "Here we make Italy, or we die." He spoke of the noble aspirations of Rome's ancient heroes. He flattered his audience and challenged them, daring them to be worthy of their great antecedents. He wrapped his provocative politics and his own perverse appetite for bloodshed in the gorgeous grandeur of liturgical rhythms. He was vatic, inspirational. His audience adored him and he adored their adoration. Crowds gathered outside his hotel in Genoa. His carefully prepared oration was rapidly followed by others, delivered extempore. The city was full of fervent nationalists who had assembled there in the hope of patriotic adventure and violent action and who were all calling upon D'Annunzio to give them a lead. Again and again he addressed them: in four days he spoke seven times.

A week later he moved on to Rome. Contemporary photographs show the streets and squares around the railway station packed solid with people who had turned out to welcome him. He narrowly escaped being trampled to death by his admirers before he was hustled to safety through a hotel kitchen. Repeatedly, over the next few days, he addressed the increasingly hysterical crowds. He spoke from his balcony. He interrupted a performance at the Constanzi Theatre to speak from the stage. He spoke on the Capitol.

D'Annunzio's rhetoric was profoundly subversive of both the new institutions of Italian democracy and the old aristocratic politics. "The command passes to the people," he announced, and he proclaimed himself, the "armed poet," the people's mouthpiece. His language was increasingly violent, his sentiments increasingly seditious. He attacked the government, still intent on appeasement, in vitriolic terms. They had betrayed their country. The very air of Rome stank of their treachery. Those who still hung back from war were traitors, assassins of the *patria*, Italy's executioners. He was openly challenging established authority: "If it is considered a crime to incite citizens to violence then I boast of committing that crime." He called upon the Roman mob to take the law into their own hands, urging them not just to reject their unworthy leaders but to hunt them down. "Proscribe them. Form squads. Lie in wait to take them, to capture them . . . Be pitiless. You have the right." An observer reports that the applause when he paused was like a storm. When he resumed, "the storm was transformed into a cyclone."

For days on end Rome was in a state of riot. Urged on by D'Annunzio the mob attempted to storm the parliament building. They attacked the prime minister's house using a fire engine as a tank. They rang all the church bells, by ancient tradition a general summons to arms in the case of grave emergency. Hundreds of people were arrested. D'Annunzio was beside himself, beyond himself. His notebooks describe the delirium, his own and the mob's: "There is nothing of myself left in me. I am like the demon of the tumult, I am like the genius of the free people . . . I am no longer intoxicated with myself alone, but with all my race." On May 13 the prime minister resigned, and eleven days later the new government declared war on Austria and Germany.

Among the rioters that month was the ex-soldier and journalist Benito Mussolini. Formerly the editor of the Socialist newspaper *Avanti!* Mussolini had been expelled from the Italian Socialist Party for calling on his country to enter the war. In his new paper, *Il Popolo d'Italia*, he inveighed furiously against "dead" neutralists and appeasers, urging his readers to shoot members of parliament in the back and recommending the ennobling and purifying effects of killing foreigners. A latter-day Clodius, he encouraged the formation of *fasci*, groups which, like Clodius's *collegia*, were ostensibly designed for the protection and benefit of the community but which were dedicated in fact to violence and to the aggrandizement of their leader. He welcomed D'Annunzio's intervention. A decade later he described the events of May 1915 as a "revolution" and boasted that in that glorious month the Italian people had risen up against their corrupt and lily-livered rulers, clamoring for the right to prove their honor and the collective heroism of their race.

In 1919, the war over, D'Annunzio led a volunteer army of deserters and mutineers on the Croatian port city of Fiume (now Rijeka) and in direct disobedience to Italy's elected rulers annexed it in the name of Italy, as Garibaldi had taken the Two Sicilies for Italy in defiance of Italy's king. He held it for over a year, thus drastically undermining the authority of the legitimate government. Meanwhile Mussolini's *fasci* were reducing the nation to a condition of lawlessness as desperate as that which had persuaded Cato that even Pompey's tyranny would be better than a prolongation of the chaos. Three years later Mussolini finished the political demolition job D'Annunzio had begun, bullying the demoralized and discredited government into offering him the prime ministership.

Dandy-poet and demagogue alike invoked the irreproachable and inspirational name of Garibaldi as patron of their attacks on the nation-state he had created. Garibaldi had appeared in Europe in 1848 in the character Mazzini had assigned to him of a latter-day paladin, an anti-Christian crusader, emissary from an simpler and grander era, his long hair streaming, his principles unsullied by contemporary reality. Two generations later the two showmen—D'Annunzio and Mussolini were both consummate performance artists—vying for leadership of Italy's disaffected majority each attempted to claim his antique grandeur for themselves. Both of them adopted his oratorical style—the chanted questions and responses which transformed a political rally into a liturgy. Each of them designed a salute derived from the one-fingered "Garibaldi sign." Both of them repeatedly referred to him, appropriating his glory to their own causes. In 1862 Garibaldi called for the formation of armed bands of citizen enforcers modeled on the *fasci* of ancient Rome: Mussolini adopted both the concept and the name. In 1915, at the climax of one of his speeches on the Capitol, D'Annunzio dramatically produced the sword of Garibaldi's comrade Nino Bixio and kissed it as he swore to continue the fight Garibaldi had begun. Again and again he invoked Garibaldi's Thousand, who had "set out, drunk on the beauty of Death, for Palermo." He flattered the crowds with Garibaldi's famous words "Soldiers of Italian liberty, with companions like you I can attempt anything." Four years later, as he set off on his march for Fiume—the demoralized Italian army giving way before him or turning to follow behind him much as the Neapolitan army had melted before Garibaldi's advance through Calabria—he proclaimed exultantly that the sunrise was suffusing the sky with Garibaldian red.

Garibaldi was not much of a democrat. He talked a lot about "the people," but he also said, "Liberty itself must sometimes be forced on the people for their future good." In Rio Grande do Sul, as his own account makes plain, he was fighting to impose independence on a populace who would manifestly have preferred to be left in peace. In 1849 he got himself elected to the Roman Assembly by finagling: he was voted in by his Garibaldini, few of whom were Roman citizens. In 1860, when a referendum was being held in Nice over the city's proposed annexation to France, he conceived a plan of sailing into the harbor, raiding the polling stations, and destroying the ballot boxes. A year later, after his attack on Cavour in the Piedmontese parliament, a former comrade wrote him an open letter: "You are not the man I thought you were, you are not the Garibaldi I loved . . . You place yourself above Parliament, heaping with vituperation the Deputies who do not think as you do; above the country, desiring to drive it where and how it suits you best." There is truth in the charges.

He was by nature an autocrat. His followers called him "*il Duce*," a title Mussolini was to borrow from him. When established governments failed to satisfy him he acted against or outside them. When his redshirts first appeared on the European scene they seemed as quaintly colorful as a consort of ancient warriors or a fraternity of medieval knights. With hindsight they look less like throwbacks to a picturesque past, more like presages of an ugly future. Garibaldi meant well. He was as high-minded and disinterested as Cato, of whom Dio Cassius had written that he was the only one of his contemporaries who "took part in public life from pure motives and free from any desire of personal gain." He was selfless, devoted, altruistic. When he sought power or raised irregular armed forces it was only so he could more effectively serve his cause. Yet a clearly visible line of descent connects him—his Million Rifles Fund; his illegal Armed Nation, which he called "the dream of my life"; his Rifle Clubs— with despotism and murderous brutality.

In 1922 Mussolini came to power after a mass demonstration which he himself grandiosely dubbed the "March on Rome." He was fascinated by past great men (he wrote a play about Napoleon which was staged in London in 1932) and he liked to borrow their personae. Marching on Rome he was following the lead of Julius Caesar (whom he thought "the greatest man who ever lived"), and simultaneously laying claim to the glamour of a second Garibaldi, in imitation of whom he was to assume the archaic title of dictator. A man with an acute understanding of the paramount importance of presentation in gaining and keeping political ascendancy, Mussolini noted: "Words have their own tremendous magic power" and "Only the myth can give strength and energy to a people about to hammer out its own destiny." When his moment of destiny came, he chose to model himself on Italy's favorite hero. Garibaldi arrived by rail in Naples, way in advance of his army, to conquer a kingdom by the power of his personality. So Mussolini took the train to Rome a day ahead of the Fascists who were trailing in from all over Italy, his blackshirts tagging along behind their glorious leader as Garibaldi's redshirts had followed theirs.

A hero is helpless to choose in which causes his charisma will be employed once he is dead and gone. Rebecca West, an outspoken opponent of Fascism in all its forms, once wrote: "The men who excite adoration, who are what is called natural leaders (which means that people feel an unnatural readiness to follow them) are usually empty. Human beings need hollow containers in which they can place their fantasies and admire them, just as they need flower vases if they are to decorate their homes with flowers." Neither Garibaldi nor any of the other heroes whose stories have been told in this book were actually hollow vessels, but all of them were to be used during the first half of the twentieth century as showcases for the display of others' fantasies.

In Alfred Noyes's epic Francis Drake addresses his crew in nationalist terms which would have seemed bizarre to an Elizabethan; like modern sports players they are understood to represent their country.

> The world's wide eyes are on us, and our souls
> Are woven together into one great flag
> Of England

Noyes's Drake is intent on planting that flag all over the globe. In California he has a vision of his country as she will one day be:

> A Power before the lightning of whose arms
> Darkness should die, and all oppression cease

It's a vision which closely echoes the prophecy Virgil has Aeneas's father, Anchises, make for Rome. Virgil gave solemn validation to his master Augustus's imperial ambitions by invoking a figure of the legendary past. So Britons of the imperial age lent themselves extra luster by remodeling Francis Drake into a figure they could admire—one patriotic and dutybound like the *pius* Aeneas, swayed by no personal emotion but love of his country—and crediting him with having foreseen and helped to found their empire. In his lifetime grandees of the ruling class had looked down on the vulgar pirate their queen so irritatingly favored, but in 1933 Winston Churchill was at pains to point out in his biography of his ancestor, the first Duke of Marlborough, that the latter was distantly related to Drake (and so, therefore, was Churchill himself).

While Drake became a British imperialist, Rodrigo Díaz became a Spanish one. Immediately after his death his lifeless corpse was led on horseback back to Castile, there to add to the splendor of the monarchy which had rejected him and the prestige of the religion to which he may or may not have subscribed. The unassailable warlord who was twice outcast from Castile became the emblematic hero of a state which did not come into existence for some four hundred years after his death. One of the Cid's daughters had married the king of Aragon: through her the first monarchs of a unified Spain were able to claim the Cid as their ancestor.

The Emperor Charles V ordered that his remains should be removed from Cardeña to the more illustrious site of Burgos cathedral and reinterred in a tomb appropriate to "the fame, nobility and deeds of the Cid, from whose valour honour redounds to all Spain."

That tomb took on the significance, menacing or consoling depending on one's viewpoint, of the only-temporary resting place of one who (ever "ware and waking" like Drake) might rise again. As the centuries went by the Cid's historical reality was called into question. Miguel de Cervantes thought that although "it is not to be doubted that such men as the Cid existed, yet we have reason to question whether they ever performed those great deeds ascribed to them." When Napoleon's troops used his tomb for target practice in deliberate desecration of a shrine of Spanish nationalism, their general, anxious about the probable damage to relations with the local populace, offered to make amends, only to be reassured by a Spanish historian that there was no cause for concern: the Cid was a mythical figure and the tomb was empty. But, occupied or not, the Cid's tomb was the repository of Spain's military pride and its will to conquest and domination. In 1898, after Spain's defeat by the United States and the loss of its American empire, when the liberal Joaquin Costa called upon all Spaniards to accept their country's reduced status pacifically, he employed its image. "Let us lock the tomb of the Cid with seven keys." In the next generation Francisco Franco was to employ it again in reverse. It was the great fear of cowards and mediocrities, he said, "that el Cid might arise from his tomb and be incarnated in the new generation." That fear had been realized, for Franco was—or claimed to be—the spirit of the Cid once more made flesh.

In 1936, when Franco and his fellow Falangists launched their rebellion against the elected government of the socialist Popular Front they could be sure of support in the Cid's birth and burial place, Burgos, where as one citizen proudly declared, "The very stones are nationalist." A journal named *Mio Cid* was launched there. Its first editorial, urging the people to support Franco, called for the "Raising of the standard of the Cid throughout Spain." Franco understood as well as Mussolini did the importance of propaganda and presentation. Throughout the civil war ballads emanating from his public relations office circulated, coupling his name with that of the never-defeated Rodrigo Díaz, while his publicists ensured that he was everywhere hailed by his supporters as the "Cid of the 20th century." The tomb, it seemed, had opened. The hero was once more among his people.

In 1939 Franco made his triumphal entry into Madrid, after first issuing a press release declaring the occasion would "follow the ritual observed when Alfonso VI, accompanied by the Cid, captured Toledo in the Middle Ages." (When Alfonso took Toledo, Rodrigo was actually still in exile, serving the kings of Zaragoza.) Franco's victory parade lasted five hours and extended over a sixteen-mile processional route illuminated by towering bonfires. Two hundred thousand troops, some carrying huge crucifixes, marched past the general. The climactic moment came when Franco proceeded to the cathedral of Santa Barbara and solemnly laid his sword on the high altar "following in the tradition of the Cid Campeador after the liberation of Toledo." That there was no such tradition was unimportant. The substantial fact was that the general had identified himself as the new incarnation of the qualities which for him the Cid epitomized, "all the mystery of the great Spanish epics: service in noble undertakings: duty as norm; struggle in the service of the true God."

A ruler with unprecedented and unconstitutional powers needs a title with illustrious precedents to lend the authority he has grabbed the semblance of legitimacy. Mussolini appropriated Garibaldi's epithet "*il Duce.*" Franco dubbed himself "*Caudillo,*" a title he borrowed from the medieval kings of Asturias. A primary-school textbook authorized for use under his regime explained that "a *Caudillo* is a gift that God makes to nations that deserve it . . . an envoy who has arisen through God's plan to ensure the nation's salvation."

Alcibiades attempted to persuade the Athenian Assembly that all Athenians should feel themselves magnified and empowered by his personal glory; similarly, it was a tenet of twentieth-century Fascism and its allied political creeds that a great man's greatness is something for which his followers should feel reverently thankful, and which makes them great by association. "Honour comes to all through him / Who in a happy hour was born," wrote the author of the *Poema de Mío Cid*, a line which Ramón Menéndez Pidal—the nationalist historian whose tremendously influential book *La España del Cid* was first published in 1929 and was required reading in military training colleges throughout Franco's ascendancy—took to express the "mystic union of the hero with his Spain." In acquiescing in such a man's assumption of almost unlimited power, an entire people can participate in his splendid destiny. One of Franco's associates told the Cortés, "God granted us the immense mercy of an exceptional *Caudillo* as one of those gifts which, for some really great purpose, Providence makes to nations every three or four centuries." As Hegel had written, great men's "aims embody the will of the world spirit." The very existence of such a man puts his followers beyond criticism. They are divinely privileged, and uniquely licensed. His appearance among them is the manifestation of God's blessing upon them, and proof that their actions, however deplorable, are means towards a manifest destiny, a "really great purpose."

In Germany, too, a new superman was borrowing the persona of a past one. In Wallenstein's lifetime there had been prophecies abroad about a great Teutonic hero who would enforce peace and unify all Europe under a German emperor. "And in the hour of Mars," proclaimed Simplicissimus, "Vulcan shall forge him a sword, with which he will subdue the whole world." At the zenith of his success Wallenstein had envisioned the empire transformed. All power would be centralized, all petty princelings terrorized into docility and vast new territories annexed. Secure within its enormously extended borders, the once ramshackle Holy Roman Empire would have metamorphosed, had he been allowed to realize his vision, into a new and far more awe-inspiring institution, a brand-new Reich.

Friedrich Schiller's *Wallenstein* trilogy was first performed in 1800, a year after Napoleon Bonaparte seized power as France's first consul: several critics understood it to be a veiled allusion to this latter-day generalissimo with imperial aspirations. During the First World War Alfred Döblin wrote an epic in which Wallenstein is a modern industrialist and speculator, "a wild marauder who makes a profit from inflation," but he was also accorded a more august character. In 1918 Oswald Spengler saluted him as the personification of the "emperor-idea." There was no emperor anymore, but that idea persisted. "Germany's search for a leader is a part of history," wrote an English biographer of Wallenstein in 1938, "and it is natural that now more than ever she should turn back to the lonely figure of Wallenstein, probing his plans, exalting the *Führerprinzip* which he may be thought to represent, investing his vast ambitions with a mysticism." The new *Führer* agreed. "We Germans should learn by Wallenstein's example," Adolf Hitler told his aides.

The British historian C. V. Wedgwood, whose classic account of the Thirty Years' War was published in 1938 and is full of echoes of the time in which it was written, noted that "Wallenstein, first perhaps among European rulers, had conceived of a state organised exclusively for war." Now he had an emulator. Wallenstein had started a school for gentlemen's sons, training his own future followers in his own way; Hitler had his Hitler Youth. Wallenstein had made of his country estates a vast factory for the provisioning of his armies; Hitler transformed all Germany into a "*Wehrwirtschaft*," an economy organized expressly for the support of his war machine. Wallenstein had told the emperor that although a moderate-size army would be a financial liability an enormous one would feed itself; Hitler, expansive and expansionist, declared his intention to follow Wallenstein's lead—"Like him we Germans must learn to free ourselves of half-measures, and set our course towards greatness."

"Among men I hate most of all soft-walkers and half-and-halfers," wrote Nietzsche. It is heroic to despise half measures, to be absolute in one's pursuit of greatness, or racial purity, or world domination, or whatever one's aim may be. It is also, if human society is to survive, impermissible. Shakespeare's Ulysses eloquently denounces Achilles' heroic insubordination. It has untuned the string of "degree" and so made a cacophony where there should be the harmony of a group organized for the benefit of all. In refusing to take his place in the orderly structure of his community the hero has ruptured the delicate bonds of duty and responsibility which link one individual to another and opened the way to a Nietzschean chaos where

> Everything includes itself in power,
> Power into will, will into appetite,
> And appetite, an universal wolf,
> So doubly seconded with will and power,
> Must makes perforce an universal prey
> And last eat up himself.

Sophocles' Antigone chose death, and we are moved by her nobility. But Ismene, in choosing life, took the harder option. The European dictators of the 1930s chose death and set their course towards greatness. Their understanding of the latter concept was crude—all three of those I have mentioned equated it more or less exactly with grandiosity—but their pursuit of it was recognizably heroic. Carlyle's *On Heroes* was required reading for German students under the Nazi regime. "Better to live one day as a lion than a hundred years as a sheep," declared Mussolini, endorsing Achilles' dreadful choice and echoing Addison's Cato, whose first words are "A day, an hour, of virtuous liberty, is worth a whole eternity in bondage." They were as inflexible as Cato, as solipsistic as Alcibiades, as violent and furious as the splendid Achilles, as lawless as Drake. Britons had laundered Drake's image to make an acceptable national hero of him, but abroad he was still the criminal adventurer who, at Port San Julian, had abolished all legitimate authority and made himself a despot ruling what one of his mariners called a "society without class or law." Mussolini had the highest regard for him. On meeting

Neville Chamberlain he was greatly disappointed to find the British prime minister so unlike "Francis Drake and the other magnificent adventurers who created their Empire." In 1938 an editorial writer in the London *Daily Mail* paid him a compliment which he must have found particularly pleasing: "Mussolini is an Elizabethan. He stands to modern Italy as Raleigh and Drake did to England in Elizabeth's day."

In 1846 Carlyle and Mazzini spent an evening together in London. Carlyle, who set such store by taciturnity, was himself notoriously garrulous. That night his talk "was a defence of mere force, success the test of right. If people would not behave well, put collars round their necks. Find a hero and let them be his slaves. It was very Titanic and Anticelestial." Mazzini, listening, "became very sad." Carlyle is not to be blamed for the political uses to which his valorization of hero worship was to be put, any more than Nietzsche—who disliked Germans and especially disliked German anti-Semitism—can be blamed for the fact that the Nazis approved of him. (It has been plausibly suggested that Hitler never actually read further than the title page of any of Nietzsche's books.) But that there is a link between hero worship and the kind of political abjection which opens the way to authoritarianism is evident. Even Emerson, who wrote, "Life is sweet and tolerable only in our belief in great men," who urged his readers to "serve the great. Stick at no humiliation. Grudge no office thou canst render. Be the limb of their body, the breath of their mouths," acknowledged that a hero can be "a monopoliser and usurper of other minds," that his worshipers are "intellectual suicides." Simone Weil, reading Homer in the 1930s, saw the *Iliad* through the prism of contemporary events as "the poem of force" and recognized a connection between Achilles (the paramount wielder of the heroic power which gives the strong liberty by annulling the rights of the weak) and the strong rulers then intent on purging their nations of "decadent" weakness. "With every growth of man in greatness and height there is also a growth in depth and dreadfulness," wrote Nietzsche. "The hero is an affliction and a terror."

There are two Homeric epics, two models of heroism. Odysseus is a warrior like Achilles but there are fundamental differences between the two of them. Achilles values prizes only for the honor they represent, but Odysseus wants to get rich: he is a looter and pillager like the Cid, an unprovoked raider of peaceful settlements like Drake, who boasts that he has "been to Hell and back for plunder." Achilles is a truth teller. He says he hates the man "who says one thing but hides another in his heart" as he hates the Gates of Death, and he means it. Odysseus says the same thing in almost identical words but even as he says it we know that he is lying. He is a trickster, a shape-shifter, a compulsive fabulist. He is not morally better than Achilles—quite the reverse—but he is more humane. Achilles is an avatar of Thanatos. Odysseus serves Eros. Achilles stands superbly alone; Odysseus defines himself within his community and longs to be a part of it once more. At the opening of the *Odyssey* he is living at ease on a beautiful island, cherished by a loving nymph. He has everything a man could wish for, except that he is isolated. He lacks relationships. He lacks responsibilities. He longs to be husband, father, son, and householder again. He is tired of being a hero, a godlike beast: he wants to be human. His story leads not, like Achilles', to a splendid tomb but to his wife's bed.

After Achilles' death the war for Troy ground grimly on until Odysseus heard of a prophecy that the city would not fall until the Greeks recovered the miracle-working bow of Heracles. Heracles had given the bow to Philoctetes, a warrior who had been bitten by a snake years before and then abandoned on a desolate rock of an island because his shipmates could stand neither his ceaseless cries of agony nor the disgusting smell emanating from his incurable wound. Sophocles continues the story. Knowing that while Philoctetes has the bow he cannot be overpowered by force and that he will never voluntarily surrender it to those who so cruelly abandoned him, Odysseus goes to the island, taking with him Achilles' son Neoptolemus, whom Philoctetes has never seen. Once there he explains to the boy that he must conceal his true identity and trick the wounded man into handing over the bow. True son to his father, Neoptolemus is appalled. He asks, "Don't you believe it wrong to tell a lie, sir?" "No," replies the devious Odysseus, "if success and safety depend upon it," and he justifies himself with the simple declaration "I am what I need to be." Neoptolemus must choose between the way of Achilles, the way of violence and honor, and the Odyssean way of guile and expediency. He vacillates, recoiling from both, and eventually he is spared his impossible decision when Heracles descends from Olympus to resolve the problem. The conclusion Neoptolemus draws from the experience is one in which both the deathly honor of Achilles and the evasiveness of Odysseus are implicitly rejected. "Each one of us must live the life God gives him; it cannot be shirked."

To do so is not easy. The song the sirens sing is about "the pains that

Achaeans and Trojans once endured / On the spreading plain of Troy."
The temptation they offer is that of evading the hard work of becoming
once more a member of civilian society and dwelling forever among the
grand simplicities of warfare. It is almost irresistible. Few Homeric
heroes make it home. Even for those who escape shipwreck the moment
of reentry to civilian life is as perilous and traumatic as anything they have
faced in battle. Agamemnon survives ten years of war and returns with his
spoils and trophies only to be slaughtered, naked and defenseless in his
bath, by his own wife. For Odysseus, Ithaca, his longed-for home, is
infested with enemies: before he can reclaim his place in it he has to
drench its floors with their blood.

Nietzsche advocated living dangerously. He exhorted his readers to
"build on the slopes of Vesuvius," to be "robbers and ravagers," to seek
out conflict in order to experience grandeur. But excited as he was by risk
and the proximity of death he also wanted desperately to love life, and it
seemed to him (troubled, lonely man that he was) that to do so would be
the most heroic achievement conceivable. A generation earlier Charles
Baudelaire enthused about the peculiar glamour of military men—"a singular mixture of serenity and audacity; a beauty arising from the need to
be prepared to die at any moment"—but to Nietzsche it was a prepared-
ness to live that seemed truly courageous, truly sublime.

Like Achilles, like everyone perhaps, Nietzsche craved immortality.
He proclaimed the death of God. He exposed the consoling vision of an
afterlife as an illusion. He insisted repeatedly and vehemently that the
finite span of consciousness that is corporeal life is all that we can look for.
All the same, he elaborated a theory which held out a promise of life everlasting. He called it "eternal recurrence": "Now I die and decay . . . and in
an instant I shall be nothingness. Souls are as mortal as bodies. But the
complex of causes in which I am entangled will recur—it will create me
again! . . . I shall return, with this sun, with this earth . . . not to a new life
or a better life or a similar life: I shall return eternally to this identical and
self-same life."

He never made explicit how this "return" would be effected. But he
was clear as to how it should be welcomed. To the inferior majority, he
assumed, the prospect of living the same life over and over again would be
as appalling as it apparently was to him. But "higher men" would embrace
it with joy. "Joy wants itself, wants eternity, wants recurrence, wants
everything eternally the same." The superman, the hero, is hungry for all
experience, however dreadful. He "wants honey, wants dregs, wants
intoxicated midnights, wants graves. . . . So rich is joy that it thirsts for

woe . . . for the world." He is capable of an unreserved and absolute acceptance of the human lot, not a soft-hearted love of life because it is lovable but a grand and steely readiness to love it even though it is not. "Did you ever say Yes to one joy? O my friends, then you said Yes to *all* woe as well. All things are chained and entwined together, all things are in love." Nietzschean heroism is not a matter of sacrifice and denial and stoic self-repression; it is the ecstatic fortitude of unconditional affirmation, the heroism not of an Achilles who surrenders life, but of an Odysseus who goes to the ends of the earth to get it back.

Nearly four decades after Nietzsche's Zarathustra had spoken, James Joyce sent his latter-day Odysseus strolling through Dublin. There was a war on: Joyce was writing the first fragment of *Ulysses* while D'Annunzio was speaking at Quarto. The novel's first publication, in serial form, began in 1918. While Joyce was writing, Europe was convulsed and the spirit of Achilles—tragic, ferocious, and brilliant—was abroad. Patrick Shaw Stewart, killed in action in Flanders in 1916, wrote shortly before his death a poem that was also a prayer: "Stand in the trench, Achilles, / Flame capped, and shout for me."

It is customary now to look back on the First World War with horror, to remember the landscape transformed into a sea of mud deep enough to drown in, the rats, the wounded hanging screaming on tangles of barbed wire, the blunders of the generals, the appalling numbers of young men dead. But for some of the combatants that atrocious war afforded, however briefly, the same kind of elation as that with which the young Spartan warriors had gone into battle singing, the same the poet had ascribed to the Cid and that Garibaldi had found under the French barrage on the walls of Rome. "It is all the most *wonderful* fun: better fun than one could ever imagine," wrote the aristocratic young Englishman Julian Grenfell in a letter from the front. "The fighting-excitement vitalises everything, every sight and word and action." For all the squalor and pain and stupid slaughter men of a certain temperament found themselves enraptured. Soldiers, wrote the Hungarian Aladar Schöpflin in 1914, "are going into the totality of life." The painter Max Beckman wrote after a month at the front, "I have in this short time lived more than I have done for years." Fear was intoxicating and the omnipresent danger of its extinction gave a brilliant intensity to consciousness. "Living through war is living deep," wrote the British novelist Ernest Raymond. "It's crowded, glorious living. If I'd never had a shell rush at me I'd never have known the swift thrill of approaching death." This was the conflict over which Nietzsche—in his more familiar, death-besotted mood—had rhapsodized, the ennobling violence which could transform a dull civilian into a superman. "The war of 1914," declared the German sociologist Werner Sombart in 1915, "is the war of Nietzsche." "Nietzsche is our Bible," confirmed Rupert Brooke.

While these ecstatic warriors, Achilles' heirs, fought and—most of them—died in fact, in Joyce's fiction a new Odysseus, Leopold Bloom, cuckold and advertising salesman, moved his bowels, fried his breakfast-time kidney, and went about his day's business in a world as yet undisturbed by the conflict through which his creator was living (Joyce set his novel in 1904). "I am a part of all that I have met," announces Ulysses in Tennyson's 1833 poem. It was Joyce's artistic mission to make his hero equally comprehensive, to acknowledge and affirm every aspect of subjectivity, to include the obscene and the trivial along with the grand, the fleeting impression along with the positive action, to exclude or deny nothing, to "drink life to the lees," as Tennyson had made Ulysses boast that he had done, "for always roaming with a hungry heart." Joyce knew his Nietzsche. His last great novel, which takes its title from the rhyme "Poor old Michael Finnegan begin again," is a structure all made of repeated and interlocking cycles of downfalls and resurrections, of leave-takings and homecomings, of eternal recurrence. And *Ulysses*, too, like Homer's *Odyssey*, is the story of one who finds that in his end is his beginning, that the greatest adventure is the one that takes him at last to the very place from which he came.

Joyce's Odysseus/Ulysses/Bloom comes stumbling home drunk at three in the morning to pass out lying diagonally across the marital bed, snoring while his wife Molly—carnal, self-indulgent, a wholehearted embracer of what the world has to offer—delivers herself of the soliloquy in which Joyce admits his readers to every part of her imaginary consciousness and in which she surveys her life, past, present, and to come, arriving at last at a kind of rapture of affirmation: "yes and then he asked me would I yes to say yes my mountain flower and first I put my arms around him yes . . . and his heart was going like mad and yes I said yes I will Yes." So Homer's Odysseus comes home at last, to lie with Penelope in a great bed made from a living tree. He is once more, quite literally, rooted. He has resisted the siren song of martial glory and won his way back to his place in a social world where there are women as well as men, swineherds as well as soldiers, old people and children as well as warriors ready for sacrifice, where living is valued as highly as dying. He has proved himself, like Molly Bloom, a Nietzschean yes-sayer, a superman, a person heroic enough not to die but to live.

AUTHOR'S NOTE

In researching this book I have drawn entirely on published sources. It follows that I owe enormous debts to the editors and translators who have made those sources available and to the writers who have interpreted them before me. Many of those writers have been dead for hundreds, in some cases thousands, of years but a number of them are still alive and I am profoundly grateful to them.

Interested readers will find details of the books on which I have drawn in the Bibliography and References, but there are certain authors to whom I owe especial thanks:

For Achilles—Robert Fagles for his superb translations and Bernard Knox for his illuminating critical essays: my reading of Homer has been greatly influenced by his.

For the Cid—I would have been lost without Richard Fletcher's magisterial book, from which I have drawn far more than simple references can indicate.

For Drake—John Hampden's collection of contemporary documents has been invaluable. I have also made extensive use of the biographies by John Sugden, John Cummins, and Harry Kelsey and two excellent books on the Armada, one by Felipe Fernández-Armesto, the other by Colin Martin and Geoffrey Parker.

For Wallenstein—I have depended at every turn on Golo Mann's encyclopedic and evocative biography. I am also indebted to Geoffrey Parker's narrative of the war.

For Garibaldi—I have made copious use of two admirable biographies, by Jasper Ridley and Christopher Hibbert. The former is more comprehensive, the latter more colorful: my debt to each of them is immense.

In spelling proper names I have chosen, in each case, the variant which I believe to be most familiar to Anglophone readers. To those irritated by the numerous anachronisms and inconsistencies into which that policy has led me I offer my apologies.

REFERENCES

PROLOGUE

4 "the only person living":
Thucydides, *History of the
Peloponnesian War*, translated by Rex
Warner (Harmondsworth, 1972),
8.53.

4 "born in a lucky hour":
Anonymous, *The Poem of the Cid*,
translated by W. S. Merwin (1959),
p. 70.

4 an unhappy land: Bertolt Brecht,
The Life of Galileo, translated by
Desmond Vesey (London, 1960),
scene 13.

4 "The Argonauts left": Aristotle,
Politics, translated by T. A. Sinclair,
revised by Trevor J. Saunders
(Harmondsworth, 1986), III, xiii.

4 "divine stupidity": Christopher
Hibbert, *Garibaldi and His Enemies*
(Harmondsworth, 1966), p. 340.

5 "heartfelt prostrate admiration":
Thomas Carlyle, *On Heroes, Hero-
Worship, and the Heroic in History*,
introduction by Michael Goldberg
(Oxford, 1993), p. 11.

5 "Beware of the pursuit": George
Bernard Shaw, *Man and Superman*
(Harmondsworth, 2000), p. 171.

5 "Life is sweet": Ralph Waldo
Emerson, *English Traits,
Representative Men and Other Essays*
(London, 1908), p. 169.

5 "indemnification for

populations . . .": Emerson, pp. 169
and 157.

6 "no name comes down": Charles
Sprawson, "Et in Arcadia: A
Defence of Sparta," in *The London
Magazine*, October 1987, p. 45.

6 "Alcibiades, leaning": Plutarch,
Makers of Rome, translated by Ian
Scott-Kilvert (Harmondsworth,
1965), p. 10.

6 "There is no law": Aristotle, III, xiii.

7 "This people has no cities":
Herodotus, IV, 46, 298.

7 "a non-co-operator": Aristotle, I, ii.

7 "a fearful tyranny": R. J.
Hollingdale, *Nietzsche* (London,
1973), p. 118.

7 "like a star . . .": Friedrich
Nietzsche, *Thus Spoke Zarathustra*,
translated and with an introduction
by R. J. Hollingdale
(Harmondsworth, 1969), p. 89.

8 "a hero of antiquity": Jasper Ridley,
Garibaldi (London, 1974), p. 324.

9 "It is the finery": Colin Martin and
Geoffrey Parker, *The Spanish
Armada* (London, 1988), p. 33.

11 "Go tell the people": Lytton
Strachey, *Eminent Victorians*
(Harmondsworth, 1975), p. 305.

11 "defeat in battle": quoted in
Sprawson, p. 39.

11 "What is he": William Shakespeare,
Troilus and Cressida, 2.3.144–145.

11 "thou picture of what": Ibid., 5.1.6

12 "his usual sickness": Christian Meier, *Caesar,* translated by David McLintock (London, 1996), pp. 326 and 423.

13 "Madam . . . the wings": Geoffrey Madan, *Notebooks* (Oxford, 1984).

13 "You chose life": quoted in Bernard Knox, *The Heroic Temper* (Cambridge, 1964), p. 34.

13 "Many men": Sallust, *The War with Catiline,* translated by J. C. Rolfe (London, 1965), ch. 2.

13 "They shall not": Laurence Binyon, *For the Fallen (1914–1918).*

13 "Being dead . . .": quoted in Peter Parker, *The Old Lie* (London, 1987), p. 217.

ACHILLES

15 Yes, says the beast: Homer, *The Iliad,* translated by Robert Fagles, introduction by Bernard Knox (London, 1990), 19.483–498.

16 "dank moldering horrors": Ibid., 20.78–79.

16 "Like the generations": Ibid., 6.171.

17 "Let that man": Ibid., 1.164.

18 "so you can learn": Ibid., 1.219.

18 "because he rules": Ibid., 1.329.

18 "hands like Ares'": Katherine Callen King, *Achilles: Paradigms of the War Hero from Homer to the Middle Ages* (Berkeley and London, 1987), p. 64.

18 "You are nothing": *Iliad,* 1.213.

19 "the same honour": Ibid., 9.386.

20 "I say my honour": Ibid., 9.741.

20 "the famous deeds": Ibid., 9.228.

20 "hungry as wolves": Ibid., 16.187.

20 "sudden, plunging death": Ibid., 16.333.

21 "Twelve of their finest": Ibid., 18.265.

21 "The man who is incapable": Aristotle, I, ii, 1253.

21 figure from a nightmare: *Iliad,* 20.554–569.

22 "form a wall": Ibid., 21.674.

22 "the bloody grind": Ibid., I.210.

22 "whose purpose is": Sigmund Freud, "Civilisation and Its Discontents," in *Civilisation, Society, and Religion,* translated by James Strachey (Harmondsworth, 1987), p. 313.

23 "Come friend": *Iliad,* 21.119–126.

23 "The salt grey sunless ocean": Ibid., 16.39.

23 "Don't talk to me": Ibid., 22.309–310.

23 "that hindrance": Tacitus, *The Annals of Imperial Rome,* translated by Michael Grant (Harmondsworth, 1996), p. 369.

23 "Die, die!": *Iliad,* 22.429.

24 "You are the best": Ibid., 23.988.

25 "cut the knot": Ibid., 18.585.

25 "disease of mean-spirited": Plato, *The Republic,* translated by Robin Waterfield (Oxford, 1993), p. 391.

25 "To be seen of all": Sallust, ch. 7.

25 "Any man will accept": *Iliad,* 9.772.

26 Curtius: St. Augustine, *The City of God,* V.xviii.

27 "You'd think me": Ibid., 21.527.

27 "winging down": Ibid., 16.1003 and 22.427.

27 "a man's life's breath": Ibid., 9.495–497.

27 "Oh my captains": Ibid., 11.975.

28 "The dogs before my doors": Ibid., 22.77–89.

28 "There is nothing": *Iliad,* 17.515.

28 "You can all turn": Ibid., 7.113.

28 "Ah my friend": Ibid., 12.374–381.

29 "like some boy": Ibid., 21.319–369.

29 "windy praise": Augustine, 5.8.

29 "Even in death": Homer, *The Odyssey*, translated by Robert Fagles, introduction by Bernard Knox (London, 1996), 24.101.

30 "journey-book": Robin Lane-Fox, *Alexander the Great* (Harmondsworth, 1986), p. 59.

30 "For that lyre": Ibid., p. 113.

30 "You are mistaken": Plato, *The Last Days of Socrates*, translated by Hugh Tredinnick and Harold Tarrant (Harmondsworth, 1993), p. 51.

31 "I am not going": Ibid., p. 53.

31 " 'Let me die' ": Ibid., p. 51.

31 "Nothing can harm": Ibid., p. 67.

32 "Become who you are!": Hollingdale, p. 96

ALCIBIADES

33 "That night": Xenophon, *A History of My Times*, translated by Rex Warner (Harmondsworth, 1979), 2.2.3.

33 "began to show": Ibid., 2.3.15.

33 "in the midst": Plutarch, *The Rise and Fall of Athens*, translated by Ian Scott-Kilvert (Harmondsworth, 1960), "Alcibiades," ch. 38.

34 "The people thought": Nepos, *Alcibiades*, ch. 7.

34 "noble lie": Plato, *Republic*, 414b.

34 "No one ever": Nepos, *Alcibiades*, ch. 1.

34 the fertile soil: Plutarch, *The Rise and Fall of Athens*, "Nicias," ch. 9.

35 "The splendour": Quoted in Donald Kagan, *The Fall of the*
Athenian Empire (Ithaca, N.Y., and London, 1987), p. 107.

36 "we need say": Plutarch, "Alcibiades," ch. 1.

36 "surrounded and pursued": Ibid., ch. 4.

36 "heroic choice": Plato, *Symposium*, p. 44.

36 two great loves . . . : Plato, *Gorgias*.

36 "was such that": Plutarch, op. cit., ch. 24.

37 "some of the athletes": Isocrates, *De Bigis*, 32.

37 "You appear to me": Plato, "Alcibiades," I, 4.

38 "Love of distinction": Plutarch, op. cit., ch. 6.

38 "but yet, so soon": Nepos, *Alcibiades*, 1.

38 "I am really quite scared": Plato, *Symposium*, p. 97.

39 "and not a soul": Plutarch, op. cit., ch. 8.

39 "You are doing well": Plutarch, op. cit., ch. 16.

39 "No sooner": Plutarch, "Nicias," ch. 9.

40 "His enthusiasm": Thucydides, bk. 6, ch. 15.

40 "beware of [Alcibiades]": Ibid., 6.12.

40 who urged Pericles: Diodorus Siculus, 12.38.

41 "in time of war": Ibid., 12.39.

41 "The fact was": Plutarch, "Alcibiades," ch. 16.

41 "with the highest hopes": Nepos, op. cit., 3.

42 "Victory shines": Euripides, *Odes*.

42 "The people of": Plutarch, op. cit., ch. 12.

42 "as if they were": Andocides, *Against Alcibiades*, 29.

42 "There was a time": Thucydides, 6.16.

42 "This much is clear": Aristotle, p. 69.

43 "thought it a sight": Plutarch, op. cit., ch. 16.

43 "Men of sense": Andocides, op. cit., 24.

43 "dazzled the imagination": Plutarch, "Nicias," ch. 12.

43 "My view is": Thucydides, 6.18.

44 "by a long way": Ibid., 6.31.

44 "its astonishing daring": Ibid.

45 "Neither then": Ibid., 6.60.

45 staged a mock murder: Donald Kagan, *The Peace of Nicias and the Sicilian Expedition* (Ithaca, N.Y., and London, 1981), p. 196.

46 "All the soldiers": Plutarch, "Alcibiades," ch. 19.

46 "people whose brilliance": Thucydides, 6.16.

47 as ill proportioned: Aristotle, p. 215.

47 "They employ this measure": Plutarch, op. cit., ch. 13.

47 "The people were ready": Plutarch, "Nicias," ch. 6.

47 "Let me seize": Homer, *Iliad*, 18.144.

48 "to fill the mouths": Plato, "Alcibiades," I, 4.

48 "might very easily": Plutarch, "Alcibiades," ch. 21.

49 "I will show them": Ibid., ch. 22.

49 "It was this": Ibid., ch. 23.

51 It has been argued . . . : I. F. Stone, *The Trial of Socrates* (London, 1988), passim.

52 "They would be armed": Plutarch, "Lycurgus," ch. 28.

52 "The Spartans are": Pausanias, quoted in Robert Calasso, *The*

Marriage of Cadmus and Harmony (London, 1993), p. 251.

52 "They did not understand": Aristotle, p. 149.

52 "neither the time": Plutarch, op. cit.

53 "When the Spartans": quoted in Calasso, p. 250.

54 "a system which is": Thucydides, 6.89.

54 "In time of war": Plutarch, op. cit., ch. 22.

54 "who says one thing": Homer, *Iliad*, 9.378, and *Odyssey*, 14.182.

54 "thievery": Homer, *Odyssey*, 19.449.

55 "one special gift": Plutarch, "Alcibiades," ch. 23.

56 "possessed in a higher degree": Plutarch, op. cit., ch. 10.

56 "The generals who": Thucydides, 6.91.

56 "One can only": Kagan, *The Peace of Nicias and the Sicilian Expedition*, p. 256.

57 "that he had not done": Plutarch, op. cit., ch. 23.

57 "He said he would easily": Thucydides, 8.12.

59 "The most powerful": Plutarch, op. cit., ch. 24.

59 "who was naturally": Ibid.

59 "became his adviser": Thucydides, 8.45.

59 "Let the Hellenes": Ibid., 8.46.

60 "gave this advice": Ibid., 8.47.

60 "thought that this": Ibid., 8.1.

61 "we must bring": Ibid., 8.53.

62 "and put everything": Ibid., 8.82.

62 "a very exaggerated idea": Ibid., 8.81.

63 "there was not a man": Ibid., 8.82.

63 "There was not another": Ibid., 8.86.

64 "the soldiers who": Plutarch, op. cit., ch. 29.

64 "Thrasybulus accomplished": Nepos, *Thrasybulus*, 1.

64 "the Spartans turned": Xenophon, op. cit., 1.1.6.

65 "with a great deal": Plutarch, op. cit., ch. 31.

65 "He had thought": Ibid., ch. 27.

65 "as though he were": Ibid., ch. 32.

65 "all men thronged": Diodorus Siculus, 13.68.

65 "for they reflected": Plutarch, op. cit., ch. 32.

65 "practically all men": Diodorus Siculus, 12.68.

67 "it had been another": Nepos, *Alcibiades*, 7.

68 "in solemn order": Plutarch, op. cit., ch. 34.

69 "rid them of those": Ibid.

69 "We do not know": Ibid., ch. 35.

70 "If ever a man": Ibid.

70 "He had entrusted": Ibid., ch. 36.

70 "in drunkenness and lust": Nepos, op. cit., 11.

72 "that if they were defeated": Diodorus Siculus, 13.105.4.

72 "We are in command": Xenophon, op. cit., 2.126.

72 "he so captivated": Nepos, op. cit., 9.

73 "none of the arrangements": Ibid., 10.

74 "Although in a public": Thucydides, 6.15.

74 "the entrails of lions": Quoted in King, p. 131.

74 "were convinced": Nepos, op. cit., 6.

74 "Most people became frightened": Thucydides, 6.15.

CATO

76 "Cato was not so much": Peter Smithers, *The Life of Joseph Addison* (Oxford, 1954), p. 256.

76 "Solus, sitting in a": Joseph Addison, *The Works*, vol. 4 (London, 1804), p. 278.

77 "fierce heart": Horace, *Odes* 3.3.

77 "the prince of": Quoted in Robert J. Goar, *The Legend of Cato Uticensis from the First Century BC to the Fifth Century AD* (Brussels, 1987), p. 84.

77 "which could neither": Ibid.

77 "And what man": Ibid., p. 104.

77 as immovable as a rock: Knox, pp. 9, 16.

77 "those marvellously incomprehensible": Nietzsche, *Beyond Good and Evil*, translated by R. J. Hollingdale (Harmondsworth, 1990), ch. 200.

78 "alone outweighs": Cicero, *Ad Atticus* 2.5.

78 "I crawl": Michel de Montaigne, *The Essays of Michel de Montaigne*, translated by M. A. Screech (London, 1991), p. 260.

79 "in whose sight": Ibid., p. 278.

79 "the more clearly": Plutarch, "Cato," ch. 8.

79 "were hostile to Cato": Ibid., ch. 45.

79 "Pompey admired him": Ibid., ch. 14.

80 "unbending, dogmatical fool": Theodor Mommsen, *The History of Rome*, translated by William Purdie Dickson (London, 1901), bk. 5, ch. 5, p. 510.

81 "I do not know": Seneca, *Letters from a Stoic*, translated by Robin Campbell (Harmondsworth, 1977), "De Providentia," 2.9–12.

81 nine thousand . . . : Orosius, quoted in H. H. Scullard, *From the Gracchi to Nero: A History of Rome 133 BC–68 AD* (London, 1959), p. 81.

82 "effeminacy and luxury": Plutarch, op. cit., ch. 9.

82 "never embraced": Ibid., ch. 139.

82 "and devoted himself": Ibid., ch. 4.

82 "as though to honour": Ibid., ch. 14.

82 "one of the strangest": Meier, p. 289, and L. R. Taylor, *Party Politics in the Age of Caesar* (Berkeley, Calif., 1949), p. 129.

85 "read the law": Plutarch, op. cit., ch. 16.

85 "instead of modesty": Sallust, ch. 3.

85 "they levelled mountains": Ibid., ch. 13.

86 "you should be seeking": Diodorus Siculus, 12.38.

86 "All men hated them": Plutarch, op. cit., ch. 17.

86 " 'This is not' ": Ibid., ch. 19.

87 "stimulating his associates": Cicero quoted in Anthony Everitt, *Cicero: A Turbulent Life* (London, 2001), p. 85.

88 "any politician who seeks": Plato, *Republic*, 8–9.

89 "as if he were living": Cicero, *Pro Murena*, 29.61.

90 "troops of criminals": Sallust, ch. 14.

91 "You, who have always": Ibid., ch. 52.

92 "hideous and fearsome": Ibid., ch. 55.

92 "For a long time": Ibid., ch. 53.

93 "that while he lived": Plutarch, op. cit., ch. 26.

93 "great dejection": Ibid., ch. 25.

94 "What a bold man . . .": Ibid., ch. 27.

94 "They urged one another": Ibid., ch. 27.

94 "that his followers": Ibid., ch. 29.

96 "Tell Pompey that Cato": Plutarch, op. cit., ch. 30.

97 "always ready": Mommsen, op. cit., bk. 5, p. 455.

97 "with downcast looks": Plutarch, op. cit., ch. 33.

97 "I prefer to be": Dio Cassius, 28.3.

97 "Let him deny": Quoted in King, p. 128.

97 "that they themselves": Plutarch, op. cit., ch. 33.

98 "the blood that streamed": Quoted in Everitt, p. 143.

98 "a colossal bore": Ibid., pp. 181, 183.

99 "For this reason": Plutarch, op. cit., ch. 36.

100 "District by district": Quoted in Fergus Millar, *The Crowd in Rome in the Late Republic* (Ann Arbor, Mich., 1998), p. 127.

100 "The Tiber was full": Quoted in Everitt, op. cit., p. 143.

102 "and that when he began": Ibid., ch. 43.

102 "What pleasure is there": Quoted in Everitt, p. 159.

103 "indeed a most horrifying": Plutarch, "Pompey," ch. 52.

103 "pedantically stiff": Mommsen, op. cit., bk. 5, pp. 496, 455.

103 "stood alone": Seneca, "De Constantia," 2.

103 "He fared as fruits": Plutarch, "Comparison of Cato and Phocion," ch. 3.

104 "all Rome clamoured": Lucan, *Pharsalia*, translated by Robert Graves (London, 1961), p. 177.

104 "Every day the Forum": Plutarch, "Cato," ch. 47.

104 "The city was left with": Plutarch, "Caesar," ch. 28.

105 "any government": Plutarch, "Cato," ch. 47.

106 "I would rather have noise": Nietzsche, *Zarathustra*, p. 185.

107 "it is a much more splendid": Quoted in Taylor, p. 169.

107 "was weeping": Plutarch, *Cato*, ch. 54.

109 "the unflinching steadiness": Seneca, *Epistles*, 95.

110 "The majority": Plutarch, op. cit., ch. 60.

111 "and could not carry": Ibid., ch. 64.

112 "broke in with vehemence": Ibid., ch. 67.

112 "the happiest men": Lucan, p. 178.

112 "cast away": Plutarch, op. cit., ch. 69.

113 "He drew forth": Seneca, "De Providentia," 2.

113 "No man of that day": Dio Cassius, 37.57.

114 "even if Cato": Plutarch, op. cit., ch. 32.

114 "torn out his tongue": Millar, p. 144.

114 "O Cato, I begrudge": Plutarch, op. cit., ch. 72.

114 "All the world": Seneca, "De Providentia."

115 "Why didst thou not": Plutarch, op. cit., ch. 3.

115 "more than any": Plutarch, "Brutus," ch. 2.

115 "god-like and unique": Cicero, "De Finibus," 3.7.

115 "remained ever true": Cicero, "De Officiis," 1.112.

115 the just man: Horace, *Odes*, 3.3 and 3.2.

116 "fills us with loves": Plato, *Phaedo*, p. 119.

116 "I almost think": Seneca, "De Constantia," 2.

116 "a voracious appetite": Cicero, "De Finibus," 3.

117 "accustoming himself": Plutarch, "Cato," ch. 6.

117 "endowed by nature": Cicero, "De Officiis," 1.112.

117 "even affect the expression": Seneca, *Epistles*, 104.

117 "He had to endure": Seneca, "De Constantia," 2.

117 "He is a great": Seneca, "De Ira," 2.32.

117 "were the sky itself": Horace, *Odes*, 3.3.

118 "as noble soil": Plutarch, *Cato*, ch. 25.

118 "The woman was set": Ibid., ch. 52.

118 "vile": Quoted in Goar, pp. 80, 87.

118 "all the women": Plato, *Republic*, 457–459.

119 "taken care of": Epictetus, *Encheiridion*, 11.

119 "high-souled philosophy": Appian, *Roman History: The Civil Wars*, translated by Horace White (London and New York, 1913), 2.99.

119 "Roman morals": Charles Oman, *Seven Roman Statesmen of the Later Republic* (London, 1902), p. 221.

119 "whether acting or speaking": Plato, *Republic*, 382e.

119 "but what he once": Plutarch, *Cato*, ch. 1.

119 "No-one ever saw": Seneca, *Epistles*, 104.

120 "Whoever wishes to preserve": Macrobius, *Saturnalia*, 2.4.

120 "As this faction-loving": Tacitus, 16, p. 391.

120 "Look, young man!": Tacitus 16, p. 396.

121 "a model for living": quoted in Goar, p. 41.

121 "The two whom heaven": Seneca, "De Constantia," 2.

121 "One day": Lucan, p. 188.

121 "With Cato's eye": Ibid., p. 95.

122 "conferring on the victim": Ibid., p. 195.

122 "It behoves all men": Sallust, 1.

122 "a fault not so far": Ibid., 11.

122 "The span of life": Ibid., 1.

122 "One trusts": Oman, p. 225.

122 "That to which Cato": Plutarch, *Cato*, ch. 9.

123 "not with a view": Dio Cassius, 37.22.

123 "He preferred rather to be": Sallust, 54.

123 "Cato did all this": Plutarch, op. cit., ch. 46.

123 "resembled Virtue herself": Velleius Paterculus, 2.35.

124 "favourable judgement": Augustine, 5.12.

124 "People commit suicide": Paul Plass, *The Game of Death in Ancient Rome* (University of Wisconsin, 1995), p. 89.

125 "undefeated, death-defeating Cato": Boethius, *The Consolations of Philosophy*, 4.87.

125 "if a man has trained": Plato, *Phaedo*, p. 121.

125 "Either reason or the rope": quoted in J. M. Rist, *Stoic Philosophy* (Cambridge, 1969), p. 237.

125 "Do you ask": Seneca, "De Ira," quoted in Rist, p. 249.

125 "the wide road . . .": Seneca, "De Providentia," quoted in Rist, p. 246.

126 "the enslavement": Augustine, 1.22.

126 "not to self-respect": Ibid., 1.23.

127 "to seek death": Seneca, "De Providentia," 2.

127 "in his most exalted": Montaigne, p. 691.

127 "virtue reaches such": Ibid., p. 475.

128 "to which all ages": Jonathan Swift, *Gulliver's Travels*, "Laputa," ch. 7.

128 "patriot, obstinately good": Addison, p. 197.

128 "defending the cause": Smithers, p. 256.

128 "The town is so fond": Ibid., p. 255.

129 "the work mentioned": Ibid., p. 265.

129 "stern and awful": Addison, p. 282.

129 "His towering soul": Ibid., p. 245.

129 "obstinately brave": Ibid., p. 273.

129 "one of the most beautiful": Smithers, p. 267.

129 "There fled the greatest": Addison, p. 285.

129 "One's way of dying": Ivan Morris, *The Nobility of Failure* (Harmondsworth, 1980), p. 14.

129 "A brave man": Addison, p. 201.

129 "You chose to cringe": Quoted in Knox, p. 38.

130 "His resolution defeated": Lucan, p. 181.

130 "a national sin-offering": Lucan, p. 31.

130 "My blood would purge": Ibid.

130 "The dying Roman": Addison, p. 198.

EL CID

Abbreviations—

Poem: *El Poema de Mío Cid*. I have quoted most frequently from the translation by W. S. Merwin (1959), and sometimes from that by Rita Hamilton and Janet Perry (Manchester, 1975).Ballads: *The Cid Ballads*, translated by James Young Gibson (London, 1887).

131 all Christendom: Quoted in Ramón Menéndez Pidal, *The Cid and His Spain*, translated by Harold Sutherland (London 1971), p. 407.

131 "he who was born": Poem, passim.

131 "This man was": Richard Fletcher, *The Quest for El Cid* (London, 1989), p. 185, and Stephen Clissold, *In Search of the Cid* (London, 1965), p. 18.

132 "How well he rewarded": Poem, 1.45.

133 "won by force": Homer, *Odyssey*, 1.456.

133 "roving the waves": Ibid., 3.81–83.

133 "This occupation": Quoted in Knox, introduction to *Odyssey*, p. 29.

133 "It is according": Aristotle, *Politics*, p. 79.

134 "I hope you will": Anonymous, *Beowulf*, translated by Kevin Crossley-Holland (London, 1973), p. 57.

134 "In Heaven's name": Poem, 2.90.

134 "Today you will all": Fletcher, 84.

134 "All who scented": Poem, 2.74.

134 "God and his Holy Mother": Poem, 2.77.

134 "He captures": Quoted in Fletcher, p. 93.

135 "every commander": Ibid., p. 27.

137 "Men must endure": Anonymous, *The Song of Roland*, translated by Dorothy L. Sayers (Harmondsworth, 1967), p. 95.

137 "Without my men": R. Dozy, "Le Cid d'Apres des Nouveaux Documents," in vol. 2 of *Recherches sur L'Histoire et la Littérature de L'Espagne Pendant le Moyen Âge* (Leyden, 1860), p. 198.

138 "Then Rodrigo": Pidal, p. 90.

138 "Oh God!": Poem, 1.40.

139 "Well it becomes": *Song of Roland*, op. cit., p. 96.

139 "My God, how great": Poem, 1.29.

140 "That which Rodrigo": Dozy, p. 113.

140 "As vassals true": Anonymous, *The Cid Ballads*, translated by James Young Gibson (London, 1887), p. 78.

142 "After the death": Fletcher, p. 118.

143 "a real prodigy": Ibid., p. 133.

143 "protection": Ibid., p. 69.

144 "many men became jealous": *Historia Roderici*, quoted in Fletcher, p. 130.

144 "He pillaged": Ibid., pp. 131–132.

145 "What a good vassal": Poem, 1.3.

145 "proud and free": Ballads, pp. 17–18.

145 In another ballad: Ballads, p. 149.

146 "Don Quixote replied": Miguel de Cervantes, *The Adventures of Don Quixote*, translated by J. M. Cohen (Harmondsworth, 1970), p. 42.

146 "How can we": Clissold, p. 104.

146 "Strong men": *Beowulf*, pp. 25, 76.

147 "an immense hoard": Fletcher, p. 75.

147 "a man without faith": Dozy, p. 219.

147 "as the fingernail": Poem, 1.18.

148 "[a]nd for dessert": Ballads, p. 178.

148 "a lion wild": Ballads, p. 57.

148 *Carmen Campi Doctoris:* in Fletcher, p. 93.

148 "Spain, the evangeliser": Fletcher, p. 203.

149 "Rodrigo, God doth love": Ballads, p. 44.

149 "Ride out, good Cid": Poem, 1.19.

149 "besiege Valencia": Ibid., 2.72.

149 "God so loves": Fletcher, p. 198.

149 "riding a white": Clissold, p. 204.

150 "he took auguries": Ibn 'Alqama, "La Prise de Valence par le Cid," in

Islam d'Occident by E. Lévi Provencal (Paris, 1948), p. 211.

150 "It is remarkable": Dozy, p. 253.

150 At his parties: Fletcher, p. 127.

151 Ibn Bassam records: Dozy, p. 25.

151 "who brought him out": Ibid., p. 18.

151 "showered him with": *Historia Roderici*, quoted in Fletcher, p. 135.

151 "accompanied by a crowd": *Historia Roderici*, quoted in Dozy, p. 122.

152 "sent a great tremor": Quoted in Fletcher, p. 149.

153 "Had I been able": Ibid., p. 148.

154 "co-operate with one another": 'Abd Allah, quoted in Fletcher, p. 152.

154 "Many were the sturdy": Poem, 2.104.

155 "he would always serve": Poem, 2.96.

155 "whose vassal I": Ballads, p. 142.

155 "all the lands": Fletcher, p. 153.

156 "to do battle": Clissold, p. 101.

156 "recruited a force": Plutarch, "Alcibiades," ch. 36.

156 "We keep alive": Poem, 1.62.

156 "a great gain": Ibid., p. 25.

157 "We have settled": Ibid., 2.66.

157 "because they fight": Maurice Keen, *Chivalry* (London, 1984), p. 234.

158 "Now honour lies": Ibid.

158 "one and all": Poem, 2.104.

158 A Latin song: Quoted in Pidal, p. 182.

158 "proudly adorned": *Beowulf*, p. 76.

159 "in order that": Fletcher, p. 137.

159 "Certain of his knights": Ibid., p. 154.

159 "much gold and silver": Ibid.

159 "a victory ever": Ibid., p. 157.

160 "drove those petty kings": Dozy, p. 16.

160 "see how Rodrigo": Clissold, p. 117.

161 "many and various": Fletcher, p. 161.

161 "the Cid's mission": Beatriz Pastor Bodmer, *The Armature of Conquest*, translated by Lydia Longstreth Hunt (Stanford, Calif., 1992), p. 82.

162 "so the King": Poem, 3.117.

163 "the bitter herb": Ballads, pp. 5–6.

163 "very great and innumerable": Fletcher, p. 97.

163 "He swore": Ibn 'Alqama, p. 205.

164 "as the sick man": Pidal, p. 296.

164 "That tyrant Rodrigo": Dozy, p. 21.

164 "They ate rats": Ibn 'Alqama, pp. 209, 218.

164 "By the look": Dozy, p. 193.

165 "The moors": Ibid., p. 194.

165 "using fraud": Ibid., p. 22.

165 "I am a man": Clissold, p. 142, and Dozy, p. 198.

165 "When my Cid": Poem, 2.74.

165 "He began to extort": Dozy, p. 175.

166 "Each Muslim had": Ibid.

166 "If you could see": Dozy, p. 12.

166 "Or at least": Ibid., p. 23.

167 "shrieking and shouting": Fletcher, p. 173.

167 "He stands out": Pidal, p. 290.

168 "By God's clemency": Fletcher, p. 173.

168 "the year when": Ibid.

168 "Swords have brought": Ibid., p. 182.

169 "Victory always followed": Dozy, p. 25.

169 "Rodrigo is full": Poem, pp. 194–195.

169 "While he lived": Fletcher, p. 185.

169 "The plight": Clissold, p. 208.

170 "until his flesh": Ibid., p. 204.

170 "You oppressors": Barber, p. 254.

170 "Let those who have been": Keen, p. 48.

170 "In our own time": Ibid.

170 "Behold": Ibid., p. 62.

171 "He began to polish": Salvador de Madariaga, *Hernán Cortés* (London, 1942), p. 96.

171 "Have a care": Ibid.

171 "Forgive me sir": Ibid., p. 99.

172 "What I have desired": Ibid., p. 446.

172 a mass to the memory: Anthony Pagden, *Lords of All the World* (London, 1995), p. 74.

173 "with his cloak": Poem, 3.112.

173 "We see two lions": Ballads, p. 213.

173 "Oh God!": Dozy, p. 38.

DRAKE

174 "finer than has ever": Alison Weir, *Elizabeth the Queen* (London, 1998), p. 36.

174 "the master-thief": John Hampden (ed.), *Francis Drake, Privateer: Contemporary Narratives and Documents* (London, 1972), p. 244.

174 "I have not to do": Ibid., p. 231.

174 "Drake is a man": John Sugden, *Francis Drake* (London, 1996), pp. 188–189.

174 "He was low": Hampden, p. 13.

176 "It is the delight": Charles Baudelaire, *My Heart Laid Bare and Other Prose Writings*, translated by Norman Cameron (London, 1950), p. 56.

174 "the greatest and strongest": Martin and Parker, *The Spanish Armada* (London, 1998), p. 13.

174 "That's not much": Felipe Fernández-Armesto, *The Spanish Armada* (Oxford, 1988), p. v.

177 "He is one": John Cummins, *Francis Drake* (London, 1995), p. 259.

177 "in his deep": Ibid., p. 305.

177 "more skilful": Sugden, p. 156.

177 "the only man that": Hampden, p. 235.

178 "a thing hardly": Sugden, p. 143.

179 "demi-Moor, bound": Payne, p. 5.

179 "would call down": Peter Vansittart, *In Memory of England* (London, 1998), p. 92.

179 "they came simply": Beatriz Pastor Bodmer, *The Armature of Conquest* (Stanford, Calif., 1992), p. 52.

179 "I came to get gold": Salvador de Madariaga, *Hernán Cortés* (London, 1942), p. 32.

179 Walter Raleigh: Charles Nicholl, *The Creature in the Map* (London, 1995), passim.

181 "lost us": Hampden, p. 37.

181 "forsook us": Ibid.

181 "when contrary to": Ibid., p. 177.

181 "wrongs received": Hampden, p. 27.

181 "commissions of reprisal": Hampden, p. 39.

182 "had easily persuaded": William Camden, *Annales* (London, 1635), p. 219.

182 "loss of all": Ibid., p. 46.

182 "that he feared": Harry Kelsey, *Sir Francis Drake: The Queen's Pirate* (London, 1998), p. 409.

183 "We are surprised": Sugden, p. 50.

183 "It is plain": Hampden, p. 51.

184 "a pile of bars": Edward Arber (ed.), *An English Garner* (Birmingham, 1882), p. 503.

184 "how we might": Hampden, p. 64.

184 "of a thousand negroes": Hampden, p. 47.

184 "entered daily": Cummins, p. 37.

185 "above two hundred": Hampden, p. 103.

185 "many sorts of dainty": Ibid., p. 73.

185 "if we had been": Ibid., p. 70.

187 "strangely changed": Ibid., p. 92.

188 "through hatred of": Sugden, p. 73.

188 "they made off": Hampden, p. 98.

189 "how all his company": Ibid., p. 100.

190 "abundantly rich": Camden, p. 220.

190 "one Drake": Sugden, p. 82.

190 "This realm is at": Ibid., p. 77.

191 "vast in body": Ffiona Swabey, *A Mediaeval Gentlewoman* (Gloucestershire, 1999).

191 "for fear of my lord": Hampden, p. 171.

191 "a sweet orator": Ibid., p. 208.

192 "great goodwill": W.S.W. Vaux (ed.), *The World Encompassed by Sir Francis Drake* (London, 1854), p. 148.

192 "a fit man": Sugden, p. 95.

192 "became so inflamed": Camden, p. 220.

193 "not under the obedience": Sugden, p. 97.

193 "diverse injuries": Hampden, p. 237.

193 "The Lord Guide": Weir, p. 30.

193 "The gentleman careth": Sugden, p. 98.

193 "affirming that her Majesty": Hampden, p. 237.

194 "my practice and": Ibid.

194 "I did never give": Kelsey, p. 95.

194 "a man well travelled": Vaux, p. 26.

194 "And so we take": Ibid., p. 27.

195 "whence departed": Bodmer, op. cit., p. 27.

196 "From this time": Hampden, p. 222.

196 "the effects of": Vaux, p. 31.

196 "would have been hanged": Hampden, p. 243.

196 "Aristotle, Pythagoras, Thales": Vaux, p. 27.

196 "aptness to anger": Cummins, p. 305.

197 "a very bad couple": Ibid., p. 227.

197 "sea of graves": Ian Cameron, *Magellan* (London, 1974), p. 100.

198 "would suffer no man": Vaux, p. 277.

198 "so hideous and horrible": Ibid., p. 60.

198 "for I will be safe": Hampden, p. 229.

198 "This is not law": Ibid., p. 230.

198 "God's will!": Ibid.

199 "Therefore my masters": Ibid., p. 231.

199 "Lo, this is the end": Hampden, p. 233.

199 Island of True Justice: Cummins, p. 84.

199 "that place where will": Hampden, p. 231.

199 Malicious gossip: Kelsey, p. 110.

199 "cut him off": Camden, p. 221.

199 "longing to explore": Dante, *Inferno*, 26.

200 "At any time": Hampden, p. 224.

201 "I have taken that": Ibid., p. 236.

202 "dark corners," "others that hide": Nicholl, p. 108.

202 "scum of men": Ibid.

202 "unruly without government": Hampden, p. 235.

202 "a company of desperate": Ibid., p. 232.

203 "I gained them": *The Cid Ballads*, translated by James Young Gibson (London, 1887), p. 147.

203 "They all bestrode": Ibid., p. 17.

203 "Here is such controversy":
Hampden, p. 235.

203 "he in tyranny . . .": Ibid., p. 228.

203 "whether they could": Ibid., p. 236.

204 "high and steep": Vaux, p. 71.

204 "many of Drake's": Ibid., p. 154.

205 "swallowed up": Ibid., p. 156.

205 "a man who has cast": Kelsey,
p. 126.

205 "cast himself down": Hampden,
p. 159.

205 "our troubles did make": Ibid.,
p. 160.

206 "That world-dividing gulf": Quoted
in Nicholl, p. 166.

206 "In many places": Zelia Nuttall
(ed.), *New Light on Drake: A
Collection of Documents Relating to His
Voyage of Circumnavigation* (London,
1914), pp. 217–219.

207 "which otherwise perhaps":
Hampden, p. 167.

207 "We could not endure": Ibid.

207 "made somewhat bold": Ibid.,
p. 108.

207 "somewhat lighter": Ibid., p. 170.

207 "certain emeralds": Kelsey, p. 155.

207 "running as dogs": Hampden,
p. 165.

208 "God would receive": Kelsey, p. 22.

209 "he took forty": Hampden, p. 216.

210 "ornament and delight": Ibid.,
p. 128.

210 "perfumed waters": Ibid., p. 214.

210 "He takes advice": Ibid.

210 "all his men trembled": Ibid., p. 215.

210 "like a shameless": Cummins, p. 106.

212 "Come on board": Nuttall, p. 158.

212 "We found in her": Hampden,
p. 170.

213 "that he would take": Ibid., p. 172.

214 "This people which": Ibid., p. 241.

214 "bountifully rewarded": Ibid.,
p. 164.

215 "as men ravished": Ibid., p. 177.

215 "they did not understand": Stephen
Greenblatt, *Marvellous Possessions*
(Oxford, 1991), p. 13.

217 "not to hurt": Hampden, p. 187.

217 but according to John Drake:
Sugden, p. 138.

218 "and those at present": Hampden,
p. 193.

218 "to decorate that sea": Sugden,
p. 140.

218 "found a settlement": Hampden,
p. 196.

218 "a proper . . . wench": Vaux, p. 183.

218 "a fair negress": Camden, p. 223.

218 "there being no probability":
Hampden, p. 197.

219 "Every thief": Vaux, p. 185.

219 "the falsest knave": Sugden, p. 143.

219 a just punishment: Ibid.

219 the last half pint: Hampden, p. 204.

220 "How was the Queen?": Nuttall,
p. 54.

221 "red Indians," "vulgar sort":
Camden, p. 224.

221 "The commons": Hampden, p. 245.

221 "His name and fame": Ibid.

221 "The adventurers who": Sugden,
p. 146.

222 next to nothing: Kelsey, p. 30.

222 "the portion," "taken notice": Ibid.,
p. 214.

222 "a mean subject": Hampden, p. 53.

223 "universal and sole": Anthony
Pagden, *Lords of All the World*
(London, 1995), p. 40.

223 "How brilliant": Fernández-
Armesto, p. vi.

224 In South America: Kelsey, pp. 142,
165, 168, 217.

225 "New mariners": Frances Yates, *Astraea* (London, 1975), p. 55.

225 "No one who guides": Hampden, p. 215.

225 "putting out different": Kelsey, p. 177.

225 "seriously dealt withal": Ibid., p. 447.

225 "hitherto have been": Hampden, p. 51.

225 "squandering more": Sugden, p. 150.

226 Lord Arundel told him: Kelsey, p. 217.

226 "In Sir Francis": Cummins, p. 305.

226 "too much pleased": Kelsey, p. 13.

226 "the master thief": Hampden, p. 244.

226 "Nothing angered worse": Hampden, p. 245.

226 "The actions which": Cummins, p. 292.

226 "commons applauded": Hampden, p. 245.

227 "many princes": Hampden, p. 13.

227 "who seeks to gain": Sugden, epigraph.

228 "Sir Francis was": Hampden, p. 13.

228 "God alone knows": Sugden, p. 191.

228 "Sir Francis Drake is a": Ibid., p. 200.

228 "to enter forcibly": Cummins, p. 164.

229 "being of a lively": Ibid., p. 305.

229 "with more speed": Ibid., p. 167.

229 "confidence that no": Sugden, p. 208.

229 "smoke and flames": Ibid., p. 210.

230 "as well": Ibid.

230 "Thus were the thresholds": Cummins, p. 170.

230 "Just look at Drake!": Sugden, p. 211.

230 "committed their usual": Kelsey, p. 296.

230 "The English are masters": Sugden, p. 214.

231 "the greatest and strongest": Martin and Parker, pp. 13, 23.

232 "like a high wood": Fernández-Armesto, p. 157.

232 "the winds grew": Martin and Parker, p. 195.

232 "far the lesser": Camden, p. 369.

232 half as large again: Martin and Parker, p. 59.

233 not a single vessel: Ibid., p. 195.

233 "so fast and so nimble": Hampden, p. 250.

234 "must depend": Fernández-Armesto, p. 134.

234 "had no more care": Ibid., p. 75.

234 "the saints in heaven": Fernández-Armesto, p. 39.

234 "Since it is": Martin and Parker, p. 107.

234 "This is a matter": Fernández-Armesto, p. 42.

234 "in the confident hope": Ibid.

235 "as one body": Cummins, p. 164.

235 "God will help": Fernández-Armesto, p. 43.

235 "If we can come": Ibid., p. 141.

235 "We pluck their feathers": Hampden, p. 150.

236 "He made the winds": Fernández-Armesto, p. 238.

237 "My brother Bartolo": Cummins, p. 262.

237 "it was not convenient": Fernández-Armesto, p. 74.

237 "He reporteth": Cummins, p. 191.

237 "Have you heard": Sugden, p. 261.

238 "officers and others": Cummins, p. 290.

239 "There was never seen": Sugden, p. 247.

239 "I know not": Ibid., p. 245.

240 "profitable also": Fernández-Armesto, p. 48.

241 "I will make him spend": Sugden, p. 245.

241 "valour and felicity": Fernández-Armesto, p. 175.

242 "By death": Hampden, p. 253.

242 "the soldiers": Martin and Parker, p. 170.

242 "much disliked": Cummins, p. 193.

242 "endless atrocities": Ibid., p. 149.

242 "With the seamen": Kelsey, p. 271.

243 "untameable wolf" . . . "further centuries": Cummins, pp. 262–265.

244 "spoke disgracefully": Camden, p. 283.

244 "The leaders were": Kelsey, p. 363.

244 "Drake was much": Cummins, p. 222.

245 "service done": Hampden, p. 51.

245 "self-willed": Kelsey, p. 380.

245 "I will bring": Sugden, p. 309.

246 "as it were": Ibid., p. 313.

246 "did untie his clothes": Robert Southey, *The Life of Nelson* (London, 1927), p. 235.

246 "the trumpets": Hampden, p. 257.

246 "It is good news": Vansittart, p. 96.

246 "his steely sides": Cummins, p. 271.

247 "this new Attila": Ibid., p. 273.

247 "This pirate blind": Ibid., p. 264.

247 "brought back heaps": Sugden, p. 115.

247 "the bleached ribs": Hampden, p. 246.

247 "With gold there": Arber, vol. 2, p. 269.

247 "He who alive": Cummins, p. 283.

248 "laughing come back rich": Terry Coleman, *Nelson, the Man and the Legend* (London, 2001), p. 137.

248 "for the stirring": Vaux, epigraph.

248 "Without having any": Southey, p. 11.

248 "Animal courage": Coleman, p. 7.

249 "conscious rectitude": Southey, p. 7.

249 "first upon the deep": Alfred Noyes, *Collected Poems* (London, 1965), p. 12.

249 "about a hundred": Cummins, p. 298.

249 General Zizka: Francis Watson, *Wallenstein, Soldier Under Saturn* (London, 1938), p. 27.

250 "out of their entire": Camden, p. 369.

250 "There at his side": Robert Nathan, "The Ballad of Dunkirk."

250 "When Drake went down": Rudyard Kipling, "The Song of the Dead."

251 "mighty conquests": Charles Kingsley, *Westward Ho!* (London, 1896), p. 34.

251 "let Orlando-Furioso": Ibid., p. 549.

251 "Of such captains": Ibid., p. 3.

252 "There came sounds": Noyes, p. 108.

WALLENSTEIN

253 "When all around": Golo Mann, *Wallenstein*, translated by Charles Kessler (London, 1976), p. 249.

253 "In the night": Friedrich Schiller, *Dramatic Works: Wallenstein's Camp*, translated by James Churchill; *The Piccolomini* and *Wallenstein's Death*, translated by Samuel Taylor Coleridge (London, 1894), p. 224.

254 unhappy land: Brecht, *Galileo*, scene 13.

254 "Some nations": Ronald G. Asch, *The Thirty Years War* (London, 1997), p. 1

254 "One may travel": Robert Ergang, *The Myth of the All-Destructive Fury of the Thirty Years' War* (Pocono Pines, Pa., 1956), p. 4.

254 "such a great": Kenneth Negus, *Grimmelshausen* (New York, 1974), p. 77.

254 "Numerous were the dark": Gustav Freytag, *Pictures of German Life*, translated by Mrs. Malcolm (London, 1862), p. 14.

256 "he maintained": Francis Watson, *Wallenstein: Soldier Under Saturn* (London, 1938), p. 160

256 "Let him be": Ibid., p. 356.

256 "the dark and sinister": Wolfgang Menzel, *The History of Germany*, vol. 2, translated by Mrs. George Horrocks (London, 1849), p. 337.

257 "several devout": Gerhard Benecke (ed.), *Germany in the Thirty Years War* (London, 1978), p. 12.

257 "He believed himself": Watson, p. 26.

257 "as a block of marble": Ibid., p. 67.

257 "Better a desert": Ibid., p. 66.

258 "reeks of atheism": Mann, p. 247.

258 "often utters": Ibid.

258 "he who does not": Menzel, p. 365.

258 "to alchemy, sorcery": Mann, p. 79.

260 "when he had exhausted": Watson, p. 56.

260 Oliver Cromwell: Geoffrey Parker, *The Thirty Years' War* (London, 1984), p. 266.

261 "vicious treason": Mann, p. 126.

261 "There sits": Ibid., p. 125.

261 "Scoundrel!": Watson, p. 23.

262 "all they crave": Mann, p. 150.

262 "He often speculated": Franz Christoph Khevenhüller, *Conterfet Kupfertisch derenjenigen vornehmen Ministren und Hohen Officiern* (Leipzig, 1722).

262 "We will not sell": Parker, p. 89.

262 "It was then": Ibid., p. 90.

264 Some of the houses": Herbert Langer, *The Thirty Years' War*, translated by C.S.V. Salt (Poole, 1980), p. 154.

264 "melancholy, always": Ibid., p. 79.

264 "He had a marked": J. Mitchell, *The Life of Wallenstein, Duke of Friedland* (London, 1853), p. 322.

265 "The Duke of Friedland": Mann, p. 220.

265 "When he commanded": Albert E. J. Hollaender, *Some English Documents on the Death of Wallenstein* (Manchester, 1958), p. 389.

265 "I cannot haggle": Mann, p. 461.

265 "I have no longer": Ibid., p. 219.

265 "It is our desire": Ibid., p. 240.

266 "He was not pleased": Hollaender, p. 389.

266 "I have a harder fight": Watson, p. 193.

266 von Pfuel: Mann, p. 357.

267 "eighteen ells," "a robe": Ibid., p. 212.

267 "In the field": Mitchell, p. 321.

267 painted his lips: C. V. Wedgwood, *The Thirty Years War* (London, 1938), p. 171.

267 "A captain of horse": Friedrich Schiller, *The History of the Thirty Years' War*, translated by A.J.W. Morrison (London, 1901), p. 292.

267 "men of mean": Hollaender, p. 389.

268 "He is a mere": Mann, p. 689.

268 "Our General": Ibid., p. 220.

268 150,000 animals: Parker, p. 225.

268 "and by each manger": Mann, p. 219.

269 "if they travel": Ibid., p. 233.

269 "of stone or brick": Ibid., p. 239.

269 "red in colour": Ibid., p. 234.

269 "lack brotherly": Ibid., p. 79.

270 "and when he comes": Schiller, *Dramatic Works*, p. 60.

272 "War must nourish": Ibid., p. 49.

272 "I have made": Watson, p. 132.

272 "a restless desire": Parker, p. 195.

272 "company of desperate": John Hampden (ed.), *Francis Drake, Privateer: Contemporary Narratives and Documents* (London, 1972), p. 232.

272 "swallowed without chewing": Parker, p. 195.

273 When he fought: Ibid., p. 204.

273 "famished and untended": Wedgwood, p. 323.

274 "No matter how": Mann, p. 352.

275 "we entered killing": Wedgwood, p. 217.

275 "The boors cruelly": Parker, p. 200.

275 "*il grand economo*": Ibid., p. 383.

276 "Had I served God": Ibid., p. 295.

276 "loyalty is in doubt": Ibid., p. 316.

276 "One must avoid": Watson, p. 210.

277 "They are as strangers": Schiller, *Dramatic Works*, p. 53.

277 "mean curs": Mann, p. 298.

277 "His armies flourished": Schiller, *History of the Thirty Years' War*, p. 105.

277 "take a different": Mann, p. 310.

278 "These are demands": Watson, p. 202.

278 "for I would not": Mann, p. 362.

278 In England: For Buckingham see Roger Lockyer, *Buckingham* (London, 1981), passim.

279 "whereby he perhaps": Watson, p. 251.

280 "I am wont": Ibid., p. 14.

280 "ordain and command": Mann, p. 376.

280 "he ordered red-hot": Mitchell, p. 115.

280 "so daring": Watson, p. 242.

280 "I see that they": Mann, p. 408.

281 "Stralsund must down": Watson, p. 264.

282 "to come out": Mann, p. 414.

282 "He is soused": Ibid., p. 444.

282 "the thought of": Ibid., p. 474.

283 "I see what impertinences": Ibid., p. 423.

283 "Come again": Ibid., p. 434.

283 "A general state": Ibid., p. 226.

284 A Silesian mystic: Asch, p. 1.

284 "castles battered": Benecke, p. 99.

284 "Priests slain": Parker, plate 23.

285 "scourge," "oppressor": Schiller, *History of the Thirty Years' War*, p. 203.

285 "Better a ruined": Watson, p. 201.

285 "through rising seas": Henry Glapthorne, *The Tragedy of Albertus Wallenstein*, in *The Old English Drama* (London 1824), p. 6.

285 "*allen ein Stein*": Langer, p. 239.

285 "the raving dog": Mann, p. 251.

285 "The arrival of": Watson, p. 222.

286 "territorial rulers": Parker, p. 101.

286 "The Duke of Friedland": Ibid.

286 "All Electors": Watson, p. 293.

286 "Had Wallenstein": Oswald Spengler, *The Decline of the West*, translated by C. A. Atkinson (London, 1980), p. 389.

286 "*Radix Omnium Malorum*": Parker, p. 98 and plate 7.

287 "I know not": Watson, p. 142.

287 "Better a desert": Ibid., p. 66.

287 "The Edict must": Parker, p. 113.

287 "The Edict cannot": Mann, p. 462.

287 "He holds the": Ibid., p. 384.

287 "that Friedland": Ibid., p. 385.

287 "those ancients": Ibid., p. 383.

288 "when sovereigns": Ibid., p. 373.

288 "extremely apprehensive": Ibid., p. 377.

288 "whose clothes": Mitchell, p. 296.

288 "not one of them": Mann, p. 222.

288 "Before Wallenstein": Ibid., p. 222.

288 "The common false": Ibid., p. 400.

289 "the greatest authority": R. Mousnier, "The Exponents and Critics of Absolutism," in *The New Cambridge Modern History* (Cambridge, 1970), p. 109.

290 "intensely hazardous": Mann, p. 499.

290 "who durst defy": John Milton, *Collected Works* (Oxford, 1969), p. 79.

290 "transcendent glory": Ibid., p. 109.

290 "the soldiery": Peter Limm, *The Thirty Years War* (London, 1984), p. 107.

290 "a man of restless": Mitchell, pp. 149 and 152.

290 "such a captain-general": Mann, p. 521.

290 "a change": Ibid., p. 525.

291 "persuade him": Watson, p. 303.

291 "Gladder tidings": Mann, p. 527.

291 "though it grieves": Watson, p. 303.

292 "snatched up his": Glapthorne, pp. 18 and 6.

292 "That I am hated": Watson, p. 293.

293 "displays excessive": Mann, p. 528.

293 "for I perceive": Ibid., p. 310.

293 "send you out": Mitchell, p. 148.

293 "The tale passes": Mann, p. 517.

293 "in the Swedes": Watson, p. 188.

296 "Your Princely Grace": Mann, p. 545.

296 "shaking belly": Elmer A. Beller, *Propaganda in Germany During the Thirty Years War* (Oxford, 1940), p. 124.

296 "hunger-wolves": Schiller, *Dramatic Works*, p. 76.

296 "It was his maxim": Schiller, *History of the Thirty Years' War*, p. 261.

297 "What is 'neutrality' ": Elmer A. Beller, "The Thirty Years' War," in *The New Cambridge Modern History*, vol. 4 (Cambridge, 1970), p. 330.

297 "wholly perplexed": Parker, p. 128.

297 only one man: Schiller, *History of the Thirty Years' War*, p. 203.

297 "I did it": Schiller, *Dramatic Works*, p. 226.

297 The Duke of Brunswick: Hans Speier, introduction, in Hans Jacob Christoffel von Grimmelshausen, *Courage the Adventuress*, edited by Hans Speier (Princeton, N.J., 1964), p. 14.

297 "enchained Victory": Menzel, p. 337.

299 "an outrage": Mann, p. 616.

299 a clear prelude: Schiller, *History of the Thirty Years' War*, p. 215.

299 "all the wild": Thomas Carlyle, *Life of Friedrich Schiller* (Columbia University Press, 1992), p. 113.

299 "a venal Italian": Mann, p. 363.

299 disgraceful murder: Hollaender, p. 370.

300 "Peasants do not": Langer, p. 90.

300 "the object": Carlyle, p. 115.

300 "Leaving a hundred": Menzel, p. 365.

300 "crept with a stick": Mann, p. 618.

301 "scorch and ravage": Ibid., p. 620.

301 "that in accordance": Ibid., p. 609.

301 "All eyes": Ibid., p. 351.

301 "His Electoral Highness": Ibid., p. 624.

302 "The combat started": Ibid., p. 634.

302 "'Twas all to no": Ibid., p. 637.

302 "plough up the wars": Shakespeare, *Troilus and Cressida*, 2.1.110.

302 "We expect": Mann, p. 648.

303 "with such a fury": Ibid., p. 655.

303 "Beloved Son": Ibid., p. 665.

303 "It is well": Mitchell, p. 311.

304 "The blood-bath": Mann, p. 663.

304 "cruel, and famous": Khevenhüller.

304 "His Princely Grace": Mann, p. 671.

305 "contempt and disregard": Ibid., p. 79.

305 "One of the maxims": Watson, p. 381.

306 "concealed under": Schiller, *History of the Thirty Years' War*, p. 204.

306 "Wallenstein fell": Ibid., p. 294.

307 "in mounting to the": Watson, p. 384.

307 "The Duke of Friedland's": Mann, p. 702.

307 "those to whom we entrust": Mitchell, p. 124.

307 "All the court": Watson, p. 381.

307 "The train announced": Mitchell, p. 321.

308 "a pretty train": Mann, p. 706.

308 "The wars of mankind": Parker, p. 220.

309 "Would it be better": Mann, p. 716.

309 "fixed mind": Milton, p. 80.

309 "Certain it is": Mitchell, p. 335.

309 "Since he is": Mann, p. 728.

309 "a waste of time": Ibid., p. 495.

310 apothecary's bills: Benecke, p. 91.

310 "Are we not arch-fools": Mann, p. 687.

311 "request": Watson, p. 387.

311 "that his Imperial": Mann, p. 717.

311 "was much honoured": Hollaender, p. 389.

311 "I shall know": Mann, p. 721.

311 "The Bavarian started": Ibid., p. 707.

312 "publicly and without": Watson, p. 394.

313 "the most pernicious": Mann, p. 742.

313 "This is my definite": Ibid., p. 748.

314 "the mighty when": Ibid., p. 669.

314 "We must regard": Ibid., p. 297.

315 "He is now so far": Ibid., p. 772.

315 "blinded by": Menzel, p. 365.

315 "I see well": Mann, p. 750.

316 "this business": Mitchell, p. 357.

316 "Salvation lies": Mann, p. 754.

316 "Oh, peace!": Watson, p. 399.

316 "were he not": Mann, p. 789.

316 "Why this delay?": Menzel, p. 365.

317 "swiftly strangled": Mann, p. 791.

317 "First he is": Ibid., p. 301.

319 "I would sooner": Ibid., p. 765.

319 "we had flooded": Ibid., p. 766.

320 "extreme remedies": Ibid., p. 796.

320 "with every day": Ibid., p. 803.

320 "the Emperor furnished": Ibid., p. 797.

320 "whether obedience": Mousnier, p. 120.

321 "letting it be heard": Mann, p. 812.

321 "one thousand": Parker, p. 139.

322 "Do you know": Mann, p. 882.

322 "how it really": Watson, p. 113.

323 "to live and die": Mann, p. 821.

323 "like a corpse": Ibid., p. 822.

324 "in the greatest": Ibid., p. 827.

324 "I hope, and": Ibid., p. 831.

326 "so heinous": Ibid., p. 842.

326 down the stairs: Wedgwood, p. 360.

327 "marvellous deed": Parker, p. 139.

327 haloes: Hans Schultz, *Wallenstein* (Leipzig, 1912), p. 131.

328 "As he lay stretched": Mann, p. 252.

328 "so fearful": Hollaender, p. 384.

328 "Presumably it was": Mann, p. 846.

328 "That's what happens": Langer, p. 154.

328 "Admiral of ships": Mann, p. 857.

328 "Who but Wallenstein": Ibid., p. 856.

329 "perjured, godless": Ibid., p. 858.

329 "the prompt and noble": Mitchell, p. 374.

329 "whether it be": Mann, p. 854.

330 "I have been": Glapthorne.

330 "at which I marvel": Hollaender, p. 373.

330 "this great Monarch-spirit": Schiller, *Dramatic Works*, p. 151.

330 "I had peace": Wedgwood, p. 357.

331 "the very disgrace": Sir Thomas Browne, *Urn-burial*.

331 "after his death": Mann, p. 855.

331 "wasted and depressed": Richard Holmes, *Coleridge: Early Visions* (London, 1989), p. 267.

331 "When the play ends": Hegel, *Über Wallenstein*.

GARIBALDI

332 "The Uncrowned king": Adam Zamoyski, *Holy Madness: Romantics, Patriots, and Revolutionaries, 1776–1871* (London, 1999), p. 411.

332 "It seemed to me": Augusto Vecchi, *Garibaldi at Caprera*, with an introduction by Mrs. Gaskell (London, 1862), p. 55.

332 "his fortune never": George Macaulay Trevelyan, *Garibaldi's Defence of the Roman Republic* (London, 1907), p. 23.

333 "He who cares": Morris, p. 244.

334 "denies the existence": Carlyle, p. xxxv.

334 "deep, rude, earnest": Ibid., p. 18.

334 "Have you ever": Trevelyan, *Garibaldi's Defence*, p. 64.

335 "the heart": Hibbert, p. 328.

335 "Sincerity": Carlyle, p. 41.

335 "rugged honesty": Ibid., p. 119.

335 "huge granite masses": Ibid., p. liv.

335 "the Wrath of God": Fray Pedro Simón, *The Expedition of Pedro de Ursua & Lope de Aguirre*, translated by William Bollaert (London, 1861), p. 49.

337 "The man who defends": Alexandre Dumas (ed.), *Garibaldi: An Autobiography*, translated by William Robson (London, 1860), p. 37.

337 "My God, I am": John Parris, *The Lion of Caprera* (London, 1962), p. 47.

339 "They sacked and destroyed": Ridley, p. 126.

339 "which proves": Ibid., p. 78.

340 "When a woman": Giuseppe Garibaldi, *Autobiography*, translated by A. Werner, three volumes with a supplement by Jessie White Mario (London, 1889), vol. 3, p. 449.

340 "In the immense": Dumas, *Garibaldi*, p. 95.

340 "We both remained": Ridley, pp. 88–89.

340 "She looked upon": Ibid., p. 97.

342 "if I had had no other": Dumas, *Garibaldi*, p. 46.

342 "the boundless confidence": Ibid., p. 114.

342 "These men are coarse": Ridley, p. 174.

342 "He knows how": Ibid., p. 213.

343 "I blow his brains": Ibid., p. 212.

343 "I have today": Hibbert, p. 291.

343 "low and veiled": Trevelyan, *Garibaldi's Defence*, p. 29.

343 "a true hero": Ridley, p. 159.

343 "sons of heroism": Ibid., p. 183.

344 "He cannot be won": Ibid., p. 223.

344 "a disinterested": Ibid., p. 218.

345 "The enemy are numerous": Dumas, *Garibaldi*, p. 210.

347 "Virgil would have": Ridley, p. 324.

347 "The age of chivalry": Keen, p. 1.

348 "The great and only": Ridley, p. 238.

348 "There you can ply": Parris, p. 73.

348 "The King": Ibid., p. 246.

348 "with a crew": Dumas, *Garibaldi*, p. 50.

349 "as if they wished": Ridley, p. 27.

349 "The body keeps pace": Dumas, *Garibaldi*, p. 243.

349 "used to visit": Graham Robb, *Victor Hugo* (London, 1997), pp. 35 and 560.

350 "Organising troops": Garibaldi, *Autobiography*, vol. 2, p. 129.

350 "Three or four": Hibbert, pp. 60–61.

351 "the very scourge": Ibid., p. 105.

351 "Rome to me": Dumas, *Garibaldi*, p. 33.

351 "Are the descendants": Ridley, p. 268.

352 "It was then": Dumas, *Garibaldi*, p. 251.

352 "I went after him": Zamoyski, p. 364.

352 "This mysterious conqueror": Dumas, *Garibaldi*, p. 251.

352 "Oh isn't he": Parris, p. 93.

353 "There is no religion": Dumas, *Garibaldi*, p. 41.

353 "The foes are": Parris, p. 89.

353 "erect on horseback": Dumas, *Garibaldi*, p. 263.

354 "Come to me": Parris, p. 96.

355 "He laid his hand": Hibbert, p. 295.

355 "go, with twenty": Ibid., p. 75.

355 "Those hurrying past": Ibid., p. 74.

355 "Even with the certainty": Ridley, p. 122.

355 "he was utterly": Ibid., p. 295.

356 "opened his eyes": Hibbert, p. 83.

357 "Here they live": Ibid., p. 85.

357 "Garibaldi was greater": Dumas, *Garibaldi*, p. 324.

357 "At every moment": Hibbert, p. 94.

357 "Within those walls": Ibid., p. 80.

358 "Women stormed him": Ibid., p. 95.

358 "They wrong man": Carlyle, p. 61.

358 "as sad as death": Dumas, *Garibaldi*, p. 326.

359 "I have decided to act": Ridley, p. 208.

359 "I ask will you take": Ibid., p. 258.

359 "It is not possible": Ibid., p. 292.

359 "propitous": Hibbert, p. 147.

359 "as sometimes in my life . . .": Garibaldi, *Autobiography*, vol. 2, p. 14.

360 "throw myself in the midst": Ibid., p. 23.

360 "a *tour de force*": Hibbert, p. 102.

362 "Soldiers, I release": Ibid., p. 107.

362 "could be made": Garibaldi, *Autobiography*, vol. 2, p. 32.

365 "I was ashamed": Ibid., p. 23.

365 "the only hope": Dumas, *Garibaldi*, p. 63.

366 "We love to associate": Emerson, p. 168.

366 "Great natures": Aristotle, *Problems*, 30.1.

367 "A great heart": Dumas, *Garibaldi*, p. 15.

367 "I have led": Hibbert, p. 123.

367 "present no points": Garibaldi, *Autobiography*, vol. 2, p. 68.

368 "There is around the name": Ridley, pp. 364 and 381.

369 "They use men": Ibid., p. 262.

369 "His face was radiant": Ibid., p. 399.

369 "The adherence": Hibbert, p. 137.

369 "I was kept as a flag": Ibid., p. 150.

370 "We intend": Ridley, p. 403.

370 "*Sono nella poesia*": George Macaulay Trevelyan, *Garibaldi and the Thousand* (London, 1949), p. 99.

370 "the head of a new": Ibid., p. 107.

370 "Come! He who stays": Hibbert, p. 159.

370 "Red Devil": Trevelyan, *Garibaldi and the Thousand*, p. 104.

372 "like a lovely": Garibaldi, p. 104.

372 "Oh that I might": Hibbert, p. 167.

374 "Now that Nice": Ibid., p. 190.

375 "at the outset": Ridley, p. 441.

375 "The Great Man": Carlyle, p. 66.

376 "The insurrection suppressed": Ridley, p. 437.

376 "Those who remember": Trevelyan, *Garibaldi and the Thousand*, p. 195.

377 "Poor Garibaldi": Hibbert, p. 186.

378 "What shall we do": Ibid., p. 213.

379 "Man is heaven-born": Carlyle, p. xxxv.

380 "Viva l'Italia," "Talia": Trevelyan, *Garibaldi and the Thousand*, p. 302.

380 "A miserable sight": Ridley, p. 448.

380 "ministers of falsehood": Hibbert, p. 105; Garibaldi, *Autobiography*, vol. 2, p. 26.

381 "One must know": Hibbert, p. 226.

382 "tomorrow will be": Ibid., p. 235.

383 "If he were to say": Hibbert, p. 239.

383 "This man, almost alone": Alexandre Dumas, *Memoires de*

Garibaldi (Brussels, 1860–1862), p. 15.

383 "liberate Italy": Ridley, p. 460.

383 "Garibaldi is a demi-god": Ibid., p. 458.

384 "at all costs": Hibbert, p. 271.

384 "but I am also": Ibid., p. 273.

384 "THE THE <u>THE</u>": Ridley, p. 459.

384 "To thee Giuseppe": Hibbert, p. 238.

384 "heroic action is paralysed": Carlyle, p. lx.

384 "We cannot struggle": Hibbert, p. 242.

385 "apostolic legateship": Denis Mack Smith, *Modern Italy* (London, 1997), p. 15.

386 "Garibaldi is here": Ridley, p. 468.

386 "Finance, taxation, police": Hibbert, p. 240.

387 "He will become": Ibid., p. 255.

387 "Your Majesty knows": Ibid., p. 256.

388 "The population was frantic": Ibid., p. 266.

388 "The Great Man": Carlyle, p. 96.

390 "the power of the State": Hibbert, p. 277.

390 "demonstrations of welcome": Ibid., p. 278.

390 "What is fear?": Dumas, *Autobiography*, p. 35.

391 "If he were not": Hibbert, p. 344.

391 "Not only was all": Ibid., p. 280.

391 "Here and there": Ibid., p. 281.

391 "The town was running": Ibid., p. 282.

392 "The stories told in Naples": Ibid.

392 "The weakness of the man": Ibid., p. 504.

393 "He was like thunder": Ibid., p. 298.

394 "insolent ultimatum": Ridley, p. 495.

395 "all were alike averse": Hibbert, p. 306.

395 "This is your king!": Ibid., p. 307.

395 "countenance was full": Ibid., p. 308.

396 "and perhaps something": Ibid., p. 311.

397 "His whole manner": Ibid., p. 314.

397 "Mankind have": Emerson, p. 165.

398 "who believed": Ibid., p. 523.

399 "a prophet . . .": Ibid., p. 518.

399 "Politics were not": Ibid., p. 431.

399 "The effect was": Ibid., p. 518.

400 "voice from the": Carlyle, p. 194.

400 "Arrogant toward": Hibbert, p. 327.

400 "like a bear": Ridley, p. 525.

401 "superhuman being": Vecchi, p. 1.

401 "the shoemaker": Hibbert, p. 321.

402 "In the name": Zamoyski, p. 408.

403 "A nation like France": Ridley, p. 535.

403 "Death if they like": Ibid.

404 "individual, however": Hibbert, p. 319.

404 "But what of": Unpublished letter from Ivan Turgenev to Alexander Herzen, Baden-Baden, August 1862.

407 "None of you": Thucydides, 6.92.

408 "It is Garibaldi's": Dumas, *Memories*, p. 238.

408 "gloomy, hoarse": Ridley, p. 589.

408 "What remains of me": Ibid., p. 602.

409 "Prologue: Flourish of": Alexander Herzen, *My Past and Thoughts*, translated by Constance Garnett (Oxford, 1968), p. 119.

410 "It was more": Hibbert, p. 340.

410 "What a noble": Ridley, p. 286.

411 "un-charlatan-like": Hibbert, p. 343.

411 "The people of England": Ridley, p. 551.

412 "He came": Hibbert, p. 341.

412 "Honest, disinterested": Ridley, p. 551.

412 "half-ashamed": Ibid., p. 289.

413 "My friend": Ibid., p. 290.

413 "because I am not": Ibid., p. 557.

414 "It is not with flowers": Dumas, *Autobiography*, p. 114.

414 "simple nobility": Hibbert, p. 243.

414 "Garibaldi has all": Ridley, p. 557.

414 "Your visit was": Hibbert, p. 351.

415 "mercilessly to sweep": Ridley, p. 262.

415 "days of shame": Garibaldi, *Autobiography*, vol. 2, p. 41.

416 "All whose brilliance": Thucydides, 6.16.

416 "Of course it would be": Ridley, p. 440.

416 "It was a different": Zamoyski, p. 444.

ODYSSEUS

417 "a landmark": Homer, *Odyssey*, 24.90.

417 "burnt-out wraiths" . . . "breathless dead": Ibid., 11.540–558.

418 "Garibaldi, last": Adam Zamoyski, *Holy Madness: Romantics, Patriots and Revolutionaries, 1776–1871* (London, 1999). p. 426.

418 "the most violent": Homer, *Iliad*, 1.172.

418 Euripedes . . . Catallus: King, pp. 115–116 and 120–121.

418 "so vain and silly . . .": Coleman, p. 315.

419 "Really": Oscar Wilde, *An Ideal Husband*, act 2.

420 In Vienna: Sigmund Freud, *The Interpretation of Dreams*, translated by Joyce Crick (Oxford, 1999), p. 273.

421 "A Titan": Noyes, p. 94.

421 Quintus of Smyrna: King, p. 134.

421 "dirt and miserable": Nietzsche, *Thus Spoke Zarathustra*, p. 42.

422 "to whom nothing": Hollingdale, p. 13.

422 "Mankind in the": Ibid., p. 94.

422 "I teach that": Ibid., p. 99.

422 "For the sake": Ibid., p. 95.

422 "It is a crime": Giuseppe Garibaldi, *Autobiography*, translated by A. Werner (London, 1889), vol. 2, p. 129.

422 "the desire": Günter Berghaus, *Futurism and Politics* (Oxford, 1996), p. 21.

422 "So let them come": Federico Tomaso Marinetti, *Selected Writings*, edited by R. W. Flint (London, 1972), p. 43.

423 "the world's": Ibid., p. 41.

423 "One has renounced": Hollingdale, p. 109.

423 "The command passes": Michael A. Ledeen, *The First Duce: D'Annunzio at Fiume* (London, 1977), p. 62.

423 "If it is considered": Gabriele D'Annunzio, *Prose did Ricerca, di Lotta e di Commando* (Milan, 1947–50), p. 43.

423 "Proscribe them": Woodhouse, p. 290.

424 "There is nothing": Ibid., p. 257.

425 "set out, drunk": D'Annunzio, p. 55.

425 "Liberty itself": Zamoyski, p. 398.

425 "You are not": Hibbert, p. 327.

426 "the greatest man": Mack Smith, p. 357.

426 "Words have their own": Piers Brendon, *The Dark Valley* (London, 2000), p. 23.

426 "The men who excite": Rebecca West, *Survivors in Mexico* (London, 2003), p. 20.

428 "the fame, nobility . . .": Clissold, p. 212.

428 "Let us lock": Paul Preston, *Franco* (London, 1993), pp. 640–641.

428 "The very stones": Brendon, p. 318.

428 "Cid of the twentieth": Preston, pp. 345 and 382.

429 "following in the": S.F.A. Coles, *Franco of Spain* (London, 1955), p. 37.

429 "all the mystery": Preston, p. 641.

429 "a Caudillo is": Ibid., p. xvii.

429 "mystic union": Pidal, p. 445.

429 "God granted us": Preston, p. xvii.

429 "aims embody the will": Meier, p. 13.

430 "And in the hour": Negus, p. 77.

430 "a wild marauder": Langer, p. 12.

430 "Germany's search": Watson, p. 416.

430 "We Germans": H. Picker (ed.), *Hitlers Tisch Gespräche* (Stuttgart, 1976), p. 217.

430 "Wallenstein, first": Wedgwood.

431 "Like him we Germans": Picker, p. 217.

431 "Everything includes itself": Shakespeare, *Troilus and Cressida*, 1.3.

431 "Better to live": Mack Smith, p. 354.

432 "Francis Drake": Ridley, p. 300.

432 "Mussolini is": Foot, p. 20.

432 "was a defence": Carlyle, p. lxx.

432 "Life is sweet": Emerson, pp. 169, 170, 261.

433 "Don't you believe": Sophocles, *Philoctetes*, translated by E. F. Watling (Harmondsworth, 1969), p. 167.

433 "I am what": Ibid., p. 198.

433 "Each one of us": Ibid., p. 207.

433 "the pains": Homer, *Odyssey*, 12.200.

434 "a singular mixture": Baudelaire, p. 52.

434 "Now I die": Nietszche, *Thus Spoke Zarathustra*, p. 237.

434 "Joy wants": Ibid., pp. 331–332.

435 "It is all the most": Joanna Bourke, *An Intimate History of Killing* (London, 1999), p. 140.

435 "are going into": Hew Strachan, *The First World War*, vol. I (Oxford, 2001), p. 137.

435 "I have in this": Ibid., p. 141.

435 "Living through war": Peter Parker, *The Old Lie* (London, 1987), p. 199.

436 "The war of 1914": Strachan, p. 1128.

436 "Nietzsche is": Ibid., p. 137.

436 "drink life to": Tennyson, *Ulysses*.

436 "yes and then": James Joyce, *Ulysses* (London, 1997), p. 690.

BIBLIOGRAPHY

Works referred to at several points in this book are listed in the section to which they are most relevant. For classical texts not listed here I have used the Loeb Classical Library edition.

PROLOGUE

Aristotle. *The Politics*, translated by T. A. Sinclair, revised by Trevor J. Saunders (Harmondsworth, 1986).

Carlyle, Thomas. *On Heroes, Hero-Worship, & the Heroic in History*, introduction by Michael Goldberg (Oxford, 1993).

Emerson, Ralph Waldo. *English Traits, Representative Men and Other Essays* (London, 1908).

Hollingdale, R. J. *Nietzsche* (London, 1973).

Knox, Bernard. *The Heroic Temper* (Cambridge, 1964).

Madan, Geoffrey. *Notebooks* (Oxford, 1984).

Sprawson Charles. "Et in Arcadia: a Defence of Sparta," in *The London Magazine*, October 1987 (London, 1987).

Strachey, Lytton. *Eminent Victorians* (Harmondsworth, 1975).

ACHILLES

Freud, Sigmund. "Civilisation and Its Discontents" in *Civilisation, Society and Religion*, translated by James Strachey (Harmondsworth, 1987).

Homer, *The Iliad*, translated by Robert Fagles, introduction by Bernard Knox (London, 1990).

———. *The Odyssey*, translated by Robert Fagles, introduction by Bernard Knox (London, 1996).

King, Katherine Callen. *Achilles, Paradigms of the War Hero from Homer to the Middle Ages* (Berkeley and London, 1987).

Lane Fox, Robin. *Alexander the Great* (Harmondsworth, 1986).

Logue, Christopher. *The Husbands* (London, 1994).

———. *Kings* (London, 1991).

———. *War Music* (London, 1981).

Nagy, Gregory. *The Best of the Achaeans* (John Hopkins University Press, Baltimore, 1980).

———. *Pindar's Homer* (Baltimore and London, 1990).

ALCIBIADES

Calasso, Roberto. *The Marriage of Cadmus and Harmony* (London, 1993).

Davidson, James. *Courtesans and Fishcakes* (London, 1998).

Green, Peter. *Achilles, His Armour* (London, 1955).

Kagan, Donald. *The Fall of the Athenian Empire* (Ithaca and London, 1987).

———. *The Peace of Nicias and the Sicilian Expedition* (Ithaca, N.Y., and London, 1981).

Pindar. *The Odes*, translated by John Sandys (London, 1968).

Plato. *The Last Days of Socrates*, translated by Hugh Tredinnick and Harold Tarrant (Harmondsworth, 1993).

———. *The Republic*, translated by Robin Waterfield (Oxford, 1993).

———. *The Symposium*, translated by Walter Hamilton (Harmondsworth, 1985).

Plutarch. *Lives*, translated by Bernadotte Perrin (London, 1919).

———. *The Rise and Fall of Athens*, translated by Ian Scott-Kilvert (Harmondsworth, 1960).

Stone, I. F. *The Trial of Socrates* (London, 1988).

Thucydides. *History of the Peloponnesian War*, translated by Rex Warner (Harmondsworth, 1972).

Xenophon. *A History of My Times*, translated by Rex Warner (Harmondsworth, 1979).

CATO

Addison, Joseph. *The Works*, vol. 4 (London, 1804).

Appian. *Roman History: The Civil Wars*, translated by Horace White (London and New York, 1913).

Everitt, Anthony. *Cicero: A Turbulent Life* (London, 2001).

Gelzer, Matthias. *Caesar, Politician and Statesman*, translated by Peter Needham (Oxford, 1968).

Goar, Robert J. *The Legend of Cato Uticensis from the First Century BC to the Fifth Century AD* (Brussels, 1987).

Lintott, Andrew. *Violence in Republican Rome* (Oxford, 1968).

Lucan. *Pharsalia*, translated by Robert Graves (London 1961).

Meier, Christian. *Caesar*, translated by David McLintock (London, 1996)

Millar, Fergus. *The Crowd in Rome in the Late Republic* (Ann Arbor, 1998).

Mommsen, Theodor. *The History of Rome*, translated by William Purdie Dickson (London, 1901).

Montaigne, Michel de. *The Essays of Michel de Montaigne*, translated by M. A. Screech (London, 1991).

Morris, Ivan. *The Nobility of Failure* (Harmondsworth, 1980).

Oman, Charles. *Seven Roman Statesmen of the Later Republic* (London, 1902).

Plass, Paul. *The Game of Death in Ancient Rome* (University of Wisconsin, Madison, 1995).

Plutarch. *Fall of the Roman Republic*, translated by Rex Warner (Harmondsworth, 1972).

———. *Makers of Rome*, translated by Ian Scott-Kilvert (Harmondsworth, 1965).

Rist, J. M. *Stoic Philosophy* (Cambridge, 1969).

Scullard, H. H. *From the Gracchi to Nero: A History of Rome 133 BC–AD 68* (London, 1959).

Seneca. *Letters from a Stoic*, translated by Robin Campbell (Harmondsworth, 1977).

Smithers, Peter. *The Life of Joseph Addison* (Oxford, 1954).

Suetonius. *The Twelve Caesars*, translated by Robert Graves (Harmondsworth, 1986).

Syme, Ronald. *The Roman Revolution* (Oxford, 1939).

Tacitus. *The Annals of Imperial Rome*, translated by Michael Grant (Harmondsworth 1996).

Taylor, L. R. *Party Politics in the Age of Caesar* (Berkeley, Calif., 1949).

Veyne, Paul. *Bread and Circuses*, edited by Oswyn Murray, translated by Brian Pearce (London, 1990).

EL CID

Anonymous. *Beowulf*, translated by Kevin Crossley-Holland (London, 1973).

———. *The Cid Ballads*, translated by James Young Gibson (London, 1887).

———. *The Poem of the Cid*, edited by Ian Michael with a translation by Rita Hamilton and Janet Perry (Manchester, 1975).

———. *The Poem of the Cid*, translated by W. S. Merwin (London, 1959).

———. *The Song of Roland*, translated by Dorothy L. Sayers (Harmondsworth, 1967).

Barber, Richard. *The Knight and Chivalry* (Woodbridge, U.K., 1995).

Cervantes, Miguel de. *The Adventures of Don Quixote*, translated by J. M. Cohen (Harmondsworth, 1970).

Clissold, Stephen. *In Search of the Cid* (London, 1965).

Corneille, Pierre. *Le Cid*, in *Oeuvres* (Paris, 1862).

Dozy, R. "Le Cid d'Apres des Nouveaux Documents," in vol. 2 of *Recherches sur l'Histoire et la Littérature de l'Espagne Pendant le Moyen Âge* (Leyden, 1860).

Fletcher, Richard. *The Quest for El Cid* (London, 1989).

Heredia, José-Maria de. *Oeuvres Poétiques Complètes* (Paris, 1984).

Ibn 'Alqama. "La Prise de Valence par le Cid," in *Islam d'Occident*, by E. Lévi Provencal (Paris, 1948).

Keen, Maurice. *Chivalry* (London, 1984).

Lévi Provencal, E. *Islam d'Occident* (Paris, 1948).

Lockhart, J. G. *Ancient Spanish Ballads* (London, 1823).

Madariaga, Salvador de. *Hernán Cortés* (London, 1942).

Menéndez Pidal, Ramón. *The Cid and His Spain*, translated by Harold Sutherland (London, 1971).

Pastor, Beatriz Bodmer. *The Armature of Conquest*, translated by Lydia Longstreth Hunt (Stanford, Calif., 1992).

Prescott, William H. *History of the Conquest of Mexico* (London, 1843).

FRANCIS DRAKE

Anonymous. *Sir Francis Drake Revived* (London, 1626).

Arber, Edward (ed.). *An English Garner*, vol. II (Birmingham, 1882).

Baudelaire, Charles. *My Heart Laid Bare and Other Prose Writings*, translated by Norman Cameron (London, 1950).

Camden, William. *Annales*, translated by R. N. Gent (London, 1635).

Cameron, Ian. *Magellan* (London, 1974).

Coleman, Terry. *Nelson, the Man and the Legend* (London, 2001).

Cummins, John. *Francis Drake* (London, 1995).

Fernández-Armesto, Felipe. *The Spanish Armada* (Oxford, 1988).

Greenblatt, Stephen. *Marvellous Possessions* (Oxford, 1991).

Hakluyt, Richard. *Voyages of the Elizabethan Seamen to America* (London, 1880).

Hampden, John (ed.). *Francis Drake, Privateer: Contemporary Narratives and Documents* (London, 1972).

Hanson, Neil. *The Confident Hope of a Miracle* (London, 2003).

Kelsey, Harry. *Sir Francis Drake: The Queen's Pirate* (London, 1998).

Kingsley, Charles. *Westward Ho!* (London, 1896).

Martin, Colin, and Geoffrey Parker. *The Spanish Armada* (London, 1988).

Maynarde, Thomas. *Sir Francis Drake: His Voyage* (London, 1849).

Nicholl, Charles. *The Creature in the Map* (London, 1995).

Noyes, Alfred. *Collected Poems* (London, 1965).

Nuttall, Zelia (ed.). *New Light on Drake: A Collection of Documents Relating to His Voyage of Circumnavigation* (London, 1914).

Osborne, Roger. *The Dreamer of the Calle San Salvador* (London, 2001).

Pagden, Anthony. *Lords of All the World* (London, 1995).

Pastor Bodmer, Beatriz. *The Armature of Conquest*, translated by Lydia Longstreth Hunt (Stanford, Calif., 1992).

Southey, Robert. *The Life of Nelson* (London, 1927).

Sugden, John. *Francis Drake* (London, 1996).

Swabey, Ffiona. *A Mediaeval Gentlewoman* (Stroud, Gloucestershire, 1999).

Vansittart, Peter. *In Memory of England* (London, 1998).

Vaux, W.S.W. (ed.). *The World Encompassed by Sir Francis Drake* (London, 1854).

Weir, Alison. *Elizabeth the Queen* (London, 1998).

Yates, Frances. *Astraea* (London, 1975).

———. *The Occult Philosophy in the Elizabethan Age* (London, 1979).

WALLENSTEIN

Asch, Ronald G. *The Thirty Years War* (London, 1997).

Beller, Elmer A. *Propaganda in Germany During the Thirty Years War* (Oxford, 1940).

————. "The Thirty Years' War," in *The New Cambridge Modern History*, vol. 4 (Cambridge, 1970).

Benecke, Gerhard (ed.). *Germany in the Thirty Years War* (London, 1978).

Brecht, Bertolt. *The Life of Galileo*, translated by Desmond Vesey (London, 1960).

Burton, Robert. *The Anatomy of Melancholy*, edited by Floyd Dell (New York, 1927).

Carlyle, Thomas. *Life of Friedrich Schiller* (Columbia University Press, New York, 1992).

Ergang, Robert. *The Myth of the All-Destructive Fury of the Thirty Years' War* (Pocono Pines, Pa., 1956).

Freytag, Gustav. *Pictures of German Life*, translated by Mrs. Malcolm (London, 1862).

Glapthorne, Henry. *The Tragedy of Albertus Wallenstein*, in *The Old English Drama* (London, 1824).

Grimmelshausen, Hans Jacob Christoffel von. *Courage the Adventuress*, edited by Hans Speier (Princeton, N.J., 1964).

Hollaender, Albert E. J. *Some English Documents on the Death of Wallenstein* (Manchester, 1958).

Holmes, Richard. *Coleridge: Early Visions* (London, 1989).

Khevenhüller, Franz Christoph. *Conterfet Kupfertisch derenjenigen vornehmen Ministren und Hohen Officiern* (Leipzig, 1722).

Langer, Herbert. *The Thirty Years' War*, translated by C.S.V. Salt (Poole, 1980).

Limm, Peter. *The Thirty Years War* (London, 1984).

Lockyer, Roger. *Buckingham* (London, 1981).

Mann, Golo. *Wallenstein*, translated by Charles Kessler (London, 1976).

Menzel, Wolfgang. *The History of Germany*, vol. 2, translated by Mrs. George Horrocks (London, 1849).

Milton, John. *Collected Works* (Oxford, 1969).

Mitchell, J. *The Life of Wallenstein, Duke of Friedland* (London, 1853).

Mousnier, R. "The Exponents and Critics of Absolutism," in *The New Cambridge Modern History* (Cambridge, 1970).

Negus, Kenneth. *Grimmelshausen* (New York, 1974).

Parker, Geoffrey. *The Thirty Years' War* (London, 1984).

Polisensky, J. V. *The Thirty Years' War* (London 1974).

Schiller, Friedrich. *Dramatic Works: Wallenstein's Camp*, translated by James Churchill; *The Piccolomini* and *Wallenstein's Death*, translated by Samuel Taylor Coleridge (London, 1894)

Schiller, Friedrich. *The History of the Thirty Years' War*, translated by A.J.W. Morrison (London, 1901).

Schultz, Hans. *Wallenstein* (Leipzig, 1912).

Spengler, Oswald. *The Decline of the West*, translated by C. A. Atkinson (London, 1980).

Srbik, Heinrich Ritter von. *Wallenstein's Ende* (Vienna, 1920).

Watson, Francis. *Wallenstein: Soldier Under Saturn* (London, 1938).

Wedgwood, C. V. *The Thirty Years War* (London, 1938).

GARIBALDI

Abba, Giuseppe Cesare. *The Diary of One of Garibaldi's Thousand*, translated by E. R. Vincent (London, 1962).

Corneille, Pierre. *Le Cid*, in *Oeuvres* (Paris, 1862).

Dumas, Alexandre. *Memoires de Garibaldi* (Brussels, 1860–1862).

Dumas, Alexandre (ed.). *Garibaldi: An Autobiography*, translated by William Robson (London, 1860).

Foot, Michael. *The Trial of Mussolini* by "Cassius" (London, 1943).

Garibaldi, Giuseppe. *Autobiography*, translated by A. Werner, 3 volumes with a supplement by Jessie White Mario (London, 1889).

Herzen, Alexander. *My Past and Thoughts*, translated by Constance Garnett (Oxford, 1968).

Hibbert, Christopher. *Garibaldi and His Enemies* (Harmondsworth, 1966).

Mack Smith, Denis. *Modern Italy* (London, 1997).

Parris, John. *The Lion of Caprera* (London, 1962).

Ridley, Jasper. *Garibaldi* (London, 1974).

Robb, Graham. *Victor Hugo* (London, 1997).

Simón, Fray Pedro. *The Expedition of Pedro de Ursua and Lope de Aguirre*, translated by William Bollaert (London, 1861).

Trevelyan, George Macaulay. *Garibaldi's Defence of the Roman Republic* (London, 1907).

———. *Garibaldi and the Making of Italy* (London, 1948).

———. *Garibaldi and the Thousand* (London, 1949).

Vecchi, Augusto. *Garibaldi at Caprera*, with an introduction by Mrs. Gaskell (London, 1862).

Zamoyski, Adam. *Holy Madness: Romantics, Patriots, and Revolutionaries, 1776–1871* (London, 1999).

ODYSSEUS

Berghaus, Günter. *Futurism and Politics* (Oxford, 1996).

Bourke, Joanna. *An Intimate History of Killing* (London, 1999).

Brendon, Piers. *The Dark Valley* (London, 2000).

Churchill, Winston. *Marlborough: His Life and Times* (London, 1933).

Clark, Martin. *Modern Italy* (London, 1996).

Coles, S.F.A. *Franco of Spain* (London, 1955).

D'Annunzio, Gabriele. *Prose di Ricerca, di Lotta e di Commando* (Milan, 1947–50).

Freud, Sigmund. *The Interpretation of Dreams*, translated by Joyce Crick (Oxford, 1999).

Huch, Ricarda. *Defeat* (London, 1928).

Joyce, James. *Ulysses* (London, 1997).

Ledeen, Michael A. *The First Duce: D'Annunzio at Fiume* (London, 1977).

Marinetti, Federico Tomaso. *Selected Writings*, edited by R. W. Flint (London, 1972).

Mussolini, Benito. *Napoleon: The Hundred Days*, adapted by John Drinkwater (London, 1932).

Newby, Eric (ed.). *A Book of Travellers Tales* (London, 1985).

Nietzsche, Friedrich. *Beyond Good and Evil*, translated by R. J. Hollingdale (Harmondsworth, 1990).

———. *On the Genealogy of Morality*, translated by Carol Diethe (Cambridge, 1994).

———. *Thus Spoke Zarathustra*, translated and with an introduction by R. J. Hollingdale (Harmondsworth, 1969).

Parker, Peter. *The Old Lie* (London, 1987).

Picker, H. (ed.). *Hitlers Tisch Gespräche* (Stuttgart, 1976).

Preston, Paul. *Franco* (London, 1993).

Ridley, Jasper. *Mussolini* (London, 1997).

Sophocles. *Philoctetes*, translated by E. F. Watling (Harmondsworth, 1969).

Stanford, W. B. *The Ulysses Theme*, introduction by Charles Boer (Dallas, 1992).

Strachan, Hew. *The First World War*, vol. 1 (Oxford, 2001).

Weil, Simone. *An Anthology*, edited by Sian Miles (London, 1986).

West, Rebecca. *Survivors in Mexico* (London, 2003).

Woodhouse, John. *Gabriele D'Annunzio: Defiant Archangel* (Oxford, 1998).

INDEX

ILLUSTRATION CREDITS

The Leave-Taking of Cato Uticensis by Ercole Gennari (1597–1658)
Galleria e Museo Estense, Modena, Italy / www.bridgeman.co.uk

Death of Cato by Giambattista Langetti (1625/35–1676)
Ca' Rezzonico, Museo del Settecento, Venice / www.bridgeman.co.uk
The Mocking of Christ with the Virgin and St Dominic, 1442 (fresco), by Fra Angelico
   (Guido di Pietro) (*c.*1387–1455)
San Marco, Florence, Italy / www.bridgeman.co.uk

Ms 282/491 fol.214, *Dialogue between Cato, Atticus, Lelius and Scipio* (vellum) by French
   School (15th century)
Musée Condé, Chantilly, France / www.bridgeman.co.uk
Giraudon / Bridgeman Art Library

Ms Royal 16 G viii fol.1476, "Julius Caesar at the Head of his Army" from *Les
   Commentaires de César*, translated by Jean de Choiseul, by French School (15th
   century)
By permission of the British Library

El Cid in an image based on his monument in Burgos, from *In Search of the Cid* by
   Stephen Clissold (1965)
We have been unable to trace the copyright holder of this image and would be grateful
   to receive any information.

El Cid woodcut from *In Search of the Cid* by Stephen Clissold (1965)
By permission of the British Library

"Socrates (470–399 BC) and his Students," from *The Better Sentences and Most Precious
   Dictations* by Al-Moubacchir (vellum), Turkish School (13th century)
Topkapi Palace Museum, Istanbul, Turkey / www.bridgeman.co.uk

Monument to El Cid (*c.*1043–99) (bronze)
Avenida del Cid, Seville, Spain / www.bridgeman.co.uk

Map charting Sir Francis Drake (*c.*1540–96)'s circumnavigation of the globe, engraved
   by Frans Hogenburg (1535–90) (colored engraving), English School (16th century)
Private Collection / www.bridgeman.co.uk

Sir Francis Drake, 1581, by Nicholas Hilliard (1547–1619)
Kunsthistorisches Museum, Vienna, Austria / www.bridgeman.co.uk

A 16th-century chart showing Drake's raid on St. Augustine, Florida, in 1585
Getty Images / Hulton Archive

Drake in California
Getty Images / Hulton Archive

SECOND PLATE SECTION

Albrecht von Wallenstein by Anthony Van Dyck
Courtesy of Artothek, Bayerische Staatsgemäldesammlung, Munich

Wallenstein in a caricature dating from 1629
Getty Images / Hulton Achive

Cartoon of Wallenstein's assassination
Getty Images / Hulton Archive

Garibaldi by M. Lorusso
Courtesy of Museo Nazionale del Risorgimento, Rome

The Battle of Sant'Antonio, Uruguay, in which Garibaldi participated, in 1846 (litho)
Colezzione Bertarelli, Milan, Italy / www.bridgeman.co.uk
Index / Bridgeman Art Library

Portrait of Giuseppe Garibaldi (1807–82) (b/w photo) by French School (19th century)
Archives Larousse, Paris, France / www.bridgeman.co.uk

Garibaldi in England
Getty Images / Hulton Archive

Label for "Elixir Garibaldi" (color litho) by French School (19th century)
Bibliotheque des Arts Decoratifs, Paris, France / www.bridgeman.co.uk
Archives Charmet

Portrait of Giuseppe Garibaldi (1807–82) (b/w photo) by Italian School (19th century)
Private Collection / www.bridgeman.co.uk
Bridgeman Art Library / Alinari

THIRD PLATE SECTION

Statue of Achilles by Richard Westmacott, in a photograph from 1919
Getty Images / Hulton Archive

The Poet in Exile, 1912 (oil on canvas), by Romaine Brooks (1874–1970)
Musée National d'Art Moderne, Centre Pompidou, Paris, France /
www.bridgeman.co.uk
Giraudon / Bridgeman Art Library

Benito Mussolini with a pet lion
Getty Images / Hulton Archive

A scene from *Napoleon: The Hundred Days* by Benito Mussolini
Getty Images / Hulton Archive

Francis Drake being knighted by Queen Elizabeth I
Getty Images / Hulton Archive

Dominique Vivant Denon (1747–1825) *Replacing the Bones of Le Cid in His Tomb* (oil on canvas) by Alexandre Evariste Fragonard (1780–1850)
Musée Antoine Lecuyer, Saint-Quentin, France / www.bridgeman.co.uk

Still from *El Cid*, starring Charlton Heston
Courtesy of Carlton International

A waxwork figure of General Franco is moved into place at Madame Tussaud's
Getty Images / Hulton Archive

Adolf Hitler photographed in 1925 by Heinrich Hoffman
Getty Images / Hulton Archive

Ulysses and the Sirens, from *The Odyssey* by Homer, Roman mosaic (3rd century AD)
Musée du Bardo, Tunis, Tunisia / www.bridgeman.co.uk

The Return of Ulysses, 1973 (oil on canvas), by Giorgio de Chirico (1888–1978)
Private Collection / www.bridgeman.co.uk
Peter Willi
We have been unable to trace the copyright holder of this image and would be grateful to receive any information.